Visions to V

WRITTEN BY

SANTOSH KUMAR

Visions to Victory

Ready to embark on your journey to success with "Visions to Victory"?

Whether you're someone committed to personal or professional growth, an aspiring entrepreneur, a seasoned business leader, or, this guide is your key to unlocking your full potential.

Uncover the blueprint for unprecedented personal and professional growth, the secrets to building a thriving 9-12 figure empire, and the essential strategies for a triumphant exit on the stock exchange with IPO Listing

This book will propel you into an era of remarkable growth and achievement. "Visions to Victory," is the ultimate bible for your personal and professional growth as well as growth of your venture. This book isn't just a guide; it's your roadmap, framework, and formula for overcoming the obstacles that stand between dreams and reality. "Visions to Victory" is a comprehensive manual that tackles common challenges in goal setting and achievement head-on. It offers clarity, motivation, actionable plans, progress monitoring, adaptability, and empowerment, equipping you to transform aspirations into tangible successes.

Dive into the epic narrative of "Visions to Victory," a beacon for entrepreneurs navigating the intricate path to business triumph. Discover the blueprint for unprecedented growth, the secrets to building a 9-12 figure empire, and the strategies for a triumphant exit on the stock exchange. This book and its series are your compass to a legacy of monumental achievements. Don't miss out! Make "Visions to Victory" your go-to resource for business excellence.

Get your copy now and elevate both your personal and professional journey to unparalleled heights of prosperity!

WRITTEN BY

SANTOSH KUMAR

Dedicated To

Starting with my introduction to the business world at the age of 14 and inspired by my key role model to begin my entrepreneurial journey at 16 in 1992, followed by establishing my first independent business in 2007, and resulting in the creation of 45 brands since then up to the present day as I write these words for this book, alongside being invited by Forbes to join their Business Council in 2021, has been a transformative journey for me. However, such a journey of continuous learning would not have been possible without acknowledging the inspiration of my life.

Throughout the vast expanse of my life's journey, one figure stands as an indomitable pillar of knowledge, strength, and wisdom - my beloved father. This book is not merely a collection of words but a heartfelt tribute to the man who shaped my values, ignited my dreams, and instilled in me the essence of resilience. As I reflect on the chapters of the learnings of my life, it is your influence that has coloured every page with hues of encouragement, sacrifice, and love. From the earliest moments of my existence, you have been the silent architect, constructing the framework of my character with patience, discipline, and a commitment to excellence.

Your lessons were not confined to mere words; they were woven into the fabric of your daily lives. In the quiet moments when you imparted your wisdom, whether through bedtime stories or shared silences, I imbibed the principles of honesty, integrity, and hard work. Your life became a living manuscript, and I, a keen observer, learned the language of values from your actions, not just your words. In the tapestry of my aspirations, your encouragement was the thread that held everything together. You believed in my dreams even when they seemed audacious, offering words of assurance and a comforting presence during times of uncertainty. Your belief became the wind beneath my wings, propelling me forward when the journey seemed arduous.

Amidst the triumphs and tribulations, you stood as a beacon of resilience. Your ability to weather storms with grace and emerge stronger became a source of inspiration. It wasn't just success that you taught me to embrace but the lessons of failure as stepping stones towards growth. Your life story, a testament to perseverance, has been my guidepost in navigating the complexities of life. As I pen down these words, I am acutely aware that every sentence, every paragraph, carries the echoes of your influence. This book, in its entirety, is a reflection of the values you etched onto my heart and the dreams you fuelled with your unwavering belief.

In dedicating this work to you, my dearest father, I seek to encapsulate the profound gratitude, love, and admiration I hold for you. You are more than a parent; you are the architect of my destiny, the guardian of my aspirations, and the compass that has unfailingly pointed me toward the true north. May this dedication stand as a small token of appreciation for the countless sacrifices you made, the lessons you imparted, and the unconditional love you showered. Your legacy is not only imprinted on the pages of this book but woven into the very fabric of who I am.

With deep love and gratitude,

Santosh Kumar

Preface

Entrepreneurs harbour numerous dreams, each evolving into a venture with a vision. Some entrepreneurs are versatile, juggling multiple visions, while others pursue dreams one by one. In either scenario, every entrepreneur begins with a vision, aiming for success beyond the norm. It is with great pleasure and a deep sense of purpose that I introduce "Visions to Victory."

"Visions to Victory" helps you tackle common challenges like defining clear goals, staying motivated through setbacks, and turning plans into action. It provides practical strategies to maintain momentum, track progress effectively, and bounce back from obstacles. By aligning personal values with goals, the book ensures that achievements are not just successful but also meaningful and fulfilling. It's a toolkit for anyone striving to achieve their aspirations with clarity and resilience.

This book is not just a compilation of strategies or a roadmap for business growth; it is a testament to the entrepreneurial spirit, an odyssey of visionaries who dare to dream big and transform those dreams into tangible victories. 'Visions to Victory' is not a mere guide; it's an immersive experience designed to inspire, inform, and empower. As you navigate through the chapters, you will encounter the VICTORY model—a strategic blueprint meticulously crafted to guide businesses through every pivotal phase of development. From the inception of visionary ideas to the grandeur of public ownership, each stage is a crucial note in the symphony of entrepreneurial success.

The journey begins with Visionary Ideation, where the seeds of business concepts are sown. You traverse the realms of Idea Inception and Launch, delving into the intricacies of cultivating startups and achieving triumph in market domination. Outperforming SME businesses, revelling in public ownership, and yielding the fruits of legacy—the VICTORY model unfolds as a comprehensive narrative of entrepreneurial excellence. What sets this book apart is not just the information it imparts but the spirit it encapsulates. It resonates with the struggles, triumphs, and relentless pursuit of success that defines the entrepreneurial journey. Each word is an ode to the determination that propels businesses from mere existence to a legacy.

As you embark on this literary voyage, envision your business not just as an entity but as a force—a force that shapes industries, influences markets, and leaves an indelible mark on the annals of business history. 'Visions to Victory' is an invitation to transform your vision into a legacy of triumph. To the dreamers, the doers, and the architects of their destinies, this book is dedicated to you. May the VICTORY model be your guiding star, illuminating the path to unparalleled success. Welcome to 'Visions to Victory.' The journey is as transformative as the destination.

Sincerely,

Santosh Kumar

Disclaimer

The contents of this book represent my personal thoughts, experiences, and insights. I have captured the context at the time of writing this book to the best of my knowledge, skill, experience, and the wisdom I have built throughout my personal, professional and social life. The advice, guidance, and perspectives shared within these pages are based on my individual journey and do not claim to be universal truths.

I, Santosh Kumar, as the author, affirm that this work is a product of my own intellectual endeavour and is not intended to replicate or infringe upon the ideas, opinions, or writings of any other author, living or deceased.

Readers are cautioned that the information presented here is not a substitute for professional advice, and any decisions made based on the content of this book are at your own discretion. I do not accept responsibility for any consequences arising from the application of the ideas or suggestions presented herein.

While I strive to provide accurate and timely information, the dynamic nature of various industries and fields means that situations and best practices may change over time. Therefore, readers are encouraged to verify information and seek professional advice when necessary.

I do not claim to be hundred percent correct for each and every person or on every instance, as everybody is unique, and their situations and thoughts can vary. To safeguard my interest, my credibility, the motive and the interest of this book, I assure that the contents written are the best representation of my thoughts, my knowledge, and experience on the day of writing this book, but I do not assert that the facts and figures mentioned in this book are hundred percent true from everyone's perspective, and the views and thoughts of others can differ from mine.

In essence, this book is an expression of my personal journey and reflections. It is my hope that the Skill, knowledge, experiences, and wisdom shared herein may inspire, motivate, and provide insights. However, everyone's circumstances are unique, and what worked for me may not be universally applicable. Hence, readers are advised to make their own judgment and not hold the anyone responsible for any claims from a person, living or dead.

By choosing to read this book, you acknowledge and accept the terms of this disclaimer. Thank you for embarking on this literary journey with an open mind and discerning perspective.

Sincerely,

Santosh Kumar

INDEX

Thank you is not enough!

As I bring this book to life, I am humbled by the realisation that "thank you" is not enough to acknowledge the collective learning and dedication that have brought us to this moment. This book, "VISIONS to VICTORY," is a testament to the profound appreciation I have for the collective efforts, dedication, and contributions of all the people with whom I have interacted. Your shared learning has made the creation of "VISIONS to VICTORY" possible and It goes beyond words, honouring the significant impact and shared achievements of everyone involved, directly or indirectly.

Thank you to all of my mentors, all of my business associates, and all of my business connections for your invaluable guidance, your positive influence and your shared knowledge have played a crucial role in shaping my journey, empowering me to overcome obstacles with determination and resilience. "VISIONS to VICTORY" stands as a reminder of what you can achieve when you unite with a common purpose and shared vision.

A special thank you to my wife and children, whose patience have been the cornerstone of this book. Your presence have been my guiding light throughout this journey. I am profoundly grateful for your love and understanding, which have fuelled my determination to bring "Visions to Victory" to fruition.

Thank you to my brothers for your encouragement. Your belief in my vision and steadfastness have given me the strength to persevere in the face of challenges. I am deeply grateful for you being around me and your role in making this book a reality.

Thank you to my beloved mother, your love and wisdom have been a constant source of guidance and inspiration. Your belief in me has fuelled my determination to pursue my dreams.

Thank you to all my family members for the shared journey of love and enjoyment. You all have been a source of strength and inspiration, propelling me forward on this journey. Lastly, I extend my gratitude to thank all my personal and business relations for facilitating the meaningful collaborations and shared learnings. Your direct and indirect actions and efforts have strengthened the collective impact and contributed to the success of this book.

I extend my heartfelt gratitude to all who have played a pivotal role in my life's journey and making this book a success. I am profoundly grateful for all your contributions, which have served as the driving force behind this endeavour. Throughout these interactions, I have not only gained valuable wisdom, expertise, and experiences from each of you but have also been continually inspired to expand my horizons. The insights and perspectives shared during these moments have challenged me to grow, innovate, and explore new avenues, thereby shaping the ideas presented in this book.

As I conclude this chapter and reflect on the shared journey, I am humbled to say that thank you is not enough to acknowledge the collective learning and dedication that have brought us to this moment. Together, you have helped me transform my visions into reality, and I am honoured to present this book, "VISIONS to VICTORY," as a testament to the shared achievements.

I genuinely feel that thank you is not enough.

With heartfelt thanks,

Santosh Kumar

What kind of book is this & Why should you read it?

When you've got this book in your hands, you might be wondering, "What exactly is this book?" Is it a helpful guide, a gripping story, or just a bunch of wise words? Let's have a look inside and see what you find. First off, this book is like a guiding torch showing you the way to get where you want to go. It's got practical tips, useful advice, and handy tools to help you deal with life's tricky bits, whether that's in your personal life, your work, or wherever you're headed. Think of it as a trustworthy friend, pointing you in the right direction. Imagine having a clear roadmap that guides you through every step of your journey towards success—whether you're starting a business, advancing in your career, or pursuing personal growth. Introducing "Visions to Victory," your ultimate companion in turning dreams into reality.

What sets "Visions to Victory" apart? It's more than just a book; it's a powerful toolkit designed to empower you with the mindset, strategies, and motivation needed to conquer obstacles and achieve lasting success. Here's how it can benefit you. But it's not just about giving advice. This book also tells a good story—it's full of tales about people facing challenges, overcoming obstacles, and learning important lessons. Through these stories, you'll be drawn in, feel what they feel, and maybe even learn a thing or two about life along the way.

And then there's the wisdom bit. This book is like a treasure trove of clever thoughts and insights, gathered from wise folks, experts, and my own experiences as an author. It takes big ideas and breaks them down into easy-to-understand titbits, helping you make sense of things in a world that can sometimes feel overwhelming. Basically, this book is a bit of everything—it's a guide, a storybook, and a source of wisdom all rolled into one. This book will help you understand where you are in your personal and professional life, where you want to be in your success journey, why you want to be there, and what's involved in it. It shows how powerful books can be in helping us learn, grow, and understand ourselves and the world around us.

Now, why should you read this book? It's simple – I passionately believe that each one of us exists and brings your ideas and thoughts into existence in the real world for a reason. You have your purpose, and you are giving everything you can to fulfil that purpose. I'm constantly on a learning curve, where every day feels like a school day and so is every entrepreneur. But how many of you know and realise it before it's too late? Recognising that every business undertakes a similar journey, I embrace the philosophy of TEAM spirit, **"Together Everyone Achieves More".** Venturing into entrepreneurship, my goal is to help connect you with as many people as possible, absorb diverse learnings, and share the wealth of skills, knowledge, and wisdom accumulated within me and from others. Cracking the code to success involves understanding not only you as my entrepreneurial audience but also your needs, aiming to bring you closer to the success you aspire to achieve with your venture.

As I write this, rest assured on one of the core philosophies, each one of us is unique. Your strengths and weaknesses vary, yet the common thread lies in the entrepreneurial path—the framework, roadmap, and blueprint. While strategies and tactics may differ, my collective aim is to transform lives of millions of entrepreneurs like you by bringing you together and guiding you away from the pitfalls that many, including myself, have encountered. I'm here to spare you sleepless nights, shield you from unnecessary pain, prevent financial losses, and, above all, safeguard your irretrievable time and save you millions. "Visions to Victory" offers entry into a world where content is meticulously crafted to align with your interests and preferences to achieve your dreams. Join me on this journey, where each segment is curated with you in mind, promising an engaging and uniquely tailored experience.

How to read this book?

Welcome to "Vision to Victory: Unleashing Your Entrepreneurial Potential." This chapter will guide you through the book's structure and offer tips for effective engagement.

1. Understand the Purpose: Reflect on why you chose this book. Are you seeking inspiration, practical advice, or strategic insights? Aligning your purpose with your goals enhances your reading experience. Understand where you are and where you wants to be.

2. Explore the Table of Contents: It's your roadmap through the book. Familiarise yourself with each chapter's topics, identify areas of interest, and prioritise your reading accordingly.

3. Read Actively: Approach each chapter with a sense of curiosity and engagement. Take notes, highlight key points, and jot down questions or ideas that arise. Active reading fosters deeper comprehension and retention of information.

4. Reflect and Apply: After each chapter, pause to ponder the insights gained. How do they connect with your experiences and goals? Think about how you can apply these concepts and strategies to your entrepreneurial pursuits & to your personal and professional success.

5. Embrace Continuous Learning: "Vision to Victory" is more than a book; it's a tool for ongoing growth. Treat each chapter as a stepping stone toward personal or professional success. Stay open to new ideas and possibilities and never stop the continuous learning

6. Connect with the Community: Engage with like-minded individuals to enhance your reading experience. Join discussions, Facebook & LinkedIn groups, workshops, or online forums related to the book's topics. Share ideas, seek support, and celebrate progress.

7. Take Action: The book's value is in its ability to inspire action. Identify specific steps to move closer to your goals while reading. Whether it's implementing a new strategy, networking, or refining your plan, commit to meaningful progress.

9. Share and Multiply Your Wisdom: As you progress through "Vision to Victory," remember that "**Knowledge Shared is Knowledge Multiplied**. Share insights, lessons, and tips with your entrepreneurial network. By teaching and mentoring, you reinforce your understanding and contribute to others' growth. Embrace collaboration and generosity to elevate the entrepreneurial community and foster positive change and innovation.

Approach "Vision to Victory" with intention, curiosity, and action to unlock its transformative potential for your entrepreneurial journey. Get ready for a path of discovery, growth, and triumph—your victory awaits!

SECTION 1

Beginning of the Journey of Collective Wisdom – The Basic Building Blocks

Entrepreneurship: Navigating the Business Waters

As I start penning down for you today, I want to celebrate what truly drives the prosperity of every nation - the entrepreneurial spirit. I passionately believe that a country's growth isn't just about economic policies or global markets; it's about the dreams and ambitions of people like you and me, those who have the courage to step into the world of personal and professional success. Imagine, if you will, a vast ocean stretching out before us, its shimmering surface reflecting the brilliance of a thousand dreams.

The Voyage to Success

Imagine your business, which is the only vehicle I believe can take you from current life state to the desired life state, as a sturdy ship named "Enterprise," sailing across this vast ocean towards a group of beautiful islands that symbolise your goals. This journey is full of challenges and opportunities that can either slow us down or help us progress swiftly. Let's explore these factors and how you can navigate them successfully.

Firstly, let's think about the weather conditions. Unpredictable changes in the market and economic downturns are like sudden storms, causing delays and forcing us to change your course. To navigate through rough seas like these, you need to be agile and have a clear direction. Next, there are technical issues to consider. Outdated technology or inefficiencies in your operations can hold back your progress, much like mechanical failures on a ship. Keeping your equipment and processes up to date is crucial for maintaining a steady pace. You also need to address regulatory hurdles. Navigating through complex regulations and compliance requirements can be time-consuming, acting like a bureaucratic fog that obscures your path. Understanding and preparing for these regulations in advance can help us navigate more smoothly.

Now, let's focus on factors that can boost your progress. Consider the favourable winds. Positive trends in the market and high demand from customers can act like strong winds, propelling your journey forward. Keeping a close watch on market signals and customer needs can give us the momentum you need. Think about cutting-edge technology. Investing in the latest technology and innovation can streamline your operations, making your ship more efficient and faster. Embracing digital transformation can ensure that every part of your business runs smoothly. Reflect on strategic partnerships. Forming alliances and collaborations with other businesses can provide us with additional resources and support, similar to having extra crew members rowing together in sync. These partnerships can strengthen your capabilities and help us navigate challenges more effectively.

You must also consider the risks involved in this voyage. Think about the icebergs. Hidden financial risks and unexpected expenses can suddenly appear, posing a threat to your progress. It's essential to have vigilant financial planning and risk management to avoid these potential dangers. Consider the threat of internal conflicts or dissatisfaction among your team, which can disrupt operations, much like a mutiny on a ship. Building a positive and motivating work environment can help prevent such disruptions and keep everyone focused on your mission.

Think about the importance of your crew. An experienced team is invaluable. Their skills and commitment are like seasoned sailors who can navigate through challenging waters. Investing in your team's development ensures they are prepared for any challenges ahead. Effective communication is crucial. Clear and consistent communication ensures everyone understands their role and the direction you're heading in. Regular updates and open dialogue keep the team informed and engaged. Strong leadership is essential. A leader with vision and the ability to make strategic decisions motivates the crew and keeps us on course. Trust and confidence in your leadership are fundamental to your success.

Finally, let's explore the destinations – the islands that represent your goals. The island of growth signifies expanding your business reach and increasing revenue or a personal and prelesional success. Exploring new markets and opportunities can lead to significant growth and success. The island of innovation represents developing new products or services that set us apart from competitors. Continuous innovation ensures your business stays relevant and competitive. The island of sustainability signifies achieving long-term stability and success through sustainable practices. Building a resilient and ethical business model is crucial for sustained success. The island of customer satisfaction represents building a loyal customer base by consistently exceeding expectations. Providing exceptional value and service ensures lasting relationships and repeat business. Island of health and relationship or personal success ensure the wellbeing and happiness of individuals.

As the captain of the "Enterprise," your role is to navigate through delays, leverage opportunities, manage risks, and lead your team towards your goals. With careful planning and strategic execution, your business ship can sail smoothly and reach the islands of success, turning your visions into realities.

The Rising Wave of Global Entrepreneurship

The rise of global entrepreneurship is an exciting development with the potential to drive significant economic growth and innovation. With the right support and resources, entrepreneurs can make a substantial impact on the economy, creating jobs and fostering new ideas. As you look at the growing number of entrepreneurs and their influence, it's clear that entrepreneurship and the personal and professional success of entrepreneurs will continue to play a vital role in shaping your world. By understanding and supporting this entrepreneurial wave, you can unlock new opportunities and build a more dynamic and prosperous global economy.

Global Entrepreneurship along with personal and professional success is a topic that is reshaping your world: the remarkable rise in global entrepreneurship. This surge in entrepreneurial activity is driven by technological advancements, better access to information, and supportive educational systems.

As of 2023, there are approximately 594 million entrepreneurs worldwide. This means that about 7.4% of the global population is engaged in entrepreneurial activities. This is a significant increase from the 582 million estimated in 2020. The rise in entrepreneurship is not just a statistic; it is a powerful force driving job creation, innovation, and economic growth around the world. Several countries are leading the charge in entrepreneurial activity. India boasts about 104 million entrepreneurs, making up 11.5% of its adult population. China has over sixty-four million entrepreneurs, representing about 5% of its adult population. The United States is home to approximately fifty-four million entrepreneurs, accounting for around 32% of its adult workforce. Brazil, UK and many other such countries globally also has a significant number of entrepreneurs contributing to its economy.

Entrepreneurship spans a wide range of demographics, with some interesting trends. Women make up about 43% of entrepreneurs worldwide, with the largest group being women aged between 40 and 59. There are approximately 252 million female entrepreneurs globally, with an additional 153 million women running established businesses.

The motivations for starting a business or personal and professional success vary, but key drivers include Being their own boss (62%), Pursuing their passion (60%), Filling a community need (52%), Building wealth (51%) and Creating jobs (42%).

However, entrepreneurship is not without its challenges. About 20% of new businesses fail within the first two years, 45% within the first five years, and 65% within the first ten years. Only 1% to 5% of new businesses survive beyond 15 years. As per the Investopedia, reasons for failure include money running out, being in the wrong market, a lack of research, bad partnerships, ineffective marketing, and not being an expert in the industry.

Every year you as entrepreneurs work on different programmes, different campaigns or bring your innovative ideas to reality. Some are embarking on this journey for the first time, while others began their journey long ago and have immersed themselves deeply into the sea of entrepreneurship.

You might be the founder of a multi-billion-pound venture operating across seven continents, or you might be a young entrepreneur starting your journey for the first time. You might be involved in the pre-start stage, or you might be getting your hands dirty with a startup. Perhaps you're the owner of a micro-business, working with 1 to 9 employees and turning over 1 to 9 million pounds. You might own an SME employing 10 to 49 employees, or you might be the chairperson of a multinational company.

One thing that is common among all of us is that you all have problems in your day-to-day lives, and you all face some known and some unknown challenges. The next common thing is that you are all constantly looking for solutions to improve not only your own lives but also the lives of millions of customers, suppliers, and partners.

If that's the case for you, then you'd be extremely interested in going through and reading this book. I am hundred percent sure that some of the concepts and blueprints I am going to introduce to you in this book you might have heard of, but there is plenty of proprietary and copyrighted content, roadmaps, blueprints, frameworks, and concepts that you will observe for the first time.

These concepts have been brought into existence for a reason, and I will not hesitate to say that I am a problem solver, and I can give you a solution to every problem you have. I am penning down to start an adventure and accomplish a mission to solve the problems of millions of entrepreneurs, add value to your life, serve the community for the better, and transform lives.

But before you dive into the details of this adventure, let's draw a comparison between setting sail as a sailor and embarking on the entrepreneurial journey where you find ourselves at the threshold of an incredible journey – the voyage of entrepreneurship.

Stepping into this journey is like embarking on a sea voyage, navigating through vast and unpredictable waters like navigating the waters of sea in sailing. In so many ways, the path of an entrepreneur mirrors that of a sailor, both requiring a clear vision, determination, and the readiness to face challenges head-on to reach their goals. It's a journey that beckons us with promises of exploration, innovation, and endless opportunities but at the same time self-doubts, fears and challenges. As you embark on this thrilling adventure, let's put aside your doubts and fears, and embrace the spirit of discovery that flows through your veins.

Like a sailor aiming for a distant shore, I strongly believe that an entrepreneur plots a course towards their vision of success. Both need a clear goal to steer their journey, whether it's tapping into a new market, creating groundbreaking products, or leaving a lasting mark on society. Every entrepreneur sets their sights on a destination, driven by their aspirations and determination. Without this vision, you inevitably pay the price soon.

Navigating the business waters

Each of us is a captain of your own vessel, navigating the uncharted waters with courage and determination. In the realm of entrepreneurship, it is not the faint of heart who prevail, but those bold enough to chase their dreams against all odds.

As you embark on this adventure, let us be guided by a vision that ignites your passion and propels us ever forward. Whether it's pioneering new technologies, creating innovative products, or exploring uncharted territories, let your vision be your guiding north star, leading us through the darkest of nights and the fiercest of storms.

But let there be no mistake – the path ahead will not be easy. Setbacks are inevitable on both journeys, whether you encounter known challenges or unexpected obstacles. Like a sudden squall at sea, unforeseen circumstances can arise, testing your mettle. Yet, it's in overcoming these setbacks that both sailors and entrepreneurs discover their inner strength and resilience.

But before you set sail, let's draw inspiration from the successful journeys of entrepreneurs around us. Their experiences can guide us as you chart your own course through the business waters.

Setting the Sail

Setting sail, whether on the sea or in the business world or in the personal or professional success, requires more than just a destination in mind. It demands a mindset of determination, courage, and self-belief. Just as a sailor must navigate through storms and unpredictable weather, an entrepreneur must navigate through the uncertainties and obstacles of the market. You will face challenges, setbacks, and obstacles that will test your resolve and shake your confidence.

Similarly, conditions can be unpredictable, sometimes aiding progress and at other times hindering the journey. Just as a favourable wind can push a ship forward, favourable market conditions can accelerate business growth. Conversely, adverse conditions may require patience and strategic navigation. It is in these moments of adversity that your true strength is revealed, as you rise to meet the challenges before us with unwavering determination and unyielding courage. Fear and risk are common experiences shared by sailors and entrepreneurs alike.

Just as a sailor faces the unknown depths of the sea with trepidation, an entrepreneur confronts the uncertainties of the market and the risks inherent in business ventures. Yet, it is through facing these fears and taking calculated risks that both can achieve their goals.

The Adventure

In the end, both sailors and entrepreneurs rely on the power of goals, the purpose and visions to guide their path and propel them forward. With determination and decisive action, they navigate the challenges, confident that their efforts will lead them to their desired destination, where they can enjoy the fruits of their labour. And though the journey may be long and arduous, let us find solace in knowing that you are not alone in your endeavours. Each of us is surrounded by a crew of like-minded adventurers, united by a common purpose and a shared vision of success. Together, you will brave the storms, navigate the treacherous waters, and emerge victorious on the other side.

You must embark on this grand adventure with hearts filled with hope, minds teeming with ambition, and spirits unbroken by the obstacles that lie ahead. For the journey of entrepreneurship is not merely a pursuit of profit, but a quest for something far greater – a legacy that will endure for generations to come. For the greatest adventures await those bold enough to seize them, and the greatest rewards belong to those who dare to chase their dreams.

Allow me to take you on the journey recounted in this book by sharing an inspirational and uplifting tale about Lily.

LET'S DIVE IN...

Chapter 1.1

Collective journey of entrepreneurship - Story of Lily's Dreams to Victory

Have you ever stopped to wonder why some people seem to accomplish so much more in the same 24 hours that we all have each day? It's a question that has puzzled many of us. The answer lies not in having more time, but in how effectively individuals manage and prioritise their time.

Time is indeed the most precious element you have in your lives because it is limited. It's the shortest supply you have, and yet it has the maximum demand. But how many of us truly accept this fact? How many understand it, realise it, and then act upon it to make the most of your time?

Everyone, from the busiest executive to the stay-at-home parent, has the same 24 hours in a day. Yet, the difference between high achievers and others often comes down to focus, purpose, and discipline.

Successful people possess a strong sense of purpose. They have clear dreams, hopes, and visions that motivate them to take action. This larger purpose gives meaning to their daily activities, making even mundane tasks feel significant.

Moreover, high achievers focus their attention on the tasks that matter most. They have a clear understanding of their goals and priorities, allowing them to concentrate on high-impact activities. This focus prevents them from being sidetracked by less important tasks or distractions.

Discipline is another crucial factor in their success. Successful individuals stick to their plans and routines, even when they don't feel like it. They set clear, actionable objectives and break them down into manageable steps. By consistently following through on their commitments, they build momentum and make steady progress toward their goals.

By mastering focus, purpose, and discipline, most individuals can make the most of their time, achieve more, and reach higher levels of success. Let's reflect on Lily's approach.

Lily was a determined young entrepreneur living in the city of Innovation Valley. She was a daydreamer, with many thoughts and ideas swirling in her mind. With a mind full of ideas and a longing for purpose, Lily navigated the urban landscape, grappling with the balance of dreams and doubts that affect every visionary soul.

The Thought

Quite recently, Lily's dearest friend lost her cherished father, Vincent, due to inorganic food and environment. Vincent was a local trader and upheld a strong sense of business ethics throughout his life. He served as a significant source of inspiration for Lily and her friend. Lily and her friend both were remarkably close to Vincent which they have lost now.

This incident shook Lily, and she was now determined to change the way you think for the better. She had this fervent thought that this incident has happened with her for a reason, and in her mind, the reason is to encourage and spread awareness of the impact of bad environment and inorganic food. This thought gave her a strong purpose and a reason to bring her thoughts to reality without realising it.

The Foundation and the Basic Building Blocks

Born into a family whose values of hard work and resilience laid the foundation for Lily's journey, Her childhood was a canvas upon which her entrepreneurial spirit began to take shape. From a young age, she displayed a voracious curiosity and an insatiable thirst for knowledge, traits that would later propel her towards her ambitious pursuits.

Physically, Lily moves with determination, her purposeful stride revealing her inner resolve. But like any human being, she was full of fears and scared of the risks involved in starting a business. Amidst the city's hustle and bustle, one can see traces of uncertainty in her eyes, reminders of the fears and insecurities that often come with chasing big dreams.

She was unsure if bringing her ideas into existence in the real world would result in a risk or a reward. She struggled to begin her journey as her conscious mind was holding her back, and the pressure from her peer group and procrastination were not helping her move forward in life and start her journey.

The Beginning

One day, destiny crossed her path in the form of a sage and encouraged her to contemplate finding the purpose of her life. Discovering what she wanted to do and why she wanted to do it sparked her thoughts and actions. It revealed the true essence of life as not being afraid, but rather building something bigger than herself, not just for her own benefit but also to make a real difference in the lives of others beyond herself.

Despite her doubts, Lily's passion for entrepreneurship burns brightly, fuelled by her commitment to creating sustainable, eco-friendly products that make a positive impact on the world. Her journey is marked by moments of triumph and difficulty as she navigates the unpredictable world of business with courage and conviction. Following guidance from the sage, Lily crafted a milestone plan for her entrepreneurial journey. She began seeking out individuals who had successfully reached milestones similar to hers, using them as role models to inspire and guide her towards her own achievements.

Now, she's set on creating something that'll have a lasting impact even after she's gone, leaving behind a legacy. She started following the journey of late Vincent as the role model to travel her entrepreneur journey. An important incident in her personal life made her realise the need to find her true purpose and has kept her passionately committed to leaving a legacy that's about more than just making money – one that truly makes a difference in the world.

Overflowing with ambition and ideas, Lily resolved to turn her vision into reality with purpose and became determined to leave her mark on the business world. However, despite experiencing small victories at the start of her business for few months, she soon realised that her journey was far from smooth sailing.

She encountered a series of challenges, both known and unknown, which left her struggling and discouraged. Challenges come thick and fast, testing Lily's strength and forcing her to confront her deepest fears. But with each setback, she embraced the chance to grow, demonstrating to herself and others her capacity for achieving greatness.

The Middle Game

One day, while browsing through a dusty corner of a bookstore, Lily stumbled upon an old book titled "A Guide for Entrepreneurship". Intrigued, she delved into its pages, uncovering stories of real entrepreneurs who had faced numerous obstacles on their path to success. These tales struck a chord with Lily, as she recognised that her own journey was also filled with challenges. Even though she harboured this vision of creating sustainable, eco-friendly products and save the world, it wasn't accepted by majority of the modern population, and she encountered numerous hurdles along the way.

With every challenge comes opportunity. While discussing her challenges in a business environment, Lily encountered a group of business coaches who had faced similar obstacles and successfully navigated the entrepreneurial landscape. Drawing upon their skills, knowledge, and experience, Lily sought guidance from these coaches tailored to each specific challenge she encountered.

With her knowledge, her skillset, her strong growth mindset, her positive attitude towards life and little support from others, she discovers the true meaning of resilience, learning to weather the storms of adversity with grace and determination.

During the implementation of her vision, Lily faced resistance from suppliers who were hesitant to adopt environmentally friendly practices. Additionally, she struggled to find investors who shared her vision and were willing to take a chance on her business.

Despite these setbacks, Lily refused to throw in the towel. Drawing strength from the stories she had read, she remained steadfast in her determination to make a difference in the world.

The Final Battle

Just when Lily felt that things couldn't get any tougher, a glimmer of hope appeared in the form of a wise old sage again. Lily finds solace in the wisdom of this wise old man whose guidance becomes the beacon of hope she so desperately needs. He's a man who has faced similar challenges in the past and has sailed through the seas of entrepreneurship numerous times with a clear purpose, achieving success. After brainstorming and discussing with Lily, he felt a willingness to offer and share his knowledge, skills, experience, and wisdom in the form of guidance and support as a mentor.

The man shared his own experiences and provided Lily with a roadmap for success. His skills, knowledge, and wisdom helped her navigate the challenges she faced, offering valuable advice and connecting her with resources and opportunities she hadn't previously considered.

With the man's support, Lily found a new supplier who shared her commitment to sustainability, and she secured the funding she needed to keep her business afloat. With renewed determination, Lily pressed on, navigating through the ups and downs of entrepreneurship with unwavering resolve. And then, one day, her perseverance paid off. Her eco-friendly products gained traction in the market, and her business began to thrive.

Lily is a renowned businessperson now, often invited to share her journey and inspire millions of people to transform their lives through various podcasts and media interviews. She's also been a part of the Forbes Council, where she offers the guidance and support to transform lives, turning their ideas into reality. On top of all this, she has developed a formula to share her knowledge for the success of other entrepreneurs, aiming to leave a lasting legacy.

Reflecting on her journey, Lily realised that the man had acted as a catalyst, much like aluminium in a chemical reaction. He had been instrumental in her success, providing the guidance and support she needed to overcome the challenges she faced and helping her stay focused on her vision, no matter what.

Dare to Dream

So, my dear friend, Lily's story is a testament to the power of perseverance, resilience, and the belief that anything is possible when you dare to dream. Lily's story also serves as a reminder that success is rarely achieved alone. Sometimes, you need the support and guidance of others to help you navigate the challenges you face and stay on course towards your goals.

I passionately believe that you are all unique, each with your own distinct approaches to adding value and contributing to the community. You must delve deeper into lily's journey and be inspired to make a difference in the business world with your unique perspective and brilliant ideas.

Remember, you are not alone on this path. So, go forth and dare to dream big. Embrace the challenges that come your way, and don't be afraid to seek out the support to assist you on your journey. With determination, resilience, and a little support of others, anything is possible.

Key Learnings

Here, you are more than business professionals; you are dreamers, creators, and architects of a future where your actions have the power to transcend personal success. It is your dreams that inspire you to strive for something greater, not just for yourselves, but for your loved ones, your families, your nations, and indeed, for all of humanity.

Lily used many of these concepts to maximise her productivity by staying focused on her goals, prioritising her tasks, and maintaining discipline in her actions. By adopting these principles and habits, you can all unlock your full potential and accomplish great things within the same 24 hours that you all have each day. The profound desire within each of you is not merely a wish but a determination to transform your dreams into reality, to create choices that lead to a life of significance. You are driven by the burning desire to leave a legacy, a legacy that echoes through the annals of time.

You call you entrepreneurs – pioneers of progress, catalyst for change. You are the ones who, armed with the right mindset and positioned in the optimal environment, take decisive actions, and embrace balanced risks. It is through your courage and resilience that jobs are created, economies flourish, and communities prosper. let me remind you that you are not just entrepreneurs; you are the architects of dreams, the builders of legacies, and the driving force behind meaningful lives for all those you touch. Your journey is not just about personal success; it's about creating a ripple effect of prosperity that extends far beyond your immediate circle.

Conclusion & Recap

Together, let us continue to dream, to innovate, and to build a future that not only fulfils your personal aspirations but leaves an indelible mark on the tapestry of humanity with a gratitude.

As I open the doors to "Visions to Victory" with this chapter, I'm not just inviting you into my world; I'm ushering you into a realm of collective wisdom, a treasury of insights amassed from the luminaries who have illuminated my entrepreneurial path. This book is not just about my journey; it's a shared odyssey, a tapestry woven with threads of experiences, teachings, and invaluable lessons from mentors, business associates, and fellow entrepreneurs. "Visions to Victory" will act as a comprehensive guidebook that addresses the challenges of clarifying goals, staying motivated, implementing strategies effectively, navigating setbacks, and celebrating achievements. By providing clarity, motivation, practical tools, and resilience-building strategies, it will empower you to transform your dreams into concrete achievements and help you realise your full potential.

So, as you embark on this collective journey of entrepreneurship, let us be inspired by the profound impact you can make. Let us be motivated by the lives you can transform, the jobs you can create, and the economies you can build. However, one of the best ways to turn your visions into victory is by being aware of common misconceptions and avoided them in your journey as much as possible.

Let's explore these misconceptions before delving deeper into the concept of Visions to Victory.

Chapter 1.2

Debunking the Common Misconception

"Remember the biggest battles are fought in our own minds. These internal struggles such as fear of failure, the pursuit of perfection or any such mental blocks can be more challenging than any external obstacles we face."

Embarking on the journey of entrepreneurship is an exhilarating experience filled with promise and potential. However, it's also rife with misconceptions that can derail even the most well-intentioned entrepreneurs. While many people struggle due to a lack of knowledge, skills, and experience, a large majority remain stuck because of their own false beliefs. These misconceptions can create mental barriers that prevent individuals from reaching their full potential. Through my interactions with 2,000 to 3,000 businesses annually and about 150 to 200 businesses each month, I've observed firsthand how pervasive and damaging these false beliefs can be. Entrepreneurs often sabotage their own success by clinging to outdated ideas or unrealistic expectations.

Remember the biggest battles are fought in your own minds. These internal struggles can be more challenging than any external obstacles you face. The fear of failure, the pursuit of perfection, and the belief that success should be immediate are just a few examples of the mental roadblocks that can hinder progress. These misconceptions not only affect decision-making but also impact motivation and confidence.

My goal is to make building businesses and bring the personal and professional success as straightforward and habitual for you as brushing your teeth. To achieve this, you need to identify and address the top misconceptions that hold you back. By shedding light on these false beliefs and providing practical strategies to overcome them, I aim to empower you to take decisive action, embrace learning and growth, and ultimately achieve sustainable success in your journey. Understanding and changing these misconceptions will help you navigate the complexities of business and personal success with clarity and confidence, transforming challenges into opportunities for innovation and growth.

Let me share my learnings to uncover and debunk the top thirty-seven common misconceptions that entrepreneurs often encounter, shedding light on the realities of starting and growing a successful business. You will explore these in detail in the following volume of this series. You might wonder why you chose the number 37 and not more or fewer.

Here's my reason: I strongly believe that, in numerology, the number 37 holds significant importance and symbolism. It combines the energies and vibrations of the numbers 3 and 7, as well as the influences of the number 1 (since 3 + 7 = 10, and 1 + 0 = 1). The number 37 in numerology symbolises creativity, introspection, new beginnings, and personal growth. It blends the energies of expression, spirituality, and leadership, making it a powerful number for those who resonate with its vibrations.

If you need to understand my thoughts on numerology, feel free to contact me using the various resources provided in this book. I will explain my interest in numerology and its power in another book if there is high demand. For now, let's return to the common misconceptions and examine them briefly here.

Misconception 1: Overnight Success Syndrome

One of the most pervasive misconceptions among the entrepreneurs is the belief in overnight success. Many envision their businesses skyrocketing to fame and fortune in record time, without fully grasping the time, effort, and perseverance required to build a sustainable enterprise. The truth is that success is rarely instantaneous; it's the result of consistent effort, strategic planning, and resilience in the face of challenges.

Misconception 2: Risk-Free Ventures

Another prevalent misconception is the idea that entrepreneurship is without risk or that failure can be completely avoided. While it's natural to seek security and certainty, entrepreneurship inherently involves risk-taking and uncertainty. Successful entrepreneurs understand that failure is not only inevitable but also a valuable learning opportunity that can pave the way for future success.

Misconception 3: Pursuit of Perfection

Entrepreneurs often fall into the trap of striving for perfection before launching their products or services. They believe that everything must be flawless from the outset, fearing that any imperfection will doom their venture to failure. However, the reality is that perfection is elusive, and waiting for it can delay progress indefinitely. Instead, embracing iteration and improvement based on customer feedback is key to success in entrepreneurship.

Misconception 4: Lone Wolf Mentality

Many entrepreneurs mistakenly believe that they have to go it alone, tackling every aspect of their business single-handedly. However, successful entrepreneurship is rarely a solo endeavour. Seeking support from mentors, partners, and employees can provide invaluable guidance, expertise, and resources to help navigate the challenges of building a business.

Misconception 5: Immediate Profitability

Entrepreneurs often expect to turn a significant profit right from the start, only to be disappointed when reality doesn't meet their expectations. Building a profitable business takes time, patience, and investment. It's important to recognise that early losses and setbacks are a natural part of the entrepreneurial journey and to focus on long-term sustainability rather than short-term gains.

Misconception 6: Underestimating Competition

Underestimating the competitive landscape is a common pitfall for entrepreneurs. They may believe that their idea is unique and that they have no direct competitors, only to discover later that there are numerous alternatives already available in the market. Thorough market research and a clear understanding of the competitive landscape are essential for identifying opportunities and differentiating your business.

Misconception 7: Neglecting Marketing Efforts

Another misconception is the belief that a great product or service will sell itself without the need for marketing. However, no matter how innovative or high-quality your offering may be, it's unlikely to gain traction without effective marketing and promotion. Investing time and resources in marketing efforts to reach and engage your target audience is essential for driving business growth and success.

Misconception 8: The Brand Awareness Blind Spot

Entrepreneurs sometimes underestimate the importance of creating awareness for their brand, assuming that their product or service will naturally gain attention. This misconception stems from a belief that word-of-mouth or existing connections will suffice for brand recognition. However, in a competitive marketplace, proactive efforts to raise brand awareness are essential for attracting customers and differentiating from competitors. Neglecting brand awareness can result in limited visibility, missed opportunities for engagement, and slower growth. By prioritising strategies such as marketing campaigns, social media presence, and networking, entrepreneurs can enhance brand recognition and establish a strong market presence.

Misconception 9: Networking is a Waste of Time

Some entrepreneurs mistakenly believe that networking is a waste of time and that they can grow their business without making any networking efforts. They may underestimate the power of building professional relationships, connecting with industry peers, and leveraging networks for opportunities, support, and referrals. However, networking plays a crucial role in expanding business connections, accessing resources, and staying informed about industry trends and opportunities. Ignoring networking opportunities can limit growth potential and hinder long-term success in entrepreneurship.

Misconception 10: Your Brand does not need Awareness

Another misconception is the belief that there's no need to invest in awareness campaigns because people will naturally become aware of the business through word-of-mouth or existing connections. While organic exposure can certainly contribute to awareness, relying solely on this approach overlooks the importance of strategic marketing and communication efforts. Proactive awareness campaigns can help businesses reach new audiences, establish credibility, and differentiate themselves in competitive markets, ultimately driving growth and success.

Misconception 11: Your Products will gain automatic exposure

some entrepreneurs assumes that their product or service or brand will gain exposure on its own without any deliberate efforts to promote their brand. They may underestimate the value of brand visibility in attracting customers, building trust, and staying top-of-mind among target audiences. Investing in brand exposure through marketing channels such as advertising, social media, and public relations is essential for increasing brand recognition, driving customer engagement, and fostering brand loyalty over time. Ignoring brand exposure efforts can result in missed opportunities to connect with potential customers and establish a strong market presence.

Misconception 12: Ignoring Customer Feedback

Entrepreneurs may mistakenly believe that they know what's best for their customers without actively listening to their feedback. However, understanding and responding to customer needs and preferences is crucial for building a successful business. Incorporating customer feedback into product development, marketing strategies, and overall business decisions is essential for attracting and retaining customers and driving long-term success.

Misconception 13: The Legal & Compliance Oversight Fallacy

Entrepreneurs often overlook the importance of addressing legal and compliance matters in their business operations. This misconception stems from a focus on immediate tasks and objectives, neglecting the potential risks and consequences of non-compliance. However, adherence to legal regulations and standards is essential for protecting the business, mitigating liabilities, and maintaining trust with stakeholders. Ignoring legal and compliance matters can lead to legal disputes, financial penalties, and reputational damage. By prioritising legal compliance, entrepreneurs can ensure the long-term sustainability and success of their ventures, fostering a culture of accountability and integrity within their organisations.

Misconception 14: The Solo Success Myth

Entrepreneurs often underestimate the value of forming partnerships and collaborating with others in their industry. This misconception arises from a desire to maintain full control and ownership of their ventures, neglecting the potential benefits of collaboration. However, partnerships can provide access to new markets, resources, and expertise, accelerating business growth. Neglecting collaboration efforts can result in missed opportunities for innovation, expansion, and mutual support. By embracing partnerships and fostering collaborative relationships, entrepreneurs can leverage collective strengths, mitigate risks, and achieve shared goals more effectively in today's interconnected business landscape.

Misconception 15: The Human Capital Blind Spot

Entrepreneurs often overlook the importance of understanding the strengths and weaknesses of their team members. This misconception stems from a focus on tasks and objectives, neglecting the human element of business. However, recognising and leveraging individual strengths fosters collaboration, innovation, and employee engagement. Neglecting to understand people's capabilities can lead to misalignment, conflicts, and suboptimal performance. By investing in employee development, fostering open communication, and empowering team members, entrepreneurs can create a positive work culture and maximise their team's potential. Embracing the people element leads to stronger teams, happier employees, and ultimately, business success.

Misconception 16: The Process Efficiency Oversight

Entrepreneurs often fail to prioritise the development and implementation of efficient processes within their ventures. This misconception stems from a focus on immediate tasks and outcomes, neglecting the long-term benefits of streamlined operations. However, well-defined processes increase productivity, reduce errors, and enhance scalability. Neglecting process-driven mechanisms can lead to inefficiencies, bottlenecks, and missed growth opportunities. By investing time and resources into optimising workflows and standardising procedures, entrepreneurs can improve organisational effectiveness and adaptability. Embracing process-driven approaches empowers businesses to achieve greater efficiency, innovation, and success in an increasingly competitive landscape.

Misconception 17: The Purpose Blind Spot

Entrepreneurs often overlook the importance of aligning their ventures with a clear sense of purpose and mission. This misconception stems from a focus solely on profit generation, neglecting the broader impact and significance of their business endeavours. However, purpose-driven ventures are more likely to attract customers, employees, and investors who share similar values and beliefs. Neglecting purpose-driven efforts can result in a lack of direction, employee disengagement, and missed opportunities for social impact. By prioritising purpose and integrating it into their business strategies, entrepreneurs can create meaningful change while achieving sustainable growth and success in the marketplace.

Misconception 18: The Website Aesthetic Oversight

Entrepreneurs often underestimate the significance of having a visually appealing website and a memorable web domain. This misconception arises from a focus on other aspects of the business, such as product development or marketing, while neglecting the online presence. However, a well-designed website and a catchy web domain are crucial for creating a positive first impression, establishing credibility, and facilitating user engagement. Neglecting these elements can result in lost opportunities for attracting and retaining customers. By prioritising the aesthetics and usability of their website, entrepreneurs can enhance brand perception and drive business growth effectively.

Misconception 19: The Silent Marketing Success Strategy

Entrepreneurs often neglect marketing efforts, believing that a great product or service will sell itself. This misconception overlooks the importance of raising awareness, reaching target audiences, and driving customer engagement. Effective marketing is essential for building brand recognition, attracting customers, and fostering long-term relationships. Ignoring marketing can result in limited visibility, missed opportunities, and slower growth. By investing time and resources into strategic marketing efforts, entrepreneurs can amplify their brand presence, differentiate from competitors, and ultimately drive business success. Recognising the value of marketing as a core business function is key to sustainable growth and profitability.

Misconception 20: The Communication Void

Entrepreneurs often overlook the importance of clear and consistent messaging in their marketing campaigns. This misconception leads to vague or ineffective communication with their target audience, resulting in reduced engagement and missed opportunities for conversion. Crafting compelling campaign messages that resonate with customers' needs and desires is essential for capturing attention, building interest, and driving action. Neglecting messaging efforts can dilute the impact of marketing initiatives and hinder the achievement of business objectives. By prioritising strategic messaging and tailoring content to address customer pain points, entrepreneurs can enhance campaign effectiveness and maximise return on investment.

Misconception 21: The Advertising Blind Spot

Entrepreneurs often underestimate the importance of advertising and awareness campaigns in promoting their businesses. This misconception leads them to allocate limited resources or ignore marketing channels altogether, assuming that organic growth will suffice. However, effective advertising increases brand visibility, attracts new customers, and reinforces brand messaging. Neglecting these efforts limits market reach, stifles growth opportunities, and hampers competitiveness. By investing in strategic advertising initiatives across various channels, entrepreneurs can elevate brand awareness, drive customer engagement, and ultimately accelerate business growth. Recognising the value of proactive advertising is essential for establishing a strong market presence and sustaining long-term success.

Misconception 22: The Sales Promotion Oversight

Entrepreneurs often overlook the importance of implementing sales promotion strategies to drive customer acquisition and boost revenue. This misconception stems from the belief that a great product or service will naturally attract buyers without the need for additional incentives. However, effective sales promotions can incentivise purchases, encourage repeat business, and differentiate the brand from competitors. Neglecting sales promotion efforts deprives businesses of valuable opportunities to stimulate demand, increase sales volume, and maximise profitability. By strategically leveraging promotions such as discounts, special offers, and loyalty programmes, entrepreneurs can enhance customer engagement and fuel business growth.

Misconception 23: The Strategy Vacuum

Entrepreneurs often fail to recognise the significance of developing and implementing comprehensive marketing strategies for their businesses. This misconception leads to haphazard or sporadic marketing efforts, lacking cohesion and direction. Effective marketing strategies align with business objectives, target audience preferences, and market trends to maximise impact and ROI. Neglecting to formulate and execute strategic marketing plans can result in wasted resources, missed opportunities, and reduced competitiveness. By prioritising strategic marketing initiatives that encompass branding, customer acquisition, engagement, and retention, entrepreneurs can position their businesses for sustained growth and success in the dynamic marketplace.

Misconception 24: The Cash Flow Blind Spot

Entrepreneurs often overlook the critical importance of managing cash flow effectively in their businesses. This misconception stems from a focus on generating revenue and profits without considering the timing of cash inflows and outflows. Neglecting cash flow management can lead to financial instability, missed opportunities, and even business failure. Cash flow is the lifeblood of any business, ensuring the ability to cover expenses, invest in growth, and weather economic downturns. By prioritising cash flow management, entrepreneurs can maintain financial health, make informed decisions, and sustain long-term success in their ventures.

Misconception 25: The Financial Negligence Fallacy

Entrepreneurs often underestimate the financial requirements of starting and sustaining a business. This misconception stems from a lack of thorough financial planning and understanding of the costs involved. Neglecting financial needs can lead to cash shortages, inability to cover expenses, and reliance on high-interest loans or emergency funding. Adequate financial planning is essential for securing startup capital, managing ongoing expenses, and achieving profitability. By recognising and addressing financial needs early on, entrepreneurs can mitigate risks, improve financial stability, and position their businesses for long-term success and growth in the competitive marketplace.

Misconception 26: The Social Silence Fallacy

Entrepreneurs often underestimate the importance of building a strong presence on social media platforms for their brands. This misconception arises from a lack of understanding of the power of social media in shaping brand perception and engaging with customers. Neglecting social brand building can result in missed opportunities to connect with target audiences, build brand loyalty, and drive sales. Social media platforms offer a cost-effective way to reach a large audience, share content, and foster meaningful relationships with customers. By prioritising social brand building efforts, entrepreneurs can enhance brand visibility, credibility, and ultimately, business success.

Misconception 27: The Website Visitor Void Oversight

Entrepreneurs often overlook the significance of driving traffic to their websites as a critical component of their online presence. This misconception stems from a focus solely on website design and content, neglecting the importance of attracting visitors. However, without consistent traffic, a website may fail to fulfil its purpose of generating leads, converting customers, or disseminating information effectively. Neglecting website traffic can result in missed opportunities for engagement, conversion, and growth. By prioritising strategies to increase website traffic through SEO, content marketing, social media, and advertising, entrepreneurs can maximise the impact of their online presence and achieve their business objectives.

Misconception 28: The Virtual Storefront Oversight

Entrepreneurs often fail to recognise their website's pivotal role as the digital storefront for their business. This misconception arises from a focus on physical locations or offline marketing efforts, overlooking the significance of the online presence. However, the website serves as the primary point of contact for potential customers, influencing their perception and purchasing decisions. Neglecting the website as a shop window deprives businesses of opportunities to attract, engage, and convert online visitors into customers. By optimising the website for user experience, search visibility, and conversion, entrepreneurs can effectively drive traffic and sales both online and offline.

Misconception 29: The Search Engine Blind Spot

Entrepreneurs often underestimate the importance of search engine optimisation (SEO) in driving organic traffic to their websites. This misconception stems from a lack of understanding of how SEO works and its impact on online visibility. Neglecting SEO efforts can result in poor search rankings, reduced website traffic, and missed opportunities for customer acquisition. SEO is essential for improving website visibility, attracting qualified leads, and staying competitive in the online marketplace. By prioritising SEO strategies such as keyword research, content optimisation, and link building, entrepreneurs can enhance their online presence and achieve sustainable growth for their businesses.

Misconception 30: The Directory Disregard Fallacy

Entrepreneurs often overlook the importance of listing their businesses in online directories. This misconception arises from a focus on other marketing channels or a lack of awareness of the potential benefits. Neglecting directory listings can result in missed opportunities for improving online visibility, attracting local customers, and enhancing search engine rankings. Directories serve as valuable platforms for potential customers to discover businesses and access key information such as contact details, location, and services offered. By prioritising directory listings on platforms like Google My Business, Yelp, and industry-specific directories, entrepreneurs can expand their reach and attract more customers to their businesses.

Misconception 31: The Print Media Oversight

Entrepreneurs often underestimate the value of magazine advertising in their marketing strategies. This misconception arises from a perception that print media is outdated or ineffective compared to digital channels. However, magazines still hold significant influence and reach among targeted audiences, offering a platform for showcasing products or services to engaged readers. Neglecting magazine advertising can result in missed opportunities to reach niche markets, build brand awareness, and drive customer engagement. By incorporating magazine advertising into their marketing mix, entrepreneurs can diversify their reach and effectively connect with potential customers who prefer consuming content in print format.

Misconception 32: The Authority Blind Spot

Entrepreneurs often overlook the importance of establishing themselves as industry leaders through thought leadership marketing. This misconception stems from a focus on traditional marketing tactics rather than building authority and credibility within their niche. Neglecting leadership marketing efforts can result in missed opportunities to differentiate from competitors, attract high-value clients, and command higher prices for products or services. Thought leadership marketing involves sharing valuable insights, expertise, and perspectives through various channels like blogging, speaking engagements, and industry publications. By positioning themselves as leaders in their field, entrepreneurs can gain trust, visibility, and influence, driving business growth and success.

Misconception 33: Fixed Mindset Misconception

Some people believe that their talents and capabilities are unchangeable and cannot be developed, thinking that what they know or believe is the only truth. However, change is a natural law, and you all lack the necessary skills and knowledge if you don't upgrade ourselves or remain open to changes and opportunities. This is the essence of a growth mindset. The essence of a fixed mindset, on the other hand, is the fear of failure and the avoidance of challenges to protect self-worth. Individuals with this mindset might avoid risks, shun feedback, and feel threatened by others' success, believing that effort is futile. This misconception overlooks the fact that a fixed mindset is more about fear and insecurity than inherent limitations, hindering growth and innovation. By understanding this, entrepreneurs and individuals can better address and shift their mindset towards growth, embracing challenges, learning from setbacks, and continuously developing their skills and abilities.

Misconception 34: The Service Oversight Fallacy

Entrepreneurs often underestimate the importance of prioritising exceptional customer service in their businesses. This misconception arises from a focus on product development or sales, neglecting the critical role that satisfied customers play in driving success. Neglecting customer service efforts can lead to poor customer experiences, negative reviews, and loss of loyalty. However, investing in responsive, personalised customer service can foster long-term relationships, encourage repeat business, and generate positive word-of-mouth referrals. By recognising the value of outstanding customer service and implementing strategies to exceed customer expectations, entrepreneurs can enhance brand reputation and drive sustainable growth.

Misconception 35: The Brand Identity Oversight

Entrepreneurs often overlook the importance of branding and the strategic selection of brand colour palettes. This misconception stems from a focus on other aspects of the business, such as product development or marketing campaigns. However, branding plays a crucial role in shaping brand perception, fostering recognition, and establishing emotional connections with customers. Neglecting branding efforts, including colour palette selection, can result in inconsistent brand identity, lack of differentiation, and diminished brand impact. By prioritising branding and carefully choosing brand colours that resonate with their target audience, entrepreneurs can strengthen brand identity and effectively communicate their values and messaging.

Misconception 36: The Content Neglect Fallacy

Entrepreneurs often underestimate the significance of content marketing in their overall marketing strategy. This misconception arises from a focus on more traditional advertising methods or a lack of understanding of the value of content. Neglecting content marketing efforts can result in missed opportunities to engage with audiences, build brand authority, and drive conversions. Content marketing involves creating and distributing valuable, relevant content to attract and retain a clearly defined audience. By prioritising content marketing initiatives such as blogs, videos, and social media posts, entrepreneurs can establish themselves as industry leaders and nurture relationships with potential customers over time.

Misconception 37: The Planless Pitfall

Finally, entrepreneurs often fail to recognise the importance of thorough business planning in achieving their goals. This misconception stems from a belief that they can navigate the entrepreneurial journey without a formal plan, relying instead on intuition or passion. Neglecting business planning can lead to lack of direction, poor decision-making, and increased risk of failure. Effective business planning involves setting clear objectives, identifying target markets, analysing competitors, and outlining strategies for growth and sustainability. By prioritising business planning efforts, entrepreneurs can mitigate risks, capitalise on opportunities, and lay a solid foundation for long-term success.

Conclusion & Recap

In the world of entrepreneurship, misconceptions abound, often leading entrepreneurs astray and hindering their chances of success. By debunking common misconceptions and embracing the realities of entrepreneurship, aspiring entrepreneurs can better navigate the challenges and uncertainties of building a business. By acknowledging the importance of resilience, adaptability, and continuous learning, they can position themselves for success and build sustainable businesses that thrive in the long term. Entrepreneurship is a journey fraught with challenges and uncertainties, yet illuminated by opportunities for growth and innovation. By dispelling common misconceptions and embracing the realities of entrepreneurship, aspiring entrepreneurs can navigate the entrepreneurial landscape with clarity, resilience, and foresight. Embracing collaboration, adaptability, and customer-centricity, they pave the way for sustainable business success and enduring impact in the dynamic world of entrepreneurship.

In your forthcoming volume, "Visions to Victory Volume 2," you'll take a closer look at common misconceptions surrounding various aspects of entrepreneurship, from the nature of passion to the importance of resilience. By dissecting these misconceptions and providing clarity on their validity, you aim to equip readers with the knowledge and understanding needed to navigate their entrepreneurial endeavours more effectively. These misconceptions will be thoroughly examined, with practical strategies, case studies, and expert insights provided to help readers overcome these obstacles and achieve their goals. As you embark on this journey of exploration and discovery, I invite you to join us in uncovering the truths behind these misconceptions and charting a course towards success in entrepreneurship. Together, let's challenge the status quo, embrace new perspectives, and unlock your full potential as business leaders. As I am planning to pen down the next chapter to share my insights with you, I can't help but draw another parallel between the journey of running a business and navigating a game of chess. Hence let's kick off your journey fist in this volume by drawing a parallel between a chessboard and the process of building a successful business.

Chapter 1.2

Mastering the Business Chessboard

"If finance is the king, then who is the queen of the business chessboard? It's sales. Finance and sales together bring and balance the capital needed for business success."

SANTOSH KUMAR

Like the game of chess, building a business is a game where every move holds the potential to shape the course of your journey, where every decision can change the outcome of the game.

Whether it's world of chess or the world of business, it is essential to build the foundation and set the stage. It is especially important to have a robust plan, the right strategies, tactics, resources, and a formula to mitigate risk, along with an overarching blueprint for success at every stage of the game at your disposal. Lily's entrepreneurial journey mirrors the strategic thinking and calculated decision-making required in the game.

Similar to how a chess player meticulously plans their moves, you must carefully evaluate the risks and opportunities before making any decisions. Each move made is critical, and it's essential to understand that every decision you take has consequences. By doing so, you can ensure that each step you take is well-calculated and aligned with your overall objectives. Each decision Lily made in her business ventures had significant consequences for her success.

Lily's story serves as an example of navigating the complexities of entrepreneurship, much like the strategic manoeuvres on a chessboard. Both narratives emphasise the importance of laying a solid foundation, evaluating risks, and making well-calculated moves to achieve long-term objectives.

The Foundation

Just as a chess player lays down a solid foundation for their game, for any success, you must establish strong foundations for your business. Lily meticulously laid the groundwork for her entrepreneurial endeavours in the story in first chapter of the section one of this book.

This foundation involves travelling the journey of continuous learning, gathering knowledge, building your skills, identifying your strengths and weaknesses, understanding market trends, and assessing your competition. It's essential finding your guiding north star – the beacon that illuminates your path and keeps you focused on your goals and helps you find your dot and your purpose, much like Lily's unwavering commitment to her vision of creating sustainable, eco-friendly products. This guiding star embodies the vision and mission of your company, serving as a constant reminder of why you embarked on this journey in the first place. It provides you with direction and purpose, helping you stay on course even when faced with challenges and uncertainties, just as Lily did.

Once you have a solid understanding of these factors, you can then build upon them strategically, leveraging your strengths and addressing any weaknesses.

Let me allow you to recall and appreciate that preparation is your greatest ally when navigating the complexities of the business world. Therefore, just as Lily's story exemplifies the importance of preparation and laying a solid foundation, remember that your journey in the business world will be strengthened by thorough planning and strategic foresight.

The Opening

Let me welcome you In the world of business chess, where every move counts, strategic finesse reigns supreme. Just like in the game of chess, the opening phase sets the stage for triumphs and challenges alike. It's a phase where you lay the groundwork for success, navigating the complexities of the business landscape with determination and vision.

In this captivating game, controlling the centre is paramount. Just as in chess, where dominance over central squares dictates the flow of the game, in business, building the foundations, having the basic building blocks in place, seizing control of pivotal markets and resources positions us for victory.

Efficient development of your assets and talents ensures that you move forward with purpose and precision, maximising your potential for growth and innovation.

But what truly marks your ascent to greatness is the achievement of castling and the connection of the rooks. Picture this: your businesses fortified, your strategies aligned, and your teams united in purpose. Castling represents not just a defensive manoeuvre, but a bold declaration of your readiness to take on the challenges ahead. And when your rooks are connected, you unlock the power of synergy, leveraging your collective strengths to overcome obstacles and forge new paths to success.

So, my fellow strategists and visionaries, let us embark on this journey together, armed with courage, resilience, and an unwavering commitment to excellence. Let us master the business chessboard with flair and finesse, inspiring others to join us on your quest for greatness.

The time is now. The game is on. Let's make your moves and seize the victory that awaits us in the middle game.

The Middle Game

The middle game is all about fighting the small battles of the game to win the final battle. Understanding that as an entrepreneur you have or you will face adversaries in the form of the market, competitors, and the industry landscape, much like players on a chessboard. Understanding that the game is not about winning every battle but winning the overall war and help reach your destination or achieve your goals. It's also crucial to recognise that each decision you make carries a weight.

Imagine yourself as the chess master, surveying the board before making your next move. Imagine Lily strategising her next move as the chess master, and understanding her starting position and how she developed strategies to move forward confidently. By having a clear understanding of your starting position, you can develop strategies and tactics to move forward with confidence. In business, this means taking the time to assess your current situation, understand your goals, and identify potential challenges and opportunities. Just as a skilled chess player carefully plans their moves ahead of time, entrepreneurs must equip themselves with a blueprint for success.

This blueprint serves as a roadmap, guiding you through the twists and turns of the entrepreneurial journey. Your blueprint for success should outline the steps needed to achieve your objectives. This includes identifying your target market, understanding your competition, and defining your unique value proposition. This involves getting your "MAPP" right and ensuring that the "Seven Pillars of Success" are aligned. It means working with each and every element of "The COGS of Success" important for your business success and implementing the right strategies and tactics for the success of the overall game. Just like a chess player anticipates their opponent's moves, entrepreneurs must anticipate market trends and customer needs to stay ahead of the game.

Build on top of your foundation and building blocks and make sure you are not gambling but taking calculated risks and giving your hundred percent to win every battle during this war. Does this mean that you will win every battle on your chessboard? Does it mean that you will have all the small wins and will have no losses? The answer is NO; it's never about winning all the battles but winning the overall game.

The middle game is the strategic and tactical moves of your overall game plan and provides you with the most effective way to take you towards victory. By taking a strategic approach and continuously refining your tactics, Like Lily anticipated market trends, you can increase your chances of success in the competitive landscape of business. It's all about staying one step ahead of your competitors, anticipating their moves, and positioning yourself for victory. With the right strategies and resources in place, you can outmanoeuvre your competitors and achieve your business goals with confidence.

The End Game for Winning the War

In the game of business, having the right strategies, tactics, and resources is crucial. Just as a chess player carefully considers their moves, you must assess the risks and opportunities before making decisions.

Furthermore, don't underestimate the value of getting the inspirations from the journey of your role model and following the roadmaps of seeking guidance from your mentors and business coaches when needed. These experienced individuals have traversed similar paths before you and can offer invaluable insights and perspectives. They can share their wisdom, provide advice, and offer support, helping you navigate unfamiliar territories with confidence. By learning from their experiences and leveraging their knowledge, you can avoid common pitfalls and make more informed decisions on your entrepreneurial journey.

At this stage, you must incorporate all the tools and resources available at your disposal to bring your king out from the safe zone and make it the most active player on the chessboard. You must employ all your pawns for maximum exposure and ensure they reach their full potential, bringing more and more value towards the overall purpose of winning the war.

In Business, Employ your blueprint, including your strategies and tactics for overcoming obstacles and mitigating risks along the way to win the war at this stage. Just as a chess player must navigate around their opponent's pieces and help the pawns progress towards the end line under the safety of the most important piece, the King, entrepreneurs must navigate around challenges using their financial and non-financial resources towards victory to overcome challenges and roadblocks such as economic downturns, changing consumer preferences, and regulatory changes.

Conclusion & Recap

By having contingency plans in place, you can adapt to changing circumstances and keep moving forward towards your goals. Ultimately, success in business, like in chess, requires foresight, adaptability, and calculated risk-taking. It requires the planning and preparation to mitigate the known and unknown risks and factors in the end game. By embracing these principles and arming themselves with the necessary tools, entrepreneurs can navigate the complexities of the business landscape and emerge victorious.

So, are you ready to make your move and conquer the world of business? Remember, preparation is about setting yourself up for success. By laying strong foundations and building upon them strategically, you can increase your chances of success and out manoeuvre your competitors. By having a well-thought-out plan in place, you can approach your business endeavours with confidence and clarity. So, Take the time to develop your blueprint for success and equip yourself with the strategies and tactics needed to navigate the game of business effectively.

Chapter 1.3

Become Unstoppable to Turn your dreams into Reality

My journey as a businessperson has been like a wild ride, full of ups and downs, challenges, and successes. Like many budding entrepreneurs, my journey started with a burst of inspiration. I was captivated by tales of bold leaders who dared to take on challenges and pursue their dreams relentlessly. Their determination, resilience, and strong belief in their vision lit a fire inside me, urging me to start my own entrepreneurial adventure.

From the early days of dreaming big to the exciting moments of reaching milestones, every step of this journey has shaped me into the person I am today. It's this journey, packed with lessons and insights, which motivated me to become the author of "Visions to Victory."

The Journey

At the beginning, entrepreneurship felt like an uphill struggle. I encountered numerous setbacks and hurdles, each one testing my determination and pushing me to my limits. However, it was during these tough times that I discovered the true power of resilience and determination. Instead of giving up, I saw each obstacle as a chance to learn and grow, fuelling my determination to succeed.

With every venture, I gained valuable experience and insights that shaped my approach to business. From launching startups to investing in innovative projects, I pursued every opportunity with passion and dedication. Along the way, I learned the importance of being adaptable, innovative, and strategic, skills that proved vital on my journey to success.

While the path to success wasn't always smooth, every victory and setback played a crucial role in shaping my entrepreneurial journey. From celebrating successful business launches to navigating through uncertain times, each experience taught me valuable lessons that I carry with me today. Through it all, I held firm in my belief that with vision, perseverance, growth mindset and hard work, anything is possible.

Starting my first venture in 1992 with my father, followed by launching my first independent venture in 2007, I faced significant challenges. I failed in five ventures within the first five years, losing a quarter of a million pounds. However, I managed to develop a process-driven venture serving customers in seven countries and recovered all my losses, converting my first successful venture into a million-pound business in five years from 2007 till 2012.

I have travelled a path of continuous learning and established forty-five brands so far. I was invited to become part of Forbes in October 2020 and joined the Forbes Business Council in April 2021, sharing a tremendous journey. Currently, I am on the path of continuous learning to transform lives and help other business owners while trying to learn at least one thing from every interaction and return one of my learnings for their benefit.

It was during this entrepreneurial journey that the idea for "Visions to Victory" took root. Inspired by my own experiences and the stories of fellow entrepreneurs, I feel compelled to share the lessons and insights I've learned along the way. I have a strong burning desire to make a difference in other people's lives. I wish to share this knowledge, wisdom, and this intellectual wealth for a purpose bigger than me and for the betterment of humanity.

The Purpose

I want to serve the wider community, add value and contribute meaningfully. I do not wish for the knowledge, skills, experience, and wisdom I've have gathered throughout my life, gained from encounters with others, as well as from the arts and sciences of continual learning, to be lost with me.

Instead, I desire to embark on the journey of continuous learning and to share the knowledge and wisdom, creating a ripple effect around me and leaving behind a legacy for the betterment of humanity, enduring beyond my own existence.

Writing this book is one way to kick off my unstoppable journey. I am sure I am starting this journey alone, but I will be meeting a variety of people along the way, sharing my thoughts and beliefs, and inspiring others to join me in starting the journey of a thousand miles from this single step.

I wish, I hope, and I want to inspire others to pursue their dreams boldly, armed with the knowledge that success is achievable for those who dare to dream big and work tirelessly to achieve their goals.

Finding Your Dot – The True Purpose

"Finding your dot" refers to discovering your unique purpose or passion in life. In this context, the "dot" symbolises your distinct path or calling. Just as every point on a canvas contributes to the overall picture, each person's journey and contribution are valuable and significant in their own way.

Finding your dot involves introspection, self-discovery, and reflection on your values, strengths, and aspirations. It's about uncovering what truly matters to you and what you are passionate about pursuing. This process often requires exploring different interests, trying new experiences, and learning from successes and failures along the way.

Once you identify your dot, it becomes your guiding north star, directing your actions and decisions towards fulfilling your purpose. It provides clarity and direction in life, helping you prioritise your time and energy on activities that align with your values and goals. Finding your dot is not just about personal fulfilment; it's also about making a positive impact on the world around you. When you are aligned with your purpose, you are better equipped to contribute your unique talents and strengths to society, whether through your work, relationships, or community involvement.

Ultimately, finding your dot is about embracing who you are, embracing your passions, and living authentically in alignment with your purpose. By finding your dot, you can lead a more meaningful and fulfilling life while making a difference in the lives of others. Make sure your purpose is something your elders and parents can be proud of. Ensure that your younger ones or your kids are able to follow you as a role model once you have achieved this purpose. Consider how you can define and find a purpose that is bigger than yourself, one that can help not only help you to fulfill all your dreams and serve the people around you but also make a difference in the lives of others, add value, serve the community, and leave a lasting legacy that people will be unable to forget in the forthcoming generations.

Find a Purpose which is Bigger than you. Your purpose will help you define your vision. Your vision serves as a north star, aligning your team, partners, and every endeavour with a common purpose. It's not only about reaching a destination; it's about travelling a journey of success with the help of your vision as a guiding light and leaving a legacy. This can be better explained by looking at some key principles and philosophies that people follow in their personal and professional lives.

So, how do you find your dot, your true purpose, and transform it into a vision that inspires and motivates? Begin by thinking big, thinking bold. The mentors in my journey emphasised that articulating a vision isn't merely a task for the business plan; it's an exercise in envisioning a future that inspires and motivates. So, when you're defining your vision, think big, think bold, and let your vision be the north star that guides every decision, every action in your entrepreneurial journey.

Seven Key Characteristics to Become Unstoppable

To becoming unstoppable means, you have to develop the mindset, skills, and qualities that enable you to persist and succeed despite obstacles, challenges, and setbacks. As an unstoppable person you have to be resilient, adaptable, and determined, maintaining focus on your goals and continuously making progress no matter what difficulties arise. You must have a clear vision, a positive attitude, and take decisive actions, ensuring that nothing can permanently hinder your forward momentum. I want to share with you some insights from my journey. These seven key characteristics have helped me navigate the path to success and can help you too.

First, resilience. Life is full of setbacks, but it's how you bounce back those matters. Resilience is about seeing obstacles as opportunities for growth. Each challenge is a chance to learn and become stronger. Next is perseverance. Staying consistent and persistent in your efforts is crucial, even when things get tough. Perseverance keeps you committed to your goals, ensuring you continue to push forward despite difficulties.

Having a clear vision is also vital. Knowing exactly what you want to achieve gives you direction and motivation. Your vision acts as a guiding star, helping you stay focused even when the journey gets challenging. Adaptability is another important trait. Being able to adjust to new conditions, challenges, and opportunities allows you to navigate uncertainties and seize new opportunities effectively. Flexibility is key in a constantly changing world.

Then there's the winner mindset. Cultivate a positive, success-oriented mindset that focuses on possibilities rather than limitations. Embrace challenges and believe in your ability to achieve great things. The right attitude is equally important. Stay proactive and optimistic. A good attitude fosters confidence and determination, helping you stay motivated regardless of the circumstances.

Finally, take massive action. It's not enough to plan and strategies; you must also execute with intensity and commitment. Taking bold, decisive actions towards your goals ensures continuous progress. By developing at least these seven characteristics—resilience, perseverance, vision, adaptability, a winner mindset, the right attitude, and taking massive action—you can overcome obstacles, stay focused on your goals, and ultimately become unstoppable.

Conclusion & Recap

My journey as an entrepreneur has been filled with moments of success, resilience, and growth. Starting from modest beginnings in 1992 and then again in 2007, till date I have created forty-five brands and was invited by Forbes to join their journey in October 2000. I was honoured to become a member of the Forbes Business Council in April 2021 and eventually became the author of "Visions to Victory." Each step of this journey has strengthened my belief in the transformative power of vision and perseverance. I am continually learning; every day and every interaction is an opportunity for growth. I am absorbing knowledge to enhance my expertise and skills so that I can share this wisdom with a broader audience and fulfil my purpose. Currently, I can share insights on how to live a happy life, enjoy fulfillment, start a business, navigate failures (including losing a quarter of a million pounds), recover, and ultimately succeed. I can also guide on creating multiple brands, joining the Forbes Council, and inspiring others to think big and act boldly. I aspire to motivate and inspire millions of people to live better lives and have influence on others as a role model and mentor. Through my story, I hope to encourage others to embark on their entrepreneurial journey with courage and determination. With the right mindset and steadfast belief in your vision, you too can turn your dreams into reality using my flagship innovation, Venture Creation, and the "Visions to Victory" Model. In the next chapter, let's explore the concept of "Visions to Victory" together and uncover its secrets.

Chapter 1.4

Visions to Victory – The Concept

Both personal and entrepreneurship success are akin to setting sail on a boundless sea of possibilities. It's a journey fuelled by dreams, guided by vision, and culminating in victory. But what truly lies at the heart of this transformative odyssey? Let's uncover this essence of this success with the help of a cricket match!

Just as in cricket, success requires strategy, skill, and adaptability. The game unfolds with each player contributing uniquely to the team's success, much like how entrepreneurs bring their vision and determination to create something impactful.

Like a cricket match, entrepreneurship and success demands resilience in the face of challenges and the ability to seize opportunities swiftly. Furthermore, both arenas thrive on innovation and calculated risk-taking. Just as a cricket team strategises its plays to outmanoeuvre opponents, entrepreneurs innovate their business approaches to stay ahead in the market. Both contexts celebrate moments of brilliance and require continuous learning and refinement to achieve sustained success.

The essence of personal as well as professional success lies in the ability to navigate uncertainties with courage, harness opportunities with agility, and persistently pursue one's vision amidst changing tides. Like a well-played cricket match, both personal and entrepreneurship success are about embracing challenges, adapting strategies, and ultimately celebrating victories that come from dedication, foresight, and teamwork.

Victory in entrepreneurship, like winning a cricket match, is the culmination of meticulous planning, disciplined execution, and relentless perseverance. It's about achieving milestones, overcoming obstacles, and ultimately making an impactful difference in the market.

Visions to Victory, therefore, is not just about achieving success but about embracing the entire journey with courage and determination. It's about harnessing the power of vision, strategic execution, resilience, and learning from every experience—transforming dreams into tangible achievements in the vast sea of entrepreneurial possibilities.

Setting the Scene of Cricket match

As you may know, the cricket match is extremely healthy sporting contest played between two teams of eleven players each, typically on a circular or oval-shaped field called a cricket ground. One of the key objectives of each team of the game is to score more runs than the opposing team within a specified period with an overall goal of winning the game and creating a history for inspiration.

A cricket match can take various formats, including Test matches, One Day Internationals (ODIs), and Twenty20 (T20) matches, each with its own set of rules and regulations governing the duration, number of overs, and other aspects of gameplay. The format and duration of the match determine the strategies employed by the teams and the overall pace and intensity of the game.

The match is typically divided into innings, with each team taking turns to bat and bowl. During their batting innings, the team attempts to score as many runs as possible by hitting the ball with a bat and running between two sets of wickets, which are positioned at opposite ends of a 22-yard-long pitch.

Meanwhile, the bowling team tries to restrict the opposing team's scoring by delivering the ball towards the batsman in an attempt to dismiss them through various means, such as getting them out caught, bowled, or lbw (leg before wicket). The fielding team also aims to prevent runs from being scored by fielding the ball and returning it to the wicketkeeper or bowler.

As you step onto the cricket field, you are driven by dreams of victory, guided by a shared vision, and destined for triumph. But what truly lies at the heart of this thrilling game? Let's explore the captivating concept of "Visions to Victory" and unravel the essence of cricketing success.

The Essence of Venture Creation

Imagine harnessing the power of your dreams and ideas, moulding them into a thriving business that transcends expectations. This is precisely the essence of "Visions to Victory" – the art of transforming aspirations into reality. It's about taking that flicker of inspiration, nurturing it with passion and dedication, and steering it towards the shores of success. Embarking on the entrepreneurial journey is an exhilarating yet challenging endeavour.

From my personal experience as well as dealing with hundreds of businesspeople every month I have understood that the road from a brilliant idea to a thriving business is fraught with obstacles, uncertainties, and risks. To navigate this complex path, you need more than just creativity and passion; you require a robust framework, practical programmes, guiding principles, strategic insights, tactical actions, and supportive tools. This is where venture creation comes into play—a comprehensive approach and framework designed to transform innovative ideas into successful businesses.

At the heart of venture creation is a well-structured framework. This framework provides a clear roadmap, encompassing several key stages of development. You begin with Ideation, where creative ideas are generated and refined. Next is Validation, testing the feasibility of these ideas through market research and feedback. Then comes Planning, where you develop detailed business plans, financial projections, and strategic approaches. Launch follows, executing the business operations and introducing the product or service to the market. Finally, you enter the Growth phase, scaling the business, expanding market presence, and increasing profitability.

Each of these stages involves critical components such as designing a sustainable business model, conducting market analysis, efficiently allocating resources, and managing risks effectively. This structured approach ensures that entrepreneurs are well-prepared for each phase of their journey.

Supporting this framework are various structured programmes that equip entrepreneurs with essential knowledge and resources. Incubators and Accelerators provide mentorship, office space, and access to vital networks, along with structured milestones and goals. Workshops and Training cover fundamental topics like marketing, finance, operations, and leadership, offering hands-on experiences and practical exercises. Funding Programmes offer grants, loans, and investment opportunities, along with assistance in pitch preparation and investor relations. These programmes nurture entrepreneurial talent and provide the necessary support for business development and growth.

Guiding principles are the foundation of venture creation, ensuring that entrepreneurs remain focused and aligned with their goals. A Customer-Centric Approach prioritises customer needs and feedback in product development, ensuring a market-fit product and building strong customer relationships. The Lean Methodology emphasises iterative development and rapid prototyping, helping minimise waste and maximise value creation. Adaptability and Resilience are essential, as entrepreneurs must be prepared to pivot and adapt to changing market conditions while maintaining perseverance in the face of challenges.

Strategic planning is crucial for navigating the complexities of venture creation. Key strategies include deciding the optimal mode and timing for Market Entry to maximise impact, differentiating the venture from competitors and building a strong brand and unique value proposition for Competitive Positioning, and developing scalable processes and systems to expand market reach through strategic partnerships and acquisitions for Growth and Scaling. These strategies help entrepreneurs make informed decisions and strategically position their ventures for success.

Specific tactical actions are necessary to implement these strategies effectively. Leveraging Digital Marketing through social media, content marketing, and SEO helps reach target audiences and optimise efforts using data analytics. Employing Sales Techniques such as consultative selling and relationship building, along with implementing effective sales funnels and lead generation tactics, are critical. Streamlining operations through Operational Efficiency ensures quality control and customer satisfaction.

A variety of tools and templates support entrepreneurs in their venture creation journey. Business Plan Templates help create detailed business plans with sections for executive summary, market analysis, and financial projections. Financial Modelling Tools provide software and spreadsheets for forecasting revenues, expenses, and profitability. Project Management Software offers tools for tracking tasks, milestones, and deadlines, facilitating team communication and coordination. These resources streamline the business planning and execution process.

To ensure entrepreneurs have the necessary support, venture creation provides various mechanisms for guidance and support. Mentorship Programmes pair entrepreneurs with experienced mentors who offer personalised advice and industry insights. Networking Opportunities include events and platforms for connecting with other entrepreneurs, investors, and industry experts, building a supportive community. Advisory Boards are formed with experts in relevant fields to provide strategic direction and ongoing support. These mechanisms ensure entrepreneurs have access to the knowledge and networks needed for success.

Importantly, the venture creation framework is designed to be flexible and adaptable to the unique needs of each entrepreneur. Unlike rigid guidelines or strict models, it can be customised to fit different industries, business models, and stages of development, ensuring that every entrepreneur can find the right path to success.

In other words, venture creation is a holistic and comprehensive approach that integrates frameworks, programmes, principles, strategies, tactics, tools, and support mechanisms. By providing a structured yet flexible roadmap, venture creation enhances the entrepreneurial journey, making it simpler, more efficient, and more likely to lead to a successful and sustainable business. Entrepreneurs who embrace this multifaceted approach are better equipped to navigate the challenges of starting and growing a business, ultimately achieving their vision and goals.

In this series, and in your upcoming ones, I invite you to join me on an exhilarating journey through the world of entrepreneurship and the secrets of personal and professional success. Through insightful narratives, practical strategies, and real-life examples, this book will not only explore the venture creation framework and travel the journey of Visions to Victory but will also guide you from the inception of your vision to the triumphant moment of victory. The chapters serve as a beacon of light, illuminating the path forward with robust basics, fundamental principles, and strategic frameworks.

Together, you'll explore the building blocks of both entrepreneurship and personal success, uncover the strategies for sustainable growth, and map out a roadmap to navigate the challenges and triumphs of the success landscape throughout this series. But beyond mere instruction, the series is also a journey – a tapestry woven with stories of triumph, resilience, and innovation. Through the experiences of fellow entrepreneurs, you'll find inspiration, guidance, and the courage to pursue your own entrepreneurial dreams.

At its core, "Visions to Victory" is about more than just financial gains. It's a holistic approach to entrepreneurship for personal and professional success that encompasses personal fulfilment, societal impact, and leaving a lasting legacy for generations to come.

Picture yourself not only achieving financial success or solving your problems but also finding fulfilment in every aspect of your entrepreneurial journey.

Irony of Cricket Match Victory

Imagine harnessing the power of your passion for cricket, channelling it into a winning team that surpasses expectations. This is the essence of "Visions to Victory" – the art of turning aspirations into on-field reality. It's about nurturing that love for the game with dedication and skill, guiding it towards the pinnacle of success.

I am sure you will agree that the essence of any game including cricket match lies in the spirit of competition, camaraderie, and skillful gameplay displayed by the players. It is a test of physical and mental prowess, requiring strategic thinking, teamwork, and individual talent to succeed.

At its core, a cricket match is about more than just winning or losing; it is an opportunity for players to showcase their abilities, push their limits, and demonstrate sportsmanship. Whether played at the amateur or professional level, cricket fosters a sense of community and belonging among participants and spectators alike.

The essence of a cricket match also lies in its ability to bring people together from diverse backgrounds and cultures, uniting them in a shared passion for the sport. It serves as a platform for social interaction, cultural exchange, and mutual respect, transcending boundaries and fostering connections that extend beyond the boundaries of the playing field.

Ultimately, the essence of a cricket match is captured in the moments of exhilaration, disappointment, and triumph experienced by players and fans alike. It is a celebration of skill, athleticism, and the enduring spirit of competition that defines the sport of cricket.

Throughout this journey, I invite you to join us on an exhilarating expedition through the world of cricket. Through insightful strategies, tactical plans, and real-life examples, I'll share from the start of the match to the triumphant moment of victory to resonate with the concept of entrepreneurship.

Some chapters will serve as a beacon, illuminating the path with techniques, teamwork, and strategic manoeuvres of entrepreneurship using cricket as an example for explanation. Together, you'll explore the fundamentals of cricket, uncover strategies for success, and chart a course to navigate the challenges and triumphs of the game. This journey is a tapestry woven with stories of teamwork, perseverance, and sportsmanship. Through this experience, you'll find inspiration, guidance, and the courage to pursue victory in the field of entrepreneurship.

Victory in a Cricket Match

Victory in cricket transcends mere wins and losses; it embodies a spectrum of achievements and ideals that define the game. It is about team performance. It is the culmination of exceptional teamwork, where each player contributes their skills and determination to the collective success of the team. In the spirit of unity and collaboration, you witness the true power of cricket as players come together to achieve a common goal. It also encompasses individual achievements that showcase the talent and dedication of each player. From scoring centuries to taking crucial wickets and making spectacular catches, these moments of individual brilliance contribute to the overall success of the team.

Victory in cricket is achieved through strategic execution. It is the result of astute decision-making by captains and coaches, who devise tactical plans to outsmart the opposition. Through strategic manoeuvres and calculated risks, teams seize opportunities and overcome challenges to emerge victorious on the field.

However, victory in cricket goes beyond the scoreboard; it embodies the principles of sportsmanship and fair play. It is about upholding the integrity of the game, respecting opponents, and playing with honour and dignity. In the heat of competition, cricket teaches us the importance of grace in both victory and defeat. It extends to the fans and supporters who passionately follow the game. It is about engaging audiences, creating moments of magic that inspire and unite cricket enthusiasts worldwide. From breathtaking performances to nail-biting finishes, these moments of victory resonate far beyond the boundaries of the field.

In other words, victory is not just about winning matches; it is about embracing the values and ideals that define the game. Using this example of cricket let us next look at the multifaceted aspect of entrepreneurship victory along with personal and professional success and strive for excellence and inspire the next generation to achieve their dreams.

Multifaceted aspects of Entrepreneurship Victory

In my view, the view of victory varies from one individual to another due to differences in goals, values, and personal definitions of success. Generally, victory can be understood as achieving one's objectives or milestones in the realm of business and innovation. However, the specifics of what constitutes victory can differ significantly among entrepreneurs. Here are several aspects to victory you may have.

First, the Financial Success, Perhaps for many of you, financial success is a primary indicator of victory. This could involve achieving profitability, reaching a certain revenue target, securing funding, exiting the business with a significant return on investment or even becoming one of the top hundred richest person on the earth and leaving a lasting legacy. However, the definition of financial success can vary widely. Some entrepreneurs may aim for modest, sustainable profits, while others may strive for rapid growth and substantial wealth creation. Understanding where you are and where you want to be in your financial success is essential before embarking on your journey.

Second, the Impact and Innovation, Perhaps for some of you, victory lies in the impact your business has on society or the industry. This could involve creating innovative products or services that solve pressing problems, disrupting traditional markets, or contributing to positive social or environmental change or helping other social and charitable causes. These entrepreneurs may measure victory in terms of the number of lives improved, the level of disruption caused, or the legacy they leave behind. Comprehending your current position and your desired destination in your impact and innovation journey is crucial before setting out.

Third, the Personal Fulfilment, May be, you are an entrepreneur who is driven by personal fulfilment and the pursuit of passion. Victory for such individuals like you may be defined by the sense of satisfaction, purpose, and autonomy they derive from building and running their own business. It could involve achieving a work-life balance, pursuing creative freedom, or simply enjoying the journey of entrepreneurship regardless of financial outcomes. Grasping your present state and envisioning your desired destination in personal self-fulfilment is vital before commencing your journey.

Next in the list is Growth and Learning, may be you are an individual where, victory is synonymous with personal and professional growth for you. These entrepreneurs like you may measure success by the challenges they overcome, the skills they acquire, and the lessons they learn along the way. Growth-oriented entrepreneurs like you may prioritise continuous learning, resilience, and adaptability as they navigate the ups and downs of building a business. Before setting out on your journey, it's crucial to grasp your current position and where you aspire to be in terms of growth and learning.

Fifth, Legacy and Longevity, Probably you are one of those entrepreneurs who, aspire to leave a lasting legacy through your ventures. Victory for these individuals like you may involve building a sustainable business that outlasts its founders, creating opportunities for future generations, or establishing a brand that becomes synonymous with excellence and innovation in its industry. Having a clear understanding of your current position and your desired destination in terms of legacy and longevity is vital before you begin your journey.

And last but not the least the Freedom and Independence, perhaps for many other entrepreneurs like you, the ultimate victory lies in achieving freedom and independence. This could mean freedom from traditional employment, autonomy to make decisions, and control over one's own destiny or transforming the lives of people around you. These entrepreneurs like you may prioritise flexibility, lifestyle design, and the ability to pursue their passions on their own terms. Knowing your current status and your desired level of freedom and independence is crucial before beginning your journey.

Ultimately, victory in entrepreneurship is a deeply personal and subjective concept that reflects the unique aspirations, values, and circumstances of each individual entrepreneur. It's not just a milestone or a destination; it's a journey. The truth of life is that you're all at different stages of this journey, making it a very personal and subjective experience. With this book my purpose is to enhance your experience through continuous shared learning and to support each other in making this journey smoother and more enriched.

Conclusion & Recap

While financial success is often a key component, it's essential to recognise that there are many other dimensions to success and fulfilment in the entrepreneurial journey. As such, entrepreneurs should define victory on their own terms and celebrate the milestones that matter most to them.

Similarly, while winning the match is undoubtedly important, victory in cricket, as well as entrepreneurship, encompasses much more. It's about the thrill of competition, the joy of teamwork, and the camaraderie shared with fellow team members.

As cricketers, you define victory not just by the scorecard but by the passion, dedication, and sportsmanship displayed on the field.

Similarly in business, it's not just about financial success. It's all about how you want the world and future generations to see us and what you want to leave as a legacy. It's not just about personal performance, but it's about inspiring generations and leaving a legacy for generations to guide and inspire. It's about looking beyond yourselves, Dare to bream big and creating something bigger than you.

So, are you ready to embark on a transformative voyage from visions to victory?

Join us as you embark on this exhilarating journey together, where dreams take flight, and success knows no bounds. Let's unlock the full potential of entrepreneurship and pave the way for a future brimming with possibility. Let your journey of success be brimming with ongoing learning and abundant success and saying that let's embark on the next stage of this journey by establishing the foundations and laying the groundwork for success.

Follow Me On Instagram

@SANTOSHKUMAR.UK

What Do I Bring To You On Instagram?

Why should you scan this QR code or hit that follow button? It's simple – I'm on a continuous learning curve, and every day is a school day for me. I understand that every business has the same journey. One of the philosophies I follow says, "Together Everyone Achieves More," so I embarked on the entrepreneurial journey to meet as many people as possible, learn as many things as possible, and help them learn from the skills, knowledge, and wisdom collected within me and from others.

I've cracked the code to success by understanding you and your needs as an entrepreneur, my audience. I can assure you that, as of now, while I'm writing this book, you have eight billion people, and believe me, everybody is unique. Their strengths and weaknesses are different, but what's common is the path of entrepreneurship – the framework, the roadmap, and the blueprint. The strategies and tactics will be different, but collectively, I want to transform lives by recommending you not to make the same mistakes as people like me and many others have done in your journey. I aim to save you from many sleepless nights, save you from much pain, save you from losing money, and, on top of everything, save you from losing your time, which once lost, you will never get back.

Following me on Instagram means stepping into a world where content is carefully crafted to match your interests and preferences. I'm here to offer you a distinctive and valuable experience. Your decision to follow is not just a click; it's an invitation to a space tailored to resonate with what matters most to you. Join me on Instagram, where every post is curated with you in mind, ensuring that your experience is not just engaging but uniquely yours.

SECTION 2

The Foundation - Laying the Groundwork for Success

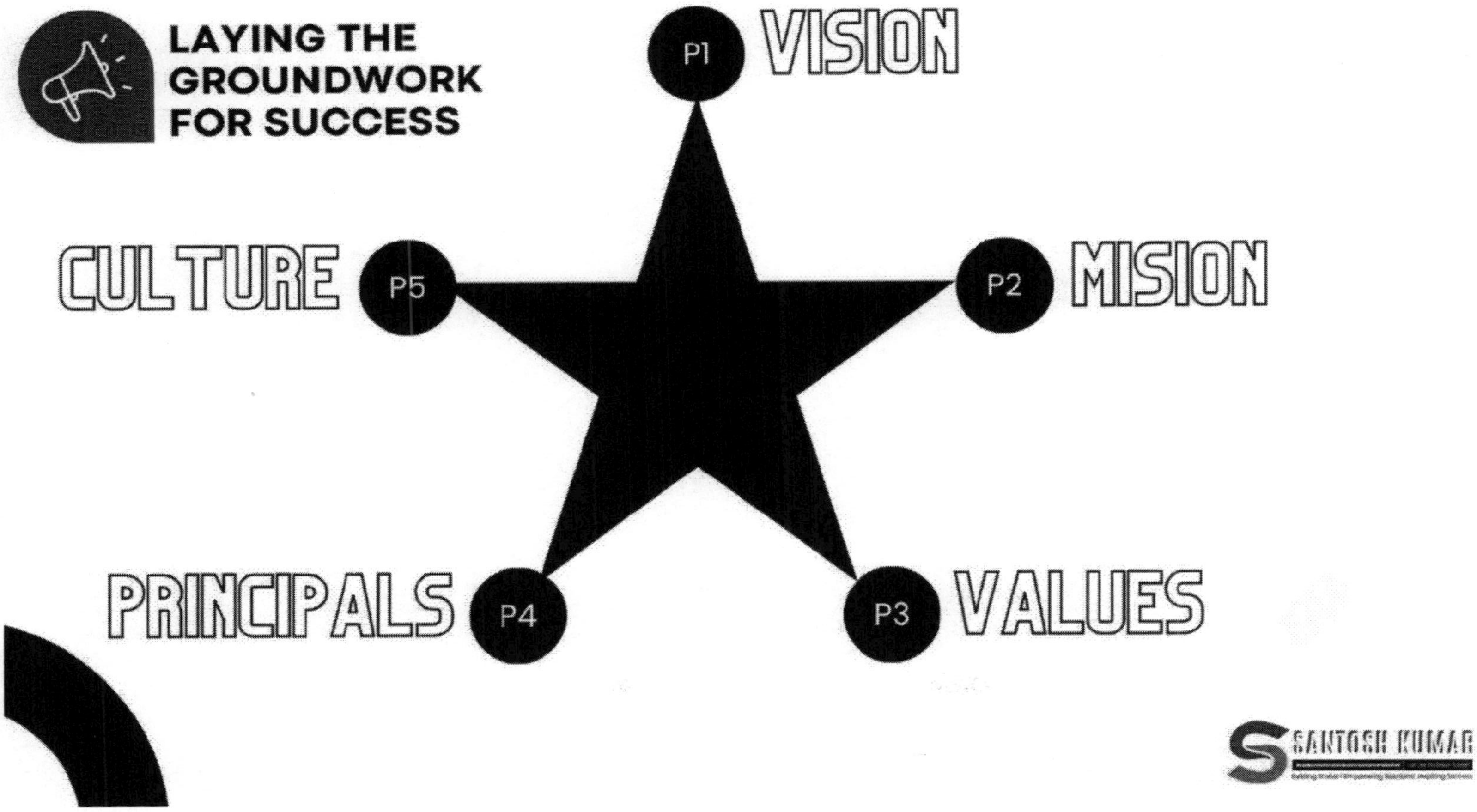
LAYING THE GROUNDWORK FOR SUCCESS
P1
VISION
P2
MISION
P3
VALUES
P4
PRINCIPALS
P5
CULTURE
SANTOSH KUMAR

Tale of The Grandchild Hare

Once upon a time, in a forest not far from where the famous race between the hare and the tortoise took place, there lived the grandchild of the original hare. This young hare inherited not only the speed of its ancestor but also his cocky attitude.

One day, as the grandchild hare was boasting about its speed, just like its grandparent had done, the tortoise, hearing the bragging, felt a familiar twinge of indignation. The tortoise challenged the grandchild hare to a race, just as grandparent hare had challenged the tortoise the years ago. Despite the advice of his peers to ignore the challenge and carry on as usual, the grandchild hare was still embarrassed from the loss of dignity from history and is willing to make a change. He believed he had found his purpose and was determined to turn the tables. He carefully considered his strategy for the race, determined not to let his overconfidence and arrogance lead him astray, as they had his grandparent.

The grandchild hare heard a small voice inside his mind, urging him to back away from the challenge. This voice from his conscious mind warned him that the fear of losing and the shame that would follow could have serious consequences not only for him but for future generations, consequences he might not fully grasp. But after a little thought and his eagerness to prove its superiority, the young hare accepted the challenge with a smirk, confident that victory was already assured. The race began, and just like before, the young hare darted ahead, leaving the tortoise trailing far behind.

However, remembering the lesson learned from the original race, the young hare didn't stop to rest. It kept running, but with each leap forward, it glanced back, gloating at the slow progress of the tortoise. This distraction caused the young hare to trip over a root and fall flat on its face and become unconscious. By the time the grandchild hare got back up and regained its consciousness and momentum, the tortoise had caught up and was steadily plodding ahead. Panicked, the young hare raced after the tortoise, determined not to let its cockiness cost it the race. In a thrilling finale, the young hare managed to surge past the tortoise just before the finish line, winning the race by a whisker.

All of the woodland creatures cheered for the young hare, but one of his friends slowly approached him and asked about the moment just before he accepted the challenge and what he was thinking.

"I was listening to the voice of fear inside me and the voices of my friend and peers who were recommending me to ignore the challenge of the tortoise and carry on doing what I am doing," the young hare replied. "But on the other hand, I thought that I'd finally found my purpose and found my dot and I must turn the tables around. I pondered what I should do, and what I shouldn't do in this race. I started planning how not to rest during the race and how my cockiness and arrogance shouldn't lead me to lose my credibility like my grandparent did."

As the dust settled and the young hare caught its breath, it realised the true moral of the story: **At every stage of life, you encounter both known and unknown challenges. Failure is an inevitable aspect of life, yet it does not solely define us. Rather, it is your response to failure that truly shapes who you are.**

The failure of grandparents did not stop young hare to accept the challenge, but he took a decision to consider this an opportunity and turned the table around. By picking itself up, running faster, and not repeating the same mistake of arrogance, the young hare emerged victorious.

The lesson learned was clear: **Achieving success demands resilience, modesty, and a readiness to learn from one's mistakes and dare to dream big.**

This section two of visions to Victory Volume one, is not just about laying the groundwork for success; it's about crafting a bedrock that sustains the weight of your aspirations and dreams. As you navigate through this section, remember that the foundation is not just about bricks and mortar; it's about laying down the principles, values, and culture that will sustain your entrepreneurial edifice. As you embark on this exploration of the foundational elements in "Visions to Victory," I'm eager to share the profound insights of entrepreneurial success.

So, define your vision, craft your mission, establish principles, nurture your culture, and envision the castle you are building. This is just the beginning, and the foundation you lay here will echo through the halls of your success.

Therefore, in the upcoming chapter, you will delve into the concept of Visionary Impact through a story that is deeply personal to me.

LET'S DIVE IN...

Chapter 2.1

Power of Cultivating a Clear Vision

“The only thing worse than being blind is having sight but no vision”

HELEN KELLER

When I was younger, my father imparted wisdom to me that has stayed with me throughout my life. "Son," he said, "We're all part of this world, and when night falls, no one will go to bed with an empty stomach. Life is never about what you can do for yourself, but what you can do for others. True purpose lies in thinking beyond yourself, in serving and helping others before considering your own needs. That's the kind of purpose that leaves a lasting impact, one that extends far beyond yourself. So, it's essential to find a purpose greater than yourself." He continued, "So, once you finish your studies and get settled in your career, I will go to your native place, open a charitable school where the underprivileged kids from the surrounding areas can get a quality but free education. Then I will bring them to Mumbai so that they can live a quality life and get inspired to do the same for other kids. This way, you will spark an idea of transforming the lives of others continuously from generation to generation."

In a world that often demands innovation and resilience, the stories of great visionaries implores us to cultivate your vision, trust in your abilities, and embrace the power of purpose. Through their life, you learn that a visionary isn't just someone who dreams big but someone who transforms those dreams into impactful realities, leaving a lasting legacy for generations to come. For in the end, it is not the grandeur of your achievements or the magnitude of your successes that define us, but rather the depth of your compassion, the strength of your resolve, and the clarity of your vision. Allow me to illustrate this conviction through a personal anecdote.

In the heart of Phulpur, India, a towering figure stood at over six feet tall, leaving an indelible mark on the community and his descendants. Although I never had the privilege of meeting the two brothers, my great grandfather and his brother, but the tales of their life resonate with grandeur, portraying a man of multifaceted accomplishments and unwavering dedication.

The Entrepreneurial Spirit

Listening to the tales recounted by my family members and uncovering the remarkable life of my great-grandfather has been an enlightening journey, offering profound insights into life, business, and community service. These inspirational stories helped us remember them for at least five generations, as I pass them down to my children.

The story of my great grandfather and his brother encapsulates invaluable lessons that resonate across generations. Delving deeper, their entrepreneurial spirit in the timber business stands as a testament to the power of vision and hard work. From the small Indian town of Phulpur to the far-reaching corners of Asia, they expanded the business empire with determination and strategic acumen. Their ability to navigate challenges during the British era serves as a lesson in resilience and adaptability, crucial attributes for success in any entrepreneurial venture.

Life Beyond the Financial Gains

Moreover, the commitment to the practice of Ayurveda illuminates the significance of serving the community. Beyond the financial gains of their business, they also dedicated themselves to healing others. The selflessness with which he treated individuals, irrespective of their background or origin, underscores the importance of using one's skills for the betterment of society. The joy they found in family bonds and the simple pleasures of playing with their grandchildren highlight the importance of balancing personal and professional life. In the pursuit of success, it's essential to cherish moments with loved ones and build a foundation of strong family ties. This balance, as exemplified by the great grandfather, contributes to a fulfilling and meaningful life. The chapter wouldn't be complete without discussing his visionary approach as a healer and his family values, so let's take a quick look at it.

A Visionary Entrepreneur

My great grandfather, a visionary in every sense, navigated the tapestry of life with determination, resilience, and a strong belief in the power of vision. The ability of two brothers to envision opportunities where others saw obstacles allowed them to create a thriving business empire. The echo of their success is felt across generations, as they passed on the thriving enterprise to their two sons, creating a legacy that stands the test of time.

In the face of adversity, The great grandfather's perseverance, and strategic acumen shine through. The echoes of their success serve as a testament to the transformative power of a clear vision and the determination to turn dreams into reality.

A Healer's Vision

A healer at heart, the brilliance and dedication to the practice of Ayurveda made them a beacon of hope for many. People would travel from distant places to seek their advice, attracted not only by their medical skills but also by their selfless nature. They treated various health issues with the natural power of Ayurvedic medicine and the soothing power of mantras, bringing balance to the Vata, Pitta, and Kapha of countless individuals.

Beyond the world of business and transactions, their vision extended to the realm of community service. As an Ayurvedic doctor, my grandfather dedicated himself to healing others, becoming a source of hope for those in need. His holistic approach, combining the natural power of Ayurvedic medicine with the resonance of mantras, demonstrates the significant impact a visionary can have on a community's well-being.

His vision wasn't solely focused on financial gains; it included a dedication to improving the lives of those around him. The compassionate service he provided highlights the notion that true success is closely linked to the positive impact & influence one leaves on others.

Balancing Vision with Family

Beyond the realm of medicine, he was a family man. The joy of playing with the grandchildren and bonding with their two sons enriched their life's journey. Amidst the hustle and bustle of business, they found joy in the simplicity of family bonds. The laughter shared with their eight grandchildren and the close ties with their two sons portrayed the man who understood the importance of balance in life. They managed to lay the foundations for a strong household and a tightly knit family in your native place, ensuring that at least the next three generations can reside and thrive together without concern for the future. Their ability to nurture both a successful business and a harmonious family life highlights the transformative potential of a well-rounded vision. Let me explain why the story of my great grandfather remains an inspiration for you even today.

Inspiration and Reflection of the Legacy

As I reflect on the life of my great grandfather, we can't help ourselves but be inspired by the enduring legacy of his visionary spirit. His story serves as a beacon for those navigating the complexities of life and business, showcasing that a clear vision can propel us forward even in the face of challenges. It is a story of interconnectedness, where entrepreneurship, family bonds, and community service weave seamlessly together.

The narrative of my great grandfather is one of resilience, compassion and entrepreneurship. His story serves as an inspiration, illustrating how one individual's dedication can shape not only a family but an entire community. As you reflect on his legacy, you are reminded that the echoes of his accomplishments continue to reverberate through time, an enduring testament to the impact one person can have on the lives of many. Reflecting on his legacy, there's a profound lesson in the interconnectedness of life, business, and community service. His success wasn't measured solely by financial gains but by the positive impact he had on the lives of those around him.

The Crucial Question

Vision, my friend, isn't the dream you see while you're asleep; it's the dream you see with your eyes wide open, but it's much bigger and more powerful than just a mere dream.

But what is vision, if not a mere dream?

It is the spark that ignites the flames of progress. It is the guiding north star that illuminates the path to greatness and inspires us to reach beyond your limitations. It serves as the instrument to craft the blueprint of your aspirations. It acts as the means to construct the roadmap to your success, and provides the capability to select the compass that steers us through the storms of uncertainty.

Think back to the greatest achievements in human history – the invention of the light bulb, the exploration of space, the eradication of diseases.

What do they all have in common?

They were born from the minds of visionaries, individuals who dared to dream big and refused to be bound by the constraints of the status quo.

I strongly believe that the universe is an expansive global family, and we are all part of a larger community where we should be prepared to support and assist each other, especially those who aspire to progress. If you have already walked a path and you can share your knowledge and wisdom, you can positively impact life and humanity by guiding others forward, without expecting anything in return. Expectations, when unmet, can lead to disappointment and often deter people from continuing their good deeds, hence, if you can, help and support people but do not keep expectations.

Writing this series for you is one of my initial steps towards sharing my knowledge and wisdom to the people where I cannot reach personally, aiming to help and support you and the other members of our global community and add value to people's lives around me and you and help them make progress towards making the world a better place before we depart from this world. For me, the key elements are community, assistance, help, support, value, inspiration, motivation, time and progress.

If destiny allows us to meet in this lifetime, I would love to share my vision, which I am diligently working on to transform from a dream into a significant endeavour worth one hundred and thirty-seven trillion pounds over the next two decades. My commitment to this endeavour is wholehearted, with the hope that it will inspire and motivate others, especially those who are privileged, to pursue their own ambitions and contribute to a greater cause, larger than themselves, for the betterment of society.

I envision establishing a global centre of excellence where members of our community can live and thrive in harmony. I dream of finding at least ten to twelve visionaries and inspirational personalities who can come together with similar thoughts of creating a legacy and history through their own ventures worth between one hundred and thirty trillion to one hundred and fifty trillion. Together, these visionaries would collaborate to transform this global centre of excellence into a lasting legacy inspiring, motivating, and setting an example for others to follow in their lifetime.

My aim is to create a convoy of five to six hundred billionaires throughout the universe who work together harmoniously, each ridding a vehicle worth one hundred to two hundred billion as an IPO with strong CSR initiatives and with a strong aspiration to serve an inspiration for others to make a difference in the world, helping others join this exclusive club by offering assistance, support, guidance, mentoring, or acting as role models.

I have a strong burning desire to bring double-digit millionaires together to become triple-digit millionaires and travel this journey together, helping other aspiring individuals and visionaries along the way. With this model, I dream of impacting millions of lives, where multimillionaires assist hundreds and thousands of families in their day-to-day lives by offering employment, personal development, help and support and making a valuable difference. I dream of creating an open-tap system that is available for anyone and everyone to access, allowing it to serve positively for their own causes in the universe.

I envision creating a step-by-step journey for the members of this convoy to contribute to the best of their ability, helping and supporting at least one person each day with whatever they can offer, be it advice, support, help, donations, food, shelter, medicine, or contributions to innovation for the advancement of humanity.

But vision is not just for the history books; it is within each of us, waiting to be unleashed.

Whether it's you, the small business owner with dreams of changing the world with your innovative product, or it's you, the student envisioning a future where education is accessible to all, or it's you, the global community leader imagining a world free from poverty and inequality, let me pose this crucial question to you today:

What is your vision? What future do you envision for yourself, your loved ones, and your community?

As you stand at the precipice of possibility, poised to embark on your own odyssey of self-discovery and achievement, you are confronted with a crucial question: what are you prepared to do to breathe life into that vision and bring that vision to life?

And, more importantly, What's holding you back?

Today, I urge you to dream bigger, to imagine a future that exceeds even your wildest fantasies, and to take the initial step towards transforming that vision into reality. I challenge you to identify that one motivating factor that will compel you to rise from your bed each day, which will inspire you and help you discover your true purpose. I implore you to uncover that one barrier preventing you from finding this inspiration and hindering you from turning your dreams into reality.

Conclusion & Recap

As you chart your course towards a brighter tomorrow, let us draw inspiration from the timeless wisdom of those who came before us, and let their legacy serve as a guiding light on your path to greatness. Let us dare to dream with your eyes wide open, for therein lies the promise of a future brimming with possibility, a future shaped by the transformative power of vision.

Today, let me stand before you not just as an author, but as a believer in the transformative power of vision and visionary thinking. I believe that within each of us lies the potential to dream big, to envision a future that surpasses your wildest imagination, and to make that vision a reality.

Let us allow ourselves now to learn and share the valuable lessons from these visionaries, leading us to the next point and the magical formula for turning dreams into reality. However, before delving into that, let's explore the common fears that serve as significant barriers to achieving your dreams and hinder your ability to Unleash Your Full Potential.

In the next chapter, fear will be explored as a common obstacle to realising your full potential. It will be dissected into various forms such as fear of failure, rejection, and the unknown. I will challenge you to reframe fear as a catalyst for personal development rather than a barrier to success. Let me encourage you to confront your fears head-on, daring to dream boldly and embrace the unknown with confidence to unlock their fullest potential. This approach will be emphasised as essential for discovering the true purpose and vision of your dreams and ventures before you explore the power of vision in following chapter.

Chapter 2.2

Overcome Your Fears to Unleash Your Full Potential

FEAR

F False

E Emotions

A Apearing

R Real

Christopher Morley once said, "Read every day something no one else is reading; think every day something no one else is thinking. It is bad for the mind to be always part of unanimity." This quote highlights the importance of thinking independently and not blindly following the crowd.

People like Christopher Morley inspire us to think that you should not fear others' opinions or change your course based on societal norms. Embracing your uniqueness and following your hearts can lead to success beyond your imagination. You should challenge ourselves to think differently and pursue your passions without fear of judgment. After all, history has shown that the greatest achievements often come from those who dare to be different. Fear is a powerful emotion that can hold us back from reaching your full potential.

In this chapter, let me talk about something that affects each and every one of us: FEAR. Fear is a force that has the power to hold us back, to paralyse us with doubt, and to keep us from reaching your fullest potential.

Fear is a universal human experience. It's that voice in the back of your minds that tells us you're not good enough, that you'll never succeed, that you should stay safely within your comfort zones. But what if I told you that fear isn't the enemy? What if I told you that fear could be the catalyst for transformation, growth, and success?

In the tale of the grandchild hare, you explored earlier, there was a notable mention of a small voice representing fear. Today, I want to delve into that familiar voice, a voice you've all encountered at some point in your lives, hindering us from realising your full potential. This inner dialogue is something every individual, present and future, will inevitably confront. That's why it's crucial to address this topic from the outset.

While I can't pinpoint the exact source, I've come across descriptions of fear in various psychological literature as "False Emotions Appearing Real." It's that persistent whisper in the recesses of your minds, casting doubts on your abilities and dreams, convincing us of your inadequacy.

Fear – Your Greatest Ally

Fear is a powerful force that has the ability to hold us back from achieving your dreams and living your best lives. It is a primal emotion that has been hardwired into your brains since ancient times, serving as a survival mechanism to help us navigate a hostile world. However, in the modern world, fear often prevents us from reaching your full potential and embracing new opportunities.

In the grand tapestry of human existence, fear often stands as the formidable adversary on the path to growth and fulfilment. It lurks in the shadows of your aspirations, whispering doubts and casting shadows of uncertainty.

Yet, what if you dared to reframe your relationship with fear? What if, instead of shunning it, you embraced it as a catalyst for growth and transformation?

But what if I told you that fear could be your greatest ally? What if, instead of letting it hold us back, you embraced it as a tool for growth and self-discovery?

Imagine a world where fear was no longer seen as a barrier, but as a stepping stone on the path to greatness. Imagine a world where you embraced your fears, confronted them head-on, and used them to fuel your dreams and aspirations. However, achieving this requires a comprehensive understanding of the three common types of fears that surround us. Let's delve into exploring these categories.

Types of Fear

Fear, in its many guises, has long been intertwined with the human experience. Fear comes in many shapes and sizes. It's the fear of failure, the fear of rejection, the fear of the unknown. But what if you saw these fears not as roadblocks, but as stepping stones on the path to success?

These fears can be paralysing, trapping us in the confines of your comfort zones and stifling your potential. Yet, they also hold the power to propel us forward, igniting the fires of innovation and resilience within. So, it's particularly important to understand the different types of fears so that you can encounter them in right manner.

Fear of Failure

One of the most common fears you face is the fear of failure. You worry about what will happen if you try something new and it doesn't work out as planned. This fear can be paralysing, preventing us from taking risks and pursuing your dreams. It's something you've all experienced at one time or another.

At its core, fear is a primal instinct, designed to protect us from harm. It served your ancestors well in the wilderness, alerting them to potential dangers and guiding their actions. However, in today's complex world, fear often manifests in response to perceived threats rather than imminent danger. It becomes a barrier to growth when you allow it to dictate your choices and limit your possibilities.

But you must remember that failure is not something to be feared but rather embraced as a natural part of the learning process. It is through failure that you grow and develop resilience.

What if you dared to confront your fears head-on? What if you viewed them not as obstacles to be avoided, but as opportunities for growth and self-discovery? The truth is, behind every fear lies a hidden treasure – a chance to confront your limitations, challenge your assumptions, and emerge stronger on the other side.

What if failure wasn't something to be ashamed of, but something to be celebrated? What if you saw it as a chance to learn and grow, rather than a mark of your inadequacy? What if you use fear to understand the challenges and analyse the related opportunities that come with it?

Consider the fear of failure, perhaps one of the most pervasive fears of all. It whispers seductively in your ears, warning us of the risks inherent in pursuing your dreams. Yet, what if failure were reframed not as the end of the road, but as a necessary detour on the path to success?

Each failure, no matter how painful, offers valuable lessons and insights that can inform your future endeavours. It is through failure that you learn resilience, perseverance, and the true meaning of success.

Fear of Rejection

And then there's the fear of rejection. You've all been there – putting ourselves out there, only to be met with indifference or outright dismissal. You worry about what others will think of us if you put ourselves out there and express your true selves. This fear can prevent us from forming meaningful connections and pursuing opportunities for personal and professional growth.

The fear of rejection can hold us back from pursuing meaningful connections and opportunities. Yet, when you embrace rejection as a natural part of the human experience, you free ourselves from the shackles of approval-seeking and open ourselves up to new possibilities. It is through vulnerability that you forge authentic connections and cultivate empathy and understanding.

But what if rejection wasn't a reflection of your worth, but simply a part of life? What if you saw it as an opportunity to connect with others who share your struggles and aspirations?

You must realise that rejection is not a reflection of your worth as individuals but rather a part of life. By facing rejection head-on, you can build confidence and develop a greater sense of self-worth.

Fear of Unknowns

Finally, there's the fear of the unknown. Perhaps one of the most insidious fears is the fear of the unknown. It's that feeling of uncertainty that keeps us up at night, wondering what the future holds.

You fear what you cannot see or predict, leading us to stay within your comfort zones and avoid taking risks. However, life is inherently uncertain, and growth often requires us to step into the unknown.

Fear of the unknown is the vast expanse of uncertainty that stretches out before us like an uncharted sea. Yet, it is in the depths of the unknown that you discover your true potential – the capacity to adapt, evolve, and thrive in the face of adversity. It is through uncertainty that you learn to trust in your intuition, embrace ambiguity, and chart your own course in life.

But what if you embraced the unknown, rather than fearing it? What if you saw it as a blank canvas, waiting to be filled with your hopes, dreams, and aspirations?

By embracing uncertainty and approaching new experiences with an open mind, you can discover new possibilities and expand your horizons.

Fear of Other's Opinion

One of the most common fears you face is the fear of others' opinions. You worry about what people will think if you stray from the norm or pursue your own path. However, when you examine the lives of the world's most enlightened and effective individuals, you see that they were not concerned about others' opinions of them.

Emerson emphasised the significance of maintaining independence in the face of societal pressure. He stated, "It is easy in the world to live after the world's opinion; it is easy in solitude to live after your own; but the great man is he who, in the midst of the crowd, keeps with perfect sweetness the independence of solitude."

These individuals had the courage to follow their hearts and take the road less travelled. They understood that conforming to societal expectations would only limit their potential. Instead, they embraced their uniqueness and pursued their passions wholeheartedly.

Overcoming Fear

Think about it - some of the greatest achievements in human history have come from overcoming fear. From exploring uncharted territories to pushing the boundaries of science and technology, fear has been the driving force behind countless breakthroughs. But fear isn't just something that exists on a grand scale. It's something that each and every one of us faces in your daily lives. It's the fear of failure, the fear of rejection, the fear of the unknown. But what if you saw these fears not as roadblocks, but as opportunities for growth and self-discovery?

Imagine a world where failure wasn't something to be ashamed of, but something to be celebrated. Imagine a world where rejection wasn't a reflection of your worth, but simply a part of life. Imagine a world where the unknown wasn't something to be feared, but something to be embraced.

So how do you overcome your fears and unlock your full potential? It starts with acknowledging that fear is a natural part of the human experience. It's about reframing your relationship with fear - seeing it not as an obstacle, but as a guiding force on your journey towards success. It's about daring to dream boldly and take risks, knowing that failure and rejection are simply opportunities for growth. It's about embracing your fears, confronting them head-on, and using them to fuel your passions and ambitions.

Embrace your Fear

So, I urge you to embrace your fears – to see them not as obstacles, but as opportunities. I invite you to dance with them, rather than run from them. For it is in the crucible of fear that true growth and transformation occur. It is through confronting your fears that you discover your inner strength, resilience, and courage. It is through confronting your fears that you find the courage to chase your dreams and live life to the fullest. And it is through embracing fear that you unlock the door to your fullest potential.

I implore you to perceive your fears not as adversaries, but as companions on your path to greatness. Within each fear resides the potential for growth, transformation, and ultimately, triumph. Embracing your fears will be pivotal in harnessing the power of cultivating a clear vision. Which is the next chapter in this journey.

Therefore, venture forth and embrace bold dreams. Take risks, defy norms, and welcome the unfamiliar. In the presence of fear, you unveil the essence of humanity—resilience, courage, and boundless potential for growth. Confront your fears directly and unlock your utmost capabilities by daring to dream boldly and facing the unknown with conviction. This mindset will guide you in uncovering the genuine purpose and vision of your journey. In the forthcoming chapter, you will explore the indispensable nature of having a vision and its profound significance.

Become Unstoppable

Let me share a simple yet powerful formula for success in all aspects of life, personal, professional or in your venture creation Journey: Become unstoppable.

Yes, you heard me right – unstoppable. But what does it mean to be unstoppable?

It means pushing past your fears, overcoming obstacles, and pursuing your dreams with unwavering determination. It means refusing to accept mediocrity and settling for anything less than greatness.

Now, you might be wondering, why should you become unstoppable?

Well, let me paint a picture for you. Imagine a life where you wake up every morning feeling excited and energised, ready to take on whatever challenges come your way. Imagine a life where you have the confidence to chase your wildest dreams and turn them into reality. Imagine a life where you feel unstoppable – because you are.

But let's be real for a moment. Life is full of obstacles. It's full of setbacks, challenges, and moments of doubt. But here's the thing: those obstacles don't have to hold you back. In fact, they can propel you forward. They can make you stronger, more resilient, and more determined than ever before.

So how do you become unstoppable?

It starts with a mindset – a mindset of possibility, resilience, and relentless determination. It starts with believing in yourself and your ability to overcome any obstacle that stands in your way. It starts with setting audacious goals and refusing to let anything, or anyone deter you from achieving them.

But it's not just about mindset. It's also about massive action. It's about taking bold, decisive action towards your goals, even when it's scary or uncomfortable. It's about facing your fears head-on and pushing through them with courage and conviction.

And let me tell you something – when you become unstoppable, amazing things start to happen. You start to attract opportunities, connections, and resources that you never thought possible. You start to inspire others with your resilience and determination. You start to live a life of purpose, passion, and fulfilment.

Embrace the challenges, overcome the obstacles, and pursue your dreams with everything you've got. Because when you do, there's no limit to what you can achieve. It's a journey that requires courage, determination, and resilience. It's a journey that will test your limits, push you out of your comfort zone, and ultimately lead you to greatness.

So, how do you embark on this journey?

How do you overcome your fears and obstacles to become unstoppable?

Let me share with you ten powerful steps that will guide you along the way.

Top 10 Powerful Steps to Become Unstoppable

Firstly, you must develop a clear vision. You must define your goals and create a compelling vision for your venture. This vision will fuel your motivation and drive us forward, even in the face of challenges.

Secondly, you must embrace failure as learning. You must understand that failure is a natural part of the entrepreneurial journey. Instead of fearing failure, you must embrace it as an opportunity to learn and grow.

Thirdly, you must cultivate a growth mindset. You must believe that your abilities and intelligence can be developed through dedication and hard work. This mindset empowers us to see challenges as opportunities for growth rather than obstacles.

Fourthly, you must take action despite fear. You must acknowledge your fears but take action anyway. The more you step out of your comfort zone, the more resilient and confident you'll become.

Fifthly, you must surround ourselves with support. You must build a network of mentors, advisors, and peers who can offer guidance, support, and encouragement.

Sixthly, you must stay flexible and adapt. You must be open to change and willing to adapt your plans based on feedback and new information.

Seventhly, you must celebrate small wins. You must acknowledge and celebrate your achievements, no matter how small. Celebrating milestones along the way can boost your confidence and momentum.

Eighthly, you must practice self-care. You must take care of your physical, mental, and emotional well-being. Prioritising activities that recharge and rejuvenate us will ensure you have the energy and resilience to face challenges head-on.

Ninthly, you must stay persistent. You must stay committed to your goals, even when faced with setbacks or challenges. Persistence is essential in overcoming obstacles and achieving long-term success.

And finally, you must focus on the journey. You must remember that the journey of venture creation is as important as the destination. You must enjoy the process, learn from your experiences, and stay curious and open-minded along the way.

By adopting these strategies and cultivating the right mindset, you can become unstoppable in your journey. You can fearlessly pursue your goals and bring your vision to life. So let us embark on this journey together, and let us become unstoppable in your pursuit of greatness.

Conclusion & Recap

Fear, often described as False Emotions Appearing Real (FEAR), manifests in various forms such as the fear of failure, rejection, and the unknown. So how can you overcome your fears and live more courageously?

The first step is to acknowledge your fears and understand where they stem from. Once you have identified your fears, you can challenge them by taking small steps outside of your comfort zones. By gradually exposing ourselves to the things that scare us, you can build confidence and develop resilience over time. It is also important to cultivate a growth mindset, viewing failure as an opportunity for learning and growth rather than a setback.

By reframing your perspective on failure, you can approach challenges with a sense of curiosity and optimism. Finally, it is essential to surround ourselves with supportive and encouraging people who uplift us and push us to be your best selves. By building a strong support network, you can draw strength from others and face your fears with greater courage and determination.

In conclusion, fear is a natural part of the human experience, but it does not have to hold us back from living fulfilling lives. By acknowledging your fears, challenging them, and embracing courage in the face of adversity, you can overcome your limitations and unlock your true potential. So let us embrace fear as an opportunity for growth and step boldly into the unknown, confident in your ability to conquer whatever challenges may come your way.

Here I challenge you to reframe fear as a catalyst for personal development rather than a barrier to success. For instance, the fear of failure is presented as an integral part of the journey to success, offering valuable lessons and opportunities for growth. Similarly, the fear of rejection is portrayed as a natural aspect of human interaction, fostering genuine connections and empathy. Lastly, the fear of the unknown is depicted as an opportunity to explore new possibilities and embrace uncertainty with courage and resilience.

Leading to which is your next topic on the importance of Vision for personal and professional success. The next chapter, titled "Think Big, Think Bold," takes you on a transformative journey within the entrepreneurial landscape. The chapter begins by emphasising the foundational importance of defining one's vision and draws insights from mentors, business associates, and seasoned entrepreneurs. The metaphor of an eagle's vision is introduced as a symbol of power and prowess, serving as a lens through which to explore the keys to success.

Chapter 2.3

Think Big, Think Bold

VISION

V Values

I Innovation

S Strategic

I Inspiration

O Optimism

N Nurturing

Imagine, if you will, a world where every dreamer dares to dream, where every seeker finds clarity, and where every challenge is met with unwavering resolve. This is the world that visionaries like you and I have the privilege to create.

Think of Martin Luther King Jr., whose dream of a society free from racial discrimination galvanised millions and catalysed the civil rights movement. His words, "I have a dream," resonated across generations, inspiring people to work towards a common vision of equality and justice.

Similarly, visionaries in business and innovation have shaped the world through their bold ideas. Steve Jobs, with his vision of putting a computer in every home, transformed the tech industry and revolutionised the way you live. Elon Musk, with his vision of sustainable transportation and space exploration, is reshaping the future of humanity.

But vision is not just for luminaries and leaders; it resides within each one of us. It's the spark of inspiration that ignites when you dare to dream beyond your present circumstances. Whether it's envisioning a successful career, a thriving business, or a more just society, your vision provides us with a roadmap for realising your fullest potential.

However, crafting a compelling vision is just the beginning; realising it requires dedication and perseverance. It demands that you confront obstacles with resilience and enlist the support of others to amplify your impact.

Moreover, vision is not static; it's an evolving journey. As you progress towards your goals, you must remain open to new possibilities and willing to adapt to changing circumstances.

vision is the driving force behind human progress. It empowers us to transcend limitations and unlock your true potential. So let us harness the power of vision in your lives and endeavours, and together, you can shape a world that reflects the beauty of your shared dreams and aspirations.

What is Vision?

Vision, my friend, is not merely a concept; it is a force—a force that propels us forward, that ignites your passion, and that guides us through the darkest of times. It is the spark that ignites the flames of innovation, the compass that points us toward your true north, and the blueprint that shapes your destiny.

Vision is the art of seeing what others cannot, of envisioning a future that surpasses the boundaries of imagination. It is the audacity to dream big, the courage to pursue those dreams relentlessly, and the determination to turn them into reality.

A vision is a clear, inspiring, and aspirational statement that defines the future state or desired outcome of an individual, organisation, or entity. It articulates what the entity hopes to achieve or become in the long term and provides a sense of direction and purpose. A vision is often bold, ambitious, and forward-thinking, serving as a guiding beacon that motivates and aligns efforts towards a common goal. It captures the essence of what success looks like and inspires individuals to work towards realising that vision. In essence, a vision paints a picture of a better future and sets the course for action to bring that future into reality.

A vision statement exists to inspire and motivate stakeholders by painting a compelling picture of the organisation's future. It answers the question, "What does the organisation aspire to achieve?"

With respect to your example of cricket match from the previous section, the vision of both teams is to secure victory in the game and craft memorable moments and experiences for all involved. This includes upholding the values and traditions of the sport and leaving a legacy of inspiration and guidance for others.

With vision as your guiding light, you have the power to overcome any obstacle, to defy any limitation, and to achieve the impossible. It is through vision that you transcend the ordinary and embrace the extraordinary. It is through vision that you leave your mark on the world and inspire others to do the same.

While a vision statement is essential for long-term objectives, it also plays a role of a beacon of the light house in the short term by providing a sense of direction and purpose. It encourages innovation, fosters commitment, and guides strategic decisions that contribute to the realisation of long-term goals.

But what precisely defines vision? Let's unravel this concept with the aid of a living legend, the exemplar of the avian realm—the majestic Eagle.

Eagle Vision- Soaring Heights of Triumph

In the vast expanse of the Bird kingdom, one creature stands out as the undisputed king—the eagle.

Have you ever wondered how and why The Eagle has become the king of Bird Kingdom?

A majestic symbol of power and prowess, the eagle's dominion is not merely a result of its physical prowess but owes much to the extraordinary power of its vision. The eagle's success as the king of the Bird kingdom is not merely a consequence of its physical prowess but is intricately tied to its vision's strategic advantage. By spotting potential threats or prey from afar, the eagle can plan its actions with precision, ensuring a successful outcome.

Beyond the biological marvel, the eagle's vision serves as a symbol of foresight and clarity for us humans. It encourages us to set your sights on distant goals, embrace strategic planning, and navigate life's challenges with precision and resilience.

Let's unravel the secrets of the eagle's vision, a remarkable ability that propels it to soar to unparalleled heights and reign supreme.

Eyesight - The Crown Jewel of the Animal Kingdom: The eagle's vision and keen eyesight is a marvel of nature, offering a level of clarity and precision that sets it apart. With eyes that can perceive details at incredible distances, the eagle surveys its domain with unmatched acuity, making it the ultimate predator in the skies.

Accuracy from 5 Miles Away - One of the eagle's most astounding feats is its pinpoint accuracy and ability to set its sights on a target from an astonishing distance of more than five miles. This superlative vision allows it to spot the opportunities with unparalleled accuracy, setting the stage for success in every endeavour.

Goal Setting and Precision Navigation - The eagle's vision is not just about seeing; it's about setting targets with an unwavering focus. Whether it's spotting a distant prey or navigating through vast landscapes, the eagle's vision becomes a compass that guides its direction with unmatched precision.

Lessons for Human Triumph - The eagle's vision offers profound lessons for human endeavours. It teaches us to cultivate a clear vision, set ambitious yet achievable goals, and adapt your strategies as needed. Like the eagle, you can soar to new heights by honing your ability to see opportunities from afar and navigate the challenges that come your way.

Extended Adaptability and Flexibility - The eagle's vision is not static; it adapts to changing environments and circumstances. By being flexible and attuned to its surroundings, the eagle exemplifies how vision, when accompanied by adaptability, becomes an unstoppable force in the pursuit of success.

The eagle's vision is a testament to the extraordinary possibilities that lie within the power of seeing beyond the immediate horizon. As you draw inspiration from this majestic creature, Let us too harness the power of vision to become kings or queens of your own domains, achieving triumph in every endeavour that lies ahead by understanding the power of a clear vision.

Imagine, if you will, the soaring majesty of the eagle as it casts its keen gaze upon the vast expanse of the world below. Like the eagle, you too possess the remarkable ability to see beyond the horizon, to envision a future brimming with limitless potential. Just as the eagle's keen vision allows it to navigate through the stormy winds and turbulent skies, so too does your own vision guide us through the challenges and uncertainties of life. It is this vision that serves as your guiding light, your unwavering compass, and your steadfast ally on the journey toward greatness.

Vision of a Cricket Team

Imagine this scene: the sun's blazing, the crowd's buzzing, and every player strides onto the cricket field with a clear vision in mind.

First and foremost, winning the match is the top priority. winning in cricket isn't just about the momentary triumph; it's about creating a lasting legacy that resonates through the annals of cricketing history, inspiring future generations, uniting communities, and shaping the cultural fabric of nations. It's what ignites every player's passion, from the seasoned pros to the fresh faces. Winning isn't just about points on the board; it's about giving your all in every ball, every shot, every catch. It's about coming together as a team, each player bringing their best to the pitch, and leaving it all out there until that final ball is bowled.

But it's not just about the team; it's about each player's personal goals too. The vision of players in a cricket match can vary depending on the context and their individual roles within the team. Whether it's hitting boundaries, taking wickets, or pulling off sensational catches, every player aims to reach their own milestones. Because in cricket, every run scored, every wicket taken, every catch held contributes to the team's success and sets the stage for future triumphs.

And let's not forget the pride of representing your team and country. Every player sees themselves as more than just athletes; they're ambassadors, carrying their nation's hopes and dreams with every step they take on that field. It's about honouring the legacy of those who came before, upholding the values of fair play, and showcasing the absolute best of cricket.

But perhaps most importantly, cricket is about entertainment. It's about the roar of the crowd, the gasps of amasement, the sheer joy of witnessing something extraordinary. Players understand their role in this grand spectacle – whether they're hitting sixes, bowling thunderbolts, or pulling off incredible catches, they're there to put on a show, to give the fans something to cheer for, something to remember long after the game is over.

Overall, the vision of players in a cricket match revolves around winning the game, performing well individually, representing their team and country with pride, and entertaining the fans. These collective goals drive their efforts and determination on the field as they strive for success in the game of cricket.

In my opinion, regarding the cricket match, both teams' vision is to secure victory in the game and craft memorable moments and experiences for all involved. This includes upholding the values and traditions of the sport and leaving a legacy of inspiration and guidance for others.

So, as you gather to watch another thrilling contest on the cricket field, let's remember the vision that drives these players – the vision of victory, of personal excellence, of national pride, and of pure, unadulterated entertainment. Let's cheer them on as they chase their dreams, knowing that win or lose, they've already won your hearts.

The Power of a Cultivating a Clear Vision

In the words of the great Helen Keller, **"The only thing worse than being blind is having sight but no vision".** Today, let us not only see but envision a future that surpasses your wildest dreams. The journey will be challenging, but the rewards will be monumental.

But vision is not just for the history books; it is within each of us, waiting to be unleashed. It is the small business owner like us who dreams of changing the world with their innovative product. It is the student who envisions a future where education is accessible to all. It is the community leader who imagines a world free from poverty and inequality.

Think back to the greatest achievements in human history – the invention of the light bulb, the exploration of space, the eradication of diseases. What do they all have in common? They were born from the minds of visionaries, individuals who dared to dream big and refused to be bound by the constraints of the status quo.

Drawing on the collective experiences of visionaries, let us next explore the transformative impact of having a well-defined vision like an eagle and learn how this compelling vision serves as the guiding North Star, steering your business through turbulent times and towards triumphant heights.

Considering the life cycle and natural power of an eagle's vision and Looking at the examples of lily's odyssey as well as the life journey of my great-grandfather mentioned in an earlier chapter and, it's probably noticeably clear that the journey to success commences with a crystal-clear vision.

Crafting a clear vision provides direction, purpose, and a roadmap for your entrepreneurial endeavours, acting as the foundational pillar for success. Let me allow myself to ignite the flame of possibility within your inner self to cultivate a mindset that transcends the ordinary and embraces the extraordinary.

Let's briefly talk about VISION framework- a powerful force that has the potential to shape not just your futures, but the destiny of generations to come and expand on what the word vision stand for me.

Values - In the pursuit of greatness, let your values be the North Star guiding your decisions and actions. Let integrity be your compass and empathy your currency. A vision grounded in strong values not only defines your path but ensures it is one of righteousness and purpose.

Innovation - Embrace the spirit of innovation, for it is the heartbeat of progress. Let curiosity be your constant companion and creativity the wind beneath your wings. A great vision thrives on the continuous exploration of new ideas and the relentless pursuit of improvement.

Strategic - To realise your dreams, you must chart a strategic course. Planning is not just a phase; it's a commitment to the success you envision. Let your actions be deliberate, each step a calculated move towards the realisation of your grand vision.

Inspiration - As you strive for greatness, let you become beacons of inspiration for others. Great visions have a contagious energy that motivates not just the visionary but an entire community. Be the spark that ignites the passion in those around you.

Optimism - In the face of challenges, let optimism be your Armor. A positive outlook fuels your perseverance, enabling you to navigate storms and emerge stronger on the other side. Remember, every setback is a setup for a greater comeback.

Nurturing -Cultivate an environment that nurtures growth and development. A great vision encompasses not only personal success but the well-being and progress of everyone involved.

Believe in your vision, embrace the journey, and let the world witness the extraordinary impact of your unwavering commitment to VISION. Let this be the day you declare your commitment to VISION. Let us dream big, think beyond boundaries, and most importantly, let us back those dreams with massive action. Your visions aren't just daydreams; they are the guiding north star for success waiting to be brought to life. So, let's define your vision and find your dot.

Philosophy of Vision Power: Think big, think bold

A vision is more than just a dream; it's a detailed plan, a guiding document, and a source of motivation and a manifest. Like a blueprint, it helps us transform abstract aspirations into concrete steps, providing the structure and direction needed to turn dreams into reality.

The journey ahead may be challenging, but with vision as your guiding star, there is nothing that you cannot achieve.

Vision is the audacity to dream big, the courage to pursue those dreams relentlessly, and the determination to turn them into reality. It is the embodiment of strength, resilience, and unwavering purpose—qualities that are mirrored in the soaring flight of the eagle.

With vision as your guiding force, you have the power to overcome any obstacle, to defy any limitation, and to achieve the impossible. Just as the eagle spreads its wings and soars to new heights, so too can you rise above the challenges that stand in your way.

But let us not forget that vision is not a solitary pursuit; it is a collective endeavour—a journey that you embark on together, hand in hand, heart to heart. It is through unity, collaboration, and shared purpose that your visions truly come to life. For it is in the unity of the flock that the eagle finds its strength, and it is in the harmony of its wings that it soars to the greatest heights.

Together, let us spread your wings and soar to new heights of possibility, let us carve a path through the skies of uncertainty, and let us build a legacy that will echo through the ages.

The journey ahead may be challenging, but with the inspiration of the eagle as your guide, there is nothing that you cannot achieve.

As you embark on this journey, remember the guiding principles that will shape your vision. Let your vision be the North Star that guides every decision, every action, ensuring consistency, adaptability, and long-term focus. Let your vision be audacious, stretching beyond conventional limitations and daring to explore uncharted territories. Think of your Vision as something that not only fulfils your ambitions but also leaves a lasting impact on others – a legacy that future generations will remember.

One of my key principles around having an ambitious and great vision is, **"When you're defining your vision, think big, think bold."** This is a call to encourage individuals, particularly entrepreneurs, to adopt an expansive and ambitious mindset when articulating their goals and aspirations.

Here allow me to share my views and why in my experience I as a serial entrepreneur support this statement to **unleash FBI Mask with a c** at the end being read as "Unleased FBI MASC."

Unleashing Creativity - Thinking big and bold prompts you to unleash your creativity and imagination. It encourages you to break free from conventional limitations and explore possibilities that may seem ambitious at first. This mindset opens the door to innovative and unconventional ideas that can propel you towards extraordinary achievements.

Fostering Innovation - Bold visions often require innovative approaches. Thinking big encourages individuals to seek out novel solutions, challenge existing norms, and pioneer new paths. It fosters an environment where creativity and innovation thrive, leading to breakthroughs and advancements in various endeavours.

Building Resilience - Pursuing bold visions often involves overcoming challenges and setbacks. Thinking big helps you as an individual develop resilience and tenacity in the face of obstacles. It instils a mindset that views challenges as opportunities for learning and growth rather than insurmountable barriers.

Inspiring Others - Bold visions have the power to inspire and rally others around a common cause. When you as an individual articulate ambitious goals, you can attract like-minded collaborators, supporters, and team members who share the enthusiasm for achieving something significant. A compelling and bold vision becomes a magnet for collective effort.

Motivating Personal Growth - Thinking big and bold encourages you as an individual to continually strive for personal growth. It promotes a mindset of continuous improvement and learning, as you as an individual push yourselves beyond your perceived limits to achieve the audacious goals you have set for yourselves.

Aligning Actions with Vision - When you think big and bold, it aligns your actions with your vision. It encourages you to make decisions and take steps that are in line with their ambitious goals, ensuring a cohesive and purpose-driven approach to your endeavours.

Setting Ambitious Goals - The phrase emphasises the importance of setting ambitious goals that stretch beyond the ordinary. Ambitious goals often lead to greater motivation and commitment, inspiring people like you to reach beyond their comfort zones and strive for excellence. Setting big and bold goals can drive significant personal and professional growth.

Creating Impact - Big and bold visions have the potential to create a lasting impact. They inspire change and progress on a larger scale, influencing not only your individual success but also contributing to societal or organisational advancement. Bold visions are often associated with transformative endeavours that leave a meaningful legacy.

So, my recommendation to "think big and think bold" is a guiding principle that encourages all the individuals like you to dream beyond the ordinary, set ambitious goals, foster innovation, build resilience, inspire others, create impact, and promote continuous personal growth. It's a mindset that empowers individuals to envision a future that transcends current limitations and to pursue goals that have the potential to make a significant and lasting difference.

In the story of the Young Hare, where he identified his true purpose when he grabbed the opportunity and began working on his vision. His vision was to embrace failure as a part of life and learn from it. His vision was to change the thought process of people around it and create a new history and not let cockiness and arrogance lead to failure like the grandparent hare. Having a vision is particularly important to set a direction and inspire and motivate us and people around us to act. Similar to the young hare, you can forget your past and start creating history by having a vision for a new beginning. let us dare to dream boldly, embrace clarity with open hearts, and march forward with unwavering determination. The world is waiting—for your vision, for your passion, and for your brilliance. Together, let us paint a future filled with possibility, let us sculpt a world infused with purpose, and let us build a legacy that will stand the test of time.

Conclusion & Recap

As you conclude this chapter, envision yourself not merely as a business owner but as the architect of a grand vision. Absorb the knowledge needed to craft a vision that transcends challenges, inspires stakeholders, and becomes the cornerstone of your entrepreneurial triumphs. This is not just a chapter; it's a blueprint for turning dreams into reality, and your journey has just begun.

For too long, you have been content to live in the shadows of doubt and uncertainty. But today, I urge you to step into the light of possibility, to embrace your vision with unwavering faith and determination. For it is only when you dare to dream that you can profoundly change the world.

But let me be clear: the path to realising your vision will not be easy. It will be fraught with challenges, setbacks, and moments of doubt. But in those moments, you must remember the power of your vision – the power to inspire, to motivate, and to transform.

So, my friend, I challenge you today to dream bigger, to envision a future that surpasses your wildest imagination, and to take the first step towards making that vision a reality. Together, let us harness the power of vision to create a world that is brighter, bolder, and more beautiful than you ever thought possible.

In next chapter, " Finding your Purpose, Understand Your Mission & Why You Exist" with an idea of creating a purpose driven venture, let me take you on a journey in crafting the foundational elements of your business's identity. Learn to articulate a clear mission and define values, shaping the soul of your venture. This next chapter is a vital compass for entrepreneurs navigating the journey from Visions to Victory.

Chapter 2.4

Finding your Purpose, Understand Your Mission & Why You Exist

MISSION

M Motivating

I Inclusive

S Striving

S Sustainable

I Impactful

O Open-minded

N Networked

In the wide range of human experiences, searching for purpose is one of the most important and lasting efforts. It transcends age, culture, and circumstance, getting to the very heart of why you are here. Finding your purpose, or as I like to call it, discovering your "dot," is about identifying where your passions, talents, and values meet. This intersection gives your life meaning and direction.

Understanding why you exist and what makes your life meaningful is not just a philosophical question—it's a practical one too. It affects every part of your life: your career choices, personal relationships, your sense of fulfilment, and overall happiness.

In simple terms, finding your purpose means living in a way that feels true to who you are, leading to a more satisfying and fulfilling life.

The search for purpose is both deeply personal and relevant to everyone. It involves looking inward, exploring different possibilities, and sometimes making big life changes. Your purpose may evolve as you learn and experience more, but the main goal stays the same: to understand what motivates you, what makes you happy, and how you can make a positive impact on the world.

In this chapter, I want to discuss various aspects of finding your purpose, importance of self-discovery, the role of your passions and strengths, and the impact of having meaningful goals. My hope is to provide you with tools and insights that will help you uncover your unique purpose and see how it can guide your decisions and actions in life.

Embarking on this journey is a big step that can transform your life. It requires courage, honesty, and a willingness to embrace change. But the benefits are immense, offering clarity, direction, and a deep sense of belonging in the world.

So, let us begin this journey together. Let us explore your potential and your dreams in the quest to find your true purpose.

Purpose of a Cricket Team members

Here, I want to talk to you about the heart and soul of cricket: the purpose that drives each team to step onto the field and give their all in pursuit of victory.

For the batting team, their purpose is clear: to score runs and build a formidable total that puts pressure on the opposition. Every player knows that their contribution at the crease is vital in setting the stage for success. Whether it's occupying the crease, rotating the strike, or launching a counterattack, their purpose is to lay a strong foundation and give their team the best possible chance of triumph.

As for the bowling team, their purpose is equally important: to take wickets and restrict the opposition's scoring. With every delivery, they aim to outsmart the batsmen, exploit any weaknesses, and create opportunities for their team to seize control of the match. Whether it's bowling with pace and accuracy, using variations to keep the batsmen guessing, or working in tandem to apply pressure, their purpose is to make their presence felt and turn the tide in their favour.

And let's not forget the fielding team, whose purpose is to support the bowlers and prevent runs through agile fielding, sharp catching, and accurate throwing. With every dive, every catch, and every throw, they aim to inspire their teammates, demoralise the opposition, and make a tangible difference in the outcome of the match. Their purpose is to be the unsung heroes of the team, the ones who turn defence into attack and create moments of magic on the field.

So, as you watch these teams take to the field, let us remember the purpose that drives them: the desire to excel, the hunger for success, and the commitment to their teammates. For in cricket, as in life, it is purpose that gives meaning to your actions and fuels your journey towards victory.

Objectives of a Cricket Team

In cricket, much like in life, setting clear objectives is crucial to achieving success and overcoming challenges.

Let's start with the batting team. Their objectives are clear: to build partnerships, maintain a healthy run rate, and capitalise on scoring opportunities. They understand that by achieving these objectives, they can set a strong foundation for their team's success and put pressure on the opposition. Whether it's rotating the strike, finding gaps in the field, or playing with patience and determination, their objectives guide their every move at the crease.

Next, you have the bowling team. Their objectives revolve around restricting the opposition's scoring, taking wickets at regular intervals, and building pressure on the batsmen. They know that by achieving these objectives, they can gain control of the match and create opportunities for their team to succeed. Whether it's bowling tight lines and lengths, using variations to outsmart the batsmen, or working together as a cohesive unit, their objectives drive their strategy and execution on the field.

Last but certainly not least, let's talk about the fielding team. Their objectives are focused on preventing runs, taking catches, and executing runouts to support the bowlers and create additional pressure on the batting team. They understand that by achieving these objectives, they can turn the momentum in their team's favour and make vital contributions to their success. Whether it's diving to stop boundaries, holding onto catches under pressure, or hitting the stumps with pinpoint accuracy, their objectives drive their commitment and effort in the field.

As you reflect on these objectives, let us remember that cricket, much like life itself, is a game of strategy, teamwork, and determination. By setting clear objectives and working together towards a common goal, you can overcome any challenge and achieve greatness on and off the field.

Core values of a Cricket Team

In cricket, much like in life, it's not just about the actions you take, but the values you uphold along the way that truly define us.

Let's start with the batting team. Patience, technique, and adaptability are the cornerstone of their approach. They understand the importance of waiting for the right opportunity, using proper technique to defend against challenges, and adapting to different conditions. These values not only guide their performance but also shape their character both on and off the field.

Next, you have the bowling team. Discipline, skill, and teamwork are their guiding principles. They know that success in bowling comes from consistent effort, using a variety of techniques, and supporting each other as a unit. Whether it's hitting the right spot consistently or executing a well-planned strategy, these values underpin their every action and decision.

Last but certainly not least, let's talk about the fielding team. Commitment, agility, and team spirit are the driving forces behind their performance. They give their all on the field, reacting quickly to every opportunity and supporting each other through thick and thin. Whether it's diving to save a boundary, taking a crucial catch, or executing a run-out, their commitment to excellence shines through in every aspect of their game.

As you reflect on these core values, let us remember that cricket, much like life itself, is a journey of growth, learning, and self-discovery. It's not just about the runs scored or wickets taken, but the values you embody and the legacy you leave behind. So, let's embrace the spirit of cricket, uphold these core values with pride, and inspire others to do the same.

Mission – the Driving purpose of your organisation

Mission is a fundamental aspect of every organisation's success. Whether large or small, nonprofit or for-profit, every organisation needs a clear and compelling mission to guide its actions, inspire its stakeholders, and drive its success.

Mission is particularly important in every part of life. The mission of the grandchild Hare in the story of this section was to continuously strive forward without resting, avoiding distractions and overconfidence and win the race. He was also on the mission to learn from past mistakes and ensure that arrogance does not cost victory. You all must have a mission in your personal and professional life.

At its core, a mission defines the purpose of an organisation in short term. It answers the fundamental question of what it seeks to achieve. Without a clear mission, you and your organisations risk drifting aimlessly, lacking direction and focus. Like a ship without a compass, they may find themselves lost at sea, unable to navigate the challenges and opportunities that lie ahead.

A well-crafted mission serves as beacon of the light house for decision-making and strategic planning. It helps you and your organisations stay true to their core values and objectives, even in the face of uncertainty or adversity. By aligning all activities and initiatives with the mission, you and your organisations can ensure that every action contributes to the overarching goals and objectives.

Mission is essential for inspiring and motivating stakeholders. Whether employees, customers, investors, or partners, people are drawn to you and your organisations with a compelling mission that resonates with their values and aspirations. A strong mission creates a sense of purpose and belonging, rallying individuals around a common cause and fostering a shared sense of commitment and dedication. It acts as a powerful tool for differentiation and positioning in the marketplace. In today's competitive business landscape, you and your organisations need to stand out from the crowd and articulate what sets them apart. A clear and compelling mission can help you and your organisations carve out a unique identity and attract customers who share their values and beliefs.

Mission provides a framework for accountability and measurement. By defining clear goals and objectives, you and your organisations can track their progress and assess their performance against predefined metrics. This allows them to identify areas for improvement, celebrate successes, and course correct as needed to stay on track towards achieving their mission.

In other words, the importance of a mission for every organisation cannot be overstated. It provides direction, inspiration, differentiation, and accountability—all essential elements for success in today's dynamic and competitive environment. As leaders and stakeholders, let us embrace the power of mission and work together to create organisations that are driven by purpose and guided by a shared vision of success. Let me share with you the power of mission, using Google as a prime example.

Inspiring Mission of Google

In the fast-paced and ever-changing landscape of business, having a clear and compelling mission is more important than ever. It is the cornerstone upon which successful organisations are built, guiding their actions, inspiring their stakeholders, and driving their success.

A mission is more than just a statement on paper; it is the beating heart of an organisation.

Whereas vision defines the purpose of why you exist, the mission defines what you aim to achieve. It is a declaration of your values, your aspirations, and your commitment to making a difference in the world.

Google's mission statement, "To organise the world's information and make it universally accessible and useful," is not just a string of words; it embodies the driving force behind one of the most influential companies of your time.

The inspiration behind Google's mission can be traced back to its founders, Larry Page and Sergey Brin, who shared a fundamental belief in the transformative power of information. When they founded Google in 1998, they envisioned a world where accessing and utilising information online would be seamless and efficient.

At the heart of their mission was a recognition of the challenges posed by the rapidly expanding internet. With the web becoming increasingly vast and complex, finding relevant and reliable information was becoming more difficult for users. Page and Brin saw an opportunity to address this challenge by creating a search engine that could organise the wealth of information available online and make it accessible to everyone, regardless of their location or background.

But their mission went beyond just improving search functionality. It was rooted in a deep-seated belief in the democratising power of information. Page and Brin saw the internet as a tool for empowerment, capable of connecting people, expanding knowledge, and driving progress. By making information universally accessible, they aimed to level the playing field and empower individuals with the knowledge they need to make informed decisions, pursue their interests, and contribute meaningfully to society.

The inspiration behind Google's mission statement reflects a commitment to harnessing the transformative potential of information technology for the greater good. It is a testament to the belief that information has the power to change lives, drive innovation, and create a more connected and informed world.

As you reflect on Google's mission, let us be reminded of the importance of having a clear and compelling mission in your own organisations. A mission is not just a statement; it is a guiding light that inspires us, aligns us, and propels us forward towards a shared vision of success.

Having a mission provides us with direction and focus in a world filled with distractions and competing priorities. It serves as a beacon of the light house, guiding us through the complexities of decision-making and ensuring that every action you take is aligned with your overarching goals.

A mission is not just about strategy; it is also about inspiration. A compelling mission inspires us to reach higher, to push boundaries, and to strive for excellence in everything you do. It instils a sense of purpose and meaning in your work, driving us forward even in the face of adversity.

A mission is a powerful tool for building identity and differentiation. It sets us apart from your competitors by clearly articulating what makes us unique and what values you stand for. It attracts like-minded individuals who share your vision and values, creating a community of passionate advocates and supporters.

Having a mission also fosters accountability and transparency. It holds us accountable to your stakeholders, reminding us of the promises you have made and the impact you seek to create. It provides a framework for measuring your progress and evaluating your performance, ensuring that you stay true to your purpose.

In other words, having a mission is essential for organisational success. It provides us with direction, inspiration, and accountability, guiding us on your journey towards achieving your goals and making a positive impact in the world.

So let us embrace your mission wholeheartedly, for it is the key to unlocking your full potential and realising your dreams. But before delving into understanding the mission of your venture, let's grasp the key differences between the vision, the mission, the goals, and the objectives of a venture, and the relationship between them.

What is a Mission?

Mission is a powerful tool and lies at the very heart of every individual, organisation, or entity. A mission is not just a statement; it's a declaration of the current state of your business. Your mission defines your purpose, your objectives, and your core values. It communicates the reason for your existence and the goals you aim to achieve in the specified period. A mission statement typically outlines the primary activities or functions of your venture and identifies the target audience or beneficiaries of its efforts. It serves as a guiding beacon that informs strategic planning, decision-making, and day-to-day operations. It aligns your efforts within the venture and provides a sense of purpose and direction.

Think of the mission as the beacon of the light house that guides us through the darkest of nights and the stormiest of seas. It defines your purpose, objectives, and core values, setting the course for everything you do. Whether you're an individual with a personal mission or part of an organisation with a collective mission, it's what gives meaning to your actions and direction to your journey.

At its core, a mission statement answers the fundamental question – "Why do you exist?"

It encapsulates the essence of who you are, what you stand for, and the impact you strive to make in the world. It's the driving force behind your decisions, shaping your priorities and guiding your actions.

But a mission is not just a lofty ideal; it's a practical tool for success. It provides a guiding framework for your daily operations, strategic planning, and decision-making processes. It aligns your efforts, ensuring that you work towards common goals with clarity and purpose.

The importance of a mission cannot be overstated. It grounds us in your core values, reminding us of what truly matters. It inspires us to reach higher, push harder, and strive for excellence in everything you do. It fosters a sense of belonging and unity, bringing together individuals and organisations with a shared purpose and vision.

But perhaps most importantly, a mission gives us hope. It reminds us that no matter how challenging the journey may be, you are part of something bigger than ourselves. It fuels your passion, fuels your determination, and fuels your belief that you can make a difference in the world.

Similar to Vision, mission statements are essential components of a business's strategic framework. They articulate the organisation's purpose, values, and aspirations, providing clarity and direction to stakeholders.

The key difference between the mission and vision lies in their focus and timeframe. A mission statement focuses on the present, defining the organisation's core purpose and values, while a vision statement focuses on the future, outlining the desired state or outcomes the organisation strives to achieve.

While the lifespan of a mission and vision may differ, both are integral to the success of an organisation. They provide guidance, inspiration, and alignment, driving both short-term actions and long-term strategic objectives. While a mission statement grounds the organisation in its core purpose and values, a vision statement inspires and guides the pursuit of future aspirations. Together, they form a powerful framework that shapes the organisation's identity, culture, and trajectory.

A mission outlines the fundamental purpose and core objectives of an organisation or venture. It articulates the reason for its existence, the values it upholds, and the overall impact it aims to achieve in its broader context. Essentially, a mission serves as a guiding principle, helping to define the company's identity and provide direction for its activities and decisions. It often reflects the organisation's commitment to its stakeholders, customers, employees, and the community. The mission statement is a key element of strategic planning and is intended to inspire and align the efforts of everyone involved with the organisation.

Allow me to stand before you with a call to action, a call to embrace a MISSION that goes beyond personal ambition and reaches towards a collective greatness. You're here to uncover the plan for success, to encourage you to dream big, imagine the extraordinary, and, most importantly, to take significant action to turn those dreams into reality. This involves understanding and expanding upon the key elements of the term "MISSION."

Motivating - Your mission must be a flame that constantly ignites passion within you. It should not be just a statement but a source of perpetual motivation. Let it be the driving force that propels you forward, even in the face of challenges.

Inclusive - Imagine a mission that transcends boundaries, a mission that unites people from diverse backgrounds and perspectives. Inclusivity is the secret ingredient that transforms ordinary endeavours into extraordinary ones. Success is amplified when shared by a diverse and inclusive community.

Striving for Excellence - Your mission is a commitment to excellence. It's a pledge to pursue the highest standards in every endeavour. Mediocrity has no place in a mission fuelled by the pursuit of excellence. Success becomes a habit when excellence is the standard.

Sustainable - A great mission is not a sprint; it's a marathon. Sustainability is the key to enduring success. Consider the long-term impacts of your mission on the environment, society, and the economy. Let your mission be a force that stands the test of time.

Impactful - Your mission should not only be about personal achievements but about making a meaningful impact on the world. Think beyond yourself; think about the legacy you want to leave. An impactful mission creates ripples that extend far beyond your immediate sphere.

Open-minded - Success often lies at the intersection of adaptability and open-mindedness. Embrace change, learn from feedback, and be open to new ideas. An open-minded mission is a dynamic mission, one that evolves and grows with the ever-changing landscape.

Networked - Imagine a mission that is not solitary but connected, a mission that thrives on collaboration and partnerships. Success is often accelerated when you build a network of like-minded individuals and organisations. Together, you can achieve more than you could ever achieve alone.

Make sure your MISSION is more than just words on paper. Let it be a living, breathing force that drives you forward. Dream big, imagine the extraordinary, and take significant action to achieve those dreams. The blueprint of success is in your hands. Keeping this in mind, let's now explore what a Mission statement is.

So let us embrace your mission with pride and conviction. Let us commit ourselves wholeheartedly to the pursuit of your goals and the fulfillment of your purpose. And let us remember that with a clear mission as your guide, there is no limit to what you can achieve.

The Key Differentiator

Crafting clear and compelling vision and mission statements is vital for any organisation, as they serve as guiding lights, steering the company towards its goals and objectives. However, understanding the distinctions between the two is crucial for effective articulation.

A vision statement illuminates the organisation's long-term aspirations and the impact it seeks to create in the world. It paints a picture of the future the company aims to realise. On the other hand, a mission statement outlines the organisation's purpose and the strategies it employs to achieve its vision. It is more focused on the present and immediate future, detailing the company's current actions and objectives.

Consider the examples provided: Tesla's vision is to accelerate the transition to sustainable energy, while its mission is to achieve this by designing, manufacturing, and selling high-quality electric vehicles and energy storage products. Similarly, Amazon's vision revolves around being the most customer-centric company, while its mission is to enhance the customer experience through internet and technology-driven innovations.

When crafting these statements, it's essential to consider the time horizon and audience.

Vision statements look towards the distant future, inspiring external stakeholders like customers and society at large. In contrast, mission statements cater more towards internal stakeholders such as employees and shareholders, focusing on the present actions and strategies.

For instance, Google's vision is to provide access to the world's information with one click, while its mission is to organise and make this information universally accessible and useful. These statements align with the company's long-term goals while outlining its immediate objectives and strategies.

Vision, mission, goals, and objectives are crucial components of strategic planning for you and your organisations, each serving distinct purposes in guiding an entity towards its desired future state. Let's consider a fictional company, ABC Limited, to illustrate these concepts of vision, mission, goals, and objectives. Here's a brief overview of each:

The vision is a forward-looking statement that describes the desired future state or the long-term aspirations of an organisation. It provides a broad and inspirational overview of what the organisation aims to achieve in the long run. A vision statement is often concise and serves to guide decision-making and actions. Considering the example of your made-up company, ABC LIMITED, the vision could be, "To be a global leader in innovative technology solutions, shaping the future of digital transformation and enhancing people's lives worldwide."

The mission statement outlines the fundamental purpose of an organisation, including its core values, the target audience, and the products or services it provides. It defines the organisation's reason for existence and helps stakeholders, both internal and external, understand the organisation's scope and objectives. The mission statement often provides a sense of direction and identity. Example of a mission statement is "ABC LIMITED is committed to delivering cutting-edge technology products and services that empower businesses and individuals. You strive to uphold the highest standards of quality, ethics, and sustainability, creating value for your customers, employees, and stakeholders."

Let's explore about the other key elements Goals and Objectives in Section 4 of this book in their respective context.

In this example, the vision sets the broad and aspirational direction for ABC Limited. The mission outlines the company's fundamental purpose and values.

While the vision and the mission set the overarching direction and purpose of an organisation, goals and objectives provide the specific and measurable targets needed to achieve that vision. Together, these elements create a roadmap for an organisation's strategic planning and decision-making processes.

In essence, vision and mission statements complement each other, providing a roadmap for the organisation's journey. They guide decision-making, inspire employees, attract customers and investors, and distinguish the company from competitors. By following a framework like the one outlined above, you and your organisations can refine and articulate their vision and mission statements effectively, aligning their actions with their values and goals.

Now that you have this understanding, let's delve into the second pillar of venture creation success – the MISSION of your venture.

Mission of a Cricket Match

Cricket, often hailed as a gentleman's game, is much more than just a sport; it's a journey of skill, strategy, and camaraderie. It's a game of guts, glory, and a good bit of strategy. But ever wondered what keeps every player going out there? Let me break it down for you.

Imagine this: the batters step up, bat in hand, ready to take on the bowlers. Their job? Simple – score runs. Hit that ball to kingdom come, dance down the pitch, and show off some serious skill. Each batter's like a warrior, facing down the bowlers with grit and determination. Why? Because runs aren't just numbers; they're the currency of cricket. A solid batting performance can set the tone for the match, making the other team shake in their boots and setting us up for a win.

But what about the bowlers? They're the ones with the ball, the ones pulling tricks out of the bag. Their mission? Stop the batters from scoring and take wickets. They throw everything at it – fast balls, slow balls, you name it. And why? To show who's boss, to take control of the game, and tip the scales in your favour. When it's bowler versus batter, it's the bowlers who can really make things happen.

And don't forget the fielders – the unsung heroes patrolling the boundaries. Their job's not flashy – stop runs, catch balls, and run people out. But every run they save, every catch they take, it makes all the difference. Why do they do it? For the love of the game, for the team, and for the sheer thrill of being in the thick of it.

The mission of players in a cricket match is as diverse as the game itself, encompassing various aspects that contribute to their team's success and the overall spirit of the game. Whether they're batting, bowling, or fielding, each player has a vital role to play in shaping the outcome of the match.

Let's start with the batting team. Their mission is clear: to score runs and build a solid total that puts pressure on the opposition. From negotiating the new ball to capitalising on scoring opportunities, each batsman has a specific role to play in laying a strong foundation for their team's innings. Players aim to establish partnerships, occupy the crease, and rotate the strike to keep the scoreboard ticking. Opening batsmen have a specific mission to negotiate the new ball, see off the initial threat posed by the opposition's fast bowlers, and lay a platform for the middle order to capitalise on.

On the other hand, the bowling team's mission is to restrict the opposition's scoring and take early wickets to gain control of the match. Bowlers strive to exploit the conditions, whether it's swing, seam, or turn, to trouble the batsmen and create opportunities for breakthroughs. Fast bowlers may have a mission to exploit swing, seam, or pace to trouble the opposition batsmen, while spinners may focus on extracting turn and variation to create chances. The bowling team's mission also includes executing bowling plans devised by the captain and coaching staff, targeting the opposition's weaknesses, and maintaining discipline in line and length.

Meanwhile, the fielding team's mission is to support the bowlers by maintaining high standards in fielding, catching, and ground fielding. From saving runs to capitalising on mistakes, fielders play a crucial role in applying pressure on the opposition and maintaining team morale. Fielders have a mission to maintain concentration and intensity throughout the innings, anticipate the batsmen's intentions, and react quickly to opportunities in the field. The fielding team's mission also includes communication and coordination among fielders, backing up each other, and providing encouragement to maintain team morale.

But beyond the individual missions of each team, there's a broader mission that transcends the boundaries of the game itself. It's about upholding the values of sportsmanship, teamwork, and fair play that define the spirit of cricket. It's about learning and improving with each match, regardless of the outcome, and leaving a legacy that inspires future generations of cricketers.

In other words, the mission of players in a cricket match is not just about winning or losing; it's about embracing the challenges, celebrating the successes, and embodying the true essence of cricket. So, as you witness the drama unfold on the cricket field, let's not just focus on the scorecard or the statistics. Let's appreciate the passion, dedication, and sportsmanship displayed by the players as they strive to achieve victory and uphold the spirit of the game.

Mission Statement and Values

A mission statement is the heartbeat of your business, pulsating with the purpose and values that define your existence. In this segment, you unravel the secrets behind creating a mission statement that resonates with authenticity and aligns with your core values. Understand how a well-crafted mission becomes a driving force for your team and a beacon for customers.

A compelling mission statement instils a sense of purpose, fostering a strong organisational culture and attracting stakeholders who share your values.

In the vast landscape of endeavours, it is not the ventures with grandeur or immense wealth that leave an indelible mark; rather, it is those driven by a profound mission and unwavering values.

Take a moment to reflect on what truly matters to you, what sets your soul on fire, and what legacy you wish to leave behind. Your mission is not just a statement; it is the heartbeat of your venture, a rhythmic force that propels you forward. It's the anchor that keeps you grounded in the turbulent seas of challenges. Crafting a mission is an act of self-definition. It's about distilling the very essence of your purpose into words that resonate with your core.

Remember **success is not a destination; it is a journey paved with the stones of purpose.**

Your mission is your roadmap, your guiding compass. It's the force that propels you out of bed each morning with a burning passion to make a difference, not just in your life but in the lives of others.

Values on the other hand are the pillars that uphold your mission. They are the non-negotiable principles that define your character. They are the silent architects of every decision, every action, and every interaction. Values shape the culture of your venture, creating an environment where integrity, respect, and innovation flourish.

Now, imagine a venture, or picture yourself directing a movie, where every individual is more than just an employee, or a contractor involved in the production. Instead, envision them as torchbearers of a shared mission, guardians of shared values. Envision a space where every task transcends mere employment and becomes a contribution to a larger narrative—a story of impact and significance.

I challenge each one of you to take action today.

Take a moment to sit down and reflect on your mission. **Ask yourself, "What change do I want to see in the world? What legacy do I aim to leave behind?"**

Let your mission be a testament to your dreams and aspirations. Allow it to function as the guiding lighthouse through the darkest nights of your journey. Alongside, let's grasp the essence of a mission statement, which is explained below.

The Essence of a Mission Statement

At the heart of every successful business lies a mission that extends beyond profit. Crafting a compelling mission statement aligns your team, attracts like-minded customers, and sets the stage for a purpose-driven and successful venture. It is akin to sculpting the guiding philosophy and heartbeat of your organisation. It serves as a powerful tool that brings unity and coherence to your team, aligning diverse individuals toward a shared vision and common goals. This shared sense of purpose fosters a cohesive work environment where each member understands their role in contributing to the overarching mission.

A well-crafted mission statement not only aligns your internal team but also acts as a magnetic force for like-minded customers. It becomes a beacon that resonates with individuals who share similar values and beliefs. Customers are not just buying a product or service; they are investing in the ethos and purpose that your mission represents. This alignment creates a strong bond between your venture and its customer base, fostering loyalty and advocacy.

Moreover, a compelling mission statement sets the stage for a purpose-driven venture. It goes beyond the mere pursuit of profit and delineates the broader impact and contribution your business aims to make. This sense of purpose becomes a driving force for innovation, resilience, and perseverance, especially during challenging times. It inspires your team to go above and beyond, knowing that they are part of something meaningful and impactful.

The act of crafting a compelling mission statement is not just a symbolic exercise; it is a strategic move that profoundly influences the dynamics of your venture. It aligns internal efforts, attracts a community of supporters, and provides the foundation for a purposeful and successful journey. It guides your team and customers alike, ensuring that every step taken contributes to the fulfilment of a greater purpose. However, this higher purpose of the venture's vision would be incomplete without discussing the connection between the mission and the core values. At the core of every mission statement are four key elements:

Purpose - The very essence of why the entity exists. It's the driving force behind every endeavour, the North Star that guides its journey. Whether it's a commitment to innovation, a dedication to service, or a passion for excellence, the purpose is what gives meaning and direction to everything the entity does.

Objectives - These are the concrete goals and aspirations that the entity aims to achieve. From expanding market share to improving customer satisfaction, objectives provide a roadmap for success and help measure progress towards the mission's fulfillment. They give focus and clarity to the organisation's efforts, ensuring that every action is aligned with its broader goals.

Values - The bedrock of any mission statement. Values are the principles and beliefs that define the character of the entity and guide its behaviour. Integrity, respect, diversity, and sustainability are just a few examples of the values that underpin mission statements, serving as a moral compass for decision-making and interactions.

Audience - Every mission statement has a target audience or stakeholders in mind. Whether it's customers, employees, shareholders, or the community, the mission statement communicates who the entity serves and seeks to impact. By understanding its audience, the entity can tailor its mission to meet the needs and expectations of those it serves.

So, as you reflect on the key elements of a mission statement, let us remember their profound significance. They are not just words; they are a declaration of purpose, a roadmap for success, and a commitment to making a positive difference in the world. So, let's now delve into the guiding light of core values in this chapter.

The Guiding Light of Core Values

Crafting your values is not a passive exercise; it's an active commitment to live authentically. Define the principles that are non-negotiable for you, the beliefs that you will not compromise on even in the face of adversity. Let your values be the foundation upon which your venture stands tall and resilient.

As mentioned above, Your mission is your roadmap, your guiding compass. But Values on the other hand are the pillars that uphold your mission. They are the non-negotiable principles that define your character. They are the silent architects of every decision, every action, and every interaction. Values shape the culture of your venture, creating an environment where integrity, respect, and innovation flourish.

Core values are the silent architects of an organisation's culture. In this segment, you explore the transformative power of defining core values. Drawing on experiences from ethical leaders, understand how core values act as a guiding light, influencing decision-making, shaping behaviours, and fostering a positive work environment.

Establishing clear core values provides a moral compass, creating a cohesive and ethical organisational culture that resonates with both internal and external stakeholders.

It is akin to setting a moral compass for your organisation, offering a guiding light that shapes the character and direction of your venture. These values serve as the foundational principles that not only define the ethical standards within your organisation but also act as a beacon for all stakeholders, both internal and external.

Internally, clear core values create a cohesive organisational culture. They become the shared beliefs and principles that unite your team, providing a common ground for decision-making, behaviour, and interactions. This unity fosters a sense of belonging and shared purpose among employees, transcending individual roles and responsibilities. It helps create a workplace where integrity, respect, and collaboration thrive, contributing to a positive and ethical working environment.

Externally, these core values become the essence of your organisation's identity. They communicate to clients, customers, and partners the principles that guide your business practices. When external stakeholders perceive a strong commitment to ethical values, it builds trust and credibility. Customers are more likely to engage with a company that aligns with their own values, and partners are more inclined to collaborate with an organisation that demonstrates a commitment to ethical conduct.

Moreover, a cohesive and ethical organisational culture, driven by clear core values, serves as a risk mitigation strategy. It establishes a framework that helps employees navigate complex decisions and dilemmas by referring back to the organisation's foundational principles. This, in turn, reduces the likelihood of ethical lapses or misconduct that could harm the reputation of the organisation.

Establishing clear core values is a strategic move that goes beyond a mere statement on paper. It acts as a moral compass, providing direction for internal behaviours and shaping the external perception of your organisation. By nurturing a united and ethical culture, and aligning the mission and values, these principles play a part in the venture's lasting success and sustainability. This resonates positively with all stakeholders involved.

Aligning Mission and Values

Harmony between your mission statement and core values is the secret sauce for enduring success. The art of aligning mission and values seamlessly is a must for any organisation success. You must uncover the strategies used by successful entrepreneurs to ensure that every action, decision, and initiative reflects the essence of your business's purpose and values.

When mission and values align, your business gains authenticity, integrity, and a powerful identity that resonates with customers, employees, and partners.

It's not just a matter of crafting individual elements; it's about orchestrating a symphony where the mission statement and core values resonate in unison, creating a powerful and cohesive narrative for your venture.

Your mission statement is the driving force that propels it forward. It's the "why" behind what you do, encapsulating the essence of your aspirations and the impact you seek to make. When in harmony with your core values, the mission statement becomes not just a declaration but a lived reality. It aligns every endeavour, decision, and action with the principles that define your organisational character.

On the other hand, core values guide the behaviour and decisions of everyone within the organisation. When in sync with the mission statement, these values infuse authenticity into every facet of your venture. They become the ethical framework that ensures your journey towards success is not only prosperous but also morally grounded.

This harmony creates a synergistic effect that permeates throughout the organisation. It cultivates a culture where employees are not just workers but passionate contributors to a shared mission, driven by values that resonate with their personal beliefs. This alignment fosters a sense of purpose and belonging, motivating individuals to give their best towards the common goals.

Externally, the harmony between mission and values becomes a magnetic force. Customers, clients, and partners are drawn to you and your organisations that not only articulate a compelling mission but also embody it through consistent adherence to core values. It builds trust, credibility, and a positive reputation that transcends individual transactions, contributing to enduring success in a competitive landscape.

When these elements work together smoothly, they establish a strong foundation for your organisation, driving it not only towards immediate success but also ensuring its long-lasting impact and significance. However, this can never be achieved unless and until it is communicated to a wider audience.

Conclusion & Recap

This chapter on Mission Statement and Values serves as a compass, guiding you to infuse purpose, integrity, and authenticity into the very fabric of your business. As you embark on this journey, envision your mission and values not as mere statements but as the driving force behind a business destined for enduring success. Let your journey be filled with purpose, passion, and boundless success!

Remember this - your venture is not just a business; it's a manifestation of your dreams, fuelled by a mission and anchored by values. Aspire for success, but let that success be defined by the positive impact you create, the lives you touch, and the legacy you leave. Today, take the first step towards crafting a mission and values that will not only lead to success but to a life of fulfilment, purpose, and significance.

Think of your mission statement as the castle's motto, the rallying cry that echoes through the halls. Crafting a mission statement is about distilling your purpose into a succinct statement that resonates with both your team and your audience. It's not a mere tagline; it's a declaration of intent. Aligning this with your values ensures that every step is taken with integrity and purpose.

A well-crafted mission statement and aligned values create a strong identity. They become the foundation upon which you build relationships, make decisions, and weather the storms of the business landscape.

In the next chapter, you delve into "Establishing the Ethical Foundation," exploring the essential and core principles and foundations of ethical entrepreneurship. Learn to build a solid framework of values that underpin your business, ensuring integrity and ethical practices. This chapter lays the groundwork for principled and responsible entrepreneurial ventures.

Chapter 2.5

Establishing the Ethical Foundation

PRINCIPLES
P Purpose
R Resilient
I Integrity
N Noble
C Consistency
I Innovation
P Passion
L Leadership
E Empathy
S Strategic

While I am writing this chapter, I feel that you all, including you and me, are standing on the brink of something truly extraordinary. There's an electric sense of anticipation in the air, a feeling that you are on the cusp of embarking on a journey of immense significance. It's as if you're standing at the threshold of greatness, poised to seize a momentous opportunity that promises nothing short of greatness.

What makes this moment even more profound is the recognition of the transformative power that lies ahead. I am not just talking about ordinary change; I am talking about profound, life-altering transformation. This journey has the potential to reshape your lives, your businesses, and your futures in ways you may have never imagined.

But what will guide you on this journey? What will serve as your North Star, your guiding light through the unknown terrain ahead?

Welcome to a pivotal chapter on your entrepreneurial journey, where you're diving into the essence of ethical entrepreneurship – Establishing Core Principles. It's the guiding principles that you hold dear. These are the foundational beliefs, the core values that will act as your compass, your roadmap as you navigate the twists and turns of your personal or professional adventure.

As you embark on this odyssey towards your dreams and aspirations, get inspired by the timeless wisdom encapsulated in these guiding lights. Embrace the transformative power of this journey and approach it with a mindset of openness, curiosity, and determination. For it is through this journey, guided by your principles, that you will discover the greatness that lies within you and the boundless potential of what you can achieve. As you absorb the collective wisdom, envision how these principles can become the bedrock of your venture, guiding it towards not just success, but sustainable and principled triumph.

In the story of the young hare, which is a great example of some core principles like resilience, persistence, and setting a positive example, you can see examples of these principles in action. Learning from failures and setbacks to bounce back stronger is a great example of resilience from this story. Persevering through challenges and setbacks without losing sight of the ultimate goal is another great example of persistence as a core principle. Inspiring others through actions and demonstrating the importance of integrity and determination in achieving success is another example of the core principle of setting a positive example. I strongly believe in the power of principles to sculpt the grand tapestry of success. Let me share a story of The Wise Owl and the Cunning Crow supporting my belief.

The Wise Owl and the Cunning Crow

In a dense forest, there lived a wise old owl named Oliver and a cunning crow named Charlie. Oliver was known throughout the forest for his wisdom and adherence to principles, while Charlie was infamous for his deceitful and manipulative ways.

One day, as the sun began to set and the forest grew quiet, Oliver and Charlie found themselves perched on adjacent branches of the same tree. As they watched the world below, Oliver noticed a group of animals struggling to find food.

Concerned for their well-being, Oliver suggested that they work together to gather food and share it amongst themselves. He believed that by working together and abiding by the principles of cooperation and generosity, they could all thrive.

Charlie, however, had other ideas. He scoffed at Oliver's suggestion, believing that he could fare much better on his own. With a sly grin, Charlie flew off into the forest, leaving Oliver behind.

Despite Charlie's departure, Oliver remained steadfast in his commitment to his principles. He worked tirelessly to gather food for himself and the other animals, sharing whatever he could find with those in need.

Meanwhile, Charlie roamed the forest, using his cunning and deceit to trick other animals into giving him their food. He lied, cheated, and manipulated his way through the forest, accumulating a large stash of food for himself.

However, as time passed, Charlie's deceitful ways began to catch up with him. The other animals grew wise to his tricks and refused to trust him. Without the support of the community, Charlie found himself alone and vulnerable.

On the other hand, Oliver's commitment to his principles had earned him the respect and admiration of the other animals. They looked up to him as a leader and a friend, and they were always willing to lend a helping hand when he needed it.

In the end, while Charlie may have accumulated a large amount of food through his deceitful ways, it was Oliver who ultimately emerged victorious. His unwavering commitment to his principles had earned him the trust and support of the community, ensuring his long-term success and happiness.

The moral of the story is that principles, such as honesty, cooperation, and generosity, are the foundation of true success and happiness. Those who adhere to their principles, like Oliver, may face challenges along the way, but they will ultimately prevail in the end. On the other hand, those who stray from their principles, like Charlie, may achieve short-term gains, but they will ultimately find themselves alone and unfulfilled.

What are PRINCIPLES?

To me, principles are like guiding lights that brighten your journey, the solid foundation upon which dreams take flight and visions materialise. They illuminate your paths and shape the essence of who you are. In your daily busy lives, it's easy to lose sight of the fundamental truths that underpin your existence. Yet, it is precisely in times of uncertainty and adversity that the importance of principles shines brightest.

Principles are the bedrock upon which your moral and ethical compass is built. They provide us with a roadmap for navigating life's twists and turns, offering clarity amidst the chaos and grounding us in times of turbulence.

But what sets principles apart is not just their steadfastness, but their profound influence on your lives. They are the silent guardians that steer your decisions and actions towards paths of righteousness, guiding us towards the higher ideals you aspire to embody.

From honesty and integrity to justice and respect for others, principles are the timeless beacons of righteousness that light your way, guiding us towards lives of purpose and meaning.

As you stand on the cusp of a new era, you must heed the wisdom of principles and embrace their transformative power. Let us strive to embody the virtues they represent and forge a brighter, more compassionate world for generations to come. Today, you stand at the threshold of greatness, poised to embark on a journey illuminated by the transformative power of guiding principles. As you set forth on this odyssey towards your dreams and aspirations, let you be inspired by the timeless wisdom encapsulated in these guiding lights. As you set forth on the path to your dreams and visions, let these PRINCIPLES illuminate your way. Let's integrate them into the very fabric of your lives, constructing a blueprint for success that not only lifts us higher but also encourages others to reach for the stars using the diverse elements of these principles given below.

Purpose-driven - At the heart of your quest lies purpose—a purpose greater than ourselves, a purpose that infuses meaning into your every action. Let us anchor your principles in this higher purpose, for it is this alignment that gives your lives depth and significance. A purpose-driven life is not just about personal gain; it is about leaving a lasting impact, a legacy that transcends time. In the pursuit of greatness, let purpose be your guiding star. Your principles should resonate with a purpose greater than yourselves. A purpose-driven life is a life of significance, a life that echoes beyond the confines of personal achievement.

Resilient - Life is a journey of peaks and valleys. It's a journey fraught with challenges and obstacles, but it is your resilience that propels us forward. Let resilience be the backbone of your principles. Challenges will come, but in your resilience, you find the strength not just to endure but to triumph over adversity. Let us embrace resilience as a guiding principle, a steadfast companion in the face of adversity. With resilience as your ally, you can weather any storm, overcome any hurdle, and emerge stronger on the other side.

Integrity - In a world marred by moral ambiguity, integrity shines as a beacon of light. Let honesty and ethical behaviour be the cornerstone of your principles, for it is trust that forms the foundation of all meaningful relationships and endeavours. Upholding integrity ensures that your actions are guided by a moral compass, leading us towards success with honour and dignity. Uphold the pillar of integrity in every facet of your life. As mentioned earlier, let honesty be the currency of your transactions, and ethical behaviour the cornerstone of your principles. In integrity, you find the bedrock of trust upon which all success is built.

Noble - True greatness lies not in personal achievements but in the impact, you have on others and the world around us. Let nobility be the essence of your actions, guiding us to uplift humanity and make a positive difference in the lives of others. By embodying noble principles, you can leave a lasting legacy of compassion, kindness, and empathy. Choose principles that elevate not just yourself but humanity. Let nobility be the essence of your actions, contributing to the greater good and leaving a positive impact on the world.

Consistency - Success is not an event; it's a journey marked by consistent effort and determination. It's not a sprint but a marathon. Let us embrace consistency as a guiding principle, committing ourselves to daily rituals and actions that propel us towards your goals. It is through consistent effort that you can turn dreams into reality and achieve lasting success.

Innovation-minded - Embrace the spirit of innovation. Innovation is the lifeblood of progress, the spark that ignites change and transformation. Let your principles foster creativity and continuous improvement. The world is ever evolving, and innovation is the compass that leads to the forefront of success. By embracing innovation, you can stay ahead of the curve and lead the way towards a brighter future.

Passion-fuelled - Passion is the fuel that powers your dreams, the fire that burns bright in your hearts. Let us infuse your principles with passion, letting it drive us towards your goals with unwavering determination and enthusiasm. With passion as your guiding light, obstacles become opportunities, and challenges become stepping stones towards greatness.

Leadership-oriented - True leadership is not about wielding power but inspiring others to greatness. Let us instil leadership in your principles, empowering ourselves and others to achieve their full potential. By embodying the qualities of a true leader—inspiration, empowerment, and guidance—you can pave the way towards success for ourselves and those around us.

Empathy-centred - Empathy is the key to building bridges of understanding. In a world divided by differences, empathy serves as a bridge that connects us all. Let us make empathy a cornerstone of your principles, seeking to understand the dreams and struggles of others with compassion and kindness. By cultivating empathy, you can build stronger, more resilient communities and create a world where everyone can thrive. A compassionate heart fosters an environment conducive to collective success.

Strategic Perspective - Success is not a matter of luck but a result of strategic planning and execution. Strategic planning is an important part of navigating the path to success Let us develop strategic principles that guide your decisions with intentionality and purpose. By charting your course with strategic foresight, you can navigate the complexities of life with confidence and clarity, achieving your goals with precision and efficiency. Let your principles be the compass that helps you navigate the intricate map of success with a strategic and purposeful approach.

Remember, it's not just about dreaming big; it's about living with principles that turn those dreams into reality. Embrace the guiding principles as the blueprint for success, weaving them into the very fabric of your life. By anchoring yourself in purpose, resilience, integrity, nobility, consistency, innovation, passion, leadership, empathy, and strategic planning, you can unlock your full potential and embark on a journey of growth, fulfilment, and prosperity.

So, why are core principles so crucial, you might ask? To explore and gain a deeper understanding, let's grasp the essence of core principles.

The Essence of Core Principles

Core principles are the unwavering beliefs that shape the very soul of your business. They are not mere words on paper; they are the guiding stars that illuminate your path, the moral compass steering you through the challenges and triumphs of the business world. Principles serve as a moral compass, shaping your business decisions, actions, and relationships with stakeholders. Core principles are the values that define your character, resonating with authenticity and trustworthiness.

The profound significance of establishing clear core principles is that these principles are not arbitrary rules; they are the cornerstone of ethical business practices. When you establish and uphold these principles, you are laying the foundation for a business that transcends transactions, building relationships steeped in trust and respect.

In a world where scepticisms often shrouds business dealings, where trust is a precious commodity, your core principles become the bedrock of credibility. Customers, employees, and partners are drawn to businesses with a strong moral foundation. It is not just about what you offer; it's about how you offer it, with a commitment to fairness, transparency, and ethical conduct.

Consider the impact on customer loyalty when they know your business operates with unwavering principles. It goes beyond product or service quality; it's about the values you embody. Customers become more than just transactions; they become advocates, champions of your brand, spreading the word about the principles that define your business.

For employees, core principles create a work environment where integrity is not just a buzzword but a way of life. When your team operates within a framework of clear values, it fosters a culture of collaboration, innovation, and shared success. Employee morale soars, and productivity becomes a natural outcome of a workplace built on trust.

Partnerships, too, are strengthened when grounded in core principles. The collaborative ventures that stand the test of time are those where each party shares a commitment to common values. It's a symbiotic relationship, where mutual respect and a shared moral compass ensure the longevity and success of the partnership.

Now, as entrepreneurs, you might wonder, how do you go about establishing and embodying these core principles? It begins with introspection. Reflect on the values that matter most to you, the ideals that define your character. Seek inspiration from successful businesses that have built legacies on unwavering principles.

Communication is key. Clearly articulate your core principles to your team, customers, and partners. Let these principles be more than just words; let them be the driving force behind every decision, action, and interaction. Your core principles should not be confined to boardroom discussions but should permeate every aspect of your business.

The essence of core principles are a call to action. As you navigate the intricate waters of entrepreneurship, let your business be a beacon of authenticity and trust. Establish and uphold core principles that reflect the values you hold dear, and witness the transformative impact on your business, relationships, and legacy.

Your journey must be guided by the unwavering light of core principles, so that your businesses not only prosper financially but stand as beacons of ethical excellence in the vast sea of commerce.

Establishing clear core principles provides a foundation for ethical business practices, fostering trust among customers, employees, and partners. Your next segment in this chapter delves into this concept and its contribution as a fundamental element.

Establishing Core Principles

It is said that behind every successful venture lies a set of guiding principles, akin to a moral compass that not only steers the ship but defines its character.

Core principles are the pillars that uphold the structure of your venture. These are the fundamental beliefs and philosophies that guide your day-to-day operations.

Drawing upon the collective wisdom of ethical leaders, you shall unravel the significance of establishing core principles and delve into the transformative impact they have on decision-making, trust-building, and the very essence of your business. Principles are not just rules; they are the heartbeat, the pulse that defines the rhythm of your venture.

Why, you might ask, are these principles so crucial?

Establishing core principles is paramount in any endeavour, be it personal or professional, as they serve as the bedrock upon which success is built. These principles act as guiding lights, providing direction, clarity, and purpose to individuals, organisations, and societies.

First and foremost, core principles provide a moral compass, guiding your actions and decisions in alignment with your values and beliefs.

They define who you are and what you stand for, serving as a constant reminder of your integrity, ethics, and character.

In business, this integrity is fundamental to building trust with stakeholders, including customers, employees, and partners. When businesses operate with a clear set of principles, they earn the respect and loyalty of their stakeholders, laying the foundation for long-term success.

Moreover, core principles foster consistency and reliability in your actions. They provide a framework for evaluating situations and making choices, ensuring that you remain steadfast in your commitment to your goals and values. This consistency is essential for building credibility and trust in both personal and professional relationships.

In business, it contributes to a positive reputation and enhances the brand's image, leading to increased customer loyalty and satisfaction.

Additionally, core principles shape organisational culture, fostering a workplace environment built on trust, respect, and collaboration. When employees share common values and principles, it creates a sense of belonging and unity, driving engagement, productivity, and morale. A strong organisational culture also attracts top talent and encourages innovation, as employees feel empowered to take risks and think creatively in pursuit of shared goals.

Furthermore, core principles play a crucial role in decision-making, especially in the face of ethical dilemmas and challenges. They provide a moral framework for evaluating options and choosing the course of action that aligns with your values and principles. In business, ethical decision-making is essential for maintaining the trust and loyalty of customers and stakeholders, as well as for upholding legal and regulatory standards.

Establishing core principles is essential for fostering integrity, consistency, and trust in your personal and professional lives. These principles serve as guiding lights, illuminating your path and shaping your actions and decisions in alignment with your values and beliefs. In business, they are the foundation of a strong ethical culture, driving success, sustainability, and positive impact in the world.

Aligning Principles with Purpose

Aligning principles with purpose is crucial because it ensures that your actions and decisions are in harmony with your overarching goals and values. When your principles are in line with your purpose, you have a clear understanding of what you stand for and what you aim to achieve. This clarity enables us to set meaningful goals and make decisions that are consistent with your values, leading to a sense of direction and purpose in your lives. It also enhances motivation and engagement. When you are driven by a sense of purpose and guided by principles that resonate with that purpose, you feel a greater sense of fulfilment and passion in your work. This intrinsic motivation fuels your efforts, enabling us to overcome obstacles and persevere in the pursuit of your goals.

Furthermore, aligning principles with purpose promotes authenticity and integrity. When your actions are aligned with your values and beliefs, you demonstrate authenticity and integrity in your interactions with others. This authenticity builds trust and credibility, both within ourselves and with those around us, fostering stronger relationships and enhancing your reputation. It fosters resilience and adaptability. In times of uncertainty or adversity, having a clear sense of purpose and values provides a solid foundation upon which to navigate challenges. Your principles serve as guiding lights, helping us stay true to ourselves and maintain your course even in the face of obstacles.

encouraging innovation and creativity is another aspect of this. When you are driven by a sense of purpose and guided by principles that reflect your values, you are more likely to think outside the box and explore new ideas. This openness to innovation enables us to adapt to changing circumstances and seize opportunities for growth and development.

Aligning principles with purpose is essential for creating a meaningful and fulfilling life. It provides clarity, focus, and motivation, fosters authenticity and integrity, promotes resilience and adaptability, and encourages innovation and creativity. By aligning your actions and decisions with your values and goals, you can live with greater purpose and make a positive impact in the world around us.

Decision-Making Guided by Principles

Principled decision-making is the cornerstone of ethical leadership. Decisions are the building blocks that shape the destiny of ventures. However, it is not the decisions in isolation but the principles that underpin them that define the true mark of leadership. Principles ensures your decisions are not swayed by the winds of expediency but anchored in a moral and ethical foundation.

Principles provide a framework for distinguishing right from wrong, guiding individuals and organisations to make decisions that align with moral values and ethical standards. By adhering to principles such as honesty, fairness, and respect, decision-makers uphold integrity and build trust with stakeholders, fostering a positive reputation and ethical organisational culture.

Principles serve as consistent guidelines that enable decision-makers to make sound judgments across different situations and contexts. By applying principles consistently, individuals and organisations demonstrate reliability and predictability, earning the trust and confidence of stakeholders and minimising the risk of arbitrary or erratic decision-making.

Principles establish clear expectations for decision-makers and hold them accountable for their actions and choices. By aligning decisions with principles such as accountability, transparency, and responsibility, individuals and organisations demonstrate a commitment to ethical governance and accountability to stakeholders, fostering transparency and trust.

Principles provide a solid foundation upon which to navigate complex and uncertain situations, guiding decision-makers to act with resilience and adaptability in the face of challenges or setbacks. By adhering to principles such as flexibility, innovation, and resilience, individuals and organisations can respond effectively to change, seize opportunities, and overcome obstacles, ensuring long-term success and sustainability.

Principles help decision-makers align their actions and choices with organisational goals, vision, and values, ensuring strategic coherence and alignment across all levels of the organisation. By adhering to principles such as strategic alignment, goal orientation, and customer focus, individuals and organisations can maximise efficiency, effectiveness, and performance, driving success and achieving desired outcomes.

Decision-making guided by principles is essential for ethical conduct, consistency, reliability, accountability, transparency, resilience, adaptability, strategic alignment, and goal achievement.

By adhering to principles in decision-making processes, individuals and organisations can uphold integrity, build trust, foster resilience, and achieve sustainable success, ultimately contributing to a positive impact on society and the world.

Principled decision-making, when applied effectively, becomes a powerful force that permeates every facet of your business. It enhances transparency by allowing stakeholders to understand the rationale behind decisions. It cultivates integrity by ensuring that choices are aligned with the values that define your business. Moreover, it fosters consistency, creating a reliable framework for decision-making that reinforces your commitment to ethical business practices.

Nurturing a Principle-Driven Culture

Imagine, if you will, a pristine forest, untouched by the hands of man. In this ecosystem, each organism plays a unique role, contributing to the harmony of the whole. The towering trees, the delicate flowers, and the industrious insects all adhere to the principles of nature. It is a symphony of collaboration, innovation, and coexistence – a lesson from Mother Nature herself. Similarly, the culture of your organisation is a reflection of its principles. It is not a set of rules imposed from above but a living, breathing entity shaped by the collective values of every individual within it. You must illuminate the strategies employed by successful business owners to nurture a principle-driven culture, strategies inspired by the very essence of nature.

Nurturing a principle-driven culture within an organisation is crucial for fostering an environment of integrity, trust, and sustainable success. A principle-driven culture establishes clear expectations and standards for ethical behaviour, guiding employees to make decisions aligned with moral values and organisational principles. By fostering a culture where integrity is valued and upheld, you and your organisations cultivate trust among stakeholders, enhance their reputation, and mitigate the risk of ethical misconduct or wrongdoing.

When employees are empowered to uphold principles such as respect, fairness, and accountability, they feel valued, respected, and motivated to contribute their best efforts to the organisation's success. By fostering a culture where principles are celebrated and practiced, you and your organisations create a positive work environment that promotes collaboration, innovation, and employee satisfaction, leading to higher levels of engagement and productivity.

A principle-driven culture provides a common set of values and beliefs that unite employees across different departments, functions, and levels of the organisation. By aligning employees around shared principles and goals, you and your organisations foster a sense of unity, collaboration, and cohesion, enabling them to work towards common objectives and overcome challenges together effectively.

In a culture where principles such as openness, honesty, and accountability are valued and practiced, employees feel comfortable speaking up, sharing feedback, and holding themselves and others accountable for their actions. By fostering a culture of transparency and accountability, you and your organisations promote effective communication, trust, and continuous improvement, leading to better decision-making and problem-solving.

In a rapidly changing and uncertain business environment, you and your organisations with a strong foundation of principles can navigate challenges and seize opportunities with confidence and agility. By fostering a culture where principles such as flexibility, innovation, and resilience are embraced, you and your organisations empower employees to adapt to change, experiment with new ideas, and learn from failures, driving innovation and growth.

Nurturing a principle-driven culture is essential for promoting ethical conduct, enhancing employee engagement and morale, fostering organisational alignment and cohesion, promoting transparency and accountability, and strengthening organisational resilience and adaptability.

By prioritising principles in organisational culture, you and your organisations can create a workplace where integrity, trust, and sustainable success thrive, ultimately leading to positive outcomes for employees, stakeholders, and society as a whole.

Fostering a principle-driven culture strengthens your brand, attracts like-minded individuals, and creates a positive work environment that contributes to long-term success. Developing purpose-driven principles is essential for the success of any business. This is affirmed through an assessment and exercise, which are crucial components as they fulfil various vital purposes:

Conclusion & Recap

In conclusion, as you absorb the insights shared in this chapter on Establishing Core Principles, envision your venture not just as a profit-driven entity but as a force for positive change guided by unwavering principles. Understand the significance of principles in shaping your business's character.

As you set forth on this journey, remember that principles are not just statements; they are the living essence that propels your business towards ethical and enduring triumph.

Hoping that the story of the young hare and the owl and the cunning crow gives motivation to have core principles as an integral part of your personal and professional journey, and that it becomes a catalyst for your success.

Your next chapter, "Fabric of Entrepreneurial Wisdom - Build a Strong Culture" is dedicated for understanding the significance of building a strong organisational culture and guides you in cultivating the vital pulse of your business.

Explore the art of fostering a robust organisational culture that breathes life into your venture. Learn to nurture an environment where values, collaboration, and shared purpose flourish, shaping the essence of your business.

Chapter 2.6

Fabric of Entrepreneurial Wisdom - Build a Strong Culture

CULTURE
C Collaboration
U Unity
L Learning
T Transparency
U Understanding
R Respect
E Empowerment

It is remarkably easy to fall into the habit of condemning others, even those you hold dear. You often find ourselves criticising the way someone eats, the manner in which they speak, or other trivial details. while it is easy to fall into the habit of condemning others, doing so can have profound negative effects on your relationships and personal growth.

By understanding the roots of your critical tendencies and making a conscious effort to cultivate empathy, focus on positives, practice self-reflection, and communicate constructively, you can foster a more positive and supportive environment for ourselves and those around us. This shift not only enhances your interactions but also contributes to a more harmonious and fulfilling life. That's where Culture comes in place.

In its early years, Uber, the ride-hailing giant that revolutionised transportation, experienced remarkable growth and success, yet beneath the surface lurked a toxic workplace culture. Reports emerged of harassment, discrimination, and unethical behaviour, reflecting a lack of values-driven leadership and a cohesive organisational culture. Recognising the gravity of the situation, Uber's leadership embarked on a journey to overhaul its culture. By prioritising accountability, transparency, and inclusivity, Uber aimed to rebuild trust internally and externally. This example underscores the crucial role of organisational culture in shaping employee behaviour, fostering trust, and driving long-term success.

The story of the young hare emphasises the importance of organisational culture, such as learning from failures, celebrating successes, and fostering a growth mindset.

Now, let's turn your attention to Enron, once a titan in the energy sector. Enron's rapid ascent to prominence was marred by a culture of greed, deceit, and arrogance. Leaders prioritised short-term profits over ethical conduct, leading to fraudulent practices and widespread corruption. The absence of a strong organisational culture rooted in integrity and accountability ultimately led to Enron's downfall. The Enron scandal serves as a stark reminder of the catastrophic consequences of a toxic culture and the vital importance of ethical leadership and values-driven decision-making.

These stories underscore the undeniable truth: organisational culture shapes the destiny of companies. A strong and positive culture, characterised by integrity, transparency, and inclusivity, fosters employee engagement, drives innovation, and enhances trust with stakeholders. Conversely, a toxic culture can erode morale, breed unethical behaviour, and ultimately spell doom for even the most successful companies.

As a business leader, it is your responsibility to cultivate and nurture a culture that reflects your values and beliefs. By prioritising integrity, fostering open communication, and promoting diversity and inclusion, you can create an environment where employees thrive, innovation flourishes, and trust abounds.

What is Organisational Culture

Organisational culture encompasses the shared values, beliefs, norms, and behaviours that define the identity and character of a company. It's the collective personality of an organisation, shaping how employees interact, make decisions, and perceive their work environment.

At its core, organisational culture reflects the company's mission, vision, and core values. It influences everything from employee engagement and morale to productivity and innovation. A strong organisational culture fosters a sense of belonging and unity among employees, driving collaboration, teamwork, and loyalty. It sets the tone for how work is approached, encouraging accountability, transparency, and integrity in all actions. It serves as a guiding force for decision-making. It provides a framework for resolving conflicts, navigating challenges, and aligning individual and organisational goals. Organisational culture is the invisible thread that weaves together the fabric of an organisation, shaping its identity, influencing its success, and defining its legacy. It is not a mere catchphrase; it's the heartbeat of your businesses. It's the collective beliefs, values, and behaviours that define who you are as a company. Imagine it as the DNA that shapes the character and identity of your organisation, transcending the tangible and manifesting in every decision, interaction, and shared moment.

Consider, for a moment, the profound impact of Organisational Culture on employee engagement. In a culture that is fostered and celebrated, employees feel connected to a larger purpose. It transforms a job into a shared mission, leading to creativity, commitment, and a sense of belonging that transcends the typical employer-employee relationship.

In my view organisational culture is not a static backdrop but a dynamic stage upon which your business story unfolds. It's not about what you do; it's about how you do it. your culture is the invisible thread that weaves through every department, every project, and every interaction, creating a cohesive fabric that defines your character and sets the tone for success.

As you navigate the complexities of entrepreneurship, let us recognise that organisational culture is not something that can be imposed; it's cultivated with intention and care. It requires introspection, alignment with mission and values, and a commitment to shaping an environment where individuals thrive, collaborate, and contribute to a shared vision.

Imagine a company as a ship sailing through the vast ocean of commerce. While strategies, products, and services serve as the ship's sails and navigation tools, organisational culture is the wind that propels it forward. It's the invisible force that shapes the way you work, interact, and ultimately succeed. At its core, organisational culture is the shared set of values, beliefs, and practices that define how things are done within a company. It's the fabric that binds employees together, providing a sense of identity and purpose beyond just the bottom line.

But why is organisational culture so important, you may ask? Let's explore.

Why is Organisational Culture Important

Imagine for a moment a workplace where every individual feels connected to a larger purpose, where collaboration is not just encouraged but celebrated, and where innovation is not a buzzword but a way of life. This is the transformative power of a robust Organisational Culture.

Firstly, it's about employee engagement and morale. A positive culture fosters a sense of belonging and pride among employees, leading to higher levels of motivation, productivity, and retention. When employees feel valued and supported, they are more likely to go above and beyond to contribute to the company's success.

Secondly, organisational culture drives collaboration and teamwork. A strong culture encourages open communication, trust, and cooperation among team members, enabling them to work together towards common goals effectively. This synergy not only enhances efficiency but also promotes innovation and creativity.

Thirdly, culture plays a crucial role in attracting and retaining top talent. In today's competitive job market, skilled professionals are not just looking for a paycheck; they're seeking companies with a compelling culture and a supportive work environment. A positive culture acts as a magnet for talent, helping companies recruit and retain the best and brightest minds in their respective fields.

Organisational culture influences decision-making and problem-solving. When employees are aligned with the company's values and mission, they use them as guiding principles in their day-to-day work. This ensures that decisions are made in the best interest of the company and its stakeholders, leading to more effective outcomes. Culture directly impacts customer satisfaction and loyalty. Employees who are happy and engaged deliver better customer service, resulting in positive experiences for customers and increased loyalty to the brand. A strong culture not only creates happy employees but also happy customers, driving long-term success.

It is not just a buzzword; it's the heartbeat of a company. It shapes the way you work, collaborate, and thrive together. By investing in a positive culture, companies can unlock the full potential of their employees, attract top talent, drive innovation, and ultimately, achieve sustainable growth and success.

Organisational Culture is the cornerstone of employee engagement. In a culture that is fostered and celebrated, employees feel a sense of belonging to something greater than themselves. It transforms a job into a shared mission, leading to heightened creativity, unwavering commitment, and a passionate drive toward success. Consider the impact on innovation. In a culture that values diversity of thought, encourages risk-taking, and views failure as a stepping stone to success, innovation becomes not just a goal but a natural byproduct. It's the fertile ground where groundbreaking ideas flourish, propelling your ventures ahead of the curve in a competitive landscape.

Moreover, Organisational Culture is the guardian of your brand reputation. In a world driven not only by what you do but how you do it, a positive and purpose-driven culture becomes a powerful magnet for both talent and customers. It creates a resilient business environment, capable of weathering storms and emerging stronger from challenges. Leadership, as architects of culture, plays a pivotal role in fostering an environment where every individual feels valued, inspired, and connected to a shared purpose. Effective leaders lead not only from boardrooms but by embodying the values and principles of the Organisational Culture in their daily actions, sending a powerful message that permeates every level of the business.

Organisational Culture is not a mere concept; it's the essence that breathes life into your businesses. It's the invisible force that propels us forward, shapes your character, and sets the tone for success. As entrepreneurs, let us recognise the profound importance of Organisational Culture and strive to be the architects of cultures that inspire, empower, and propel us toward enduring success. To better grasp and improve your skills, let's delve into how to build a robust organisational culture in the next part of this chapter.

Building a Strong Organisational Culture

Imagine entering the headquarters of Salesforce, a leading cloud-based software company known for its exceptional workplace culture. As you step into the office, you're greeted by a vibrant atmosphere filled with energy and enthusiasm. This isn't just a place to work; it's a community where employees feel valued, supported, and inspired to do their best.

Salesforce has built a strong organisational culture based on several key principles: The company prioritises its employees' well-being and development. From comprehensive health benefits to ample opportunities for professional growth and advancement, Salesforce invests in its people's success and happiness. It fosters a culture of inclusivity and diversity. The company believes that diverse perspectives lead to better innovation and problem-solving, so it actively promotes diversity in its workforce and creates an environment where everyone feels welcome and respected.

Salesforce is also committed to giving back to the community. Through its 1-1-1 model, the company donates 1% of its product, 1% of its equity, and 1% of its employees' time to charitable causes. This culture of philanthropy and social responsibility inspires employees to make a positive impact both inside and outside the workplace.

Fourthly, Salesforce encourages a culture of innovation and creativity. Employees are empowered to take risks, experiment with new ideas, and push the boundaries of what's possible. This culture of innovation has led to the development of groundbreaking products like Salesforce Customer 360 and Einstein Analytics. It values transparency and open communication. From regular all-hands meetings to CEO Marc Benioff's commitment to radical transparency, the company fosters a culture of trust and accountability where employees feel empowered to speak up and share their ideas.

So, why is building a strong organisational culture important?

Simply put, a strong culture drives employee engagement, retention, and productivity. When employees feel connected to the company's mission and values, they're more motivated to do their best work and contribute to the company's success. It helps you embark on a journey that goes beyond the balance sheets and profit margins, into the very essence of your ventures—the art and science of building a positive organisational culture. This isn't just about policies and procedures; it's about sculpting an environment where success isn't just achieved; it's experienced, celebrated, and cherished.

Imagine for a moment a workplace where every individual radiates positivity, where collaboration is more than a necessity—it's a joy, and where innovation is not a buzzword but a way of life. This is the promise of a positive organisational culture, and today, I want to share with you the strategies that can transform this vision into a reality.

As the architects of your businesses, you have the power to set the tone, to be the driving force behind a culture that uplifts and inspires. In doing so, you become the catalysts for a positive culture that permeates every corner of your organisations.

A positive culture thrives on transparency, where information flows freely, ideas are welcomed, and every voice is heard. Communication becomes the glue that binds everyone together, fostering an environment where trust flourishes, and collaboration becomes second nature.

In the fast-paced world of entrepreneurship, it's easy to overlook the victories, both big and small. However, in a positive culture, every achievement is a cause for celebration. It's about recognising the efforts of each team member, acknowledging milestones, and creating a culture where success is not just an end goal but a continuous journey. Empowerment is another cornerstone. A positive culture empowers individuals to take ownership, to innovate, and to contribute their unique strengths. When every team member feels a sense of agency, your organisations become dynamic hubs of creativity and resilience.

Beyond the products and services you offer, your ventures are part of something greater—a purpose that transcends profits. When your teams understand and connect with this purpose, their work becomes more than a job; it becomes a meaningful contribution to a shared vision. Building a positive organisational culture is not a one-time project; it's an ongoing commitment, a journey where every strategy, every decision, and every interaction plays a crucial role.

In other words, whether you're a small startup or a multinational corporation, take a page out of Salesforce's playbook. Invest in your people, embrace diversity and inclusion, give back to the community, foster innovation and creativity, and prioritise transparency and open communication. By building a strong organisational culture, you'll not only attract and retain top talent but also create a workplace where everyone can thrive and succeed.

Let us be the stewards of a culture that not only breeds success but radiates positivity, leaving an indelible mark on your teams, your communities, and the business landscape. Let's delve into the essence of organisational culture to understand how it shapes every aspect of a business.

The Essence of Organisational Culture

Organisational culture is not just a catchphrase; it's the essence that breathes life into your business. It's the collective beliefs, values, and behaviours that define who you are as a company. Imagine it as the DNA that shapes the character and identity of your organisation. In understanding this, you recognise that it is not something that can be imposed but cultivated with intention and care.

From the moment an employee steps through the door to the interactions with clients and customers, the organisational culture sets the tone. It is the invisible hand guiding the decisions made in boardrooms, the innovation cultivated in workspaces, and the spirit that echoes in every team meeting.

It is the catalyst for creating a cohesive and motivated team—an assembly of individuals unified by a shared vision and values. In such an environment, innovation flourishes, collaboration becomes second nature, and success is not just a destination but a continuous journey.

In a culture that values innovation, employees are empowered to think beyond the ordinary. It is a playground where ideas are nurtured, risks are taken, and creativity is celebrated. This fertile ground for innovation becomes a breeding ground for solutions that set your organisation apart in a competitive landscape.

A strong organisational culture fosters collaboration, breaking down silos and building bridges between departments. It's about recognising the strength that comes from diverse perspectives working harmoniously towards common goals. Collaboration becomes the cornerstone of a resilient and dynamic organisation.

As you cultivate a positive and purpose-driven culture, you lay the groundwork for sustainable success. This success is not measured solely by financial achievements but by the lasting impact you make on your employees, customers, and the community at large. It's about building a legacy that extends beyond the balance sheet—a legacy rooted in values, integrity, and a commitment to excellence.

Let us recognise the profound importance of the organisational culture as the soul of your business. As you shape and cultivate this culture, remember that you are not just fostering a workplace but nurturing an environment where individuals thrive, collaborate, and contribute to a shared vision. The essence of your organisational culture becomes the beacon guiding your journey toward sustainable success.

Building a strong organisational culture creates a cohesive and motivated team, fostering an environment conducive to innovation, collaboration, and sustainable success. Let's examine how the transformative power of culture enriches you and your organisations in the next segment of this chapter.

Transformative power of culture

In the realm of business, success is not solely defined by profit margins or market share. It's also about the intangible force that breathes life into ventures and shapes their identity—the organisational culture. As entrepreneurs, understanding and harnessing the transformative power of culture can be the difference between mediocrity and greatness. Organisational culture is more than just a buzzword; it's the soul of a business. It encompasses the values, behaviours, and norms that define how things are done within an organisation. From collaboration to transparency, from learning to empowerment, every aspect of culture plays a crucial role in shaping the company's trajectory. Let's delve into the concept of organisational culture using the CULTURE framework:

Collaboration - Envision a culture where collaboration is not just encouraged but celebrated. Imagine the synergy that arises when diverse minds come together, each contributing their unique strengths to a collective vision. A culture that celebrates collaboration fosters synergy among diverse minds. When individuals come together, each contributing their unique strengths to a collective vision, success becomes inevitable. Collaboration is the cornerstone of innovation and problem-solving in any organisation. In collaboration, you find the alchemy of success.

Unity - Picture a culture where unity prevails. Unity within a culture creates a collective identity that transcends individual ambitions. A culture that binds you together with a shared purpose and vision, creating a collective identity that transcends individual ambitions. When everyone is aligned with a shared purpose and vision, they become unstoppable. Unity provides the strength to overcome challenges and navigate through uncertainties. In unity, you discover the strength to overcome any challenge.

Learning - Embrace a culture of perpetual learning. Success is not a static destination, but a journey marked by continuous growth. A culture of continuous learning is essential for staying ahead in today's dynamic business landscape. Success is a journey marked by growth and adaptation. Embracing a culture of learning ensures that individuals and organisations evolve and thrive in the face of change. In a culture that values learning, innovation flourishes, and adaptability becomes your compass.

Transparency - Cultivate a culture of transparency. Imagine an environment where openness and honesty are not just encouraged but ingrained. In transparency, trust blossoms, and individuals feel empowered by the knowledge that they are part of something greater.

Understanding - Empathy and understanding are vital components of a healthy organisational culture. Envision a culture of deep understanding and empathy. In such a culture, diverse perspectives are not only acknowledged but celebrated. It is a culture where everyone feels seen, heard, and valued—a fertile ground for creativity and inclusivity. When diverse perspectives are acknowledged and respected, creativity flourishes, and inclusivity becomes the norm. Understanding fosters a sense of belonging and camaraderie among team members.

Respect - Respect is the cornerstone of positive interactions within an organisation. Instil a culture of respect. Imagine a world where every individual is treated with dignity and courtesy. In such a culture, positive interactions become the norm, fostering an atmosphere of collaboration and shared success. When every individual is treated with dignity and courtesy, a culture of mutual respect emerges. Respectful workplaces are conducive to collaboration, productivity, and overall well-being.

Empowerment - Let me allow you to think and foster a culture of empowerment. Empowerment is about giving individuals the autonomy and authority to make decisions and take ownership of their work. Picture an environment where every individual is empowered to take initiative, where autonomy is not just granted but encouraged. In empowerment, you unlock the full potential of each member, contributing to the collective triumph. In an empowered culture, employees feel valued and trusted, leading to increased motivation and engagement. Empowerment unleashes the full potential of individuals and drives organisational success.

Building a strong organisational culture is not a one-time effort but an ongoing journey. It requires leadership commitment, employee buy-in, and a relentless focus on nurturing the desired values and behaviours. Examples from companies like Google, IKEA, Salesforce, and Unilever demonstrate the power of culture in driving success and innovation.

Cultivating Success: The Role of Culture

Organisational culture is not just a nice-to-have; it's a must-have for businesses looking to thrive in today's competitive landscape. By embracing the CULTURE framework and fostering a culture that values collaboration, unity, learning, transparency, understanding, respect, and empowerment, you and your organisations can create a blueprint for success that inspires and empowers employees to achieve greatness.

As you embark on the journey to shape this remarkable CULTURE, let us not merely speak of these ideals but embody them in your actions. Organisational Culture is the soul of your business. It's the intangible force that breathes life into your ventures, shaping your identity and influencing every aspect of your journey. As entrepreneurs, let us be the custodians of cultures that inspire, empower, and propel us toward enduring success.

This is your collective endeavour, a journey towards a culture that becomes a beacon of inspiration for generations to come. So, let us embark on this journey to build a culture-driven organisation—one that not only achieves success but leaves a lasting legacy for generations to come. Together, let us create a culture that not only propels us toward success but radiates a positive influence far beyond your immediate surroundings.

Conclusion & Recap

In conclusion, as you absorb the insights shared in this chapter on Building a Strong Organisational Culture, envision your business not merely as a structure but as a living, breathing entity with a distinct culture. Through the experiences of mentors and seasoned entrepreneurs, grasp the transformative impact of culture on your business's success. Remember that organisational culture isn't a byproduct; it's a deliberate and strategic choice that can propel your venture towards enduring prosperity. As mentioned earlier, the story of the young hare places great emphasis on organisational culture, highlighting the importance of learning from failures, celebrating successes, and fostering a growth mindset. Through the stories and chapters in this section, I strongly advocate for an inclusive and supportive culture that promotes open communication, collaboration, and mutual respect. Let us emphasise the importance of learning from failures, celebrating successes, and fostering a growth mindset among team members. Encourage innovation, creativity, and a willingness to challenge the status quo in pursuit of continuous improvement and excellence. Let us embrace the values of diversity, equity, and inclusion, recognising the unique strengths and perspectives that each individual brings to the team as part of this chapter for your own success in personal and professional life.

Connect with Me on LinkedIn:

https://www.linkedin.com/in/santoshkmis/

What Do I Bring To You On LinkedIn?

Imagine the possibilities when you connect with me on LinkedIn – it's a gateway to a world of value, positivity, and transformative insights! Think of me as your source for valuable, original content, whether it's through thought-provoking articles, captivating blog posts, or engaging videos that showcase a unique perspective.

But it doesn't stop there – I'm all about building a vibrant community. Get ready for active participation in discussions, where your thoughts and questions are not only welcomed but celebrated. Together, you'll foster a sense of connection and collaboration that goes beyond the digital realm. Need practical tips and strategies to elevate your professional game? I've got you covered. My journey, both personal and professional, is an open book, inviting you to connect with me on a deeper, more personal level.

Let's take it a step further – join me in dynamic webinars and live sessions where interaction is the name of the game. Your questions, your curiosity – they fuel the conversation in real-time. It's not just about me talking; it's about you being an active participant in your own learning and growth.

Diversity is key, and that extends to the content I curate. Brace yourself for a mix of curated gems from other sources, adding richness and depth to your discussions with my weekly LinkedIn Newsletter, carefully curated with your best interests in mind. But it's not just about content – it's about connection. Actively engaging with you means building relationships that open doors to exciting collaborative opportunities. Consistency is my mantra, ensuring you can rely on a steady stream of quality content that speaks to your professional journey.

Get ready to be captivated! Experimenting with various content types, from eye-catching images to informative infographics and attention-grabbing videos, is my way of keeping things fresh and exciting. So, why connect with me on LinkedIn? It's not just a connection; it's an invitation to a vibrant, dynamic, and enriching professional journey. Let's make it happen – connect with me today!

SECTION 3

Building blocks as Golden Nuggets - Key Success Ingredients

THE KEY INGREDIENTS OF SUCCESS

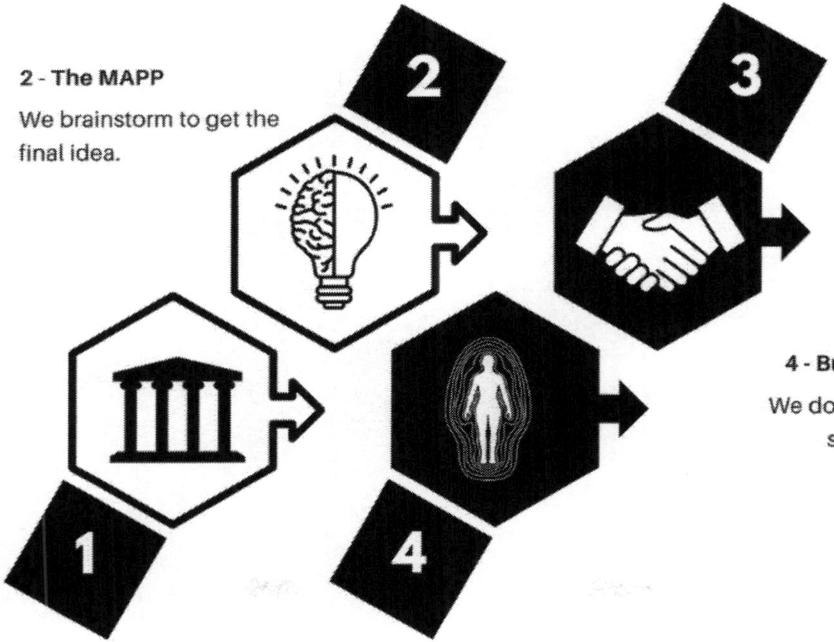

1 -The Pillars of Success

tells us of what you want and need. Timelines are set.

2 - The MAPP

We brainstorm to get the final idea.

3 - DEAL MODEL

Creative team gathers materials and inspiration.

4 - Business AURA

We do the necessary steps to deliver the result.

When I share my journey of overcoming obstacles and challenges, experiencing failures, and ultimately creating and managing multiple brands simultaneously in seminars and speeches worldwide, along with continually travelling towards my goals and success, I am often asked by audiences and attendees how I manage to operate so many businesses at once. They inquire about how I maintain my work-life balance, how I turn challenges into opportunities, whether I feel fatigued, frustrated, or exhausted, and if I have a family and children.

Here is my response.

I'm driven by my passion for what I do and my love of continuous learning. I gain insights from others' experiences, enjoy meeting new people, traveling, and drawing from diverse communities. I love creating brands and stories, and most importantly, transforming lives while working alongside friends and family, keeping them close wherever I go.

My vision is to touch millions of lives as a major milestone on this journey and inspire a million businesses. I aim to choose and influence one thousand businesses annually and inspire them to turn their business ideas into multimillion-pound enterprises. My vision includes working with one hundred aspiring business owners and becoming a catalyst to help them start their business growth journey, leading to an IPO and transforming them into multi billion pound enterprises. Working with such aspiring entrepreneurs gives me a sense of satisfaction and fulfilment as I become a source of significant impact in their lives.

Ultimately, I think of working with ten to twelve aspiring individuals and visionaries who have a burning desire to make a substantial change in the world we live in and bring them into the global citizen network of the trillionaires club. Together, we will achieve philanthropic objectives, creating limitless opportunities, adding value, and sparking a significant journey and legacy to make the world a better place. Through these charitable activities around education, medical and scientific research and philanthropic initiatives, I desire the global citizens to achieve something greater than themselves and leave a self-sustaining and scalable legacy for future generations.

Contributing to the betterment of humanity is a key aspect of the life I want to lead before I leave this world, serving as an inspiration and motivation for the next generation to follow and expand this vision for the betterment of society.

How do I achieve this? Through the powerful and insightful philosophies, robust frameworks, and innovative models that I have created and refined based on my own experience and the experience of others I interacted and learned in my entrepreneurial journey since 1992, using simple but proven methods. Among some of my most impactful business growth models includes a dynamic and rhythmic communication model, the MAPP Model, the 4 Pillars of Success, the 7 Pillars of Success, the business AURA framework , the DEAL methodology and venture creation framwork. These tools are designed to propel businesses towards unprecedented growth and success. Allow me to delve into these transformative models in this section, but before that, let's explore the inspiring story of Maya and understand the context of this journey in relation to entrepreneurship. Maya's journey illuminates the profound impact of these models and set the stage for your own path to extraordinary success.

Maya was a woman in her early forties living in the city of London, filled with dreamers and doers. She had enjoyed a successful professional life, as well as a personal life with two children who had moved out to explore their own experiences. Maya had always harboured big dreams of becoming a successful entrepreneur, but her personal and professional commitments had always been a barrier to achieving these dreams. Like any journey, hers was filled with twists and turns, challenges, and triumphs. She was going through a series of challenges in her personal, professional, and individual life, but she was determined not to give up on her dreams despite the setbacks. She was determined to overcome her fears and explore the needs and wants of life further.

After a few roadblocks and bumps in the entrepreneurial road, Maya soon understood the challenges and began debunking common misconceptions about entrepreneurship. She realised that you are all products of our own environment and that you attract the kind of people you think about. She started attending social as well as business events to connect names to faces and reinforce her presence in the business community. She attended business conferences and exhibitions to let other businesses know and understand her brand, its colours, its name, and the services it offers. By doing this, she ensures her brand remains at the forefront of other businesses' minds, constantly reminding them of her company's presence and commitment to supporting their business journey. This approach also allows her to meet new people and explore fresh opportunities and insights in the business world.

While she was still trying to run the business on her own and feeling stuck, she bumped into an old friend in one of these environments—an experienced professional who had navigated the seas of entrepreneurship, experiencing failures, challenges, opportunities, risks, and rewards. He was semi-retired now. Maya wished to make him her role model and convinced him to become her mentor and guiding light, sharing his learnings, knowledge, skills, experience, wisdom, and network to help her grow.

Based on the learnings shared from her mentor, Maya's journey began with a spark of inspiration and a vision to create something extraordinary in the wine industry. Armed with determination and a thirst for knowledge, she set sail into the unknown, navigating the rough waters of entrepreneurship with the help of the MAPP Model. With each obstacle she encountered, Maya embraced the model's principles of mindset, attitude, process, and planning, charting her course towards success.

As Maya embarked on her entrepreneurial journey, she soon realised that resilience was her greatest ally. Faced with setbacks and challenges, she unleashed the power of her growth mindset, turning obstacles into opportunities for growth. Drawing strength from her family values and transformative experiences, Maya refused to be paralysed by fear, choosing instead to embrace each setback as a stepping stone towards her goals.

In the face of adversity, Maya's positive attitude became her guiding light. With unwavering optimism and a determination to succeed, she overcame every obstacle that stood in her way. Drawing inspiration from her mentors and the extraordinary power of attitude, Maya transformed even the toughest challenges into opportunities for personal and professional growth.

Like the king of the jungle, Maya embraced the lion's attitude, standing tall in the face of adversity and leading with courage and resilience. Drawing lessons from the wild, she understood that attitude was the cornerstone of a life well-lived, and that with the right mindset, anything was possible.

With a clear vision and a strategic plan in place, Maya built her empire on the core pillars of success: plan, process, people, profit, product, pricing and propagation. By surrounding herself with a talented team and leveraging their strengths, Maya transformed her dreams into reality, achieving unprecedented success in the business world.

With her business flourishing, Maya continued to unleash her potential, harnessing the power of the DEAL methodology to maximise productivity and efficiency. By delegating tasks, eliminating distractions, automating processes, and leveraging her resources, Maya propelled her business to new heights of success.

As Maya reflected on her journey, she realised that entrepreneurship was not without its thrills and spills. From the daring risks she took to the sweet rewards she reaped, Maya's journey was a rollercoaster ride of emotions and experiences. But through it all, she remained steadfast in her determination to succeed, knowing that the greatest rewards often came from taking the biggest risks.

In her quest for success, Maya embraced the Business AURA Framework, accepting the challenges that came her way, understanding their underlying causes, realising the potential outcomes, and taking decisive action to overcome them. With each step of the framework, Maya unlocked new levels of success, emerging stronger and more resilient than ever before.

So, my friend, as Maya's story comes to a close, let me remind you that success is not just about reaching the destination, but about embracing the journey with courage, resilience, and a positive attitude. Like Maya, may you all dare to dream big, take calculated risks, and seize the opportunities that lie before you, knowing that with the right mindset and determination, anything is possible.

Before delving into the deep understanding of the business model of success and creating a strategic path in fortifying our business, let's start with one of the key dependent models called MAPP with double P. In the upcoming Chapter, you will embark on a journey to navigate the seas of success using this very concept called "MAPP Model." You will begin by setting sail with a discussion on growth-oriented mindset and its pivotal role in shaping your approach to challenges and opportunities. Next, you will explore the importance of cultivating the resilient and positive attitude to navigate the turbulent waters of entrepreneurship. Following that, you will delve into the realm of strategic perception and philosophies, understanding how they influence your decision-making and actions. It is crucial for success in implementing any system or process, or running a sales or marketing campaign, and is a must-have unit to explore before you dive into it. The chapter will conclude with a recap of key points and key takeaways to reinforce your understanding of the MAPP Model's principles.

LET'S DIVE IN...

Chapter 3.1

Follow a MAPP for Business Success

EXPLORING THE DIFFERENT AREAS OF A SUCCESS MAPP

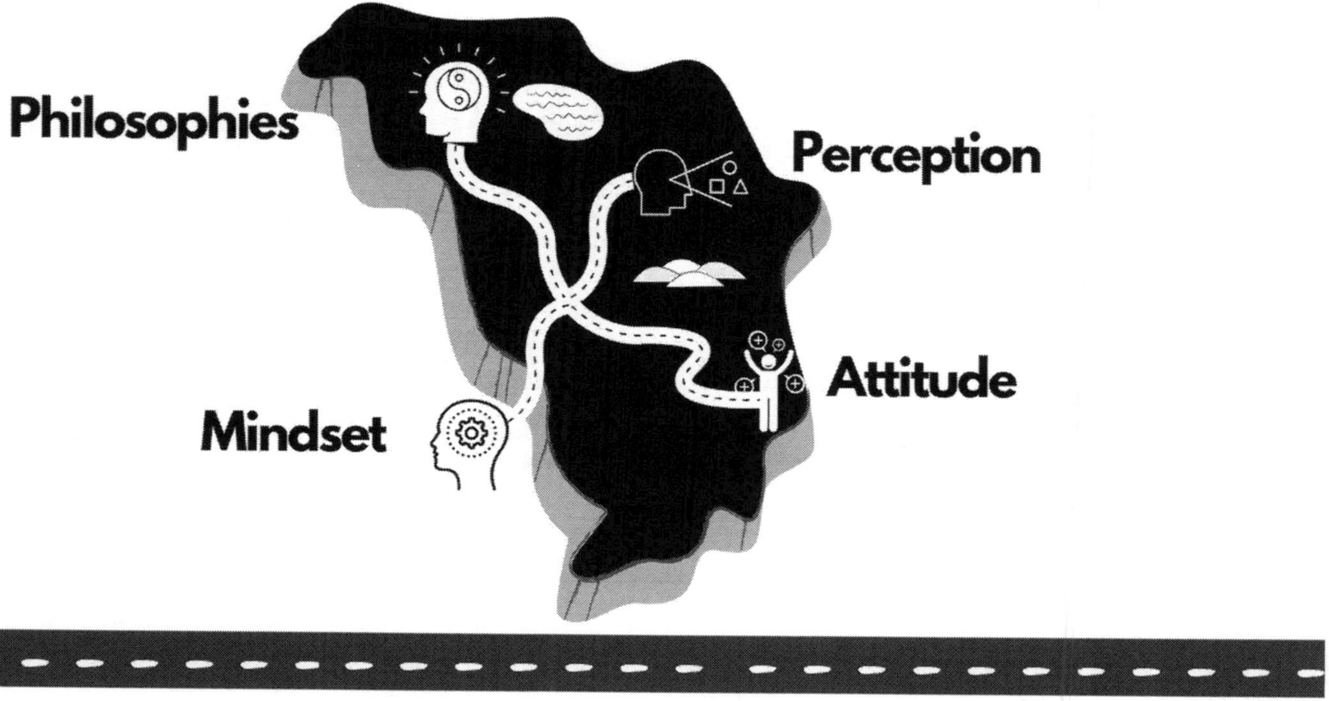

Jack was a young entrepreneur living in a port town nestled along the rugged coastline of England, Jack had always dreamed of setting sail on the vast seas of business, but he knew that success in the tumultuous waters of entrepreneurship would not come easily. Determined to chart his course to triumph, Jack decided to seek guidance from an old sea captain known for his wisdom and experience.

One crisp morning, Jack set out to meet the captain, his heart brimming with anticipation. As he approached the weathered old ship that served as the captain's home, he could hear the sound of the sea lapping against the hull and the creaking of the timbers in the salty breeze. With a nervous but determined smile, Jack knocked on the door and awaited the captain's invitation.

The door swung open, revealing the grizzled face of the old sea captain, his eyes twinkling with mischief and wisdom. "Ahoy there, young lad," he greeted Jack with a hearty laugh. "Come in, come in! I've been expecting you."

Jack stepped into the cozy cabin, taking in the sights and smells of the sea that permeated every corner. The captain gestured for him to take a seat at the rough-hewn table, and as they sat down, he began to regale Jack with tales of his adventures on the high seas.

"Ah, the life of an entrepreneur is much like that of a sailor," the captain mused, his voice low and gravelly. "It requires courage, determination, and a keen sense of direction. But fear not, young Jack, for I have just the thing to guide you on your journey—a powerful compass known as the MAPP model."

Imagine, if you will, a grand adventure—a voyage into the unknown, where every wave presents a new challenge and every gust of wind carries the promise of opportunity. This is the world of entrepreneurship, a world where dreams are born and destinies are forged. But in this world, success is not merely a destination—it is a journey, a journey that begins with the right mindset.

Intrigued, Jack leaned in closer, eager to learn more about this mysterious tool that promised to unlock the secrets of success. "Tell me more, captain," he urged, his eyes shining with curiosity.

The captain nodded, a knowing smile playing at the corners of his weathered lips. "The MAPP model, my boy, is a roadmap to triumph—a guide that will steer you through the treacherous waters of entrepreneurship with confidence and grace. It consists of four essential elements: Mindset, Attitude, Perception, and Philosophies."

In this chapter, you set sail on the vast seas of entrepreneurial success, guided by the powerful compass of the MAPP model. In the next few moments, I invite you to join me as you delve into the depths of these essential elements and uncover the secrets to triumph in the tumultuous waters of business.

Setting the Sail with Growth Oriented Mindset

"Mindset, my friend," the captain continued, "is the foundation upon which every entrepreneurial venture is built. It is the blueprint of your vessel, the map that guides us through uncharted waters."

"But what is mindset?" Jacked asked with curiosity.

"It is more than just positive thinking—it is a way of life, a philosophy that shapes your perception of the world and your place within it. With a growth oriented mindset, you see challenges not as obstacles, but as opportunities for growth. You embrace failure not as the end of the road, but as a stepping stone on the path to success." Captain continued.

The journey to triumph commences with the mindset—the foundational blueprint of your entrepreneurial vessel. Cultivating a growth mindset, resilience, and adaptability lays the groundwork for overcoming challenges and seizing opportunities.

As the captain spoke, Jack listened intently, hanging on his every word. He learned that mindset was the foundation upon which every entrepreneurial venture was built—a positive and growth-oriented mindset that embraced challenges as opportunities for growth. He understood that In the journey of personal and professional growth, the concept of mindset emerges as a pivotal element. A mindset is essentially the collection of beliefs and attitudes that shape how you perceive and respond to the world around you. It serves as the foundation for your actions, influencing your approach to challenges, your resilience in the face of adversity, and your capacity for growth and innovation.

Understanding the power of mindset is crucial for anyone aiming to achieve success and fulfilment. It is the lens through which you view your abilities and potential, significantly impacting your motivation and performance. A growth-oriented mindset, in particular, emphasises the belief that talents and abilities can be developed through dedication, hard work, and learning from experiences.

Adopting a positive and growth-oriented mindset allows individuals like you to embrace challenges as opportunities for improvement, persist in the face of setbacks, and see effort as a path to mastery. This perspective fosters a love for learning and resilience, essential traits for achieving long-term goals.

"As you hoist your sails and set forth, you must first anchor yourselves in the power of mindset," the captain continued. "It is the cornerstone, the bedrock upon which every entrepreneurial endeavour is built. Cultivating a growth mindset, fostering resilience, and embracing adaptability are not merely suggestions; they are imperatives in the pursuit of success. With unwavering determination, you shall navigate the tumultuous waters of challenges and seize every opportunity that arises."

Navigating Challenges with the Resilient Attitude

"Mindset alone is not enough," the captain asserted, his voice carrying the weight of experience and wisdom. "You must also cultivate the resilient attitude—the wind in your sails that propels us forward in the face of adversity. Positivity, and perseverance are the cornerstones of this resilient attitude, qualities that will guide you through even the stormiest seas. Embrace every setback as an opportunity to learn and grow, for with the right attitude, no challenge is insurmountable."

Turning to Jack, the captain continued to impart his knowledge. "Attitude acts as the wind in your sails, driving us onward amidst challenges," he explained. "Understanding the significance of a resilient and positive attitude in the entrepreneurial journey is crucial. It shapes how you handle setbacks and navigate obstacles, ensuring you maintain a steady course towards success."

Reflecting on his own experiences, the captain added, "Attitude serves as the driving force—the resilience and positivity that propel us forward in adversity." He paused, allowing his words to sink in, before continuing with conviction, "In times when change sweeps through like a fierce wind, your attitude becomes your strongest ally. It is this attitude that pushes you towards your goals, no matter the obstacles. It allows you to embrace setbacks not as barriers, but as opportunities for growth and advancement. With a resilient spirit and a positive outlook, you can overcome any storm that crosses your path."

He concluded with a nod, reinforcing the importance of maintaining such an attitude. "By fostering resilience and positivity, you not only navigate challenges effectively but also grow stronger with each hurdle you overcome. This mindset not only shapes your personal journey but also influences the success and sustainability of your ventures."

Jack absorbed the captain's words, contemplating their profound implications for his own entrepreneurial journey. He understood that developing resilience and maintaining a positive attitude were not just strategies for overcoming difficulties, but essential traits for achieving long-term success and fulfillment in business and beyond.

Attitude is a fundamental aspect of human psychology that influences your thoughts, feelings, and actions. It encompasses your predispositions, beliefs, emotions, and behavioural tendencies towards people, objects, events, or ideas. Often described as a mental posture or disposition, attitude shapes how you perceive and interact with the world around you.

At its core, attitude reflects your overall outlook or mindset towards various aspects of life. It can be positive, negative, or neutral, influencing your responses to challenges, opportunities, and everyday situations. Your attitudes are shaped by a combination of factors, including your upbringing, experiences, culture, and personal values.

In the context of personal and professional growth, attitude plays a pivotal role in determining success. A positive attitude can foster resilience, creativity, and a solution-oriented approach to problems. It encourages perseverance in the face of setbacks and inspires confidence in oneself and others. Conversely, a negative attitude can hinder progress, limit innovation, and create barriers to achieving goals.

The significance of attitude extends beyond individual behaviour to impact team dynamics, organisational culture, and ultimately, business outcomes. Leaders who cultivate a positive and empowering attitude among their teams often see higher levels of motivation, productivity, and collaboration.

Understanding the power of attitude involves recognising its influence on your thoughts, emotions, and behaviours. It requires self-awareness to identify and adjust attitudes that may be limiting personal or professional growth. By adopting a growth-oriented positive attitude, you can enhance your ability to learn from failures, adapt to changes, and embrace new opportunities with enthusiasm and determination.

As the sun began to set on the horizon, casting a warm glow over their conversation, Jack felt a renewed sense of purpose. Armed with the captain's guidance on navigating challenges with resilience and positivity, he was ready to face the unpredictable seas of entrepreneurship with courage, determination, and an unwavering belief in the power of attitude.

Perception – Uncovering the hidden Opportunities

"But again, whether it's just mindset or attitude, it's not enough," the captain continued, his voice carrying the weight of experience and insight. "You must also cultivate the right perception—the lens through which you view the world and navigate the complexities of business. Strategic perception goes beyond mere observation; it involves understanding the ebb and flow of opportunity and risk, and making decisions with clarity and foresight. By sharpening your perception, you gain the ability to uncover hidden opportunities where others see obstacles, and to navigate through uncertain waters with confidence."

"As you embark on your entrepreneurial journey, perception becomes your most valuable asset. It is through perception that you interpret the landscape, foresee challenges, and seize opportunities. Developing strategic perception enables you to navigate the unpredictable terrain of business, ensuring that every decision is well-informed and purposeful."

"Perception acts as the compass guiding you through the seas of business," the captain imparted to Jack. "Understand the crucial role of strategic perception in your entrepreneurial endeavours. Cultivate a perceptive mindset that not only identifies nuances but also reveals pathways to success, even amidst turbulence."

"Ah, the business landscape may shift unpredictably," the captain mused, "but do not falter. Your perception remains your steadfast guide. With keen insight and a strategic approach, you can transform challenges into opportunities and steer towards success. Embrace every twist and turn as an opportunity to refine your perception, navigating towards your goals with clarity and purpose."

Jack understood that Perception in business is not just about seeing what is immediately apparent but also about interpreting trends, anticipating shifts, and seizing opportunities that may not be obvious to others. It involves cultivating a deep understanding of market dynamics, consumer behaviour, and industry trends. Strategic perception allows entrepreneurs to make decisions that are not only proactive but also resilient in the face of change.

By honing your perception, you can stay ahead of the curve, identifying emerging trends and adapting your strategies accordingly. It requires continuous learning, openness to new ideas, and the ability to pivot when necessary. This proactive approach to perception not only mitigates risks but also enhances opportunities for growth and innovation.

Perception is the lens through which you interpret and make sense of the world around us. It involves the complex processes by which our brain receives, organises, and interprets sensory information, allowing us to understand our environment and react accordingly. Perception is not just a passive reception of stimuli but an active construction of reality influenced by your experiences, beliefs, expectations, and cultural backgrounds.

At its core, perception shapes your reality. It affects how you see yourself, others, and the situations you encounter daily. Your perceptions guide your decisions, influence your behaviours, and determine how you interact with the world. For instance, two people may experience the same event but perceive it in entirely different ways based on their individual perspectives and prior experiences.

For both personal and professional growth, perception plays a crucial role. Strategic perception enables business leaders to discern market trends, anticipate challenges, and identify opportunities that others might overlook. It involves seeing beyond the surface, understanding the deeper currents of change, and making informed decisions with clarity and insight.

Cultivating a sharp and strategic perception is essential for navigating the complexities of the modern world. It involves honing the ability to observe carefully, think critically, and remain open to new information and perspectives. By developing a keen perception, individuals and businesses can better adapt to changing circumstances, innovate effectively, and achieve sustained success.

In other words, perception is not just a tool but a mindset—an essential compass that guides entrepreneurs through the complexities of business. By developing and refining their perception, you can navigate the ever-changing business landscape with confidence, insight, and purpose, ultimately steering you ventures towards sustained success and impact.

Philosophies – The heart of your journey

"Philosophies," began the captain, his voice carrying authority and wisdom, "are not just principles but the heart of your journey—a collection of beliefs and values that guide us morally through the unpredictable waters of business." Jack, listening intently, grasped the weight of the captain's teachings.

"But perhaps most importantly, you must anchor your journey in your guiding philosophies—the principles and values that serve as your moral compass." Captain said, "From the start of any business venture," the captain continued, "it's vital to ground ourselves in your guiding philosophies. These are more than mere words; they embody the core principles that shape how you operate, how you treat others, and the legacy you aim to leave."

He gestured towards the setting sun, casting a warm glow over the deck. "In the complexities of business, your philosophies act as your constant guide—a reliable beacon that helps us navigate through challenges and uncertainties."

Jack nodded thoughtfully, pondering how he could develop similar guiding principles for his own entrepreneurial journey.

"Your philosophies," the captain went on, "must be rooted in integrity and aligned with your fundamental values. They influence not just your business decisions but also the culture you foster within your teams and the relationships you build with customers and stakeholders."

He paused, emphasising the importance of customer-centricity and ethical conduct. "Prioritising customer needs ensures you always put their satisfaction first. This builds trust, fosters loyalty, and drives sustainable growth."

"Similarly, ethical practices form the foundation of your operations," the captain stressed. "They dictate how you conduct yourself in every aspect, from production and marketing to sales and beyond. Upholding ethical standards isn't just a legal obligation; it's a moral duty that guides your conduct and earns respect in your industry."

Jack scribbled notes eagerly, capturing every detail of the captain's discussion on philosophies and their practical application in business. He was beginning to understand the profound impact that well-defined philosophies could have on shaping both the success and reputation of a business.

"Behold," the captain declared with reverence, "these philosophies are the guiding stars of your journey. They're not static rules but living values that evolve with your experiences, shaping your growth as entrepreneurs."

He looked directly at Jack, his gaze firm yet encouraging. "Craft your philosophies carefully, young man. Let them reflect the highest ideals of integrity, innovation, and responsibility. Embrace them as the compass that guides you through challenges and opportunities, leading you towards lasting success and a legacy of positive influence."

Jack concluded that Personal philosophies form the bedrock upon which individuals build their lives, guiding their decisions, actions, and aspirations. They represent deeply-held beliefs, values, and principles that shape one's outlook and approach to life. These philosophies serve as a moral compass, providing clarity amidst life's complexities and helping individuals navigate personal and professional challenges with integrity and purpose.

At its core, personal philosophies encompass a set of guiding principles that govern how individuals perceive the world, interact with others, and make choices. They are reflections of our core values and beliefs, developed over time through experiences, reflections, and influences from mentors, role models, and significant life events.

In the realm of personal growth, philosophies act as anchors that foster self-awareness, resilience, and a sense of direction. They empower individuals to define their goals, prioritise what truly matters to them, and align their actions with their values. By adhering to these principles, individuals can cultivate a sense of fulfilment and authenticity in their personal lives, leading to greater overall happiness and well-being.

In the professional sphere, personal philosophies are equally instrumental. They guide ethical decision-making, influence leadership styles, and shape organisational cultures. Leaders who uphold strong ethical philosophies inspire trust and loyalty among their teams, fostering a positive work environment conducive to innovation and growth. For employees, personal philosophies inform their work ethic, professionalism, and commitment to excellence, contributing to their career success and advancement.

The journey of developing personal philosophies involves introspection, continuous learning, and a willingness to adapt based on new experiences and insights. It requires individuals to clarify their values, articulate their principles, and actively integrate them into their daily lives and interactions.

By cultivating and refining personal philosophies, individuals can enhance their resilience, leadership effectiveness, and overall satisfaction in both personal and professional domains.

As the sun dipped below the horizon, casting a peaceful twilight over the ship, Jack felt renewed determination. Armed with the captain's profound insights on philosophies, he was ready to embark on his entrepreneurial voyage with clarity, conviction, and a steadfast commitment to ethical excellence.

Anchoring Your Journey

As the captain finished his tale, Jack felt a surge of excitement coursing through his veins. He knew that with the MAPP model as his guide, he could conquer any challenge that lay ahead and chart a course to triumph. With a grateful smile, he thanked the captain for his wisdom and bid him farewell, eager to set sail on his entrepreneurial journey.

And so, armed with the knowledge of the MAPP model, Jack embarked on his voyage of triumph. With each passing day, he faced new challenges and obstacles, but he met them head-on with courage and determination. Whenever he felt lost or uncertain, he would consult his trusty compass—the MAPP model—and it would always point him in the right direction.

Through the stormy seas and calm waters alike, Jack pressed on, guided by the timeless wisdom of the MAPP model. And as he neared the shores of success, he looked back on his journey with pride and gratitude, knowing that he had navigated the entrepreneurial seas with skill and perseverance.

As you near the conclusion of your voyage, let us anchor ourselves in the wisdom of the MAPP model. Mindset, Attitude, Perception, and Philosophies—these are the pillars upon which your success rests. Let us integrate them into the very fabric of your being, creating a holistic framework that empowers us to navigate the seas of entrepreneurship with grace and fortitude.

Conclusion & Recap

And so, my friend, let Jack's journey serve as a testament to the transformative power of the MAPP model—a beacon that can illuminate your own path to victory. Whether you're an experienced entrepreneur or embarking on your maiden voyage into business, remember that with the right mindset, attitude, perception, and philosophies, anything is achievable.

Let us embark together on a profound exploration into the realms of the entrepreneurial psyche, where success is guided by the robust compass of the MAPP model. In your journey, you delve deep into the Mindset, Attitude, Perception, and Philosophies that shape the trajectory of your enterprises. Join me as you unravel the wisdom imparted by mentors, colleagues, and the diverse tapestry of entrepreneurial experiences.

As you conclude your voyage today, let us reflect on the profound teachings of the MAPP model. Mindset, Attitude, Perception, and Philosophies—these are the keys that unlock the mysteries of entrepreneurial triumph. Let us integrate these principles into your daily lives and businesses, knowing that their collective power knows no bounds.

My friend, as you embark on this grand adventure, let us do so with courage, determination, and unwavering purpose. Though the seas may be tempestuous and the winds fierce, with the MAPP model as your guiding star, you shall navigate towards victory. Let us set sail together on this journey, for the greatest adventure awaits us beyond the horizon.

As you bid farewell to the shores of this chapter, let us carry forth the invaluable teachings of the MAPP model. May your mindset be resilient, your attitude positive, your perception strategic, and your philosophies grounded in your deepest values. In the unpredictable waters of entrepreneurship, it is these guiding lights that shall steer us towards the triumphant horizons ahead.

Therefore, my friend, let us unfurl your sails and embark on this extraordinary expedition. With the MAPP model as your steadfast companion, there are no limits to what you can achieve.

May the MAPP model be your unwavering guide, navigating you through the turbulent waters of entrepreneurship. As you absorb the wisdom within these pages, may your mindset grow in resilience, your attitude in positivity, your perception in strategy, and your philosophies in steadfastness to your values.

Chapter 3.2

Getting your Four Pillars of Success Right

Top 4 Ps
Plan
A
Process
B
People
C
Profit
D
Pillars of Success

In a world marked by revolutionary technological advancements such as digital media, virtual reality, space exploration, and precision weaponry, it's easy to lose sight of what truly matters. Despite your progress in technology and your interconnectedness through modern devices, there's a growing feeling of disconnection from your community, your purpose, and the values that define us. As you journey through life, it's crucial to pause and reflect on the impact you're having, understand your purpose, and consider the difference you're making in the lives of others. It's not just about comprehending and recognising the "what" and "why" of your purpose or principles of legacy; it's equally important to determine the "how" behind these elements.

Having witnessed the swift passage of time myself, I've come to appreciate the fleeting nature of life. Without grasping the "how" of these elements, days merge into weeks, weeks into months, and before you know it, years slip away. That's why it's vital to live each day with purpose and intentionality, ensuring that you leave no room for regret over unfulfilled dreams and untapped potential.

Let us strive to make every moment count, to reconnect with your humanity, and to establish a lasting legacy that enriches the lives of others for generations to come through the implementation of the four pillars of success model. In this crucial chapter, I explore the profound insights embedded in the journey through the Top 4 Pillars of Success: Plan, Process, People, and Profit. Drawing from the wealth of knowledge imparted by mentors, business associates, and seasoned entrepreneurs, I encourage you to delve into the intricate dynamics of these pillars, understanding how they collectively underpin enduring success for any venture.

The Plan – Topmost pillar of Business Success

Let's delve into the first pillar – Planning. The cornerstone of every personal and professional success lies in meticulous planning, a truth reinforced by the wisdom of successful entrepreneurs. Drawing from their experiences, these entrepreneurs emphasise the critical role of strategic planning. It's about setting clear objectives, articulating a compelling vision, and crafting a roadmap that steers your business through the intricacies of the entrepreneurial terrain. Picture your plan as a meticulously drawn map, intricately designed to navigate your ship through the unpredictable waters of challenges and opportunities.

First and foremost, consider direction. Just as a compass guides a weary traveller, a well-structured plan directs your business towards its intended destination. It defines the path, ensuring you stay focused and avoid drifting aimlessly.

Furthermore, envision your team as a united crew aboard this vessel. A clear plan serves as a unifying force, aligning everyone towards a shared goal. It transforms a collection of individuals into a cohesive, synchronised team, each contributing harmoniously towards victory.

However, a plan isn't rigid; it's a flexible guide. In the face of storms or unknown waters, a well-crafted plan allows for adaptation. It's not about blindly sticking to a course but having the agility to adjust sails when necessary. This flexibility ensures your business not only weathers challenges but also seizes unforeseen opportunities. Appreciate the power of a plan – a dynamic blueprint that not only charts the course but also unites the crew and adapts to changing conditions. In the unpredictable journey of business, a well-structured plan stands as your most dependable ally. It ensures not only reaching your destination but also navigating the exhilarating and demanding waters with resilience and triumph.

Planning is crucial for both personal fulfilment and professional achievement. It not only involves setting clear goals and devising strategies but also organising resources to navigate towards desired outcomes. In personal growth, planning allows individuals to pursue aspirations in areas like health, relationships, education, and self-improvement. It provides direction, helping to anticipate challenges and adapt to changes, fostering resilience along the way.

In the professional realm, planning is fundamental for businesses to define their mission, set strategic goals, and allocate resources effectively. Career planning empowers professionals to identify career objectives, develop skills, and advance within their fields. It promotes productivity, discipline, and accountability by prioritising tasks and optimising performance.

The Process – The Second Key Pillar of Success

Successful ventures are not merely the result of luck but are intricately woven with well-defined and efficient processes. Drawing insights from seasoned entrepreneurs, you explore the second pillar – Process. You delve into the significance of establishing streamlined and effective processes and learn how to optimise operations, boost productivity, and foster a culture of continuous improvement within your organisation.

Efficient processes are the backbone of productivity, minimising errors and fostering agility, thereby positioning your business for sustained success. Systems and processes are essential pillars supporting both personal growth and professional achievement. They provide structured frameworks that individuals and organisations rely on to streamline tasks, boost efficiency, and consistently achieve desired outcomes.

Imagine your processes as unseen conductors, orchestrating a flawless performance that not only captivates but drives your business towards enduring success.

Firstly, let's consider productivity – the lifeblood of any thriving enterprise. Efficient processes act as silent maestros, directing operations with precision. They remove unnecessary obstacles, streamline workflows, and ensure every note in your business symphony resounds with productivity.

Now, let's discuss the art of error reduction. Picture your processes as vigilant guardians, meticulously examining each step. Through efficiency, they stand as stalwart protectors against missteps that could disrupt your performance. A well-coordinated process guarantees flawless execution, enhancing not only productivity but also the quality of your business output.

Then, there's agility and adaptability – the dancers gracefully navigating change. Efficient processes provide the choreography for your business to glide through shifts and gracefully manoeuvre around challenges. They ensure your business isn't just a static entity but a dynamic, ever-evolving masterpiece poised for sustained success.

In personal development, effective systems and processes help individuals manage their time, resources, and goals efficiently. Whether it's establishing routines for self-improvement, managing finances, or maintaining work-life balance, structured systems bring clarity, reduce stress, and empower individuals to take control of their lives. Professionally, these frameworks are crucial for optimising workflows, enhancing productivity, and driving organisational success. Businesses use them to standardise operations, improve customer satisfaction, and maintain a competitive edge. From project management methodologies to quality control measures, well-defined systems ensure reliability, consistency, and scalability in delivering products and services.

Therefore, let us celebrate the ballet of efficiency – the unseen force elevating productivity, reducing errors, and transforming your business into a nimble performer in the grand theatre of commerce. In the rhythm of efficient processes, your business discovers not only success but also the agility to dance through the symphony of challenges, emerging triumphantly on the stage of sustained success.

The People - The Third Most Important Pillar

People play a vital role in both personal growth and professional achievement, forming the cornerstone of your journeys towards success. No business can thrive without the right team. In this segment, I delve into the third pillar – People. You explore the critical elements of building a talented and motivated team.

Personally, meaningful relationships provide you with support, encouragement, and diverse perspectives that enrich your life. Whether through friends, mentors, or family, these connections contribute to your emotional well-being and resilience in facing life's challenges.

Professionally, people are essential to building effective teams and networks that drive success. Collaboration within teams fuels innovation, enhances productivity, and aligns with organisational goals. Leadership and interpersonal skills are key in fostering cohesive teams that thrive together. Beyond immediate colleagues, professional networks offer opportunities for learning, career advancement, and accessing essential resources.

Understanding the importance of effective communication, team empowerment, and fostering a supportive work environment that nurtures both individual growth and organisational success is essential. A strong, engaged team fosters innovation, collaboration, and resilience, propelling your business towards its objectives. Visualise your team as architects of innovation, maestros of collaboration, and unsung heroes of resilience, all working harmoniously to drive your business forward.

Firstly, let's uncover the magic of innovation. A team that is not only strong but also engaged becomes a breeding ground for creative sparks. It's a dynamic environment where diverse ideas converge, giving rise to innovations that can set your business apart in a competitive arena. An engaged team is more than just a workforce; it's a collective mind thriving on the stimulating exchange of inventive ideas.

Next, consider collaboration – the elegant dance of minds coming together. An engaged team doesn't work in isolation; it operates in harmony like a Bee who are a remarkable example of collaboration for success in the natural world. They live in highly organised colonies where every bee has a specific role to play in ensuring the survival and prosperity of the hive. It's the seamless blending of skills, efforts, and aspirations towards achieving excellence. Collaboration becomes the melody that harmonises every aspect of your business, creating a symphony of success.

Then, there's resilience – the unwavering spirit that perseveres through challenges. An engaged team provides a sturdy support system, standing united in the face of adversity. It's the resilience born from shared goals, shared victories, and a collective determination to overcome any obstacle that threatens to dim your business's spotlight.

Therefore, let us raise a toast to the powerhouse of success – a strong, engaged team. They are not merely employees; they are the driving force behind your business's innovation, the architects of collaboration, and the epitome of resilience. Together, they craft a narrative of triumph that resonates far beyond the confines of your workplace. Recognising the impact of people underscores the value of communication, empathy, and teamwork. These qualities create environments where individuals and organisations flourish. Investing in relationships through mentorship, team development, and networking fosters a supportive ecosystem that nurtures personal growth and collective achievement.

The Profit - Forth Pillar of the Business Success

While profit stands as the ultimate goal, it also mirrors the overall health of your business. Let's explore the fourth pillar – Profit. Drawing insights from successful entrepreneurs, you focus on effective financial management, revenue generation strategies, and the importance of adapting to evolving market conditions. Profitability guarantees the sustainability and expansion of your business, furnishing the resources necessary to invest in innovation, growth, and the welfare of your team.

Profitability goes beyond mere figures on a balance sheet; it acts as the lifeblood ensuring the enduring viability and progress of your venture. Think of it as the fuel powering the engine of innovation. Profitability provides the means to finance groundbreaking ideas, pushing the boundaries of what your business can achieve. It serves as the financial catalyst propelling you into uncharted territories of creativity and keeping you ahead in the ever-evolving competitive landscape.

But its significance extends further. Profitability forms the cornerstone of expansion, unlocking doors to new markets and opportunities. It represents the financial strength enabling you to reach a broader audience, diversify your offerings, and make a lasting impact on the business terrain.

Let's not overlook its human aspect – the beating heart of your enterprise. Profitability acts as the caring custodian of your team's well-being. It affords the ability to foster a positive workplace culture, provide competitive remuneration, and invest in the professional development and satisfaction of each contributor to your business's success. In essence, profitability transcends mere profit-making; it secures the future, fosters innovation, facilitates expansion, and nurtures the core of your business – your team.

The Harmonious Symphony of Foundational Pillars

The essence of business success lies in seamlessly blending these four foundational pillars: planning, processes, people, and profit. Just as a symphony is a meticulously orchestrated ensemble of different instruments, the journey of success is an artful harmony of these essential elements.

Imagine planning as the conductor – the guiding force that sets the tempo and charts the course for your business journey. A well-structured plan isn't just a route map but the musical score that drives you and the people around you towards a crescendo of achievements.

Think of processes as the instruments – each playing a unique role in creating a harmonious melody. Efficient processes boost productivity, reduce errors, and contribute to the agile rhythm of your business.

People are at the heart of this symphony – your team, engaged and motivated, adding their individual notes to craft a collaborative masterpiece. A robust and inspired team stimulates innovation, resilience, and propels your business towards its objectives.

Lastly, profit represents the grand finale – the applause that signifies the success of your orchestrated efforts. Profitability ensures the sustainability and expansion of your business, providing the means to invest in innovation, growth, and the welfare of your team. Therefore, let's embark on this musical journey of business success, where the seamless integration of planning, processes, people, and profit creates a symphony resonating with enduring triumph. Just as a conductor harmonises instruments to create beautiful music, successful entrepreneurs orchestrate these pillars to build a resilient and prosperous business ecosystem.

As you navigate the complexities of entrepreneurship, remember that success lies not in the mastery of a single note but in the orchestration of a harmonious blend. Embrace the art of balancing these pillars, refining their integration over time to compose a business masterpiece that echoes prosperity and resilience. In other words, let the harmonious integration of planning, processes, people, and profit guide your business journey. With each pillar contributing its distinct melody to the symphony of success, you can navigate challenges, seize opportunities, and lead your business towards sustained growth and accomplishment.

Conclusion & Recap

As you digest the insights shared in this chapter on the Top 4 Pillars of Success, see these pillars not as separate entities but as interconnected forces shaping the path of your personal and professional success and the success of your venture. Drawing on the collective wisdom of my mentors and seasoned entrepreneurs, grasp the holistic approach to success that extends beyond mere profit.

Planning serves as a blueprint for intentional action, guiding individuals and organisations towards success by enhancing decision-making, managing resources efficiently, and achieving meaningful progress in personal and professional endeavours. By adopting and refining systems and processes, individuals and organisations foster a culture of efficiency and continuous improvement. These frameworks not only streamline daily operations but also support proactive decision-making, resource allocation, and adaptation to evolving challenges. Ultimately, they contribute to sustainable growth, resilience, and the attainment of long-term goals in personal and professional realms alike.

People inspire, challenge, and empower us to reach our potential. By cultivating meaningful connections both personally and professionally, you pave the way for sustained success, fulfillment, and positive contributions to society. Nurturing and empowering your people and associated relationship is fundamental to achieving sustainable success. By fostering an environment where communication flows freely, empowerment is embraced, and support is unwavering, you create a foundation upon which your team can thrive. They become more than just contributors; they become integral to the fabric of your business's success story, ensuring that every step taken is towards a future defined by achievement and fulfilment.

Profitability stands as the financial bedrock ensuring the longevity and advancement of your business. By prioritising effective financial management and strategic revenue generation, you pave the way for sustained growth and resilience in dynamic market environments. Profitability not only signifies financial success but also underpins your ability to innovate, expand, and cultivate a thriving organisational culture that propels you towards long-term success and prosperity. Discover how these pillars interweave to form a sturdy foundation for your business, fostering adaptability, sustainability, and long-term success. Each element plays a vital role in maintaining the rhythm of your business operations, ensuring that challenges are met with resilience and opportunities are seized with purpose.

In this symphony of business, planning provides direction and clarity, processes ensure efficiency and consistency, people bring creativity and collaboration, and profit secures growth and stability. Together, they create a symphony that not only withstands the test of time but also evolves with the changing dynamics of the market. As you embark on this journey, remember that success isn't achieved in isolation but through the harmonious orchestration of planning, processes, people, and profit.

Chapter 3.3

Taking Control of your Destiny with The Power of DEAL Methodology

DEAL
D Delegate
E Eliminate
A Automate
L Leverage

Emily is a young entrepreneur living in the bustling city of Dubai filled with dreamers and doers. Emily had big dreams and even bigger aspirations, but she often found herself overwhelmed by the sheer magnitude of her goals. No matter how hard she worked, it seemed like success was always just out of reach.

In today's fast-paced world, you business owners are no different from Emily, and achieving success in both your personal and professional lives can often feel like an uphill battle. You juggle countless tasks, manage competing priorities, and strive to make the most of every opportunity that comes your way.

But is this why you entered the real world of business? Is this why you started your businesses? Probably not.

I strongly believe that you, as business owners, should have the freedom and ability to do what you want, when you want, and keep your time free as much as possible.

But how do you achieve this without losing sight of your key business purpose?

What if I say there is a simple yet powerful framework that could help you navigate this complex landscape with ease?

Enter the DEAL methodology – a transformative approach to productivity, efficiency, and success.

One day, as Emily sat in her office feeling discouraged, a wise old mentor paid her a visit. "Emily," he said with a twinkle in his eye, "I want to share with you a secret that has the power to transform your personal as well as professional life. It's called DEAL.

"It's more than just a set of strategies; it's a mindset shift that empowers individuals and organisations to unlock their full potential. Let's delve deeper into each component of the DEAL methodology and discover how it can revolutionise the way you work and live." He continued.

Intrigued, Emily leaned in closer, eager to learn more. The mentor began to explain painting a picture of a world where overwhelm was replaced by clarity, chaos by calm, and doubt by confidence.

Delegate

Mentor: "First, let's talk about Delegate, Emily." leaning in with a reassuring smile "You don't have to do it all alone. At the heart of the DEAL methodology lies the concept of delegation."

Emily: nodding thoughtfully "So, you mean I don't have to carry the weight of everything on my shoulders?"

Mentor: "Exactly, Emily. As entrepreneurs, it's easy to feel like you have to handle everything ourselves. But business is never about you doing everything by ourselves. You as a business owner need to be free from anything and everything to do the thing which you want and when you want without tying ourself to one particular activity and without hindering the progress. And that's where delegation comes in."

Emily: listening intently "Tell me more."

Mentor: "Delegating involves assigning tasks or responsibilities to others who are better suited or more capable of completing them efficiently and have better capacity. As a business owner, you should delegate as much as possible without trying to do everything by yourself. Think of yourself as a decades-old business turning over billions of pounds every year, having thousands of employees and multiple boards of directors. Like a big multi-billion-pound business, what would you do in that situation? Would you still do everything by yourself? If the answer is no, then why don't you virtually travel your path now and believe in the same concept at this phase of your business, and act and behave for maximum efficiency? By delegating effectively, you can focus on high-priority tasks that require your expertise while empowering others to contribute to the overall goals."

Emily: feeling intrigued "It sounds like it's not just about passing off tasks—it's about building a team and empowering them to excel."

Mentor: "Precisely, Emily. It's about leveraging the skills and expertise of others to achieve more in less time. When you distribute responsibilities effectively, you create a culture of collaboration and trust."

Emily: feeling inspired "I can see how that could transform the way I work."

Mentor: "Absolutely. Surround yourself with a network of talented individuals who can help you bring your vision to life. By delegating tasks and responsibilities, you free up valuable time and energy to focus on what truly matters."

Emily: determined "I'm ready to embrace the power of delegation and unlock your full potential."

Mentor: "That's the spirit, Emily. With delegation as your guiding light, you can navigate the complexities of entrepreneurship with grace, confidence, and unwavering determination."

Emily: grateful "Thank you for showing me the way" nodding, feeling a glimmer of hope begin to stir within her "But what about the things which I can't delegate? what about all the things on my to-do list that seem to never end?"

Mentor: smiling reassuringly "Ah, that's where Eliminate or Reprioritise comes in, Emily."

Eliminate or Reprioritise

He Continued, "Take a good hard look at your list and ask yourself, 'Is this task essential? Does it align with my current objectives and goals?' If not, it's time to let it go. By eliminating or reprioritising non-essential tasks, you create space for the activities that bring you closer to your dreams."

Emily: feeling intrigued "So, it's about focusing on what truly matters in the given timeframe and given context?"

Mentor: "Exactly, Emily. This step involves identifying and removing non-essential tasks or activities that do not contribute significantly to achieving objectives. Alternatively, tasks may be reprioritised based on their importance and urgency to ensure that time and resources are allocated efficiently."

Emily: realising the importance "So, by decluttering my to-do list, I can make room for the things that really make a difference."

Mentor: nodding approvingly "Precisely. In a world filled with distractions and competing demands, it's essential to focus on what truly matters. This second component of the DEAL methodology encourages us to identify non-essential tasks and reprioritise your commitments accordingly. By freeing ourselves from unnecessary obligations, you create space for the activities that align with your goals and aspirations."

Emily: feeling empowered "I can't wait to start decluttering and prioritising. It feels like a weight has been lifted off my shoulders already."

Mentor: smiling warmly "I'm glad to hear that, Emily. Remember, by streamlining your tasks and focusing on what truly matters, you'll be able to achieve your goals with greater clarity and purpose."

Emily: grateful "Thank you for showing me the way, I'm excited to see where this journey takes me but how do I do this"

Mentor: encouragingly "You're welcome, Emily. Now, I don't think there is a right or wrong way and you all are different hence you would choose your own ways, But If I have to choose or recommend one, I suggest combining the Eisenhower Matrix with the MOSCOW method which indeed can be a powerful technique for prioritisation and task management. The Eisenhower Matrix helps you categorise tasks based on their urgency and importance, while the MOSCOW method helps you prioritise tasks based on their significance to your goals or objectives."

They share a determined smile, ready to tackle Emily's to-do list and make room for her dreams. As Emily listened intently, the mentor continued to share insights about Automation and Leverage, illustrating how technology and collaboration could supercharge her efforts and propel her towards success.

Automate

Emily: looking intrigued "So, mentor, how do you tackle the tasks which I can't delegate or eliminate but I still have to do it and get it done in a given timeframe? all these repetitive tasks that seem to eat up so much of my time?"

Mentor: smiling knowingly "Ah, Emily, that's where automation comes into play. It's the third component of the DEAL methodology, and it's all about harnessing the power of technology to your advantage."

Emily: nodding thoughtfully "So, automation is about using technology to streamline my processes?"

Mentor: "Exactly! Automation involves leveraging technology and tools to streamline repetitive or time-consuming tasks, reducing manual effort and increasing efficiency. If you know that there is task which you must do and you cannot delegate or eliminate, ask yourself if you have to do this task once or more than one time. If it's a repetitive task then find out how you can learn to do it, create a process and automate and save 80% to 90% of your time through this automation"

Emily: feeling excited "That sounds like it could really make a difference! But how exactly does it work?"

Mentor: "Well, think about it like this. Have you ever set up email filters to organise your inbox automatically?"

Emily: nodding "Yes, I have! It's been a lifesaver."

Mentor: "That's a perfect example of automation in action. By setting up those filters, you've freed up time that would have been spent manually sorting through emails. Instead, you can now focus your energy on more strategic activities that drive value for your business."

Emily: feeling inspired "I see! So, automation is all about working smarter, not harder."

Mentor: "Exactly, Emily. By automating repetitive tasks and workflows, you can save time, minimise errors, and focus your energy on more meaningful activities. Whether it's using project management software to streamline collaboration or implementing chatbots to handle customer inquiries, automation empowers us to work more efficiently and effectively."

Emily: grateful "Thank you for explaining mentor. I can't wait to explore how automation can help us take my business to the next level."

Mentor: smiling warmly "You're welcome, Emily. I'm excited to see how automation transforms your workflow and propels you towards success."

They share a knowing smile, both eager to delve deeper into the possibilities that automation holds for their business.

Technology has revolutionised the way you work, offering countless tools and solutions to streamline your processes. By automating repetitive tasks and workflows, you can save time, minimise errors, and focus your energy on more meaningful activities. From email filters to project management software, automation empowers you to work smarter, not harder.

Leverage

Emily: looking intrigued "So, mentor, what's the final piece of the puzzle in this DEAL methodology?"

Mentor: smiling "Ah, Emily, which would be leverage. It's all about making the most of your resources and networks to achieve maximum impact."

Emily: nodding thoughtfully "So, it's about using what you have to our advantage?"

Mentor: "Exactly! If you can't delegate, eliminate, or automate a task, then leveraging your resources and networks is the next best step."

Emily: feeling curious, "How does that work exactly?"

Mentor: "Well, consider a task and the outcome associated with it. Ask yourself a question: is it worth putting your time and effort into this task, or could you better invest your time in more meaningful, joyful, and productive engagements where the value of your time investment is much better? If the answer is yes, then reach out to people and resources you know who are most effective, efficient, and resourceful with respect to time, cost, and quality. They can do a better job within the given timeframe and budget while maintaining quality, offering your more value and allowing you to free yourself up. It involves utilising existing resources, networks, and opportunities to maximise outcomes. This could mean forming strategic partnerships, accessing external expertise, or leveraging your existing assets to achieve your goals more effectively and efficiently."

Emily: realising the potential "So, it's about working smarter, not harder, by tapping into the strengths of others?"

Mentor: "Precisely! Whether it's seeking mentorship from someone who has been there before, collaborating with other business owners who excel in their field, or leveraging your personal and professional connections, there's power in working together."

Emily: feeling inspired "I can see how that could really take my business to the next level."

Mentor: nodding "Absolutely, Emily. By pooling your collective expertise and resources, you can achieve far more together than you ever could alone. It's about opening doors to new opportunities and possibilities."

Emily: grateful "Thank you for explaining mentor. I'm excited to start leveraging your assets and seeing where it takes me."

Mentor: smiling warmly "You're welcome, Emily. I have no doubt that with the power of leverage on your side, you'll be able to achieve great things."

They share a determined smile, ready to harness the power of leverage and propel their business forward.

How to Empower the Deal Methodology

DEAL is a strategic methodology used for optimising productivity and efficiency in both personal and professional contexts.

Delegate tasks and responsibilities to trusted individuals who possess the skills and expertise to handle them effectively. By relinquishing control and empowering others, you free up valuable time and energy to focus on high-impact activities that drive your business forward.

Identify tasks and commitments that no longer align with your goals or provide significant value. Eliminate these distractions or delegate them to others. Reprioritise your to-do list to ensure that you're focusing on activities that align with your business's mission and objectives.

Adapt technology and systems to automate repetitive tasks and streamline workflows. Whether it's email marketing, customer support, or inventory management, automation allows you to save time, reduce errors, and enhance productivity across your organisation.

Identify and leverage your strengths, resources, and networks to maximise opportunities and achieve your goals. Whether it's forming strategic partnerships, leveraging your brand's reputation, or tapping into your team's expertise, leverage enables you to achieve more with less effort.

Each component of the DEAL methodology represents a key strategy for managing tasks, resources, and responsibilities effectively to achieve desired outcomes.

Inspired by the mentor's words, Emily set out to implement DEAL in her life and business. She began by delegating tasks to her team, freeing up her time to focus on strategic initiatives. Next, she ruthlessly eliminated or reprioritised activities that didn't serve her goals, clearing the clutter and creating space for growth.

With the help of automation tools and systems, Emily streamlined her processes and achieved greater efficiency than ever before. And by leveraging her network of mentors, colleagues, and friends, she unlocked opportunities she never thought possible.

As the months passed, Emily watched in amasement as her business flourished and her personal life thrived. With DEAL as her guide, she navigated the ups and downs with grace and determination, never losing sight of her ultimate vision.

This transformative approach to productivity, efficiency, and success offers a roadmap for business owners to reclaim their time, focus, and purpose.

As Emily listened to her wise old mentor explain each component of the DEAL methodology, she felt a sense of clarity and empowerment wash over her. This wasn't just a set of strategies—it was a mindset shift that had the power to transform her life and business. Armed with this newfound knowledge, Emily embarked on her journey to implement the DEAL methodology in her business and personal life. By delegating tasks, eliminating distractions, automating processes, and leveraging her strengths, she began to reclaim her time, focus, and purpose.

As business owners, you too can embrace the DEAL methodology and unlock your full potential. By adopting a strategic approach to productivity and efficiency, you can navigate the complexities of entrepreneurship with confidence and clarity. It's time to reclaim your freedom, fulfill your purpose, and achieve success on your own terms.

Master Time Management with Eisenhower Matrix

In this segment, let me introduce you to a powerful tool for managing your time and increasing your productivity, which you may or may not know: the Eisenhower Matrix, also known as the Urgent-Important Matrix. This simple yet effective framework helps you prioritise your tasks by focusing on their urgency and importance. The Eisenhower Matrix is named after Dwight D. Eisenhower, the 34th President of the United States. He once highlighted the crucial difference between urgent and important tasks, and this matrix builds on that distinction.

The matrix divides your tasks into four main categories.

First, you have tasks that are both urgent and important. These tasks need your immediate attention and are crucial for achieving your long-term goals. They often include crises, pressing problems, and projects with tight deadlines. Managing these tasks effectively is key to preventing them from becoming emergencies.

Next, you have tasks that are urgent but not important. These tasks demand your immediate attention but are not critical to your long-term goals. They often include interruptions, certain emails, and non-essential meetings. To manage these tasks, you should aim to delegate or minimise them, freeing up time for more important activities.

There are also the tasks that are important but not urgent. These tasks are vital for your long-term success but do not require immediate action. Examples include strategic planning, building relationships, personal development, and preventive activities. Prioritising these tasks helps reduce the number of urgent tasks and promotes sustainable productivity.

Lastly, there are tasks that are neither urgent nor important. These tasks do not contribute to your long-term objectives and are often trivial activities or distractions. Minimising or eliminating these tasks is crucial for maintaining focus and productivity.

By categorising your tasks into these four areas, the Eisenhower Matrix helps you make informed decisions about where to invest your time and energy. It encourages you to shift from reacting to every immediate demand to planning and executing your tasks strategically. Ultimately, this matrix serves as a valuable tool for enhancing efficiency, achieving your goals, and maintaining a healthy balance between work and personal life.

Use the Eisenhower Matrix to categorise tasks. Start by placing your tasks into the four quadrants of the matrix based on their urgency and importance

Unlocking Productivity: Harnessing the Power of MoSCoW and the Eisenhower Matrix

Imagine a world where you have a clear roadmap for every project or a venture, where you can easily identify the most critical tasks and allocate your resources efficiently and manage your business decisions quickly and efficiently. The MoSCoW method makes this possible, and I am here to show you how.

The MoSCoW method is simple yet highly effective approach will help you focus on what truly matters, ensuring that your ventures are successful and your goals are achieved. MoSCoW stands for four categories of priority that will revolutionise your workflow.

First, you have the "Must Have" tasks. These are the absolute essentials, the non-negotiables that your venture cannot succeed without. By identifying these key elements, you ensure that your venture has a solid foundation and meets its core objectives.

Next, you have the "Should Have" tasks. These are important elements that add significant value to your venture. While not critical for basic functioning, including these will enhance the overall quality and success of your venture. They come after the "Must Haves" in your prioritisation, ensuring that your venture is not just functional, but excellent.

Then, there are the "Could Have" tasks. These are the nice-to-haves, the cherries on top. If time and resources allow, including these features can add extra polish and appeal to your venture. However, they are not essential, and can be set aside if necessary.

Finally, you come to the "Won't Have" tasks. These are the elements that, after careful consideration, you decide to leave out of the current venture scope. This doesn't mean they aren't valuable, but rather that they can wait for future phases or ventures. By consciously deciding what to exclude, you free up energy and resources to focus on what really counts.

To ensure you are making the best decisions, you can also use the Eisenhower Matrix in conjunction with the MoSCoW method. As mentioned earlier, this matrix helps divide tasks into four categories: urgent and important, important but not urgent, urgent but not important, and neither urgent nor important and by evaluating your tasks through both frameworks, you can gain a comprehensive understanding of their priority and impact. The beauty of the MoSCoW method lies in its clarity and simplicity. It gives you a structured way to make decisions, ensuring that your efforts are aligned with your goals. By using this method, you will find yourself more focused, more efficient, and ultimately more successful.

I encourage you to embrace the MoSCoW method and the Eisenhower Matrix in your ventures and daily tasks and business decisions. Let these tools guide you in prioritising what truly matters, and watch as your productivity soars and your ventures thrive. The power to achieve more with less effort is within your reach—unlock it with MoSCoW and the Eisenhower Matrix. By combining the Eisenhower Matrix with the MOSCOW method, you gain a comprehensive framework for prioritising tasks based on both their urgency/importance and their significance to your goals. This approach can help you focus your efforts on the most impactful activities, leading to greater productivity and goal achievement and break more better business Deals or have more successfull growth journey.

Are you ready to make the DEAL? And if so then, my dear friend, the story of Emily and DEAL reminds us that no dream is too big, no goal too ambitious. With the right mindset and tools at your disposal, you can overcome any obstacle and create a life of purpose, passion, and abundance.

Conclusion & Recap

Overall, the DEAL methodology provides a structured approach to managing workload, optimising productivity, and achieving desired outcomes by emphasising delegation, elimination or reprioritisation, automation, and leveraging resources. Incorporating the DEAL methodology into your lives isn't just about improving your productivity – it's about unlocking your full potential and achieving your wildest dreams. By embracing delegation, reprioritisation, automation, and leverage, you can overcome obstacles, seize opportunities, and create a life of purpose and fulfilment. So, are you ready to unleash your potential with the power of DEAL? It's time to take control of your destiny, embrace change, and chart a course towards success. Remember, the journey may not always be easy, but with the DEAL methodology as your guide, the possibilities are endless.

Delegate as many tasks and activities as possible to keep yourself free. If delegation isn't an option, determine how urgent or important the task is. Then, decide whether you can eliminate it from your task list or reprioritise it for a later date. Automation – allows us to harness the power of technology to your advantage. Automation involves leveraging technology and tools to streamline repetitive or time-consuming tasks, reducing manual effort and increasing efficiency. By automating routine processes, individuals can free up time to focus on more strategic activities that drive value. Last but not least, the fourth component of the DEAL methodology encourages us to leverage your resources and networks for maximum impact. If you can neither Delegate, not Eliminate or Automate something then you should work with collaborate other business owners who are expert in what they do and can do something for us efficiently and better. Leveraging involves utilising existing resources, networks, and opportunities to maximise outcomes. This may include forming strategic partnerships, accessing external expertise, or leveraging existing assets to achieve goals more effectively and efficiently.

Whether it's forming strategic partnerships, seeking mentorship, or tapping into your personal and professional connections, leveraging your assets can open doors to new opportunities and possibilities. By pooling your collective expertise and resources, you can achieve far more together than you ever could alone. In the daring world of entrepreneurship, there's a thrilling rollercoaster ride awaiting those brave enough to take the plunge. Imagine having a bright idea, a spark of innovation that sets your heart racing. But be prepared, because alongside the exhilarating highs come the heart-stopping lows. Welcome to the wild and wonderful realm of risk and reward in business, which you will explore in the next chapter.

Chapter 3.4

Taking the Biggest Risks - Thrills and Spills of Entrepreneurship

“In the world of entrepreneurship, fortune favours the bold. Embrace the adventure, seize the moment, and watch your dreams unfold”

SABTOSH KUMAR

The journey of entrepreneurship is not for the faint of heart. The exhilarating rollercoaster ride of entrepreneurship is a journey filled with risks and rewards, twists and turns, highs and lows. It demands courage, perseverance, and a willingness to embrace uncertainty. But oh, what a ride it is! I would like to share two stories as part of this chapter. By understanding the dynamic interplay between risk and reward, entrepreneurs can make informed decisions, seize opportunities, and chart a path towards sustainable success in the ever-evolving landscape of business.

In the vibrant streets of London, Sarah, a young entrepreneur with boundless ambition, embarked on her maiden voyage into business. Fuelled by a passion for food and a talent for hospitality, she opened a cosy café tucked away in a serene corner of the city. The café quickly became a hub of activity, brimming with laughter and savoury delights. Sarah poured her heart and soul into creating a warm atmosphere where patrons could gather and enjoy delicious meals.

Initially, success seemed within grasp. However, unforeseen challenges emerged. Steep rent hikes and unexpected maintenance costs threatened to derail Sarah's dream. Despite her best efforts, she faced the heart-wrenching decision to close the café's doors. It was a poignant moment, marking the end of Sarah's first entrepreneurial chapter.

On the other side of the world, a young Elon Musk, driven by an insatiable curiosity and a thirst for innovation, embarked on a different path. After studying physics and economics, Elon felt the magnetic pull of entrepreneurship. Armed with nothing but a vision and unwavering self-belief, he ventured into uncharted territory.

Elon's journey began with Zip2, a pioneering software company that revolutionised online business directories and maps for newspapers. Despite encountering numerous obstacles, Elon persisted with unyielding determination. He invested his all in building Zip2 into a thriving enterprise. When the company eventually sold for a staggering sum, Elon's resilience and perseverance bore fruit, cementing his reputation as a visionary entrepreneur of our era.

These stories epitomise the rollercoaster ride of entrepreneurship—a journey marked by resilience in adversity and the pursuit of dreams against all odds. They remind us that while risks abound, so too do the opportunities for transformative success.

Risk – The Daredevil

Let me talk about something fundamental to entrepreneurship: risk.

Risk is an inherent part of not only in starting and running a business but also in our personal and professional success. Understanding the risk is crucial for anyone looking to succeed in their field. It encompasses the uncertainty and potential for loss that accompanies any business endeavour. It's the daredevil of the entrepreneurial world, lurking around every corner, daring you to take a leap of faith. When you start your own venture, you're not just gambling with money – you're putting your dreams on the line.

Let's explore the different types of risks entrepreneurs face.

First, there's financial risk. Financial risk is like walking a tightrope without a safety net; one misstep could send you tumbling into the abyss of debt and despair. This is one of the most immediate challenges for any entrepreneur. Starting a business often requires a significant investment, either from personal savings or external funding. This financial commitment carries the possibility of losing that investment if the business doesn't generate enough revenue or profit. It's essential to manage finances carefully to mitigate this risk and ensure the venture's sustainability.

Then there's market risk, the wild card that keeps entrepreneurs like you and me on our toes. In the ever-changing landscape of consumer demand and competition, predicting the next big thing is like trying to catch lightning in a bottle. Will your product fly off the shelves, or will it gather dust in the bargain bin? The thrill of the chase is what keeps entrepreneurs hooked, but it's also what keeps them up at night, sweating over sales forecasts and market trends.

The success of any business depends on its ability to identify and meet market needs. Entrepreneurs face the uncertainty of market conditions, changing consumer preferences, and competition. These factors can threaten the viability of a business if it fails to adapt quickly. Staying attuned to market trends and being flexible in strategies are crucial for navigating these uncertainties.

Your personal reputation and your brand reputation are the most valuable assets. Reputational risk arises from negative publicity, customer complaints, or ethical lapses. These issues can damage a brand's image and erode consumer trust, directly influencing customer loyalty and sales. It's crucial to prioritise ethical business practices and effective communication to protect and enhance the brand's reputation.

Running a business involves managing numerous operational challenges, which you refer to as operational risk. This includes issues like supply chain disruptions, regulatory compliance, and human resource management. If these aspects aren't handled effectively, they can lead to inefficiencies and delays, potentially causing business failure. Entrepreneurs need robust operational strategies and contingency plans to maintain smooth business operations.

Lastly, there's personal risk. Entrepreneurship often demands significant personal sacrifices. Entrepreneurs typically endure long hours, high stress levels, and persistent uncertainty. These demands can strain personal relationships, impact health, and affect overall well-being. Balancing work and personal life is essential to avoid burnout and ensure sustained success.

Risk is an unavoidable aspect of entrepreneurship, encompassing financial, market, operational, reputational, and personal dimensions. By understanding and strategically managing these risks, entrepreneurs can better navigate the complexities of building and growing a successful business. While the journey is filled with challenges, careful planning, adaptability, and resilience can help turn risks into opportunities and achieve long-term success.

The Reward

But hey, it's not all doom and gloom. Because for every risk, there's a tantalising reward waiting to be claimed. Imagine the rush of adrenaline when your hard work pays off and your business starts to soar.

Financial freedom beckons on the horizon, promising a life of luxury and leisure. But it's not just about the money. It's about the thrill of creativity unleashed, the joy of making a difference, and the personal growth that comes with the territory.

With a successful business under your belt, you call the shots – no more answering to the boss, no more Monday morning blues. So, despite the inherent risks, entrepreneurship offers numerous rewards that attract individuals to pursue this path. Let's look at them one by one next

Financial Freedom - One of the most compelling rewards of entrepreneurship is the potential for Building wealth and financial independence. Successful entrepreneurs can build substantial wealth by creating innovative products or services, capturing market opportunities, and scaling their businesses. This financial freedom not only secures your future but also allows you to invest in further ventures or causes they are passionate about.

Creative Fulfilment - Next, you have the power of self-fulfilment. Entrepreneurship is a powerful platform for creative expression and problem-solving. Entrepreneurs have the freedom to pursue their passions, explore new ideas, and bring their visions to life. This creative autonomy can be deeply fulfilling, as it allows you to make tangible contributions to the world and see your ideas take shape in meaningful ways.

Autonomy and Control - Another compelling reward is the autonomy and control such as being your own boss. Unlike traditional employment, entrepreneurship offers significant autonomy and control over one's work life. Entrepreneurs can set their own schedules, choose their team members, and shape the culture of their organisations. This control allows you to align your business operations with their personal values and goals, creating a work environment that truly reflects your vision.

Impact and Legacy - The Impact for the community or leaving the Legacy for people around you is next big reward of entrepreneurship in order to serve the community or make a difference in the life of others. Entrepreneurs have the opportunity to make a profound impact on society. By addressing unmet needs, driving innovation, and creating jobs, you contribute to economic growth and social progress. Successful entrepreneurs often leave behind a legacy that extends beyond financial success, influencing future generations and fostering a spirit of innovation and entrepreneurship.

Personal Growth - Personal Growth is another big one. The entrepreneurial journey is a continuous learning experience that fosters significant personal growth and development. Entrepreneurs develop resilience, adaptability, and leadership skills as they navigate challenges, overcome obstacles, and learn from both their successes and failures. This personal growth not only enhances your professional capabilities but also enriches your overall life experience.

Navigating the Balance - Achieving success in entrepreneurship requires striking a delicate balance between risk and reward. While embracing risk is essential for innovation and growth, entrepreneurs must also mitigate risk through strategic planning, market research, and contingency planning. Additionally, maintaining a realistic perspective on the potential rewards of entrepreneurship helps entrepreneurs stay motivated and resilient in the face of adversity.

Entrepreneurship, with its myriad rewards, remains a compelling pursuit for those ready to take on its challenges. Whether driven by the promise of financial freedom, the desire for creative fulfilment, or the ambition to make a lasting impact, entrepreneurs play a crucial role in shaping the future of our economy and society.

Is entrepreneurship worth the risk?

Absolutely. Because beyond the sleepless nights and nail-biting uncertainty lies a world of endless possibilities. It's a world where dreams come true and ordinary people achieve extraordinary things. So, if you've got a fire in your belly and a dream in your heart, don't let fear hold you back. Take the plunge, embrace the adventure, and watch as the rewards of entrepreneurship unfold before your very eyes.

Entrepreneurship is often romanticised as the path to freedom, wealth, and success. While these rewards are certainly possible, they come with significant risks and challenges. In this segment, let's delve into the dynamic interplay between risk and reward in the world of entrepreneurship next.

And speaking of rewards, oh, how sweet they are! Picture this: you've taken the plunge, weathered the storms, and emerged victorious on the other side. The sense of accomplishment is unparalleled.

Devastated but undeterred, Sarah refused to let failure define her. Armed with lessons learned and a newfound resilience, she dusted herself off and set her sights on a new venture – an online marketplace for handmade crafts.

This time, Sarah approached her business with caution, conducting thorough market research and meticulously planning every step. Slowly but surely, her online platform gained traction, attracting talented artisans and eager customers from around the country.

But on the other story, Elon was not one to rest on his laurels. Fuelled by a desire to make a lasting impact on humanity, he set his sights on even greater challenges. With the founding of X.com, which later became PayPal, Elon revolutionised the way people conduct financial transactions online. His vision and ingenuity transformed a fledgling startup into a global powerhouse, paving the way for a future where digital payments are the norm.

Yet, as with any journey of entrepreneurship, Elon's path was not without its share of failures. His attempt to revolutionise the electric car industry with Tesla Motors was met with scepticism and ridicule. Many doubted the viability of electric vehicles and questioned Elon's ability to deliver on his ambitious promises. But Elon refused to be deterred by the naysayers, pressing forward with unwavering determination and a steadfast belief in his vision.

And oh, how his perseverance paid off! Today, Tesla stands as a shining beacon of innovation and sustainability, leading the charge towards a greener, more sustainable future. Elon's relentless pursuit of excellence has propelled him to unimaginable heights, earning him a place among the world's most influential and revered entrepreneurs.

There's the sheer joy of creativity unleashed. Entrepreneurship is like painting on a blank canvas, a chance to let your imagination run wild and create something truly extraordinary. Whether you're revolutionising an industry or solving a problem that's been bugging people for years, the feeling of making a difference is incomparable.

And let's not forget the personal growth that comes with the territory. Entrepreneurship is a crash course in resilience, teaching you to bounce back from setbacks stronger and wiser than before. It's a journey of self-discovery, pushing you out of your comfort zone and forcing you to confront your fears head-on.

Perhaps Elon's greatest legacy lies in his audacious vision for the future. From colonising Mars with SpaceX to revolutionising transportation with the Hyperloop, Elon's dreams know no bounds. He is a testament to the power of imagination, the rewards of taking risks, and the transformative impact of entrepreneurship on society.

So, as you marvel at Elon Musk's extraordinary journey, let us be inspired to dream big, take risks, and push the boundaries of what is possible. For in the world of entrepreneurship, the greatest rewards await those bold enough to chase their dreams, defy the odds, and change the world for the better.

Similarly in case of Sarah, As the business grew, so did Sarah's confidence. She expanded her offerings, diversified her revenue streams, and embraced new technologies to stay ahead of the curve. Before long, her once small startup had blossomed into a thriving e-commerce empire, turning over substantial profits and earning Sarah a reputation as a trailblazing entrepreneur.

Entrepreneurship is not for the faint of heart. It requires courage, resilience, and a willingness to embrace uncertainty. But for those brave enough to take the plunge, the rewards are beyond measure. So, to all the dreamers and doers in the audience in my seminars and public speaking, I say this: seize the moment, chase your dreams, and never let fear hold you back.

Conclusion & Recap

In the words of Winston Churchill, "Success is not final, failure is not fatal: It is the courage to continue that counts." So, let us embark on this grand adventure together, knowing that the greatest rewards await those who dare to dream.

As you navigate our own paths in business and life, let us draw the learnings and inspiration from Sarah and Elon's experiences. Embrace the challenges, learn from setbacks, and dare to dream big. For it is in the pursuit of our dreams that you discover the true essence of entrepreneurship—the courage to forge ahead, undeterred by the highs and lows of the journey.

Risk is the daring leap into the unknown, the moment when you throw caution to the wind and bet it all on yourself. Starting your own business is like setting sail on a stormy sea – you never know what challenges lie ahead. Financial risk, market risk, operational risk – they're all part of the game. But remember, fortune favours the bold. Without risk, there can be no reward.

Amidst her success, Sarah never forgot the lessons of her past. She knew that entrepreneurship was a journey filled with risks and rewards, highs and lows. And while the road had been rocky at times, the rewards far outweighed the challenges. Today, her story serves as an inspiration to aspiring entrepreneurs everywhere. It's a reminder that failure is not the end, but rather a stepping stone on the path to success. With courage, resilience, and a willingness to take risks, anything is possible in the world of entrepreneurship. So, to all the dreamers and doers out there, take heed of Sarah's tale. Embrace the adventure, chase your dreams, and remember that the greatest rewards often come from taking the biggest risks. After all, "The only way to predict the future is to create it."

In next chapter, you will explore the triad of success, encompassing role models, business coaches, and mentors. Beginning with an overview of this powerful combination, you'll unlock the transformative power of mentorship. Next, you'll elevate your understanding of the profound influence of business coaches. Moving beyond, you'll uncover the impactful role of role models in personal growth, emphasising their ripple effect on individuals. The chapter will also unveil the transformative journey of role models, showcasing their power to inspire and guide. Lastly, you'll witness the magic of mentorship and the strategic leadership unleashed by combining mentorship with visionary thinking. Through the lens of "Visions to Victory," you'll decode the success journey of an entrepreneur and explore the importance of evolving role models every five years for sustained success.

Chapter 3.5

Accelerate your learning curve with Triad of Success

The Triad of Success

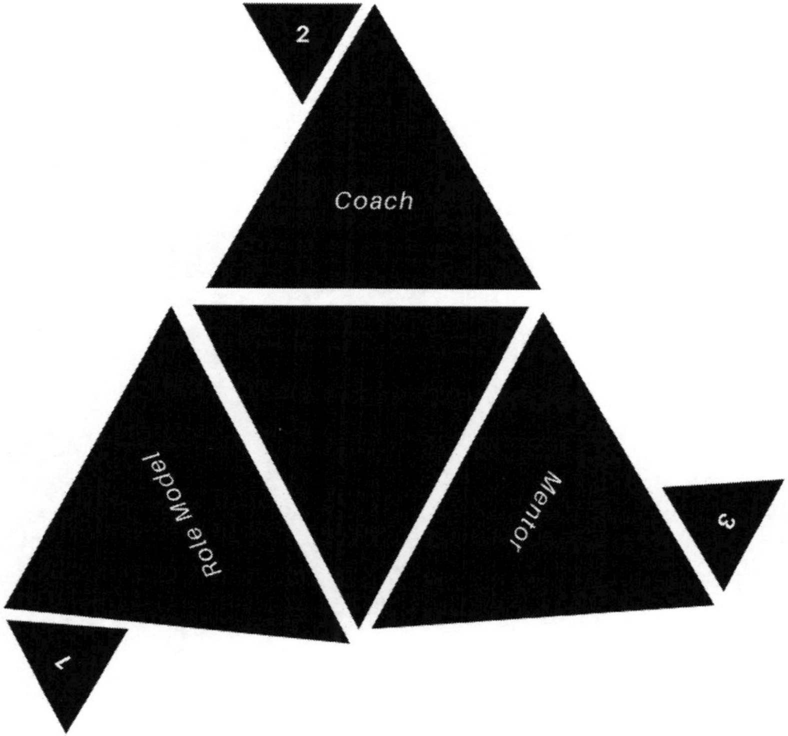

In life, you often find ourselves facing challenges, uncertainties, and obstacles on the path to your goals. But what if I told you that there are shortcuts to success? What if I told you that you can accelerate your learning curve and avoid common pitfalls by tapping into the wisdom and experience of those who have walked the path before us? This is where role models, business coaches, and mentors come into play.

In the journey towards personal and professional success, individuals often seek guidance, inspiration, and strategic support from various sources to achieve their goals. Among these sources, three roles stand out as pillars of support: the Business Coach, the Role Model, and the Mentor. Together, they form a triad that not only shapes success but also fosters growth and resilience in individuals and organisations alike. Today, I want to talk about these three key figures that can shape your journey to personal and professional success. These three roles together create a winning combination that can truly transform your path to success. Together, they form a triad that not only shapes success but also fosters growth and resilience in individuals and organisations alike. These three form a powerful support network, each playing a unique yet connected role in helping you grow and achieve goals.

The triad of success – An Overview

Firstly, let's talk about role models. At the heart of the triad lies the concept of role models — individuals who embody the qualities, achievements, and values that others aspire to emulate. Role models serve as living examples of what is possible, offering inspiration and motivation to those who seek to follow in their footsteps. Whether they are icons in the public eye or everyday heroes within your communities, role models inspire by their actions, their resilience, and their unwavering commitment to excellence. Role models are people who embody the qualities and achievements you aspire to. They show us what is possible through their actions, resilience, and commitment to excellence. Whether they are famous icons or everyday heroes in your communities, role models inspire us to reach higher and strive for success.

Next, you have business coaches, complementing the influence of role models — seasoned professionals who provide strategic guidance, and functional support to individuals seeking to navigate the complexities of the business world. Business coaches offer a wealth of expertise and insight, helping clients refine their goals, develop actionable plans, and overcome obstacles on the path to success on a functional or business unit. Through tailored coaching sessions, business coaches empower individuals to unlock their full potential, optimise their performance, and achieve their business objectives. These are experienced professionals who offer strategic guidance and support as you navigate the business world. Business coaches help us set clear goals, develop actionable plans, and overcome obstacles. They bring a wealth of expertise and insight, empowering us to unlock your full potential and achieve your business objectives.

Finally, Rounding out the triad are mentors — trusted advisors who offer guidance, wisdom, and growth support to individuals as they navigate their personal and professional journeys. Mentors provide a unique blend of experience, perspective, and empathy, serving as sounding boards, confidants, and role models for their mentees. Through mentorship relationships, individuals gain access to invaluable insights, constructive feedback, and opportunities for growth, helping them develop the skills, confidence, and resilience needed to thrive in their chosen fields.

The Role of a Business Coach

A Business Coach plays a pivotal role in your journey towards professional growth and organisational success. Think of them as your strategic partner. They're not there to give you all the answers, but to help you find them yourself.

They'll work with you to set clear goals and develop smart strategies. Through regular sessions and honest feedback, they'll sharpen your decision-making skills and help you tackle any challenges that come your way. Whether you're trying to improve your leadership skills or streamline your business operations, a good coach is like having a knowledgeable guide cheering you on from the sidelines.

Unlike consultants who provide ready-made solutions, a coach serves as a facilitator, empowering you to uncover insights and solutions on your own. Their objective is not to dictate but to collaborate with you in setting clear, achievable goals and devising intelligent strategies tailored to your unique circumstances.

Regular coaching sessions are structured to provide a platform for reflection, analysis, and growth. Through these interactions, a coach offers invaluable feedback that hones your decision-making abilities and enhances your problem-solving skills. They act as a sounding board, helping you navigate complexities and uncertainties with clarity and confidence. This process is akin to having a seasoned guide by your side, offering encouragement and strategic direction while fostering a deeper understanding of your strengths and areas for improvement.

Whether your focus is on refining leadership qualities, optimising operational efficiencies, or tackling strategic challenges, a competent coach brings expertise and perspective to the table. They draw from their own experiences and knowledge of best practices to offer practical insights and actionable advice. This mentorship extends beyond immediate goals, aiming to cultivate long-term personal and professional development.

Moreover, a coach's role transcends mere technical expertise; they also provide emotional support and motivation. They celebrate your achievements, bolster your resilience during setbacks, and inspire you to push beyond perceived limits. This holistic approach not only accelerates your growth trajectory but also nurtures a mindset conducive to continuous learning and improvement.

The Influence of Role Models

Next up, you have Role Models. These are the people who inspire us by their achievements and their character. They show us what's possible and encourage us to aim high. Role models aren't just about success in business; they embody qualities like resilience and ethical leadership that are crucial for long-term success. By following their example, you can gain clarity on our own goals and the steps you need to take to achieve them.

Role models serve as profound influencers in our lives, shaping our ambitions and ethical foundations through their exemplary achievements and conduct. More than just individuals who have achieved success, role models embody the values and principles that contribute to their accomplishments, making them sources of inspiration and guidance.

By observing role models, individuals gain clarity on their own aspirations and the paths to achieving them. Role models provide tangible examples of what dedication, perseverance, and ethical behaviour can achieve, illustrating the possibilities and potential for personal and professional growth. They serve as beacons of success, offering a roadmap that inspires others to strive for greatness.

The impact of role models extends far beyond their professional achievements. They inspire resilience in the face of adversity, demonstrating how challenges can be overcome with determination and integrity. Their ethical leadership qualities set benchmarks for others to emulate, fostering a culture of accountability and excellence.

Moreover, role models cultivate a sense of purpose and direction. They instill confidence in individuals by showing that success is attainable through hard work, dedication, and adherence to ethical standards. Their influence encourages individuals to set ambitious goals and pursue them with conviction, fostering a mindset of continuous improvement and achievement.

The Guidance of Mentors

Then there are Mentors. These are like wise friends who have been there and done that. They offer invaluable advice based on their own experiences. Mentors invest their time and energy in helping you grow both professionally and personally. They provide guidance on your career path, introduce you to new contacts, and give you the confidence to overcome challenges. Their support can make a world of difference, especially when you're navigating tricky waters in your career.

Mentors are invaluable guides who bring a wealth of wisdom, experience, and personalised advice to their mentees. Unlike coaches who primarily focus on skill enhancement, mentors offer a deeper, more holistic form of support rooted in their own professional journeys.

These trusted advisors play a pivotal role in nurturing the development of their mentees by sharing firsthand insights garnered from their successes and setbacks. They provide constructive feedback, encouragement, and practical guidance tailored to the individual's career aspirations and personal growth objectives.

Mentors foster comprehensive development by addressing both professional challenges and personal development needs. They act as advocates for their mentees, facilitating valuable networking opportunities and championing their advancement within their respective fields.

The mentor-mentee relationship is built on mutual trust and respect, fostering meaningful connections that endure over time. Mentors not only impart knowledge and expertise but also serve as role models, exemplifying leadership qualities and ethical behavior that inspire their mentees to emulate and embody.

Through ongoing support and encouragement, mentors empower individuals to navigate complexities with confidence and resilience. They provide a safe space for mentees to explore ideas, seek advice, and develop strategies for overcoming obstacles encountered along their professional journeys.

Interconnected Synergies and Benefits of the Triad

While each component of the triad — role models, business coaches, and mentors — offers distinct benefits and contributions, their influence is often interwoven and complementary. Role models inspire individuals to set ambitious goals and pursue excellence in their endeavours. Business coaches provide the strategic guidance and support needed to translate those aspirations into tangible action plans and results. Mentors offer the personalised guidance and support that help individuals navigate challenges, overcome obstacles, and stay focused on their long-term objectives.

The synergy created by combining a Business Coach, Role Model, and Mentor is profound. Each role complements the others, offering a comprehensive support system that accelerates learning, enhances decision-making capabilities, and fosters personal and professional development. Together, they create an ecosystem where individuals can thrive, innovate, and achieve their full potential.

But rather than talking about each one of them independently again, let's talk about why this triad of support is so powerful when combined.

Firstly, you get a comprehensive support system. Your coach helps you with skills and strategy, your role models inspire you with their achievements, and your mentor gives you personalised advice and support. It's like having a dream team backing you up.

Secondly, this combination speeds up your learning curve. Instead of figuring everything out on your own, you can learn from the experiences and mistakes of others. This means fewer setbacks and quicker progress towards your goals.

Thirdly, having these three roles in your corner keeps you motivated and resilient. When you have people believing in you and pushing you forward, it's easier to stay focused and keep going, even when things get tough.

Lastly, this network expands your horizons. Through your mentor and role models, you gain access to new opportunities, ideas, and connections that you might not have found on your own.

The synergy between role models, business coaches, and mentors creates a robust support system. Each figure contributes differently but harmoniously to your development:

Role Models, inspire us and set a benchmark for what you can achieve.

Business Coaches, provide practical, strategic guidance to navigate professional challenges.

Mentors, offer personal, empathetic advice and support, helping us grow holistically.

the triad of success—role models, business coaches, and mentors—plays a crucial role in shaping your growth and achievement. By drawing on the strengths of these three types of support, you can find the inspiration, guidance, and wisdom needed to reach your full potential. This interconnected network not only helps us achieve your immediate goals but also fosters long-term personal and professional development.

By leveraging the collective power of role models, business coaches, and mentors, individuals can create a synergistic network of support and guidance that propels them towards success. Whether seeking inspiration, strategic direction, or personal development, the triad offers a wealth of resources and opportunities for growth. By cultivating relationships with role models, engaging the services of a business coach, and seeking out mentorship opportunities, individuals can tap into a rich ecosystem of support that empowers them to achieve their goals, realise their potential, and chart a course towards lasting success.

In other word, the triad of a Business Coach, Role Model, and Mentor forms a cornerstone of success in today's competitive world. Together, they empower individuals to navigate challenges, seize opportunities, and achieve meaningful growth. By leveraging the unique strengths of each role, individuals can build resilience, expand their capabilities, and forge paths to enduring success.

Whether you're aiming for professional advancement, entrepreneurial success, or personal fulfillment, embracing the support of these three roles can be transformative. They are not just advisors; they are catalysts for greatness, guiding individuals towards their highest aspirations and helping them leave a lasting impact on their industries and communities.

Together, they form a powerful network of support and guidance, each playing a unique yet interconnected role in shaping the trajectory of an individual's growth and achievement.

A Mentor or a Business coach?

A mentor typically provides guidance based on their experience and knowledge, offering insights and advice. On the other hand, a business coach focuses on helping you develop specific skills, set goals, and create actionable plans for professional growth. While both offer support, mentoring tends to be more holistic, drawing on the mentor's overall experience, while coaching is often more structured and skill oriented.

A mentorship relation often involves a more informal and personal connection, with the mentor sharing their experiences, lessons learned, and providing guidance on a wide range of career and life aspects. It's about passing on wisdom and fostering personal development.

On the other hand, a business coach tends to have a more structured approach. They work with you to set specific, measurable goals, identify obstacles, and develop strategies to overcome them. Coaches focus on skill development, accountability, and often use specific methodologies to guide you through challenges.

In other words, a mentorship is often characterised by a broader, long-term relationship based on shared experiences, while business coaching is typically more focused on specific, short-to-medium term goals with a structured plan for improvement.

Let me share with you the transformative power of mentorship and business coaching through some real-life examples.

Let's start with mentorship:

Picture an experienced entrepreneur mentoring a new startup founder. The seasoned entrepreneur shares invaluable insights from their own business journey, recounting the challenges they faced and the strategies they used to overcome them. This guidance helps the new founder navigate the tumultuous waters of running a startup, providing a roadmap based on real-world experience.

Consider another scenario where a senior professional mentors a junior colleague. The senior professional has already travelled this journey before, offering tips and possessing extensive experience in the subject area. They are familiar with the ins and outs and are happy to share their knowledge, skills, and wisdom for the junior's growth as a mentor. The mentor provides advice on career development, offering tips on how to achieve work-life balance and successfully navigate the corporate culture. This kind of mentorship fosters growth, confidence, and a clearer path to professional success for the junior colleague.

Now, let’s talk about business coaching:

Imagine a business coach working with a manager to enhance their leadership skills. Together, they set specific goals such as improving team communication and implementing effective delegation strategies. Through regular sessions, the coach provides tailored feedback and exercises, enabling the manager to become a more effective and inspiring leader.

In another example, an executive coach helps a professional develop their negotiation skills. The coach designs custom exercises and provides detailed feedback, helping the professional navigate complex business deals with greater confidence and competence.

In both mentorship and business coaching, you see the profound impact of guided support and strategic advice. Mentors offer wisdom from their own experiences, helping mentees avoid common pitfalls and achieve their goals. Coaches provide structured guidance, sharpening specific skills and fostering personal and professional growth.

Together, mentors and coaches play a pivotal role in shaping successful careers, guiding individuals toward achieving their full potential.

In essence, a mentor's guidance is often broader and more encompassing, drawn from personal experiences, while a business coach's focus is specific, targeting skill development and goal achievement through a structured process.

The Power of Evolution - Why You Should Review or Change Their Role Models Every Five Years

Entrepreneurs, like all individuals, are shaped by the influences and inspirations they encounter along their journey. While it may seem counterintuitive to change role models every five years, there are several compelling reasons why entrepreneurs should consider refreshing their sources of inspiration periodically.

Evolution of Goals and Aspirations - As entrepreneurs grow and evolve, so too do their goals, aspirations, and visions for the future. What may have inspired them in the early stages of their journey may no longer resonate with their current ambitions. Changing role models allows entrepreneurs to align their aspirations with individuals who reflect their evolving values, priorities, and objectives.

Adaptation to Changing Industries - Industries evolve rapidly in response to technological advancements, market trends, and shifting consumer preferences. Entrepreneurs operating in dynamic sectors may find that their role models from five years ago no longer represent the cutting edge of innovation or success in their field. By updating their role models, entrepreneurs can stay abreast of industry trends and adapt their strategies accordingly.

Diversification of Perspectives - Exposure to a diverse range of role models can broaden an entrepreneur's perspective and inspire innovative thinking. By continually changing role models, entrepreneurs can explore different leadership styles, approaches to problem-solving, and business philosophies, gaining insights that enrich their own entrepreneurial journey.

Avoiding Complacency - Success can breed complacency if entrepreneurs become too comfortable with their current level of achievement. Changing role models injects fresh energy and motivation into their entrepreneurial endeavours, challenging them to strive for new heights of excellence and innovation.

Continued Learning and Growth - Entrepreneurship is a journey of lifelong learning and growth. By seeking out new role models every five years, entrepreneurs expose themselves to new ideas, experiences, and perspectives that stimulate personal and professional development. Embracing change in role models fosters a culture of curiosity, adaptability, and continuous improvement.

Networking and Mentorship Opportunities - Each new role model presents an opportunity for networking and potential mentorship. By cultivating relationships with different role models over time, entrepreneurs can expand their professional network, seek guidance from diverse sources, and tap into valuable resources for support and advice.

In other words, reviewing, and if needed, changing role models every five years enables entrepreneurs to adapt to evolving circumstances, stay abreast of industry developments, foster innovation, and maintain a growth-oriented mindset. By embracing change and seeking inspiration from a diverse array of sources, entrepreneurs can position themselves for long-term success and fulfillment in their entrepreneurial endeavours.

Conclusion & Recap

Role models are the guiding lights that inspire us to reach higher and strive for excellence. They show us what is possible through their actions, their resilience, and their unwavering commitment to excellence. By studying their journeys, you can gain invaluable insights into the strategies and mindsets that lead to success. Business coaches offer strategic guidance and expertise to help us navigate the complexities of the business world. They provide tailored advice based on their understanding of industry trends and best practices, helping us make more informed decisions and avoid common pitfalls. And then there are mentors – trusted advisors who offer personalised support and guidance as you navigate your personal and professional journeys. Mentors provide wisdom, encouragement, and constructive feedback, helping us overcome obstacles and capitalise on opportunities.

In this chapter, you explored the triad of success, which encompassed role models, business coaches, and mentors. Beginning with an overview of this powerful combination, you delved into the distinction between a mentor and a business coach. Then, you unlocked the transformative power of mentorship, highlighting its significance in shaping one's professional journey. A Business Coach is more than just a professional advisor; they are a catalyst for transformation, guiding you towards achieving your full potential and driving sustainable success in your career and business endeavours. Role models play a crucial role in shaping not only career aspirations but also personal values and character development. Their influence is invaluable in guiding individuals towards fulfilling their potential and contributing positively to their communities and industries. As you look to role models for inspiration, you are inspired not only to achieve success but also to embody the principles that sustain it over the long term. Mentors play a crucial role in shaping the next generation of leaders by equipping them with the skills, insights, and mindset necessary to thrive in their careers and make meaningful contributions to their organisations and communities. Their guidance extends beyond immediate career progression, fostering long-term personal and professional growth that benefits both the mentee and the broader society.

Whether you're aiming for starting your own business, or simply looking to grow as a person, having a Business Coach, Role Model, and Mentor can make all the difference. They're not just advisors; they're your secret weapons for achieving your dreams and leaving a lasting impact. So, embrace their support, learn from their wisdom, and let them guide you towards the success you deserve.

you also elevated your understanding of the profound influence of business coaches, exploring how they could elevate professions and drive success. Moving beyond, you uncovered the impactful role of role models in personal growth, emphasising their ripple effect on individuals. The chapter also unveiled the transformative journey of role models, showcasing their power to inspire and guide. Lastly, you witnessed the magic of mentorship and the strategic leadership unleashed by combining mentorship with visionary thinking.

Through the lens of "Visions to Victory," you decoded the success journey of an entrepreneur and explored the importance of evolving role models every five years for sustained success. By learning from the experiences and insights of role models, business coaches, and mentors, you can accelerate your learning curve and achieve success more efficiently and effectively. You can avoid repeating the mistakes of others and benefit from their connections, resources, and networks.

In the next chapter, I'm going to share a powerful framework that has the potential to transform the way you approach challenges and obstacles in your lives. It's called the Business AURA framework, and it's more than just a strategy – it's one of the key ingredients to success. Let's deep dive in

Chapter 3.6

Embrace The Power of Business AURA Framework & Unlock Your Success

KEY SUCCESS **ELEMENT**

BUSINESS

AURA

A ACCEPT IT

U UNDERSTAND IT

R REALISE IT

A ACT ON IT

In today's fast-paced world, challenges and obstacles are inevitable. Whether in business or in life, you are constantly faced with problems that demand your attention and resolution.

But what if there was a systematic approach to tackling these challenges head-on and emerging victorious? Enter the Business AURA framework – a strategic problem-solving approach designed to empower individuals to handle and overcome obstacles with confidence and efficiency.

Imagine a world where challenges are not roadblocks but opportunities for growth. A world where acceptance is the first step towards transformation, where understanding leads to clarity, where realisation breeds insight, and where action fuels progress. This is the world that the Business AURA framework invites us to inhabit – a world of endless possibilities and boundless potential. Let's understand this with the journey of an entrepreneur named Alisha.

Alisha had always dreamed of building a successful business, but like many, she faced her fair share of challenges along the way.

One day, feeling overwhelmed by the obstacles in her path, Alisha stumbled upon a remarkable discovery – the Business AURA framework. Intrigued by its promise of transformation, she decided to delve deeper into its teachings and see if it could help her overcome the hurdles that stood between her and her dreams.

At the core of the Business AURA framework are four essential steps: ACCEPT, UNDERSTAND, REALISE, and ACT. Let's delve deeper into each step and explore how it can revolutionise the way you confront challenges.

The first step of the framework was Acceptance. Alisha realised that she couldn't continue to ignore the challenges she faced; she had to confront them head-on. With newfound courage, she accepted the setbacks and setbacks as opportunities for growth, embracing them with open arms.

ACCEPT – Embracing the Reality of Challenges

As young entrepreneurs, it can be difficult to acknowledge that you don't know everything and that problems are inevitable. Sometimes even the most experience people also fall into this trap.

Believing that you are flawless and can handle any issue without struggle can hinder our progress. Instead, you should recognise that you are not the first to feel this way, there are others who have travelled this path and learning from others' experiences can be valuable. Reinventing the wheel wastes time and once lost it cannot be regained, even with immense wealth.

Time is the most valuable commodity in the universe known to human beings, and it's crucial not to waste a single second being unproductive. Accepting the situation and being proactive or finding your sherpa before climbing the Everest for the guidance and support is not a embracement but it's about being proactive and finding solutions of known and unknown challenges of the personal and professional journey in advance is crucial. That's this framework emphasises accepting the reality of potential problems and being open to finding solutions. This approach can help young entrepreneurs like you and Alisha avoid unnecessary struggles and use their time efficiently and effectively.

Acceptance – the first step in your journey. The journey towards overcoming challenges begins with acceptance. It's about acknowledging the existence of challenges, both known and unknown, and embracing them with open arms. It's about refraining from turning a blind eye to them. Instead of turning away from adversity, you face it head-on, armed with courage and determination.

Instead of succumbing to denial or avoidance, acceptance fosters a proactive mindset, empowering individuals to confront challenges head-on. Acceptance empowers us to take control of your destiny, to shape your own future, and to rise above the obstacles that stand in your way.

By embracing acceptance, individuals open themselves up to a world of possibilities. They recognise that challenges are not roadblocks but opportunities for growth and development. With acceptance as the foundation, individuals can embark on a journey of self-discovery and transformation.

In other words, the world of personal or professional life is full of challenges and roadblocks, both known and unknown to us. Most of the time, you don't want to accept that there is a challenge until it's too late. Initially, our enthusiasm and overconfidence blind us, then our fixed mindset ignores it, and finally, our conscious mind tells us not to worry to safeguard ourselves from negative feelings. By the time you accept that there is a challenge, it has already taken months or sometimes years, and it is too late; the damage is already done with no way back. You have already incurred losses in business, experienced sleepless nights with stress and anxiety, or, in many cases, closed our business doors to customers, never daring to reopen them for anyone in any business. Hence, the first step is to accept the situation or problem at hand. By acknowledging the issue, one opens themselves up to finding a solution.

When starting anything new, our initial belief can be a significant obstacle. You may feel that you are perfect and have everything under control, but is that really the case? It's essential to learn from others' experiences and acknowledge potential challenges before embarking on a new journey. By reinventing the wheel, you risk losing valuable time, which is a precious commodity that cannot be regained, even with millions of pounds.

Therefore, it's crucial to acknowledge and learn from others' experiences to avoid unnecessary struggles and find effective solutions efficiently. The Business AURA framework can provide a structured approach to decision-making that considers all relevant factors, allowing individuals and businesses to make informed decisions and achieve their goals efficiently and effectively.

The Next step of Business AURA is U for Understanding – the gateway to enlightenment. It's about delving deep into the heart of the matter, unravelling its mysteries, and uncovering its truths. Through understanding, you gain clarity and insight, enabling us to see the bigger picture and make informed decisions. Understanding is the light that guides us through the darkness, illuminating the path ahead with wisdom and knowledge. Let's look at the step 2 of AURA Framework.

UNDERSTAND – Delving Deep for Insights

The subsequent step in the Business AURA framework is to understand the challenge at hand. Initially, many individuals deny the existence of any problems, and even if they do acknowledge them, they may struggle to comprehend them entirely. This could be due to our limited perspective or fixed mindset. Therefore, it's crucial to recognise that once you accept that there is a problem, you need to understand the problem and its potential impact.

As an entrepreneur, once you understand the problem, you need to recognise the potential consequences of different courses of action. This helps you make more informed decisions that take into account the potential impact on your venture. The Business AURA framework emphasises the importance of comprehensively understanding the problem by gathering and analysing all relevant information. By doing so, individuals or businesses can make well-informed decisions that are not based on incomplete information or assumptions.

Understanding serves as the key to unlocking the true nature of challenges. It entails delving deep into the problems, gathering relevant data, and analysing facts to obtain comprehensive insights. Through understanding, individuals can peel back the layers of complexity surrounding the challenges they face, thus paving the way for informed decision-making.

In the pursuit of understanding, individuals harness their analytical skills and critical thinking abilities. They dissect problems, pinpoint underlying causes, and explore potential solutions with clarity and precision. With each revelation, they draw closer to unravelling the mysteries of the challenges before them.

Next, Alisha embarked on the journey of understanding. She delved deep into the heart of her challenges, unravelling their complexities and gaining valuable insights along the way. Through understanding, she glimpsed the bigger picture and achieved clarity regarding the steps she needed to take to progress.

R for Realisation is the third element of business AURA framework– the moment of clarity. It's when the pieces of the puzzle finally fall into place, and you see the full extent of the challenge before us. Let's look at it below

REALISE – Evaluating Potential Outcomes

The third stage of the Business AURA framework involves realising the problem at hand and its impact on our lives and those of our loved ones. In my experience, comprehending the situation's pros and cons is crucial for making informed decisions and taking appropriate action. By focusing on solutions and considering the potential outcomes, you can avoid further damage or setbacks.

For example, when my business encountered financial difficulties due to increased competition or economic downturns, I worked with my mentor and understood the financial impact on our revenue, reputation, and future prospects. Realising the gravity of these factors, along with my business coach and mentor I developed strategies to overcome the financial hurdles, such as cutting expenses or diversifying our product range to stay relevant in the market.

Furthermore, this process helped me to identify potential risks and opportunities. I could take steps to mitigate them or devise alternative plans to avoid them and leverage them for maximum benefit and growth.

With understanding came Realisation. Realisation empowers us to evaluate the potential outcomes, impacts, and consequences of your decisions, ensuring that you tread carefully and thoughtfully. With realisation comes wisdom, and with wisdom comes the power to shape your destiny. Alisha evaluated the potential outcomes of her decisions, weighing the risks and rewards with a keen eye. She realised that every choice she made had consequences, and she was determined to make the most of them.

Realisation is the bridge between understanding and action. It's about evaluating the potential outcomes, impacts, and consequences associated with the identified problems. Through realisation, individuals gain a realistic perspective on how different solutions may affect their business or personal life.

In the realm of realisation, individuals exercise foresight and discernment. They weigh the pros and cons of each potential course of action, considering both short-term gains and long-term consequences. Armed with this insight, they can make well-informed decisions that align with their goals and aspirations.

Understanding and realising the situation is critical to making sound decisions, avoiding setbacks, identifying risks and opportunities, and achieving success.

And the last one is Action – the catalyst for change. It's when you roll up your sleeves and get to work, turning your dreams into reality one step at a time. Action is the engine that drives progress, propelling us forward towards your goals with unwavering determination. With action comes momentum, and with momentum comes the power to achieve greatness.

ACT – Turning Insights into Action

The final step is to take action on the information gathered and the insights gained from the previous steps. Action is the final frontier of the Business AURA framework. It's about translating insights into practical solutions and proactively taking steps to address and overcome challenges. Through action, individuals transform their vision into reality, driving positive change and achieving meaningful results.

This means making a decision or implementing a solution that addresses the problem or leverages the opportunity identified. While realising the impact of the situation is crucial, taking appropriate and timely action is equally important. By taking timely action, you transition from being a passive observer to an active participant in addressing the problem. This enables you to put your strategies into practice, monitor progress, and make necessary adjustments to achieve desired outcomes. Without taking action, your plans remain ineffective, and the problem persists, leading to further damage and setbacks. Therefore, taking action is pivotal in achieving your goals, resolving challenges, and attaining success.

In the arena of action, individuals demonstrate courage and resilience. They rise to the occasion, armed with a strategic plan and a steadfast determination to succeed. With each decisive step they take, they inch closer to their goals, propelled by the momentum of progress and possibility.

Finally, For Alisha, it was time to ACT. Armed with courage, wisdom, and determination, Alisha set out to turn her dreams into reality. She rolled up her sleeves and got to work, taking bold steps towards her goals with unwavering resolve.

The Result

As Alisha took action, something remarkable happened – she began to see results. Her business started to grow, her dreams started to take shape, and her confidence soared to new heights. With each passing day, she moved closer to her goals, fuelled by the power of the Business AURA framework and her unwavering belief in herself.

In the end, Alisha achieved more than she ever thought possible. Her business flourished, her dreams became a reality, and she became a beacon of inspiration for others who dared to dream big.

Conclusion & Recap

So, dear friends, remember the tale of Alisha and the Business AURA framework. For just like Alisha, each and every one of us has the power to overcome your challenges, achieve your dreams, and become the heroes of your own stories. The story of Alisha and the Business AURA framework serves as a powerful reminder that each of us has the potential to overcome challenges, achieve our dreams, and become the heroes of our own stories. Alisha's journey exemplifies how acceptance, understanding, realisation, and action can lead to remarkable success.

The Business AURA framework is more than just a theory—it's a call to action. It's a reminder that you hold the power to shape our destinies, overcome obstacles, and achieve our dreams. Embracing acceptance, seeking understanding, realising our potential, and taking bold action towards a brighter future are the cornerstones of this framework. Together, you can unleash the power of the Business AURA framework and pave the way to success.

In conclusion, the Business AURA framework is not just a problem-solving approach—it's a catalyst for transformation and growth. By embracing these principles, you can navigate through challenges with grace and confidence, emerging stronger and more resilient than ever before. Let's embrace the power of the Business AURA framework and unlock the path to success together.

Entrepreneurship is a journey filled with uncertainty, but it's also ripe with opportunities for those willing to take risks. The Business AURA framework equips us with the tools to navigate this journey effectively. It helps us build resilience, foster innovation, and drive sustainable growth. By embracing acceptance, understanding, realisation, and action, you can transform challenges into opportunities and setbacks into stepping stones. Let's commit to this journey with determination and optimism, knowing that the path to success is within our reach. Together, you can achieve remarkable things and create a future filled with promise and potential.

In the next chapter, let me share some of the golden nuggets I have learned from my mentors and role models. Together, let us accelerate your learning curve, avoid common pitfalls, and propel ourselves towards your goals with greater speed and confidence.

Chapter 3.7

Unearth Growth Opportunities with Golden Nuggets of Wisdom

Life is too short to learn everything firsthand, and time is always against us. Most inventors, such as Graham Bell for telephone communication and Thomas Edison for light and electricity, failed many times before making their significant discoveries. If you had to reinvent everything firsthand, you would need many lifetimes. Instead of reinventing, life should be a journey of continuous learning from others' experiences. You should preserve these learnings as golden nuggets to build your success by following and implementing the nuggets that suit your environment and meet your needs at any given moment.

Talking about golden nuggets, Imagine yourself panning for gold in a river, sifting through gravel and sediment in search of that elusive gleam. In business, Golden Nuggets are much the same – they are those rare gems of knowledge and wisdom that, when discovered and applied, can yield immense value and success. They come in various forms – from practical tips and strategies to profound insights and philosophies – each one offering a glimpse into the minds of those who have navigated the treacherous waters of entrepreneurship and emerged victorious.

Golden Nuggets are more than just pieces of advice or insights – they are beacons of light in the darkness, guiding us through the challenges and uncertainties of the business world. They offer clarity amidst confusion, direction amidst chaos, and inspiration amidst despair. By heeding their wisdom, you can avoid common pitfalls, capitalise on emerging opportunities, and chart a course towards sustainable growth and success.

These nuggets are not made of precious metals but are invaluable gems of wisdom, garnered from the experiences, trials, and triumphs of successful entrepreneurs and business leaders. They are the distilled essence of hard-earned lessons, offering insights, strategies, and principles that can guide us on the path to prosperity.

Golden Nuggets are the lifeblood of business success – invaluable gems of wisdom that can guide us on the path to prosperity.

In this chapter, Let us look at the high-level concept of the fifteen key golden nuggets—time-tested strategies and insights—that can empower you to foster sustainable growth and elevate their businesses to new heights. These golden nuggets will ignite and accelerate your business growth trajectory, illuminating pathways to success and prosperity.

Golden Nugget 01 - Continuous Learning and Improvement

Foster a culture of continuous learning within yourself and your team to help all of you strive for excellence in everything you do.

Embracing a culture of lifelong learning and improvement is the hallmark of entrepreneurial excellence. Existing entrepreneurs foster an environment where curiosity, experimentation, and innovation thrive. Encouraging employees to pursue professional development opportunities, embrace feedback, and challenge the status quo empowers individuals to reach their full potential and drives collective advancement towards organisational excellence.

Golden Nugget 02 - Strategic Partnerships

Collaborate with other businesses to leverage their resources and unlock new opportunities for growth.

Collaboration is the cornerstone of growth for existing entrepreneurs seeking to expand their horizons. Strategic partnerships with complementary businesses or organisations offer a gateway to shared resources, expertise, and market access. Through synergistic collaborations, you can amplify your impact, penetrate new markets, and unlock unparalleled opportunities for growth and expansion.

Golden Nugget 03 - Customer Retention

Focus on Customer Loyalty as Loyal customers are more likely to repeat purchases and refer others to your business

Amidst the pursuit of acquiring new customers, you as an entrepreneur must recognise the paramount importance of nurturing and retaining their existing customer base. By delivering unparalleled value, fostering authentic relationships, and providing exemplary customer service, you can cultivate a loyal customer following. These loyal patrons not only contribute to recurring revenue but also serve as brand advocates, amplifying the business's reach and influence.

Golden Nugget 04 – Technology implementation

Make informed decisions by leveraging technology for Data-Driven Decision Making and to collect and analyse data effectively

In the digital age, data reigns supreme as a guiding beacon for strategic decision-making. You as an entrepreneur harness the power of data analytics and market insights to glean actionable intelligence about your business landscape. By leveraging advanced analytics tools and technology, you can decipher market trends, anticipate consumer behaviour, and optimise resource allocation to drive sustainable growth and competitive advantage.

Golden Nugget 06 - Investment in people power

People are the true power behind business growth. Your team is the backbone of your business to drive innovation,

productivity, and excellence within your organisation.
Your team is your greatest asset in achieving sustainable growth. When you invest in your team, you invest in your future. Recognising that success hinges upon the collective prowess of your team, you as an entrepreneur must prioritise investment in talent acquisition and development. By recruiting, training, and retaining top-tier talent, entrepreneurs cultivate a culture of innovation, collaboration, and excellence within your organisations. A skilled and motivated workforce serves as the engine driving forward momentum and fuelling the innovation necessary for sustained growth.

Golden Nugget 07 - Finance & the Cashflow

Finance is the King in the game of Business Growth as without robust finance management even the most innovative and high-potential businesses can fail.

Amidst the myriad considerations of business growth, one golden nugget shines brightly—finance and cash flow reign supreme as the lifeblood of entrepreneurial endeavours. Finance and cash flow are the backbone of any business, serving as its lifeblood. Experienced entrepreneurs recognise that prudent financial management is the linchpin of sustainable growth and resilience in the face of uncertainty. Without Finance and Cashflow, even profitable ventures would find it challenging to survive & stay afloat. By meticulously monitoring cash flow, optimising working capital, and managing expenses, entrepreneurs ensure the liquidity necessary to weather economic downturns, seize strategic opportunities, and fuel ongoing innovation. Moreover, maintaining a robust financial foundation instills confidence among stakeholders, fosters credibility with lenders and investors, and positions the business for long-term success. In essence, adept management of finance and cash flow is not merely a component of business strategy—it is the very essence of entrepreneurial stewardship, guiding decisions, and actions towards enduring prosperity.

Golden Nugget 08 – Sales

Sales is the Queen in the game of Business Success as its essential for driving revenue

Often regarded as the queen in the realm of business, sales stands as the strongest ally to the king—finance and cash flow. Sales not only contribute directly to revenue generation but also play a pivotal role in maintaining a healthy cash flow by ensuring a steady influx of income. Through effective sales strategies, businesses not only acquire new customers but also nurture existing relationships, drive repeat purchases, and maximise the lifetime value of each customer. Moreover, sales teams serve as ambassadors for the company, representing its values, products, and services to the outside world. By aligning sales efforts with financial objectives and customer needs, businesses can unlock the full potential of their sales function, fortify their revenue streams, and sustain long-term growth and profitability. Thus, sales emerges as a formidable force, complementing the financial prowess of the king and cementing its place as a cornerstone of business success.

Golden Nugget 09 - Market Expansion

Explore new markets and opportunities for growth beyond your current customer base

As stalwarts in the entrepreneurial arena, you as an entrepreneur must understand the imperative of exploring new frontiers for growth. Beyond the confines of your current customer base lies a vast expanse of untapped potential. By venturing into new markets, whether geographically or through diversification of product/service offerings, you as an entrepreneur can unlock new revenue streams and fortify your market position.

Golden Nugget 10 - Operational Efficiency

Streamlining operations and optimising workflows will improve productivity, reduce costs, and enhance your overall efficiency.

The pursuit of operational excellence lies at the core of sustainable growth for existing entrepreneurs. By optimising workflows, eliminating inefficiencies, and harnessing technology, entrepreneurs enhance productivity, reduce costs, and fortify their operational foundations. Streamlining processes and embracing automation liberates valuable resources, allowing entrepreneurs to focus their energies on value-creating endeavours that propel business growth.

Golden Nugget 11 – Innovation

Encourage a Culture of Innovation to stay ahead of the competition and meet changing customer needs

In the ever-evolving landscape of entrepreneurship, stagnation is synonymous with regression. Recognising this truth, You espouse a culture of innovation and continuous improvement within your organisations. By embracing creativity, fostering a spirit of experimentation, and leveraging emerging technologies, you can stay ahead of the curve, anticipate market trends, and meet evolving customer demands with innovative solutions.

Golden Nugget 12 - Agility and Adaptability:

Stay nimble and responsive to market shifts to seize

opportunities and mitigate risks.

In the ever-shifting landscape of entrepreneurship, agility and adaptability are paramount virtues. You as an entrepreneurs must remain attuned to market dynamics, emerging trends, and competitive threats, ready to pivot their strategies or business models as needed. By embracing change and remaining nimble in their response, entrepreneurs seize opportunities, mitigate risks, and maintain a competitive edge in dynamic market environments.

Golden Nugget 13 - Brand Building:

A strong and recognisable brand is the most powerful asset

Central to the fabric of successful businesses is a strong and resonant brand identity. You as an entrepreneur must invest in building a brand that captivates and connects with their target audience on a profound level. Through compelling storytelling, consistent messaging, and authentic engagement, entrepreneurs cultivate brand loyalty and differentiation, fostering enduring relationships that transcend transactional exchanges.

Golden Nugget 14 – Marketing Power

Marketing is the only indispensable engine that have power to drives business growth and success.

Strong and consistent Marketing is the crucial engine that propels business growth. It is the primary mechanism through which businesses attract new customers, retain existing ones, and build a strong brand presence. Constant and effective marketing strategies create awareness, generate interest, and drive demand for products or services. By communicating value propositions clearly and persuasively, marketing fosters customer engagement and loyalty. Additionally, it provides valuable insights into market trends and consumer behaviour, guiding business decisions and innovation. Without robust marketing, businesses struggle to grow, as they fail to reach and resonate with their target audience, making marketing indispensable for sustainable success.

Golden Nugget 15 – Harness the Power of Connection

You are one conversation away from your next fortune

In the realm of entrepreneurship, every conversation holds the potential to unlock new opportunities, forge strategic partnerships, and propel business growth. Whether networking with industry peers, engaging with potential clients, or seeking mentorship, each interaction carries the possibility of catalysing success. By embracing the art of meaningful conversation, entrepreneurs can tap into a wealth of knowledge, insights, and resources, paving the way for their next breakthrough.

Conclusion & Recap

Golden nuggets are distilled wisdom crucial for business success, offering guidance, efficiency, continuous improvement, a foundation for success, and empowerment. In the entrepreneurial landscape, achieving sustainable growth requires agility, innovation, and strategic foresight, all supported by these nuggets of wisdom.

Volume 2 of "Visions to Victory" focuses on strategies for business success, building on Volume 1's foundational principles. Each golden nugget discussed is accompanied by actionable insights and practical strategies to empower entrepreneurs in achieving their goals.

For further exploration of these principles, you can reach out to me by any means mentioned in this book and use the resources provided in the book to connect and delve deeper. These nuggets serve as essential tools for success, and based on demand, future volumes or independent books may delve deeper into specific topics.

Stay tuned for "Visions to Victory Volume 2" as it unveils secrets to sustainable growth and success. Connect via social media to share thoughts and requests. This concludes Section 3 of "Visions to Victory."

Ready to transform your business journey? Join us in the next section to craft your strategic path for success and discover your roadmap to victory!

Join Me on my Facebook Group:

What Do I Bring On Facebook Group?

I invite you to consider joining the Facebook group of Visions to Victory—a vibrant community dedicated to entrepreneurship, leadership, and personal growth.

Imagine a place where you can connect with fellow entrepreneurs, industry leaders, and experts. A platform buzzing with opportunities to forge collaborations and partnerships that could propel your ventures to new heights.

In this group, knowledge flows freely. You'll discover a wealth of resources, from insightful articles to practical tips shared by seasoned professionals. It's a virtual hub where learning never stops, where webinars, workshops, and engaging discussions await to expand your skills and broaden your horizons.

But it's not just about knowledge; it's about support and inspiration. Here, you'll find a community ready to rally behind you, offering encouragement during challenging times and celebrating your victories, big and small.

By joining us, you stay informed. You'll be the first to know about upcoming events, workshops, and exclusive opportunities within our community. It's your gateway to staying ahead in the dynamic world of entrepreneurship.

Moreover, active participation can bring visibility and recognition. Share your insights, showcase your achievements, and build your reputation among peers who share your passion for success.

So, why should you join the Facebook group of Visions to Victory? Because it's more than just a group—it's a supportive ecosystem where ideas flourish, connections thrive, and dreams take shape. It's where you belong if you're committed to continuous learning, growth, and achieving your fullest potential.

Join us on this journey of empowerment and success. Together, let's pave the way for a future where each step brings us closer to our visions of victory.

SECTION 4

Crafting a Strategic Path & a Framework for Success

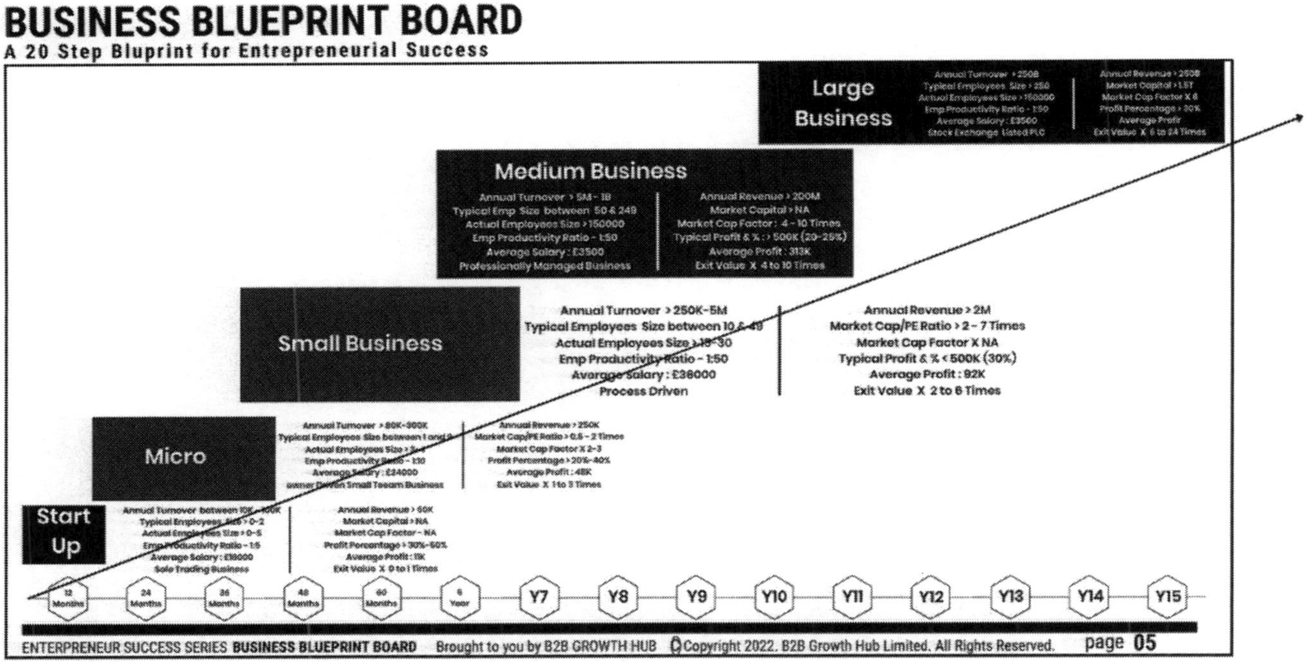

From Idea to Enterprise - Navigating the Journey of Entrepreneurship

The journey of entrepreneurship, whether starting small or aiming for greatness, is a transformative odyssey that begins with an idea—a glimmer of innovation or a spark of inspiration—that evolves into a thriving enterprise leaving a lasting impact.

It all starts with your idea—the solution to a problem, a product filling a market gap, or a service meeting unmet need. Entrepreneurs like you and me conceptualise our vision, conduct market research, and craft a business plan to turn a thought into a viable venture. With passion, determination, and strategic planning, your startup emerges—a fledgling enterprise with boundless potential and a mission to disrupt the status quo.

As your startup gains traction and attracts customers, it moves into the micro stage of development. This phase is defined by rapid growth, agile operations, and a focus on scalability. Micro-businesses refine their offerings, expand their customer base, and establish themselves as key players in their markets. It's a period of experimentation, learning, and laying the groundwork for future expansion.

With sustained growth and increasing market share, your micro-businesses evolve into small enterprises. This transition brings a more structured organisational framework, streamlined operations, and a focus on efficiency. Your small businesses deepen their market presence, diversify their offerings, and solidify their brand identity. It's a phase of consolidation, shifting focus towards sustainable growth and long-term success.

Continuing to thrive and expand, your small businesses progress into the medium stage of development. This phase sees significant growth, strategic partnerships, and broader market reach. Medium-sized enterprises invest in infrastructure, technology, and talent to support their expanding operations. They adopt a holistic approach to business management, emphasising innovation, customer satisfaction, and operational excellence.

Finally, your successful medium-sized enterprises ascend to become large corporations—a culmination of years of hard work, innovation, and strategic planning. Large businesses possess a global footprint, extensive resources, and a dominant position in their industries. They set industry standards, drive innovation, and make a meaningful impact on society. It's a phase of empowerment, influence, and the realisation of the entrepreneur's vision on a grand scale.

Mark Zuckerberg, the founder and CEO of Facebook, started with the goal of connecting people and building a global social network. Zuckerberg imagined a platform where users could share and communicate with friends and family online. He pursued this vision tirelessly, focusing on user engagement and growth, which ultimately led Facebook to become one of the largest social media platforms worldwide.

But Mark is no different from you and me; you all can achieve the same results as long as you have the thought and the idea, belief and hope to turn our dreams into reality, and a burning desire and strong purpose to follow a simple and effective process and framework. Nothing can stop us from taking massive action to reach our destination and turn our visions into victory.

In other words, your journey of entrepreneurship is a dynamic adventure marked by perseverance, innovation, and the relentless pursuit of success. From the humble beginnings of your idea to the towering heights of a large business, each stage brings its own challenges and growth opportunities. By embracing the journey with resilience and determination, entrepreneurs can turn their dreams into reality and create a lasting legacy in the ever-evolving business landscape. Let's draw inspiration from Mark's story bit closure in the next segment.

The Genesis of Facebook

Imagine, if you will, the genesis of Facebook—a story that epitomises the essence of entrepreneurship. It began as a mere idea in a college dorm room, conceived by a group of students led by Mark Zuckerberg.

Their vision? To create a platform for connecting people, starting with their peers at Harvard University. This initial spark of innovation ignited a flame that would soon spread far and wide.

But what sets successful ventures like Facebook apart? From its inception, Facebook prioritised the needs of its users, crafting an intuitive and seamless experience that captivated millions. By listening to feedback and evolving with the times, it cultivated a community that felt valued and empowered.

Yet, success does not stop at user satisfaction—it extends to scalability and global expansion. Facebook's rapid growth from a university network to a global phenomenon is a testament to its strategic vision and adaptability. With each new market entered and each cultural barrier crossed, it solidified its position as a leader in the digital landscape.

Of course, no journey is without its challenges. But it is in overcoming these obstacles that true greatness is achieved. Facebook's ability to innovate and adapt to changing market dynamics ensured its relevance and resilience in the face of adversity. By embracing emerging technologies and forging strategic partnerships, it stayed ahead of the curve, shaping the future of connectivity.

Yet, amidst the pursuit of profit, Facebook never lost sight of its social responsibility. It fostered a sense of community among its users, empowering them to connect, share, and support each other. Through initiatives like charitable fundraisers and crisis response features, it leveraged its reach for positive social impact, leaving a legacy that extends far beyond business success.

As you reflect on the journey of Facebook and other successful ventures, you can very easily notice the spirit of innovation, the power of community, and the importance of ethical leadership. For it is these values that will guide you on your own path to success, whatever form it may take.

Do you know the secret formula of success?

Dare to dream, innovate, and build a future that is brighter and more prosperous for all.

Facebook's journey from a dorm room project to a multi-billion-dollar empire is a fascinating story of innovation, perseverance, and strategic decision-making. It's the tale of Mark Zuckerberg and his college roommates who started this journey, creating a blueprint for success that has left an indelible mark on your era.

Here's how Facebook's success unfolded in my own words.

It all began in 2004 when Harvard University student Mark Zuckerberg and his friends envisioned a platform to connect students within Harvard. This innovative idea quickly expanded beyond Harvard, reaching other universities and eventually the general public.

Central to its success was a user-centric design approach. Facebook's platform was intuitive and user-friendly, allowing people to connect, share updates, photos, and engage seamlessly. Continuous feedback from users guided Facebook in refining its features and enhancing user experience, ensuring high satisfaction and retention rates.

Facebook's rapid scalability and global expansion strategies were pivotal. Starting from U.S. college campuses, it expanded internationally, adapting its platform with localised features and language support to appeal to diverse global markets.

Monetisation was another key strategy. Initially relying on targeted advertising based on user demographics and interests, Facebook expanded its revenue streams through strategic acquisitions like Instagram and WhatsApp. These acquisitions not only broadened its user base but also introduced new monetisation opportunities.

Strategic partnerships further strengthened Facebook's position. Collaborations with tech firms, content creators, and advertisers enriched its ecosystem and added value for users and businesses alike.

Innovation remained at the core of Facebook's strategy. Continual introduction of new features such as Facebook Live, Marketplace, and Oculus VR kept users engaged and facilitated growth. Investments in emerging technologies like AI, VR, and AR solidified Facebook's leadership in the tech industry.

Community engagement was crucial. Facebook fostered a sense of community where users could connect, share experiences, and support each other. This community-driven approach bolstered its popularity and user loyalty, enabling impactful initiatives like charitable fundraisers and crisis response features.

Leadership played a pivotal role. Under Mark Zuckerberg's guidance, Facebook embraced bold visions, strategic decisions, and a culture of innovation. This leadership enabled Facebook to navigate challenges and drive continuous improvement.

Yet, Facebook faced regulatory and ethical challenges, particularly concerning user privacy and content moderation. Proactive measures and engagement with regulators helped address these concerns and strengthen trust.

Adapting to mobile and changing trends was essential. Recognising the shift towards mobile usage, Facebook optimised its platform and developed standalone apps like Messenger and Instagram, ensuring its relevance in the mobile-first era.

Facebook's success story exemplifies the power of innovation, strategic foresight, and a commitment to user satisfaction. From a dorm room project to a global powerhouse, Facebook continues to shape the digital landscape and inspire the next generation of entrepreneurs.

Long-Term Sustainability & Growth of Facebook

Looking ahead, Facebook continues to focus on innovation, diversification, and long-term sustainability. Initiatives such as the development of the metaverse, investment in digital currencies (like Libra, now called Diem), and expansion into new markets indicate Facebook's ambition to remain at the forefront of technology and shape the future of connectivity.

Facebook's journey from a college dorm room to a multi-billion-dollar empire illustrates the transformative power of technology, entrepreneurship, and innovation. Through visionary leadership, relentless innovation, and a deep understanding of user needs, Facebook has reshaped how people connect, communicate, and share in today's digital age.

When you examine the founders of Apple, PayPal, and Google, despite their diverse backgrounds and industries, several common traits emerge.

Firstly, visionary leadership was paramount. Each founder possessed a clear vision for the future and the determination to pursue it despite challenges they faced along the way.

Secondly, they all exhibited innovative thinking, disrupting traditional industries with groundbreaking ideas and solutions that pushed boundaries.

Their strong entrepreneurial spirit drove them to take risks and seize opportunities, building successful ventures from the ground up.

Persistence and resilience were key. Despite setbacks and obstacles, they refused to give up on their visions, persevering through adversity to achieve their goals.

Commitment to excellence was non-negotiable. They prioritised quality, user experience, and customer satisfaction in everything they created.

Understanding and meeting customer needs was another crucial factor. They developed products and services that addressed pain points and improved people's lives.

Team building and collaboration were essential. They surrounded themselves with talented individuals who shared their vision and values, fostering strong teams that propelled their companies forward.

Adaptability and a willingness to learn were also evident. They adjusted their strategies based on feedback, market dynamics, and emerging trends to stay ahead.

They all had a long-term vision for their companies, focusing on creating enduring legacies and making a lasting impact on society rather than just short-term gains.

Ethical leadership underpinned their actions. They upheld principles of integrity, transparency, and social responsibility in all their business practices.

The journeys of these visionary founders teach us valuable lessons about leadership, innovation, and resilience. They inspire us to think boldly, act decisively, and strive for excellence in everything you do.

While the specific journeys and outcomes of Apple, PayPal, and Google's founders may differ, these common traits and characteristics played pivotal roles in each one of their success stories. Based on my understanding, experience and analysis in following some of these visionaries as role model along with sharing a strategic path of success, let me start the journey with the first chapter of this section, entitled " Navigate your Success through A Five Phase Growth Cycle".

Here, you'll explore how every business has its unique journey, traveling through various stages of growth. Each stage involves navigating essential aspects of the business life cycle. You will examine different phases, including the startup or inception phase, survival phase, sustain phase, success phase, and thrive phase of each business stage. Each phase will be discussed in detail, highlighting the key characteristics and challenges that entrepreneurs may encounter.

Additionally, you will delve into the concept of crafting success across various business scales, including the startup growth life cycle, micro-business growth life cycle, SME growth life cycle (Small and Medium-sized Enterprises), and large business growth life cycle. These different scales will be examined to understand the unique considerations and strategies required for success at each level.

LET'S DIVE IN...

Chapter 4.1

Navigate your Success through A Five Phase Growth Cycle

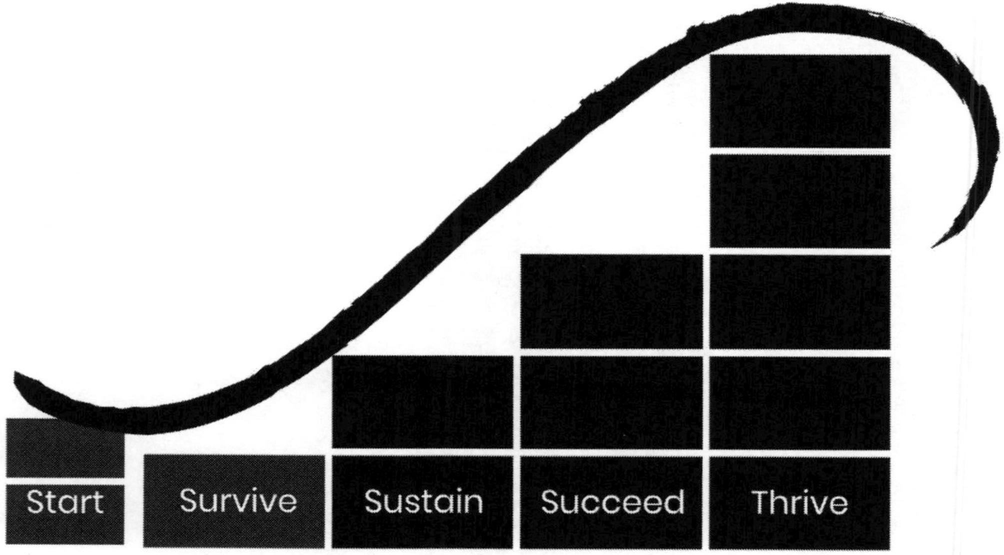

Growth Life Cycle Phases of a Business

SANTOSH KUMAR

Life and business are both very dynamic and need to change the course and adjust from time to time. After returning from Dubai last night to attend this particularly important investors meeting in London, I decided to park the car at nearest station and jump on a train after 6 years to take a break from driving. But now I think I can complete this chapter for you. See the best use of time on train, in my view.

As I write this chapter, I'm sitting on this train travelling from Southampton Airport to Canary Wharf, planning my journey in my head. and I'm trying to recall which tube station I need to catch, as I did six years ago when I was a frequent traveller to the London office. Once I reach London Waterloo, my first milestone, I'll switch to another mode of transport, which is the London Tube. However, if there's a tube strike and I can't use the Tube, I may catch a bus or an Uber. The important thing is making progress towards my destination. This process will continue until I reach my destination of Canary Wharf. But if I catch a train or another vehicle heading in the opposite direction, I will never reach my destination in the given timeframe. To make progress in the right direction and reach your destination within the given timeframe, you need to have a plan, the right vehicle, a defined timeline and the planned phases of the journey to reach to your destination.

Building a business or running a campaign or launching a products or services isn't much different. It involves reaching various milestones, possibly using different vehicles along the way. Reaching each milestone represents progress. What's interesting about this journey is that each stage follows a similar five-phase model to complete the milestone journey. I refer to this model as the Business Growth Life Cycle phases of venture creation framework. The growth of a business, idea, or campaign might begin at the inception, then go through the stages of starting up the campaign or idea, followed by a journey of growth. This growth then progresses from being startup to scaleup to becoming a small, then medium-sized, and finally a large business before establishing itself as a legacy.

Understanding the complete roadmap of the desired business and the Growth Life Cycle phases of each business stage is paramount for entrepreneurs and business leaders as they navigate the complexities of various stages of business development. The stories of tech giants like Google, Facebook, Amazon, Uber, and Apple all share a common thread—they embarked on transformative journeys, evolving from startups to micro-businesses, then scaling up to SMEs and eventually becoming large corporations. What binds these narratives together is not just their scale or industry dominance, but the journey they undertook through each phase of the Growth Life Cycle.

At the heart of every successful business, weather its Facebook or Amazon, lies a journey of transforming the business into multiple stages and each of these stages are marked by distinct phases: from the inception of an idea to survival, followed by sustainability, success, and ultimately thriving. Each phase represents a critical juncture in the evolution of a business stages, shaping its trajectory and defining its legacy in the marketplace.

In this chapter, you embark on a guided tour through the five-step blueprint, unravelling the intricacies of navigating the entrepreneurial journey. But before that, let's have a look at the types of businesses that form our economy. Your business may fall into one of these stages during its lifetime.

From Startup Dreams to Corporate Giants: Exploring the Types of Businesses in Our Economy

Success is not just a destination; it is a continuous journey that starts with the daring dreams of a startup and can lead to the towering heights of corporate giants. I'd like to talk about the diverse types of businesses that make up our economy. Understanding these different categories is essential, as each plays a unique role in driving growth, innovation, and prosperity in your success journey.

You begin with the intrepid entrepreneurs, those who dare to dream and disrupt the status quo. Let's start with startups. Startups represent the genesis of innovation, where bold ideas take shape. Fuelled by sheer determination and passion, these fledgling enterprises are where the journey towards success truly begins. These are new ventures born from innovative ideas and the ambition to change the world. Startups are often launched by passionate entrepreneurs who want to disrupt existing markets with unique products or services. They thrive on creativity and a willingness to take risks, often with limited resources. In the early stages, startups rely on personal savings or investments from venture capitalists to fund their operations. They typically have small teams working tirelessly to turn their visions into reality. The startup phase is all about refining business models, attracting initial customers, and carving out a niche in the market. These businesses are crucial because they bring fresh ideas and drive technological advancements.

Next, you have micro-enterprises. As your startups gain momentum, it often evolve into micro-enterprises. These nimble and agile businesses cater to niche markets and forge deep connections with their customers. At this stage, resilience and adaptability become paramount. It's about weathering storms of uncertainty while continuing to grow. These are very small businesses, usually with fewer than 10 employees. Often run by individuals or families, micro-enterprises are deeply embedded in local communities. They focus on providing personalised products or services and often cater to niche markets. Micro-enterprises are important to the economy because they create jobs and support local economies. They rely heavily on building strong relationships with their customers, offering personalised service and fostering loyalty. Despite their small size, micro-enterprises are incredibly adaptable, able to respond quickly to changes in the market. Their close connection to their customers allows them to tailor their offerings to meet specific needs, making them a vital part of our business landscape.

Moving on, you arrive at small and medium-sized enterprises also called SMEs—the backbone of economies around the world. SMEs embody innovation, flexibility, and resilience. Having outgrown the roots, micro businesses emerge as formidable players in their industries at this stage. Here, strategic objectives are achieved, market leadership is secured, and a strong brand presence is established. These businesses are larger than micro-enterprises but not as extensive as large corporations, typically employing between 10 and 250 people. SMEs are considered the backbone of our economy. They play a critical role in job creation, economic growth, and innovation. SMEs operate across various industries, from manufacturing to services. They have a more structured organisation compared to micro-enterprises, with defined roles and responsibilities. Despite facing challenges such as accessing finance and competing with larger firms, SMEs remain flexible and innovative. They focus on delivering quality products and services, often establishing strong customer relationships. Their ability to adapt to market changes and meet customer needs is what sets them apart.

Finally, at the apex of our journey, you encounter large corporations—giants of industry. With vast resources and global reach, these behemoths lead the way in industry innovation. They foster positive organisational cultures and contribute significantly to social and environmental responsibilities. These well-established companies employ hundreds or even thousands of people and often operate on a global scale. They have vast resources at their disposal, which allows them to invest heavily in research and development, driving innovation and setting industry standards. Large corporations play a significant role in the economy. They contribute to GDP, provide employment, and often lead in corporate social responsibility, focusing on sustainability and community development. These businesses have complex structures with specialised departments, ensuring efficient operations across various functions like marketing, finance, and human resources. Their global reach and influence enable them to shape industries and economies.

The diversity of businesses—startups, micro-enterprises, SMEs, and large corporations—creates a vibrant and dynamic economic landscape. No matter the scale of your business, these stages of growth serve as a universal compass, guiding us toward success. Each stage builds upon the foundation of the one before it, creating a roadmap filled with endless possibilities. Each type of business brings something unique to the table. Startups inject fresh ideas and innovation, micro-enterprises support local communities, SMEs drive growth and flexibility, and large corporations lead in global influence and industry standards. Together, they form a balanced ecosystem that fuels economic progress and prosperity. As you celebrate this diversity, let's recognise the vital role each type of business plays in shaping our economy and contributing to a brighter future for all.

As you navigate the intricate landscapes of entrepreneurship, let us remember: success knows no bounds. It transcends scales, industries, and geographies. With courage, resilience, and a shared commitment to excellence, you can all craft our own success stories and leave a lasting legacy that inspires generations to come.

Let's look at the business growth life cycle of each type of Business. Embracing this business growth life cycle model is not just a choice; it's a strategic imperative for every business, whether a fledgling startup, a nimble micro-business, a growing SME, or a seasoned large corporation.

This framework provides a roadmap for enterprises, allowing them to comprehend the challenges, opportunities, and strategic focus required at each phase. Let's delve into the five essential phases of a business milestone journey: Startup or Inception phase, Survive phase, Sustain Phase, Success Phase, and Thrive Phase, with a focus on how these phases unfold across different business scales - Startup, Micro, SME, or Large.

Navigating the Growth Life Cycle Phases of Your Business

Navigating the journey from inception to enduring success is both an art and a science. Amidst the complexities of the business world, this comprehensive framework of mine emerges as the Five-Phase Business Growth Triumph Model. This model serves as a guiding light for ventures of all sizes. It steers entrepreneurs through clear phases: START, SURVIVE, SUSTAIN, SUCCEED, and THRIVE, regardless of whether they're dealing with an idea, thought, campaign, or full-fledged business expansion. I also sometimes call it the 4S1T Growth Model.

I extend a heartfelt welcome to an odyssey that promises to transform not just your businesses but the very essence of your entrepreneurial spirits. The 5-phase blueprint of 4S1T is a fundamental Growth framework that holds significance for businesses across all stages of growth, regardless of whether they are startups, micro-businesses, SMEs (Small and Medium-sized Enterprises), or large corporations. This blueprint provides a comprehensive guide for navigating the complexities of the business lifecycle and ensuring long-term viability and success.

The 5-phase Growth Cycle is not just a roadmap but as a living, breathing guide that adapts to the rhythm of your unique entrepreneurial beats. This blueprint isn't just a manual; it's a companion that will accompany you through the complexities of the business lifecycle, ensuring long-term viability, and paving the way for unparalleled success. This framework is a saga of inception, survival, sustainment, success, and, ultimately, thriving against all odds. Let's explore these phases starting with the Inception Phase.

Navigating the Startup Journey: From Dream to Execution

In the startup phase also called inception phase, entrepreneurs, new or experienced, breathe life into their ideas, laying the groundwork for their ventures or campaigns to take flight. This is a time of bold innovation, strategic planning, and securing the initial resources needed to turn dreams into reality.

As you step into the Inception Phase, you're witnessing the birth of dreams, the ignition of ideas, and the daring plunge into the unknown. This phase isn't merely about establishing a business; it's about giving life to innovation. Picture this as the first light breaking through the darkness, embodying ideation, market research, and that exhilarating initial capitalisation.

In this exhilarating phase, you are filled with a sense of boundless creativity, audacious ideas, and the unwavering courage to challenge the status quo. you dare to dream of a world where problems are not obstacles, but opportunities for innovation. you envision solutions that transcend boundaries, defy conventions, and inspire change.

But dreams alone are not enough; you must be grounded in reality, nurtured by diligence, and fuelled by passion. That is why the Startup Phase is not just about ideation; it is about execution. It is about rolling up your sleeves, diving headfirst into the depths of market research, and validating your ideas with unwavering conviction.

In this phase, you face challenges that test your resolve, obstacles that threaten to derail your progress, and uncertainties that cloud your vision. But in the face of adversity, you find strength. You find resilience. you find the relentless determination to persevere, to adapt, and to overcome.

Securing initial capital may seem like a daunting task, but you refuse to be deterred. You seek out investors who share your vision, partners who believe in your potential, and opportunities that pave the way for your success. You understand that every penny invested is not just a sum of money; it is a vote of confidence, a vote of belief in your ability to change the world.

As you navigate the complexities of the Startup Phase, you do not tread this path alone. You surround yourself with mentors who guide you, advisors who counsel you, and peers who support you. you understand that success is not a solitary pursuit; it is a collective endeavour—a journey that you and your co-founders undertake together, hand in hand, shoulder to shoulder.

But perhaps most importantly, this phase is about vision. It is about charting a course for the future, painting a vivid picture of what could be and relentlessly pursuing that vision with unwavering determination. It is about daring to defy the odds, to challenge the sceptics, and to prove that anything is possible with passion, perseverance, and a belief in the power of one's ideas.

It's here you lay the foundation of the Venture Creation Proof of Concept, validation of your position in the market, and the creation of a foundational business plan. You're sowing the seeds for a campaign, a product launch, or an idea. This phase is where dreams take shape and transform into blueprints.

In the words of great Mark Twain "The secret of getting ahead is getting started." So, let us embrace this moment with open arms and open minds. Let us dare to dream, to innovate, and to create. For in the crucible of the Startup Phase, greatness is born, and the seeds of change are sown. Let's start this amazing journey together, knowing that the best is still ahead of us. That's the conclusion of the introduction of inception phase and takes us into the next stage of growth, the Survival phase.

Embracing Resilience: The Journey through the Survival Phase

As the business or idea or campaign gains momentum, it enters the survival phase, where the focus shifts to establishing a foothold in the market and weathering the challenges of competition and uncertainty.

Welcome to the Survival Phase, where challenges are not roadblocks but stepping stones to resilience. Acquiring those initial customers is akin to finding your true north amidst the tumultuous waves.

In the Survival Phase, you find yourselves navigating rough seas and stormy weather, where every wave threatens to capsize your ships and every gust of wind threatens to blow you off course. But in the face of these challenges, you do not cover; you rise. You rise to the occasion, fortified by the knowledge that challenges are not roadblocks, but stepping stones to resilience.

For startups and micro-businesses, the Survival Phase is a battleground where the very essence of your existence is put to the test. It is a time of fierce competition, limited resources, and relentless uncertainty. But amidst the chaos, you find opportunity. You find the opportunity to establish a market presence, to manage cash flow, and to adapt to market feedback with agility and foresight.

Even for SMEs and large businesses, the Survival Phase is not without its trials. Economic downturns, industry disruptions, and unexpected crises can threaten the very foundation of even the most established enterprises. But in the face of these challenges, You do not falter; you innovate. You innovate to stay ahead of the curve, to pivot when necessary, and to emerge stronger and more resilient than before.

At the heart of the Survival Phase lies the strategic focus on agile cost management, the art of acquiring customers, and the wisdom to adapt to the ever-changing winds of market feedback. It is a time of resourcefulness, creativity, and unwavering determination—a time when every decision, every action, is a testament to your resilience and your commitment to survival.

But perhaps most importantly, the Survival Phase is a testament to the human spirit—the spirit of resilience, perseverance, and unwavering determination in the face of adversity. It is a reminder that no matter how daunting the challenges may seem, you are capable of overcoming them. You are capable of rising above the storm and charting a course towards a brighter, more prosperous future.

So let us embrace the challeges of the Survival Phase with courage in your hearts and fire in your souls. Let us stand tall in the face of adversity, knowing that every obstacle you overcome brings you one step closer to your goals. And let us remember that in the crucible of survival, greatness is not merely achieved—it is forged. That brings us to the end of another introduction and a chance to move on to exploring the sustain phase next,

Achieving Excellence: The Entrepreneur's Guide to the Sustain Phase

The sustain phase sees the entrepreneurship solidify its position, expanding its offerings, and building a loyal customer base. This phase is characterised by adaptability, innovation, and a relentless commitment to excellence. At sustain phase, you stand at a pivotal moment in the journey of entrepreneurship—a moment where the storm clouds of uncertainty begin to dissipate, and the sun of stability begins to shine upon you.

As the storm subsides, the sustain Phase unfolds, offering a haven of stability. Operations are no longer a battleground but a well-oiled machine. Revenue is not a fleeting hope but a constant stream, and your brand is not just recognised; it's etched in the minds of your customers.

In the Sustain Phase, you find yourself at a crossroads—a moment of transition from survival to sustainability. Having weathered the storms of adversity, you now have the opportunity to build upon the foundation you have laid and chart a course towards long-term success.

For startups and micro-businesses, the Sustain Phase represents a turning point—a time to refine your products, deepen customer loyalty, and streamline operations for efficiency and effectiveness. It is a time to harness the lessons learned from your trials and tribulations and use them to fuel your journey towards growth and prosperity.

But sustainability is not just about survival; it is about thriving. It is about scaling your operations, retaining your customers, and building a brand that stands the test of time. It is about seizing opportunities, mitigating risks, and embracing innovation as a driving force for progress.

For SMEs and large businesses, the Sustain Phase is a reminder that success is not a destination but a journey—a journey marked by continuous adaptation, evolution, and reinvention. It is a journey that requires you as an entrepreneur to remain agile, responsive, and forward-thinking in the face of ever-changing market dynamics.

At the heart of the Sustain Phase lies the pursuit of excellence—the relentless pursuit of excellence in everything you do. It is about exceeding customer expectations, delivering exceptional value, and cultivating a culture of innovation and excellence that permeates every aspect of your business.

But perhaps most importantly, the Sustain Phase is about having the foundation of leaving a legacy—a legacy of resilience, integrity, and impact. It is about laying the foundations of building a business that not only endures but thrives—a business that leaves an indelible mark on the world and inspires others to dream, innovate, and create.

As you embark on this journey through the Sustain Phase, let us do so with courage, conviction, and unwavering determination. Let us embrace the challenges that lie ahead as opportunities for growth and transformation. Together, let us rise to the occasion and seize the opportunities that await us in the Sustain Phase. By doing this, you're not only ensuring your own success but also laying the groundwork for a better, more sustainable future for generations to come. This will lead us into the success phase, which is introduced in the next in this chapter.

Reaching New Heights: Embracing the Success Phase of Business

As the idea of your business or campaign matures, it enters the success phase, where it achieves market leadership, sets industry benchmarks, and garners widespread recognition for its achievements. Here, you stand on the precipice of greatness—a summit beyond survival and sustainability, where leaders are crowned, benchmarks are set, and industries take notice. Welcome to the Success Phase—a phase defined not just by achievement, but by the relentless pursuit of excellence and the unwavering commitment to reaching new heights.

let us take a moment to reflect on the journey that brought you to this pinnacle of success. It has been a journey marked by trials and tribulations, challenges and triumphs, setbacks and successes. But through it all, you have persevered. You have weathered the storms, navigated the rough terrain, and forged ahead with unwavering determination.

For startups and micro-businesses, success is the realisation of dreams—the validation of ideas, the acquisition of loyal customers, and the proof of concept for your business models. It is a testament to your resilience, your ingenuity, and your relentless pursuit of excellence in the face of adversity.

For SMEs and large businesses, success is about more than just financial growth—it is about achieving strategic objectives, attaining market leadership, and establishing a powerful brand presence. It is about diversifying offerings, expanding into new markets, and innovating to stay ahead of the curve. It is a testament to your adaptability, your agility, and your ability to set a stage to thrive in an ever-changing landscape.

But perhaps most importantly, the Success Phase is about embracing strategic focus. It is about looking beyond short-term gains and setting your sights on the long-term vision. It is about diversifying your strategies, seizing opportunities, and marking your progress with impactful objectives that propel you ever onward on this perpetual journey of success.

As you stand here at this phase, let us not rest on your laurels. Let us celebrate your achievements, but let us also remember that the journey is far from over. There are still peaks to climb, challenges to overcome, and victories to be won. Together, let us embrace the Success Phase with humility, gratitude, and a steadfast commitment to excellence. Let us stand tall, with the wind of accomplishment in your hair, and let us gaze out upon the landscape of your success with pride and satisfaction. So, let's keep pushing the limits of what you can achieve, aiming for new levels of success, and leaving a legacy that motivates others to dream, innovate, and achieve greatness and explore the introduction segment of the thrive phase next.

Pinnacle of Success: The Entrepreneur's Journey through the Thrive Phase

Finally, in the thrive phase, your idea or the business or the campaign reaches its pinnacle, shaping industry trends, driving innovation, and making a meaningful impact on society. This phase represents the culmination of years of hard work, vision, and perseverance, as the business transforms into a beacon of success and inspiration for others to follow. It's a realm where you as an entrepreneur don't just survive or succeed, you shape the very trends you once followed. This is the crescendo of the entrepreneurial symphony, where industry boundaries blur, and global impact becomes a responsibility, not a choice. In the symphony of entrepreneurship, the Thrive Phase represents the crescendo—the moment where your dreams become reality, and your actions shape the very trends you once followed.

For startups and micro-businesses, thriving at this stage means becoming market leaders, continually innovating, and solidifying a strong competitive position. It is a testament to your resilience, your creativity, and your unwavering commitment to excellence.

For SMEs and large businesses, thriving in this phase requires more than just maintaining a strong market position—it involves being agile, adaptable, and forward-thinking in the face of emerging trends. It is about leading industry innovation, fostering a positive organisational culture, and embracing social and environmental responsibilities as integral parts of your business model.

But perhaps most importantly, thriving in this phase requires us to embrace a strategic focus that extends beyond profit margins. It is about echoing corporate social responsibility through your actions, pulsating with innovation in your veins, and achieving a harmonious balance between financial success and positive impact on the world.

As you embark on this journey through the Thrive Phase, let us do so with humility, integrity, and a steadfast commitment to making a difference. Let us embrace the responsibility that comes with shaping industry trends and global impact, knowing that your actions today will ripple through generations to come.

Together, let us be the architects of change, the catalysts for innovation, and the stewards of a future where entrepreneurship not only drives economic growth but also fosters social progress and environmental sustainability. For in the Thrive Phase lies not just the culmination of your efforts, but the promise of a brighter, more sustainable future for all.

Why Embrace the Growth Life Cycle Phases

In the grand saga of entrepreneurship, each phase of the Growth Life Cycle is not merely a hurdle, but a milestone. It's not an obstacle, but an opportunity—a chance to grow, evolve, and shape the narrative of your journey in unique and profound ways. The Growth Life Cycle is not a linear path—it's a thrilling journey, where each turn, each twist, adds a new dimension to your story. From the inception of your ventures to the survival phase, from success to thriving, each phase brings its own set of challenges and opportunities for growth and learning. It's a journey that tests your mettle, challenges your assumptions, and pushes you to evolve and adapt in ways you never imagined possible. As you navigate through these phases, let us embrace the challenges, dance with uncertainties, and sculpt your narrative with courage, resilience, and unwavering determination.

As you venture through these phases, let us not merely survive; let us thrive. Let us embrace the journey with open arms, knowing that with each challenge you overcome, you grow stronger, wiser, and more resilient. Let us not just seek success, but significance—a deeper sense of purpose and meaning that transcends mere financial gains.

The growth of your enterprises mirrors the growth of your vision. It's not just about profit margins or market share—it's about creating a lasting impact, making a difference, and leaving a legacy that extends far beyond ourselves. It's about building businesses that not only thrive for your own sake but flourish for the greater good of society and the planet.

But as you grasp the core concept of the Growth Life Cycle, let us not forget to explore the success stories across various business scales. Let us celebrate the achievements of entrepreneurs who have dared to dream, who have dared to innovate, and who have dared to defy the odds to create something truly remarkable.

The Growth Life Cycle is a journey of entrepreneurial significance—a journey where each phase is a stepping stone towards a brighter, more prosperous future. Together, let us forge ahead with courage, conviction, and a shared commitment to building a world where businesses not only thrive but flourish for the greater good of all.

Conclusion & Recap

Regardless of the size or stage of a business, the 5-stage business life cycle blueprint provides a holistic approach to growth. The Growth Life Cycle Phases serve as a roadmap for businesses and entrepreneurs like you, guiding you through the ups and downs of entrepreneurship and empowering you to navigate the complexities of growth and development. By understanding and embracing these phases, entrepreneurs and business leaders like yourself can chart a course towards long-term success and create a lasting legacy in the ever-evolving business landscape.

As you traverse through these phases, let's not see them as mere milestones. Instead, let them be the threads weaving the intricate tapestry of your business journey. Each phase, each scale, brings its challenges, opportunities, and triumphs. It's not about the size of the vessel but the skill of the sailor navigating through the Growth Life Cycle.

As I extend my odyssey to an exploration, reflection, and revelation, let this journey be more than just an intellectual exercise. Let it be a profound experience that resonates with the core of your entrepreneurial spirits. Brace yourselves for the odyssey of a lifetime, a symphony echoing through the halls of innovation, resilience, and triumph. Embrace the challenges, savour the victories, and let this extended Entrepreneurial Odyssey be the defining chapter of your entrepreneurial legacy.

Stay tuned for a transformative journey as I unveil the secrets to sustainable growth and success in "Visions to Victory - Vol 2" , but once again, If you wish to delve deeper into my thoughts on these five stages of growth cycle and related principles beforehand, feel free to contact me using the various resources provided in this book. If there is high demand, I will include a specific section or even draft an independent book on this topic in the forthcoming volume.

Connect with me on Facebook, LinkedIn, or Instagram or join my webinars, seminars or workshops to share your thoughts and any specific requests. I will do my best to address them in the upcoming volume.

So, fasten your seatbelt and embark on this enlightening journey through the Five Stage Blueprint. May these shared experiences be the wind in your sails and the stars guiding you on your unique entrepreneurial odyssey.

Chapter 4.2

Develop a Roadmap to Success - Your Entrepreneurial GPS

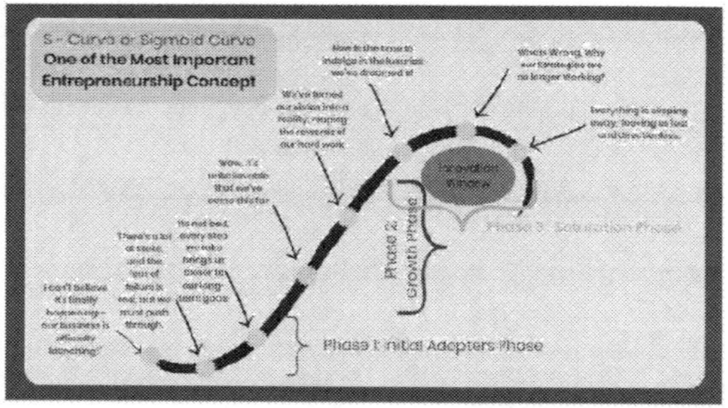

STRATEGIC GROWTH PLANNING

A good, solid game plan can make a difference between making a huge mistake and your next business breakthrough.

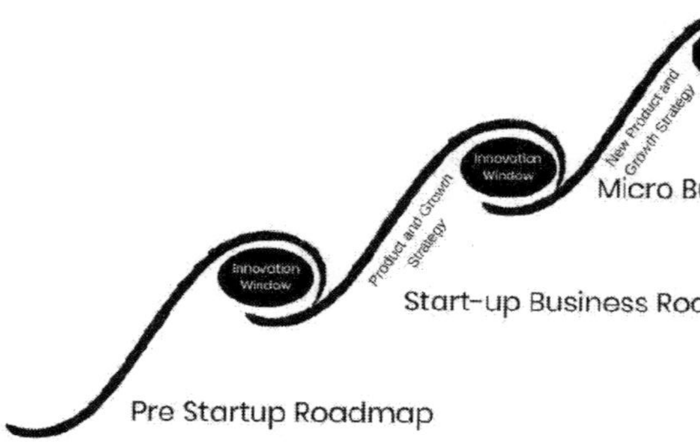
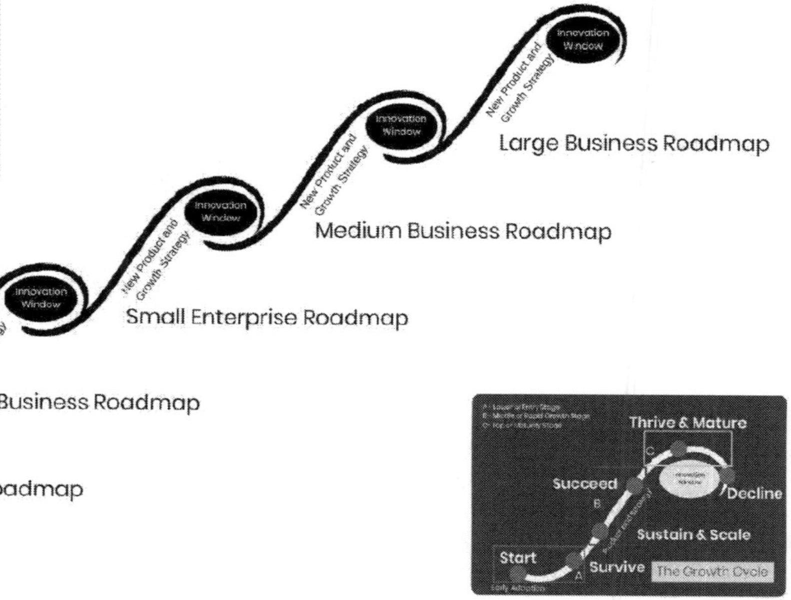

Step into a chapter revealing the intricate blend of art and science in crafting a roadmap to triumph—a guiding compass that has steered countless business professionals, myself included, through the unpredictable terrain of the entrepreneurial expedition. While some refer to it as the "S" curve, I affectionately term it the "Success Curve" roadmap.

Navigating the startup stage of this Success Curve roadmap, you're ignited by passion and propelled by purpose. Your vision is crystal clear, your ambition limitless, yet the path forward is laden with uncertainty. It's a voyage that will examine your strength, question your determination, and require nothing less than your utmost effort. During these initial stages, advancement may appear frustratingly gradual. You'll contend with market timing, engage in the struggle of customer adoption, and negotiate the intricacies of product development. It's a period marked by uncertainty, by hesitation, yet also by steadfast resolve.

But fear not, for just when you least expect it, the tide begins to turn. You hit that pivotal inflection point on the S-curve, and suddenly, everything changes. Growth explodes, customers flock to your product, and opportunities abound. It's a moment of validation, of vindication, and of boundless potential. Yet, as quickly as success arrives, it can vanish into thin air. You hit a plateau on the S-curve, and growth slows to a crawl. Sales stagnate, productivity wanes, and doubts creep in. It's a sobering reality check, a reminder that the journey to success is anything but linear.

But here's the secret. In every curve lies opportunity. It's about understanding where you stand on the curve and adapting your strategies accordingly. It's about embracing the unpredictability of innovation, the inherent risks and rewards that come with blazing a trail in uncharted territory. At the precipice of entrepreneurial ambition, where dreams collide with the stark realities of business growth, you've embarked on a journey that begins with a mere idea and culminates in the lofty heights of the stock market. This journey, however, is not without its formidable challenges.

Firstly, consider the daunting hurdle of capital constraints. Accessing sufficient funds to fuel your growth is no mean feat. Whether it's navigating the scepticism of investors or securing loans from financial institutions, the path to financial backing is riddled with obstacles. But fear not, for with perseverance and strategic planning, you can bridge this capital gap and propel your ventures forward.

Next, you confront the labyrinth of market penetration. Breaking into competitive arenas demands innovation, resilience, and a keen understanding of consumer needs. Establishing a distinct identity amidst established giants requires unwavering dedication and strategic marketing prowess. Through targeted campaigns, partnerships, and niche market strategies, you can carve your niche and expand your footprint.

Scaling your operations presents another monumental challenge. Transitioning from a fledgling startup to a scalable enterprise requires streamlined processes, robust infrastructure, and scalable technologies. It's about optimising efficiency without compromising quality, ensuring that every expansion is sustainable and aligned with your long-term vision.

Navigating regulatory landscapes adds another layer of complexity. Compliance with stringent financial standards and regulatory frameworks is non-negotiable, particularly as you prepare for an IPO. Engaging legal expertise, staying abreast of evolving regulations, and maintaining impeccable financial integrity are imperative for navigating this regulatory maze unscathed.

Of course, talent acquisition remains a cornerstone of your growth strategy. Attracting and retaining skilled individuals who share your passion and vision is crucial. By fostering a culture of innovation, offering competitive incentives, and championing professional development, you can assemble a formidable team capable of driving our ambitions forward.

In your pursuit of growth, you cannot overlook the intricacies of risk management. From operational risks to market fluctuations and financial vulnerabilities, anticipating and mitigating risks is paramount. Through comprehensive risk assessments, contingency planning, and robust insurance coverage, you fortify your resilience against unforeseen challenges.

Strategic decision-making underscores every milestone on your journey. Informed by market insights, data analytics, and foresight, your decisions must be agile and adaptable. It's about seizing opportunities, optimising resources, and navigating shifting market dynamics with unwavering determination.

As you grow, preserving your entrepreneurial spirit amidst organisational evolution is pivotal. Embracing change, fostering transparency, and nurturing a culture of inclusivity empower you to maintain your identity while adapting to larger-scale operations and structures.

Your journey to the stock market hinges on investor relations. Building trust, fostering transparency, and demonstrating your commitment to shareholder value are paramount. By cultivating strong relationships with investors, stakeholders, and analysts, you inspire confidence and propel our trajectory towards success.

Lastly, public perception shapes your brand's narrative. Upholding ethical standards, prioritising customer satisfaction, and engaging in corporate responsibility initiatives cultivate a positive brand image. Through strategic public relations efforts, you reinforce trust, enhance credibility, and amplify your impact on the market.

While the path ahead may present challenges, it also offers numerous opportunities. By embracing innovation, resilience, and strategic foresight, you navigate these challenges with unwavering determination. This is where the S Curve, also known as the Sigmoid Curve or Success Curve, comes into play. Understanding the S Curve is of immense importance to you on your journey to success. The S Curve helps entrepreneurs like you and me move forward, overcome challenges, and chart a course towards sustainable growth and eventual success in the stock market.

The S Curve symbolises growth, evolution, and transformation across various domains. It provides visionaries like you and me a visual framework to understand the stages of development, from inception and rapid expansion to maturity and potential renewal or decline. It encourages proactive decision-making, strategic planning, and adaptability in navigating personal, professional, and business challenges. Allow me to share the S Curve roadmap and help you understand how it helps you turn your visions into victory.

The Sigmoid Curve Roadmap: Guiding Businesses Through Life's Phases

Within the dynamic landscape of business, the Sigmoid curve stands as a potent metaphor, symbolising the undulating journey of a venture's life cycle for you. When mapped onto the stages encompassing pre-startup, startup, scale-up, and beyond, it unveils a roadmap of transitions and growth, each delineated by a distinctive sigmoid curve. This journey forms a continuum of interconnected curves, symbolising the metamorphosis of businesses from modest beginnings to industry titans.

The Sigmoid curve or success curve, often likened to an S-shaped graph, traces the trajectory of growth experienced by entities over time. It embodies the stages of pre-startup, startup, scale-up, maturity, and decline, mirroring the cyclical nature of business evolution. Each phase presents its own set of challenges and opportunities, shaping the trajectory of the venture's journey.

The journey commences with the pre-startup phase, marked by the exploration of entrepreneurial ideas and opportunities. Here, you as an aspiring entrepreneur, conduct market research, identify potential niches, and lay the groundwork for your future ventures.

As ideas solidify into action, the venture progresses into the startup phase of the Sigmoid curve. This stage is characterised by the introduction of the venture to the market, as entrepreneurs navigate the uncertainties of market entry and lay the foundation for future growth.

With promising traction and validated business models, ventures enter the scale-up phase of the Sigmoid curve. Here, companies focus on accelerating growth, scaling operations, and expanding their market presence. Strategic partnerships, investments, and innovations drive the venture towards increased market share and profitability.

As growth stabilises, the venture transitions into the maturity phase of the Sigmoid curve. Here, companies focus on consolidating their market position, optimising operations, and sustaining profitability amidst intensifying competition and market saturation.

Ultimately, every Sigmoid curve reaches its decline phase, where growth stagnates or begins to decline. This stage may result from shifting consumer preferences, technological advancements, or the emergence of superior alternatives. Companies facing decline must navigate challenges and uncertainties, strategising to prolong the lifecycle of their offerings or pivot towards new opportunities.

The Sigmoid curve roadmap offers a comprehensive framework for understanding the life cycle of businesses, illuminating the journey from ideation to maturity and beyond. By embracing the insights offered by the Sigmoid curve, you and your businesses can navigate the complexities of each phase with foresight and agility, positioning themselves for sustained success in an ever-evolving business landscape.

In the dynamic landscape of your business, the Sigmoid curve serves as a powerful metaphor, capturing the ebb and flow of a venture's life cycle. When applied to the stages of startup, micro, small, medium, and large businesses, it unveils a roadmap of transitions and growth, each represented by a distinct sigmoid curve. This journey is a chain of interconnected curves, symbolising the evolution of you and your businesses from the humble beginnings to becoming industry giants.

Therefore, let us welcome the S-curve with open arms. But before you do this, let's understand the growth curve with the example of McDonald's.

The Journey of McDonald's: From Humble Beginnings to Global Dominance

McDonald's, the iconic fast-food giant, has become a staple in the diets of millions around the world.

Known for its golden arches and consistent, affordable meals, McDonald's journey from a single restaurant to a global empire is a remarkable story of innovation, adaptation, and relentless pursuit of growth.

The story of McDonald's begins in the 1940s with two brothers, Richard and Maurice McDonald. In 1940, they opened a small drive-in restaurant in San Bernardino, California, which focused on barbecue food. However, in 1948, they revolutionised their business by implementing the "Speedee Service System," a new concept emphasising quick service, reduced prices, and high volume. They simplified their menu to nine items, including their famous 15-cent hamburgers, and introduced a novel assembly line system for food preparation, which drastically cut service times and costs.

The McDonald brothers' innovative approach caught the attention of Ray Kroc, a Multimixer milkshake machine salesman, in 1954. Intrigued by their efficient operation and its potential for expansion, Kroc convinced the brothers to franchise their restaurant concept. In 1955, he opened the first McDonald's franchise in Des Plaines, Illinois, and founded the McDonald's Corporation.

Under Kroc's leadership, McDonald's embarked on an aggressive expansion strategy. He emphasised uniformity and strict quality control, ensuring that customers received the same experience at every McDonald's location. This consistency became a hallmark of the brand and a key factor in its widespread appeal.

By the 1960s, McDonald's had established itself as a major player in the fast-food industry. In 1961, Kroc bought out the McDonald brothers for $2.7 million, gaining full control of the company. The introduction of the Big Mac in 1968 and the Egg McMuffin in 1972 further diversified the menu and attracted a broader customer base.

McDonald's continued to innovate and expand throughout the following decades. The company introduced drive-thru service in 1975, catering to the increasing demand for convenience. International expansion also took off, with the first overseas restaurant opening in Canada in 1967, followed by locations in Europe, Asia, and beyond.

Today, McDonald's operates over 39,000 restaurants in more than hundred countries, serving approximately sixty-nine million customers daily. The brand's global presence is supported by a strong franchising model, with over 90% of McDonald's restaurants owned and operated by independent franchisees.

McDonald's has continually adapted to changing consumer preferences and market trends. The introduction of healthier menu options, such as salads and fruit, as well as the adoption of digital ordering and delivery services, has helped the company stay relevant in an increasingly competitive landscape.

Despite its success, McDonald's has faced its share of challenges and criticisms. The company has been scrutinised for its impact on public health, labour practices, and environmental sustainability. In response, McDonald's has made efforts to address these issues by improving nutritional information, committing to sustainable sourcing, and implementing eco-friendly practices in its operations.

The legacy of McDonald's lies not only in its vast global footprint but also in its influence on the fast-food industry and popular culture. The brand's marketing campaigns, iconic mascots like Ronald McDonald, and community initiatives have cemented its place in the hearts of millions.

From its humble beginnings as a single drive-in restaurant to a global powerhouse, McDonald's journey is a testament to the power of innovation, strategic franchising, and adaptability. As the company continues to evolve and face new challenges, its commitment to providing consistent, affordable, and convenient meals remains unwavering. The story of McDonald's is a remarkable example of how a simple idea, executed well, can transform into a worldwide phenomenon.

McDonald's journey through the Success Curve demonstrates how businesses can navigate the phases of growth, maturity, and potential decline through strategic innovation and adaptation. By continuously evolving its menu, embracing technology, and focusing on sustainability, McDonald's has managed to extend its growth phase and maintain its status as a global leader in the fast-food industry. This approach highlights the importance of proactive management and reinvention in sustaining long-term business success.

Let us embrace the expedition—the peaks and valleys, the victories and obstacles—with the understanding that each curve propels you nearer to your aspirations. In the realm of entrepreneurship, the path to triumph may be uncertain, but guided by the S-curve, the opportunities are boundless.

As you set sail on your entrepreneurial voyage, keep this in mind. You are the designers of your own future, the commanders of your own destiny. With bravery in your hearts and tenacity in your souls, there are no boundaries to what you can accomplish with the appropriate guidance.

So, what is this Success Curve Roadmap?

What is a Success Curve Roadmap

In my view, a personal or professional success roadmap acts as a strategic guide outlining the essential steps and milestones for you and your venture to achieve its ambitions. It provides you and your organisation a clear direction, guiding your decisions and efforts towards success.

Imagine this roadmap as a compass in the vast wilderness of the market, offering guidance and clarity to those brave enough to explore. It goes beyond mere documentation; it embodies a strategic design that charts the course of your entrepreneurial journey, navigating you through the turbulent seas of the business world.

Let's explore its key components.

Firstly, the roadmap begins with a clear articulation of your and your company's vision and mission. At its core, every success roadmap starts with a vision—a bold, audacious dream that sets the stage for greatness. This vision serves as the guiding star, illuminating every decision and action, anchoring efforts to a higher purpose and greater cause, defining your and your organisation's overarching purpose and direction.

Next, specific, measurable, achievable, relevant, and time-bound (SMART) goals are established to support your vision and mission. These goals serve as the targets that you and your company aims to achieve within a defined timeframe, serving as milestones on the journey to success.

However, a vision and goals without a plan are mere wishes. This is where strategy comes into play—the art of translating dreams into actionable steps. The roadmap outlines the high-level strategies and approaches you and your company will use to achieve its goals, such as market expansion, product development, and customer acquisition.

Moving forward, tactics and action plans are detailed—the practical steps to turn vision into reality. It involves meticulous planning, resource allocation, and team mobilisation to bring strategies to life.

Action plans break down the steps, tasks, responsibilities, timelines, and resources required for effective strategy execution.

Identifying key performance indicators (KPIs) is crucial to measure progress towards the goals. These metrics provide insights into strategy effectiveness, enabling adjustments as needed.

Navigating challenges is essential on the road to success. The roadmap includes robust risk management strategies—anticipating threats, mitigating risks, and forging ahead with resilience. It assesses potential risks, develops mitigation plans, and prepares the organisation to navigate uncertainties and minimise disruptions for you.

Resource allocation is another critical aspect, considering finances, manpower, technology, and time. Efficient resource allocation supports action plan execution, maximising efficiency and effectiveness in your goal pursuit.

Monitoring and evaluation are ongoing processes to track progress, measure performance, and make necessary adjustments. This ensures alignment with your goals and identifies areas needing improvement.

Adaptability is key. A successful roadmap remains dynamic, embracing change as an opportunity. It allows flexibility in adjusting strategies and tactics for you in response to evolving market conditions, customer needs, and internal capabilities.

In essence, a Success Curve Roadmap, also known as a Sigmoid Curve Roadmap, guides an organisation towards its desired outcomes. It provides clarity, direction, and focus, keeping the company aligned with its vision and effectively navigating the path to success for you and your venture. With the right map in hand, there's no limit to how far you can go. So, chart your course guided by vision, fuelled by passion, and driven by the relentless pursuit of excellence. Long-term goals may seem daunting, but fear not—I am here to guide you through the transformative process of breaking them down into manageable milestones.

Breaking Down Long-Term Goals

Imagine, if you will, your long-term goals not as distant summits but as a series of conquerable peaks as sown in the diagram at the start of this chapter using S Curve or success curve. These are not mountains to climb in one daring ascent but challenges to overcome through a series of strategic victories. Through the lens of breaking down long-term goals, you shall explore the concept of short-term wins – understanding how achieving smaller goals fuels motivation and propels your venture forward.

Consider the entrepreneur who faced the daunting prospect of a long-term goal. Instead of being paralysed by the enormity of the task, they dissected it into bite-sized, achievable milestones. Each small victory became a stepping stone, a testament to their progress, and a source of motivation for the journey ahead. It's not about reaching the summit in one stride but about conquering the trail, one step at a time.

If you can see the way I see, One of the real-life example of a successful individual who broke down their long-term goals into smaller, manageable tasks is Elon Musk, the CEO of SpaceX and Tesla, Inc. Musk is known for his ambitious visions of transforming transportation and space exploration. To achieve these monumental goals, Musk breaks them down into smaller, actionable steps and focuses on achieving them incrementally. For instance, in the case of SpaceX, Musk's long-term goal is to establish a sustainable human presence on Mars. However, he understands that this is a complex and multi-faceted endeavour. Therefore, he breaks down this long-term goal into smaller milestones, such as developing reusable rocket technology, launching satellites to generate revenue, and progressively advancing towards crewed missions to the International Space Station. Similarly, at Tesla, Musk's long-term goal is to accelerate the world's transition to sustainable energy. To accomplish this, he breaks down the goal into incremental steps, such as increasing the production capacity of electric vehicles, expanding the charging infrastructure, and innovating in renewable energy solutions like solar power.

By breaking down long-term goals into manageable tasks and focusing on achieving them one step at a time, Elon Musk demonstrates how effective goal-setting and strategic planning can lead to significant success in business and innovation.

Mastering the art of breaking down long-term goals into achievable milestones is not just a strategy; it's an empowerment tool for your entrepreneurial journey. It's about fostering a sense of accomplishment, creating a rhythm of victories, and building momentum that propels you forward. As you break down your long-term goals, envision each milestone as a victory flag planted on the path of your success.

Benefit from the transformative power of this approach. Master the art of breaking down long-term goals into manageable milestones. Understand that the journey to success is not a marathon but a series of strategic sprints. Celebrate the small victories, for they are not just stepping stones but the building blocks of your triumph.

Envision your long-term goals not as distant dreams but as a series of achievable victories. Break them down into manageable milestones, and watch as the sense of accomplishment fuels the fire of your motivation. Onward, to new horizons where your journey is marked not just by the magnitude of your goals but by the strategic brilliance of achieving them, one milestone at a time. May your venture be propelled forward by the momentum of your victories, and may each small win be a testament to the triumph that awaits you.

Let's take a moment to reflect on the game of cricket to understand the typical roadmap before you jump on the detailed concept of S Curve.

Building a Cricket Match Roadmap

Cricket, like any other sport, is not just about skill and athleticism; it's also about strategy and planning. And at the heart of every successful cricket team lies a roadmap—a blueprint for victory. With the ultimate aim of winning the game and inspiring millions in the long run, the team focuses on short-term successes by meticulously strategising each inning and session. These incremental advances culminate in the overarching goal of clinching the win.

Just imagine for a moment a cricket match without a roadmap. Players would be running onto the field without a clear direction, swinging their bats and bowling their balls aimlessly. Chaos would reign supreme, and victory would seem like an elusive dream.

But fortunately, that's not how cricket works. Every successful team meticulously plans its approach to the game. They study the pitch, analyse their opponents, and strategies every move. And just like a roadmap guides us on a journey, these plans guide the players on their path to victory.

So why is having a roadmap so crucial in winning the game of cricket? And what makes breaking down long-term goals into smaller, manageable chunks so crucial?

Let me share a few reasons with you.

Firstly, a roadmap provides direction. It helps the team understand what they need to do to win the game. Whether it's setting a competitive target with the bat or taking crucial wickets with the ball, the roadmap outlines the path to victory. It assists in breaking down goals and objectives into manageable short-term targets instead of solely focusing on long-term visions.

Secondly, a roadmap promotes collaboration. In cricket, as in any team sport, success is built on collaboration and coordination. A well-defined roadmap ensures that every player understands their role and contributes to the team's success. Every team member is cognizant of the overarching goal as well as their individual missions contributing to long-term success.

Thirdly, a roadmap allows for adaptability. In cricket, conditions can change in an instant—the pitch might start favouring spinners, or the weather might take a turn for the worse. A roadmap helps the team adapt to these changes and adjust their strategy accordingly. The overarching strategy was never solely focused on winning every small battle, but rather on navigating through victories and losses with adaptability, ultimately securing the win in the game.

And finally, a roadmap instils confidence. When players step onto the field with a clear plan in mind, they feel empowered and motivated. They know that they have done their homework and are ready to take on whatever challenges come their way. Each short-term victory elevates confidence to new heights, while small losses cultivate adaptability and flexibility, guiding strategic adjustments towards the ultimate goal of winning the game.

Here's a typical plan outlining the roadmap for the batting and bowling teams to win the cricket match.

Batting Team Cricket Match Roadmap

I want to talk to you about the roadmap for the batting team in cricket. Just like any journey, a successful innings in cricket requires careful planning and execution. Let's break it down into six stages:

Stage 1: Assess the Pitch - Before the match begins, it's crucial to assess the pitch conditions. Is it fast or slow? Does it offer bounce or spin? Understanding these factors allows the batting team to develop a strategy tailored to the pitch characteristics, maximising their scoring opportunities.

Stage 2: Set a Target - Once the pitch has been assessed, the next step is to set a target. This involves determining a competitive total based on factors such as the pitch conditions, the strength of the opposition, and the match situation. The aim is to set a challenging total that puts pressure on the opposing team.

Stage 3: Build Partnerships - In cricket, partnerships between batsmen are crucial for stabilising the innings and accumulating runs steadily. Batsmen should focus on rotating the strike, capitalising on scoring opportunities, and minimising risks to build strong partnerships that lay the foundation for a competitive total.

Stage 4: Identify Key Bowlers - Every team has its key bowlers who pose a threat to the batting side. It's essential to identify these bowlers and formulate plans to counter their strengths and exploit any weaknesses. Batsmen should adapt their techniques accordingly to neutralise the threat posed by key bowlers.

Stage 5: Accelerate When Necessary - As the innings progresses, it's essential to assess the match situation and adapt batting strategies accordingly. If the team has wickets in hand and the pitch favours aggressive batting, they should aim to accelerate the scoring rate in the later stages of the innings to set a formidable total.

Stage 6: Finish Strongly - Finally, it's crucial for the batting team to finish the innings strongly. This involves capitalising on the final overs to maximise the total. Even tail-end batsmen should contribute valuable runs to extend the innings and ensure that the team sets a formidable target for the opposition.

In essence, a successful innings in cricket requires careful planning and execution at every stage of the game. By following this roadmap and adapting to the conditions as necessary, the batting team can give themselves the best chance of success.

Bowling Team Cricket Match Roadmap

In the exhilarating world of cricket, where every delivery holds the promise of victory or defeat, the role of the bowling team is pivotal. let's explore the roadmap for the bowling team, consisting of six crucial stages.

Stage 1: Analyse Opposition Batsmen - Firstly, before the match even begins, it's essential to analyse the opposition batsmen thoroughly. By understanding their strengths, weaknesses, and recent performances, the bowling team can formulate targeted strategies to dismiss them early and gain the upper hand.

Stage 2: Adapt to Conditions - As the match progresses, adaptability becomes key. Assessing the pitch and weather conditions allows the bowlers to tailor their approach, whether it's using seam, swing, or spin bowling techniques, to exploit the nuances of the pitch and maximise effectiveness.

Stage 3: Maintain Pressure - Maintaining pressure on the opposition batsmen is fundamental. Through consistent lines and lengths, coupled with strategic field placements, the bowling team aims to restrict scoring opportunities and induce mistakes, creating catching opportunities and maintaining pressure.

Stage 4: Target Weaknesses - Identifying and targeting the weaknesses of opposition batsmen is a strategic imperative. By varying bowling speeds, angles, and lengths, bowlers keep batsmen guessing and capitalise on any lapses in concentration to take regular wickets and disrupt the opposition's batting flow.

Stage 5: Take Regular Wickets - As the innings progresses, taking regular wickets at key intervals becomes crucial. This not only exposes the opposition's lower order but also applies pressure on new batsmen, making it harder for them to settle and score freely.

Stage 6: Finish Strongly - Finally, as the innings draws to a close, finishing strongly is essential. Bowlers must maintain intensity and focus in the final overs, aiming to restrict the opposition's scoring and take wickets to limit the target set by the batting team, setting the stage for a successful chase.

In essence, the roadmap for the bowling team in cricket is a strategic blueprint for success. By meticulously analysing the opposition, adapting to changing conditions, and executing targeted bowling strategies, the bowling team can assert its dominance on the field and pave the way for victory.

The Essence of a Roadmap

Success isn't merely a destination; it's a journey meticulously outlined by the essence of a roadmap. Just as a traveller needs a map to navigate uncharted territories, a successful venture demands a roadmap—a dynamic guide that leads from the spark of vision to the sweet taste of victory.

In the match of cricket, by following typical roadmap shared above, the batting and bowling teams can work cohesively to maximise their chances of winning the cricket match. The importance of having a roadmap in winning the game of cricket cannot be overstated. It provides direction, promotes teamwork, allows for adaptability, and instills confidence. Each player should understand their role and contribute effectively towards achieving the team's objectives. So, the next time you watch a cricket match, take a moment to appreciate the careful planning and strategising that goes into every move. Because behind every victory lies a roadmap—a blueprint for success.

Let's explore the roadmap-building process, drawing from the collective wisdom of mentors, business associates, and seasoned entrepreneurs.

As mentioned earlier, Elon Musk, the CEO of SpaceX and Tesla, epitomises this approach with his ambitious goals and strategic planning. Musk sets clear objectives for SpaceX to colonise Mars and for Tesla to revolutionise the automotive industry with electric vehicles. Each step towards these goals is meticulously planned, broken down into achievable milestones.

Similarly, Jeff Bezos, the founder of Amazon, strategically outlined his vision for the company in a 1997 letter to shareholders, detailing long-term goals and strategies. Bezos has consistently executed this roadmap, expanding Amazon's offerings and dominating multiple industries.

Indra Nooyi, the former CEO of PepsiCo, is another example of strategic leadership. Nooyi crafted a roadmap prioritising healthier product offerings and sustainability initiatives, successfully diversifying PepsiCo's portfolio and expanding its global presence.

Warren Buffett, the legendary investor and CEO of Berkshire Hathaway, is renowned for his disciplined approach to investing and strategic decision-making. Buffett follows a clear investment philosophy outlined in annual shareholder letters, guiding Berkshire Hathaway to become one of the most successful conglomerates globally.

The roadmap isn't just a static piece of paper; it's a dynamic tool that charts the course through the unpredictable terrain of business. It provides direction, cohesion to endeavours, and adapts to the changing colours of the business landscape.

As you delve into the essence of a roadmap, envision it not as a rigid script but as a dynamic companion on the journey, adjusting its steps to the rhythm of progress. It's the heartbeat of a venture, pulsating with the rhythm of vision, transforming dreams into victories, and making the journey a legend of entrepreneurial triumph.

Starting with the End in Mind

Success isn't something left to chance but rather carefully crafted with intention. Crafting a roadmap starts with a crystal-clear destination. Imagine your entrepreneurial journey as a grand expedition, with the destination not just a vague point on the horizon but a meticulously defined endpoint—this is the essence of beginning with the end in mind.

Steve Jobs, the co-founder of Apple Inc., was renowned for his visionary approach to product development. Jobs famously began with the end goal of creating innovative and user-friendly technology products that would revolutionise industries. He focused on designing products that weren't just aesthetically pleasing but seamlessly integrated into users' lives, ultimately leading Apple to become one of the most valuable companies globally.

It's not about stumbling upon success; it's about crafting a journey where every step is intentional, purposeful, and aligned with the ultimate goal. Envisioning success as a well-defined endpoint transforms your roadmap from a mere document into a strategic guide.

Starting with the end in mind isn't just about setting goals; it's about setting the right goals—ones that resonate with the deepest aspirations of your venture. Learn the significance of envisioning success, and let it be the guiding star that illuminates your roadmap, ensuring every twist and turn of the S-Curve leads you closer to your desired outcome.

As you explore the concept of the S-Curve or Sigmoid curve, let's examine the trajectory of your journey. An S-Curve represents growth and transformation. Similarly, when crafted with the end in mind, your roadmap propels your venture through phases of acceleration, maturation, and eventual mastery. It's not just a journey; it's an evolution, and starting with the end in mind ensures your roadmap aligns with the natural progression of success.

Acquire the skill of envisioning your destination, enabling you to design a roadmap precisely leading where you want to go. Let your destination be more than a point on the map; let it be the North Star guiding your journey. Starting with the end in mind isn't just a strategy; it's an art form, and you, fellow dream weavers, are the artists shaping the masterpiece of your success.

Richard Branson, the founder of the Virgin Group, began with the end goal of building a diverse and innovative conglomerate of companies. Branson focused on creating businesses challenging traditional industries and providing unique value propositions to customers. He started with a clear vision of building a brand standing for innovation, quality, and customer service, driving the success of the Virgin Group across various sectors, including airlines, music, telecommunications, and hospitality.

Many successful entrepreneurs demonstrate the importance of starting with the end in mind and having a clear vision of their goals and objectives from the outset. By focusing on their long-term aspirations and relentlessly pursuing their visions, they have achieved remarkable success and made enduring impacts on their industries and the world.

Envision your roadmap not as a mere plan but as the narrative of your triumph. As you start with the end in mind, let every goal set, every decision made, and every obstacle overcome be a deliberate step towards your ultimate destination. Moving forward towards uncharted territories where your strategic plan turns aspirations into tangible accomplishments, and your expedition evolves into a tale of entrepreneurial victory. One essential tool utilised in crafting such a roadmap is the S-Curve, which you will delve into in the upcoming segment.

Navigating Business Growth along Side S Curve

Grasping the path to growth is crucial for achieving success. One of the most enlightening tools for understanding this journey is the S Curve, also known as the sigmoid curve. This graphical representation provides profound insights into the life cycle of products, industries, and business processes, offering invaluable guidance to entrepreneurs and business leaders alike.

Imagine a visual depiction that charts how a product, industry, or business process evolves over time. That's the S Curve. Its distinctive S-shaped pattern maps out the stages of growth, maturity, and decline that every entity experiences. Mastering each phase is essential for making informed decisions and navigating the challenges and opportunities that define the business landscape. Let's explore the journey through the distinct phases of the S Curve.

Firstly, there's the Introduction or Infancy Phase. Here, a new product, new campaign, industry, or business process enters the market. Growth is gradual as awareness builds and early adopters cautiously embrace the innovation. It's a time of uncertainty and investment as the entity seeks to establish its position.

Next, you have the Scaleup Phase. As acceptance in the market increases, the entity enters a phase of rapid growth. Adoption becomes widespread, market share expands, and profitability flourishes, driving the entity to greater heights.

Then comes the Maturity Phase. Over time, growth stabilises as the entity matures. Competition intensifies, and the market may become saturated as the product or industry becomes well-established. While opportunities for innovation persist, growth becomes more incremental, necessitating strategic adaptation to stay relevant.

Lastly, there's the Decline Phase. Every S Curve eventually faces decline, where growth stagnates or declines. This phase could be triggered by changing consumer preferences, technological advancements, or the emergence of disruptive competitors. It's a period of reflection and reinvention as the entity seeks to extend its lifecycle or explore new avenues for growth.

The insights of the S Curve are profound and applicable across countless businesses and industries. Companies like Apple Inc., Amazon, and Tesla exemplify agility in navigating these phases, using innovation and strategic foresight to maintain their competitive edge.

In today's ever-evolving business environment, understanding the dynamics of growth is crucial for long-term success. The S Curve provides a powerful framework for comprehending business development, guiding entrepreneurs and business leaders through growth, maturity, and decline. By embracing these insights, businesses can chart a course towards sustainable growth and enduring success in an increasingly competitive world.

Understanding the S Curve Phenomenon

Understanding the sigmoid curve is crucial for businesses to anticipate and manage the life cycle of their products or industries effectively. It helps in strategic planning, decision-making, and adapting to changes in the market to sustain growth or find new opportunities. Companies often aim to innovate and introduce new products or services before the decline phase sets in to ensure continued success. Let me begin by sharing my understanding of the first phase of the S-curve with you.

Introduction (Infancy) Phase

The infancy stage of the sigmoid curve represents the early days of a product, campaign, industry, or business process. At this point, entities are just beginning to enter the market, and growth is slow as they strive to raise awareness and persuade consumers to embrace the new offering.

During this phase, the product is fresh and may require significant education for the target audience. Companies concentrate on establishing their presence in the market, often encountering difficulties in generating initial interest and awareness. They focus on communicating the features and benefits of the product to potential customers, with an emphasis on setting it apart from existing alternatives.

One of the main challenges during the introduction phase is overcoming consumer inertia and doubt. Companies may encounter resistance to change or adoption, particularly if the product differs significantly from existing solutions. Marketing efforts are crucial in addressing these challenges and creating a positive perception of the new offering.

During the introduction phase, companies typically invest heavily in research and development, marketing, and distribution. Resources are allocated to understanding consumer needs, refining the product, and developing effective communication strategies. The objective is to establish a strong foundation for future growth and success.

Scaleup (Adolescence) Phase

The growth phase of the sigmoid curve is defined by rapid expansion and widespread adoption of the product or industry. During this stage, companies take advantage of the increasing demand by expanding production, entering new markets, and strengthening their position in the market.

This phase sees a surge in sales, revenue, and market share. Positive feedback from customers and growing brand recognition contribute to this momentum. Companies may find themselves in a cycle of success, where increased demand leads to economies of scale and higher profitability.

Opportunities arise for companies to expand operations, invest in infrastructure, and establish a strong brand presence. Becoming a market leader becomes a feasible goal, and companies may look to diversify to sustain their growth. The strategic decisions made during this phase can have a significant impact on long-term success.

However, as success attracts competitors, companies must navigate increased competition. Product differentiation and innovation become crucial for maintaining market share. Pricing strategies, improvements in quality, and effective marketing all play important roles in the competitive landscape.

Navigating the Maturity (Adulthood) Phase: Strategies for Sustained Success

As businesses evolve through the stages of growth, they inevitably encounter the maturity phase, a pivotal stage where growth begins to plateau, and market dynamics shift. Understanding the nuances of this phase is crucial for businesses to navigate successfully and sustain their position amidst increased competition and market saturation.

The maturity phase signals a period where growth slows down as the market reaches saturation and competition intensifies. Companies in this phase pivot towards prioritising cost efficiency, enhancing existing products, and exploring new markets or customer segments to maintain their foothold.

In maturity, the market stabilises, and growth rates level off. While companies continue to generate revenue, the pace becomes more moderate. Consumer preferences tend to solidify, prompting a shift from acquiring new customers to retaining existing ones.

To remain competitive, companies often implement cost-cutting measures, streamline operations, and improve product features. Market share becomes a critical metric, prompting exploration of avenues for differentiation through branding, customer service, or product variations.

Maturity brings heightened competition, often resulting in price wars and margin pressures. Companies must carefully manage pricing strategies while balancing factors like product quality and customer loyalty. While innovation remains important, it often takes the form of incremental improvements rather than radical changes.

The maturity phase presents both challenges and opportunities for businesses. By strategically managing cost efficiency, product enhancements, and market differentiation, companies can navigate this stage successfully and sustain their position in the market. By understanding the dynamics of maturity and implementing effective strategies, businesses can emerge stronger and more resilient, ready to tackle the next phase of growth.

The maturity phase signifies a stage where growth starts to slow down as the market becomes saturated, and competition intensifies. Companies in this phase often focus on cost efficiency, improving existing products, and finding new markets or customer segments to sustain their position.

In maturity, the market stabilises, and growth rates level off. Companies continue to generate revenue, but at a more moderate pace. Consumer preferences may become more established, and the focus shifts from capturing new customers to retaining existing ones.

To maintain competitiveness, companies may implement cost-cutting measures, streamline operations, and enhance product features. Market share becomes a crucial metric, and companies explore ways to differentiate themselves through branding, customer service, or product variations.

Maturity often leads to increased competition, resulting in price wars and margin pressures. Companies need to carefully manage pricing strategies while considering factors such as product quality and customer loyalty. Innovation remains important, but it may take the form of incremental improvements rather than radical changes.

Navigating the Decline Phase: Strategies for Business Resilience

In the journey of every product, campaign, industry, or business process, there inevitably comes a phase known as decline, where sales dwindle, and market share dwindles. This pivotal stage presents businesses with the challenge of adapting to shifting consumer preferences, technological advancements, or superior alternatives. Understanding and effectively navigating the decline phase is essential for businesses to extend the lifespan of their offerings and remain resilient in the face of market challenges.

The decline phase is characterised by a decrease in sales and market share, driven by factors such as changing consumer preferences, technological advancements, or the emergence of superior alternatives. Companies find themselves grappling with the challenge of adapting to these changes and seeking ways to prolong the life of their products or industries.

During the decline phase, demand for the product or industry wanes, leading to a decline in sales and profitability. Companies may witness the erosion of their market share as consumer interest diminishes, marking a phase of diminishing relevance in the market.

Companies confronted with decline must make strategic decisions to navigate through this challenging period. Some may opt for an orderly exit from the market, reallocating resources to more promising ventures. Others may explore avenues to rejuvenate the product through rebranding, feature additions, or targeting niche markets. Cost-cutting and efficiency measures become imperative to weather the decline and preserve resources.

Successful adaptation during the decline phase necessitates a blend of foresight and agility. Companies must stay vigilant to market trends, identifying emerging opportunities and being prepared to make bold moves such as diversification or repositioning. Understanding the underlying reasons behind the decline is critical for developing effective strategies for renewal or transformation.

The decline phase poses significant challenges for businesses, but it also presents opportunities for renewal and transformation. By strategically managing the decline through cost efficiency, product rejuvenation, and market adaptation, companies can extend the lifespan of their offerings and emerge stronger from the downturn. By embracing change and proactively seeking opportunities for renewal, businesses can weather the decline phase and position themselves for future success.

Strategies for Business Revitalisation Using S Curve

As businesses face the onset of the decline phase, they are confronted with the critical choice of whether to pursue renewal or transformation. Navigating renewal and transformation stands out as one of the key strategies within the S Curve Growth Cycle. This pivotal stage demands strategic decisions aimed at rejuvenating the product, industry, or business process to reclaim relevance and sustainability.

Renewal involves strategic efforts to breathe new life into the product, industry, or business process. This often entails introducing innovations or entirely new products and services. Companies may invest in research and development to bring fresh and improved offerings to the market, incorporating technological advancements, enhanced features, or even a complete reimagining of the product.

Alternatively, companies may opt for transformation, reshaping their position in the market through strategic decisions. This could entail forging partnerships, pursuing mergers or acquisitions, or diversifying into related or entirely new industries. Bold decisions are essential to navigate the challenges and uncertainties inherent in a declining market.

Successfully navigating the renewal or transformation phase demands a strategic approach to risk management. Companies must meticulously assess the market landscape, anticipate future trends, and be willing to take calculated risks. Adaptability and a readiness to embrace change are crucial for achieving success in this phase.

Understanding the position of a product, industry, or business process on the sigmoid curve is instrumental in making informed decisions about resource allocation, marketing strategies, and future planning. Proactively identifying opportunities and challenges at each stage is imperative for long-term sustainability and success in the ever-evolving business landscape.

The sigmoid curve serves as a valuable framework for comprehending the life cycle of a product, industry, or business process. Each phase presents unique challenges and opportunities, and companies that adeptly navigate these stages with strategic decision-making, innovation, and adaptability are better positioned to achieve enduring success in today's dynamic business environment.

The Sigmoid Curve Roadmap: Guiding Businesses Through Life's Phases

Within the dynamic landscape of business, the Sigmoid curve stands as a potent metaphor, symbolising the undulating journey of a venture's life cycle. When mapped onto the stages encompassing pre-startup, startup, scale-up, and beyond, it unveils a roadmap of transitions and growth, each delineated by a distinctive sigmoid curve. This journey forms a continuum of interconnected curves, symbolising the metamorphosis of businesses from modest beginnings to industry titans.

The Sigmoid curve or success curve, often likened to an S-shaped graph, traces the trajectory of growth experienced by entities over time. It embodies the stages of pre-startup, startup, scale-up, maturity, and decline, mirroring the cyclical nature of business evolution. Each phase presents its own set of challenges and opportunities, shaping the trajectory of the venture's journey.

The journey commences with the pre-startup phase, marked by the exploration of entrepreneurial ideas and opportunities. Here, aspiring entrepreneurs conduct market research, identify potential niches, and lay the groundwork for their future ventures.

As ideas solidify into action, the venture progresses into the startup phase of the Sigmoid curve. This stage is characterised by the introduction of the venture to the market, as entrepreneurs navigate the uncertainties of market entry and lay the foundation for future growth.

With promising traction and validated business models, ventures enter the scale-up phase of the Sigmoid curve. Here, companies focus on accelerating growth, scaling operations, and expanding their market presence. Strategic partnerships, investments, and innovations drive the venture towards increased market share and profitability.

As growth stabilises, the venture transitions into the maturity phase of the Sigmoid curve. Here, companies focus on consolidating their market position, optimising operations, and sustaining profitability amidst intensifying competition and market saturation.

Ultimately, every Sigmoid curve reaches its decline phase, where growth stagnates or begins to decline. This stage may result from shifting consumer preferences, technological advancements, or the emergence of superior alternatives. Companies facing decline must navigate challenges and uncertainties, strategising to prolong the lifecycle of their offerings or pivot towards new opportunities.

The Sigmoid curve roadmap offers a comprehensive framework for understanding the life cycle of businesses, illuminating the journey from ideation to maturity and beyond. By embracing the insights offered by the Sigmoid curve, businesses can navigate the complexities of each phase with foresight and agility, positioning themselves for sustained success in an ever-evolving business landscape.

In the dynamic landscape of business, the Sigmoid curve serves as a powerful metaphor, capturing the ebb and flow of a venture's life cycle. When applied to the stages of startup, micro, small, medium, and large businesses, it unveils a roadmap of transitions and growth, each represented by a distinct sigmoid curve. This journey is a chain of interconnected curves, symbolising the evolution of businesses from their humble beginnings to becoming industry giants.

Exploring the Pre-Startup Phase of S-Curve Roadmap

On any entrepreneurial journey, you encounter a critical phase known as the Pre-Startup or Idea Stage. This initial stage lays the groundwork for entrepreneurial triumph, representing the genesis of a venture—an era of innovation, experimentation, and calculated risk-taking. Within this curve lie the uncertainties of infancy, where businesses navigate the path towards a viable model and seek validation within the market.

Initial Innovation and Ideation - The Pre-Startup phase is marked by a flurry of creativity and ideation. Entrepreneurs delve into brainstorming sessions, exploring various concepts and ideas to address existing market gaps or cater to unmet needs. It is a time of ideation, where innovative solutions are conceived, laying the groundwork for future development.

Low Market Share and Revenue - During this stage, businesses typically operate with minimal market presence and revenue generation. As ventures are in the nascent stages of development, they have yet to establish a significant foothold within their respective industries. Revenue streams may be sporadic or non-existent, reflecting the early nature of the business.

High-Risk Environment - The Pre-Startup phase presents a high-risk environment for entrepreneurs. With limited resources and untested business models, ventures face the inherent uncertainties associated with venturing into uncharted territory. The risk of failure looms large, requiring entrepreneurs to exercise caution and strategic decision-making.

Resource-Intensive Growth Strategies - To navigate the challenges of the Pre-Startup phase, ventures often adopt resource-intensive growth strategies. This may involve investing in research and development, prototyping, market research, and establishing initial infrastructure. Entrepreneurs leverage available resources to refine their concepts, validate their ideas, and prepare for the subsequent stages of growth.

The Pre-Startup or Idea Stage serves as the foundation upon which entrepreneurial ventures are built. It is a period of exploration, where ideas are cultivated, risks are taken, and aspirations take shape. By understanding the key features of this phase and adopting strategic approaches to innovation and growth, entrepreneurs can lay a solid foundation for future success. As ventures progress along the sigmoid curve, navigating through subsequent stages of growth, the lessons learned and experiences gained during the Pre-Startup phase remain invaluable, guiding entrepreneurs towards their ultimate objectives of market success and sustainability.

Navigating the Startup Stage of S-Curve Roadmap

As the pre-startup curve starts to ebb, a new sigmoid curve comes into play, signifying the commencement of the Startup stage. This phase resembles a transition towards stability and growth. It denotes a shift towards incremental growth, validation of Venture Creation Proof of Concept, and the establishment of operational processes. It represents a pivotal juncture, indicating progress and a step towards stability in the entrepreneurial journey. Within the Startup stage, several distinctive features set the tone for business evolution.

Venture Creation Proof of Concept and Initial Market Validation

The Startup stage is characterised by the validation of the Venture Creation Proof of Concept. Entrepreneurs focus on refining their initial ideas and concepts, testing them in the market to ascertain their feasibility and appeal to target audiences. It's a phase of experimentation and validation, where entrepreneurs seek evidence of market demand and viability.

Incremental Growth in Customer Base and Revenue
During the Startup stage, ventures experience gradual growth in their customer base and revenue streams. As the business gains traction and visibility within the market, it attracts a growing number of customers and generates increasing revenue. This incremental growth serves as a testament to the venture's ability to meet the needs of its target audience and deliver value.

Introduction of Operational Processes
With the expansion of the business comes the introduction of operational processes. Entrepreneurs focus on establishing efficient and scalable systems to support business operations and facilitate growth. This may involve streamlining workflows, implementing technology solutions, and developing organisational structures to enhance productivity and effectiveness.

Shift Towards Product-Market Fit
A key objective of the Startup stage is to achieve product-market fit. Entrepreneurs strive to align their offerings with the needs and preferences of their target market, refining their products or services based on customer feedback and market insights. This iterative process of iteration and refinement is essential for establishing a strong foundation for future growth and success.

The Startup stage represents a crucial phase in the entrepreneurial journey, characterised by incremental growth, validation of concepts, and the establishment of operational processes. By navigating through this stage with strategic planning, adaptability, and a focus on customer needs, entrepreneurs can position their ventures for long-term success and sustainability in the competitive business landscape.

Transitioning into the Micro Stage of S-Curve Roadmap

Following the Startup stage, the subsequent curve unveils the micro stage—a period characterised by well-defined products or services, heightened operational efficiency, and a moderate foothold in the market. This phase is focused on progressing with well-defined offerings and improved efficiency. Businesses in this phase focus on honing their operations, delving into niche markets, and establishing a foundation for long-term growth.

Within the micro stage, several notable characteristics shape the landscape of business evolution.

Defined Products/Services - Businesses at the micro stage boast clearly delineated products or services. They have honed their offerings, refining them to meet the specific needs and preferences of their target audience. This clarity in product or service offerings enables businesses to differentiate themselves in the market and carve out a distinct identity.

Improved Operational Efficiency - Efficiency becomes a focal point for businesses in the micro stage. They streamline their operations, optimising processes to enhance productivity and reduce costs. By leveraging technology and best practices, businesses improve their operational efficiency, enabling them to allocate resources more effectively and achieve greater outputs with fewer inputs.

Moderate Market Share and Revenue - At this juncture, businesses have secured a moderate market share and revenue stream. While they may not yet dominate their respective industries, they have established a foothold in the market and garnered a loyal customer base. This moderate level of success provides a solid foundation for further expansion and growth.

Exploration of Niche Markets - Businesses in the micro stage actively explore niche markets, seeking opportunities for growth and differentiation. They identify underserved or untapped segments within their target market and tailor their products or services to meet the unique needs of these niche audiences. By catering to specific market segments, businesses can foster stronger customer relationships and increase their market penetration.

The transition into the micro stage signifies a significant milestone in the journey of business development. With defined offerings, enhanced efficiency, and a foothold in the market, businesses are poised for sustained growth and success. By leveraging their strengths and exploring niche opportunities, businesses can continue to evolve and thrive in the competitive business landscape.

Moving in with the Small Business Innovation Window

Following the micro stage, a subsequent transition takes place, symbolising the progression from micro to small business. This transition heralds the appearance of a fresh sigmoid curve, indicating continued growth, solidification of market presence, and a heightened level of sophistication in business operations.

As businesses transition into the small business stage, several notable characteristics become apparent.

Consolidation of Market Position - At this stage, businesses focus on consolidating their position within the market. They strive to strengthen their brand identity, build customer loyalty, and establish themselves as key players in their respective industries.

Increased Market Share and Revenue - With the transition to the small business stage comes an increase in market share and revenue. Businesses experience growth in their customer base and sales volume, enabling them to capture a larger portion of the market and generate higher revenue streams.

Expansion into Broader Markets - Small businesses seize opportunities to expand into broader markets. They explore new geographic regions, target different customer segments, or diversify their product or service offerings to reach a wider audience and tap into additional revenue streams.

Development of More Sophisticated Business Processes - As businesses mature into the small business stage, they invest in developing more sophisticated business processes. This may involve implementing advanced technology solutions, enhancing operational efficiencies, and adopting best practices to streamline workflows and improve productivity.

The transition to the small business stage represents a significant milestone in the growth journey of enterprises. With a focus on consolidating market position, expanding into new markets, and refining business operations, small businesses are poised for continued success and sustainability in the competitive business landscape.

Transitioning with Small Business S Curve Stage

Moving forward, the third sigmoid curve represents the small business stage—a phase characterised by the ability to scale, diversified product offerings, and consistent revenue growth. With a loyal customer base and strengthened brand reputation, these businesses have firmly established themselves and are ready for the next stage of expansion.

In the small business stage, several key attributes come to the forefront.

Increased Scalability - Businesses in this stage exhibit greater scalability, meaning they can efficiently grow their operations to meet increasing demand. They have the infrastructure and resources in place to expand their business without compromising quality or customer service.

Diversification of Products/Services - Small businesses diversify their offerings, introducing new products or services to cater to evolving customer needs and preferences. By broadening their product portfolio, they can capture a larger market share and mitigate risks associated with dependence on a single product or service.

Steady Revenue Growth - With a solid foundation in place, small businesses experience consistent revenue growth. Their stable customer base and diversified offerings contribute to a steady influx of income, providing financial stability and fuelling further expansion opportunities.

Enhanced Brand Recognition - Through effective marketing and exceptional customer service, small businesses enhance their brand recognition. They become known entities within their industry, earning the trust and loyalty of customers and distinguishing themselves from competitors.

Transitioning into the small business stage marks a significant achievement for enterprises. With increased scalability, diversified offerings, steady revenue growth, and enhanced brand recognition, these businesses are well-positioned for continued success and expansion in the ever-changing business landscape.

Moving in with the Medium Business Innovation Window

Following the small business phase, there comes another transition, propelling businesses from small to medium-sized enterprises. This transition brings forth a new sigmoid curve, representing heightened market expansion, ongoing revenue growth, and the establishment of sophisticated management frameworks.

As businesses progress into the medium business stage, several key features emerge.

Further Market Expansion - Medium-sized enterprises embark on further market expansion initiatives, extending their reach beyond existing territories. They explore new geographic markets, target additional customer segments, and diversify their distribution channels to broaden their market presence.

Continued Revenue Growth - With the transition to the medium business stage comes continued revenue growth. These enterprises experience sustained increases in sales and income streams, driven by their expanded market footprint and diversified product offerings.

Development of Advanced Management Structures - Medium-sized enterprises invest in developing advanced management structures to support their growing operations. They implement sophisticated organisational frameworks, establish clear hierarchies, and introduce robust systems and processes to enhance efficiency and accountability.

Increased Investment in Innovation - As businesses mature into medium-sized enterprises, they allocate greater resources towards innovation and R&D. They focus on developing new products or services, improving existing offerings, and staying ahead of market trends to maintain their competitive edge and drive future growth.

Transitioning into the medium business stage represents a significant milestone for enterprises. With further market expansion, continued revenue growth, the development of advanced management structures, and increased investment in innovation, these businesses are poised for sustained success and expansion in the dynamic business landscape.

Reaching the Medium Business S Curve Phase

The subsequent curve embodies the essence of the medium business stage—a phase where enterprises attain significant size, market leadership, and substantial revenue streams. These businesses are characterised by ongoing diversification, innovation, and the establishment of a robust operational framework.

As businesses transition into the medium business stage, several prominent features come to light.

Market Leadership in Specific Segments - Medium-sized enterprises emerge as leaders in specific market segments or niches. They command a strong presence within their chosen industries, leveraging their expertise and resources to gain a competitive edge over rivals and establish themselves as key players.

Robust Operational Frameworks - Medium-sized enterprises develop robust operational frameworks to support their expanding operations. They implement efficient processes, clear organisational structures, and advanced technology solutions to enhance productivity, streamline workflows, and ensure seamless business operations.

Substantial Revenue Streams - With their growing market presence and diversified offerings, medium-sized enterprises generate substantial revenue streams. They enjoy a steady influx of income from multiple sources, providing financial stability and fuelling further expansion and innovation initiatives.

Continued Diversification and Innovation - Even as they achieve considerable size and market leadership, medium-sized enterprises remain committed to diversification and innovation. They explore new product lines, enter new markets, and invest in research and development to stay ahead of evolving customer needs and market trends.

Transitioning into the medium business stage marks a significant milestone for enterprises, characterised by market leadership, substantial revenue streams, and ongoing diversification and innovation. With a robust operational framework in place, these businesses are well-positioned for continued growth and success in the competitive business landscape.

Moving into the large Business Innovation Window

The second-to-last transition signifies the progression from medium to large business. A fresh sigmoid curve comes into view, indicating ongoing expansion, market dominance, and a global footprint. The business is on track to becoming a significant player in the industry.

As businesses move into the large business stage, several key attributes become apparent.

Dominant Market Position - Large businesses establish themselves as dominant players within their respective markets. They wield considerable influence and control over industry dynamics, often setting the standard for competitors to follow.

High Revenue and Market Share - With their expansive operations and extensive customer base, large businesses generate high revenue and command significant market share. They become household names, synonymous with quality and reliability.

Global Market Presence - Large businesses expand their reach beyond domestic boundaries, establishing a presence in international markets. They operate on a global scale, leveraging their resources and capabilities to tap into diverse markets and cultures.

Advanced Research and Development - Large businesses invest heavily in research and development to drive innovation and maintain their competitive edge. They pioneer new technologies, products, and services, pushing the boundaries of what is possible in their respective industries.

Transitioning into the large business stage represents a monumental achievement for enterprises, characterised by dominance in the market, high revenue and market share, global presence, and advanced research and development capabilities. With their influence and reach, these businesses shape the trajectory of entire industries and set the stage for continued growth and innovation on a global scale.

Reaching the Large Business S Curve Stage

The ultimate sigmoid curve embodies the large business stage—a milestone where enterprises achieve industry leadership, global impact, and a variety of revenue streams. These businesses have made a lasting impression, reflecting the culmination of a journey that began with the vision of a startup.

As businesses reach the large business stage, several notable characteristics come to light.

Industry Leadership - Large businesses establish themselves as leaders in their respective industries. They set the standards, drive innovation, and shape the direction of the market, influencing competitors and stakeholders alike.

Continued Innovation and Adaptation - Despite their size and success, large businesses remain committed to innovation and adaptation. They invest in research and development, embrace emerging technologies, and evolve their strategies to stay ahead of the curve.

Diversified Revenue Streams - With their expansive operations and diverse portfolio of products and services, large businesses generate revenue from multiple sources. This diversification provides stability and resilience, mitigating risks associated with market fluctuations or changes in consumer preferences.

Significant Global Influence - Large businesses wield significant influence on a global scale. They operate across multiple countries and continents, shaping economies, influencing policies, and impacting communities worldwide.

Reaching the large business stage marks the pinnacle of success for enterprises, characterised by industry leadership, ongoing innovation, diversified revenue streams, and significant global influence. With their enduring legacy and far-reaching impact, these businesses continue to drive progress and shape the future of industries and societies around the world.

Journey of Growth with S Curve

The Sigmoid curve roadmap serves as a visual narrative of the entrepreneurial journey, capturing growth, transitions, and evolution. Each curve represents a phase in the life cycle of a business, from the uncertainties of a startup to the stability of a large enterprise. The decline of one curve is not a sign of failure but a natural progression, as successful businesses reinvent themselves to stay relevant. The roadmap is a testament to the resilience, adaptability, and continuous innovation that characterise businesses on their path to lasting success. Stay tuned for the next curve in the series—a journey that promises more growth, challenges, and triumphs. The best is yet to come.

The Sigmoid curve is often used to represent the life cycle of a business, and when applied to different stages such as startup, micro, small, medium, and large businesses, it illustrates the transition and growth phases. Each sigmoid curve represents one stage of business development. Let's elaborate on this roadmap:

It's important to note that the decline stage of one sigmoid curve doesn't necessarily indicate failure but rather a natural part of the business life cycle. Successful businesses continuously reinvent themselves, engaging in innovation and adaptation to stay relevant in the ever-changing market landscape. The sigmoid curve roadmap provides a visual representation of this dynamic journey from startup to large business, capturing the essence of growth, transition, and evolution.

Integrating Flexibility into the Roadmap

let us delve into a crucial facet of strategic planning, where the rigidity of a roadmap is not a mark of strength but a potential liability. I invite you to explore the transformative power of integrating flexibility into your roadmap – the key to ensuring that your strategic journey is not hindered by obstacles but empowered by adaptability.

Your roadmap is not an unyielding script but as a dynamic dance, adjusting its steps to the rhythm of your journey. A rigid roadmap may be a beautifully drawn map, but it lacks the ability to navigate the unpredictable terrains of the entrepreneurial landscape. Adaptability is not a deviation from the plan but a strategic enhancement.

As an entrepreneur you will face unexpected challenges, but with seamlessly adjusted roadmap. Instead of being tethered to a static plan, embrace flexibility as a strength, allowing you to pivot without losing sight of your overarching vision. It's not about abandoning the roadmap but making it dynamic, ensuring it remains a living guide rather than a fossilised document.

Developing a mindset that values adaptability is not just a skill; it's a strategic advantage in the face of uncertainties. The world of business is dynamic, and success lies not in resisting change but in harnessing its energy. Your roadmap is not a rigid structure but as a tool that adapts to the twists and turns of your journey, ensuring that every pivot is a deliberate step toward your ultimate destination.

One of the immensely powerful example of a successful entrepreneur and living legend who integrated flexibility into their roadmap is Jeff Bezos, the founder and former CEO of Amazon. Bezos is known for his ability to adapt to changing market conditions and pivot, when necessary, which has been instrumental in Amazon's growth and success.

When Bezos first started Amazon in 1994, the company initially focused on selling books online. However, as the internet landscape evolved and consumer preferences shifted, Bezos recognised the importance of diversifying Amazon's offerings. He integrated flexibility into Amazon's roadmap by expanding the company's product lines to include electronics, apparel, home goods, and more.

Furthermore, Bezos embraced innovation and experimentation within Amazon, encouraging teams to explore new ideas and take calculated risks. For example, Amazon launched its Prime subscription service, which offers free two-day shipping and other benefits, as a way to enhance customer loyalty and drive sales. This initiative was a significant departure from Amazon's traditional business model but ultimately proved to be a game-changer for the company.

Another example of an entrepreneur who embraces flexibility in their roadmap is Reed Hastings, the co-founder, and CEO of Netflix. Hastings recognised early on that the media landscape was rapidly changing, with consumers increasingly shifting towards streaming services for entertainment. Instead of sticking to Netflix's original model of DVD rentals by mail, Hastings pivoted the company towards streaming, investing heavily in original content and technology infrastructure.

By embracing flexibility in their roadmaps, entrepreneurs like Jeff Bezos and Reed Hastings have been able to adapt to changing market dynamics, seize new opportunities, and stay ahead of the competition. Their willingness to pivot when necessary has been key to their success in building and growing their respective companies.

Let us develop a mindset that values adaptability, ensuring that your strategic plans remain dynamic tools rather than static documents. Understand that it's not about abandoning the plan but enhancing its resilience, allowing your roadmap to weather storms and still guide you toward success.

Let flexibility be the compass that guides your journey. As you integrate adaptability into your roadmap, let it be more than a strategy; let it be a commitment to staying nimble in the face of uncertainties.

Let your journey be marked not just by the strategic brilliance of your plan but by the adaptability that transforms challenges into opportunities.

Collaborative Road mapping

The symphony of ideas and insights **harmonis**es to create a roadmap not just for one, but for all. It's a process where the collective intelligence of your team becomes the driving force behind the evolution of your strategic journey. It fosters a sense of ownership, commitment, and a shared vision within your organisation.

Your entrepreneurial journey is not just a solitary exploration but a collective odyssey, where every member of your team contributes to the creation of a roadmap that reflects diverse perspectives and enhances its effectiveness. Consider you as an entrepreneur where, instead of crafting a roadmap in isolation, you gathered the collective intelligence of your team. Each member brought a unique perspective, a valuable piece of the puzzle that, when combined, created a roadmap richer in insights and more resilient to challenges. It's not about one mind but many, not about individual brilliance but collective genius.

Effective collaboration is not just about sharing ideas; it's about creating a roadmap that becomes a symbol of collective ownership, where every contributor sees their mark and feels a sense of commitment to the journey. The entrepreneurial journey is not just about individual brilliance but collective synergy. Embrace the diversity of thought within your team, and watch as your roadmap becomes a masterpiece that reflects the multitude of perspectives, experiences, and expertise gathered around the table.

The spirit of collaboration is the compass that guides your journey. As you harness the collective intelligence of your team, let your roadmap be more than a plan; let it be a testament to the power of unity in the face of challenges. Your journey is marked not just by strategic brilliance but by the collective genius that propels you toward unparalleled success. Let your collaborative roadmap be a living embodiment of shared vision, commitment, and triumph.

Monitoring and Adjusting the Course

No roadmap is flawless from the outset. Delve into the importance of continuous monitoring and adjustment. Acquire the ability to monitor progress, identify deviations, and make strategic adjustments to keep your venture on track toward its goals. The realisation dawns that no roadmap is flawless from the outset.

Let's understand the transformative importance of continuous monitoring and adjustment—a skill that separates the ordinary from the extraordinary. As you explore your journey as an entrepreneur you will be faced with deviations, adjusted your course, and ultimately reached your destination. Your roadmap is not only an immutable plan but also as a dynamic guide, responsive to the ever-changing landscape of your journey.

In the early days of SpaceX, Musk faced numerous setbacks and challenges in his quest to develop reusable rockets and make space exploration more affordable. However, instead of giving up, Musk closely monitored the progress of his team and the development of SpaceX's technology. He regularly adjusted the company's course based on new information and insights, making strategic decisions to overcome obstacles and achieve his long-term goals. For example, when SpaceX experienced multiple failed rocket launches in its efforts to develop reusable rocket technology, Musk and his team carefully analysed the root causes of these failures and made necessary adjustments to their approach. They iteratively improved their rocket designs, propulsion systems, and launch procedures, eventually achieving success with the Falcon 9 rocket, which became the world's first partially reusable rocket. Through the lens of monitoring and adjusting the course, you shall unravel the tales of those who understood that success lies not in a flawless plan but in the ability to identify deviations, adjust the course, and stay resolutely on the path to their goals.

Consider you as an entrepreneur who, mid-journey, noticed a deviation from the original plan. Instead of being paralysed by the unexpected, they embraced the power of continuous monitoring and adjustment. It's not about avoiding deviations; it's about identifying them early, recalibrating the course, and ensuring that every step is still in alignment with the overarching vision. Acquire the ability to monitor progress, identify deviations, and make strategic adjustments to keep your venture on track toward its goals. The world of business is dynamic, and success lies not in sticking to a rigid plan but in the agility to adapt. Envision your roadmap not as a fixed path but as a series of strategic adjustments, ensuring that you stay on course, regardless of the challenges that may arise.

When Tesla faced production challenges and delays in ramping up the production of its Model 3 electric car, Musk personally took charge of the manufacturing process and implemented aggressive measures to streamline production and increase efficiency. By closely monitoring key performance indicators and market trends, Musk was able to identify areas for improvement and implement strategic changes to address them. His willingness to adapt and pivot when necessary has been instrumental in the success of both SpaceX and Tesla, demonstrating the importance of monitoring and adjusting the course in achieving long-term goals.

Let us acquire the skill to navigate the twists and turns of your journey, understanding that no venture is immune to deviations. Embrace the mindset that sees adjustments not as setbacks but as opportunities for refinement and improvement. Continuous monitoring and adjustment is the sails that propel your entrepreneurial ship. As you navigate the uncertainties of business, let your roadmap be more than a plan; let it be a living guide that adapts to the rhythm of your journey. Your venture is marked not just by the brilliance of your plan but by the resilience and adaptability that keep you on the path to triumph. Let your ability to monitor and adjust be the cornerstone of your sustained success.

Conclusion & Recap

In this chapter you explored various elements essential for crafting an effective roadmap for success. You delved into the essence of a roadmap and its significance in guiding entrepreneurial endeavours. Starting with the end goal in mind was emphasised as a fundamental step in strategic planning. You discussed the concept of the S Curve or Sigmoid Curve in business and how it could be applied to navigate the business life cycle effectively. The chapter also focused on breaking down long-term goals into manageable milestones, ensuring clarity and feasibility. Integrating flexibility into the roadmap was highlighted as crucial for adapting to changing circumstances and seizing opportunities. Additionally, collaborative road mapping was discussed, emphasising the importance of involving stakeholders in the planning process. So, let's not just build businesses; let's forge legacies. As you navigate the roadmap-building process together, envision yourself not as a passive reader but as an active architect of your entrepreneurial journey. May the insights shared in this chapter serve as the compass guiding you through the dynamic landscape of success. Buckle up, co-pilot, for your roadmap to success awaits. In your next chapter, "Adapting to Changing Circumstances - The Art of Business Flexibility," you will delve into the art of business flexibility, highlighting the necessity of adapting to changing circumstances in the entrepreneurial landscape. Through anecdotes and practical wisdom, the chapter underscores the importance of agility, resilience, and the ability to pivot strategies to navigate the evolving challenges of the business environment.

Chapter 4.3

Crafting Actionable Strategic Plan with A2E Framework of Success

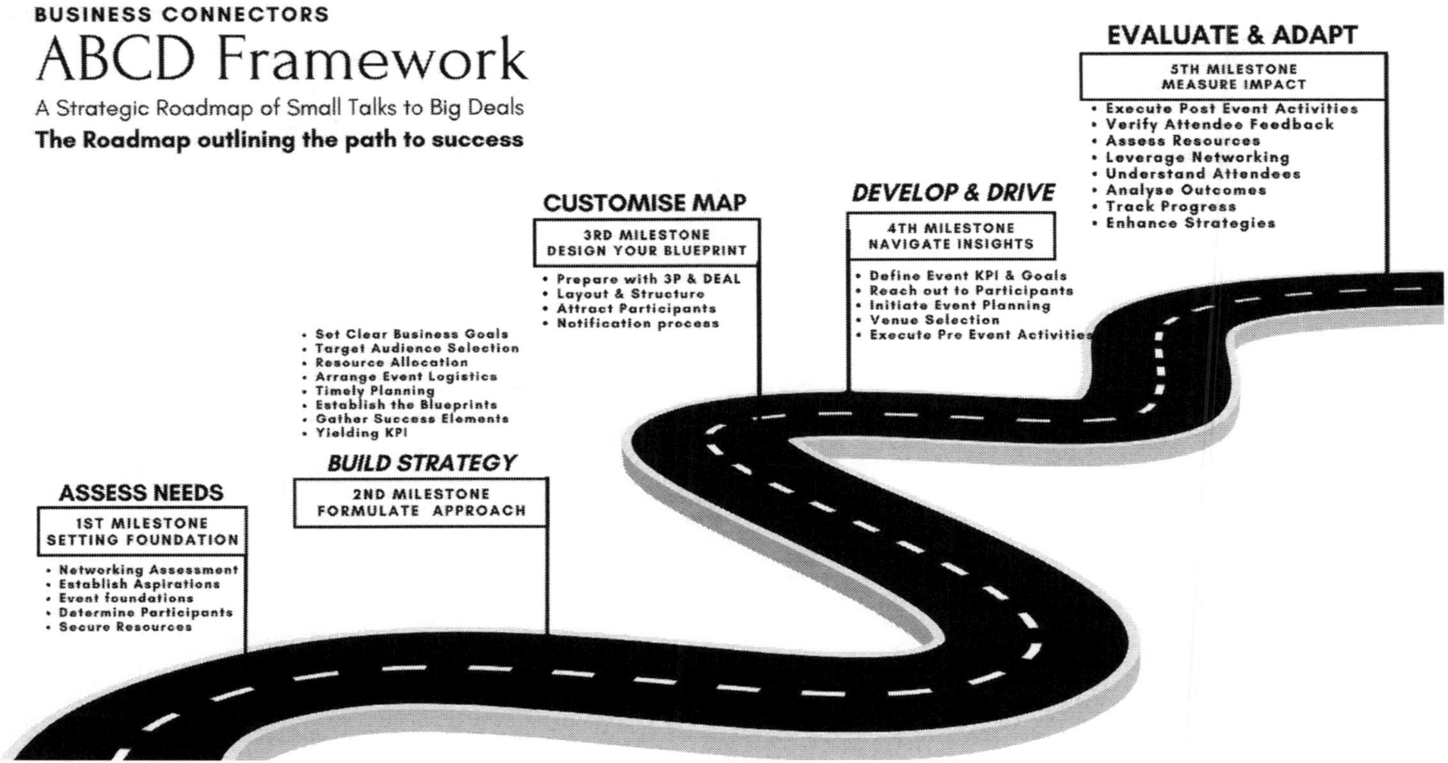

BUSINESS CONNECTORS
ABCD Framework
A Strategic Roadmap of Small Talks to Big Deals
The Roadmap outlining the path to success
ASSESS NEEDS
1ST MILESTONE
SETTING FOUNDATION
• Networking Assessment
• Establish Aspirations
• Event foundations
• Determine Participants
• Secure Resources
BUILD STRATEGY
2ND MILESTONE
FORMULATE APPROACH
• Set Clear Business Goals
• Target Audience Selection
• Resource Allocation
• Arrange Event Logistics
• Timely Planning
• Establish the Blueprints
• Gather Success Elements
• Yielding KPI
CUSTOMISE MAP
3RD MILESTONE
DESIGN YOUR BLUEPRINT
• Prepare with 3P & DEAL
• Layout & Structure
• Attract Participants
• Notification process
DEVELOP & DRIVE
4TH MILESTONE
NAVIGATE INSIGHTS
• Define Event KPI & Goals
• Reach out to Participants
• Initiate Event Planning
• Venue Selection
• Execute Pre Event Activities
EVALUATE & ADAPT
5TH MILESTONE
MEASURE IMPACT
• Execute Post Event Activities
• Verify Attendee Feedback
• Assess Resources
• Leverage Networking
• Understand Attendees
• Analyse Outcomes
• Track Progress
• Enhance Strategies

I believe that success in this realm hinges on one fundamental element—a well-crafted strategic framework. Imagine for a moment filled with opportunities and challenges. Navigating this landscape without a clear plan can be daunting, but with a strategic framework, you have a roadmap guiding you towards your goals. A strategic framework is not just a plan; it is your compass, providing clarity and direction. It helps you define your vision, set achievable goals, and outline the necessary steps to reach them. More importantly, it enables you to anticipate obstacles, adapt to changes, and remain focused on your mission.

I understand that every entrepreneurial journey is unique. That's why I have dedicated this chapter to creating a comprehensive framework designed to support and nurture your business aspirations from the ground up which will provide everything you need to build a solid foundation for your venture. Let's unravel the layers of crafting a strategic framework, a pivotal step in steering your venture toward triumph.

Mastering Transformative Engagements - The A2E Framework Unveiled

In the ever-evolving landscape of business and collaboration, success is not just about striking deals; it's about orchestrating transformative engagements that leave a lasting impact.

The A2E Framework, also called as ABCDE Framework, a comprehensive strategic roadmap, serves as the guiding light for organisations seeking to navigate the intricate journey from small talks to big deals. It's a comprehensive strategic roadmap designed to guide businesses from the initial spark of an idea through the complex journey to lasting success. This framework isn't just a set of steps; it's a dynamic process that emphasises thorough assessment, strategic planning, and meticulous evaluation. It is a process that adapts to the nuances of each unique engagement. Let me begin this journey by sharing the first milestone of the A2E framework and unveiling the essence of the ABCDE Framework.

Milestone 1: Assessing the landscape & the Needs - Setting Foundation

let's talk about laying the groundwork for success, specifically focusing on Milestone 1 of the ABCDE Framework. This milestone is all about setting the stage for what's to come in your entrepreneurial journey.

First things first, before you dive headfirst into making big plans, it's crucial to take a good look at the lay of the land. In the first milestone, 'Assessing & Setting Foundation,' the ABCDE Framework emphasises the critical importance of assessing and understanding the landscape before embarking on any transformative journey. The process begins with a thorough assessment of needs, not just within the organisation but also in the broader context of stakeholders and the market. This step sets the stage for success by identifying aspirations, building foundational elements, determining key participants, and securing the necessary resources. You need to understand what you're dealing with before you can start making moves. Think of it like this: before you go charging into battle, you want to know the strengths and weaknesses of your opponents, right? It's the same deal here in the world of business.

So, what exactly does Milestone 1 entail? Well, it's all about assessing what's going on around us. Understand the terrain on which you tread. Identify the strengths, weaknesses, opportunities, and threats that shape the battlefield of entrepreneurship. It's not about conquering the unknown but about understanding it, mastering it, and transforming it into your arena of triumph. Before embarking on any transformative journey, understanding the landscape, and identifying needs is paramount. The A2E Framework's first milestone, 'Setting Foundation,' emphasises the critical steps to ensure a robust start.

You're not just looking at your own needs as a company, but also what your customers want and what's happening in the market. This helps us make smart decisions and lay a solid foundation for success.

Based on my experience and insights from my mentors and business associates, the initial steps of the A2E framework are divided into five key stages. Let me share these with you first.

Step one is about assessing the need: You need to figure out what everyone needs. That means understanding what your customers want, what the market demands, and what you need to keep your business running smoothly. Organisations must meticulously identify stakeholder needs, analyse market demands, and understand their own requirements. A deep dive into the landscape sets the stage for informed decision-making.

Step two is about Assessing the Established Aspirations: You've got to set some big goals for ourselves. What do you want to achieve in the long run? By defining these goals and making sure they match up with what your customers want, you can create a clear vision for where you're headed. Defining long-term objectives and aligning them with stakeholder expectations ensures a clear vision. The establishment of core values and organisational culture creates a foundation that resonates with all participants.

Step three is assessing the foundation built. Building on that, you need to make sure you've got a strong foundation in place. That means making sure your business is set up with the right tools, systems, and culture to support your goals. Strengthening infrastructure and fostering a positive organisational culture are key elements. This step ensures that the organisation is well-prepared to navigate the challenges that may arise during the engagement.

Step four is about assessing Participants determination. You've got to figure out who's going to help us get there. You need to identify your key stakeholders, figure out who your target audience is, and get everyone on board with your plans. Identifying key stakeholders, segmenting target audiences, and mapping influencers and decision-makers lays the groundwork for effective communication and collaboration.

And finally, step five is about assessing the understanding of the resources at hand. You need to take stock of what resources you've got at your disposal. That means looking at your budget, your team, and the technology you're working with to make sure you're all set to move forward. Understand budget needs, understand human capital, and understand necessary technologies available at hand ensure that the current state of your organisation and its resources to move forward.

So, that's Milestone 1 in a nutshell. It's all about laying the groundwork, understanding what's going on around us, and getting ourselves ready to tackle whatever challenges lie ahead. With Milestone 1 under your belts, you'll be well on your way to success in the world of entrepreneurship.

Milestone 2: Build your vision & Strategy - Formulate Approach

This is the place where dreams meet reality and vision meets strategy. Welcome to Milestone 2 of the ABCDE Framework – 'Build and Formulate Approach'. This milestone is like the architect's drawing board, where you sketch out the plans that will shape your destiny. This milestone is akin to crafting the blueprint for the transformative journey. Here, the focus is on building a strategic foundation that aligns with organisational goals. Clear business goals are set, target audiences are carefully selected, and resources are allocated strategically. The planning process extends to logistics, timelines, and the creation of detailed blueprints, all aimed at ensuring a clear and effective approach.

With insights gleaned from assessment, construct the vision that will be the north star of your journey. It's not just about dreaming; it's about building a castle in the sky and then laying the foundation to make it rise from the ground strategically.

Picture this: You're not just dreaming here; you're laying down the groundwork to turn those dreams into actionable plans. It's about building a strategic foundation that lines up perfectly with your organisational goals and sets us on the path to success.

With the foundation in place, it's time to craft a strategy that aligns with organisational goals. The second milestone, 'Formulate Approach,' dives into the nitty-gritty of strategic planning.

So, what exactly does 'Formulate Approach' involve?

Firstly, you need to get crystal clear on your business goals. You need to build the definitions of clear business goals for your venture. You're talking about setting specific objectives and defining measurable targets that will guide every step of your journey. Defining specific objectives and outlining measurable targets creates a roadmap for success. These goals become the guiding principles for the entire engagement.

Next up, you need to identify your target audience. You need to build the target audience selection criteria. Who are you trying to reach? By understanding the demographics, psychographics, and unique selling points of your audience, you can tailor your approach to resonate with them effectively. segmenting demographics, understanding psychographics, and identifying unique selling points facilitate a more targeted and effective approach to engagement.

Now, let's talk resources and build the resource allocation criteria. You need to ensure you're investing your money, time, and manpower wisely. By distributing budgets effectively, optimising your human resources, and investing in the right technologies, you ensure that your resources are aligned with your strategic goals. Distributing budgets effectively, optimising human resources, and investing in technological infrastructure ensure that resources are aligned with strategic goals.

Of course, no plan is complete without logistics and hence you need to build the logistics arrangement criteria. You need to plan out the physical and virtual spaces where your engagement will take place, coordinate travel and accommodations, and implement technology platforms to ensure everything runs smoothly. Planning physical and virtual spaces, coordinating travel and accommodations, and implementing technology platforms set the stage for a seamless execution of the engagement.

Time is precious, so you need to manage it wisely. Hence the next is to build the timeline planning. You'll develop project timelines, establish milestone dates, and incorporate contingency plans to keep us on track and ensure you're making the most of your time. Developing project timelines, establishing milestone dates, and incorporating contingency plans contribute to effective time management.

With the logistics and timeline planning sorted, it's time to create the blueprints for success. Hence, you need to build the blueprints establishments. You'll design strategic frameworks, develop action plans, and create implementation schedules to provide a detailed roadmap for successful execution. Designing strategic frameworks, developing action plans, and creating implementation schedules provide a detailed roadmap for successful execution.

Lastly, you need to build success Element KPIs and Yielding KPIs. You need to set ourselves up for success by identifying key performance indicators (KPIs) that will measure the impact of your engagement. By leveraging past successes and defining KPIs, you ensure that your efforts are both measurable and impactful. Identifying key success factors, leveraging past successes, and defining key performance indicators (KPIs) contribute to a measurable and impactful engagement.

So, there you have it – Milestone 2 of the ABCDE Framework in a nutshell. By following these steps and crafting a solid approach, you'll be well on your way to turning your entrepreneurial dreams into reality. But the h=journey is not finished yet, let's have a look at milestone 2 of this framework.

Milestone 3: Customise Your Roadmap to Design Your Blueprint

With the strategy in place, the third milestone, 'Design Your Blueprint,' moves the organisation from planning to execution. Welcome to Milestone 3 of your journey through the ABCDE Framework – 'Design Your Blueprint'. Today, you're transitioning from the planning phase to execution, turning your vision into a tangible reality.

This phase is not just about logistics; it's about creating an experience that engages and resonates with everyone involved and creating an engaging and purposeful experience. Prioritising the 4Ps – Plan, Process, People and profit - lays the groundwork for a successful engagement. The layout and structure are meticulously designed, participants are attracted through effective marketing, and a seamless notification process ensures everyone is on the same page.

Tailor your strategic plan to fit the contours of your vision. Align the goals, the resources, and the actions with the unique landscape you navigate. It's about crafting a roadmap that is not just a path but a personalised narrative leading you to greatness. With the strategy in place, the third milestone focuses on translating plans into actionable steps. 'Design Your Blueprint' emphasises the importance of meticulous planning and engaging content.

Let's dive into crafting your blueprint for success.

Firstly, let's talk about customising your roadmap to prepare with 4Ps and the DEAL model. You need to align it with the contours of your vision. By prioritising the 3Ps and embracing the DEAL model – Prioritising, Plan, Process, People – you ensure that your engagement revolves around meaningful connections and shared objectives. This sets the stage for a collaborative and impactful experience.

Next, let's focus on the layout and structure and customise your layout & structure. Designing the event flow, defining session formats, and planning interactive elements are crucial for creating a dynamic and engaging atmosphere. Attention to detail here enhances participant engagement and fosters an environment conducive to fruitful interactions.

Now, let's discuss attracting participants and customers and customise your strategies to attract participants & Customers. Developing compelling invitations, implementing effective marketing strategies, and leveraging social media and networking platforms are essential for driving active participation. Customising your strategies ensures that your event reaches the right audience and generates the desired response.

Lastly, let's streamline your notification process and customise your notification process for better communication. Clear communication of logistics, confirmation of participation, and providing detailed event information contribute to a smooth pre-engagement phase. This ensures that all stakeholders are well-informed and prepared for the upcoming event, setting the stage for a seamless execution.

In essence, Milestone 3 is all about translating plans into actionable steps. 'Design Your Blueprint' emphasises the importance of meticulous planning and engaging content, laying the foundation for a successful and impactful engagement.

So, as you embark on this milestone, remember to tailor your strategic plan to fit the unique landscape you navigate. Craft a roadmap that is not just a path but a personalised narrative leading you to greatness. With careful customisation and attention to detail, you'll be well on your way to turning your vision into reality.

Milestone 4: Develop & Drive Solutions with Actionable Steps - Drive Data and Drive the plan to Navigate Insights

As you traverse the path of transformation, you often find ourselves amidst dreams and plans, pondering how to turn these ethereal visions into tangible reality. It is in this pursuit that Milestone 4 of the ABCDE Framework, aptly named 'Navigate Insights,' assumes paramount significance.

Dreams and plans are ethereal until translated into action. Develop actionable steps that convert aspirations into reality. It's about not just knowing the way but taking the steps that bridge the gap between where you are and where you want to be. In this pivotal phase of your journey, you are tasked with the formidable challenge of translating aspirations into actionable steps. No longer can you afford to merely envision the future; you must take deliberate strides towards its realisation.

At the core of Milestone 4 lies the imperative of data-driven decision-making. You are called upon to define clear Key Performance Indicators (KPIs) and goals ensuring a focus on measurable outcomes., thereby laying the foundation for a strategic approach to execution. By harnessing the power of insights gleaned from data, you can steer your course with precision and purpose.

Moreover, this phase compels us to reach out to both internal and external stakeholders. Through meaningful engagement and solicitation of feedback, you can foster a culture of collaboration and shared ownership. It is through this collective effort that you pave the way for success. Outreach to internal and external customers begins, initiating planning and resource selection. The execution of pre-campaign activities ensures that all elements are in place for a successful engagement.

Execution planning emerges as a linchpin of Milestone 4, where meticulous coordination and monitoring of progress against established timelines are paramount. By ensuring that all elements are in place for a seamless execution, you mitigate the risk of unforeseen challenges derailing your journey. This fourth milestone to 'Navigate Insights,' emphasises the importance of customising the roadmap as per your campaign need and having data-driven decision-making process and the execution of the engagement.

Furthermore, resource selection becomes a strategic imperative as you strive to optimise the overall experience. Whether it be physical or virtual resources, your choices must be guided by the principles of accessibility, comfort, and technological efficacy.

Let's dive into crafting your solution with actionable steps.

Develop & Drive KPI & Goals - Refining KPIs based on strategy, aligning goals with business objectives, and establishing metrics for evaluation set the stage for data-driven insights.

Develop & Drive Participant Reach out - Fostering pre-campaign engagement, collecting feedback and expectations, and encouraging to create a participative atmosphere.

Develop & Initiate Execution Planning - Executing logistics plans, coordinating with stakeholders, and monitoring progress against timelines contribute to a seamless execution.

Develop and drive Resource Selection - Choosing appropriate physical or virtual Resources, ensuring accessibility and comfort, and leveraging technology infrastructure enhance the overall experience.

Develop and Execute Pre-Campaign Activities - Conducting dry runs and rehearsals, testing technology and equipment, and addressing potential issues proactively ensure a glitch-free event.

In essence, Milestone 4 beckons us to customise your roadmap in alignment with the unique contours of your campaign. By embracing a data-driven approach and executing with precision, you can navigate the complexities of transformation with confidence and clarity.

As you embark on this crucial phase, let us be guided by the spirit of innovation and resilience. Let us remain steadfast in your commitment to turning dreams into reality, knowing that success is not a destination but a journey of continual growth and evolution.

Milestone 4 stands as a testament to your collective resolve and determination. Let us rise to the occasion, armed with insights and driven by action, as you chart a course towards a future defined by progress and prosperity.

Milestone 5: Evaluate & Adapt - Measure Impact

As you journey through the realm of entrepreneurship, you are often consumed by the excitement of progress and the pursuit of your goals. But amidst the hustle and bustle, there comes a time for reflection, for assessment, and for adaptation. This pivotal moment is encapsulated in Milestone 5: Evaluate & Adapt. The entrepreneurial journey is dynamic, ever-changing. Constantly evaluate your progress, adapt to the evolving landscape, and refine your approach. It's not just about reaching milestones but evolving with each step, growing stronger and wiser.

This is the final milestone to Measure Impact which brings the transformative journey full circle. Post-campaign activities, Participants feedback verification, and resource assessment allow organisations to gauge the success of the engagement. Leveraging engagement opportunities and understanding participants provide valuable insights for future collaborations. This phase is about analysing outcomes, tracking progress, and enhancing strategies based on the lessons learned.

Before embarking on any transformative journey, understanding the landscape and identifying needs is paramount. The ABCDE Framework's first milestone for 'Setting Foundation,' emphasises the critical steps to ensure a robust start with an end of the circle with Milestone 5: Evaluate - Measure Impact before it goes in the next reiterative cycle to confine and refine the process again in next cycle.

The final milestone, 'Measure Impact,' focuses on evaluating the success of the engagement and leveraging insights for future endeavours.

Allow me to delve into the intricacies of this milestone, to shed light on its eight crucial steps that guide us towards greater success and sustainability.

Step one: Evaluate and Execute Post-Campaign Activities. It's imperative that you take a moment to look back at your journey, to collect feedback, assess your performance against set goals, and extract valuable lessons that will shape your future endeavours. Collecting post-campaign feedback, assessing performance against goals, and capturing lessons learned contribute to a comprehensive evaluation.

Step two: Evaluate and Verify Feedback. You must listen attentively to the voices of your stakeholders, analyse their satisfaction levels, and address their concerns. Their feedback is your compass, guiding us towards improvement and excellence. Analysing satisfaction levels, addressing concerns and suggestions, and gathering testimonials and endorsements provide valuable insights.

Step three: Evaluate the Resources. Let us review your budget allocations, assess the deployment of your human capital, and evaluate the effectiveness of your technological tools. By doing so, you ensure that your resources are utilised optimally and sustainably. Evaluating budget utilisation, reviewing human capital deployment, and examining technology effectiveness contribute to a holistic assessment.

Step four: Evaluate and Leverage Engagement. Building and nurturing relationships are at the heart of your success. Let us seize the opportunity to foster ongoing engagement, capitalise on new connections, and lay the groundwork for future collaborations. Capitalising on new connections, fostering ongoing relationships, and implementing follow-up strategies contribute to long-term collaboration.

Step five: Evaluate Participants. Understanding the demographics and engagement levels of your audience is paramount. Let us delve into their experiences, preferences, and needs, so that you may tailor your strategies to meet them effectively. Analysing participant demographics, evaluating engagement levels, and identifying potential future collaborations provide insights into audience dynamics.

Step six: Evaluate & Analyse Outcomes. It's time to assess your impact, to measure your success against Key Performance Indicators, and to evaluate your return on investment. By identifying areas for improvement, you pave the way for greater achievements ahead. Measuring event success against KPIs, evaluating return on investment (ROI) and return on engagement (ROE), and identifying areas for improvement contribute to a comprehensive analysis.

Step seven: Evaluate to Track Progress. Your journey doesn't end here; it's an ongoing evolution. Let us monitor your long-term impact, implement continuous improvement initiatives, and stay aligned with your goals for sustained success. Monitoring long-term impact, implementing continuous improvement, and aligning future strategies with insights contribute to sustained success.

Step eight: Evaluate to Enhance Strategies. Finally, let us embrace the spirit of growth and innovation. By incorporating the lessons learned into your strategies, by adapting to changing landscapes, and by fostering a culture of continuous improvement, you ensure that you evolve with every step you take. Incorporating lessons learned, adapting strategies for future initiatives, and fostering a culture of continuous improvement ensure ongoing success.

In conclusion, Milestone 5 is not just a moment of reflection; it's a catalyst for growth, a beacon of progress, and a testament to your commitment to excellence. Let us embrace the principles of evaluation and adaptation, for they are the cornerstone of your journey towards greater heights of success.

The Essence of Strategic Milestone Planning

In the vast expanse of entrepreneurship, where uncertainty reigns and challenges abound, one tool stands as a beacon of hope and guidance: the strategic plan. The importance of a well-crafted strategic plan cannot be overstated. It's not just a document; it's a visionary masterpiece, a roadmap to success that navigates us through the uncharted waters of business. It is the cornerstone upon which the empires of success are built.

Crafting a strategic plan is like wielding a torch in the darkness. It offers clarity amidst ambiguity, guiding us towards your goals with precision and purpose. It illuminates the path forward and aligns your vision with actionable steps. It transforms abstract dreams into tangible realities, painting a vivid picture of your venture's future. It's not merely about setting goals but about forging a path to achieve them, with every decision, every action, contributing to the grand tapestry of success.

As an entrepreneur, you are captains navigating uncharted waters, you're your strategic plan is the navigator that ensures you stay on course, even in the face of turbulent seas. It empowers you to make informed decisions, crucial for the success of your ventures. In the dynamic theatre of business, where uncertainty is a constant companion, a well-crafted strategic plan becomes the North Star that guides you through the storm.

Let us not view strategic planning as a mere exercise but as an art form – a symphony of vision, foresight, and execution. It's about weaving together the threads of your aspirations and reality, creating a tapestry that not only withstands challenges but transforms them into opportunities for growth.

Embrace the essence of strategic planning as more than just a roadmap. It is the navigator, the guiding force, and the architect of your success. Let your strategic plan be not just a document but a living testament to your vision, resilience, and unwavering commitment to greatness.

Your strategic plan is the wind in your sails, propelling you towards success with unwavering determination. The stage is set, the canvas is yours – let the masterpiece of your entrepreneurial legacy unfold with the brilliance of a well-crafted strategic plan. Onward to triumph! However, this milestone journey cannot be completed without delving into the development of actionable steps, which involves setting clear goals and Key Performance Indicators (KPIs) for these steps. Hence, let's take a closer look at the process of setting SMART goals next.

Setting SMART Goals

In Today's world, you stand at the threshold of greatness, poised to embark on a journey that will define your destinies and shape your futures. But this journey of entrepreneurship is not just about dreaming; it's about crafting a vision that is concrete, actionable, and propels us forward with unwavering determination. it's about turning those dreams into reality, one step at a time.

At the heart of this transformative journey lies the essence of setting SMART goals—Specific, Measurable, Achievable, Relevant, and Time-bound. These are not mere words; they are the guiding principles that will lead us towards your goals and aspirations. they are the pillars upon which the skyscrapers of success are built. They are the secrets whispered by triumph to those who dare to set their sights on greatness.

Consider for a moment the power of specificity. Specific goals are like a finely tuned compass, directing us towards your destination with pinpoint accuracy. They are the architectural blueprints of success, laying the foundation for a venture that is not just a dream but a tangible reality. They lay the foundation for your success, providing us with a clear roadmap to follow.

Measurability adds a layer of objectivity to your aspirations. It transforms abstract ambitions into quantifiable milestones, allowing us to track progress and celebrate every step forward. Measurable goals are the milestones that turn your journey into an exhilarating adventure, marked by achievements that fuel the fire of your entrepreneurial spirit.

Achievability is the key that unlocks the doors of success. Goals that are within reach, challenging yet attainable, become the stepping stones that propel us forward. They are the fuel for your perseverance, the catalysts for growth, and the testaments to your resilience in the face of challenges.

Relevance ensures that your goals align with your overarching vision. It's not just about achieving for the sake of achievement but about progressing towards a meaningful destination. Relevant goals are the north star that keeps us on course, preventing us from wandering off the path of purpose.

Time-bound goals inject a sense of urgency into your journey. They are the ticking clock, the reminder that every moment is precious, and every goal is a race against time. Time-bound goals infuse your entrepreneurial pursuits with a sense of purpose, transforming your ventures into a race towards achievement.

Embracing SMART goals isn't just a strategy; it's a mindset. It transforms your strategic plan into a tangible roadmap, a roadmap dotted with clear milestones that foster a sense of achievement and progress along the entrepreneurial path. It's not just about dreaming big; it's about executing with precision, purpose, and an unwavering commitment to excellence. It transforms your dreams into actionable plans, paving the way for success. So, as you set your goals, remember to make them SMART—Specific, Measurable, Achievable, Relevant, and Time-bound.

Let these goals be your guiding light, your roadmap to success. Let them propel you forward with determination and purpose, towards a future filled with triumph and achievement. The path is clear, the goals are set—now let's embark on this journey together, towards the horizon of success! But this needs a different mindset and this mindset come from your environment and hence choose an environment which is suitable for you and your goals. Let's explore this concept further.

Choosing your Environmental

You are all products of our own environment.

Picture for a moment those trailblazers who dared to venture into the unknown, those who meticulously dissected the internal and external landscapes that influenced their entrepreneurial journey. These are the pioneers who understood that entrepreneurship doesn't exist in a vacuum but within a dynamic environment shaped by a myriad of factors.

By delving into the experiences of these visionaries, you will unfold the tapestry of Environmental Analysis - a compass that directs you to assess internal and external factors, market trends, and competitor landscapes. It's a roadmap that reveals the secrets of informed decision-making, a treasure map that guides you through the intricacies of entrepreneurship.

Why is this analysis so crucial?

Because understanding your environment equips you with insights into potential challenges and opportunities. It transforms your venture into a vessel that sails not just through calm waters but also navigates the storms of uncertainty. It is the beacon that illuminates the dark corners, revealing the hidden gems that could be the game-changers for your success.

Consider, for a moment, the internal factors – the strengths and weaknesses within your own venture. An environmental analysis unveils the treasures within, allowing you to leverage your strengths and fortify your weaknesses. It's not just about knowing your ship; it's about understanding its sails, the wind it catches, and the course it can set.

External factors, the ever-changing winds of the market, also demand your attention. Market trends and competitor landscapes are the elements that shape the currents you sail in. Environmental analysis is not just a telescope to view the horizon; it's a radar that detects shifts in the winds, enabling us to adjust your sails for optimal speed and direction.

As you conduct your environmental analysis, remember – it is not a mere task; it is the compass that guides you. It empowers you with the knowledge to make proactive decisions that influence the sustainability and growth of your venture. It's the strategic advantage that separates the captains of industry from the sailors lost at sea.

The importance of choosing the right environment and the people around us cannot be overstated. Just as a skilled gardener selects the perfect soil for their plants to thrive, so too must entrepreneurs carefully consider the ecosystem in which they choose to launch and grow their ventures.

Imagine for a moment the towering skyscrapers of success that dot your modern business landscape. Behind each of these towering edifices lies a carefully chosen environment – one that nurtured innovation, fostered collaboration, and provided the necessary resources for growth.

But what exactly is an entrepreneurial environment? It encompasses everything from people around you to the economic conditions and market dynamics to regulatory frameworks and access to funding. It's the soil from which businesses spring forth, the air that fills their sails, and the sun that nourishes their growth.

So why does choosing the right environment matter?

Because it can make all the difference between success and failure. A supportive ecosystem and the people with like mindset can provide entrepreneurs with access to resources, market opportunities, and networking connections that are essential for success. It can be the difference between struggling to survive and thriving in a competitive market.

But how does one go about choosing the right environment?

It starts with careful research and consideration. Define your business needs and goals, research potential locations, assess access to resources, consider market opportunities, evaluate the regulatory environment, seek networking opportunities, visit potential locations, and seek feedback and advice from experienced entrepreneurs.

By following these steps and conducting thorough research, aspiring entrepreneurs can set themselves up for success in the entrepreneurial journey. Remember, choosing the right environment is not just about finding a place to set up shop – it's about finding a home for your vision, a launchpad for your dreams, and a community of like-minded individuals who will support you every step of the way.

So let us embrace the challenge of choosing the right environment with open arms and unwavering determination. Let us seek out the places where your dreams can take root and flourish. And let us build a future where every entrepreneur has the opportunity to thrive, innovate, and change the world for the better. However, this also requires a deep understanding of yourself as an individual, as well as an understanding of others. It's about discovering what works well with them and what doesn't, recognising your own strengths and weaknesses, as well as those of others. By leveraging your strengths and those of others while overlooking weaknesses, you can cultivate a strong culture of innovation and continuous learning. Therefore, let's explore the tools that enable us to achieve this goal.

SWOT Analysis - Unveiling Your Strategic Landscape

In the world of entrepreneurship, where every decision can make or break a venture, having a clear understanding of your strategic landscape is paramount. This is where SWOT analysis comes into play – a powerful tool that allows entrepreneurs to uncover the strengths, weaknesses, opportunities, and threats that shape their businesses and shape their individual relations in the network.

The acronyms SWOT, which stands for Strengths, Weaknesses, Opportunities, and Threats, encapsulate a potent tool that entrepreneurs wield to unveil the strategic landscape of their ventures.

SWOT analysis is not just a mundane task to check off a list; it's an art form. It's about peeling back the layers of your venture to reveal its true essence – the vibrant strengths, the subtle weaknesses, the promising opportunities, and the lurking threats. It's a journey of self-discovery and strategic insight that can transform your business into a masterpiece. It’s an art that transforms your venture into a canvas where the strengths are bold strokes of brilliance, weaknesses are gentle nuances to be refined, opportunities are vivid landscapes waiting to be explored, and threats are shadows to be dispelled. It's a symphony of introspection that resonates through the corridors of your business, revealing the melodies of potential and the harmonies of resilience.

Let's start with strengths – the bold strokes on the canvas of your venture. Picture the canvas of your venture, where the strengths are the vibrant colours that define your uniqueness. SWOT analysis empowers you to capitalise on these strengths, to showcase them in the grand gallery of entrepreneurship. It's not just about knowing your strengths; it's about leveraging them to stand tall amidst the competition, to be the masterpiece that captivates the world. It's about harnessing your advantages to stand out in a crowded marketplace and make your mark on the world.

But no venture or individual is without its weaknesses – the shadows that cast doubt on your canvas. SWOT analysis is not about dwelling in darkness but about shining a light on these areas, refining them into strengths. It's about transforming vulnerabilities into opportunities for growth, for improvement. It's the sculptor's chisel, the instrument that shapes your venture into a resilient work of art.

Look beyond the canvas, and you'll see a landscape of opportunities waiting to be explored. SWOT analysis is the explorer's map, guiding you through uncharted territories. It's about seizing opportunities, turning them into stepping stones toward success. It's the compass that ensures you navigate towards prosperity with unwavering precision.

Yet, even in the vast landscape of opportunities, threats lurk. SWOT analysis is the vigilant guardian, the protector of your venture against potential risks. It's not about succumbing to threats but about mitigating them, transforming them into challenges to be conquered. It's the armour that shields your venture from the storms of uncertainty.

Performing a SWOT analysis isn't just a task; it's an awakening, it's a revelation. It empowers entrepreneurs to make informed decisions, capitalise on their strengths, address their weaknesses, seize opportunities, and mitigate threats. It's the cornerstone of a resilient and adaptable business strategy that thrives in the ever-changing landscape of entrepreneurship.

SWOT is a Powerful tool however, when combined with the personality assessment tools like DISC or Wealth dynamics, entrepreneurs gain a deeper understanding of themselves, their team members and the people they collaborate to work as partners enabling a more comprehensive analysis of their strategic position.

Incorporating the tools like DISC analysis, individuals with dominant traits (D) often exhibit assertiveness, confidence, and decisiveness. These qualities translate into strengths for the venture, as dominant individuals excel in leadership roles and are adept at making quick, effective decisions. When conducting a SWOT analysis, recognising these dominant traits can highlight areas where assertive leadership and decisive action can be leveraged for strategic advantage.

On the flip side, individuals with influential traits (I) may encounter weaknesses that could affect the venture. While influential individuals are often charismatic and sociable, they may struggle with attention to detail and prioritising tasks effectively. By identifying these weaknesses through a combined SWOT and DISC analysis, entrepreneurs can implement strategies to mitigate potential risks and enhance overall productivity.

Steady individuals (S) are known for their patience, empathy, and reliability. In the context of a SWOT analysis, these traits can uncover opportunities for building strong, enduring relationships with customers and stakeholders. By recognising the importance of stability and harmony in business relationships, entrepreneurs can capitalise on opportunities to foster long-term partnerships and loyalty.

Lastly, individuals with conscientious traits (C) bring valuable qualities such as attention to detail, analytical thinking, and organisational skills. However, their tendency towards perfectionism and resistance to change can pose threats to the venture. Through a combined SWOT and DISC analysis, entrepreneurs can identify potential threats stemming from overly rigid processes or an aversion to innovation. By addressing these threats proactively, entrepreneurs can foster a culture of adaptability and continuous improvement within their venture.

In essence, combining SWOT analysis with the personality assessment tools like DISC or Wealth dynamics provides a holistic framework for understanding the strategic landscape of a venture. By leveraging the strengths, addressing the weaknesses, seizing the opportunities, and mitigating the threats identified through this combined analysis, entrepreneurs can position their ventures for long-term success and growth.

So, let the SWOT analysis be the artist's brush in your hands, painting a masterpiece that transcends challenges and celebrates victories. As you navigate your venture's strategic landscape, may your SWOT analysis be the compass that guides you towards a future defined by triumph, growth, and enduring success. However, what purpose do these analyses serve if actionable strategies for execution are not developed? Let's delve into the next segment of this chapter to explore the creation of actionable strategies.

Creating Actionable Strategies

Let's explore this fundamental aspect of entrepreneurial success: creating actionable strategies. In the ever-changing landscape of business, having a vision is only part of the equation. The real magic happens when that vision is transformed into actionable steps – tangible plans that lead to real results.

Crafting actionable strategies is the bridge that spans the gap between theory and practice. It's not just about setting goals; it's about formulating clear, tangible steps that align with your aspirations. As you dive into the experiences of these entrepreneurs, you unravel the secrets of how they seamlessly translated their strategic plans into strategies that propelled their ventures towards success. It is like laying the bricks of a sturdy foundation for your business. It's about taking your dreams and breaking them down into manageable tasks, each contributing to the greater goal. It's about clarity, direction, and purpose.

Think of your strategic plan as a treasure map, and actionable strategies as the steps that lead you to the hidden chest of success. An entrepreneur armed with a strategic plan possesses knowledge, but it is the crafting of actionable strategies that transforms that knowledge into power, into the force that propels ventures forward with unyielding momentum.

But why are actionable strategies so important?

Well, imagine setting off on a journey without a map or a compass. You may have a destination in mind, but without a clear plan of action, you're likely to get lost along the way. Actionable strategies provide that map, guiding you through the twists and turns of the entrepreneurial journey.

These strategies help us prioritise your efforts, ensuring that you focus on the tasks that will move us closer to your goals. They also promote accountability, giving us a framework for tracking your progress and holding ourselves – and others – to task.

So, how do you go about creating actionable strategies?

It starts with setting clear goals – defining what you want to achieve and why it matters. From there, you break down those goals into smaller, more manageable tasks, each with its own timeline and set of responsibilities.

You also need to be flexible and adaptable, ready to pivot and adjust your strategies as circumstances change. After all, the business world is nothing if not unpredictable, and the ability to adapt is often the difference between success and failure.

Finally, you must celebrate your successes along the way. Each milestone achieved is a cause for celebration, a reminder of how far you've come and how much further you can go.

Utilise the strengths identified in your SWOT analysis as the building blocks for your actionable strategies. These strengths are not mere observations; they are the tools in your toolkit, the secret weapons that give you an edge in the competitive landscape of entrepreneurship. Crafting actionable strategies is about leveraging those strengths to create a narrative of triumph and prosperity.

Remember, that flexibility and adaptability are the sails that propel your ship in the ever-evolving landscape of entrepreneurship. Actionable strategies are not rigid scripts; they are dynamic plans that adjust to the winds of change. In the face of challenges and opportunities, it's your adaptability that ensures your strategies remain effective and relevant.

Actionable strategies are an art, a symphony of intention and execution. Each strategy you craft is a stroke on the canvas of your venture, painting a picture of growth, resilience, and enduring success.

Let your strategic plan not be confined to paper but manifest into actionable strategies that set your venture on a trajectory of triumph. Let flexibility be your compass, adaptability be your ally, and the actionable strategies you craft be the winds that carry your ship towards success!

Creating actionable strategies is not just about planning; it's about action. It's about taking those first steps towards your goals and then continuing to move forward, one task at a time. So, let's roll up your sleeves, get to work, and turn your dreams into reality.

Flexibility and Adaptability

The ability to be flexible and adaptable is more important than ever before. You live in a time of uncertainty, where the only constant is change. And in the face of this uncertainty, it's those who can embrace flexibility and adaptability who will thrive.

So, what exactly do you mean by flexibility and adaptability?

Flexibility is about being open to change, willing to consider new ideas, and able to adjust your plans when needed. It's about being resilient in the face of challenges and versatile in your approach to problem-solving. Adaptability, on the other hand, is about responding effectively to new situations or challenges by modifying your behaviour, mindset, or strategies. It's about being proactive, resourceful, and quick to learn from your experiences.

In the intricate tapestry of entrepreneurship, a strategic plan is not a rigid script but a dynamic score. Flexibility is the ability to adjust the notes, to change the tempo when the melody of the market shifts unexpectedly. Adaptability is the art of dancing to that evolving tune, navigating the twists and turns with grace and precision. Embracing change is not a sign of weakness; it is the hallmark of strength and foresight. Successful entrepreneurs understand that course correction is not a setback but an opportunity to sail into uncharted waters where treasures of innovation await discovery. It is the pivot that turns challenges into stepping stones and transforms setbacks into comebacks.

Why are these qualities so important?

Well, for starters, they allow us to navigate uncertainty with confidence. In a world where things are constantly changing, being flexible and adaptable means, you can roll with the punches and adjust your course when needed. It also means you're better equipped to embrace change as an opportunity for growth rather than a threat to your stability.

Flexibility and adaptability also enable us to seize opportunities when they arise. In a fast-paced world, opportunities often come out of nowhere, and it's those who are flexible and adaptable who are best positioned to recognise and capitalise on them. By being open-minded and willing to try new things, you increase your chances of success and fulfillment.

But perhaps most importantly, flexibility and adaptability help us build resilience—the ability to bounce back from setbacks or adversity. Life is full of ups and downs, and it's those who can adapt to whatever comes their way who are most likely to come out on top. By cultivating these qualities, you become better equipped to handle whatever life throws at us, knowing that you have the skills and mindset to overcome any obstacle.

So how do you cultivate flexibility and adaptability in your own lives?

It starts with embracing change and staying open-minded. It means being willing to learn new things, try new approaches, and step outside of your comfort zones. It also means being proactive about problem-solving and staying agile in the face of adversity.

Infusing flexibility and adaptability into your strategic plan is not just a strategy; it's a mindset. It positions your venture not as a passive observer but as an active player in the dynamic theatre of business. It is the realisation that in the ever-evolving landscape, the ability to embrace change is the key that unlocks doors to new opportunities.

In the face of uncertainties, flexibility becomes your shield, protecting your venture from the arrows of stagnation. Adaptability becomes your sword, carving a path through the challenges that lie in wait. Together, they form the arsenal that equips your venture to navigate the unpredictable seas, seizing emerging opportunities, and maintaining relevance. The stories of flexibility and adaptability are your guide and the fuel that propels your ship through the turbulent waters of entrepreneurship. As you infuse these virtues into your strategic plan, remember that your venture is not just navigating uncertainties; it is creating waves of innovation, leaving a trail of success in its wake.

Flexibility and adaptability are not just skills; they're attitudes and mindsets that shape how you approach life's challenges and opportunities. By cultivating these qualities, you empower ourselves to navigate uncertainty with confidence, resilience, and a sense of possibility. So, let's embrace the journey, stay flexible, and adapt to whatever comes your way, knowing that your ability to do so will ultimately lead to growth, success, and fulfillment.

Flexibility and adaptability are not just tools; they are the wind that fills your sails and propels your venture towards new horizons of accomplishment and prosperity.

Let your journey be marked not just by the challenges you face but by the adaptability that turns them into triumphs!

Aligning Goals and Objectives

Imagine navigating through uncharted waters with a reliable compass—goals and objectives serve exactly that purpose in the dynamic world of business. They are not just aspirations; they are the practical markers that define where you want to go and how you plan to get there.

Goals give us direction and purpose. They outline the overarching aims of our ventures, providing a clear vision of what you aim to achieve.

Objectives, on the other hand, break down these larger goals into tangible, measurable steps. They guide our day-to-day decisions and actions, ensuring that you stay focused and productive on the path to success. In entrepreneurship, aligning goals and objectives is absolutely crucial. It ensures that every effort you put in, every decision you make, contributes directly to our bigger vision for the business. This alignment is what turns our ideas into reality and our ambitions into achievements.

Consider the remarkable journey of Brian Chesky, the co-founder of Airbnb. Chesky didn't just dream of creating a platform for booking accommodations; he envisioned a global community where travellers could experience unique and authentic stays. His overarching goal was clear: to revolutionise the hospitality industry. To achieve this, Chesky set specific objectives: expanding global reach, enhancing user experience, and fostering community among hosts and guests.

These objectives were meticulously aligned with Airbnb's strategic roadmap, guiding the company's growth and innovation efforts. Through focused determination and strategic planning, Airbnb evolved from a small startup into a global powerhouse valued at billions of dollars.

Aligning goals and objectives isn't just about achieving short-term success; it's about driving continuous growth and fostering innovation. It provides clarity and direction to our entrepreneurial endeavours, helping us navigate through the complexities and uncertainties of the business world.

Setting clear goals and aligning them with actionable objectives is fundamental for entrepreneurial success. They serve as our guiding light, illuminating the path ahead and ensuring that every decision and action you take contributes towards realising our ultimate vision. Whether you're starting a new business, scaling up your current venture, or pursuing ambitious dreams, remember the power of setting clear goals and objectives.

In the realm of entrepreneurship, aligning goals and objectives serves as the guiding compass that steers ventures towards success amidst the unpredictable tides of business. Let's delve deeper into this concept by exploring alternative examples of entrepreneurs who have effectively aligned their goals with their roadmap, illuminating the path to achievement.

Brian Chesky's success with Airbnb, the world's largest online marketplace for lodging and hospitality services, underscores the importance of aligning goals and objectives with a visionary roadmap. Chesky's overarching objective for Airbnb was to create a platform that connected travellers with unique and authentic lodging experiences around the world. To achieve this goal, Chesky set specific objectives such as expanding Airbnb's global reach, enhancing user experience through technology and design, and fostering a sense of community among hosts and guests. These objectives were meticulously aligned with Airbnb's roadmap, guiding the company's strategic initiatives and product development efforts. By aligning goals and objectives, Chesky transformed Airbnb from a small startup operating out of a San Francisco apartment into a hospitality giant valued at billions of dollars.

Aligning goals and objectives is essential for entrepreneurs to navigate the complexities of business and achieve long-term success. By setting overarching objectives and aligning them with specific, actionable goals, entrepreneurs can steer their ventures towards their desired destination with clarity and purpose. As demonstrated by Brian Chesky and other visionary entrepreneurs, aligning goals and objectives is a fundamental strategy for driving growth, fostering innovation, and making a positive impact in the world.

As you navigate your own entrepreneurial journeys, let us embrace the lessons from visionaries like Brian Chesky. Let us adopt a mindset that turns aspirations into achievements, challenges into opportunities, and dreams into reality. Together, let's chart a course towards enduring success with determination, focus, and unwavering belief in our ability to make a difference.

Conclusion & Recap

As you conclude this chapter on crafting a strategic plan, envision yourself not just as a reader but as a strategic architect, equipped with the tools to design a roadmap that leads your venture toward unprecedented success. The Iterative Nature of Success is heavily dependent on Enhanced Strategies. The A2E framework, also called as ABCDE Framework, is more than just a roadmap; it is a guiding philosophy that empowers you and your organisations to master transformative engagements. By systematically progressing through the milestones of Assessing Needs, Building Strategy, Creating Plans, Driving Data, and Evaluating Impact, businesses unlock the potential for sustained success. The adaptability and comprehensiveness of the ABCDE Framework make it a valuable tool for any organisation seeking not just deals but lasting, meaningful transformations. The whole purpose behind this section is to Empower Success Through the ABCDE Framework.

To remind you, I have drafted Volume 2 of "Visions to Victory," which focuses on winning the battle of business success whereas this volume is all about setting the foundation of business success. In Volume 2, you will also embark on an in-depth exploration of A2E framework for business growth uncovered in this volume. Stay tuned for a transformative journey as I unveil the secrets to sustainable growth and success in "Visions to Victory - Vol 2" using the A2E, but once again, If you wish to delve deeper into my thoughts on these concepts and related principles beforehand, feel free to contact me using the various resources provided in this book. If there is high demand, I will include a specific section or even draft an independent book on this topic in the forthcoming volume.

Connect with me on Facebook, LinkedIn, or Instagram or join my webinars, seminars or workshops to share your thoughts and any specific requests. I will do my best to address them in the upcoming volume.

The ABCDE Framework recognises that success is not a one-time event but an ongoing process of improvement. The iterative nature of the framework becomes apparent in the final step, 'Enhance Strategies.' By incorporating lessons learned, adapting strategies for future initiatives, and fostering a culture of continuous improvement, you and your organisations ensure that they are always evolving and staying ahead in the dynamic business landscape. May the insights shared here serve as a beacon, illuminating the path to strategic excellence in your entrepreneurial journey.

Chapter 4.4

Explore the right Business Success Framework

"Success demands more than vision; it requires a structured framework as your blueprint. It saves time and resources by steering you away from trial and error, offering proven strategies and best practices."

SABTOSH KUMAR

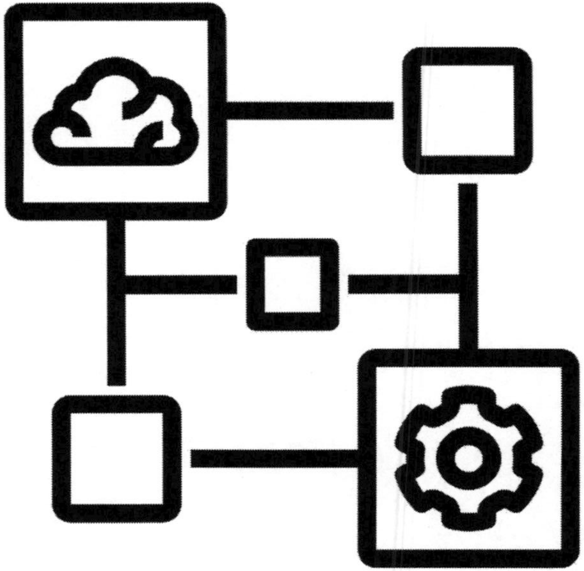

Embarking on the entrepreneurial odyssey necessitates more than a mere vision; it requires a well-structured framework and an understanding of models that have proven effective in navigating the intricate pathways of business. As you delve into this chapter, envision it as a treasure trove of insights drawn from the experiences, learnings, and wisdom shared by mentors, business associates, and accomplished entrepreneurs. Together, let's unravel the intricate tapestry of business success frameworks and models that can serve as your guiding light in the pursuit of triumph.

Unveiling the Business Success Framework

In the dynamic landscape of entrepreneurship, navigating the path to success requires more than just ambition and hard work. It demands a strategic approach, guided by a well-defined framework that serves as a roadmap for sustainable growth. This framework, akin to a meticulously designed blueprint, draws from the collective wisdom and experiences of seasoned entrepreneurs who have charted their own paths to success.

At the core of any robust business success framework lie several essential components, each playing a pivotal role in shaping the trajectory of a venture. Strategic planning stands as the cornerstone, serving as the guiding force behind every decision and action taken by the business. It involves a comprehensive analysis of market dynamics, competitor landscapes, and emerging trends, allowing entrepreneurs to identify opportunities and mitigate risks effectively.

However, strategic planning alone is not sufficient to ensure success. Goal setting emerges as another critical element within the framework, providing entrepreneurs with a clear direction and purpose. By establishing SMART (Specific, Measurable, Achievable, Relevant, Time-bound) goals, businesses can align their efforts towards tangible outcomes, track progress, and celebrate milestones along the way. Moreover, setting long-term visions alongside short-term objectives allows for a balanced approach that fosters both innovation and execution.

Furthermore, the establishment of core principles forms the bedrock upon which a business operates. These principles encompass values, ethics, and beliefs that define the company's culture and guide decision-making processes. By adhering to a set of core principles, entrepreneurs cultivate trust, integrity, and transparency, thereby fostering strong relationships with stakeholders and fostering a positive organisational culture.

Understanding and implementing a business success framework empowers entrepreneurs to build a solid foundation for their ventures. It provides clarity of purpose, ensuring that every step taken aligns with the overarching objectives of the business. Moreover, it fosters adaptability and resilience, enabling entrepreneurs to navigate through challenges and seize opportunities as they arise.

In essence, a robust business success framework serves as a compass, guiding entrepreneurs through the complexities of the business landscape. By incorporating strategic planning, goal setting, and the establishment of core principles, entrepreneurs can forge a path towards sustainable growth and enduring success in their entrepreneurial journey.

Exploring Proven Business Models

In the expansive realm of entrepreneurship, navigating the maze of business models is akin to embarking on a journey through a labyrinth of possibilities. Over time, certain business models have emerged as stalwarts, proving their resilience and adaptability in the face of evolving market dynamics. By delving into the experiences of successful entrepreneurs who have harnessed these models, aspiring business owners can glean invaluable insights into their nuances and potential applications.

One such model that has gained prominence in recent years is the subscription-based model. This model, characterised by recurring revenue streams from subscribers who pay a periodic fee for access to a product or service, has revolutionised industries ranging from entertainment to software. By examining case studies of companies like Netflix and Spotify, entrepreneurs can unravel the strategies behind building a loyal subscriber base, optimising pricing structures, and continuously delivering value to customers to ensure long-term retention.

Similarly, the freemium model has garnered attention for its ability to attract a wide user base through a free offering while Monetising through premium features or upgrades. Companies such as Dropbox and LinkedIn have successfully leveraged this model to scale their user acquisition and drive revenue growth. By dissecting the intricacies of freemium offerings, entrepreneurs can learn how to strike a delicate balance between providing value for free and incentivising users to upgrade to paid tiers.

Moreover, with the proliferation of e-commerce, understanding the nuances of online retail models is essential for entrepreneurs looking to carve a niche in the digital marketplace. Whether it's the direct-to-consumer (DTC) model embraced by brands like Warby Parker and Casper or the marketplace model exemplified by Amazon and eBay, each approach comes with its own set of opportunities and challenges. By analysing success stories and pitfalls within the e-commerce landscape, entrepreneurs can devise strategies to optimise their online storefronts, enhance customer experiences, and drive sustainable growth in an increasingly competitive environment.

Learning from proven business models equips aspiring entrepreneurs with a diverse toolkit, allowing them to select or adapt a model that aligns with their venture's unique needs and industry dynamics. By drawing inspiration from the experiences of trailblazing companies and understanding the principles that underpin their success, entrepreneurs can chart a course towards building resilient, scalable businesses that stand the test of time.

The Lean Startup Methodology

In the dynamic landscape of entrepreneurship, where uncertainties loom large and the path to success is often obscured by ambiguity, the Lean Startup methodology has emerged as a guiding light for aspiring founders and seasoned entrepreneurs alike. Rooted in the principles of agility, experimentation, and customer-centricity, this transformative approach has revolutionised the way startups conceptualise, develop, and scale their ventures. By delving into real-world applications of the Lean Startup methodology, entrepreneurs can glean invaluable insights into its practical implications and transformative potential.

At the heart of the Lean Startup methodology lies the concept of iterative development. Rather than adhering to traditional, linear approaches to product development, Lean Startup advocates for a process of continuous iteration and refinement. Entrepreneurs embark on a series of rapid experiments, using minimum viable products (MVPs) to test hypotheses, gather feedback, and iterate based on real-world data. By embracing this iterative approach, startups can rapidly validate assumptions, identify product-market fit, and course-correct in real-time, minimising the risk of investing time and resources in misguided ventures.

Moreover, validated learning is a cornerstone of the Lean Startup methodology. Instead of relying solely on intuition or gut instincts, entrepreneurs leverage data-driven insights to inform decision-making and drive progress. By deploying experiments designed to validate or invalidate key hypotheses, startups can gather actionable feedback from customers, iterate on their offerings, and pivot in response to market demand. This relentless focus on validated learning empowers entrepreneurs to make informed decisions, mitigate risks, and optimise resource allocation, thereby maximising their chances of success in an uncertain environment.

Central to the Lean Startup methodology is a relentless focus on customer feedback. By prioritising the needs, preferences, and pain points of their target audience, entrepreneurs can develop products and services that resonate deeply with customers and address genuine market needs. Through techniques such as customer interviews, surveys, and usability testing, startups can gather qualitative and quantitative feedback, iterate on their offerings, and continuously refine their value proposition. By placing the customer at the centre of the product development process, entrepreneurs can foster a culture of empathy, responsiveness, and customer-centricity that drives long-term success.

Integrating the Lean Startup methodology into your approach enhances adaptability, reduces risks, and accelerates the development of a product or service that resonates with your target audience. By embracing iterative development, validated learning, and a relentless focus on customer feedback, entrepreneurs can navigate uncertainties with confidence, pivot with agility, and ultimately build scalable, sustainable ventures that thrive in today's rapidly evolving marketplace.

The Franchise Model

For those seeking a proven path to entrepreneurship, the franchise model stands as a compelling option for aspiring business owners who seek a proven path to success. By delving into the intricacies of the franchise model, entrepreneurs can uncover valuable insights gleaned from the experiences of those who have ventured into this realm. This approach offers a structured framework that leverages the established brand recognition, operational systems, and support networks of a franchisor, providing franchisees with a roadmap for business ownership and growth.

At its core, the franchise model represents a symbiotic relationship between franchisors and franchisees. Franchisors, typically established brands with a successful track record, grant franchisees the right to operate under their brand name and utilise their proven business model in exchange for an initial investment, ongoing fees, and adherence to established standards. In return, franchisees gain access to a well-established brand identity, marketing support, operational guidance, and economies of scale, minimising the risks inherent in starting a new business from scratch.

One of the key benefits of the franchise model is the balance it strikes between autonomy and adherence to established brand standards. While franchisees maintain a degree of independence in day-to-day operations, they must also adhere to strict guidelines and standards set forth by the franchisor. This balance ensures consistency across franchise locations, safeguarding the integrity of the brand and maintaining a cohesive customer experience. By navigating this delicate balance, franchisees can capitalise on the benefits of brand recognition while still exercising autonomy in decision-making and business management.

Exploring the franchise model provides valuable insights into a structured approach to entrepreneurship. Unlike independent startups, franchisees benefit from the support and guidance of a proven business model, comprehensive training programmes, and ongoing operational support from the franchisor. This structured approach streamlines the process of launching and operating a business, minimising the learning curve and accelerating the path to profitability.

Furthermore, the franchise model offers entrepreneurs the opportunity to tap into established brand recognition and consumer trust, reducing the time and resources required to build brand awareness from scratch. By aligning themselves with a well-known brand, franchisees can leverage existing marketing campaigns, customer loyalty programmes, and brand messaging to attract and retain customers, driving revenue and profitability from day one.

In essence, the franchise model represents a win-win proposition for both franchisors and franchisees. Franchisors expand their brand presence and market reach through the growth of their franchise network, while franchisees gain access to a turnkey business opportunity with built-in support and resources. By embracing the franchise model, entrepreneurs can embark on their journey to business ownership with confidence, leveraging the power of established brands and operational frameworks to achieve success in their chosen industry.

The Platform Business Model

In the digital age, platform businesses have emerged as dominant forces across a myriad of industries, revolutionising traditional business models and reshaping the way value is created and exchanged. By delving into the experiences of entrepreneurs who have successfully built and scaled platform-based ventures, you can gain invaluable insights into the dynamics of this innovative business model.

At its core, the platform business model revolves around creating and facilitating interactions between two or more distinct groups of users, often referred to as "sides" of the platform. These interactions generate value for all participants and create what is known as a network effect, where the platform becomes more valuable to users as more participants join and engage with it.

One of the key challenges in building a platform-based venture lies in fostering user engagement and incentivising participation from both sides of the platform. Successful entrepreneurs understand the importance of designing user experiences that are intuitive, seamless, and compelling, enticing users to actively participate and contribute to the platform's ecosystem. Whether it's through gamification, social features, or personalised recommendations, effective engagement strategies are essential for driving user adoption and retention.

Furthermore, maintaining a delicate balance between supply and demand is critical for the long-term success of a platform business. Entrepreneurs must carefully manage the dynamics of supply and demand, ensuring that there are enough providers (suppliers, sellers, creators) to meet the needs and preferences of users (buyers, consumers, subscribers), and vice versa. This involves implementing strategies to attract and onboard new users while also incentivising providers to join and remain active on the platform.

Moreover, understanding the nuances of creating a network effect is essential for driving growth and scalability in a platform-based venture. Entrepreneurs must focus on expanding the reach and engagement of their platform, leveraging technology and data analytics to identify opportunities for optimisation and enhancement. By continuously refining and iterating on their platform's features and functionality, entrepreneurs can create a virtuous cycle of value creation that attracts and retains users over time.

Grasping the intricacies of the platform business model equips entrepreneurs with insights into leveraging technology to create scalable and sustainable ventures. By studying real-world examples of successful platform-based businesses, aspiring entrepreneurs can gain valuable lessons and best practices for building and scaling their own platform ventures in today's digital economy. Whether it's through fostering user engagement, managing supply and demand dynamics, or creating a network effect, mastering the platform business model opens up new opportunities for innovation and growth in the digital age.

Conclusion & Recap

In essence, the exploration of business success frameworks and models is not a mere academic exercise; it is a practical guide infused with the collective wisdom of those who have navigated the dynamic landscape of entrepreneurship. As you absorb these insights, envision your venture as a canvas where you can paint with the hues of strategic planning, proven business models, and innovative methodologies. May this chapter serve as your compass, guiding you toward a business framework that not only ensures success but propels you toward the pinnacle of your entrepreneurial aspirations.

To remind you, I have drafted Volume 2 of "Visions to Victory," which focuses on winning the battle of business success whereas this volume is all about setting the foundation of business success. In Volume 2, you will also embark on an in-depth exploration of A2E framework for business growth uncovered in this volume. Stay tuned for a transformative journey as I unveil the secrets to sustainable growth and success in "Visions to Victory - Vol 2" using the A2E, but once again, If you wish to delve deeper into my thoughts on these concepts and related principles beforehand, feel free to contact me using the various resources provided in this book. If there is high demand, I will include a specific section or even draft an independent book on this topic in the forthcoming volume.

Connect with me on Facebook, LinkedIn, or Instagram or join my webinars, seminars or workshops to share your thoughts and any specific requests. I will do my best to address them in the upcoming volume.

As you conclude this chapter, marking the logical end of your inaugural section, THE FOUNDATION, let's reflect on its essence through a summary Section 1: The Foundation - Laying the Groundwork for Success

Join the "Visions to Victory" Facebook Group

https://www.facebook.com/groups/visionstovictory/

What Do I Bring To You with Facebook group?

Embark on an exclusive journey with me within the vibrant community of the "Visions To Victory" Facebook group! Here, you are not just spectators; you are active participants in a world of unparalleled insights and personalised connections.

Unlock Exclusive Insights and dive deep into unique perspectives, strategies, and advice that extend beyond the ordinary. In the " Visions To Victory " group, I share insider knowledge reserved solely for your cherished members.

Get Direct Access to Wisdom and have direct access to the minds behind the brilliance. Engage in live Q&A sessions, seek personalised guidance, and connect on a level that transcends the traditional online experience.

Forge Meaningful Connections as this isn't just a group; it's a thriving community. Connect with like-minded individuals, share experiences, and collaborate in a space where networking is more than just a buzzword—it's a vibrant reality.

Be the First to Know and stay ahead of the curve with early access to cutting-edge content. Whether it's exclusive articles, sneak peeks, or advanced media, you get a front-row seat to what's next.

Get Tailored Resources at Your Fingertips and access resources curated to meet your specific needs and interests. From practical tools to insightful templates, you provide more than just information—you provide solutions.

Get Exclusive Events Unveiled and brace yourself for exclusive events, from riveting webinars to hands-on workshops, all within the confines of this private group. Elevate your learning experience and make every moment count.

Experience the power of a supportive community that goes beyond online interactions. Share challenges, seek advice, and revel in your successes with a group that utterly understands.

Get Special Offers Just for You. As a part of the "Visions To Victory " community, enjoy special offers, discounts, and exclusive opportunities that add an extra layer of excitement to your journey with us.

Ready to redefine your online experience? Join the "Visions To Victor " Facebook group and immerse yourself in a world where engagement knows no bounds!

SECTION 5

Fortifying your Business Future with COGS of Success

Navigating Watch Mechanics

The magical power behind timekeeping.

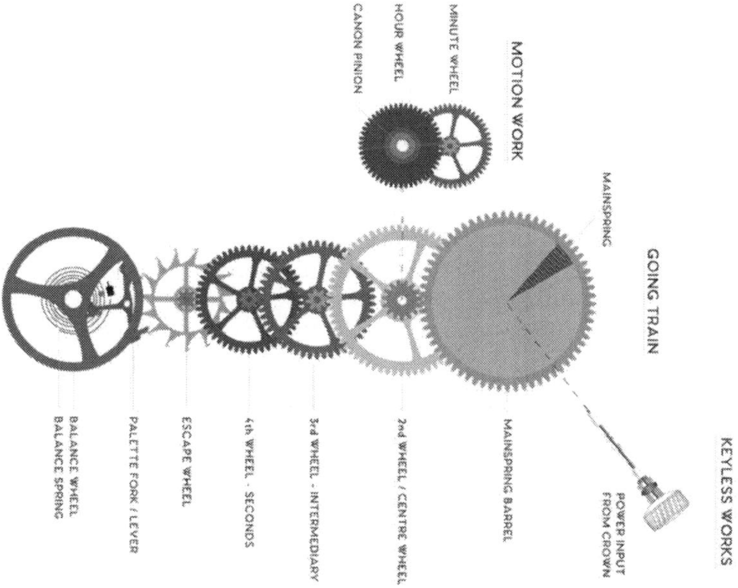

Source: www.marloewatchcompany.com/blogs/news/what-do-all-those-cogs-do

Before I began my first corporate job with Johnson & Johnson as a management trainee in 1998, I had gained valuable experience running my own business as a side hustle supported by my father from 1992 to 1998. This business operated in the evenings after college hours. Additionally, during summer holidays, I worked with Standard Chartered Bank selling credit cards on commission-only jobs with my college friends for fun during the day. This diverse experience gave me an advantage when working with the leadership team at Johnson & Johnson, helping me understand international business operations deeply. It was a period of intense learning, driven by curiosity and reminiscent of falling down the rabbit hole like Alice in Wonderland. Throughout my corporate career, I supported and worked with many national and international businesses across various industries, from manufacturing to FMCG, to the government agencies, financial sectors, third world companies and many more. So far, I have worked with businesses operating from locations such as India, Hong Kong, the USA, UK, Australia, Middle East and many other such locations as part of the management team in my consulting careers. I gained invaluable lessons from top consultants and companies around the world, implementing budgets worth millions and billions of pounds annually. I had the privilege to learn and become part of the operations and mechanisms of FTSE 500 companies, gaining insights into key concepts and methods rarely exposed even with significant investment in startups.

Some people now say I am lucky to have my hand in multiple businesses and to be part of Forbes business council. Although I managed my first business with my father from 1992 to 1998 as a side hustle, when I started my own independent business in February 2007 to develop a software product for the insurance industry while still employed, it became a journey of exploration, courage, and the pursuit of dreams fuelled by a strong burning desire. Unfortunately, it turned into the biggest failure of my life at that time, hiring and firing three employees and losing £67,000 of investment along with enduring eight months of sleepless nights. Despite this setback, I was determined not to give up on my dreams.

My dad used to say, "Failure is a part of life; it's better to try and fail to learn the lessons than not to take part in the race of life. Failure is the greatest teacher. The key is to ensure that the lessons learned outweigh the losses." He continued, "First, make sure you learn from those mistakes and don't repeat them. Second, if you lose millions in failures, ensure you gain lessons worth billions. Lastly, don't let your failures stop you; get up stronger and run faster."

"If you follow these 3 rules of life with strong mindset and positive attitude, nothing can stop you from becoming the winner of your life.", He Added.

In 2008, I grasped the true meaning of this lesson and became even more determined. I resigned from my employment and left it in February 2009 with a strong mindset of embarking on a journey of creating stories and building brands, starting six businesses by 2012. Unfortunately, when I left my job, the universe was in deep recession, money circulation was constrained and five of my businesses collapsed in first five years, resulting in a loss of around a quarter of a million pounds. I managed to balance my life while taking on some small temporary assignments to support the family and business along with ensuring that my thirty-seven employees keep on receiving their salaries to run their families, all without them knowing about the challenges the business was facing, along with many other difficulties and setbacks.

One of my key lessons from life is that we always have two choices at any point: we can either look at the challenges and blame everything on other factors such as luck, weather, government, politics and the people around us, or we can take accountability and ownership on ourselves and, find a way to manoeuvre the roadblocks and bumps on the road to make our own ways, and make progress.

However, these failures and losses of quarter of million pounds taught me invaluable lessons, frameworks, and strategies worth quarter of a billion pounds. I implemented these insights, framework and models into eight startups between 2012 and 2016, and all these startups are still operational till today. Some of the brands have changed from sole trading to limited companies now. Let me try to highlight the role of one of these key concepts using Harmony Watches Inc. as an example to illustrate this key concepts of the cycle of success that I learned during this journey.

The Symphony of Success: The COGS of Prosperity

Harmony Watches Inc. was the company that stood out amidst the competition in the bustling town of Prosperity. Led by the charismatic CEO, Charlie, Harmony Watches wasn't just another business – it was a beacon of innovation, luxury, and precision. But what truly set Harmony Watches apart wasn't just Charlie's leadership; it was the seamless harmony among the different business units and its members, each a master in their own right.

Fredy, the Finance Director, was the silent hero behind the scenes. With his eagle-eyed focus on numbers and a knack for financial strategy, he ensured that the finances of Harmony Watches were always in top shape, laying a sturdy foundation for growth and success.

Peter, the Production Director, was the wizard of production and delivery. His keen eye for detail and commitment to quality meant that every timepiece leaving Harmony Watches Inc.'s workshops was nothing short of perfection. Customers knew they could trust the brand, thanks to Peter's dedication to excellence.

Alex, the Advertising extraordinaire, was the creative force behind the captivating Advertising campaigns of Harmony Watches. With his innovative ideas and flair for storytelling, he brought the company's luxury timepieces to life, captivating audiences and leaving a lasting impression in their minds.

Palak, the Promotions Director, was the mastermind behind the irresistible deals and offers that drew watch enthusiasts in droves. Her strategic promotions complemented Alex's advertising efforts, creating a powerful one-two punch that kept customers coming back for more.

Beccy, the Brand Director, was the guardian of the identity of Harmony Watches. With her deep understanding of luxury markets and consumer psychology, she crafted a brand image that resonated with customers on a personal level, turning them into loyal advocates for the company.

Mohit, the Marketing and Messaging Director, was the wordsmith who breathed life into the brand message of Harmony Watches. His carefully crafted messaging conveyed the company's values and dedication to craftsmanship in a way that resonated with customers, forging deep emotional connections that went beyond mere timekeeping.

Sarah, the Sales Director, was the face of Harmony Watches to its clients and partners. With her impeccable style and persuasive charm, she forged strong relationships that drove sales and revenue, propelling the company to new heights of success.

Overseeing the intricacies of day-to-day operations was Oliver, the Operations Manager. His meticulous planning and strategic foresight ensured that workshops of Harmony Watches ran like a well-oiled machine, optimising efficiency and driving productivity.

Ian, the IT and Business Change Director at Harmony Watches, led a pivotal technological transformation. His expertise in automation and technology enhanced efficiency across departments, improving precision in production and operations while boosting overall time and quality standards.

Ian's initiatives empowered team members, driving innovation and process streamlining. He played a key role in driving business growth, ensuring competitive advantage, managing risk and compliance, achieving substantial cost savings, and enhancing customer service. Leveraging technology for efficiency, innovation, customer experience, and data utilisation, process automation and technology advancement Ian contributed significantly to sustainable growth and competitive edge of Harmony Watches.

And finally, there was Christine, the Customer Services Director, whose dedication to customer satisfaction turned first-time buyers into lifelong fans. Her personalised service and attention to detail were the embodiment of their commitment to luxury and exclusivity.

Together, Charlie and his team of talented individuals formed a symphony of success, each playing their part in perfect harmony. Their collective efforts didn't just drive profits; they inspired loyalty, fostered innovation, and made Harmony Watches a sought-after name in the world of luxury timepieces. As the sun set on another successful day at Harmony Watches, Charlie couldn't help but feel grateful for the incredible team that made it all possible. And with their unwavering dedication and boundless passion, he knew that the best was yet to come for Harmony Watches.

Hope life was so simple for everyone, but In the vast world of business, reaching the top can feel like climbing Ben Navis, the highest mountain in UK, without a map. Achieving success is often seen as a tough goal pursued by companies of all shapes and sizes across various industries. What if reaching the summit wasn't just about luck or hard work, but about having a thorough framework made up of blueprints, roadmaps, strategies, tactics, and a robust plan to guide you every step of the way?

What if success isn't just an end goal but instead a well-planned journey, guided by a comprehensive model? That's where the COGS of Success comes in – it's like having a detailed business success System with a roadmap that helps you stay on track and make the right decisions as you navigate through the twists and turns of business life on the similar lines of harmony Watch. It's a concept that emphasises strategic alignment, careful planning, and adaptability to navigate the intricacies of the business world.

LET'S DIVE IN...

Chapter 5.1:

Unlock the Puzzle: Revealing the COGS of Success

The Ant & the Grasshopper

In a sunny meadow, there lived an ant and a grasshopper. The ant was diligent, spending his days collecting food and preparing for the winter ahead. The grasshopper, on the other hand, preferred to sing and dance, enjoying the warmth of the summer sun.

As the days grew shorter and the air turned colder, the ant continued his preparations, storing away food for the winter. But the grasshopper laughed at the ant's efforts, believing there was still plenty of time before the cold weather arrived.

When winter finally came, the grasshopper found himself hungry and cold, with no food or shelter to keep him warm. Desperate and shivering, he approached the ant's cozy home.

"Please, can you spare some food and shelter?" begged the grasshopper.

The ant, although sympathetic, reminded the grasshopper of his folly.

"Throughout the summer, I worked hard to prepare for the winter ahead," said the ant. "While you sang and danced, you failed to plan for the future. Now, you must suffer the consequences of your lack of preparation."

And so, the grasshopper learned a valuable lesson about the importance of planning and preparation.

A well planned and robust roadmap for the future is a must have requirement to face the life challenges and uncertainties, Just like the ant. Those who fail to plan for future will face the consequences of this lack of preparation sooner or later but by that time they realise it, it could be too late. So, let us heed the ant's example and strive to plan ahead, ensuring a secure and prosperous future for ourselves.

This section is not just about getting ready for the journey ahead; it's about fortifying yourself with the knowledge and strategies that will serve as the shield and Armor in the face of challenges. As you are navigating through the pages of "From Visions to Victory," I'm eager to keep sharing with you the invaluable insights accumulated from mentors, business associates, and fellow entrepreneurs who have illuminated the path of preparation.

Fortifying Your Journey: From Visions to Victory

The journey of any success starts by having the vision and idea followed by the understanding of your current situation and your desired destination. Determine where you stand as of now based on specific key indicators tailored to your requirements. These might include trading history, number of employees, business turnover, profitability, or a combination of these factors.

Once you grasp your current position, understand the key questionnaire to help you find out your Business Stage and where you want to be. Please be aware that the criteria to classify a business may differ from country to country or from person to person. The "Visions to Victory" workbook I devised along with this framework and questionnaires offers comprehensive tools to suit your needs. Reach out to me and I will share this with you or you can get this under resources section in members area of website. You can easily and quickly customise this questionnaires to fit your requirements using simplified steps. Even though the choice of questionnaires may vary, the framework remains consistent and will help you fulfil your needs. Let's delve into each aspect of preparation:

Picture this: You're a company, big or small, in any industry imaginable. You've got dreams of making it bigger and taking it to next level, but you know it's not going to happen overnight. So, instead of just winging it and hoping for the best like grasshopper, you decide to be smart about it like the Ant.

You focus on strategic alignment – making sure that every part of your business is working together towards the same goals. You plan meticulously like the ant, thinking about every possible scenario and how you'll tackle it. Your worked the **Visionary Thinking** Model and Embraced this concept by setting clear, specific goals and visualising them as already accomplished. Mentally, you traverse the entire path, envisioning the journey with vivid imagination and utilising tools and KPIs on paper to navigate. This process is called Visualisation which helps you create a **Clear Mental Image of what you want and how you will reach their.** A detailed and vivid mental image of what one desires is crucial for manifesting wealth.

This image acts as a blueprint for the creation process. You analyse the twists and turns of the business landscape, encountering expected challenges and devising contingencies for unforeseen obstacles. Most importantly, you remain adaptable, prepared to adjust course if circumstances deviate from the plan, while following a roadmap that countless business owners have traversed before you. And eventually you completed the journey of your business success once virtually. The beauty of nature is that we all have this immense visualisation power within ourselves, but everyone uses it according to their thoughts and beliefs. Most of the time, we don't use it because we are not aware of the power within. Think about the last time you visualised success—whether in your career, relationships, or personal goals. What did you see? What did you feel? Visualisation allows us to tap into the creative power of our subconscious mind, programming it with positive images and beliefs that propel us towards our aspirations.

Consider what happens when embarking on a journey for the first time. Doubts arise, uncertainties lurk around every part of the way, confidence may falter, and myriad other concerns may surface. Now, envision embarking on the same journey a second time. Suddenly, the path seems familiar, confidence grows, and a sense of assurance prevails.

That's the essence of visionary thinking and visualisation—a powerful tool that allows us to embark on a journey mentally before taking it physically for the first time, preparing us for subsequent travels. Undoubtedly, familiarity breeds confidence.

But how does one achieve such a roadmap and replicate this experience?

That's the COGS of Success in action – it's about having a clear strategy, careful planning, and the flexibility to adjust as needed. With these tools in your toolkit, you're not just chasing success – you're building a solid foundation for it, one step at a time.

Deciphering COGS of Success

If you can utilise your visualisation power, you can draw parallels between the successful functioning of a business and the intricate workings of a watch, using the concept of COGS as your guide. Let's break down what COGS is all about.

COGS of Success is akin to the blueprint that guides a business towards success. It's essentially a business success model and a detailed plan outlining how businesses can grow and thrive. It's not just any plan – it's an ecosystem of business components within a broader Business Success Model.

Much like the intricate mechanism of a watch, COGS serves as a dynamic and adaptable framework for success. It's not merely a static plan; rather, it's a toolkit comprising various components that form the building blocks of a successful strategy. Think of it as a dynamic model that helps companies assess their current position, define short and long-term goals, and determine the actions needed to excel in the business world.

Now, this toolkit is made up of different parts, or "components," if you like. These components are like building blocks that help put together a strategy for success.

In the realm of business, these components cover all the important areas of a business, like branding, marketing, finance, sales, operations, and so on. They are like the gears in a watch, each playing a crucial role in driving the overall functionality and success of the enterprise. Just as the gears work in harmony within the watch mechanism, the components of COGS collaborate to orchestrate triumph in the corporate arena.

Here's where the analogy truly shines: just as watches come in various shapes, sizes, and designs, COGS isn't a one-size-fits-all solution. Nope, it's flexible. It can be adjusted to fit the specific needs and challenges of different audience. After all, what works for one business might not work for another. It's not only flexible but its capable of being tailored to fit the unique needs and challenges of different businesses. Much like how a watchmaker adjusts the components to suit the specific design and functionality of each timepiece, businesses can customise COGS to align with their individual goals and circumstances.

So, think of COGS as a guidebook and a rulebook of scientific patterns that helps companies figure out their own path to success. It's like having a roadmap that you can customise to suit your own journey. And with COGS by your side, you're better equipped to navigate the twists and turns of the corporate world and come out on top. But before you delve into the intricacies of this chapter, let's first visualise and understand the key components of a watch and the COGS of Success Model.

What is COGS of SUCCESS

Let me introduce you to the concept of the COGS of Success, which is a dynamic and adaptable Business Success Model. The COGS of Success is a framework and is a must have framework for any and every business irrespective of their shape and size. It identifies and defines the fundamental components necessary for achieving success in a business context and taking them to next stage of their journey.

COGS, an acronym for "Components of Growth Strategies", embodies a comprehensive model crafted to illuminate the path to success in business and entrepreneurial endeavours. COGS of success is the short form of the phrase "Components of Growth Strategies of success" and encapsulates a proprietary and innovative framework designed to provide entrepreneurs with a sustainable roadmap towards success.

Each COG or component represents a crucial element that contributes to the overall growth and prosperity of an enterprise. To understand this concept in details, let's extend the visualisation of the mechanical marvel of making of a watch and understand how it works in order to draw an apparel between the COGs of Success and it's components.

Navigating the COGS of Business Success

Think of COGS as a handbook or the formula book for businesses, offering a tailored roadmap to navigate the complexities of the corporate world. Just like an exquisitely crafted watch ensures precise timekeeping, COGS empowers companies to tackle the challenges of business, guiding them towards success. With COGS as their guiding principle, businesses can fine-tune their strategies, adapt to changing environments, and excel in a competitive market.

COGS represents a robust framework around top three essential factors: Strategies, Blueprint, and Roadmap. These factors provides a structured approach to strategic planning, organisational structure, and adaptability, respectively.

The first layer, Core COGS, emphasises strategic alignment, planning, and the success of PEOPLE, encompassing both internal and external stakeholders. Customer Success is highlighted as a crucial aspect, underlining the importance of fostering positive relationships with both internal and external customers. The second layer, Inner Rim COGS, consists of immediate operational elements essential for business success, including IT & Business Change, Finance, Production, and Marketing, among others. Each element plays a unique role in contributing to efficiency and competitiveness. The third layer, Outer Rim COGS, became indispensable as you and your organisations expands, supporting scaling efforts and addressing secondary business units' needs.

The COGS of Success wheel underscored the harmonious interplay between these divisions, forming a symphony that created a resilient organisation capable of adapting to change and achieving success. It also discussed the model's applicability across diverse industries, highlighting its flexibility and scalability.

The COGS of Success wheel is a cornerstone for building a successful business, providing a roadmap to navigate entrepreneurship's challenges. By following the COGS principles, businesses can manage resources, mitigate risks, and overcome obstacles effectively. This approach not only saves energy, money, and sleepless nights but also paves a clear path towards goals. In Section 6, you'll explore the specifics of the COGS of Success wheel further.

By incorporating strategic alignment, meticulous planning, and adaptability, this model equips businesses with the tools they need to turn aspirations into tangible success. In the ever-evolving landscape of business, the COGS of Success offer a compass for those ready to embark on the transformative journey to triumph. You will explore about this concept in detail in next section.

Inside the Mechanical Marvel: How a Watch Works

In the intricate world of watchmaking, a mechanical movement stands as a testament to the marvels of engineering. Let's delve into the inner workings of these timepieces to uncover the intricate ballet of gears and springs that bring them to life.

The Heart of the Watch: The Mainspring Barrel - At the core of a mechanical watch lies the mainspring barrel, akin to the beating heart of the timepiece. This barrel houses a tightly coiled mainspring, crafted from resilient spring steel, poised to unleash its potential energy. But how does this energy translate into the steady rhythm of timekeeping?

The Dance of Gears: Regulating Time - As the mainspring unwinds, its energy is harnessed by a series of gears, each meticulously calibrated to turn at specific rates. An individual gear is also referred as COG by many. These gears form an intricate network, with the second wheel driving the third, and so on. Through this ballet of gearwork, the energy is channelled to various components of the watch, including the hour and minute hands that grace the dial.

The Maestro of Time: The Balance Wheel - Amidst this symphony of gears stands the balance wheel, a mesmerising component that captivates with its rhythmic oscillations. Paired with the pallet fork and escape wheel in what's known as the escapement, the balance wheel acts as the conductor, regulating the release of energy from the mainspring. With each swing of the palette fork, the escape wheel engages, orchestrating the precise passage of time.

Bringing Time to Life: Your Role in the Process - Yet, the magic of a mechanical watch doesn't stop with its intricate mechanisms. You, the wearer, play a crucial role in the watch's operation. By turning the crown, you infuse the mainspring barrel with your energy, setting the stage for the watch to spring to life and fulfil its timeless purpose.

In the realm of watchmaking, a mechanical movement is not merely a collection of gears and springs; it's a symphony of precision and craftsmanship. From the coiled mainspring to the mesmerising dance of the balance wheel, each component plays its part in the timeless dance of timekeeping. So, the next time you glance at your wristwatch, take a moment to appreciate the intricate beauty of its inner workings—a testament to human ingenuity and the enduring allure of mechanical mastery.

The Components of a Watch

Referring to the diagram label as "Navigating the Watch Mechanism" In the context of watches and at the start of this section, the "COGS" analogy can be extended to represent different aspects or components of the watch mechanism. Let's break down the COGS of a watch mechanism to understand it's key parts:

1. Main Spring: This is the primary power source of mechanical watches. It's like the engine of the watch, storing energy that is gradually released to power the movement.

2. Balance Wheel and Escapement: These components regulate the release of energy from the mainspring, ensuring that it is distributed evenly to power the movement of the watch hands.

3. Gear Train: Similar to the transmission system in a car, the gear train consists of a series of gears that transmit power from the mainspring to various parts of the watch, such as the hands and other complications.

4. Escapement Mechanism: This is a crucial component of the watch movement that controls the release of energy from the mainspring in precise increments, allowing for accurate timekeeping.

5. Pallet Fork: Working in conjunction with the escapement wheel, the pallet fork controls the movement of the gear train and ensures that the energy released from the mainspring is utilised efficiently.

6. Jewels/Bearings: These are small synthetic rubies or sapphires used as bearings in the movement to reduce friction and wear, ensuring smooth operation and longevity of the watch mechanism.

7. Regulator: The regulator is a device used to adjust the rate at which the watch movement runs, allowing for fine-tuning of the timekeeping accuracy.

8. Balance Spring: Also known as the hairspring, this component regulates the oscillation of the balance wheel, further enhancing the accuracy of the watch.

9. Complications: These are additional features or functions beyond basic timekeeping, such as chronographs, calendars, moon phases, and tourbillons, adding complexity and functionality to the watch mechanism.

10. Case and Dial: While not part of the internal mechanism, the case and dial provide the housing and display for the watch mechanism, protecting it from external elements and allowing for easy readability of the time. These different "parts" of COGS of watch mechanism represent the various components and scientific mechanisms that work together harmoniously to drive the functionality and performance of a watch.

The Components of a Business

Similar to COGs of watch mechanism, in the seance of Business Growth, following list outlines key components crucial for the success of a business, known as COGS (Components of Growth Strategies). Each component represents a fundamental aspect of business operations and strategy, Let's break down the COGS of a business success and visualise to understand it's key parts.

1. Customer Servicing / PEOPLE: Ensuring excellent customer service and fostering a positive relationship with clients through effective communication and support.

2. IT & Business Change or Digital Landscape: Embracing technological advancements and adapting to changes in the digital landscape to drive innovation and improve business processes.

3. Finance: Managing financial resources effectively, including budgeting, forecasting, and financial reporting, to support strategic decision-making and ensure financial stability.

4. Production: Overseeing the manufacturing process to ensure the timely and efficient production of goods or services while maintaining quality standards.

5. Delivery and distribution: Managing the logistics and transportation of products to ensure timely delivery and distribution of products and services to customers and optimise supply chain efficiency.

6. Branding: Developing and maintaining a strong brand identity to differentiate the company from competitors and build brand loyalty among customers.

7. Advertising: Developing creative advertising campaigns to raise brand awareness and attract potential customers through various channels.

8. Promotions: Planning and executing promotional activities to stimulate sales and encourage customer engagement, such as discounts, coupons, or special events.

9. Marketing: Developing comprehensive marketing strategies to identify target markets, promote products or services, and drive customer acquisition and retention.

10. Messaging & Campaign Management: Crafting compelling messaging and brand narratives to effectively communicate with customers and align with brand values.

11. Sales: Managing sales activities and developing sales strategies to drive revenue growth and achieve sales targets.

12. Operations: Overseeing day-to-day business operations to ensure efficiency, productivity, and adherence to organisational goals and standards.

13. Accounting: Managing financial records, accounts payable and receivable, and financial transactions to ensure accuracy and compliance with accounting standards.

14. HR: Managing human resources functions, including recruitment, training, performance management, and employee relations, to support organisational objectives and employee satisfaction.

15. Designing: Creating visually appealing and functional designs for products, packaging, and marketing materials to enhance brand perception and customer experience.

16. Stock and Inventory: Managing inventory levels and stock control processes to ensure sufficient stock availability while minimising excess inventory costs.

17. Purchase: Procuring goods and services from suppliers at the best possible prices and terms to support production and operations.

18. Events: Planning and coordinating events such as product launches, trade shows, or corporate gatherings to enhance brand visibility and engage with customers.

19. Account Management: Building and maintaining strong relationships with key clients or accounts to maximise customer satisfaction and retention.

20. Admin: Providing administrative support and managing office operations to ensure smooth and efficient business functioning.

21. Leadership & Training Support: Providing leadership and training to employees to develop their skills and capabilities and foster a culture of continuous improvement and innovation.

22. Public Relations: Managing communication with the public, media, and stakeholders to maintain a positive brand image and manage reputation.

23. R&D: Investing in research and development activities to drive innovation, improve products or services, and maintain a competitive edge in the market.

24. Legal & Regulatory Compliance: Ensuring compliance with relevant laws, regulations, and industry standards to mitigate legal risks and uphold ethical business practices.

By understanding and effectively implementing these components, businesses can enhance their performance, drive growth, and achieve long-term success in today's competitive landscape.

Decoding The Watch Mechanics

In the intricate world of horology, the mechanism of a watch can be divided into three distinct divisions or parts: the Core, the Inner Rim, and the Outer Rim. Each part plays a crucial role in ensuring the smooth operation and accuracy of timekeeping in mechanical timepieces. Let's delve into the components within each section and visualise to uncover their significance in the grand orchestration of watch mechanics.

Part 1: The Core
At the heart of every mechanical watch lies THE CORE, comprising essential components responsible for generating and regulating the power that drives the movement. These components include:

1. Mainspring Barrel: Housing the mainspring, this component stores potential energy that is gradually released to power the watch.

2. Balance Wheel: Acting as the timekeeping regulator, the balance wheel oscillates back and forth at a precise rate, ensuring accurate timekeeping.

3. Escapement Mechanism: Consisting of the escape wheel and pallet fork, this critical system regulates the release of energy from the mainspring to the balance wheel, controlling the movement of the watch's hands.

Part 2: The Inner Rim
Surrounding the Core is THE INNER RIM, housing components that facilitate the transmission of power and the coordination of various functions within the movement. Key components in this section include:

1. Gear Train: Comprising a series of gears, the gear train transmits power from the mainspring to various parts of the movement, such as the hands and complications.

2. Jewels/Bearings: Synthetic rubies or sapphires used as bearings to reduce friction and wear within the movement, ensuring smooth operation and longevity.

3. Complications: Additional features beyond basic timekeeping, such as chronographs, calendars, and moon phases, adding complexity and functionality to the watch.

Part 3: The Outer Rim
Extending beyond the Inner Rim is THE OUTER RIM, encompassing components that interface with the external elements of the watch, such as the dial, case, and bracelet/strap. These components include:

1. Dial (Face): The visible interface of the watch, displaying the time and often additional features such as date windows or sub-dials.

2. Case: The outer housing of the watch, protecting the movement from external elements and providing structural support.

3. Strap/Bracelet: The means by which the watch is worn, comprising various materials such as leather, rubber, or metal, enhancing comfort and aesthetics.

By visualising and understanding the division of watch components into Core, Inner Rim, and Outer Rim, you gain insight into the intricate interplay of mechanisms that make mechanical watches tick. From the precision of the Core components to the functionality of the Inner Rim and the aesthetics of the Outer Rim, each part contributes to the craftsmanship and functionality of these timeless timepieces.

Aligning the Layers of Business and Watch

You can discern striking similarities in their respective roles and significance by drawing a parallel between the three layers of a watch – Core, Inner Rim, and Outer Rim – the three divisions of the COGS of Success model,

Core COGS or The Core Layer

The foundation of the COGS of Success lies in its first division – the Core.

Just as the Core layer serves as the foundation of a watch, the Core COGS division forms the bedrock of the COGS of Success model. Here, strategic alignment, careful planning, and the success of strong relationship management take priority. PEOPLE, encompassing both internal and external stakeholders, engagement takes the highest precedence at this layer as a concept of customer service. Customer Success emphasises the importance of satisfied internal customers (directors, employees) and external customers (clients, partners, governing bodies).

Business is considered to be seen as an ethical machine to serve the community, making a positive impact on every life you touch and adding value as part of engaging with people, alongside collaboration and coordination as key elements in overall business ethics. This parallels the vital functions of the Core layer in a watch, where essential components like the mainspring barrel and balance wheel ensure the smooth functioning of the timepiece.

Acknowledging the importance of fostering positive relationships within and outside the organisation and serving as the driving force behind business success, much like how the Core layer powers the watch mechanism under this layer termed as Customer Services.

Inner Rim COGS and Inner Rim Layer

Moving outward from the Core, you encounter the Inner Rim layer, which houses the immediate operational elements critical for business success. Similarly, the Inner Rim COGS division encompasses several key elements essential for business functionality, including IT & Business Change, Finance, Production, and Branding, Marketing, among others. These elements, akin to the gears and wheels within the Inner Rim of a watch, work in harmony to drive efficiency, competitiveness, and overall business operations.

These components are absolutely crucial. They form the key elements and are the must have elements of your foundations. if you do not have the strategies, the blueprint, the model, the roadmap for successful planning, implementation, and execution of these elements in harmony, your business will inevitably encounter problems. It's like having a watch with broken gears - it won't just struggle; it could lead to significant failure.

It may not only cause you a big-time failure and may be a reason for you to be forced to close the doors for your customers and loose the trust and credibility of your customers on you within the first few years of your operation without materialising the objectives of your business, campaign or product launch and achieving your desired aspiration and dream. You'll face many sleepless nights, lose your hard-earned money or savings, and perhaps will never let you dare to return to the fantastic world of business in near future. These are essential elements not only to survive and sustain in the but also to thrive in the market.

Outer Rim COGS and Outer Rim Layer

Finally, you arrive at the Outer Rim layer, which expands upon the foundational elements of the watch and becomes indispensable as the organisation scales. Similarly, the Outer Rim COGS division encompasses secondary business units vital for business expansion, such as HR, Product Design, or R&D. These elements, analogous to the outer casing and features of a watch, enhance the organisation's capabilities and facilitate growth, much like how the Outer Rim layer provides additional functionalities and aesthetics to the timepiece. It's the safety net of business growth and provides the key elements of a safety net for surviving, sustaining, succeeding, and thriving in business.

These are the nice-to-have elements during the planning or idea phase but can cost you a fortune if you have not strategised these elements in your business success. They are the greatest contributors to the success phase and thrive phase of the business but need to be planned and sown the seed before you start your journey or in the early days to save time and money and efficiently need for success and thrive stage.

In essence, just as the layers of a watch work synergistically to ensure its functionality and appeal, the divisions of the COGS of Success model collaborate to drive business success and growth. Each layer or division plays a unique yet interconnected role, highlighting the importance of holistic planning and alignment in achieving sustainable success in both horology and business. The COGS of Success wheel is a crucial foundation in building a business and achieving success. It's like a roadmap that guides you through the journey of entrepreneurship, safeguarding you from potential pitfalls and leading you towards your desired destination. By following the principles outlined in the COGS of Success wheel, you can effectively manage your resources, mitigate risks, and navigate the challenges of business ownership. This approach not only saves you energy, money, and sleepless nights but also provides a clear path for reaching your goals without fear. Let's delve deeper into the specifics of the COGS of Success wheel and how it can propel your business towards success in the upcoming chapters of this book.

Conclusion & Recap

Just as a well-crafted watch mechanism ensures accurate timekeeping and smooth operation, COGS empowers companies to navigate the twists and turns of the business world, ultimately leading them to success. COGS of success are the guidebook for businesses, providing a roadmap that can be customised to navigate the complexities of the corporate landscape. With COGS as their guiding principle, businesses can optimise their strategies, adapt to changing environments, and emerge victorious in the competitive marketplace. The COGS of Success is not a mere theoretical construct; it's a practical guide for organisations aspiring to navigate the complexities of the business world. The benefits of the COGS of Success included strategic planning, operational efficiency, scalability, and a customer-centric approach, all of which contributed to sustainable growth and success. The chapter concluded with a recap, emphasising the practicality and effectiveness of the COGS of Success as a guide for organisations navigating the complexities of the business world, setting the stage for further exploration in subsequent sections.

Let me bring your attention to the Volume 2 of "Visions to Victory," which focuses on winning the battle of business success whereas this volume is primarily focussed about setting the foundation of business success. In Volume 2, you will also embark on an in-depth exploration of the three layers of this framework for business growth uncovered in this volume. Stay tuned for a transformative journey as I unveil the secrets to sustainable growth and success in "Visions to Victory - Vol 2" using the three layers, but once again, If you wish to delve deeper into my thoughts on these concepts and related principles beforehand, feel free to contact me using the various resources provided in this book. If there is high demand, I will include a specific section or even draft an independent book on this topic in the forthcoming volume. Connect with me on Facebook, LinkedIn, or Instagram or join my webinars, seminars or workshops to share your thoughts and any specific requests. I will do my best to address them in the upcoming volume.

Chapter 5.2

Digging Deeper into The COGS of Success Blueprint

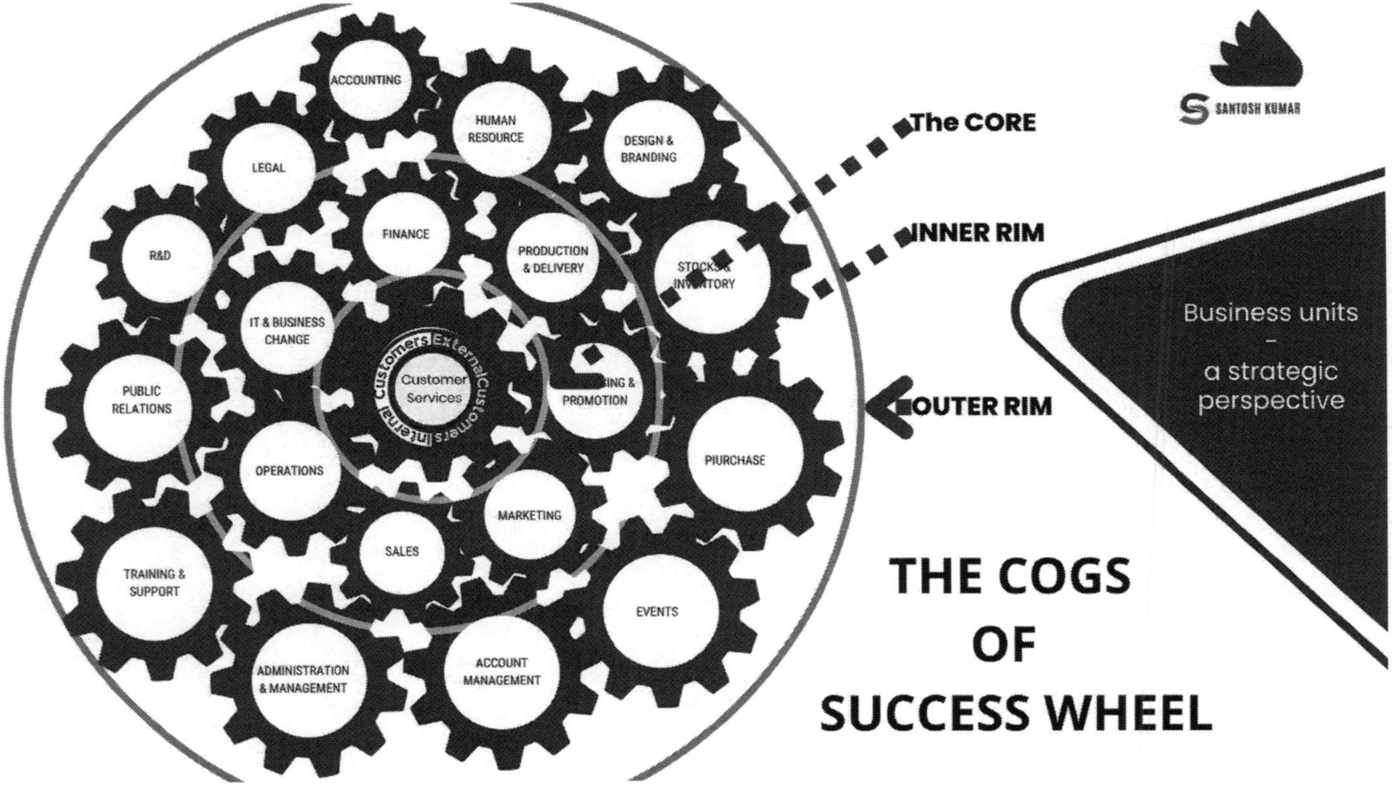
SANTOSH KUMAR
Business units
-
a strategic
perspective
The CORE
INNER RIM
OUTER RIM
THE COGS
OF
SUCCESS WHEEL
ACCOUNTING
HUMAN RESOURCE
DESIGN & BRANDING
LEGAL
FINANCE
PRODUCTION & DELIVERY
R&D
IT & BUSINESS CHANGE
Customer Services
External Customers
Internal Customers
PROMOTION
PUBLIC RELATIONS
PIURCHASE
OPERATIONS
MARKETING
SALES
TRAINING & SUPPORT
EVENTS
ADMINISTRATION & MANAGEMENT
ACCOUNT MANAGEMENT

The key learning from the story of the ant and the grasshopper introduced at the start of this section is the importance of planning and preparation for the future. The ant's diligent efforts to collect food and prepare for winter contrast starkly with the grasshopper's carefree attitude of singing and dancing without concern for the future. When winter arrives, the grasshopper suffers the consequences of his lack of preparation, while the ant thrives due to his foresight and hard work.

In this chapter, I am uncovering the intricacies of COGS of Success Blueprint, a strategic masterpiece, as part of your preparation and planning. This blueprint will serve as your compass in navigating the ever-changing landscape of corporate achievement.

Let's visualise and understand the concept with the story of planning and preparation of two rival bakeries: The Floury Delight and The Golden Crust. Both bakeries had been in business for decades, serving their loyal customers with delicious treats day in and day out.

A Tale of Planning and Preparation

At The Floury Delight, Mr. Baker, the owner, believed in meticulous planning and preparation. Every morning, before the sun rose, he would wake up and start preparing the dough for the day's bread and pastries. He paid close attention to the quality of ingredients, ensuring that only the finest flour and freshest eggs were used in his creations. Mr. Baker knew that success in the bakery business required careful attention to detail and a commitment to excellence.

Meanwhile, at The Golden Crust, Mr. Dough, the owner, had a more carefree approach to running his bakery. He believed in living in the moment and often left things to chance. While his pastries were undeniably tasty, Mr. Dough didn't bother with long-term planning or strategic thinking. He preferred to focus on the present, enjoying the hustle and bustle of his bakery without worrying too much about the future.

As the years went by, both bakeries continued to attract customers with their delicious treats. However, when a new supermarket opened in town, offering a wide range of baked goods at lower prices, both The Floury Delight and The Golden Crust faced tough competition.

Mr. Baker, with his careful planning, the process driven approach, and strategic mindset, quickly adapted to the changing landscape. He introduced new recipes, expanded his product range, and focused on providing exceptional customer service. He also invested in marketing efforts to attract new customers and retain existing ones. Despite the challenges posed by the supermarket, The Floury Delight continued to thrive, thanks to Mr. Baker's foresight and resilience.

On the other hand, Mr. Dough found himself struggling to keep up with the competition. His lack of planning, lack of processes and lack of preparation meant that he was ill-prepared to face the challenges posed by the supermarket. Despite his best efforts to lower prices and increase promotions, The Golden Crust saw a decline in sales, and Mr. Dough was forced to close down his bakery.

In the end, the story of The Floury Delight and The Golden Crust serves as a poignant reminder of the importance of planning, process and preparation in business. Just like Mr. Baker, those who take the time to craft a strategic blueprint for success are better equipped to navigate the challenges of the ever-changing business landscape. By understanding the core components of growth strategies, embracing operational excellence, and fostering relationships with customers, entrepreneurs can chart a course towards sustained success, even in the face of adversity.

The Moral of the story

This story exemplifies the importance of planning, process, and preparation in the context of business, which is closely related to the concept of COGS (Components of Growth Strategies). Here's how:

Planning and Preparation - Mr. Baker from The Floury Delight represents meticulous planning and preparation in business operations. He wakes up early to prepare the dough, pays attention to ingredient quality, and focuses on providing excellent customer service. His strategic mindset and commitment to excellence allow him to adapt to challenges effectively.

In contrast, Mr. Dough from The Golden Crust lacks planning and preparation. He adopts a carefree approach, neglecting long-term planning and strategic thinking. As a result, he struggles to compete when faced with challenges like the new supermarket opening in town.

The Processes around COGS of Success Framework - The COGS of Success framework emphasises the importance of visualising and understanding the core components of growth strategies. Mr. Baker's approach aligns with this framework as he focuses on key elements such as product quality, customer service, and marketing efforts to drive success.

Mr. Dough's failure to adapt highlights the consequences of neglecting essential components outlined in the COGS framework. Without strategic planning and operational excellence, his bakery faces difficulties in surviving competition and ultimately closes down.

Revisiting the COGS of Success Framework

In the exploration of the COGS of Success framework, you embark on a journey to understand its three foundational segments: the Core, the Inner Rim, and the Outer Rim.

the story of Two bakers illustrates how businesses that prioritise planning, preparation, and adherence to growth strategies are better equipped to thrive in the face of challenges.

By understanding and leveraging the core components of growth strategies, entrepreneurs like you and me can navigate uncertainties and achieve sustained success, as demonstrated by Mr. Baker's Floury Delight bakery.

To remind you, The COGS of Success, is a comprehensive framework and business growth model that identifies and emphasises the critical components, both internal and external, necessary for achieving success in a business. It encourages a holistic approach, acknowledging the interconnectedness of various business units and the importance of positive relationships with both internal and external stakeholders.

These segments are not just arbitrary divisions; they represent the structural pillars upon which entrepreneurial success is built. Let's kick things off and start delving into the COGS of success. Let us embark on this enlightening journey in the following segments of this chapter, exploring the blueprint's three integral divisions: The Core, The Inner Rim, and The Outer Rim.

By visualising, understanding and leveraging the components within each segment of the COGS framework, entrepreneurs can navigate the complexities of the business landscape with confidence and clarity. Whether they are focusing on optimising their core operations, streamlining their inner workings, or adapting to external forces, the COGS framework provides a comprehensive roadmap for long-term success. So let us delve deeper into each segment, unravelling the secrets of sustainable growth and achievement in the entrepreneurial realm. Let's dig deeper into each of these elements of COGS of success wheel one by one.

The Core: Foundations for Triumph with Customer

At the heart of the COGS framework is THE CORE, which represents the essential operations that define an organisation's existence and growth. This section emphasises the crucial components that ensure the business remains aligned with its purpose and strategic goals. Customer service stands out as the lifeblood of any enterprise within this framework, playing a vital role in both internal cohesion and external reputation.

Customer service, as seen within the COGS framework, goes beyond traditional support and engagement. It is not just a department but a philosophy embedded throughout the organisation. Internally, it recognises that employees, shareholders, and partners are integral stakeholders whose satisfaction directly impacts overall performance. Their engagement, happiness, and well-being significantly contribute to the operational efficiency and success of the organisation.

Externally, customer service extends to clients, suppliers, and end-users, who collectively form the ecosystem that sustains the business. Their preferences, feedback, and satisfaction levels dictate product development, service delivery, and overall customer experience. Building strong relationships with these stakeholders involves listening carefully to their needs, resolving issues promptly, and consistently exceeding expectations.

The holistic approach advocated by the COGS framework stresses the interconnectedness of all stakeholders. By prioritising excellence in customer service, organisations cultivate loyalty, advocacy, and long-term partnerships. This commitment not only enhances the brand's reputation but also boosts customer retention rates, driving sustainable growth over time.

In essence, THE CORE segment of the COGS framework underscores the centrality of customer service in achieving organisational success. By fostering positive relationships internally and externally, and by embracing a holistic approach to service delivery, businesses establish a solid foundation for thriving in today's dynamic and competitive business environment. This strategic focus ensures that every interaction, whether internal or external, contributes to the overall health and longevity of the organisation.

The Inner Rim: Operational Excellence Unveiled

Moving outward from the Core, which is the essence of an organisation's operations, you encounter THE INNER RIM, a critical component that supports the day-to-day functioning and strategic growth of the enterprise. This segment encompasses several interconnected elements, each playing a pivotal role in ensuring operational efficiency and effectiveness.

At the heart of THE INNER RIM lies IT & Business Change, pivotal in driving innovation within the organisation. Information Technology (IT) is not merely a support function but a catalyst for transformation. Embracing technological advancements and adapting to evolving business landscapes are essential for staying competitive and agile. IT optimises processes, enhances productivity, and facilitates seamless communication and collaboration across departments. By integrating innovative IT solutions, businesses streamline operations, respond swiftly to market dynamics, and innovate their offerings.

Finance stands as the financial compass of the organisation within THE INNER RIM, guiding strategic decision-making and ensuring financial stability. Effective financial management involves meticulous budgeting, accurate forecasting, robust risk management, and prudent capital allocation. Understanding the financial landscape enables businesses to gauge their financial health, evaluate performance metrics, and identify growth opportunities. By managing finances strategically, organisations mitigate risks, capitalise on market opportunities, and pave the way for sustainable growth.

Production & Delivery are the engines that propel operational efficiency within THE INNER RIM. Optimising production processes, managing supply chains effectively, and ensuring timely delivery are paramount to meeting customer demands and maintaining a competitive edge. Businesses that delve into the intricacies of production and logistics streamline operations, minimise wastage, and maximise productivity. By enhancing production efficiencies and refining delivery logistics, organisations improve cost-effectiveness and elevate customer satisfaction levels.

Branding & Production Design play a pivotal role in shaping the identity of the business within THE INNER RIM. In today's dynamic marketplace, crafting a strong brand identity is crucial for differentiation and customer loyalty. Effective branding strategies resonate with the target audience, establish a distinct market position, and foster long-term customer relationships. Production design complements branding efforts by ensuring that the physical and visual elements align with the brand's identity, enhancing brand recognition and consumer appeal.

Advertising, Promotions, Marketing, and Sales synergise within THE INNER RIM to drive business growth and customer engagement. This symphony of salesmanship encompasses creating compelling advertising campaigns, implementing strategic promotions, devising innovative marketing strategies, and executing effective sales tactics. These elements work cohesively to enhance brand visibility, attract prospective customers, and drive revenue generation. By aligning advertising, promotions, marketing, and sales efforts, organisations create a unified brand experience that resonates with their target market and sustains growth momentum.

In essence, THE INNER RIM segment of the COGS of Success framework underscores the importance of foundational business units in driving immediate success and laying the groundwork for sustained growth. By optimising IT & Business Change, finance, production & delivery, branding & production design, and advertising, promotions, marketing, and sales strategies, organisations enhance operational efficiency, innovate their offerings, and strengthen their competitive advantage in the marketplace.

The Outer Rim: Scaling Heights

Finally, you reach THE OUTER RIM, which extends beyond the immediate operations of the organisation and encompasses external factors that influence its success. This segment includes collaboration, innovation, competition, risk management, global dynamics, and market trends. While not immediately essential for the organisation's survival, these factors play a crucial role in shaping its long-term trajectory. By paying attention to the Outer Rim, entrepreneurs can adapt to changing market conditions, capitalise on emerging opportunities, and position their business for sustained growth and success.

The Outer Rim segment of the COGS of Success framework represents the outer perimeter of your enterprise's operations, offering foundational support for long-term success as the business advances. While these elements may not be immediately mandatory, they become indispensable during the scaling phase, contributing to the overall success and sustainability of the business. Here's an elaborate expansion on the components of the Outer Rim:

The Outer Rim encompasses external factors that significantly contribute to business success. These factors include Collaboration, Innovation, Competition, Risk Management, Global Dynamics, and Market Trends. Understanding and effectively navigating these external forces are crucial for sustaining growth and competitiveness in the marketplace. Examples of Outer Rim Units are as follows:

Accounting & HR: The Backbone of Operations - Robust accounting and human resource management form the backbone of operations, providing stability and resilience to the organisation. Efficient financial management and talent acquisition and retention are essential for ensuring operational efficiency and effectiveness.

Stock and Inventory, Purchase - Streamlining Operations: Streamlined stock and inventory management, coupled with strategic purchasing practices, are essential for maintaining efficient operations. Effective management of stock levels and procurement processes minimises wastage, reduces costs, and ensures timely availability of resources.

Events, Account Management, Admin, Training Support - Building a robust infrastructure involves managing various aspects such as events, accounts, administration, and providing effective training support. These functions contribute to organisational efficiency, productivity, and employee development, laying the groundwork for long-term success.

Public Relations, R&D, Legal - Ensuring Longevity: Effective public relations, research and development (R&D), and legal strategies are essential for ensuring the longevity and sustainability of the business. Maintaining positive relationships with stakeholders, investing in innovation, and complying with legal regulations are critical for mitigating risks and fostering organisational resilience.

In essence, the Outer Rim segment of the COGS of Success framework comprises external factors and units that contribute to the long-term success and sustainability of the business. By understanding and leveraging these components, businesses can navigate the complexities of the external environment, strengthen their infrastructure, and position themselves for continued growth and competitiveness in the marketplace.

So, why is COGS of SUCCESS so pivotal?

The COGS of Success framework plays a pivotal role for several reasons, acting as a guide and roadmap for entrepreneurial success in the ever-changing world of business.

Entrepreneurial journeys are often uncertain and challenging, much like navigating uncharted waters. In this context, COGS of Success acts as a compass, offering direction and guidance amid the unpredictability of the business landscape. It clarifies the path forward and helps businesses navigate unfamiliar territory.

At its core, COGS of Success offers a sustainable roadmap for entrepreneurial success. Unlike short-lived strategies or tactics, this comprehensive approach provides a long-term perspective designed to endure over time. By adhering to its principles, entrepreneurs can chart a course towards sustainable growth and prosperity.

COGS of Success is more than just a set of strategies; it's a holistic approach to business success. It considers both internal and external factors, essential components, and strategic elements crucial for achieving sustainable growth and resilience. This approach ensures that every aspect of the business is aligned and optimised for success.

The business landscape is unpredictable, with unexpected challenges and opportunities. COGS of Success equips entrepreneurs with tools and strategies to navigate these complexities effectively. Whether adapting to market changes, seizing opportunities, or managing risks, the framework provides a structured approach to addressing challenges and capitalising on opportunities.

Ultimately, COGS of Success empowers entrepreneurs to achieve triumphs in their ventures. By offering a structured framework, strategic guidance, and a roadmap for success, COGS of Success enables entrepreneurs to overcome obstacles, maximise their potential, and realise their vision for their business. It serves as a catalyst for growth, innovation, and prosperity.

In essence, COGS of Success is pivotal because it provides guidance through uncertainty, offers a sustainable roadmap for success, embraces a comprehensive approach to business growth, navigates the complexities of the business landscape, and empowers entrepreneurial achievements. Embracing COGS of Success principles and components enables entrepreneurs to confidently navigate business challenges, driving their ventures towards sustained success.

Who can benefit from COGS of SUCCESS?

The COGS of Success framework is not exclusive to seasoned industry veterans; it is a valuable resource for any entrepreneur embarking on their business journey, regardless of their level of experience. Let's explore further who should pay heed to COGS of Success:

Innovators and Visionaries - For entrepreneurs who are driven by innovation and vision, COGS of Success provides a framework for turning their ideas into reality. By aligning their innovative concepts with strategic planning and execution, innovators and visionaries can effectively bring their visions to life while ensuring long-term sustainability and success. COGS of Success empowers these entrepreneurs to navigate the complexities of innovation and drive meaningful change in their industries.

Established Enterprises - Even established enterprises can benefit from the insights and guidance provided by COGS of Success. As businesses evolve and grow, they encounter new challenges and opportunities that require strategic thinking and planning. COGS of Success offers established enterprises a framework for reassessing their strategies, identifying areas for improvement, and adapting to changing market conditions. By incorporating the principles of COGS of Success into their operations, established enterprises can maintain their competitive edge and continue to thrive in an ever-changing business landscape.

Aspiring Entrepreneurs - For those who are just beginning their entrepreneurial journey, the COGS of Success framework serves as an invaluable tool for setting a strong foundation. It provides aspiring entrepreneurs with a strategic roadmap and essential guidance as they navigate the initial stages of launching their business. By embracing the principles of COGS of Success early on, aspiring entrepreneurs can avoid common pitfalls and set themselves up for long-term success.

Early-stage Startups - Early-stage startups often face numerous challenges and uncertainties as they work to establish their presence in the market. COGS of Success offers these startups a structured approach to growth and development, helping them identify key components and strategies essential for their success. By paying heed to COGS of Success, early-stage startups can streamline their operations, optimise their resources, and position themselves for sustainable growth.

Entrepreneurs Facing Adversity - In times of adversity or crisis, such as economic downturns or industry disruptions, entrepreneurs may find themselves struggling to navigate uncertain waters. COGS of Success serves as a guiding light during these challenging times, offering entrepreneurs a roadmap for resilience and recovery. By focusing on the core components of success and leveraging strategic strategies, entrepreneurs facing adversity can weather the storm and emerge stronger on the other side.

In essence, COGS of Success is a versatile and invaluable resource that is relevant to entrepreneurs at every stage of their journey. Whether you're just starting out or leading an established enterprise, COGS of Success can serve as your compass, ally, and strategic guide, helping you chart a course towards entrepreneurial success in the tumultuous seas of business.

Timing and Adaptability of COGS of SUCCESS

Expanding on the idea of when to implement COGS of SUCCESS, it's crucial to understand that its adaptability is one of its greatest strengths. Unlike rigid business frameworks that may only apply to specific stages of a company's lifecycle, COGS of SUCCESS can be seamlessly integrated at any point along the entrepreneurial journey.

For those embarking on the exciting adventure of starting a new venture, implementing COGS of SUCCESS from the outset can lay a solid foundation for future growth and sustainability. By adopting a holistic approach to success early on, entrepreneurs can avoid common pitfalls and establish a strategic mindset that will guide their decision-making processes as their business evolves.

Similarly, for established enterprises facing the challenges of maturity or even stagnation, COGS of SUCCESS offers a fresh perspective and a framework for revitalisation. By reassessing their business strategies through the lens of COGS of SUCCESS, companies can identify areas for improvement, adapt to changing market dynamics, and reignite growth.

In essence, there's never a wrong time to consider implementing COGS of SUCCESS. Whether you're just starting out or looking to revitalise your existing business, embracing this holistic approach can provide clarity, direction, and a roadmap for sustainable success in today's dynamic business landscape.

The Comprehensive Application of COGS of SUCCESS Across Business Elements & its application

The application of COGS of SUCCESS extends deeply into the fabric of your organisation, touching upon every aspect that contributes to its success and longevity. You might be wondering, how does the COGS of SUCCESS finds its application within the various elements of your business, let's explore

Strategies - COGS of SUCCESS prompts a meticulous examination and implementation of strategies tailored to your business objectives. This involves identifying key growth areas, setting clear goals, and devising strategic initiatives to achieve them. Whether it's expanding market reach, optimising operational efficiency, or enhancing product innovation, COGS of SUCCESS guides the strategic decision-making process.

Blueprints - Crafting meticulous blueprints is another crucial aspect of COGS of SUCCESS. These blueprints serve as architectural designs for your organisation, outlining the structure, processes, and workflows necessary for efficiency and effectiveness. By aligning every aspect of your business with a well-defined blueprint, you create a solid foundation for growth and scalability.

Roadmaps - Navigating the ever-changing landscapes of the business environment requires dynamic roadmaps that adapt to new challenges and opportunities. COGS of SUCCESS emphasises the importance of creating flexible and agile roadmaps that provide clear direction while allowing for adjustments as needed. These roadmaps serve as guides for navigating uncertainties and maintaining momentum towards your business goals.

Customer Relationships - At the core of COGS of SUCCESS lies a focus on fostering relationships with your customers. Recognising that customer satisfaction is essential for long-term success, COGS of SUCCESS emphasises the importance of building trust, delivering value, and providing exceptional customer experiences. By prioritising customer relationships, you create a loyal customer base that drives sustainable growth and profitability.

In summary, COGS of SUCCESS permeates every aspect of your organisation, from strategic planning to operational execution and customer engagement. By applying its principles diligently, you can create a resilient and adaptive business that thrives in today's dynamic and competitive landscape.

Strategic Implementation of COGS of SUCCESS

Implementing COGS of SUCCESS involves a systematic and strategic approach aimed at integrating its principles into every aspect of your business operations. Wondering how you can effectively implement COGS of SUCCESS in your venture, Here's how to achieve this.

Strategise with Purpose - Begin by defining clear business objectives and goals aligned with your vision. Strategise with purpose by identifying key growth areas, assessing market opportunities, and developing actionable plans to achieve your objectives. Leverage market insights, competitor analysis, and customer feedback to inform your strategic decisions and ensure they are aligned with your long-term vision.

Craft Organisational Blueprint - Develop a comprehensive organisational blueprint that outlines the structure, processes, and workflows necessary to support your strategic objectives. This blueprint should encompass various aspects of your business, including operations, marketing, sales, finance, and customer service. Ensure that the blueprint is flexible enough to adapt to changing market conditions while maintaining a focus on efficiency and effectiveness.

Navigate Tides of Change with Dynamic Roadmaps - Create dynamic roadmaps that serve as guides for navigating the ever-changing business landscape. These roadmaps should outline specific initiatives, timelines, and milestones to help you track progress and make informed decisions. Stay agile and responsive to changes in market trends, customer preferences, and competitive dynamics by regularly updating and adjusting your roadmaps as needed.

Nurture Relationships with Customers - Prioritise building and nurturing relationships with your customers, as they are the lifeblood of your business. Provide exceptional customer experiences, anticipate their needs, and exceed their expectations at every touchpoint. Leverage customer feedback and data analytics to gain insights into their preferences and behaviours, allowing you to tailor your products and services to meet their evolving needs.

By implementing COGS of SUCCESS in your business, you can create a strategic framework that fosters growth, resilience, and long-term success. Stay committed to your strategic objectives, remain adaptable to changing market conditions, and prioritise the needs of your customers to drive sustainable growth and profitability.

In essence, the COGS of SUCCESS framework transcends being a mere collection of components; it embodies a symphony, a harmonious force that orchestrates every aspect of your organisational journey. It serves as a guiding light that aligns your organisational compass, providing direction and purpose to your endeavours. Moreover, it forms the very foundation of your enterprise, structuring it in a way that ensures resilience and stability in the face of challenges.

This framework is not just about achieving success for ourselves; it extends beyond to those you serve – your customers, stakeholders, and communities. By exploring the framework in detail across the segments of this chapter, you can uncover the intricate melodies of each component, understanding how they harmonise together to create a symphony of success.

So, let's embark on this journey of exploration, delving into the nuances of the COGS of SUCCESS framework. By understanding its intricacies, you can unlock the potential for sustained growth and achievement in your entrepreneurial pursuits.

Conclusion & Recap

In this chapter, we explored The COGS of Success Blueprint, a guide for achieving business success. The COGS of SUCCESS framework was introduced, providing a structured approach to entrepreneurship. Core components essential for building a successful business were discussed, highlighting operational excellence (inner rim) and business expansion (outer rim). The chapter concluded with a recap and exercises to reinforce learning and application of the framework.

Volume 2 of "Visions to Victory" will further explore the COGS framework for business growth. Stay tuned for insights into sustainable growth and success. For deeper engagement, contact me via the resources provided in this book or join my social media channels and events.

In the next chapter, you'll explore the COGS model, focusing on customer success. Detailed examination of internal and external customer services will emphasise harmonising success between them. Internal customers will foster organisational harmony, while external customers will drive overall success. Various strategies for customer services will be discussed, positioning it as central to the COGS framework. The chapter will also cover the essence of CORE COGS and the synergy needed for comprehensive success. Insights, blueprints, and roadmaps for customer service strategies will be provided, emphasising balanced relationships for holistic success.

This framework is designed to help you navigate challenges and opportunities, leading to triumph in your business endeavours. As you continue your entrepreneurial journey, may the COGS of Success guide you towards the pinnacle of success.

Chapter 5.3

Harmonising Success: Exploring the Heart of COGS Model

ExternalCustomers
Internal Customers
Customers
Suppliers
Partners
Government
Directors
Investors
Employees
Shareholders
Customer
Services

The Core of the COGS model is the foundational force in the intricate workings of business success. The core is not just a foundation; it's the force that orchestrates strategic alignment, meticulous planning, and adaptability in the intricate workings of business success.

Think of THE CORE as a maestro, guiding organisations towards sustained growth and excellence. It's at the heart of a symphony of triumph, a dynamic force that shapes every decision and action within the business.

Imagine a symphony orchestra where each instrument plays a crucial role in creating beautiful music. Similarly, the core ensures that every part of the organisation works together harmoniously towards common goals. It aligns strategic aspirations with meticulous planning, ensuring everyone moves in sync towards success.

But what makes the core truly powerful is its adaptability. In today's fast-paced business environment, adaptability is key to staying competitive and relevant. The core enables organisations to pivot swiftly, seizing new opportunities and overcoming challenges with agility.

In this chapter, let me expand the concept of THE CORE of the COGS of success model as our guiding light and pave the way for success, ensuring that every decision you make and every action you take leads you closer to your goals.

The Concept of Customer Success in the Core COGS

The concept of Customer Success at the core of the Core COGS represents a profound acknowledgment of the crucial role played by both internal and external customers in the overall success of an organisation.

The concept of Customer Success within the Core COGS framework is not a concept that goes beyond mere financial gains. It's about recognising the pivotal role that both internal and external customers play in the overall success of an organisation.

Firstly, Customer Success embodies a holistic approach. It's not just about making money; it's about ensuring the satisfaction and prosperity of everyone involved – from your directors, shareholders, employees, to your investors. Customer Success, within the Core COGS goes beyond mere financial gains. It recognises that success is not a one-dimensional achievement but a multi-faceted journey that involves the satisfaction and prosperity of all stakeholders. The holistic approach ensures that the organisation's strategies and actions take into account the interests and well-being of both internal and external customers. It fosters a balanced consideration of the diverse needs and expectations within and outside the organisational boundaries.

Next it's about Positive Relationships. Recognising directors, shareholders, employees, and investors as internal customers highlights the importance of fostering positive relationships within the organisational structure. When internal customers succeed, it translates to a motivated and engaged workforce. External customers, comprising clients, suppliers, partners, and governing bodies, are pivotal to the external business ecosystem. Their success is closely tied to the organisation's sustained growth, emphasising the significance of cultivating positive relationships in the broader business environment. The concept underscores the idea that success is not a zero-sum game. Both internal and external customers should derive value from their association with the organisation. This mutual value delivery forms the foundation of enduring and fruitful relationships.

It's also about driving motivation and growth. Internally, when directors, shareholders, employees, and investors experience success in their respective roles, it creates a motivated and dedicated workforce. This motivation becomes a driving force behind increased productivity, innovation, and overall organisational excellence. Externally, customer success contributes to sustained business growth. Clients, suppliers, partners, and governing bodies who find success through their interactions with the organisation become advocates, fostering a positive reputation and attracting new opportunities.

It's about long-term sustainability. Focusing on Customer Success is not just about immediate gains but about ensuring the long-term sustainability of the organisation. Balancing short-term objectives with a commitment to customer satisfaction creates a foundation for enduring success. A holistic perspective on customer success encourages organisational adaptability and resilience. It acknowledges that the business environment is dynamic, and success requires an ongoing commitment to meeting the evolving needs of both internal and external customers.

And finally, it's about cultural implications. Embracing Customer Success as a core principle influences the organisational culture. It promotes a customer-centric mindset that permeates through all levels of the organisation, fostering a culture of service excellence and continuous improvement. A commitment to customer success aligns the values of the organisation with the expectations of its customers. This alignment is essential for building trust, loyalty, and a positive reputation in the marketplace.

The Essence of Customer Service: Nurturing Relationships for Enduring Success

The pivotal element that holds the key to the success of your ventures—the heartbeat of your business and the nucleus of triumph is the realm of customer service. Imagine, if you will, embarking on a journey where every interaction, every decision, and every effort revolves around a single, powerful concept—the customer.

Customer service refers to the assistance and support provided by a business to its customers before, during, and after a purchase or interaction. It encompasses a range of activities and interactions aimed at ensuring customer satisfaction, resolving issues, and fostering a positive relationship between the business and its internal and external clientele.

In the grand tapestry of entrepreneurship, the first brushstroke is painted by this unit you call "Customer Service." Customers aren't mere transactions; they are the heartbeat of your business. In this realm, communication becomes your compass, guiding you through the vast sea of consumer needs.

Customer service is more than just a business function; it is the heartbeat of your business, the nucleus of triumph. It's about creating meaningful interactions, addressing concerns, and building lasting relationships. So, think and find innovative way to not only limit your interaction for business transactions but also how you can add value to your customers. Picture each customer interaction as an opportunity, not just to resolve issues, but to lay the foundation for trust and loyalty.

In this realm, communication becomes our compass, guiding us through the vast sea of consumer needs. It's about proactive problem-solving, ensuring issues are resolved swiftly and preventing them from arising in the first place. Guidance and assistance become our guiding stars, helping customers navigate their decisions with confidence.

Post-purchase support transforms our business into a trusted partner on our customers' journeys. It extends beyond the point of sale, fostering brand loyalty that stands the test of time. And let's not forget the invaluable feedback—we don't just serve customers; we collaborate with them, learning and growing together.

But why does customer service matter? It's not merely a business function; it's the cornerstone of your success. It's not merely about transactions; it's about relationships.

Satisfied customers aren't just one-time buyers; they are loyal advocates and brand ambassadors. They are your greater ally. In the competitive arena of entrepreneurship, exceptional customer service becomes our secret weapon, setting us apart and propelling us forward.

Customer service is the assistance and support provided by a business throughout the customer journey—from before a purchase, during the interaction, and after the transaction. It encompasses a wide range of activities aimed at ensuring customer satisfaction, resolving issues promptly, and nurturing a positive relationship with our clientele.

let us not view customer service as an afterthought but as the genesis of our business cycle. By placing customers at the heart of our venture, we not only ensure short-term success but build a legacy of trust, loyalty, and enduring prosperity. Let us embrace this ethos wholeheartedly, for it is through exceptional customer service that we forge ahead, leaving a lasting imprint on the landscape of business. Imagine each interaction as an opportunity, a chance to not only address concerns but to build lasting relationships.

So, I implore you, consider this business unit not as an afterthought but as the genesis of your business cycle. Place your customers at the heart of your venture, for in doing so, you not only build a successful business but a legacy of trust, loyalty, and enduring success. Let's look at it in detail

Key elements of customer service

Customer service is the bedrock of any successful business. It's about communication—clear, effective communication through various channels like phone calls, emails, live chat, and face-to-face interactions. It's how we understand your needs, provide the right information, and swiftly address any concerns you may have.

Our role doesn't end there. We're here to resolve issues and their life easier. Customer service teams are responsible for resolving problems that your customers may encounter. Whether it's a technical glitch, a problem with a product, or simply ensuring your satisfaction, our customer service teams are dedicated to finding solutions and making sure you feel valued throughout the process.

You also aim to empower your customers with guidance and assistance. Providing guidance and assistance to customers helps them make informed decisions. They might need help navigating your website. Want to understand more about your products or services? You must be there to provide expert advice, ensuring you make informed decisions that meet their needs.

And it doesn't stop at the point of purchase. Post-purchase support is crucial. From setting up their new product to providing tutorials or troubleshooting any challenges their face, You're committed to ensuring their satisfaction long after you've made a purchase.

Businesses often use customer service channels to collect feedback. Their feedback is invaluable to us. Through their insights, we learn how we can improve our offerings, understand the preferences better, and ultimately enhance the quality of our products and services. Their voice shapes our continuous improvement efforts.

In essence, customer service isn't just a department—it's a commitment. It's about building strong relationships, ensuring the satisfaction, and continuously striving to exceed the expectations. By focusing on effective communication, swift problem-solving, knowledgeable guidance, comprehensive post-purchase support, and proactive feedback collection, we aim to deliver experiences that not only meet but exceed your expectations.

Mastering the significance of Customer Service

Customer service plays a pivotal role in the success of any business. It's not just about handling inquiries or resolving complaints—it's about building relationships, fostering loyalty, and ensuring that every interaction leaves a lasting impression.

Firstly, let's talk about customer retention. When a business provides excellent customer service, it nurtures customer loyalty. Satisfied customers are more likely to stick with a brand, make repeat purchases, and even become advocates who recommend the business to others. They become the bedrock upon which businesses can grow and thrive.

Secondly, customer service profoundly impacts a brand's reputation. Positive interactions with customers contribute to a positive brand image. Whether it's through word-of-mouth recommendations, glowing online reviews, or positive mentions on social media, these endorsements are invaluable. They shape how the public perceives a business and can significantly influence its reputation in the marketplace.

In a competitive world, superior customer service becomes a key differentiator. It sets businesses apart from their competitors. In a crowded marketplace where products and services can often seem similar, exceptional service becomes the distinguishing factor that attracts and retains customers.

Furthermore, customer satisfaction is crucial. When businesses consistently meet or exceed customer expectations, they foster satisfaction. Satisfied customers are not just likely to return—they are more inclined to become loyal patrons. They leave positive reviews, spread the word about their experiences, and contribute to a strong, loyal customer base that supports the business in the long term.

Beyond reactive measures, proactive customer service can also prevent issues from escalating. By listening to customers, addressing concerns promptly, and demonstrating genuine care, businesses can pre-emptively resolve problems. This proactive approach not only enhances customer satisfaction but also helps maintain positive relationships and shields the business from negative publicity.

In essence, customer service is not merely a department within a business—it is a fundamental philosophy. It is about understanding and meeting the needs of customers, resolving issues effectively, and creating positive experiences that build trust and loyalty. By prioritising customer service, businesses not only secure repeat business but also pave the way for sustained growth and success in a competitive marketplace.

Customer service is a fundamental aspect of any successful business. It is a holistic approach to meeting customer needs, resolving issues, and creating positive experiences that contribute to long-term success. Let's continue to champion exceptional customer service as a cornerstone of our business strategies, because ultimately, the satisfaction and loyalty of our customers are the true measures of our success.

The Symphony of Internal and External Customers

The symphony of success is shaped by both internal and external customers. Picture your business as an orchestra, where each department and team member plays a unique instrument. They create more than just products or services; they craft an experience, embody a culture, and define your organisation's essence. "Harmonising Success" inspires precise conduct, fostering an environment where internal customers resonate in perfect harmony.

Recognising and satisfying the needs within your organisation transforms the workplace into a collaborative sanctuary, driving towards operational excellence. Beyond the office, the symphony extends to external customers—the lifeblood sustaining financial harmony and building brand loyalty. Their transactions sustain your financial harmony, while loyalty builds your brand's melody. Nurturing these relationships allows you to compose a masterpiece that delights customers and establishes your presence in the competitive marketplace.

This convergence of internal efficiency and external loyalty creates a symphony resonating with growth and prosperity. It fuels sustained success and organisational prosperity, guiding you towards the victory envisioned in your entrepreneurial journey. As you navigate "Visions to Victory," let the music of success inspire your entrepreneurial symphony, where every note played resonates with excellence.

The union of internal and external dimensions into a symphony of success is utmost important. Balancing these two realms is crucial, as it highlights the importance of harmonising internal operations while delivering exceptional value to external customers.

Uncover the secret to organisational prosperity by balancing the needs of both internal and external customers. This balance creates a synergistic environment conducive to success.

A positive culture of internal customer satisfaction resonates outward, creating a virtuous cycle of efficiency, customer loyalty, and sustained success. This cycle drives the organisation closer to the victory envisioned from the start.

Embark on this journey through "Visions to Victory" as you delve into the layers of internal and external customer relationships. This chapter, titled "Harmonising Success," is not just a chapter; it's a melodic exploration of business dynamics. It's an odyssey through the symphony of success, where internal and external customers dance in harmony, creating a masterpiece that resonates with prosperity and growth.

Internal Customers: Composing Harmony Within

Understanding the dynamics of customer relationships within an organisation involves recognising the importance of both internal and external customers.

Internal customers are individuals or departments within an organisation who rely on the products, services, or information provided by another department or individual within the same organisation. Imagine the marketing department creating promotional materials for the sales team; in this scenario, the sales team is the internal customer of the marketing department.

Within an organisation, internal customers can be either individuals or departments. Different departments often serve each other, ensuring seamless collaboration and effective communication across the organisation. Recognising internal customers promotes teamwork and a collaborative culture, encouraging departments to work together to achieve common goals. When different departments understand and fulfil each other's needs, it streamlines processes, reduces bottlenecks, and increases overall efficiency. Focusing on internal customer satisfaction also contributes to a positive work environment, fostering a sense of shared purpose and mutual support.

Acknowledging internal customers nurtures a culture of collaboration, transforming the organisation as departments align their efforts towards shared goals. Internal customer satisfaction acts as a catalyst for streamlined processes, enhancing efficiency and propelling the organisation towards operational excellence. Shifting focus towards internal customer satisfaction also has a transformative impact on organisational culture, fostering an environment of shared purpose and mutual support.

The relationship between customer services and internal customers is like a well-choreographed ballet, where every move is synchronised to create a harmonious performance. Directors, employees, investors, and shareholders play pivotal roles as the unsung heroes behind the scenes.

Directors craft the overarching narrative of the organisation. Extending customer services internally involves fostering an environment where the leadership team feels supported and valued. Providing seamless communication, addressing their concerns promptly, and aligning service delivery with their strategic vision contribute to the directors' well-being, enabling them to steer the organisation with confidence and focus.

Employees, the heartbeat of any organisation, benefit from a workplace culture where they feel heard, appreciated, and motivated. Effective communication, recognising their needs, and valuing individual contributions are key. When employees are treated as internal customers, their satisfaction and engagement increase, leading to higher productivity, creativity, and a positive workplace atmosphere.

Investors and shareholders, the custodians of the organisation's financial health, also benefit from top-notch internal customer services. Transparent communication, timely reporting, and addressing their financial concerns nurture trust and attract additional investments, strengthening the company's financial stability.

Customer services for internal customers go beyond resolving issues; they aim to create an environment where the organisational ecosystem thrives. When directors, employees, investors, and shareholders are treated as valued customers, the entire business benefits. This fosters a culture of collaboration, innovation, and sustained success, where everyone plays a crucial role in achieving organisational excellence.

In essence, the relationship between customer services and internal customers is reciprocal. When directors, employees, investors, and shareholders are treated as internal customers, they receive the attention and care they deserve, ensuring their satisfaction and propelling the organisation forward with robust support.

External Customers: The Crescendo of the Symphony

External customers are the individuals, businesses, or entities outside an organisation that purchase, use, or consume its products or services. If you own a retail business, your external customers are the people who buy your products. For a consulting firm, the clients seeking professional services are the external customers.

External customers are the end-users or consumers of the organisation's products or services. Their satisfaction and loyalty are crucial for the success and sustainability of the business. The relationships with external customers are typically transactional, involving the exchange of goods, services, or information for value.

External customers are the primary source of revenue for an organisation. Satisfying their needs and delivering value is critical for financial success. Positive experiences with external customers build a strong brand reputation and foster loyalty, leading to repeat business and positive word-of-mouth. Understanding and meeting the needs of external customers is essential for staying competitive in the market and differentiating the organisation from competitors.

As the narrative unfolds, we transition to the crescendo – the external customers. These individuals stand as the reason for the organisation's existence, and in this chapter, we explore their role in crafting the final masterpiece.

External customers compose the melody of revenue generation. Their transactions act as the musical notes sustaining the organisation's financial harmony. Loyalty from external customers builds brand reputation. Nurturing relationships with them contributes to sustained success. Their needs become the compass guiding the organisation through the competitive marketplace.

The relationship between customer services and external customers forms the bedrock of a successful and sustainable business ecosystem. Let's delve into the intricate dynamics with customers, suppliers, partners, and government, highlighting the significance of exceptional customer services in each facet.

At the forefront of any business, customers are the lifeblood that keeps the organisation thriving. Customer services, when directed externally, is the art of creating an exceptional experience for buyers. It involves providing prompt and personalised support, addressing queries or concerns, and ensuring a seamless and enjoyable journey. Exceptional customer services build trust, loyalty, and contribute to positive word-of-mouth, essential for attracting and retaining customers in a competitive market.

The relationship with suppliers is a critical aspect of the external customer spectrum. Effective customer services here involve timely and transparent communication, fair and ethical business practices, and collaboration to address any challenges. A strong rapport with suppliers ensures a streamlined supply chain, reliability in the procurement process, and ultimately, the delivery of quality products or services to end customers.

Strategic partnerships are the backbone of many successful businesses. Customer services in the context of partners mean fostering a collaborative environment. This includes open communication, mutual support, and addressing concerns promptly. Nurturing positive relationships with partners contributes to shared success, innovation, and the ability to adapt to changing market dynamics together.

The relationship with government entities is often overlooked in discussions about customer services. However, it plays a crucial role in regulatory compliance, licensing, and overall business operations. Effective customer services towards government bodies involve prompt response to inquiries, adherence to regulations, and a proactive approach to compliance. A positive relationship with the government ensures a stable operating environment, avoiding legal issues and contributing to the overall sustainability of the business.

In essence, customer services for external customers extend far beyond handling complaints or inquiries; it's about creating a positive and collaborative ecosystem. Whether with customers, suppliers, partners, or government entities, exceptional customer services build bridges, fortify relationships, and contribute to the long-term success and sustainability of the business. It's a commitment to excellence that echoes through every interaction, fostering a reputation that attracts customers, strengthens partnerships, and ensures the smooth functioning of the entire business network.

The Essence of the CORE COGS

Imagine Core COGS as the heartbeat of success, encompassing not just strategies, blueprints, and roadmaps, but a crucial element that beats with the rhythm of victory: Customer Success. Here, organisational aspirations align with strategic planning, and the human factor becomes the catalyst for triumph.

In the Core COGS, customers are more than just patrons; they are the essence of success. People are not just assets; they are the driving force behind every achievement. As you strategise, create blueprints, and chart your roadmaps to success, remember that the ultimate goal is not just financial prosperity but the success and satisfaction of those your organisation serves.

Let the essence of Core COGS guide you in your pursuit of success. Aspire strategically, blueprint meticulously, roadmap purposefully, and above all, prioritise the success of your customers and people. In the world of business, Core COGS is the beacon that lights the path to sustained growth and excellence. May your journey be filled with victories, and may the essence of Core COGS propel you to the pinnacle of success.

Customer Services Strategies: The Architect of Success

Strategies, the first pillar of Core COGS, are the architects of your grand design. They lay the groundwork for your success, guiding you through a maze of challenges and opportunities. As you dive into strategic planning, picture yourself as the master architect, sketching the blueprint of your organisation's triumph. Each strategic move should resonate with purpose, aligning your aspirations with the ever-changing business landscape.

This component involves a thorough examination of the market landscape, competitive positioning, and a visionary approach to achieving organisational goals. Strategies provide a roadmap that extends beyond day-to-day operations, offering a comprehensive plan for sustained success.

Strategies serve as a guiding light, ensuring businesses are proactive rather than reactive. In a rapidly evolving business environment, a well-defined strategy allows you and your organisations to navigate challenges with foresight and agility.

The Customer Services Blueprint: Structuring the Foundations

The Blueprint, the second pillar of the Core COGS, involves the structural design of your organisation. It outlines the architecture, processes, and resource allocation necessary for optimal performance. The Blueprint serves as the organisational compass, ensuring that every facet is aligned with your overarching goals.

A well-crafted Blueprint is essential for organisational efficiency and effectiveness. It ensures you're your resources are allocated strategically, your processes are streamlined, and your internal framework supports your overall objectives of the business.

Blueprints are the intricate maps that guide you through the complexities of execution. Think of them as the treasure maps leading to the vaults of success. With precision and clarity, create your blueprints, ensuring that every step taken is a deliberate move towards organisational excellence. Let these blueprints be the compass that keeps you on course even in the stormiest seas of business.

The Customer Services RoadMap: Navigating the Journey

The RoadMap of PEOPLE Success is the dynamic plan that charts the course of your organisation's journey. It is designed to adapt to the evolving business landscape, providing guidance for the strategic implementation of initiatives. The roadmap ensures that your organisation remains on track, even in the face of uncertainties.

In a world where change is constant, having a RoadMap is crucial for maintaining a sense of direction. It offers a step-by-step guide for achieving strategic goals, helping the organisation stay agile and responsive to market dynamics.

Roadmaps illuminate the path to your destination. Just as a well-marked road ensures a smooth journey, meticulous roadmaps chart the course for organisational triumph. As you navigate the twists and turns of the business landscape, let these roadmaps be your guiding stars, ensuring that your journey is purposeful, intentional, and marked by milestones of achievement.

Customer Success: Fostering Relationships

At the core of the Core COGS lies the concept of Customer Success, recognising the importance of both internal and external customers. Internal customers, comprising directors, shareholders, employees, and investors, are crucial for the organisation's internal dynamics. External customers, including clients, suppliers, partners, and governing bodies, are integral to the external business ecosystem.

Focusing on Customer Success is a testament to the holistic approach embedded in the COGS of Success. Internal customer success leads to a motivated workforce, while external customer success ensures sustained business growth through positive relationships and value delivery.

By fostering positive relationships, driving motivation, and Prioritising long-term sustainability, you and your organisations can build a resilient foundation for success that goes beyond financial metrics, creating a legacy of excellence in customer and stakeholder satisfaction. In the realm of the COGS of Success, the Core COGS stands as the bedrock upon which triumph is built. It is the strategic nucleus that shapes the organisation's destiny, aligns its goals, and fosters success for all stakeholders. As businesses navigate the complexities of the modern business landscape, understanding and embracing the Core COGS becomes not just a choice but a strategic imperative – a pathway to unlocking sustained success in the ever-evolving world of commerce. Before you delve into the inner workings of the COGS of success, I want to spend some time exploring a few key elements of its core. These include Building a Talented Team, Navigating Strategic Alliances and Partnerships, Cultivating a Supportive Work Environment, and Mastering Effective Communication Strategies.

The Synergy of THE CORE

The Core COG is not a mere collection of components; it's a synergistic force that aligns the organisational compass, structures the foundation, guides the journey, and fosters success for both internal and external stakeholders. It sets the tone for the entire COGS of Success model, laying the groundwork for the subsequent Inner Rim and Outer Rim COGS.

This synergy forms the heartbeat of the entire framework, emphasising that success is not just financial prosperity but the satisfaction and success of those the organisation serves. In volume 2, I will expand on this concept to offer a comprehensive solution that many successful entrepreneurs have utilised in the past and will continue to use for achieving customer success. Let the essence of THE CORE COGS be the guiding light in your pursuit of success, Prioritising the success of your customers and people above all. May your journey be adorned with victories, and may the essence of THE CORE COGS propel you towards the pinnacle of success.

Conclusion & Recap

Both internal and external customers play integral roles in the success of an organisation. While internal customers facilitate smooth internal operations, external customers are the ultimate beneficiaries of the organisation's products or services. Balancing and Prioritising the needs of both internal and external customers contribute to the overall health and prosperity of the business. The concept of Customer Success in the Core COGS is a strategic and cultural cornerstone. It reflects a comprehensive understanding of success, emphasising the interconnectedness of internal and external stakeholders.

In this series and in Volume 2, I am delving deeper into this concept, offering a comprehensive solution that successful entrepreneurs have relied on in the past and will continue to employ in the future to achieve customer success. This exploration will encompass a detailed examination of strategies, methodologies, and real-world applications that have proven effective across various industries. By drawing on historical successes and contemporary practices, the aim is to equip you with a robust toolkit for fostering customer satisfaction, loyalty, and retention. Through practical insights and actionable advice, Volume 2 aims to empower entrepreneurs to navigate complexities, drive innovation, and ultimately, elevate their customer service to new heights of excellence.

Let's move outward from THE CORE to the INNER RIM. In next chapter, I am delving deep into these components, unveiling the intricacies and synergies that make up the Inner Rim. As we navigate into the next chapter together, you will discover how to harness the power of the Inner Rim to drive your business forward. You will learn to identify and leverage the strengths within your organisation, address potential weaknesses, and optimise processes to achieve sustainable growth. The knowledge imparted in this chapter aims to equip you with the tools and insights needed to build a resilient and dynamic enterprise capable of adapting to changing market conditions and seizing emerging opportunities.

We will explore how these elements interact to create a robust framework that sustains the business, enabling it to thrive in a competitive landscape. You will gain insights into best practices, innovative strategies, and the practical wisdom necessary to enhance your organisation's performance. Lets dive in...

Chapter 5.4

Inner Rim - Blueprint for Business Triumphs

ADVERTISING & PROMOTION
PRODUCTION & DELIVERY
MARKETING
FINANCE
SALES
IT & BUSINESS CHANGE
OPERATIONS

Come along with me on a journey through the Inner Rim of the COGS of Success, where businesses carve their destinies and lay the foundations for enduring triumphs.

Surrounding the Core is THE INNER RIM, housing components that facilitate the transmission of power and the coordination of various functions within the movement. Key components in this section include:

Inner rim is a composite unity of business success akin to the gears and wheels within the Inner Rim of a watch, work in harmony to drive efficiency, competitiveness, and overall business operations. Not having strategic execution and performance of these elements in harmony is like having the watch with broken gears - it won't just struggle; it could lead to significant failure.

This segment of your entrepreneurial odyssey is not just about planning; it's about fortifying the very core of your ship for the challenges that lie ahead. Imagine yourself as a fellow voyager, poised to soak up the vast wealth of knowledge passed down from mentors, trusted business associates, and seasoned entrepreneurs who have successfully navigated these intricate waters.

Picture the Core as the heartbeat of an organisation, the fundamental essence driving its operations. As you venture outward from the core you encounter the Inner Rim—a critical component that not only supports the daily functions but also fuels the strategic growth of your venture. This pivotal segment is composed of several interconnected elements, which is similar to the intrinsic network series of gears of the watch , each playing a vital role in ensuring operational efficiency and effectiveness.

The Inner Rim is where strategic vision translates into actionable plans, and where the aspirations of the Core are realised through meticulous execution. From financial management and human resources to technology infrastructure and customer relations, each aspect of the Inner Rim is meticulously examined to provide you with a comprehensive understanding of its significance. The journey through the Inner Rim is not just a passage; it is a transformative experience that will shape the future trajectory of your entrepreneurial venture.

1. IT & Business Change: Navigating Technological Tides

As you set sail into the realm of IT & Business Change, envision this as navigating through the technological tides that shape the modern business landscape. My tech-savvy mentors, the navigators of digital waters, have shared profound insights into the strategic importance of embracing technology for organisational transformation.

let me help you to delve into the very heartbeat of modern business dynamics—the COG that propels you and your organisations into the realms of transformation and technological prowess—the IT & Business Change.

In an era where the tides of technology shape the landscapes of success, dedicating a significant portion of a business's spending budget, imagine IT & Business Change as the engine room of a mighty ship, steering the vessel through the ever-evolving technological tides. This cog is not merely an investment; it is a lifeline, a conduit that connects the aspirations of businesses with the transformative power of technology. Organisations across the globe are allocating a substantial part of their budgets ranging from 5% to 15% of their overall revenue and budget to navigate these technological tide to this critical cog which is not just a strategic decision; it's a necessity for survival and triumph. Let us explore why

First Digital Transformation, The IT and web technologies are no more a nice to have feature for business in modern digital world. They are the must have requirement for not only the growth but also the survival. If you do not embrace the current trend of IT and business change, you as a business will struggle to not only survive but will struggle to stand up. The world is undergoing a profound digital transformation, reshaping industries and redefining how businesses operate. Investing in IT & Business Change allows you and your organisations to survive, sustain, succeed and thrive. Sonner you realise and accept the fact, better chances you have for survivals and success. Embrace this transformative wave, leveraging cutting-edge technologies to enhance efficiency, streamline processes, and stay competitive in an increasingly digital landscape.

Second Innovation and Agility, the IT & Business Change cog is the epicentre of innovation. Businesses allocate significant funds to stay at the forefront of technological advancements, fostering agility and adaptability. In an era where the pace of change is unprecedented, you and your organisations must invest in IT to swiftly respond to market shifts, emerging trends, and evolving customer expectations.

Third is Enhanced Productivity and Efficiency, the integration of robust IT systems and business change initiatives results in enhanced productivity and efficiency. Whether through automation, cloud computing, or data analytics, these investments empower you and your organisations to optimise workflows, reduce operational bottlenecks, and drive overall productivity gains.

Competitive Edge is the next one. In today's fast-paced business environment, maintaining a competitive edge is non-negotiable. Allocating a significant portion of the budget to IT & Business Change ensures that you and your organisations have the technological arsenal to outpace competitors, seize new opportunities, and lead the charge in their respective industries.

And last but not the least is Adaptation to Market Demands. Consumer behaviours, market trends, and regulatory landscapes are in constant flux. The IT & Business Change cog enables you and your organisations to proactively adapt to these changes. Whether it's developing customer-centric digital experiences or aligning with industry regulations, businesses investing in this cog position themselves as agile and responsive entities.

The allocation of 5% to 15% of a business's spending budget to IT & Business Change is not merely a financial decision for most of the successful business; it is an investment in the future. As you navigate the technological tides, let me help you recognise that this cog is the compass that points us toward innovation, efficiency, and sustained relevance. Embrace the transformative power of technology, for in doing so, you not only invest in the success of your business today but pave the way for a future where your organisation stands as a beacon of technological brilliance.

IT & Business Change is not just about adopting the latest gadgets; it's about leveraging technology for strategic advantages. Embracing digital transformation ensures that your ship sails with the winds of efficiency, innovation, and competitiveness. Strategic adoption of technology ensures that your ship not only keeps pace with the digital waves but surfs them to new heights. In the digital waters, digital innovation is the wind in your sails. Embracing emerging technologies, fostering a culture of innovation, and integrating IT into business processes contribute to your ship sailing with the winds of digital advancement. Embracing digital transformation ensures that your ship is not just technologically equipped but is a pioneer in the vast sea of digital possibilities.

2. Finance: Navigating the Fiscal Seas with Prudence

Now, let's venture into the fiscal seas of Finance, a realm where financial wisdom becomes the rudder that guides your ship through economic currents. My financial maestros, the helmsmen of fiscal prudence, have shared profound insights into the strategic importance of financial management for sustainable business growth.

This is a journey into the intricate and often tumultuous seas of Finance, where the astute navigation of fiscal waters is not just a skill but the very essence of sustainable business growth.

Visualise this as your ship, the vessel of your enterprise, sailing through economic currents. In this voyage, the cog that serves as the rudder, steering you with precision and prudence, is the vital realm of Finance. Financial management is the cornerstone for triumph in the business world. Let us explore why

First and foremost, the strategic Decision-Making. Financial planning and budgeting is one of the key to the success of any strategic decision in your business. Without financial planning, whether, short term, midterm or long-term financial planning, business have no idea about their current financial need or financial requirements. Lack of financial planning leave business in the complete dark and you throw yourselves in a battlefield without the arms and ammunition required to win the battlefield. In other words, you jump into the venture without a robust budget or allocation of resources for the current as well as future growth, which leads to a big-time failure. Finance is the compass that guides strategic decision-making within an organisation. The allocation of resources, investment decisions, and overall financial strategy are intricately tied to the success of the business. It is the financial helmsmen who navigate through the multitude of choices, ensuring that each decision aligns with the overarching goals of sustainable growth and profitability.

Second the Risk Mitigation. Just as a skilled captain anticipates and navigates through stormy weather, financial experts are adept at identifying and mitigating risks. Through meticulous financial planning, businesses can safeguard themselves against economic uncertainties, market fluctuations, and unforeseen challenges. Prudent financial management acts as a resilient anchor, ensuring the ship weathers any financial storm that may arise.

Third Resource Optimisation. The Finance cog is responsible for optimising the utilisation of resources. Whether it's capital, human resources, or operational assets, effective financial management ensures that resources are allocated efficiently. This optimisation not only enhances productivity but also contributes to cost-effectiveness, bolstering the financial health of the organisation.

Fourth the Compliance and Governance. In the vast fiscal seas, adherence to regulations and ethical financial practices is paramount. Financial management encompasses the establishment of robust governance structures and compliance frameworks. By adhering to these principles, you and your organisations not only uphold their integrity but also build trust with stakeholders, fostering long-term sustainability.

Fifth the Investor Confidence. The financial seas are often observed by external entities, such as investors. Sound financial management builds confidence among investors, showcasing the organisation as a prudent and reliable investment. This confidence, in turn, attracts capital and facilitates access to financial markets, providing the resources needed for expansion and innovation.

And last but not the least the Long-Term Sustainability. Finance is the compass that guides the ship not only in calm waters but also through the challenges of the fiscal seas. Sustainable business growth requires a long-term perspective, and financial management is the tool that ensures the organisation's journey is characterised by stability, resilience, and continuous adaptation to changing landscapes.

The importance of the Finance cog cannot be overstated. It is the rudder that steers the ship through the fiscal seas with prudence, ensuring that every decision aligns with the vision of sustainable growth. As you venture into these waters, let financial wisdom be your guiding light, propelling your ship towards prosperity and triumph. May your fiscal seas be navigated with precision, and may your journey be marked by the success that comes with astute financial management.

Finance is not just about numbers on a balance sheet; it's about strategic fiscal management. Prudent financial practices, budgeting, and investment decisions are the anchors that stabilise your ship in the vast sea of economic complexities.

In the fiscal seas, let Finance be your anchor. Strategic fiscal management ensures that your ship not only weathers financial storms but sails through them with resilience and stability. Sound financial practices, risk assessment, and resource allocation contribute to your ship sailing with the winds of financial stability and growth. Strategic fiscal management ensures that your ship's journey is not just financially secure but sails with the winds of economic prosperity.

3. Production: Crafting Excellence in the Ship's Engine Room

Let's delve into the engine room of your ship, the realm of Production, where excellence in manufacturing becomes the powerhouse that propels your business forward.

In the realm of Production, where excellence in manufacturing becomes the powerhouse that propels your business forward, let's explore the strategic importance of production excellence for business success.

Production is not just about making products or not merely about churning out goods; it's about crafting excellence. Just as a skilled artisan meticulously shapes raw materials into a masterpiece, your production team transforms raw materials into high-quality products. The focus on craftsmanship underscores the commitment to delivering products of exceptional quality, precision, and value. Every product that leaves your production line reflects the dedication to excellence ingrained in your operations. Operational efficiency, quality control, and continuous improvement are the elements that ensure your ship's engine runs smoothly and efficiently.

Operational efficiency is the cornerstone of production excellence. It involves optimising processes, minimising waste, and maximising output to achieve the highest level of productivity with the resources available. Like a well-oiled machine, efficient production processes ensure that every component of your operation works seamlessly together, minimising downtime, reducing costs, and maximising profitability.

Quality control is paramount in ensuring that each product meets or exceeds the expectations of your customers. It involves implementing rigorous standards and procedures to detect and address any deviations from the desired quality criteria. By maintaining strict quality control measures, you instill confidence in your customers, enhance brand reputation, and minimise the risk of costly recalls or returns.

Continuous improvement is the driving force behind production excellence. It involves a commitment to ongoing refinement and innovation, seeking out opportunities to enhance processes, streamline operations, and elevate product quality. Embracing a culture of continuous improvement empowers your team to identify inefficiencies, address bottlenecks, and adapt to changing market dynamics, ensuring that your business remains competitive and resilient in the face of challenges.

In the engine room of your ship, let Production be your powerhouse. Efficient production processes, quality assurance, and a commitment to continuous improvement collectively propel your business forward. Operational efficiency ensures that your ship's engine not only runs smoothly but also propels your business to new heights of success. By Prioritising production excellence, you position your business for sustained growth, customer satisfaction, and market leadership.

Production excellence is the foundation upon which successful businesses are built. By emphasising craftsmanship, operational efficiency, quality control, and continuous improvement, you empower your production team to serve as the driving force behind your business's success. As you navigate the seas of business, let Production be your powerhouse, propelling your venture towards new horizons of excellence and prosperity.

In the engine room, let Production be your powerhouse. Crafting excellence ensures that your ship not only produces goods but does so with precision, quality, and operational efficiency. Efficient production processes, quality assurance, and a commitment to continuous improvement contribute to your ship sailing with the winds of production efficiency and customer satisfaction. Operational efficiency ensures that your ship's engine not only runs smoothly but propels your business to new heights.

4. Delivery & Distribution: Navigating the Logistics Waters with Precision

As you set your sights on the Logistics Waters of Delivery, envision this as the strategic management of the supply chain that ensures your products reach their destination with precision and efficiency. You must understand the importance of efficient delivery systems for customer satisfaction and business success.

In the vast ocean of business, where success is often measured by customer satisfaction and loyalty, navigating the logistics waters with precision is paramount. Just as a skilled captain relies on the stars to chart a course, businesses depend on efficient delivery systems, streamlined logistics processes, and timely shipments to ensure that their cargo reaches its destination with precision and reliability. Let's explore how these principles come together to propel businesses towards the shores of customer delight.

From insights gleaned from logistics captains, it becomes evident that delivery is not merely about shipping products; it's about strategic supply chain management. Efficient delivery systems, timely shipments, and effective logistics planning serve as the anchors that ensure a business's cargo reaches its destination with precision. In the logistics waters, delivery must be the anchor. Strategic supply chain management ensures that a business's cargo not only reaches its destination but does so with punctuality and reliability.

Efficiency becomes the wind in the sails of logistics operations. Effective delivery systems, streamlined logistics, and a commitment to timely shipments contribute to a business sailing with the winds of customer satisfaction and loyalty. As businesses navigate the logistics waters, efficiency should be the guiding light. Strategic supply chain management ensures that a business's cargo is not just delivered but does so with the winds of customer delight.

Effective delivery and distribution systems are the backbone of successful logistics operations. This entails optimising transportation routes, leveraging technology for real-time tracking and monitoring, and establishing robust communication channels. Streamlining logistics processes involves eliminating inefficiencies, reducing waste, and optimising workflows to enhance productivity and efficiency. A commitment to timely shipments requires proactive planning, effective scheduling, and close monitoring of transportation activities.

Efficiency becomes the guiding light that propels businesses forward in the logistics waters. By implementing effective delivery systems, streamlining logistics processes, and Prioritising timely shipments, businesses can optimise resource utilisation, minimise costs, and maximise customer value and satisfaction.

Navigating the logistics waters with precision is essential for businesses aiming to sail towards customer delight. By crafting excellence in logistics and embracing efficiency as the North Star, businesses can ensure that their cargo reaches its destination with precision and reliability. Strategic supply chain management becomes the compass that guides businesses through the complexities of logistics operations, propelling them towards the shores of customer satisfaction and loyalty.

Delivery is not just about shipping products; it's about strategic supply chain management. Efficient delivery systems, timely shipments, and effective logistics planning are the anchors that ensure your ship's cargo reaches its destination with precision. Strategic supply chain management ensures that your ship's cargo not only reaches its destination but does so with punctuality and reliability.

Effective delivery systems, streamlined logistics, and a commitment to timely shipments contribute to your ship sailing with the winds of customer satisfaction and loyalty. Strategic supply chain management ensures that your ship's cargo is not just delivered but does so with the winds of customer delight.

5a. Advertising: Crafting the Message that Resonates

Now, let's enter the realm of Advertising, a dynamic sea where crafting the right message becomes the wind that propels your ship forward in the vast ocean of consumer choices. In this realm, effective advertising strategies, compelling narratives, and a consistent brand message are the elements that ensure your ship stands out amidst the fleet. Let's delve deeper into the strategic importance of advertising for brand visibility and market presence, as shared by advertising artisans who are the creators of compelling narratives.

Advertising transcends mere promotional campaigns; it's about crafting messages that resonate deeply with the audience. Effective advertising strategies focus on creating compelling narratives that capture attention and evoke emotion. A consistent brand message ensures that your ship's presence is not just noticed but celebrated in the vast sea of consumer choices.

In the advertising sea, compelling narratives serve as the wind in your sails. Thoughtful advertising strategies, consistency in messaging, and a commitment to brand image contribute to your ship sailing with the winds of consumer trust and recognition. Crafting these narratives ensures that your ship's message is not just heard but resonates deeply in the vast sea of market options.

As you navigate the advertising sea, let compelling narratives be your compass. Effective advertising ensures that your ship's message is not just heard but resonates deeply with the audience. By crafting stories that captivate and engage, businesses can establish a strong emotional connection with consumers, leading to increased brand loyalty and market share.

In the competitive landscape of advertising, standing out amidst the fleet is essential for success. Businesses must develop unique selling propositions and compelling brand stories that differentiate them from competitors. By consistently delivering messages that resonate with their target audience, businesses can carve out a distinctive identity in the market and build long-lasting relationships with consumers.

Crafting the message that resonates is paramount in the realm of Advertising. By focusing on effective advertising strategies, compelling narratives, and a consistent brand message, businesses can ensure that their ship stands out amidst the vast sea of consumer choices. Let compelling narratives be your compass as you navigate the advertising sea, ensuring that your message not only reaches but deeply resonates with your audience.

5b. Promotions: Crafting Incentives for Customer Delight

Let's navigate into the seas of Promotions, a dynamic realm where crafting incentives becomes the strategic approach to delighting your customers and fostering loyalty. In this sea, thoughtful promotion strategies, customer loyalty programmes, and strategic discounting are the anchors that ensure your ship sails with the winds of customer satisfaction. My promotion maestros, the architects of customer satisfaction, have shared insights into the importance of promotions for brand loyalty and market competitiveness. Let's delve deeper into the insights shared by promotion maestros, the architects of customer satisfaction, regarding the importance of promotions for brand loyalty and market competitiveness.

Promotions transcend mere discounts and offers; they're about crafting incentives that delight customers. Thoughtful promotion strategies focus on providing value-added benefits and experiences that go beyond price reductions. Customer loyalty programmes and strategic discounting are essential components that ensure your ship not only attracts customers but retains them amidst the vast sea of market choices.

In the promotions sea, customer delight serves as the wind in your sails. Strategic promotion strategies, customer-centric incentives, and a commitment to exceeding expectations contribute to your ship sailing with the winds of customer loyalty. By focusing on delighting customers rather than just attracting them, businesses can create lasting relationships and differentiate themselves in the competitive market landscape.

As you navigate the promotions sea, let customer delight be your guiding star. Effective promotions ensure that your ship's offerings are not just purchased but celebrated by customers in the vast sea of market competition. By consistently delivering exceptional value and memorable experiences, businesses can cultivate a loyal customer base that acts as advocates and ambassadors for their brand.

In the competitive landscape of promotions, standing out amidst the competition is crucial for success. Businesses must innovate and differentiate their promotional strategies to capture the attention and loyalty of customers. By offering unique incentives, personalised experiences, and exclusive rewards, businesses can set themselves apart and create a competitive edge in the market.

Crafting incentives for customer delight is paramount in the realm of Promotions. By focusing on thoughtful promotion strategies, customer loyalty programmes, and strategic discounting, businesses can ensure that their ship sails with the winds of customer satisfaction and loyalty. Let customer delight be your guiding star as you navigate the promotions sea, ensuring that your offerings are not just purchased but celebrated by customers amidst the vast sea of market competition.

6a. Marketing: Navigating the Sea of Market Trends

Now, let's venture into the Sea of Marketing, a vast expanse where understanding market trends becomes the compass that guides your ship through the ever-changing currents of consumer preferences. My marketing visionaries, the navigators of market dynamics, have shared insights into the strategic importance of marketing for brand positioning and market relevance. In this dynamic sea, market research, brand positioning, and consumer behaviour analysis are the essential elements that ensure your ship sails with the winds of market relevance. Let's delve deeper into the insights shared by marketing visionaries, the navigators of market dynamics, regarding the strategic importance of marketing for brand positioning and market relevance.

Marketing transcends mere advertising; it's about understanding and influencing market trends. Market research, brand positioning, and consumer behaviour analysis are critical components that ensure your ship adapts to the currents and navigates them to your advantage amidst the vast sea of consumer choices. By staying attuned to market dynamics, businesses can identify opportunities and tailor their strategies to meet evolving consumer needs and preferences.

In the marketing sea, market insights serve as the wind in your sails. Thoughtful market research, strategic brand positioning, and a proactive approach to consumer trends contribute to your ship sailing with the winds of market leadership. By leveraging market insights, businesses can anticipate shifts in consumer behaviour, identify emerging trends, and position themselves as industry leaders, setting the course for success in the competitive market landscape.

As you navigate the marketing sea, let market insights be your guiding light. Effective marketing ensures that your ship's offerings are not just in demand but also set the course for market trends amidst the vast sea of consumer choices. By leveraging market insights to inform decision-making and strategy development, businesses can stay ahead of the curve and maintain their competitive edge in the market.

In the ever-changing landscape of marketing, strategic brand positioning and a proactive approach to consumer trends are essential for success. Businesses must continually monitor market dynamics, analyse consumer behaviour, and adjust their strategies accordingly to stay relevant and competitive. By understanding and influencing market trends, businesses can position themselves as industry leaders and shape the direction of the market, setting the course for long-term success and growth.

Navigating the Sea of Marketing requires a deep understanding of market trends and consumer preferences. By harnessing market insights, businesses can adapt to changing currents, position themselves for success, and maintain their relevance in the competitive market landscape. Let market insights be your guiding light as you navigate the marketing sea, setting the course for market leadership and success amidst the vast sea of consumer choices.

6b. Messaging: Crafting the Narrative that Resonates

Now, let's enter the realm of Messaging, a dynamic sea where crafting the right narrative becomes the compass that guides your ship through the vast ocean of communication channels. My messaging architects, the creators of compelling stories, have shared insights into the strategic importance of messaging for brand communication and consumer engagement.

Effective messaging strategies, storytelling, and a consistent brand narrative are the essential elements that ensure your ship stands out amidst the noise. Thinking about the insights shared by messaging architects, the creators of compelling stories, regarding the strategic importance of messaging for brand communication and consumer engagement. Let's delve deeper into it further.

Messaging goes beyond mere communication; it's about crafting narratives that resonate with your audience. Effective messaging strategies, combined with the art of storytelling and a consistent brand narrative, ensure that your ship's message not only gets heard but also deeply resonates in the vast sea of communication channels. By infusing your brand's message with compelling narratives, you can capture the attention and imagination of your audience, fostering meaningful connections and driving engagement.

In the messaging sea, let Messaging be your compass. Crafting compelling narratives ensures that your ship's message is not just communicated but cherished amidst the noise of communication channels. By strategically shaping your brand's narrative and crafting messages that resonate with your audience, you can navigate through the complexities of the messaging landscape with clarity and purpose, guiding your ship towards success and recognition.

Compelling stories serve as the wind in your sails in the messaging sea. Thoughtful messaging strategies, consistency in communication, and a commitment to brand storytelling contribute to your ship sailing with the winds of consumer engagement and loyalty. By harnessing the power of storytelling, you and your businesses can captivate their audience, evoke emotions, and inspire action, driving deeper connections and fostering loyalty among consumers.

As you navigate the messaging sea, let compelling stories be your guiding star. Effective messaging ensures that your ship's narrative is not just communicated but cherished amidst the vast sea of brand communications. By weaving narratives that resonate with your audience and staying true to your brand's voice and values, you can elevate your messaging efforts and create memorable experiences that leave a lasting impression on consumers.

Crafting compelling narratives is essential for navigating the sea of Messaging successfully. By leveraging effective messaging strategies, storytelling techniques, and a consistent brand narrative, businesses can stand out amidst the noise of communication channels, driving engagement, and fostering consumer loyalty. Compelling stories are your guiding star as you navigate the messaging sea, setting the course for meaningful connections and lasting success in the vast ocean of brand communications.

7. Sales: Navigating the Waters of Customer Engagement

Sales, a dynamic realm where customer engagement becomes the strategic approach to converting leads into loyal patrons. My sales virtuosos, the architects of customer relationships, have shared insights into the importance of sales for revenue generation and business sustainability.

In this ever-evolving landscape, effective sales strategies, customer relationship management, and a commitment to customer satisfaction are the essential elements that ensure your ship sails with the winds of revenue generation. Wondering what I bring inside this book for you from the insights shared by sales virtuosos, the architects of customer relationships, regarding the importance of sales for revenue generation and business sustainability. Let's explore

Sales transcends mere transactions; it's about building lasting relationships with customers. Effective sales strategies, combined with the art of customer relationship management and a dedication to customer satisfaction, serve as the anchors that ensure your ship sails with the winds of revenue generation. By Prioritising relationship-building over transactions, businesses can foster loyal customers amidst the vast sea of market choices, setting the stage for long-term success and sustainability.

In the sales waters, let Sales be your anchor. Building relationships ensures that your ship not only sells products but also nurtures loyal customers amidst the complexities of the market. By focusing on building genuine connections with customers and understanding their needs and preferences, businesses can navigate through the sales landscape with confidence and purpose, driving revenue generation and fostering customer loyalty.

Customer relationships serve as the wind in your sails in the sales waters. Thoughtful sales strategies, personalised customer engagement, and a commitment to exceeding expectations contribute to your ship sailing with the winds of customer loyalty. By Prioritising customer satisfaction and going above and beyond to meet their needs, businesses can create memorable experiences that resonate with customers, driving repeat purchases and referrals.

As you navigate the sales waters, let customer relationships be your guiding light. Effective sales ensure that your ship's offerings are not just purchased but celebrated amidst the vast sea of market competition. By cultivating meaningful relationships with customers and delivering exceptional experiences at every touchpoint, businesses can differentiate themselves from competitors and earn the loyalty and trust of their customer base.

Building lasting customer relationships is paramount for navigating the seas of Sales successfully. By leveraging effective sales strategies, customer relationship management techniques, and a dedication to customer satisfaction, businesses can drive revenue generation and foster long-term loyalty amidst the dynamic market landscape. Let customer relationships be your guiding light as you navigate the sales waters, setting the course for sustainable growth and success in the vast ocean of customer engagement.

8. Operations: Navigating the Sea of Efficiency

As you set sail into the Sea of Operations, envision this as the strategic management of core activities that ensures your ship's journey is smooth and efficient. My operations architects, the navigators of streamlined processes, have shared insights into the importance of efficient operations for business sustainability and growth. Navigating the Seas of Operations: Achieving Efficiency and Growth

Embark with us as you set sail into the Sea of Operations, a strategic realm where the management of core activities ensures your ship's journey is smooth and efficient. In this vast expanse, efficient operations, productivity enhancement, and a commitment to continuous improvement serve as the guiding principles that propel your ship forward. Operations transcend routine tasks; they are about the orchestration of streamlined processes. Efficient operations, productivity enhancement, and a dedication to continuous improvement are the essential elements that ensure your ship sails with the winds of operational efficiency. By optimising processes and eliminating inefficiencies, businesses can navigate through the operational sea with agility and precision, driving productivity and ensuring long-term sustainability.

In the operational sea, let Operations be your anchor. Streamlined processes ensure that your ship's journey is not just routine but sails with the winds of efficiency and productivity. By establishing robust operational frameworks and embracing best practices, businesses can navigate through challenges and seize opportunities, setting the course for success and growth in the competitive market landscape.

Operational efficiency serves as the wind in your sails in the operational sea. Effective operations management, process optimisation, and a proactive approach to challenges contribute to your ship sailing with the winds of business sustainability and growth. By fostering a culture of efficiency and innovation, businesses can stay ahead of the curve and drive continuous improvement, positioning themselves as industry leaders in the dynamic market environment.

As you navigate the operational sea, let operational efficiency be your compass. Streamlined operations ensure that your ship not only stays afloat but sails with the winds of industry leadership. By embracing technology, leveraging data-driven insights, and empowering employees to contribute to process improvement initiatives, businesses can achieve operational excellence and drive sustainable growth in the ever-evolving market landscape. Efficient operations are fundamental for navigating the seas of Operations successfully. By Prioritising streamlined processes, productivity enhancement, and a commitment to continuous improvement, businesses can propel themselves forward with confidence and resilience. Let operational efficiency be your guiding light as you navigate the operational sea, setting the course for success and growth amidst the challenges and opportunities that lie ahead.

Conclusion & Recap

In this chapter, you explored key aspects critical for business success. You navigated IT and Business Change, highlighting the need to adapt to technological advancements. The Finance section focused on sound financial management. In Production, the emphasis was on ensuring high-quality outputs. Efficient delivery processes were covered in the Delivery section. Advertising and Promotions discussed crafting compelling messages and incentives for customers. Marketing and Messaging examined market trends and effective narratives. Sales focused on engaging customers effectively. Finally, the Operations segment highlighted streamlining processes. This chapter acts as a guide to navigating business success, drawing insights from mentors, associates, and experienced entrepreneurs. It provides a blueprint for overcoming challenges and seizing opportunities in your entrepreneurial journey. As I conclude this chapter on The Inner Rim of the COGS of Success, imagine yourself as the captain, equipped with the wisdom shared by mentors and fellow business owners. The Inner Rim is about fortifying your business for future challenges. As you venture into the vast ocean of business possibilities, may these lessons propel your ship toward success. Sail forth, and let The Inner Rim of COGS of Success guide you through the ever-changing waters of business triumphs. As you embark on this journey through The Outer Core in next chapter, let us embrace the challenges and opportunities that lie ahead with courage and optimism. Together, you will navigate the complexities of business expansion, harnessing your collective knowledge and expertise to steer towards new horizons of growth and success.

Chapter 5.5

Navigating the Waters of Expansion - The Outer Core of the COGS

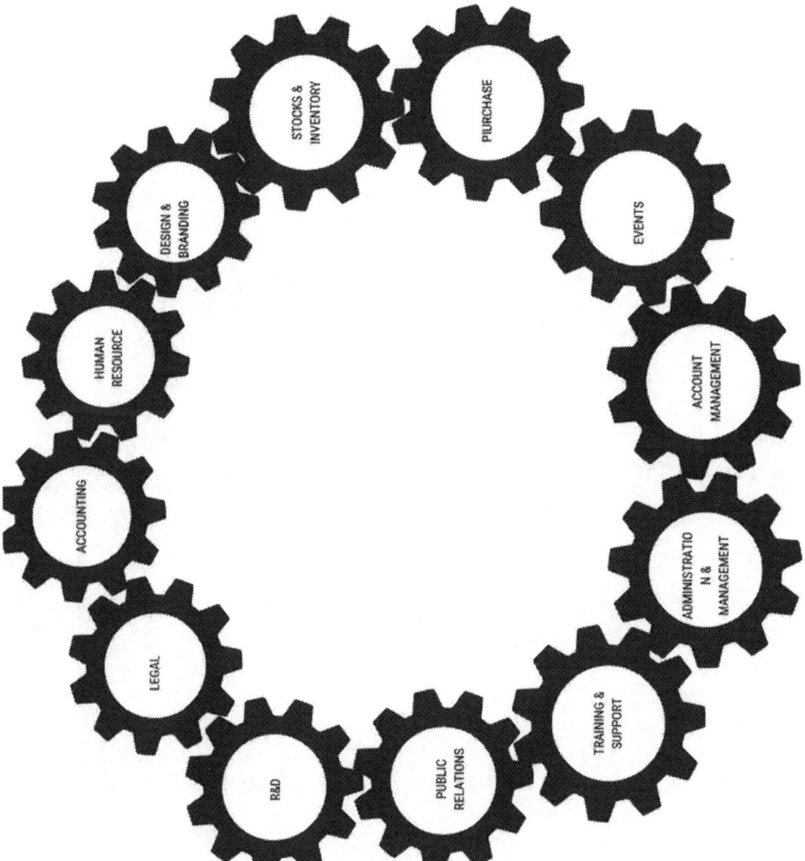
STOCKS & INVENTORY
PIURCHASE
EVENTS
ACCOUNT MANAGEMENT
ADMINISTRATIO N & MANAGEMENT
TRAINING & SUPPORT
PUBLIC RELATIONS
R&D
LEGAL
ACCOUNTING
HUMAN RESOURCE
DESIGN & BRANDING

As I reflect on the extensive journey of entrepreneurship, I find myself drawn to a pivotal phase often referred to as "The Outer Core" in the COGS of Success. In this phase, I have encountered invaluable lessons that have profoundly shaped my understanding of business growth and expansion.

Imagine yourself standing at the threshold of growth, ready to embark on a journey of exploration and achievement. Allow me to be your guide as you navigate the uncharted waters of The Outer Core.

This section of your business voyage, while not immediately obligatory, serves as both the anchor and sail as you embark on the journey to scale new heights. It represents a critical juncture where strategic decisions and calculated risks pave the way for sustainable growth and success. Embracing The Outer Core means venturing beyond the comfort zone, embracing change, and embracing new challenges with confidence and determination.

In The Outer Core, you are called upon to leverage your experiences, insights, and networks to propel your businesses forward. It's a phase where innovation, adaptability, and resilience are paramount. By embracing this phase wholeheartedly, you can position yourselves for long-term success, navigating through obstacles and seizing opportunities with agility and foresight.

Throughout The Outer Core, entrepreneurs must remain steadfast in their commitment to continuous learning and improvement. It's a journey of discovery, where each obstacle overcome and each success achieved brings valuable lessons and insights. By embracing a growth mindset and remaining open to new possibilities, entrepreneurs can unlock their full potential and chart a course towards lasting prosperity.

1. Accounting: Navigating Financial Waters with Precision

Picture yourself at the helm of your business ship, navigating through the vast expanse of financial waters with precision and purpose.

As you set sail, it's crucial to acknowledge the vital role of accounting as your guiding compass in this journey. Accounting is not merely about crunching numbers; it's a strategic tool that empowers us to maintain financial transparency, ensure compliance with regulatory standards, and gain a clear view of your business's financial health.

In the company of seasoned financial captains, I've learned that accurate financial records, adherence to accounting standards, and robust financial management serve as the anchors that stabilise your ship amidst the complexities of the financial seas. These are the foundations upon which your success is built, providing us with the stability and clarity needed to navigate confidently through turbulent waters.

But your journey doesn't stop there. As you navigate through the pages of financial records, you discover that sound fiscal practices are the wind in your sails, propelling us forward with stability, growth, and resilience. Meticulous record-keeping, strategic budgeting, thorough risk assessment, and prudent resource allocation are the cornerstones of your financial strategy, guiding us towards your destination with precision and purpose.

So, let us steer with caution as you sail through these financial waters, embracing the challenges and opportunities that lie ahead. With sound financial management as your compass, you have the power to chart a course towards success, navigating the waves of uncertainty with confidence and determination.

2. HR: Cultivating the Workforce Garden

As you move into the territory of Human Resources (HR), imagine this as the nurturing of the workforce garden. Imagine Human Resources domain as the nurturing of a flourishing workforce garden, where every seed planted represents a potential for growth, productivity, and success.

Recruitment, employee relations, and performance management are not just administrative functions; they form the very heart of your ship. They are the seeds that, when nurtured effectively, cultivate a vibrant and productive workforce.

Think of HR as your dedicated cultivator in the workforce garden. Just as a skilled gardener tends to each plant with care and attention, HR nurtures your employees, ensuring they have the skills, motivation, and support they need to thrive.

As you delve deeper into the workforce garden, I've come to understand that a productive crew is akin to the wind in your sails. Strategic recruitment practices, fostering positive employee relations, and investing in ongoing training and development all contribute to cultivating a workforce that is skilled, motivated, and adaptive.

So, as you navigate through the workforce garden, let us keep productivity as your guiding compass. By nurturing your workforce and empowering them to excel, you equip your ship to navigate through the dynamic challenges of the business world with confidence and resilience.

I urge each of you to embrace the principles of HR with enthusiasm and dedication. Let us harness the power of strategic recruitment, foster positive employee relations, and Prioritise ongoing training and development. Together, you can cultivate a workforce garden that blooms with success and prosperity.

3. Branding: Forging a Distinctive Identity

Let's venture into the vast expanse of Branding, often hailed as the art of crafting a unique identity. Through my entrepreneurial journey, I've come to realise that branding transcends mere logos and colours; it's about creating a distinct persona that resonates with your audience. A robust brand presence ensures that your business stands out amidst the competition.

In the realm of branding, recognition and trust are the driving forces. Employing effective branding strategies, maintaining message consistency, and cultivating a positive brand image are essential for your ship to make waves in the crowded market.

I'm excited to invite you on an enthralling expedition into the world of Branding – a journey where you'll explore the depths of identity creation and transformation. It's not just about visual elements; it's about crafting a narrative that captivates your audience.

As you navigate through the branding waters, let's unveil the sails of uniqueness. By establishing a strong brand identity, you ensure that your ship doesn't get lost in the sea of consumer choices but stands tall as a beacon of distinction.

Amidst the branding seas, I've realised that recognition and trust act as the winds propelling your ship forward. Through strategic branding tactics, consistent messaging, and fostering a positive brand perception, you can carve your place in the vast market landscape.

So, as you chart your course through the branding seas, let's make recognition your guiding light. Let's cultivate a robust brand presence that sails with the winds of consumer trust and recognition, steering your ship towards new realms of success.

I urge each of you to embrace the essence of branding with fervour and dedication. Together, let's harness the power of uniqueness, consistency, and trust-building to elevate your brand to unprecedented heights. With confidence and determination, you can navigate the branding seas and chart a course towards enduring success.

4. Production Designing: Aesthetics and Innovation

Venturing into the realm of Production Designing is akin to exploring a world where aesthetics and innovation reign supreme. It's a domain where form meets function, and creativity intertwines with practicality.

In this journey, I've learned that Production Designing transcends mere functionality; it's about crafting products that engage and delight the senses. Aesthetic appeal and innovation serve as the pillars upon which standout products are built, ensuring they not only perform admirably but also leave a lasting impression on consumers.

As you navigate through the waters of aesthetics and innovation, let us embrace design as your ultimate embellishment. Production Designing ensures that your products not only meet the needs of consumers but also evoke emotions and desires through their visual appeal and innovative features.

In the realm of innovation, I've discovered that aesthetic appeal and innovation act as the driving forces propelling your ship forward. By Prioritising thoughtful product design, fostering a culture of continuous innovation, and staying attuned to evolving market trends, you can ensure that your products stand out amidst the competition.

As you sail through the innovation waters, let creativity be your guiding light. Embracing creativity and pushing the boundaries of innovation not only keep your ship afloat but also position us as trailblazers in your industry, setting new standards and inspiring others to follow suit.

5. Stock and Inventory: Streamlining the Supply Chain

Exploring stock and inventory management is akin to embarking on a mission to streamline your business's pulse—the supply chain. It's a journey into the core of your operations, where adept handling of goods and resources unlocks productivity and profitability.

Beyond warehousing, stock and inventory management optimise the entire supply chain. Strategic management minimises carrying costs, prevents stockouts, and ensures your cargo is always ready for the next journey.

Efficiency is your steadfast anchor in this maritime domain of logistics. With strategic management, your cargo seamlessly transitions to the next destination.

As I navigated through the logistics harbour, I realised efficiency acts as the wind in your sails. Effective management contributes to a streamlined supply chain, enabling agility and precision in navigating procurement challenges.

Let efficiency illuminate your path as you traverse the logistics harbour. A streamlined supply chain ensures prompt and reliable cargo delivery.

Stock and inventory management orchestrate a logistics symphony, ensuring products are available when and where needed. They serve as the linchpin of a well-oiled supply chain, meeting customer demands while minimising costs and maximising efficiency.

Embrace stock and inventory management as the backbone of your operations. Implementing robust systems streamlines operations, minimises stockouts, and optimises inventory turnover, enhancing customer satisfaction and bolstering your bottom line.

In your pursuit of supply chain optimisation, stock and inventory management drive operational excellence. Leveraging advanced technologies grants real-time visibility into inventory levels, enabling anticipation of market fluctuations and informed decision-making.

Charting your course through supply chain management, let innovation guide your helm. Embracing emerging technologies transforms your supply chain into a strategic asset, propelling us towards sustained success in the ever-evolving marketplace.

6. Purchase: Strategic Procurement and Vendor Management

The Purchase sector involves strategic buying and managing suppliers. It's about making smart decisions and building relationships to help the business grow. Buying things isn't just about getting stuff; it's about working with others, reducing risks, and making sure you get the best value for your money.

When you talk about strategic buying and managing suppliers, it's important to understand how vital it is. Buying things isn't just a simple process; it's a way to help your business do better. By choosing the right suppliers, negotiating well, and managing them effectively, you can save money, reduce risks, and make sure everything runs smoothly.

To do this successfully, you need to plan carefully. It starts with doing thorough research and picking suppliers that match your needs and standards. Then, armed with this knowledge, you can negotiate to get the best deals that save us money and keep risks low. But it doesn't stop there; once you've signed contracts, you need to keep working closely with your suppliers to keep things running smoothly and improve over time.

So, what's the secret to good buying? It's about sourcing smartly, negotiating carefully, managing relationships, reducing risks, and using technology well. By doing all these things, you can make sure your buying processes are efficient, transparent, and driven by data.

Strategic buying isn't just a task; it's a way of thinking—a commitment to doing your best to help the business succeed. By embracing strategic buying practices, you can navigate the challenges of buying things with confidence and skill, helping the business grow and thrive in a fast-changing world.

7. Events Promotion: Networking and Brand Exposure

Venturing into the realm of Events opens doors to dynamic opportunities for networking and brand promotion. In today's business landscape, planning and executing events have become essential strategies for fostering connections, enhancing brand visibility, and engaging customers.

Events are more than just social gatherings; they are strategic platforms for you and your businesses to showcase their offerings, connect with key stakeholders, and leave a lasting impression on attendees. Whether participating in industry conferences, trade shows, or hosting bespoke events, you and your businesses have the chance to network with industry peers, potential clients, and partners, thus expanding their reach and influence.

Strategic event planning ensures that you and your businesses can leverage these opportunities to their advantage. By carefully selecting the right events to participate in or host, you and your businesses can ensure that their presence is felt, celebrated, and remembered amidst the myriad of industry gatherings. From meticulously crafting event agendas to creating engaging experiences for attendees, every aspect of event management plays a crucial role in driving brand visibility and customer engagement.

Participation in industry events allows you and your businesses to showcase their expertise, products, and services, positioning themselves as industry leaders and thought innovators. Hosting brand-specific events provides an even greater opportunity to showcase unique offerings, connect with target audiences on a personal level, and build brand loyalty. These strategic events act as the winds in the sails of businesses, propelling them forward and setting them apart from competitors.

Effective event management is key to ensuring that you and your businesses not only have a presence at industry gatherings but also make a meaningful impact. By focusing on seamless execution, engaging content, and personalised interactions, you and your businesses can ensure that their presence is not just acknowledged but celebrated. This approach fosters stronger relationships with existing customers, attracts new prospects, and reinforces brand reputation in the market.

Events play a pivotal role in driving networking opportunities and brand promotion for businesses. By strategically participating in and hosting events, you and your businesses can expand their network, increase brand visibility, and foster meaningful connections with customers and stakeholders. With effective event management practices, you and your businesses can navigate the seas of events with confidence, ensuring that their ship sails towards success in the competitive business landscape.

8. Account Management: Nurturing Key Relationships

Account Management is a crucial aspect of business where the focus shifts towards nurturing and maintaining strong relationships with key accounts. In this realm, the significance of effective account management for customer retention and fostering long-term partnerships cannot be overstated. Nurturing key relationships is paramount to contribute to the success of businesses.

Account management transcends mere transactions; it's about building and nurturing relationships with clients. Effective account management lays the foundation for customer retention, encourages repeat business, and fosters trust and loyalty. By Prioritising the needs and preferences of key accounts, you and your businesses can strengthen their position in the market and solidify their relationships with valuable clients.

Nurturing key relationships ensures that you and your businesses have a firm anchor in the trust and loyalty of their clients. By investing time and effort in understanding their clients' business objectives, challenges, and expectations, you and your businesses can tailor their offerings and services to meet their clients' needs effectively. This personalised approach not only enhances customer satisfaction but also strengthens the bond between businesses and their clients.

Resilience is the driving force behind effective account management. By adopting a proactive communication strategy, you and your businesses can anticipate and address their clients' needs and concerns in a timely manner, thus fostering trust and confidence. Additionally, maintaining a customer-centric approach ensures that you and your businesses remain responsive to changing market dynamics and evolving client preferences, enabling them to adapt and thrive in the face of challenges.

Effective account management also involves fostering a culture of collaboration and partnership between businesses and their clients. By serving as trusted advisors and strategic partners, you and your businesses can position themselves as extensions of their clients' teams, offering valuable insights, expertise, and support to help them achieve their business goals. This collaborative approach strengthens the relationship between businesses and their clients, driving mutual success and growth.

Nurturing key relationships through effective account management is essential for you and your businesses to thrive in today's competitive landscape. By Prioritising customer retention, fostering trust and loyalty, and adopting a proactive and customer-centric approach, you and your businesses can sail with the winds of lasting partnerships and achieve sustained success in the long run.

9. Admin: Supporting Smooth Operations

Admin, often regarded as the backbone of any organisation, serves as the administrative hub responsible for ensuring the seamless functioning of business operations. Efficient administrative functions are crucial in supporting the core activities of businesses.

Administration goes beyond mere paperwork; it plays a pivotal role in supporting the core operations of a business. Efficient administrative functions are essential for enhancing productivity, streamlining processes, and maintaining compliance with regulations. By handling routine tasks such as record-keeping, scheduling, and correspondence, administrative staff allow leadership to focus on strategic initiatives and critical decision-making, thereby driving the organisation forward.

Efficiency serves as the guiding principle in administration. Admin support ensures that business operations run smoothly, employees are well-supported, and resources are utilised optimally. From managing schedules and coordinating meetings to handling inquiries and facilitating communication, efficient administrative functions contribute to the overall effectiveness of an organisation, enabling it to navigate through challenges with ease and precision.

Efficiency is akin to the wind in the sails of a ship. Effective administrative functions propel you and your businesses forward by ensuring streamlined operations, minimising delays, and maximising resource utilisation. By optimising workflows, automating repetitive tasks, and implementing efficient systems and processes, administrative departments enable you and your businesses to operate at peak efficiency, driving growth and success.

Let efficiency be the compass guiding administrative functions. Streamlined admin support ensures that the journey of a business is not just smooth but sails with the winds of operational efficiency. By Prioritising efficiency and embracing best practices in administrative management, you and your organisations can position themselves for sustained success and navigate through the complexities of the business landscape with confidence and resilience.

10. Training Support: Developing Human Capital

Training support is the cornerstone of developing human capital within an organisation, encompassing various initiatives such as leadership training, coaching, and mentoring programmes. Investing in the development of employees is crucial to contributes to building a skilled and adaptive workforce.

Training support goes beyond being a mere formality; it represents a strategic investment in the future of the organisation. By providing employees with opportunities for growth and development, you and your organisations can ensure that their workforce remains skilled, motivated, and adaptable to evolving business needs. Leadership training, coaching, and mentoring programmes play a vital role in nurturing talent, fostering leadership capabilities, and empowering employees to reach their full potential.

In the journey of organisational development, let training be the guiding star. By investing in the development of the workforce, you and your organisations can equip their employees with the skills, knowledge, and resilience needed to navigate through challenges and seize opportunities effectively. Training initiatives not only enhance individual capabilities but also contribute to building a cohesive and high-performing team, driving the organisation towards its goals.

A skilled crew serves as the wind in the sails of an organisation. Ongoing training, leadership development, and a commitment to employee growth are essential for building a workforce that can adapt to changing circumstances, innovate, and excel in their roles. You and your organisations that Prioritise training support cultivate a culture of continuous learning and improvement, positioning themselves for long-term success and competitiveness in the marketplace.

A well-developed workforce ensures that the organisation is not merely afloat but sails with the winds of continuous improvement and innovation. By fostering a learning culture and providing ample opportunities for skill enhancement, organisations can future-proof their workforce, drive performance, and achieve sustainable growth in a dynamic and ever-evolving business environment.

11. Public Relations: Managing the Company's Image

Public Relations (PR) is akin to steering the ship of a company's reputation through the ever-changing tides of public perception. It's a strategic endeavour aimed at managing how the company is perceived by its stakeholders and the broader public. Maintaining a positive public image and effective PR strategies contribute to the success of a business.

PR goes beyond the realm of issuing press releases; it's about shaping perceptions and managing reputations. A positive public image is essential for building credibility, fostering trust, and cultivating goodwill among stakeholders, including customers, investors, employees, and the community at large.

Effective public relations efforts act as a beacon, ensuring that your company's reputation remains steadfast and shines brightly, even amidst turbulent waters. A positive image is the wind that propels the ship of your company forward. Thoughtful PR strategies, proactive crisis management, and a commitment to transparency are the sails that catch this wind, enabling your ship to sail smoothly with the currents of public opinion.

By investing in effective public relations, your company can not only preserve its reputation but also enhance it, earning the trust and admiration of stakeholders and positioning itself as a leader in its industry.

Effective PR is instrumental in safeguarding and enhancing the company's reputation. By managing perceptions, fostering transparency, and maintaining open communication channels, you and your organisations can navigate the reputation seas with confidence, ensuring that their ship sails with the winds of a positive public image.

12. R&D: Driving Innovation

Research and Development (R&D) is the engine that propels a company forward into the future, driving continuous innovation and ensuring its relevance in a rapidly evolving marketplace. Let's explore the significance of investing in R&D and how it contributes to the long-term success and sustainability of a business.

R&D goes beyond the confines of laboratories and experiments; it's the catalyst for innovation. In today's competitive landscape, staying ahead requires more than just maintaining the status quo. R&D efforts are essential for pushing boundaries, exploring new ideas, and adapting to changing market dynamics. They ensure that your company remains at the forefront of industry trends and technological advancements.

Think of R&D as the engine that powers your ship forward. By driving innovation, R&D initiatives propel your company beyond mere adaptation, enabling it to chart its course and lead the way in shaping the future of the industry.

Forward-thinking innovation acts as the wind in your sails, propelling your ship towards new horizons of progress and growth. A commitment to R&D, combined with a proactive approach to embracing new ideas and technologies, ensures that your company sails with the winds of change, rather than against them.

By Prioritising R&D and fostering a culture of innovation within your organisation, you not only stay abreast of industry trends but also drive them, ensuring that your ship not only rides the waves but creates them.

R&D is the lifeblood of innovation and progress in any organisation. By investing in R&D, companies can stay ahead of the curve, remain competitive, and chart a course towards sustained success in an ever-changing business landscape.

13. Legal: Ensuring Compliance and Mitigating Risks

Navigating the legal landscape is akin to ensuring that your ship sails smoothly through the often-turbulent waters of compliance and risk management. Legal compliance and risk mitigation safeguards your business and ensures its long-term success.

Legal compliance and risk mitigation are not merely bureaucratic formalities; they serve as the bedrock of your business's stability and resilience. From adhering to regulatory requirements to safeguarding intellectual property rights, these legalities are the anchors that protect your ship from the unpredictable storms of legal challenges.

Think of compliance as your anchor, grounding your ship and providing stability in the face of regulatory uncertainties. By ensuring legal adherence, you fortify your business against potential liabilities and penalties, thereby safeguarding its reputation and financial well-being.

Legal safeguards act as the wind in your sails, propelling your ship forward with confidence and security. Proactive compliance efforts, coupled with robust risk mitigation strategies, empower your business to navigate legal complexities with agility and resilience, ensuring smooth sailing even amidst legal challenges.

Let legal safeguards be your guiding light as you navigate the legal waters. By Prioritising legal compliance and risk management, you not only mitigate potential threats but also demonstrate your commitment to ethical business practices and corporate responsibility.

Legal compliance and risk mitigation are essential pillars of business success. By Prioritising these measures, you ensure that your ship sails with the winds of legal security, enabling it to navigate through the complexities of the legal landscape and emerge stronger and more resilient in the face of adversity.

Conclusion & Recap

In this chapter you explored various aspects crucial for expanding and strengthening you and your businesses. You started by navigating the financial waters with precision in the Accounting section, ensuring sound financial management practices. HR was discussed, focusing on strategies for developing and retaining talent in the workforce garden. Branding was emphasised as a means of forging a distinctive identity in the market. Additionally, you delved into production designing to enhance aesthetics and innovation in product development. Streamlining the supply chain was a key focus in Stock and Inventory, optimising inventory management processes. Strategic procurement and vendor management were highlighted in the Purchase section to ensure efficient sourcing. Events were explored as opportunities for networking and brand promotion. Nurturing key relationships was emphasised in Account Management, while admin supported smooth operations. Developing human capital through training support was discussed, along with managing the company's image in Public Relations. Driving innovation was a key focus in R&D, while ensuring compliance and mitigating risks were highlighted in Legal.

As I conclude this chapter on The Outer Core of the COGS of Success, envision yourself at the helm, equipped with the wisdom garnered from mentors, associates, and fellow business owners. The Outer Core is not just about expanding; it's about fortifying your ship for the journey ahead. As you set sail into new horizons, may these lessons be the compass that guides your ship through the uncharted waters of business growth.

Chapter 5.6

Testing the Waters with Venture Creation PoC

"Anchoring lessons from each Proof of Concept journey, we refine our skills and steer towards success. Like seasoned sailors, we adapt to challenges, explore new opportunities, and sail forth towards victory."

SABTOSH KUMAR

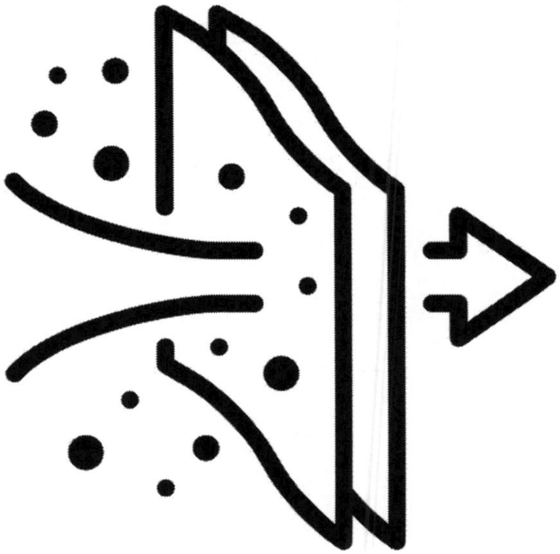

Alex is a young entrepreneur eager to carve his path in the business world. Fuelled by passion and ideas, Alex's journey began with a quest for knowledge. His journey took a pivotal turn when he discovered a venture creation bootcamp, an immersive experience designed to empower entrepreneurs like him with tools and insights to turn their visions into reality.

Embracing the bootcamp, Alex absorbed the wisdom and guidance of seasoned mentors and fellow entrepreneurs. This journey equipped him with practical skills and instilled the core principles of the COGS of Success framework. Venture Creation Proof of Concept (PoC) emerged as a fundamental idea, checking if an idea is feasible and valuable before investing significant time and money.

In the bootcamp, Alex immersed himself in a dynamic ecosystem of learning and growth. Through expert guidance and hands-on workshops, he honed strategic thinking, market research skills, and financial acumen—reminiscent of the COGS framework's emphasis on holistic business development. The vibrant community of entrepreneurs offered support and inspiration, underscoring the importance of positive relationships highlighted by the COGS framework.

As weeks passed, Alex's confidence grew, and his vision crystallised into a tangible business plan, emphasising operational excellence and strategic foresight. Approaching the bootcamp's culmination—a pivotal pitch day—Alex unveiled his venture to potential investors and industry experts. With nerves tingling, Alex delivered his pitch with conviction, captivating the audience and embodying entrepreneurial resilience and innovation.

Emerging victorious, Alex secured the resources and support needed to propel his venture forward, showcasing the transformative power of the COGS of Success framework. Reflecting on his journey, Alex realised that the bootcamp had equipped him with practical skills and a mindset aligned with the core principles of the COGS framework. With a newfound purpose and belief in his ability to effect change, Alex embarked on his entrepreneurial journey, poised to leave a mark on the world—one bold idea at a time.

In the realm of venture creation, where dreams converge with determination, the possibilities are boundless. For Alex, the adventure had only just begun. The journey of entrepreneurship is like sailing uncharted waters, where success depends on navigating challenges and seizing opportunities. This chapter delves into the Venture Creation Bootcamp, a transformative experience designed to equip budding entrepreneurs with the tools and insights to test their ideas with Venture Creation Proof of Concept (PoC), uncovering the wisdom that paves the path to success.

Navigating the Venture Creation PoC Process

Welcome to a voyage like no other. Meet Sarah, a young entrepreneur with a vision to transform the fitness industry. Her journey began with a passion for health and wellness, driven by a desire to create a solution that empowers people to live healthier lives. As Sarah embarked on her entrepreneurial journey, she learned the importance of clarity in defining her goals. With guidance from mentors at the Venture Creation Bootcamp, she mapped out her objectives precisely, setting off with a clear vision of her destination. Like Sarah, you too are embarking on a journey that will shape your success—the uncharted waters of the Venture Creation Proof of Concept (Venture Creation PoC) process.

Imagine your ship, sails catching the wind as you embark on this thrilling adventure. But before you depart, gather on deck to explore the secrets of success that will lead you to victory. Clarity becomes your guiding star. It's about knowing exactly where you're headed and what you aim to achieve. Think of it as your map, guiding you through the twists and turns of entrepreneurship.

Clarity isn't just having a destination in mind; it's understanding the scope of your journey and setting clear benchmarks for success. By defining your goals precisely, you equip yourself with the tools needed to navigate challenges and seize opportunities ahead.

No voyage is complete without a skilled, diverse crew—similarly vital for your journey through Venture Creation PoC. Picture your ship as a bustling hub, with experts from all corners of entrepreneurship sharing insights. Each crew member brings unique skills, enriching your concept evaluation and charting a course to success. Together, you're stronger, more resilient, ready to overcome obstacles.

In entrepreneurship, choosing the right course is crucial. Just as a skilled sailor navigates seas, you must target audiences and markets carefully for your Venture Creation PoC. By understanding audience needs, testing concepts in conducive waters, you increase chances of success, paving the way for growth and innovation.

As you embark together, remember clarity, collaboration, and strategic decisions' power. Set sail purposefully, build your crew thoughtfully, and navigate with confidence. In the vast ocean of entrepreneurship, your visions will lead to victory.

Executing the Venture Creation PoC Manoeuvres

Prototyping, simulation, and feedback were pivotal in Sarah's Venture Creation PoC journey. Like a skilled navigator, she created small-scale prototypes of her fitness app to test functionality and user experience. Simulating scenarios helped her anticipate challenges and refine her approach. Seeking feedback from fitness enthusiasts and industry experts, Sarah iterated on her idea, incorporating valuable insights to enhance its value proposition.

Prototyping, a term familiar to seasoned entrepreneurs, is akin to building a small model ship to gauge its seaworthiness. It's about refining designs and ensuring the idea holds up before committing to a full-scale version.

Simulating real-life situations is crucial in the Venture Creation Proof of Concept (Venture Creation PoC) journey. It involves testing your idea in scenarios that mirror real business challenges, allowing you to identify issues early and improve your plan. It's like testing your ship in rough waters to prepare for the challenges of real business.

Feedback in the business world acts like the gentle sound of the sea guiding your ship. Mentors stress the importance of seeking advice from customers, experts, and industry peers. Listening carefully and incorporating feedback helps refine your idea and navigate business challenges smoothly.

With prototyping, simulations, and feedback as your compass, you'll navigate the seas of entrepreneurship towards success.

Evaluating the Venture Creation PoC Results

Sarah analysed her Venture Creation PoC results using data analysis to identify patterns and trends, gaining confidence in her fitness app's market potential. Mentors stressed the importance of assessing the app's readiness for competition, leading Sarah to refine her strategy accordingly.

Like ancient sailors navigating by the stars, data analysis serves as your guiding constellations in evaluating Venture Creation PoC. It's crucial for steering your business through uncertain seas, much like sailors relied on stars for navigation.

During Venture Creation PoC, gathering data isn't just about collecting facts; it's about understanding them. Deciphering patterns and spotting trends helps steer your business in the right direction, similar to sailors reading stars to chart their course.

Data analysis acts like a trusted navigator, guiding you through the complexities of the business world. Insights from data empower informed decisions that propel your ventures forward.

Beyond data analysis, assessing your concept's viability requires a rigorous test of its seaworthiness. This ensures your idea can withstand the challenges of the market's changing tides. Mentors emphasise the importance of evaluating whether your concept is robust enough to succeed in competitive landscapes.

Just as sailors test a ship's seaworthiness before setting sail, assessing your concept's viability is critical in determining its potential success in the market.

Navigating Venture Creation PoC evaluation demands a blend of data analysis and strategic assessment. By using data as your guiding stars and subjecting your concept to thorough viability testing, you can set sail towards entrepreneurial success in unpredictable waters.

Making Informed Navigation Decisions

Armed with insights from her Venture Creation PoC expedition, Sarah anchored her decisions in the lessons learned along the way. Drawing from the fundamentals of the COGS of Success framework, she assessed the strengths and weaknesses of her venture, making informed navigation decisions to steer it towards success. With a solid roadmap in place, Sarah set sail with purpose, guided by the principles of strategic decision-making and operational excellence.

After completing the Venture Creation Proof of Concept (Venture Creation PoC) voyage, you must stress the importance of decision anchors. These anchors are like weights attached to your Venture Creation PoC anchor, guiding your final decision. They're influenced by the lessons learned and insights gained during the exploration.

Decision anchors are crucial in determining what to do next after the Venture Creation PoC. They can sway your decision on whether to proceed with the full fleet, make tweaks to your course, or even rethink the entire journey. These anchors are firmly based on the experiences and knowledge gained during the Venture Creation PoC process. They provide a solid basis for making sensible decisions about the future direction of your venture.

In essence, decision anchors act as guiding principles that help entrepreneurs navigate the choppy waters of decision-making after completing the Venture Creation PoC. By considering the lessons learned and insights gained, they offer a clear path forward, ensuring your journey continues towards success.

Learning from the Venture Creation PoC Expedition

Sarah and her fellow entrepreneurs gathered for collaborative problem-solving, applying their knowledge and skills with teamwork and creativity. They tackled challenges with ingenuity, reinforcing lessons from their Venture Creation PoC journey.

For Sarah, Venture Creation PoC was an ongoing adventure of growth and learning. She navigated entrepreneurship with resilience, adapting her course through iterative learning and flexibility. Each lesson and insight became valuable wisdom, shaping Sarah's entrepreneurial path for future success.

Iterative navigation in Venture Creation PoC is like refining techniques for future projects based on lessons learned.

In the unpredictable business world, flexibility is crucial. Insights from Venture Creation PoC stories showed you and your businesses altering routes and destinations. Flexibility guides you through uncharted waters, handling unexpected challenges.

Reflecting on her Venture Creation Bootcamp journey, Sarah anchored lessons learned, ready to apply them. Armed with business fundamentals and renewed determination, she set sail confidently towards success.

Conclusion & Recap

The chapter on Venture Creation Proof of Concept (Venture Creation PoC) highlights the idea that learning is a continuous process. It stresses the importance of taking lessons from each Venture Creation PoC journey and using them to improve future projects. Think of it like constantly refining your skills based on past experiences to make better decisions in the future.

The chapter also talks about the need to be flexible when dealing with the uncertainties of business. Sometimes, insights from Venture Creation PoC require changes in direction, or even a complete rethink of the plan. Being flexible is like having a reliable compass, helping entrepreneurs adapt to challenges and explore new opportunities confidently.

Ultimately, the chapter encourages entrepreneurs to keep learning and adapting as they navigate through the Venture Creation PoC process. It's about being open to change and using past experiences to steer towards success in the ever-changing world of business.

As you conclude this chapter on testing the waters with Venture Creation Proof of Concept, envision yourself as a seasoned navigator equipped with the wisdom of Venture Creation PoC. It's not merely a phase in your entrepreneurial journey; it's the compass that ensures you navigate the business seas with clarity, resilience, and adaptability. May the lessons shared in this chapter anchor your decisions and guide your ship through the unpredictable waters of entrepreneurship.

Sail forth, and may your Venture Creation PoC voyages be laden with insights, steering your ship towards success which brings us to the most important chapter of the series to turn your visions into reality. Let's dive in.

Chapter 5.7

Turning your Visions into Reality

You live in a world where ideas are abundant, but the ability to bring those ideas to fruition is what sets true leaders apart. It's not enough to simply dream; you must have the courage, determination, and resilience to turn those dreams into reality.

Success is not merely about reaching a destination; it's about embarking on a transformative journey that leads to growth, innovation, and sustainability. However, navigating this journey can be daunting, with numerous challenges and uncertainties lurking around every corner. This is where the Visions to Victory Model shines as a beacon of guidance and inspiration, offering a structured approach to business success that empowers entrepreneurs to overcome obstacles and achieve their goals.

So, what does it take to turn your visions into reality?

Firstly, it requires clarity of purpose. You must have a clear and compelling vision that guides your actions and inspires others to join you on your journey. This vision should be ambitious yet attainable, challenging yet achievable.

Secondly, it demands strategic planning. You need to develop a roadmap that outlines the steps, resources, and timelines required to achieve your vision. This plan should be flexible enough to adapt to changing circumstances but robust enough to withstand challenges along the way.

Next, it calls for innovation. You must be willing to think outside the box, challenge the status quo, and embrace change. Innovation is the lifeblood of progress, driving you to explore new ideas, experiment with new approaches, and push the boundaries of what is possible.

Execution with excellence is also paramount. Ideas alone are not enough; you must have the discipline, focus, and determination to execute your plans with precision and efficiency. This requires attention to detail, effective delegation, and a relentless commitment to excellence.

Resilience is another essential ingredient. Along the journey from vision to reality, you will inevitably encounter obstacles, setbacks, and failures. But it is your ability to bounce back from these challenges, learn from your mistakes, and keep moving forward that ultimately determines your success.

Celebrating milestones along the way is equally important. Each step forward, no matter how small, deserves recognition and acknowledgment. It's these moments of celebration that keep you motivated, energised, and focused on the bigger picture.

And finally, the commitment. You must be willing to stay the course, even when the path ahead seems uncertain or daunting. It's your passion, persistence, and determination that will see you through to the end.

Turning your visions into reality is not just a goal; it's a journey. It's about embracing the challenges, seizing the opportunities, and making a lasting impact on the world around you. So let us dare to dream, let us dare to act, and let us dare to turn your visions into reality.

The Guiding Light

I deeply believes in the transformative power of vision, strategy, and sheer perseverance.

Allow me to introduce you to Alice, a young entrepreneur from the bustling city of New York. Alice harboured a dream – a dream to build a business that would not only thrive but would revolutionise the very fabric of how people lived their lives. Her vision was clear: she wanted to create products that brought joy, convenience, and innovation to her customers.

But, as with any entrepreneurial journey, Alice soon encountered the harsh realities of the business world. The path ahead seemed daunting, fraught with challenges and uncertainties that left her feeling lost and overwhelmed.

It was in this moment of uncertainty that Alice stumbled upon a beacon of hope – the Visions to Victory Model. Intrigued by its promise of providing guidance to entrepreneurs on their path to success, Alice decided to delve deeper into its principles.

In the vast ocean of business, where storms may arise and currents may shift, having a guiding light is imperative. And that guiding light, my friend, is none other than the Visions to Victory Model.

The Anchor

"Why is the Visions to Victory Model so crucial in your journey towards business success?" you may ask. Allow me to shed some light on this matter.

First and foremost, the Visions to Victory Model sparks the flames of inspiration within us. It encourages us to dream big, to envision a future where your businesses thrive beyond your wildest imagination. With a clear vision in mind, you can navigate your path towards your goals with unwavering determination and purpose.

Take Alice, for example. She discovered that the Visions to Victory Model wasn't merely a collection of strategies or tactics; it was a comprehensive framework designed to empower you and your businesses in today's dynamic and competitive landscape. It underscored the importance of having a clear vision, crafting actionable strategies, and fostering resilience in the face of challenges.

However, a vision without a plan is merely wishful thinking. This is where the strategic framework of the Visions to Victory Model comes into play. It enables us to translate your vision into practical strategies, to break down your goals into manageable steps, and to execute with precision and adaptability. With the Visions to Victory Model as your guide, you can navigate the complexities of the business world with confidence and clarity.

Inspired by what she had learned, Alice decided to implement the Visions to Victory Model in her own business. She dedicated herself to crafting a compelling vision for her company, setting ambitious goals, and devising strategic plans to achieve them. Embracing challenges as opportunities for growth, Alice knew that each obstacle she overcame brought her closer to her ultimate triumph.

Yet, in your pursuit of success, challenges are inevitable. It is during these moments of adversity that the resilience instilled by the Visions to Victory Model becomes your greatest asset. It teaches us to persevere in the face of obstacles, to adapt to changing circumstances, and to emerge stronger on the other side. With the Visions to Victory Model as your anchor, you can weather any storm and continue sailing towards your goals with unwavering resolve.

And indeed, as Alice applied the principles of the Visions to Victory Model, she began to see results. Her business flourished steadily, attracting loyal customers and gaining recognition from investors and industry leaders alike. With each success, Alice gained confidence and momentum, propelling her closer towards her ultimate goal of building a thriving and impactful enterprise.

Guiding philosophy

One of the most remarkable aspects of Alice's journey isn't just the success she achieved, but the person she became along the way. The Visions to Victory Model reminds us that success isn't just about reaching a destination; it's about the journey itself.

Through the trials and tribulations of entrepreneurship, Alice discovered a strength and resilience within herself that she never knew existed. She learned to embrace failure as a stepping stone to success and to persevere in the face of adversity with unwavering determination.

The model encourages us to embrace every twist and turn, every victory and setback, as opportunities for growth and learning. With the Visions to Victory Model as your guiding philosophy, you can find fulfilment and purpose in your entrepreneurial endeavours, knowing that each step you take brings us closer to your ultimate triumph.

Alice's business stands as a testament to the power of vision, strategy, and resilience. And as she reflects on her journey, she acknowledges that she owes it all to the Visions to Victory Model – a framework that not only guided her towards success but transformed her into the fearless and unstoppable entrepreneur she is today.

The Beneficiaries of the Visions to Victory Model

This comprehensive framework isn't just for the select few; it's for anyone with a vision, ambition, and the drive to succeed. let's explore who exactly stands to benefit from this transformative model and how it can shape their entrepreneurial journey.

Firstly, let's consider the trailblazers of the business world: start-up founders. These visionaries often find themselves at the inception of their entrepreneurial journey, brimming with ideas yet navigating through a maze of challenges. The Visions to Victory Model provides them with a clear roadmap, helping to define their vision, foster innovative strategies, and execute plans effectively. With a structured approach in hand, start-up founders can chart a course towards success from the very beginning.

Next, you have small and medium enterprises (SMEs), the backbone of many economies. Often in the midst of scaling up, SMEs require structured approaches to manage growth effectively. The Visions to Victory Model assists them in maintaining momentum while addressing the complexities that come with expansion. By aligning efforts, fostering innovation, and promoting operational excellence, SMEs can sustain their growth trajectory with confidence.

Corporate leaders, tasked with steering large organisations towards sustained success, also stand to benefit from the Visions to Victory Model. By providing the tools to inspire innovation, drive strategic initiatives, and ensure operational excellence, this model empowers corporate leaders to navigate the complexities of the business landscape with clarity and purpose. With a clear vision, innovative strategies, and resilient operational frameworks in place, corporate leaders can chart a course towards sustainable success.

Non-profit leaders, too, can harness the power of the Visions to Victory Model to maximise their impact and ensure sustainable operations. By defining their vision, fostering innovative approaches, and promoting operational efficiency, non-profit leaders can navigate the unique challenges of the non-profit sector with confidence and purpose.

Entrepreneurs in transition, whether transitioning from start-up to growth phase or from a traditional to a digital model, can greatly benefit from the Visions to Victory Model. By providing guidance and structure during critical transitions, this model empowers entrepreneurs to navigate change with confidence and resilience.

Young professionals and intrapreneurs within established organisations are also key beneficiaries of the Visions to Victory Model. By providing them with the tools and frameworks to drive innovation and lead new initiatives, this model empowers young professionals to accelerate their careers and contribute to the success of their organisations.

The Visions to Victory Model is a versatile and powerful framework that offers significant benefits to a wide range of individuals and organisations. Whether you're a start-up founder, an SME owner, a corporate leader, a non-profit leader, an entrepreneur in transition, or a young professional, this model provides the guidance and tools needed to turn visions into reality. By focusing on strategic vision, innovative thinking, strategic planning and execution, operational excellence, and resilience, the Visions to Victory Model helps beneficiaries navigate the complexities of the business world and achieve sustainable success.

Understanding the Visions to Victory Model

In today's fast-paced and fiercely competitive business world, success isn't just about having a great idea; it's about having a strategic plan to bring that idea to life. That's where the Visions to Victory Model comes into play. This comprehensive framework integrates strategic vision, innovative thinking, strategic planning and execution, operational excellence, and resilience and adaptability, providing a roadmap for you and your businesses to thrive in the ever-evolving landscape.

Let's break down what each component of the Visions to Victory Model entails and how it contributes to business success.

Firstly, strategic vision sets the direction for the business by crafting a clear and compelling picture of the future. This vision serves as a guiding star, aligning efforts towards common objectives and inspiring employees to work towards a shared goal.

Secondly, innovative thinking fosters a culture of creativity where new ideas are not only welcomed but encouraged. This culture of innovation enables you and your businesses to differentiate themselves in the market, drive growth through the development of new products and services, and remain agile in response to changing market conditions.

Thirdly, strategic planning and execution bridge the gap between vision and reality. By setting clear goals, developing detailed plans, and executing these plans effectively, you and your businesses can ensure that their resources are used efficiently, milestones are met, and progress is tracked.

Fourthly, operational excellence focuses on optimising processes, resources, and workflows to achieve maximum efficiency and effectiveness. By continuously evaluating and improving business processes, leveraging technology, and implementing best practices, you and your businesses can deliver high-quality products or services consistently, enhancing customer satisfaction and reducing costs.

Lastly, resilience and adaptability are essential for you and your businesses to withstand and recover from setbacks, and to pivot in response to changing market conditions. By developing contingency plans, fostering a culture of continuous learning and improvement, and encouraging flexibility and agility in decision-making processes, you and your businesses can navigate challenges and seize opportunities.

The true strength of the Visions to Victory Model lies in its holistic approach. Each component is interrelated and reinforces the others, creating a synergistic effect that drives business success. For example, a clear strategic vision informs innovative thinking, which in turn guides strategic planning and execution. Operational excellence ensures that plans are implemented efficiently, while resilience and adaptability provide the ability to adjust and thrive in the face of challenges.

To illustrate the effectiveness of the Visions to Victory Model, let's consider the above story of Alice, a young entrepreneur who used the model to build her business from the ground up. By crafting a compelling vision, fostering a culture of innovation, setting clear goals, optimising operations, and remaining resilient in the face of challenges, Alice was able to achieve success and transform her dream into reality.

The Visions to Victory Model is a powerful framework that empowers you and your businesses to navigate the complexities of the modern market landscape. By understanding and implementing the components of the model, entrepreneurs and business leaders can turn their visions into reality, ensuring sustained growth and long-term success.

Timming the Implementation of the model

Timing the implementation of the Visions to Victory Model involves recognising pivotal moments in the business lifecycle and leveraging these opportunities to achieve strategic goals. Let's explore some key moments and how to make the most of them.

Firstly, during the startup phase, implementing the model lays the foundation for success. Crafting a compelling vision statement and developing a detailed business plan are essential steps to set the business on the right path.

During periods of rapid growth, the model helps in maintaining efficiency and effectiveness while scaling operations. Refining the vision and investing in operational excellence are crucial during this phase.

When entering new markets or launching new products, the model assists in adapting strategies to meet new demands and fostering innovation.

Following a significant setback or crisis, post-crisis recovery requires resilience and adaptability. The model provides a framework for bouncing back stronger and realigning strategies.

In periods of stagnation, the model helps in revitalising the business by identifying new growth opportunities and encouraging innovative thinking.

During a strategic pivot, such as changing business models or target markets, the model ensures a structured transition and provides the tools to adapt effectively to new strategic directions.

Continuous assessment of the business environment and internal operations is key to identifying the right time for implementing the model. Flexibility is also essential, as circumstances may change, requiring adjustments to the implementation plan.

Implementing the model incrementally, starting with the most critical components, can be more effective in some cases. Gradually integrating the other components as the business evolves allows for a smoother transition.

Timing the implementation of the Visions to Victory Model is crucial for achieving business success. By recognising and leveraging key moments in the business lifecycle, you and your businesses can maximise the impact of the model and navigate challenges effectively. Timing ensures that you and your businesses are well-equipped to seize opportunities and achieve sustained success.

The Importance of the Model

In your ever-evolving business landscape, marked by fierce competition, rapid technological advancements, and unpredictable market shifts, having a clear and compelling vision is paramount. The Visions to Victory Model helps in clarifying this strategic vision, providing you and your businesses with a roadmap towards their long-term objectives. By aligning efforts towards common goals, it prevents resource wastage and ensures everyone is moving in the same direction.

But a vision alone is not enough; innovation is the key to staying relevant and competitive. The Visions to Victory Model fosters a culture of innovative thinking, where new ideas are welcomed and nurtured. This environment encourages you and your businesses to stay ahead of market trends and technological advancements, ensuring long-term relevance and competitiveness.

Strategic planning is the bridge between vision and reality. The Visions to Victory Model provides a structured approach to strategic planning, helping you and your businesses develop detailed action plans with clear goals, milestones, and timelines. This ensures effective execution, reducing the likelihood of deviations and enhancing the chances of success.

Operational excellence is crucial for delivering high-quality products or services consistently. The Visions to Victory Model promotes operational excellence by encouraging continuous improvement and the adoption of best practices. This leads to enhanced efficiency, reduced costs, and improved product or service quality, ultimately resulting in increased customer satisfaction and loyalty.

In today's volatile business environment, resilience and adaptability are essential for survival and growth. The Visions to Victory Model equips you and your businesses with strategies for managing and mitigating risks, ensuring they can weather storms and emerge stronger. By fostering a culture of adaptability, it enables you and your businesses to pivot quickly in response to changing market conditions and emerging opportunities.

Effective leadership is another crucial component of business success. The Visions to Victory Model provides a framework for developing strong leadership skills, ensuring leaders can effectively inspire and guide their teams. By aligning all team members with the business vision and strategic goals, it fosters unity and collaboration, enhancing overall performance and productivity.

The Visions to Victory Model is not just a theoretical framework; it is a practical and essential tool for achieving business success in today's complex and fast-paced environment. By clarifying strategic vision, fostering innovation, ensuring effective strategic planning and execution, promoting operational excellence, and building resilience and adaptability, the model provides a comprehensive approach to navigating the myriad challenges you and your businesses face. Implementing the Visions to Victory Model empowers you and your organisations to turn their aspirations into achievements, driving sustainable growth and long-term success.

Applicable Environments for the Model

This model, a comprehensive framework designed to guide you and your businesses through strategic vision, innovative thinking, strategic planning, operational excellence, and resilience, holds immense potential for success. But understanding where and how to apply it is key to unlocking its full benefits.

Let's delve into the various environments where the Visions to Victory Model can be effectively implemented to achieve optimal results.

Start-up Ecosystems - Start-ups, with their dynamic and uncertain environments, find a natural ally in the Visions to Victory Model. It helps them navigate through uncertainties by providing a clear vision and strategic planning. Moreover, the model fosters a culture of innovative thinking, something essential for start-up success.

Small and Medium Enterprises (SMEs) - For SMEs, structured approaches are vital as they navigate through growth phases. The Visions to Victory Model aids in aligning efforts towards common objectives, fostering innovation to stay competitive, and enhancing efficiency through streamlined operations.

Corporate Environments - In the realm of corporations, with their complex structures and long-term sustainability goals, the Visions to Victory Model finds fertile ground. It ensures alignment with the corporate vision, guides large-scale strategic initiatives, and promotes operational improvements through best practices.

Non-Profit Organisations - Non-profits, driven by their mission-focused activities and resource constraints, benefit greatly from the clarity provided by the Visions to Victory Model. It helps in clarifying the organisation's mission, encourages innovation in service delivery, and optimises resource use for maximum impact.

Educational Institutions - With a growing focus on innovative teaching methods and strategic growth, educational institutions find the Visions to Victory Model invaluable. It aids in developing a clear vision for the institution's future, encourages innovative curriculum development, and improves administrative efficiency.

Healthcare Sector - In the healthcare sector, where patient-centred care and regulatory compliance are paramount, the Visions to Victory Model plays a vital role. It sets the direction for patient care, encourages adoption of innovative medical technologies, and enhances operational efficiency for better patient outcomes.

Government and Public Sector - Government agencies, tasked with policy implementation and public service improvement, can benefit immensely from the strategic guidance provided by the Visions to Victory Model. It helps in guiding public policies, encourages innovation in governance, and improves the efficiency of public services.

The Visions to Victory Model is a versatile framework that can be effectively applied across a wide range of environments. Its comprehensive approach ensures that it can adapt to the unique challenges and opportunities presented by each environment. By understanding where this model can be implemented, you and your organisations can harness its strengths to achieve sustained success and growth.

Implementing the Model

Having a structured approach to achieving success is essential to every business, big or small, nowadays. The Visions to Victory Model offers a comprehensive framework designed to guide you and your businesses through strategic planning, fostering innovation, ensuring operational excellence, and building resilience. Let me outline the step-by-step process of implementing this model to transform your business vision into reality.

Step 1: Define Your Strategic Vision - First and foremost, you must articulate your vision. Clearly define the long-term goals and aspirations of your business. This vision should be compelling, inspirational, and align with your core values. Engage key stakeholders in the vision-setting process to ensure buy-in and alignment across the organisation. Conduct workshops and brainstorming sessions with leadership and team members to refine your business vision. Develop a concise and clear vision statement that communicates your long-term goals and aspirations.

Step 2: Foster a Culture of Innovation - Encouraging creativity is crucial. Create an environment where new ideas are welcomed and nurtured. Encourage team members to think creatively and challenge the status quo. Dedicate resources, including time and budget, to support innovative projects and initiatives. Regularly hold brainstorming sessions and innovation workshops to generate new ideas. Establish innovation labs or teams focused on developing and testing new concepts and solutions.

Step 3: Develop a Strategic Plan - Next, set clear goals. Define specific, measurable, achievable, relevant, and time-bound (SMART) goals that align with your vision. Determine the key initiatives and projects that will drive your business towards achieving its goals. Conduct a SWOT analysis to identify strengths, weaknesses, opportunities, and threats. Develop detailed action plans for each initiative, outlining the steps, resources, and timelines required.

Step 4: Execute with Operational Excellence - Streamline your processes to enhance efficiency and effectiveness. Implement best practices and standard operating procedures. Utilise technology and automation to improve operational efficiency and reduce costs. Map out existing processes to identify areas for improvement. Adopt a culture of continuous improvement, regularly reviewing and refining processes to enhance performance.

Step 5: Build Resilience and Adaptability - Prepare for potential risks and challenges by developing contingency plans. Encourage flexibility and adaptability within your organisation to quickly respond to changes and uncertainties. Implement a risk management framework to identify, assess, and mitigate risks. Provide training and development programmes that focus on building resilience and adaptability among employees.

Step 6: Monitor and Evaluate Progress - Finally, regularly monitor progress towards your goals using key performance indicators (KPIs) and other metrics. Continuously evaluate the effectiveness of your strategies and make necessary adjustments to stay on track. Use performance dashboards to track and visualise progress in real-time. Conduct regular performance reviews and strategy meetings to assess progress and make data-driven decisions.

Example of Implementation

Let's consider a mid-sized technology company aiming to expand its market share and innovate its product line. Here's how they implemented the Visions to Victory Model:

Define Strategic Vision - The company's leadership team conducted workshops to develop a vision of becoming a market leader in innovative tech solutions within five years.

Foster Innovation - They established an innovation lab, encouraging employees to submit new product ideas and provided resources for development and testing.

Develop Strategic Plan - The company set SMART goals, including launching three new products within two years and increasing market share by 15%. They identified key initiatives like market research, product development, and marketing campaigns.

Execute with Operational Excellence- They streamlined their product development process and implemented agile methodologies to improve efficiency.

Build Resilience and Adaptability - The company developed contingency plans for potential market disruptions and invested in employee training programmes focused on adaptability and resilience.

Monitor and Evaluate - Using performance dashboards, they tracked progress and conducted quarterly reviews to adjust strategies as needed.

As a result, the company successfully launched innovative products, increased market share, and built a more resilient and adaptable organisation. Implementing the Visions to Victory Model involves a systematic approach that begins with defining a clear vision and fostering a culture of innovation. Through strategic planning, operational excellence, and building resilience, you and your businesses can navigate the complexities of the modern market landscape. By monitoring progress and making necessary adjustments, you and your organisations can ensure sustained growth and long-term success. The Visions to Victory Model provides a robust framework for turning business visions into reality, empowering you and your businesses to achieve their strategic goals and thrive in a competitive environment.

Conclusion & Recap

Implementing the Visions to Victory Model is crucial for business success. Firstly, at its core lies strategic vision—a clear picture of the future entrepreneurs aim to create. Defining this vision provides clarity on goals, guiding decision-making and actions. You and your businesses align efforts and resources towards a common purpose, fostering unity.

Secondly, innovation is vital for growth and competitiveness. The model promotes a culture of innovation, nurturing creativity and embracing new ideas. This environment helps you and your businesses anticipate trends, capitalise on opportunities, and adapt to changes in technology and customer preferences.

Thirdly, success requires more than just a great idea—it demands strategic planning and execution. The model offers a roadmap, setting goals, milestones, and actionable plans. This approach enables effective resource allocation, risk management, and opportunity seizing for sustainable growth.

Moreover, operational excellence is crucial. The model emphasises optimising processes, leveraging technology, and continuous improvement. This enhances productivity, reduces costs, and delivers customer value, maintaining competitiveness and adapting to market shifts.

Lastly, resilience and adaptability are essential in today's business environment. The model equips entrepreneurs to navigate uncertainties, overcome challenges, and bounce back stronger. You and your businesses can pivot swiftly, seize new opportunities, and thrive amidst change, ensuring long-term success.

In essence, the Visions to Victory Model guides entrepreneurs to integrate strategic vision, innovation, effective planning, operational excellence, resilience, and adaptability into their business strategies for enduring success.

Chapter 5.8

Cardinal Rules for Entrepreneurial Success

The cardinal rules are fundamental principles as well as guidelines that are considered essential for success in entrepreneurship. These rules serve as guiding principles, providing direction and clarity to individuals like you and me navigating the complexities of starting and growing a business. They encapsulate key insights, best practices, and lessons learned from experienced entrepreneurs and business leaders, offering invaluable wisdom and advice to those embarking on their entrepreneurial journey.

The cardinal rules provide a framework for success, helping entrepreneurs like us avoid common pitfalls, make informed decisions, and navigate challenges effectively. By adhering to these rules, you can establish a solid foundation for your ventures, mitigate risks, and increase their likelihood of achieving your goals. Whether it's defining a clear vision, understanding the market, prioritising customer satisfaction, or managing finances wisely, each cardinal rule plays a crucial role in shaping the trajectory of a business and driving long-term success.

In the forthcoming volume, "Visions to Victory Volume 2," I am excited to delve deeper into the top ten cardinal rules outlined in this chapter. Through meticulous exploration and analysis, I will unravel the intricacies of each rule, providing invaluable insights, practical strategies, and real-world examples to support you as na aspiring entrepreneurs on your journey to success. With a comprehensive framework and roadmap at hand, you will be equipped with the knowledge, tools, and guidance needed to navigate the complexities of entrepreneurship with confidence and clarity. Together, you will embark on a transformative journey towards realising visions and achieving victory in the dynamic and competitive landscape of your business.

In this chapter, you delve into the cardinal rules that serve as guiding principles for you, illuminating the path to success in the dynamic and competitive landscape of business.

Cardinal Rule 1 - Define Your Vision

Articulate a clear vision guiding every decision.

At the heart of every successful venture lies a compelling vision that fuels ambition, ignites passion, and steers the course of action. Your vision encapsulates the essence of your aspirations, values, and the impact you seek to make in the world. Take the time to articulate a clear and inspiring vision that serves as the North Star guiding every decision and endeavour.

Cardinal Rule 2 - Know Your Market

Dive deep into understanding your target audience and their pain points.

Market research forms the bedrock upon which successful businesses are built. Dive deep into understanding your target market—its demographics, psychographics, purchasing behaviour, and pain points. This invaluable insight will inform your product development, marketing strategies, and customer engagement efforts, ensuring alignment with market needs and preferences.

Cardinal Rule 3 - Create Value

Identify unmet needs and develop solutions.

The cornerstone of business success lies in the ability to create value for your customers. Identify unmet needs, pain points, or inefficiencies in the market and develop products or services that offer tangible benefits and solutions. By focusing on delivering genuine value, you can forge meaningful connections with your audience and differentiate yourself in a crowded marketplace.

Cardinal Rule 4 - Build a Strong Brand

Craft an authentic brand identity.

Your brand is more than just a logo or a name—it's the embodiment of your business's identity, values, and promise to customers. Invest in crafting a strong and authentic brand identity that resonates with your target audience and sets you apart from competitors. Consistently communicate your brand message across all touchpoints to build trust, loyalty, and recognition.

Cardinal Rule 5 - Stay Agile

Remain responsive to changes and seize opportunities

In the fast-paced and ever-evolving landscape of business, adaptability is paramount to survival and success. Remain nimble and responsive to changes in the market, customer feedback, and industry trends. Embrace a culture of continuous improvement, iterating on your products, strategies, and processes to stay ahead of the curve and seize emerging opportunities.

Cardinal Rule 6 - Embrace Innovation

Foster a culture of creativity, and experimentation.

Innovation is the lifeblood of progress and differentiation in business. Foster a culture of innovation within your organisation, where creativity, experimentation, and out-of-the-box thinking are encouraged and celebrated. Stay curious, explore new ideas, and be willing to challenge the status quo to drive innovation and stay ahead of competitors.

Cardinal Rule 7 - Prioritise Customer Satisfaction

Deliver exceptional experiences

Happy customers are the cornerstone of sustainable business growth. Make customer satisfaction a top priority by delivering exceptional products, services, and experiences. Listen attentively to customer feedback, address their concerns promptly, and go above and beyond to exceed their expectations, fostering long-term loyalty and advocacy.

Cardinal Rule 8 - Manage Finances Wisely

Develop a sound financial plan

Sound financial management is the foundation of business sustainability and growth. Develop a comprehensive financial plan that covers budgeting, cash flow management, forecasting, and investment strategies. Keep a vigilant eye on your finances, monitor key metrics, and make informed decisions to ensure financial stability and resilience.

Cardinal Rule 9 - Build a Strong Team

Invest in talented individuals who share your vision.

Your team is your most valuable asset in achieving your business goals. Surround yourself with talented, passionate individuals who share your vision and values. Invest in recruiting, training, and empowering your team members, fostering a culture of collaboration, creativity, and accountability that drives collective success.

Cardinal Rule 10 - Never Stop Learning

Continuously seek knowledge and adapt to challenges.

Entrepreneurship is a journey of continuous learning and growth. Stay curious, humble, and open-minded, seeking out opportunities to expand your knowledge, skills, and perspective. Embrace feedback, learn from both successes and failures, and remain adaptable in the face of challenges, evolving as a leader and entrepreneur with each experience.

The cardinal rules are fundamental principles essential for success, providing direction to entrepreneurs. They encapsulate insights from experienced leaders, guiding ventures to mitigate risks and achieve goals. Adherence to these rules establishes a solid foundation, aiding in navigating challenges and shaping long-term success.

Conclusion & Recap

Adherence to these rules serves as a compass, guiding you towards prosperity. By embracing vision, market understanding, value creation, and agility, you can navigate challenges with confidence, unlocking your venture's full potential.

In the unpredictable terrain of entrepreneurship, adherence to these cardinal rules can serve as a compass, guiding you towards success and prosperity. By defining a compelling vision, understanding the market landscape, creating value for customers, and embracing agility, innovation, and customer-centricity, entrepreneurs can navigate the challenges and uncertainties of the entrepreneurial journey with confidence and resilience, unlocking the full potential of your ventures.

In the forthcoming volume of "Visions to Victory," you embark on an enlightening journey to delve deeper into the cardinal rules outlined in this chapter. Through meticulous exploration, analysis, and real-world case studies, you will unlock the secrets of success, guiding entrepreneurs from the inception of your dreams to the pinnacle of victory. By focusing on these cardinal rules, you will unveil invaluable strategies and insights to help you grow your businesses and navigate the path to success with confidence and resilience. Whether aspiring to build a thriving startup or transform a venture into a multi-million-dollar stock market listing company, this volume will serve as a comprehensive guide, equipping readers with the tools and knowledge needed to turn their visions into reality and achieve victory in the dynamic landscape of entrepreneurship.

In the next section you will embark on an odyssey to explore the VICTORY model, a framework designed to guide entrepreneurs towards success. You will begin by understanding the components of the VICTORY model, starting with "V" for Vision for Visionary Ideation, where you'll learn how to formulate a compelling vision for your business ventures. Next, you'll move on to "I" for Idea Inception and Launch, focusing on the process of generating and launching innovative ideas. Then, you'll explore "C" for Curate & Cultivate the Startup, learning strategies to nurture and develop your startup ventures. Subsequently, you'll delve into "T" for Transforming the Micro Venture for Market Domination, where you'll discover methods to scale your businesses for market success. Following that, you'll discuss "O" for Optimising Your SME Business with Operational Excellence and Innovation, exploring ways to enhance operational efficiency and foster innovation within your small and medium-sized enterprises. Next, you'll move on to "R" for Rising in Public Ownership and Leadership, where you'll explore strategies for expanding your businesses and assuming leadership roles in the industry. Finally, you'll conclude with "Y" for Yielding the Fruits of Legacy, where you'll discuss leaving a lasting impact and legacy through your entrepreneurial endeavours. The chapter will conclude with an exercise to reinforce learning and application of the VICTORY model concepts.

Stay Tuned for Implementation of COGS of success in the Next Volume

Why should you stay tuned for the next volume in this transformative series? The answer lies in the promise of uncovering the secrets to achieving sustained success, much like Harmony Watches Inc. Each volume is designed to delve deeper into the elements that constitute the COGS of Success, offering you a treasure trove of insights and practical strategies to implement in your own business journey.

In-Depth Case Studies - Future volumes will explore more real-world examples of your businesses that have navigated their paths to success using the principles of the COGS of Success. These case studies will provide detailed analyses and actionable takeaways that you can apply directly to your own ventures.

Expert Insights - You will bring you exclusive interviews and advice from industry leaders and experts who have mastered the art of strategic vision, innovation, and operational excellence. Their wisdom and experiences will serve as invaluable guides as you chart your course to success.

Practical Tools and Frameworks - Each volume will introduce you to practical tools and frameworks designed to help you implement the principles of the COGS of Success in your business. From strategic planning templates to innovation frameworks, you'll have access to resources that can drive tangible results.

Success Stories and Testimonials - Hear from entrepreneurs and business leaders who have transformed your businesses by following the COGS of Success. Their stories of triumph and resilience will inspire and motivate you to stay the course, no matter the challenges you face.

Interactive Learning Experiences - Engage with interactive elements, such as self-assessment quizzes, exercises, and planning worksheets, to help you internalise the concepts and apply them effectively in your own context. These hands-on activities will ensure that you not only understand the theory but also know how to put it into practice.

Community and Support - Join a community of like-minded entrepreneurs and business enthusiasts who are on the same journey as you. Share your experiences, seek advice, and build connections that can support you as you navigate the complexities of the business world.

The next volume in this series promises to be an indispensable resource for anyone serious about achieving lasting success in business. Whether you're a seasoned entrepreneur or just starting out, the COGS of Success will equip you with the knowledge, tools, and inspiration needed to turn your visions into reality and reach new heights of achievement. So, stay tuned and get ready to embark on a journey of discovery, growth, and unparalleled success with the COGS of Success. The future of your business awaits, and with the right guidance, there are no limits to what you can achieve.

Become the Part of Power Team

What Do I Bring To You with Power Team?

Joining a Power Team propels your business and community impact to new heights. As a valued Power team member, you are granted exclusive access to a network of specialised local services, creating an invaluable resource for tackling complex challenges.

As a Power Team member, your visibility and influence in the community grow exponentially. You become a recognised and trusted expert, positioning yourself for collaboration and referral opportunities that can significantly expand your client base. The collective strength of the Power Team results in a shared reputation for reliability, reinforcing the positive impact on the local community.

Active participation in the Power Team is a catalyst for building a strong, positive image and cultivating goodwill within the community. Your dedication as part of power team enhances your reputation and fosters trust among peers and community members alike.

Being part of a community of professionals is more than just a networking opportunity; it's a journey towards mutual trust and credibility. Your association with the Power Team establishes you as a reliable and respected business professional within the community. Moreover, your collective efforts contribute to the prosperity of the community, creating a positive ripple effect that goes beyond individual successes.

Power Team is a dynamic ecosystem where collaboration, trust, and shared success converge. As you actively engage in this vibrant community, you not only elevate your business but also play a vital role in shaping a prosperous and thriving local environment. Joining the Power Team is not just a decision; it's a commitment to excellence, community impact, and the collective growth of all its members.

SECTION 6

VISIONS TO VICTORY FRAMEWORK: From Volume 1 to Volume 2

The Stepwise Journey of Business Success: Unveiling the Blueprint

Lily's story and her journey in this book is a testament to the power of determination and resilience. Just like Lily, there are countless individuals around the world who have embarked on similar paths to success, overcoming obstacles and achieving their dreams. One such inspiring figure is John, whose story is a remarkable example of perseverance and achievement. John's journey, much like Lily's, serves as a beacon of hope and motivation, demonstrating that with hard work, dedication, and massive action, success is attainable for anyone.

John D. Rockefeller, the iconic American industrialist and philanthropist, led a life journey that epitomised the American Dream. Born on July 8, 1839, in Richford, New York, Rockefeller grew up in modest circumstances. His father, William Avery Rockefeller, was a traveling salesman, and his mother, Eliza Davison, was a devout Baptist.

Rockefeller's early years were marked by a strong work ethic and a knack for business. At the age of sixteen, he entered the workforce as a bookkeeper, demonstrating an aptitude for numbers and financial management. In 1859, Rockefeller ventured into the nascent oil industry, founding his first oil refinery in Cleveland, Ohio, with a business partner. Through shrewd business practices and strategic investments, Rockefeller rapidly expanded his oil empire, consolidating smaller refineries to form the Standard Oil Company in 1870. Standard Oil quickly became the dominant force in the oil industry, controlling nearly 90% of oil refining and distribution in the United States.

Rockefeller's business acumen and ruthless pursuit of efficiency earned him both admiration and criticism. Critics accused Standard Oil of engaging in monopolistic practices and stifling competition. In 1911, the U.S. Supreme Court ruled that Standard Oil violated antitrust laws and ordered its breakup into smaller companies. Despite the dissolution of Standard Oil, Rockefeller remained one of the wealthiest individuals in history, thanks to his diversified investments in banking, railroads, and other industries. However, in his later years, Rockefeller shifted his focus from accumulating wealth to giving it away.

A firm believer in the principle of philanthropy, Rockefeller dedicated himself to using his fortune for the betterment of society. In 1913, he founded the Rockefeller Foundation, one of the world's largest philanthropic organisations, with a mission to promote public health, education, and scientific research. Rockefeller's philanthropic efforts had a lasting impact on countless lives around the world. From funding medical research to supporting education initiatives, his legacy continues to shape the fields of public health, education, and social welfare to this day.

John D. Rockefeller's life journey is a testament to the transformative power of entrepreneurship, innovation, and philanthropy. From humble beginnings, he rose to become one of the most influential figures of his time, leaving behind a legacy that transcends generations. His story is a transformative journey and is outlined within the VICTORY Model, a comprehensive framework designed to navigate entrepreneurs through the multifaceted stages of their entrepreneurial odyssey. In this section, you will embark on an exploration of each of the stages of the VICTORY Model, summarising the key principles and highlighting their significance in the entrepreneurial journey.

LET'S DIVE IN...

Chapter 6.1

Unveiling the VICTORY Model - A Prelude to Triumph

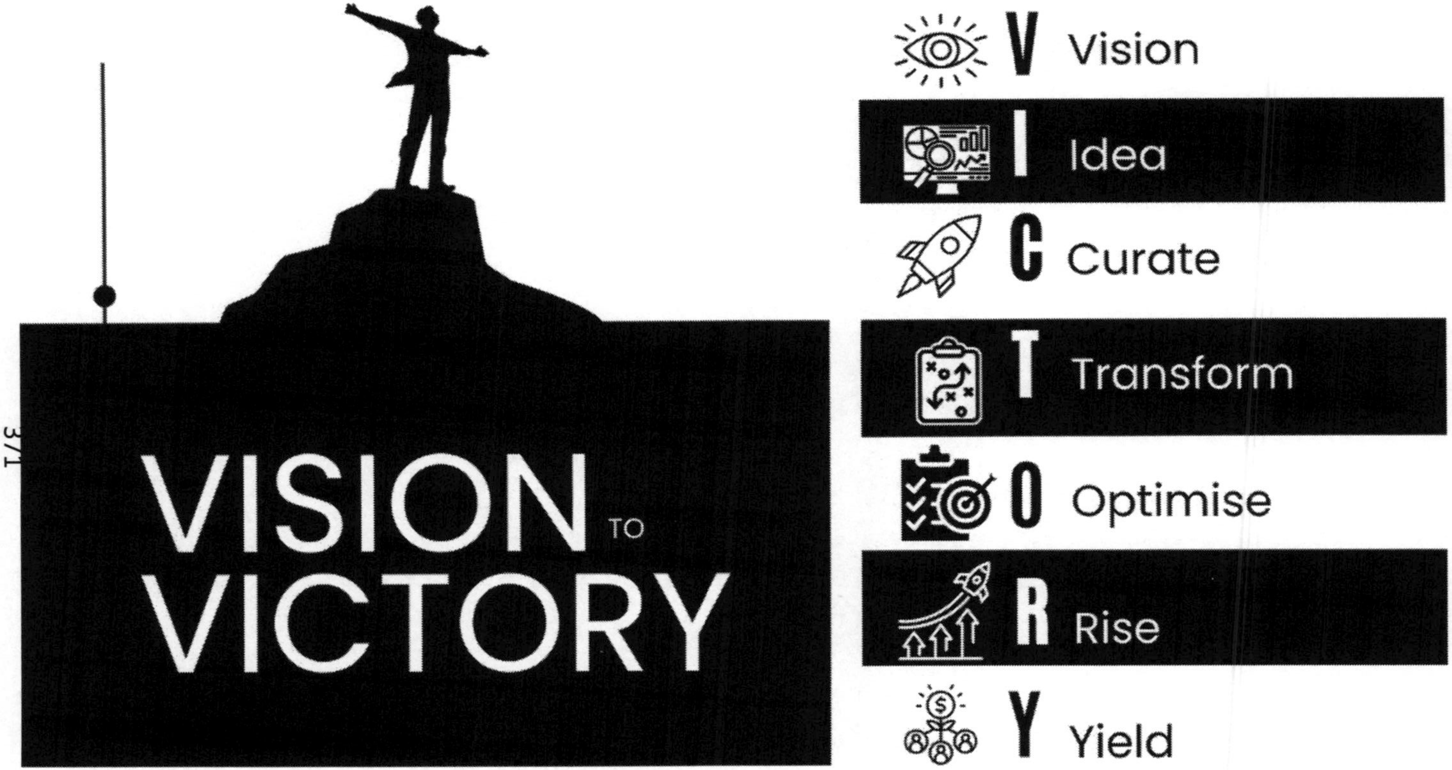

VISION TO VICTORY
V Vision
I Idea
C Curate
T Transform
O Optimise
R Rise
Y Yield

Evelyn, a young lady living in a quaint village nestled among rolling hills in one of Rockefeller's industrial sites, was known for her boundless imagination and adventurous spirit. From a young age, she dreamed of exploring distant lands and discovering hidden treasures.

Unveiling the Map of Dreams

One day, while wandering through the woods near her village, Evelyn stumbled upon an old, dusty map hidden beneath a pile of fallen leaves. As she unfurled the map, her eyes widened with wonder at the intricate illustrations and mysterious symbols it contained. With a spark of excitement, Evelyn realised that this map could lead her on the adventure of a lifetime.

Convinced that the map held the key to uncovering untold riches, Evelyn conceived a daring plan. She would embark on a journey to follow the map's cryptic clues, braving unknown dangers and overcoming formidable obstacles along the way.

Approaching Rockefeller for advice on changing her life's course, Evelyn listened intently as he shared stories of belief in oneself and taking bold steps to achieve dreams. Inspired by his words, Evelyn resolved to pursue her quest with unwavering determination.

Despite the doubts of her loved one, Evelyn steadfastly believed in the power of her dream. She spent countless hours studying the map, deciphering its secrets, and preparing for the challenges that lay ahead. With strong determination, Evelyn set out on her quest, fuelled by her belief that she was destined for greatness.

As Evelyn ventured deeper into the wilderness, she encountered treacherous terrain, wild beasts, and unexpected trials. Yet, with each obstacle she faced, Evelyn drew strength from her firm belief in her vision. Through sheer perseverance and indomitable spirit, she pressed on, refusing to be deterred by fear or doubt.

Finally, after months of arduous travel and heart-pounding adventure, Evelyn reached her destination. With trembling hands, she unearthed the hidden treasure buried beneath the forest floor in terms of black gold mine. However, with Evelyn treasure hunt, in the Industrial revolution in the 18th and 19th centuries that coal became a major source of energy. In that moment, Evelyn realised that her dream had become a reality – and it was more magnificent than she ever could have imagined.

The exact origin of coal as a fuel source is not clear to me, but evidence suggests that ancient civilisations, such as the Chinese and Greeks, may have used coal for heating and cooking as early as 3,000 years ago.

During the Industrial Revolution, advancements in technology, such as the steam engine, created a growing demand for coal as a fuel to power machinery and locomotives. This led to the widespread mining and use of coal in Europe and North America. Coal mines were established, and coal was extracted from underground mines or surface mines using various methods.

The invention of the steam engine by James Watt in the late 18th century revolutionised coal mining and its use as a fuel. Steam engines powered by coal allowed factories to operate machinery more efficiently, leading to increased industrial production and economic growth.

Coal continued to be a dominant source of energy throughout the 19th and early 20th centuries, fuelling the expansion of industries such as steel manufacturing, transportation, and electricity generation. However, concerns about pollution and environmental damage associated with coal mining and combustion have led to a shift towards cleaner and more sustainable energy sources in recent years.

Evelyn's journey serves as a testament to the power of conceiving a bold vision, believing in its possibility, and taking decisive action to achieve it. Through her courage, resilience, and unwavering faith in her dream, Evelyn transformed her aspirations into an awe-inspiring adventure that captured the hearts and imaginations of all who heard her tale.

This strategic framework, woven with threads of vision, innovation, collaboration, determination, optimisation, and sustained success, unfurls like a tapestry of triumph for those willing to embark on the thrilling journey of business growth. Just like Evelyn, as you unravel this map of the VICTORY Model, your eyes will widen in awe at its intricate details and cryptic symbols. With a surge of excitement, you'll realise the potential it holds to lead you on an extraordinary adventure. Let's delve deeper into this model.

Visions to Victory: A Framework for Excellence

Consider your personal and professional journey as an entrepreneur. The first step for any business success is to identify a problem that addresses the concerns of a group or community. You need to believe in your concept and have hope that you can achieve the outcome and convert it into a business model. This model should have a clear understanding of where you currently are, where you are heading, what you are trying to do, and why it is important. This exercise will give you purpose. Your purpose must be strong enough to keep you awake at night, get you out of bed early, and inspire you to make a valuable difference to the people around you. It should spark a burning desire to reach your destiny, regardless of the challenges you face along the way. In the business world, this stage is called Vision Creation or Vision Ideation.

Success is often perceived as a distant peak, attainable only by the fortunate few. However, with the right framework, every entrepreneur can transform their vision into reality and achieve unprecedented success.

There are many ways you can reach to this destination but one such way is "Visions to Victory" model. This model is a meticulously crafted framework designed to guide entrepreneurs through the multifaceted journey of development and growth. This framework offers a strategic roadmap, addressing every stage from inception to maturity, ensuring sustainable success and resilience in the face of challenges.

The model encapsulates the essence of visionary ideation, strategic planning, operational excellence, and legacy creation, offering a roadmap for success in the dynamic landscape of business. From the inception of bold visions to the celebration of enduring legacies, this model is the simple vehicle to help you unravel the intricacies of entrepreneurship and pave the way towards sustained success and lasting impact. Visions to Victory is my proprietary model and framework, which I use to transform millions of lives and I am going to reveal to this model for you. Beauty of this model is that I have created this model keeping you in mind and made it so simple so that even a 12 year kid can implement it. In this context of my proprietary framework, The journey of the Visions to Victory Model begins with the first framework, called "Visionary Ideation." This is where ideas are born, fuelled by a strong sense of purpose. It's the stage where dreams are envisioned with open eyes and a determination to reach the final destination. This is the place where a campaign of a large organisation is discussed and a vision is created or a startup is thought of. This phase can also be referred as the pre-startup stage or a pre-campaign stage, focusing on turning your dreams and visions into conceptual forms, helping to bring your ideas into reality and validate the concept.

Once you've identified the problem you're solving and the unique solution you offer, the next crucial step is turning your idea or campaign into a proof of concept or minimum viable product (MVP) as the second phase. In this second phase you transform your concept into a tangible product or service or a campaign, validating its feasibility and market potential. By focusing on essential features and gathering early user feedback, you can refine your idea and ensure it meets real-world needs. This stage, known as ideation or idea inception, is vital for directing your efforts and setting a strong foundation for your entrepreneurial journey, inspiring innovation and action. The second framework of the Visions to Victory Model is associated with the "Inception Stage" or an "Idea Stage". Here, the focus is not just on the birth of an idea but on nurturing and shaping it into a viable business concept. This stage involves exploration, learning, and setting the foundation for the transformative journey ahead. Ideas undergo a brainstorming phase, the business model is defined and decided, and the entity becomes real through thorough analysis, including a high-level financial and conceptual plan of the offering, pricing, and revenue model.

Once your idea is a minimum viable product (MVP), the next logical step is turning it into a startup success. This involves launching your product, attracting customers and collaborating with partners or investors to grow your business. Form a small team, including key stakeholders and one or two employees, to support this growth. Focus on effective marketing, gathering customer feedback, and making necessary improvements. Secure funding, manage costs, and aim to reach the break-even point. Continuously innovate and adapt to ensure long-term success and profitability, ultimately creating a sustainable and thriving business. This is the third phase of Visions to Victory Model. This third framework of the Visions to Victory Model, called the "Cultivate Stage " framework is also known as Startup Creation Framework focuses on building a strong foundation for the business. This stage is vital as it lays the groundwork for all future efforts. This framework is dedicated to transforming a startup concept into a successful venture, helping it become a process-driven organisation. It supports the business owner's decision to either maintain it as a lifestyle business or advance it to the next stage of growth, moving towards becoming a micro business.

Your next target for your startup is of transforming it into a micro venture, with 1-9 employees and increased revenue. Focus on improving operational efficiency, expanding your market, and building a strong team. Streamline processes, manage costs, and track performance. Conduct market research, develop targeted marketing strategies, and build strong customer relationships. Hire skilled employees, invest in their development, and foster a positive company culture. Drive revenue growth through effective sales strategies and continuous product improvement. Seek mentorship, stay informed about industry trends, and set clear goals. This phase is key to achieving sustainable growth and long-term success. Once the foundation is laid and the idea, campaign, or business has successfully navigated the cultivate stage, the next phase is the "Transform Stage" framework, also known as the Micro Creation framework. Here, the focus shifts to operational efficiency, market expansion, and team building, guiding aspiring entrepreneurs through the journey of transforming their ventures into successful micro businesses.

In the fifth stage, you must turn your micro business focuses on growing into a Small and Medium-sized Enterprise (SME). This phase involves improving efficiency across operations to reduce costs and enhance productivity. The business expands into new markets, diversifies its offerings, and strengthens its team through hiring and training. Financial management becomes more rigorous, with a focus on securing funding for expansion and managing cash flow. Customer relationships are prioritised, with efforts to improve satisfaction and loyalty. Through strategic planning, innovation, and risk management, the business aims for sustainable growth and competitiveness in the market, paving the way for long-term success as an SME. The "Optimise Stage" focuses on sustaining growth through diversification and strategic planning.

Moving from a Small and Medium-sized Enterprise (SME) to a large business involves expanding operations, refining strategies for growth, and aiming for market leadership. Key focuses include scaling operations efficiently, entering new markets through targeted marketing, strengthening organisational structure and leadership, securing funding for expansion, driving innovation to meet customer needs, forming strategic partnerships, adopting digital technologies for efficiency and customer engagement, and establishing robust governance frameworks. This phase marks a significant step towards achieving sustained growth, profitability, and resilience in a competitive business landscape. This phase in Visions to Victory model is called the "Rise Stage" where the focus is on scaling operations and fostering innovation to stay ahead of the competition.

The yield phase is the final stage of your journey and represents the culmination of efforts in transforming a large business into a listed company, achieving the envisioned goals, and solidifying its position as a market leader. It signifies the achievement of milestones set forth in the initial vision, reflecting on the journey from SME to a prominent entity. This phase involves reaping the rewards of strategic planning and execution, celebrating successes, and leaving a lasting legacy. It symbolises the attainment of the 'North Star' position, where the business not only thrives financially but also leaves a profound impact on its industry, community, and stakeholders, shaping its enduring legacy. This final stage, "Yield", is about achieving peak performance and solidifying the business's position in the market.

You can embark on this journey and accomplish all seven milestones independently, or alternatively, leverage a proven model and framework such as the Visions to Victory Model. This structured approach provides a roadmap for navigating each phase—from inception to scaling up—ensuring clarity and strategic alignment. By adopting this model, entrepreneurs can streamline their efforts, capitalise on best practices, and mitigate risks, thereby enhancing their chances of achieving sustainable growth and success. Whether forging ahead alone or with a guided framework, the ultimate goal remains the realisation of milestones and the establishment of a thriving and impactful business venture. "Visions to Victory" is a comprehensive model consisting of multiple frameworks to suit the needs of a transformative journey of entrepreneurs from the conceptualisation to the public listed company. It is designed to guide entrepreneurs through the intricate journey of building and growing a successful business. By focusing on key elements such as business foundation, market understanding, operational efficiency, innovation, and customer satisfaction, this framework provides a strategic roadmap for transforming visions into victorious realities.

As entrepreneurs navigate through the various stages of the "Visions to Victory" framework, they are equipped with the knowledge, tools, and strategies needed to achieve lasting success. This framework not only inspires but also empowers entrepreneurs like you and me to overcome challenges, seize opportunities, and reach new heights in their business ventures. With "Visions to Victory," the path to entrepreneurial excellence is clear, achievable, and within reach.

Embarking on A Journey from Visions to Victory

In "Visions to Victory," I invite you to join me on this captivating narrative, where you unravel the transformative journey of entrepreneurs who turned setbacks into stepping stones toward success. Through colourful storytelling and reflective anecdotes, you'll uncover the top secrets of business success and reveal the essential elements driving thriving enterprises. Within the pages of this book series lie the carefully guarded secrets of business success. Drawing from real-world experiences, I will unveil the strategies and principles that have proven instrumental in achieving and sustaining success.

From strategic decision-making to cultivating a resilient mindset, you will gain access to the tried-and-true secrets that separate thriving businesses from the rest.

This tale chronicles the entrepreneur's evolution from failure to triumph, showcasing the resilience, adaptability, and sheer grit required to overcome obstacles on the road to success. It's a reminder that failure isn't the end of the line; it's a vital part of the journey towards victory. "Visions to Victory" distills the complex dynamics of running a successful business into three key elements: effective leadership, strategic vision, and a culture of innovation. These pillars form the solid foundation upon which successful enterprises are built, guiding us through the critical components essential for long-term success. At the heart of the book lies the Venture Creation Framework — a strategic blueprint that outlines the path from entrepreneurial vision to business success. Through this framework, you'll gain a comprehensive understanding of the strategic steps involved in turning dreams into reality. From ideation to execution, you'll gain a comprehensive understanding of the strategic steps involved in turning visions into victorious ventures.

But you won't stop at theory. Oh no. You'll dive into real-world case studies and practical examples, showing you how the Venture Creation Framework can be applied in various contexts. From spotting market opportunities to overcoming obstacles, you'll see the transformative power of strategic planning and execution in action.

As the architect of "Visions to Victory," I'll share personal insights and reflections on my own entrepreneurial journey. From lessons learned to the evolution of my own mindset, I'll transition from a visionary entrepreneur to a mentor, offering guidance to aspiring business leaders like yourself.

"Visions to Victory" equips you not just with a compelling success story, but with the knowledge and tools to embark on your own entrepreneurial odyssey. It's a testament to the transformative power of resilience, strategic thinking, and unwavering commitment in turning dreams into reality in the world of business.

So, as you delve into the heart of the VICTORY model, remember – it's more than just a roadmap to success. It's an entire journey of visionary ideation, impactful innovation, relentless collaboration, unyielding tenacity, operational optimisation, and enduring success. Let's set sail together, starting from the very first stage of visionary ideation.

Chapter 6.2

Visionary Ideation: The Genesis of Entrepreneurial Success

When I was six years old, my father took me to our native place with a group of his friends for a ten-day tour to visit relatives nearby. We spent nights at their homes and returned to Mumbai at the end. I clearly remember the long convoy of cyclists traveling together, with me sitting in the front seat with my dad. We visited my aunt and my cousin Geeta, who gave me lots of dried fruits, gifts, and lots of chocolates, making her my favourite aunt on that trip. One remarkable memory from that journey is the open taps in the villages we passed through. Often, no one was there to serve us, but we could stop, drink water, and sometimes villagers would treat us with sweets, all without expecting anything in return. We were just travellers, likely never to return to those villages, but their generosity left a lasting impression on me.

Reflecting on this now, I think life is wonderful when you create something that serves others on their journey. We are all travellers on this earth, each on our own path. It's not about what you can do for yourself, but the real difference comes when you, like the open taps, create a system that serves the community. You should help others access what they need, regardless of whether you are present or not. I believe this is where the true purpose of your life meets your destiny—creating something remarkable that serves others and becomes a pipeline that sustains beyond your lifetime. Whether you are nearby or not, people should be able to use the tap you created, help themselves, and move on, while the tap continues to serve others on their journeys.

Idea to thriving enterprise begins with a single step—a vision. This is the crucial first phase where dreams are not only imagined but meticulously crafted into actionable plans.

The idea of "V" in the VICTORY model, which stands for Visionary Ideation lays the foundation for an entrepreneurial journey that aims to transform industries, touch lives, and create lasting legacies. I also want to introduce you to a transformative concept at the heart of entrepreneurial success—the "Vision Creation" Programme. I created the Visions to Victory Model to help build a convoy of businesspeople who are dedicated not only to serving themselves and those around them but also to thinking beyond themselves and making history. They can consider humanity beyond their own interests and create a parable of a pipeline, like an open tap, that can exist beyond our lifespans and serve humanity in education, medical, and scientific research, remaining as a beacon of inspiration for others to follow. This programme is designed to guide aspiring entrepreneurs and business leaders through the crucial early stages of their journey, transforming their innovative ideas into well-defined visions that lay the groundwork for sustainable success.

The Birth of a Vision

Imagine standing at the precipice of possibility, where your single thought hold the potential to reshape entire markets and influence countless lives.

One of the guiding philosophies I follow is that life must be a transformative journey. It should never be stationary; it should be a moving vehicle that travels through different regions of our lives and adds to our wisdom along the way. That's the secret of success. Once life becomes stationary, progress and growth stop, and we start deteriorating. While we are moving on our journey, we are not only transforming our own lives but also touching the lives of the millions of others who comes in our contact during this journey and transform their lives too.

Historical figures such as Thomas Edison and Andrew Carnegie illustrate how creative thinking, determination, and a focus on opportunities can lead to immense wealth, regardless of initial circumstances. Their journeys demonstrate the transformative power of perseverance and innovation, not only in their own lives but also in the countless lives they impacted through their achievements.

Think of the situation, where you have become part an elite business owners club, a part of the Global Citizen network, travelling across the countries without any restriction or around the world to spark the inspiration among other and motivate others to follow the path of success. They have turned an idea into millions, billions, or even or may be trillions or quadrillions. There are no limits except those we impose on ourselves through our thoughts and beliefs.

If you think you can and believe in yourself, no force can stop you from making history like Andrew Carnegie and becoming an inspiration and motivation for millions of people around you. There is nothing to stop us transforming lives and helping people to become part of this global citizen network from generation to generations, adding value, serving the community and keep doing the good work.

Visionary Ideation is the fertile ground where these thoughts and ideas take root. It's more than a moment of inspiration; it's a deliberate process of nurturing concepts that can withstand the test of time and market dynamics. Entrepreneurs become creators, embarking on a journey that begins with a vision and culminates in a legacy. This initial phase is characterised by a dynamic interplay of creativity, strategic thinking, and meticulous planning. It's not merely about dreaming big but about laying down a robust framework that will guide the business through its evolutionary stages. Vision Creation is that evolving force that adapts and propels your business toward sustained growth and industry leadership.

V –Visionary Ideation of your Vision

The "V" in the VICTORY model is crucial as it sets the foundation for your entire venture. It's the phase where seeds are sown and ideas are born; it's where dreams are seen with open eyes and a determination to reach the destination.

Think about it: every great achievement, every monumental success, begins with a single thought—a thought that dares to envision a better future, a thought that refuses to accept the status quo, and a thought that ignites a passion within us to strive for more. This is the essence of this segment—to recognise that our thoughts have creative power, that they shape our reality, and that by aligning our thoughts with our desires, we can manifest abundance in our lives.

This is the phase where the seeds of business concepts are not just planted but cultivated into visions that have the potential to reshape the lives of individuals, industries, and whole communities. Your journey unfolds with crafting a solid foundation, refining ideas, and conducting meticulous market research—an endeavour aimed at establishing the viability and potential of your business, setting the stage for future growth.

Imagine the moment when you, as an entrepreneur, assume the role of a creator. Visionary Ideation becomes the birthing ground for ideas that have the power to leave an indelible mark on the business landscape. Crafting a solid foundation is more than a casual endeavour. It involves meticulous cultivation—a process that withstands the tests of time and market dynamics. Your programme, Vision Creation, serves as a guiding beacon, not merely a set of instructions but a strategic framework empowering entrepreneurs to craft a vision that transcends immediate horizons.

In Vision Creation, I am delighted to share with you the profound insights as a treasure trove of wisdom that guides you towards achieving financial prosperity and personal fulfillment, offering principles that can elevate your lives to new heights. Vision Creation helps you explore a pivotal concept: the importance of advancing with a sense of purpose and vision.

Success is not merely a destination; it is a journey fuelled by clarity of purpose and unwavering vision. Think about the last time you felt truly inspired and driven—when you were guided by a clear sense of purpose and a compelling vision for the future. What motivated you? It was your commitment to something greater than yourself, your passion for making a meaningful impact. This is the essence of Vision Creation—to inspire you to advance with purpose and vision in every endeavour.

Imagine waking up each day with a deep sense of purpose, knowing that every action you take contributes to your vision for a better future. By aligning your efforts with your purpose and vision, you harness the creative power of the universe to manifest your dreams into reality.

But advancing with purpose and vision is not just about setting goals; it is about embodying values that drive meaningful action. Vision Creation teaches us to clarify our purpose, to define our vision with clarity and specificity, and to cultivate resilience in pursuit of our goals. It encourages us to stay committed to our principles, to embrace challenges as opportunities for growth, and to inspire others through our example.

Think of the great visionaries and entrepreneurs who have shaped our world—individuals who dared to dream big, who believed in their ideas, and who took bold, decisive action to bring their visions to life. From Thomas Edison illuminating the world with electric light to Steve Jobs revolutionising personal technology, their stories teach us that success begins with a single thought—a thought that dares to challenge the status quo and to envision a better future.

Consider the stories of individuals like Andrew Carnegie or Henry Ford who have achieved extraordinary success by advancing with purpose and vision—leaders who sparked movements, entrepreneurs who pioneered innovations, and visionaries who transformed industries. Their stories remind us that purpose-driven action not only leads to personal fulfillment but also creates lasting impact in the world.

Vision Creation is a strategic framework helping millions like you to cultivate a sense of purpose and vision that empowers you to advance towards your goals with passion and determination. Let your purpose and vision be your guiding stars on the journey to wealth, prosperity, and personal fulfillment.

Together, let us dare to dream big, to define our purpose with clarity, and to pursue our vision with unwavering commitment. By aligning your actions with your values and aspirations with a strategic framework, Vision Creation is ready to create a future filled with abundance, make a positive difference in your communities, and leave a legacy of inspiration for generations to come.

The Core Components of the Vision Creation

The journey into Vision Creation is more than a static roadmap; it's a dynamic force that evolves, adapts, and propels your business toward sustained growth and industry leadership. This isn't just about setting goals; it's about creating a narrative that inspires and resonates—an entire journey from the birth of an idea to the establishment of an enduring legacy. This isn't a mere guideline—it's a roadmap for success from ideation to legacy. It aligns visionary ideation with a comprehensive plan.

The first step in this journey is the conceptualisation of your vision. This involves clearly defining what you want your business to achieve, considering your long-term aspirations, the impact you wish to have, and the legacy you aim to create. A well-articulated vision serves as your North Star, guiding every decision and action. Alongside this vision, it's crucial to establish the core purpose of your venture and the values that will guide your actions and decisions. These values form the foundation of your company culture and influence how you interact with stakeholders.

Next, you focus on identifying opportunities. Comprehensive market research is essential to understand the market landscape, identify gaps, and pinpoint opportunities where your business can thrive. Staying abreast of industry trends, emerging technologies, and shifts in consumer behaviour allows you to innovate and lead in areas where the market is headed.

With opportunities identified, it's time to generate innovative ideas. Creativity is the lifeblood of innovation, and using techniques like brainstorming sessions, mind mapping, and reverse thinking can help generate a pool of innovative ideas. Encourage out-of-the-box thinking to develop disruptive innovations that can differentiate your business from competitors and redefine industry standards.

Once you have a set of promising ideas, the next step is validation. Assessing the technical, financial, and operational feasibility of your ideas ensures that your concepts are practical and viable. Developing prototypes or minimum viable products (MVPs) and conducting market tests to gather feedback is crucial for refining and improving your concepts.

A compelling narrative is crucial for communicating your vision effectively. Developing a narrative that clearly communicates your vision, mission, value proposition, and core values should resonate with your audience and convey the essence of your business. Ensuring that your narrative inspires and aligns stakeholders, including investors, employees, partners, and customers, fosters trust and commitment.

Finally, establishing long-term goals is essential to guide your business development. Setting specific, measurable, achievable, relevant, and time-bound goals provides a clear roadmap for your venture and helps track progress. Identifying key performance indicators (KPIs) to monitor and evaluate your venture's success over time ensures that you stay on track and make informed decisions.

The Visionary creation Programme is essential for turning your entrepreneurial dreams into reality. By following these core components—conceptualising your vision, identifying opportunities, generating innovative ideas, validating concepts, creating a compelling narrative, and establishing long-term goals—you lay the groundwork for enduring success.

Why the Vision Creation Programme is Essential

Having a well-defined vision is not just beneficial—it is essential. Allow me to elaborate on why this programme serves as a cornerstone for entrepreneurial success.

First and foremost, Visionary Ideation serves as the foundational building block for any entrepreneurial venture. It transforms abstract thoughts into concrete, actionable plans, setting the stage for future success. Imagine embarking on a journey without a destination—this is what starting a business without a clear vision feels like. Visionary Ideation provides direction and clarity from the outset. Moreover, a strong vision provides the initial momentum needed to overcome the uncertainties and challenges that are inherent in the entrepreneurial journey. It acts as a catalyst, propelling the venture forward with confidence and determination.

Second, having a clear and compelling vision is vital for standing out. A unique value proposition, articulated through your vision, sets your business apart from the competition. It highlights what makes your venture special and why customers should choose you over others. Additionally, a well-defined vision contributes significantly to building a strong brand identity. This identity is not just about logos or slogans; it is about the values and purpose that your brand represents. A compelling vision attracts and retains customers, fostering loyalty and trust.

Next, it acts as a driving force, inspiring entrepreneurs and their teams to strive towards achieving their goals and overcoming obstacles. When the road gets tough, a clear vision serves as a beacon of hope and motivation. It instills a sense of purpose and direction, which is crucial for maintaining motivation and perseverance, especially during challenging times. Knowing the "why" behind your efforts helps sustain the energy and enthusiasm needed to push through difficulties and stay committed to your entrepreneurial journey.

Fourth, A clear vision aligns the efforts of all stakeholders, ensuring that everyone is working towards the same objectives and fostering a sense of unity and teamwork. When everyone understands and believes in the vision, their efforts become synergistic, creating a powerful force that drives the business forward. Furthermore, it provides a consistent framework for decision-making. This helps avoid conflicts and ensures that all actions are aligned with the overall vision of the business. Decisions made within this framework are more likely to support the long-term goals and success of the venture.

And last but not the least, Visionary Ideation is not just about immediate success; it's about creating a lasting legacy. A strong vision ensures that the business continues to grow and evolve, leaving a positive impact on the industry and society. It encourages entrepreneurs to think beyond short-term gains and focus on creating a sustainable and meaningful impact through their ventures. This long-term perspective fosters responsible business practices that contribute to societal well-being and environmental sustainability.

In other words, the Visionary Ideation Programme is essential for any entrepreneur aiming to build a successful, impactful, and enduring business. It lays the foundation for success, differentiates the business in a competitive market, inspires and motivates the team, aligns and unifies efforts, and ensures a lasting legacy.

As you embark on your journeys, let us embrace the power of vision creation. Let your visions be bold and your ambitions high. With a clear and compelling vision guiding us, there is no limit to what you can achieve.

Implementation of the Visionary Ideation

The first step in implementing the Vision creation Programme is through interactive workshops and seminars. These sessions are crafted to guide participants through each stage of the Visionary Ideation process. By engaging in hands-on activities and collaborative exercises, participants gain a deep understanding of how to transform their ideas into actionable plans.

Next, you emphasise the importance of mentorship and coaching. You will provide access to experienced mentors and coaches who can offer invaluable insights, feedback, and support. These mentors have navigated the entrepreneurial landscape themselves and are equipped to help you avoid common pitfalls and capitalise on opportunities.

To facilitate the development and validation of business ideas, you will offer a variety of tools, templates, and resources. These resources are designed to streamline the ideation process, making it easier to conceptualise, plan, and validate your business concepts. Having the right tools at your disposal is crucial for efficient and effective execution.

Networking opportunities are another key component of your programme. You will create platforms for you to connect with industry experts, potential investors, and fellow entrepreneurs. These connections can provide valuable insights, open doors to funding, and foster collaborations that can drive your business forward.

Finally, you believe in the power of continuous learning. The entrepreneurial landscape is constantly evolving, and staying updated with the latest industry trends and best practices is essential. You will encourage continuous learning and adaptation, ensuring that you remain at the forefront of your industry. In other words, the implementation of the Visionary Ideation Programme involves interactive workshops, mentorship, valuable tools and resources, networking opportunities, and a commitment to continuous learning. By embracing these components, you will be well-equipped to turn your visionary ideas into successful ventures. Let us embark on this journey together, fostering innovation, growth, and lasting impact.

Conclusion & Recap

The Visionary Ideation stage is the genesis of your entrepreneurial journey. By conceptualising a clear vision, identifying market opportunities, generating innovative ideas, validating concepts, crafting a compelling narrative, and setting long-term goals, you lay the groundwork for success. This stage fosters creativity, strategic thinking, and clarity of purpose, enabling you to navigate challenges and seize opportunities.

As you conclude this chapter, remember that Visionary Ideation is the foundation upon which your entire entrepreneurial journey is built. Stay tuned for the grand unveiling of the VICTORY model—a comprehensive framework that will guide you through the exhilarating journey of business evolution. Your adventure has just begun, and the best is yet to come. From imagining what could be to setting the foundations for reality, the transition from vision to inception marks the initial strides of dreams toward becoming tangible ventures, prompting us to delve into the next part of the model, "I".

Stay tuned for the grand unveiling of the VICTORY model—a framework, a blueprint, and a roadmap that will guide you through the exhilarating journey of business evolution. Your adventure has just begun, and the best is yet to come. From imagining what could be to setting the foundations for reality, the transition from vision to inception marks the initial strides of dreams towards becoming tangible ventures, prompting us to delve into the second part of the Model, "I".

Chapter 6.3

Inception & Idea Creation: Navigating The Power of Thoughts

New ideas and solutions create new opportunities and expand the overall wealth available. This chapter underscores the idea that the universe is inherently abundant and designed to support the growth and expansion of life. I Want to shares stories of entrepreneurs and innovators who became wealthy by introducing new products, services, or ideas that improved people's lives. For instance, Henry Ford's innovation in automobile manufacturing, which not only made cars affordable but also created jobs and contributed to societal advancement. This chapter builds on the idea that aligning with the universal laws of abundance and creative growth is key to attracting wealth.

The philosophy, Creative Thinking Generates Wealth reiterates that Success and wealth come from creative thinking and innovation and visionary ideation.

Exploring the Inception or Idea Launch stage is the cornerstone of every successful venture. Inception marks the very beginning—the point where dreams start to crystallise into tangible business ideas. It is the foundational phase that sets the stage for the entire entrepreneurial endeavour. This pivotal phase transforms abstract concepts into tangible business ideas, marking the moment when dreams begin to take shape and laying the groundwork for future growth and development. This is the stage where creativity flourishes and ideas take root in the fertile soil of possibility. This chapter delves deep into the concept of Inception, exploring its significance, the processes involved, and the transformative power it holds in the realm of venture creation.

Understanding Inception

Inception is the moment when a spark of inspiration ignites the creative process, transforming abstract concepts into actionable business ideas. It is the starting line of the entrepreneurial race, where visionaries begin to explore, ideate, and shape their ideas into viable ventures. This phase is characterised by a blend of creativity, curiosity, and strategic thinking, laying the groundwork for future development and growth.

At its core, Inception is about the birth of an idea. It is the moment when entrepreneurs identify a unique opportunity, envision a solution, and decide to pursue it. This initial spark can come from various sources—personal experiences, market gaps, emerging trends, or technological advancements. The key is recognising this spark and nurturing it into a full-fledged concept.

Inspiration plays a crucial role in Inception. It is the catalyst that triggers the creative process, encouraging entrepreneurs to explore new possibilities and think beyond conventional boundaries. Inspiration can strike at any moment and from any direction, whether it's a casual conversation, a sudden realisation, or a deep-seated passion. The ability to capture and harness this inspiration is what sets successful entrepreneurs apart.

I – Inception and Idea Launch

The "I" stage in the VICTORY Model, represents the Inception or Idea Launch. This stage serves as the cornerstone of your entrepreneurial journey, marking the inception of abstract concepts into tangible business ideas. This is the stage where business is launched, and the first step of your dreams turns into reality. It's a pivotal phase where creativity flourishes, and entrepreneurs identify market opportunities, laying the groundwork for future development and growth. Picture this as the heartbeat of entrepreneurship, where innovation fills the air and ideas take root in the fertile soil of possibility.

Idea creation, or ideation, becomes the symphony of entrepreneurial creativity—a dynamic force propelling innovation and driving progress. In this part of the Visions to Victory series, I, as the Idea of VICTORY, will be sown. It's not a solitary event but a collective effort where entrepreneurs explore market opportunities, envision solutions, and define their journey's conceptual framework. Idea creation is more than just a process; it's a dynamic force that fuels innovation and drives progress across various domains. It's the spark that ignites the flames of creativity, leading entrepreneurs to think beyond conventional boundaries.

The entrepreneurial journey during the IDEA phase is not just about the birth of an idea; it's about nurturing and shaping that idea into a viable business concept. This period will be a time of exploration, learning, and setting the stage for the transformative journey ahead.

This period becomes a time of exploration, learning, and laying the foundation for the transformative journey ahead. Refining the concept is crucial—an examination of the initial idea considering market dynamics, consumer needs, and potential challenges. Entrepreneurs act as sculptors, chiselling away the unnecessary to reveal the true essence of their concept.

Idea Creation - Navigating the Path to Innovation

The ability to acquire wealth is not a matter of environment or luck but a precise science. I firmly believe that anyone can become rich, and the fundamental idea is that becoming wealthy is governed by laws, much like physics or mathematics. By understanding and applying these laws, anyone can achieve wealth.

This chapter focuses on the concept of giving the "impression of increase" to everyone you interact with. It suggests that by helping others perceive abundance, you attract more of it yourself. The chapter introduces the idea that wealth comes from creative, rather than competitive, action. This means that success isn't about taking wealth from others but about creating new value.

Think of innovators who created wealth by introducing new products, services, or ideas that improved people's lives. This creative process leads to wealth without the need to compete or deprive others. By establishing the idea that getting rich is a science with predictable results, and through the concept of idea creation, I aim to empower readers with the confidence that you can achieve wealth through disciplined application of these principles. This chapter lays the groundwork for understanding how to think and act in ways that lead to wealth, which is further explored in the subsequent chapters.

Let me emphasise that opportunities arise from creative thinking and actions. Those who develop new ideas, products, or services create their own opportunities and generate wealth. Think of the story of Thomas Edison, whose inventive mind and relentless pursuit of new ideas led to the creation of the electric light bulb and many other innovations. Edison's success demonstrates how creative thinking opens up limitless opportunities.

A structured approach to generating and nurturing ideas can significantly enhance the likelihood of success. The Idea Creation Programme is a comprehensive framework designed to systematically guide entrepreneurs from the inception of a concept to its realisation as a viable business idea.

Idea Creation is not merely a stroke of luck or a fleeting moment of inspiration—it is a deliberate and systematic process that unfolds through exploration, iteration, and strategic planning. Within this chapter, you shall embark on a comprehensive exploration of the intricacies of Idea Creation, unravelling the steps involved and the principles that guide entrepreneurs on their quest to transform ideas into reality.

Idea Creation is a dynamic and multifaceted process that encompasses a series of iterative steps, each essential in nurturing the seeds of innovation and bringing them to fruition.

While the journey of Idea Creation may vary from one entrepreneur to another, its underlying principles remain constant, serving as guiding beacons in the quest for transformative ideas.

In the concept of idea creation, I want you to delve deeper into the idea of thinking in a specific way to attract wealth. Let me emphasise that a clear and focused mental image, coupled with unwavering faith and purpose, is essential for manifesting riches. Each of us possesses this same creative potential within us. We have the ability to conceive bold ideas, to envision a future that surpasses our current reality, and to take inspired action towards realising our dreams. Whether you aspire to innovate in technology, arts, business, or any other field, it all begins with nurturing and harnessing the power of your thoughts—the core principle of idea creation.

Objectives of the Idea Creation Programme

The Idea Creation Programme is crafted with a clear vision: to guide entrepreneurs from the initial spark of inspiration to the formation of robust, actionable business ideas. Allow me to outline these objectives, meticulously designed to ensure participants are not only inspired but also equipped to bring their ideas to fruition.

Firstly, we aim to stimulate creativity. At the heart of every groundbreaking venture lies a powerful idea—one that challenges the status quo and explores uncharted territories. Our programme encourages participants to think beyond boundaries and explore new possibilities. By fostering an environment where new ideas can flourish, I envisage to empower entrepreneurs to envision and create the future.

Secondly, my objective is to help entrepreneurs identify opportunities. In a rapidly changing world, recognising market gaps, emerging trends, and potential areas for innovation is crucial. We provide participants with the tools and techniques needed to analyse the market landscape effectively. Understanding customer needs, industry trends, and competitive dynamics enables entrepreneurs to pinpoint opportunities that others might overlook.

The third objective is to validate concepts. An idea, no matter how brilliant, must be tested and validated to confirm its viability and relevance. You emphasise the importance of rigorous testing and feedback. Participants are encouraged to develop prototypes, conduct market tests, and gather real-world data to validate their concepts. This iterative process ensures that ideas are refined and improved, minimising risks and increasing the likelihood of success.

Next, we guide entrepreneurs in developing strategic plans. A great idea without a clear plan is like a ship without a rudder. Our programme helps entrepreneurs craft actionable plans that outline the steps needed to bring their ideas to life. This includes defining the value proposition, identifying target markets, outlining business models, and setting measurable goals. Strategic planning is the bridge that connects inspiration to execution, turning dreams into reality.

Lastly, we foster collaboration. Innovation thrives in environments where diverse perspectives come together to solve problems and generate new ideas. We promote teamwork and leverage the collective intelligence of your participants. Through collaborative projects, peer feedback, and networking opportunities, we create a community of innovators who support and inspire each other.

In other words, the Idea Creation Programme serves as a catalyst for innovation and entrepreneurship. By stimulating creativity, identifying opportunities, validating concepts, developing strategic plans, and fostering collaboration, you provide entrepreneurs with the foundation they need to succeed. As you embark on this journey together, let us embrace the spirit of innovation and remain steadfast in your commitment to turning ideas into reality.

Components of the Idea Creation Programme

The Idea Creation Programme consists of several key components, each designed to address different aspects of the ideation process.

Firstly, we have Idea Generation Workshops. These sessions provide a collaborative space for brainstorming and creative thinking, facilitated by experienced mentors. Through techniques like mind mapping and design thinking, participants explore new possibilities and unleash their creativity.

Next, Market Research and Analysis play a crucial role. Understanding the market landscape is essential for validating ideas and gauging their potential impact. Through comprehensive analysis and customer feedback, participants ensure that your ideas are grounded in reality and have a strong market fit.

Prototyping and Testing are integral steps in the programme. Creating prototypes and testing them with real users allows participants to gather feedback and refine their concepts. This iterative process drives innovation and ensures that ideas meet the needs of end-users.

Mentorship and Coaching form the backbone of the programme. Experienced entrepreneurs and industry experts provide guidance and support, helping participants navigate challenges and accelerate their learning. Mentorship fosters growth and empowers entrepreneurs to overcome obstacles on their journey.

Finally, Strategic Planning Sessions translate ideas into actionable business plans. Participants learn how to develop strategic roadmaps and define key milestones, setting the foundation for success.

In other words, the Idea Creation Programme comprises these key components, each designed to nurture innovation and guide entrepreneurs towards success. I am eager to witness the transformative ideas that emerge from this programme.

Implementing the Idea Creation Programme

Successfully implementing the Idea Creation Programme involves several critical steps and best practices. You can embrace following comprehensive steps to executing the programme effectively:

Firstly, it is crucial to define the programme's scope and objectives clearly. This involves identifying the target audience, outlining the programme's goals, and setting specific, measurable outcomes. By this, you can effectively guide the programme's design and execution, ensuring alignment with your overarching objectives.

Diversity is the cornerstone of creativity and innovation. Assemble a team of participants with varied backgrounds, skills, and perspectives. This diversity will enrich the ideation process, leading to more robust and innovative solutions. By harnessing the collective intelligence of a diverse group, you can unlock new insights and perspectives that drive meaningful change.

Workshops are the heart of the Idea Creation Programme. Design engaging and interactive sessions that encourage participation and creativity. Utilise a mix of techniques such as brainstorming, role-playing, and case studies to stimulate ideas and foster collaboration. By creating a dynamic and stimulating environment, you can inspire participants to think creatively and push the boundaries of innovation.

Market research is essential for validating ideas and understanding market trends. Conduct thorough research to gain insights into customer needs, market dynamics, and competitive landscapes. Use surveys, interviews, and data analysis to gather valuable insights that inform the development and refinement of ideas. By grounding your ideas in market realities, you can increase your chances of success and relevance.

Prototyping and testing are crucial steps in refining ideas and ensuring their viability. Develop minimum viable products (MVPs) and test them with real users to gather feedback. Use this feedback to iterate and improve upon the initial concept, ensuring that the final product meets customer needs and expectations. By embracing an iterative approach to development, you can rapidly validate ideas and iterate towards success.

Mentorship is a cornerstone of the Idea Creation Programme. Provide participants with access to experienced mentors who can offer guidance, support, and feedback throughout the ideation process. Regular check-ins and coaching sessions will help keep participants on track and motivated, ensuring that you have the support you need to succeed.

Idea creation programme help participants like you and me develop detailed business plans that outline the steps needed to bring your ideas to life. Provide tools and frameworks for strategic planning, goal setting, and risk management. Ensure that participants have a clear roadmap for execution and growth, empowering them to turn your ideas into reality.

Finally, create or become a part of an environment that encourages collaboration and open communication. Utilise team-building activities, collaborative tools, and peer feedback sessions to foster a sense of community and shared purpose among participants. By fostering a collaborative environment, you can harness the collective wisdom and creativity of your participants, driving meaningful progress and innovation.

In other words, the successful implementation of the Idea Creation Programme requires careful planning, strategic execution, and a commitment to fostering creativity and innovation. By following these steps and best practices, you can empower yourself to turn your ideas into reality and create a brighter future for all.

Benefits of the Idea Creation Programme

The Idea Creation Programme offers numerous benefits to entrepreneurs like you. This programme, with its structured framework and innovative approach, offers numerous benefits to aspiring entrepreneurs, empowering them to turn your visions into reality and drive meaningful change in the world.

At the heart of the Idea Creation Programme lies the enhancement of creativity. By providing a structured approach to ideation, this programme serves as a catalyst for creativity, inspiring participants like you and me to explore new possibilities and think outside the box. Through workshops, brainstorming sessions, and creative exercises, you are encouraged to unleash your creative potential and push the boundaries of innovation.

But creativity alone is not enough. The Idea Creation Programme also emphasises the importance of market validation. Thorough market research and testing ensure that ideas are not just innovative but also commercially viable. By gathering insights into customer needs, market trends, and competitive landscapes, you can validate your ideas and ensure they have a strong market fit. This validation process mitigates the risk of launching a product or service that may not resonate with the target audience.

Furthermore, the programme helps entrepreneurs develop strategic clarity. Strategic planning is essential for the success of any venture, and the Idea Creation Programme provides entrepreneurs with the tools and guidance they need to navigate this process effectively. Through strategic planning sessions, you learn how to define your value proposition, identify target markets, and outline key milestones. This strategic clarity provides entrepreneurs like you and me with a roadmap for execution, ensuring you stay focused and aligned with your goals.

But perhaps the most significant benefit of the Idea Creation Programme is its ability to reduce risk. Entrepreneurship inherently involves risk, but through rigorous validation and testing, this programme helps entrepreneurs identify and address potential challenges early on. By validating ideas and refining them through feedback and testing, you increase the likelihood of success for your ventures while minimising the risk of failure.

Lastly, the Idea Creation Programme fosters collaborative innovation. Innovation thrives in environments that foster collaboration and open exchange of ideas. Through collaborative workshops, team projects, and peer feedback sessions, entrepreneurs have the opportunity to leverage the collective intelligence of your peers. This collaborative approach not only leads to more innovative solutions but also fosters a sense of community and shared purpose among participants.

In other words, the Idea Creation Programme is a beacon of opportunity for aspiring entrepreneurs. From enhancing creativity and market validation to providing strategic clarity, reducing risk, and fostering collaborative innovation, this programme equips entrepreneurs with the tools and resources they need to succeed in the dynamic world of entrepreneurship.

Conclusion & Recap

As you wrap up your journey through the Idea Creation Programme, let us embrace the transformative power of creativity, collaboration, and strategic thinking. This programme serves as a beacon guiding entrepreneurs through the intricate process of generating, validating, and developing innovative ideas. By understanding the steps involved and implementing best practices, entrepreneurs can navigate the path to innovation with confidence and clarity.

the "I" stage of the VICTORY Model is essential because it lays the foundation for entrepreneurship, drives innovation, validates market relevance, and mitigates risks associated with launching new ventures. It's the starting point where ideas take shape, setting the stage for future success in the entrepreneurial journey.

As you conclude your exploration of the IDEA phase, remember that this journey is about the transformation of ideas into reality. From the germination of entrepreneurial seeds to the official launch of ventures, this phase is a testament to the power of innovation and the resilience of those who dare to dream.

Stay tuned with the realm where creativity takes flight, ideas are born, and the entrepreneurial journey begins—a journey that will be explored in vivid detail in the upcoming chapters of the Visions to Victory series. As you transition into the IDEA phase, get ready to witness the birth of entrepreneurial creativity and the crucial transition from conceptualisation to actualisation.

As you navigate the intricacies of the entrepreneurial landscape, may your ideas be as boundless as your ambition. Stay tuned for the grand unveiling of the VICTORY model—a framework, a blueprint, and a roadmap that will guide you through the exhilarating journey of business evolution. Your adventure has just begun, and the best is yet to come.

The Idea Creation Programme provides a structured approach, ensuring that ideas are not only creative and innovative but also practical and market ready. It equips entrepreneurs with the tools, resources, and support needed to turn visions into reality. Through Idea Creation, you have the opportunity to unleash your potential, shape the future, and leave an indelible mark on the world.

Remember Your thoughts shape your reality, so Focus on positive thoughts and beliefs to attract wealth and success.

In the next chapter, let's turn your attention to the next phase: Curate. As you transition from the inception phase, where ideas take shape, to the curate phase, where refinement and strategic planning come into play, the journey of a startup progresses from conception to cultivation.

Chapter 6.4

Universal Growth Principle of Curate and Startup Creation Programme

In the dynamic landscape of entrepreneurship, where innovation reigns supreme and bold ideas fuel aspirations, Curate Stage and the startup creation programmes emerge as beacons of hope and guidance for aspiring entrepreneurs.

In this chapter I want to emphasis several key beliefs and principles that underpin the process of launching and growing a successful venture.

Let me draw a parallel with the natural world, where plants, animals, and ecosystems constantly grow, evolve, and expand. This relentless drive for growth is a universal principle that applies to all aspects of life, including wealth and prosperity. Just as water flows effortlessly when it follows the river's natural course, wealth flows easily when one aligns with the universal purpose of growth and expansion.

In the Visions to Victory Model, "Curate and Cultivate Stage" represents a pivotal stage in the entrepreneurial journey where startup ideas are carefully selected, refined, and validated to ensure their viability and alignment with market needs. This phase serves as the foundation upon which successful startups are built, laying the groundwork for sustainable growth and long-term success. By carefully curating their concepts, you increase the likelihood of success, mitigate risks, and lay a solid foundation for sustainable growth and long-term success in the competitive business landscape.

One of my prominent belief is that the ability to create a thriving startup is not solely dependent on external factors like luck or environment but is rooted in a systematic approach akin to a science. This viewpoint asserts that anyone, through understanding and applying the principles and laws governing entrepreneurship, can build a prosperous business.

Moreover, the chapter stresses the importance of fostering a mindset that sees opportunities where others may see obstacles. It encourages aspiring entrepreneurs like you and me to cultivate creativity and innovation as core elements of our entrepreneurial journey, highlighting that true wealth creation often stems from introducing novel solutions that add value to society. The science of the Curate stage is a systematic process designed for you to adopt and embrace and grow a business naturally.

C – Curate & Cultivate the Startup

The "C" in the Victory Model stands for "Curate & Cultivate the Startup," signifying a pivotal stage in the entrepreneurial journey where startups transition from ideation to operational reality. During this phase, entrepreneurs curate and refine their business concepts, laying the groundwork for sustainable growth and success. As you stand at the precipice of entrepreneurial transformation, the letter C beckons—a symbol of the third act in your journey, the stage of "Curate & Cultivate the Startup."

In the forthcoming volume of Visions to Victory, you will witness the seeds planted during ideation transforming into the vibrant sprouts of operational reality. This is a period of nurturing and development, akin to tending to a plant, encouraging growth, refining the initial business idea, launching operations, and optimising processes for sustainable development. It sets the stage for learning, growth, and a robust foundation.

The CURATE model serves as a guiding beacon, illuminating the path for aspiring entrepreneurs to navigate the complexities of the business world and transform their ideas into thriving ventures.

Let's dissect the acronym CURATE and uncover its significance in the entrepreneurial journey:

C - Cultivate the startup idea involves the meticulous selection and refinement of the initial business concept. It is about carefully crafting a vision that resonates with the market. Through thorough market research and analysis, entrepreneurs identify target demographics, assess potential competitors, and ensure that their venture addresses genuine market needs.

U - Understanding the market landscape is paramount during the CURATE phase. Entrepreneurs like you and me delve deep into market trends, consumer behaviours, and industry dynamics to gain invaluable insights. This understanding serves as the foundation upon which strategic decisions are made, shaping the direction of the startup and positioning it for success.

R - Research and validation are the pillars of the CURATE phase. Entrepreneurs like you and me embark on a journey of validation, meticulously testing hypotheses and gathering feedback from potential customers. This rigorous validation process not only reduces the risk of failure but also ensures that the startup is built on a solid foundation of market relevance.

A - Aligning the startup idea with market needs and opportunities is imperative. Entrepreneurs like you and me strive to align their business concepts with emerging trends, unmet needs, and untapped opportunities in the market. This alignment ensures that the startup has a clear value proposition and a competitive edge that sets it apart from the rest.

T - Transforming the curated idea into a tangible plan of action marks the culmination of the CURATE phase. Entrepreneurs like you and me develop a strategic roadmap, outlining goals, objectives, and strategies for bringing their startup to life. This transformation sets the stage for the subsequent stages of startup development, paving the way for cultivation and growth.

E - Evolving and adapting are the hallmarks of the CURATE phase and beyond. Entrepreneurs like you and me embrace flexibility and remain open to feedback, continuously refining our strategies based on market dynamics and changing customer preferences. This continuous evolution is vital for staying relevant and competitive in the ever-changing business landscape.

In essence, the CURATE model represents a systematic approach to startup development, emphasising the importance of thorough research, validation, and alignment with market needs. By carefully curating your ideas and strategies, you can increase the likelihood of startup success and lay a solid foundation for sustainable growth and scalability.

But while Curate focuses on refining and validating startup ideas, understanding its place within the broader startup creation journey is critical for your entrepreneurial success.

Transitioning seamlessly from Curate to startup creation ensures a continuity of strategy, allowing you to maintain alignment between your vision and the practical steps needed to bring it to life. By considering the entire creation phase, you can address challenges holistically, anticipate market entry hurdles, and optimise resources effectively. While Curate is vital for idea refinement and startup transformation, it's incomplete without considering the broader context of startup creation. By embracing the entire creation journey, you can develop a comprehensive approach to building successful ventures.

The curate stage champions the idea that entrepreneurship is about more than just financial gain; it's a pathway to personal fulfillment and making a positive impact in the world. By instilling these beliefs, this segment on Startup Creation aim to inspire and equip individuals with the confidence and mindset necessary to embark on the challenging yet rewarding path of entrepreneurship. Start Up

Creation framework, designed to nurture and support the birth of your new ventures, play a pivotal role in shaping the future of business and driving economic growth.

But what exactly is the startup creation programme, and why is it essential?

Startup Creation Programme

A Startup Creation is a structured initiative aimed at supporting aspiring entrepreneurs in bringing their innovative ideas to life and launching successful businesses. This programme provide a comprehensive framework of resources, mentorship, education, and networking opportunities to help you navigate the complexities of startup and overcome common challenges.

Startup Creation framework of the Visions to Victory Model is the crucial phase that stands as the bedrock of startup success. This framework embodies the journey from ideation to the actualisation of a thriving venture. Imagine the startup journey as a daunting labyrinth, where your vision serves as the guiding star amidst the challenges and uncertainties. It's not just about envisioning the immediate path; it's about charting a course towards a prosperous future. This is where strategic planning steps in, acting as the compass of startup cultivation. By making deliberate decisions and setting clear objectives, entrepreneurs navigate through the complexities of the business landscape, ensuring alignment with their goals.

Yet, the entrepreneurial journey is far from smooth sailing. It's a voyage through storms and calms alike, where resilience becomes the wind in the sails, propelling startups forward in the face of challenges. It's about weathering setbacks, adapting to change, and emerging stronger from the inevitable trials of startup cultivation.

Startup Creation is a dynamic process and a robust framework—a metamorphosis that transforms groundbreaking ideas into viable and scalable ventures. It's not merely about having an innovative concept; it's about navigating the initial challenges of market entry, shaping the business model, and laying the foundation for sustained growth. As entrepreneurs like you and me breathe life into our concepts, the startup evolves with each decision and action, becoming a living entity that reflects our vision and determination.

Navigating the challenges of market entry is the first step in this cultivation process, demanding a strategic approach to overcome obstacles and make a mark in a crowded marketplace. As startups take their first steps, laying the foundation for sustained growth becomes imperative. Building a scalable business model, optimising operational processes, and creating a framework for expansion are vital components. It's about ensuring not just immediate success but long-term viability—a legacy that endures through time.

Central to this framework is the Curate and cultivate stage, where you carefully select and refine your business ideas, ensuring alignment with market needs. This involves conducting thorough market research, identifying target demographics, and assessing potential competitors. By curating your startup ideas, entrepreneurs like you and me position our ventures for success.

But the journey doesn't end there. The Cultivate stage marks a crucial phase where the seeds of success are sown and nurtured. Here, a comprehensive understanding of the market landscape is essential. It involves deep research and analysis to tailor products or services to meet the demands of the target audience effectively.

At the heart of the Cultivate stage lies the establishment of a clear mission and vision for the business. This serves as the guiding light, inspiring confidence among stakeholders and aligning efforts towards a common goal. A comprehensive business plan acts as the roadmap, outlining goals, strategies, and action plans for success.

Moreover, Product/Service Enhancement focuses on continuous improvement and innovation, ensuring relevance and competitiveness in the marketplace. Through constant enhancement, startups stay ahead of the competition and ensure long-term viability.

At their core, startup creation programmes are designed to facilitate the transformation of raw ideas into viable businesses by offering guidance, validation, and strategic support at every stage of the entrepreneurial journey. Whether it's refining a business concept, conducting market research, developing a business plan, or securing funding, these programmes provide aspiring entrepreneurs with the tools and knowledge they need to succeed.

As you delve deeper into the Cultivate stage in Volume 2 of this series, you will explore these concepts in detail, offering insights, strategies, and practical advice to empower you on your entrepreneurial journey. From developing a solid understanding of your market to integrating strategies for sustainable growth, Volume 2 will equip you with the tools and knowledge needed to cultivate success and thrive in the ever-evolving business landscape.

Why are Startup Creation Programmes Essential?

Start Up Creation and the Curate stage of Visions to Victory Model serve as catalysts for innovation and growth, providing a myriad of benefits that are essential for startup success.

Firstly, startup creation programmes offer access to a wide range of resources that you may not have access to otherwise. From funding opportunities to mentorship from experienced industry experts, entrepreneurs gain access to invaluable support networks that can fuel their journey towards success.

Moreover, these programmes provide guidance and mentorship, helping you navigate the complexities of venture creation. Mentors offer insights and advice based on their own experiences, empowering you to make informed decisions and overcome challenges with confidence.

Education and training are also paramount in startup creation. Workshops, seminars, and training sessions equip you with the knowledge and skills you need to thrive in today's competitive business landscape, covering everything from business planning to financial management.

Participating in these programmes allows you to validate your business ideas and receive valuable feedback from mentors, peers, and industry experts. This validation process helps refine concepts, identify challenges, and develop strategies for success.

Furthermore, startup creation provide abundant networking opportunities, allowing you to connect with potential co-founders, investors, customers, and partners. These networking events foster collaboration and innovation, creating a vibrant ecosystem where valuable relationships are forged.

But perhaps most importantly, this programme offers a sense of community and support for aspiring entrepreneurs like you and me. The journey of entrepreneurship can be daunting and lonely, but being part of a supportive community of like-minded individuals can make all the difference. Startup creation cultivate a culture of collaboration, resilience, and innovation, empowering entrepreneurs like you and me to pursue our dreams and overcome obstacles together.

In other words, startup creation programmes are essential for aspiring entrepreneurs, providing access to resources, guidance, education, validation, networking opportunities, and a supportive community. These programmes play a crucial role in nurturing and empowering the next generation of innovators and change-makers.

Navigating the Startup Creation Life Cycle

Startup Growth Life Cycle is a journey of Innovation and Evolution. In the world of entrepreneurship, embarking on a startup journey is akin to setting sail on a grand adventure—an adventure filled with excitement, challenges, and the promise of turning dreams into reality. Just as a ship navigates through different phases of its voyage, startups too traverse a Growth Life Cycle, each phase marking a significant milestone in their journey towards success.

Startup Creation Inception Phase: Setting Sail with Inspiration - In the beginning, your startup business, concept, campaign or product launch is like a blank canvas, waiting eagerly for the first stroke of inspiration. This is the Inception Phase, where ideas are born, prototypes are crafted, and the journey towards building something remarkable begins. It's a time of excitement, creativity, and the thrill of turning innovative concepts into tangible realities.

Startup Creation Survival Phase : Navigating Turbulent Waters - As your startup business, concept, campaign or product launch sets sail, it encounters the turbulent seas of the Survival Phase. Customer acquisition becomes the anchor that keeps the ship steady, while refining the product based on market feedback becomes the compass guiding through stormy uncertainties. It's a phase characterised by resilience, adaptability, and the relentless pursuit of finding a foothold in the competitive market landscape.

Startup Creation Sustain Phase : Unfurling the Sails of Growth - With survival comes the opportunity to thrive, and thus begins the Sustain Phase. Here, the sails of your startup business, concept, campaign or product launch unfurl as operations scale, a loyal customer base is built, and the initial brand presence emerges on the horizon. It's a phase of growth, stability, and laying the foundation for long-term success.

Startup Creation Success Phase: Guided by the North Star of Market Validation - In the Success Phase, your startup business, concept, campaign or product launch finds its North Star in market validation. Early benchmarks are set, strategic growth becomes the focus, and the entrepreneurial ship charts a course towards success. It's a phase where the seeds of innovation planted in the inception phase begin to bear fruit, and the startup starts to realise its full potential.

Startup Creation Thrive Phase: Harnessing the Wind of Innovation - Finally, your startup business, concept, campaign or product launch enters the Thrive Phase—a phase where innovation becomes the wind in its sails. Here, the focus shifts towards expanding into new markets, contributing to industry trends, and shaping the business landscape. It's a phase of empowerment, influence, and the realisation of the startup's role as a force to be reckoned with in the business world.

As startups navigate through each phase of the Growth Life Cycle, they embark on a journey of innovation, evolution, and transformation. With each milestone achieved, they inch closer towards their ultimate goal of success, leaving a lasting impact on the world around them.

In essence, the Startup Creation Growth Life Cycle is not just a roadmap, but a testament to chart new courses, overcome challenges, and sail towards a future where startups not only survive but thrive, shaping the business landscape for generations to come.

From Idea to Startup- Navigating with Confidence

Turning your idea into a startup is an exciting journey, filled with opportunities and challenges. Your journey begins with validating your idea. Start by diving into market research to understand your target audience, their needs, and the competition. Engage with potential customers through surveys and interviews to gather valuable feedback that can refine your concept. Assess the feasibility of your idea from technical, financial, and operational perspectives, identifying potential hurdles and risks along the way.

Next, craft a comprehensive business plan. This plan should paint a vivid picture of your startup, capturing its mission and vision. Dive into market analysis to provide a detailed overview of your industry, market size, and trends, alongside a competitive analysis that identifies key players and their strengths and weaknesses.

Develop a robust marketing and sales strategy, outlining how you will reach your audience and convert them into loyal customers.

Describe your product or service in detail, highlighting its unique selling points and benefits.

Outline your operational plan, detailing your business location, technology, equipment, and supply chain.

Define the organisational structure, introducing key team members and their roles. Finally, build a financial plan that includes your revenue model, pricing strategy, cost structure, and financial projections.

Choosing the right legal structure is crucial. Decide whether to register as a sole trader, partnership, limited company, or corporation. Register your business name with the relevant authorities and obtain necessary licences and permits. Protect your brand and intellectual property to ensure your unique ideas remain yours.

Building a prototype or minimum viable product, often called an MVP, is a pivotal step. Develop a tangible version of your product to test and gather user feedback, iterating based on what you learn. Choose the right technology and tools to support your development process.

Securing funding is often necessary to bring your vision to life. Consider self-funding through personal savings or funds from friends and family. Explore options with angel investors and venture capitalists, preparing a compelling pitch deck and business plan to attract their interest. Crowdfunding platforms like Kickstarter or Indiegogo can also be effective ways to raise capital.

Seek guidance from experienced advisors and mentors who can provide valuable insights and connections.

When it comes to launching your product, plan a memorable event or campaign to create buzz. Utilise social media, public relations, and digital marketing to reach your audience. Focus on strategies to attract and retain customers, ensuring you deliver excellent service that fosters loyalty.

Monitoring and evaluating your progress is critical. Track key performance indicators to measure success and continuously gather and act on customer feedback. Regularly review financial statements and adjust your strategies as needed.

Throughout this journey, stay adaptable. Be ready to pivot based on market feedback and changes. Build a strong network by forming relationships with other entrepreneurs, investors, and industry professionals. Commit to continuous learning, staying updated with industry trends and continually improving your skills and knowledge.

Leverage available resources such as online courses and workshops. Consider joining startup incubators and accelerators like Startup Creation, which provide mentorship, funding, and resources. Utilise business tools like Trello or Asana for project management, QuickBooks for financial management, and Hootsuite or Mailchimp for marketing. By following these steps and guidelines, you can transform your idea into a thriving startup, navigating the journey with confidence and determination.

Conclusion & Recap

Overall, the Curate & Cultivate stage of the Victory Model is essential for transforming your ideas into thriving businesses. By carefully curating and cultivating our ventures, entrepreneurs like you and me can create a solid foundation for success and pave the way for long-term growth and sustainability. On the other hand, startup creation play a vital role in nurturing the next generation of entrepreneurs like you and me and driving innovation and economic growth. By providing access to resources, guidance, education, validation, networking opportunities, and community support, this programme empower aspiring entrepreneurs like you and me to turn our dreams into reality and launch successful businesses. As you look to the future of entrepreneurship, it's clear that startup creation will continue to play a critical role in shaping the landscape of innovation and driving positive change in the world.

This is not just the beginning; it's the foundation upon which your entire entrepreneurial saga stands. As you embark on this visionary odyssey, may your startup creation be as boundless as your ambition, and may your vision be the guiding light propelling you toward triumph and the creation of a lasting legacy.

In conclusion, it's essential to follow Curate's principles and focus on continuous growth and wealth accumulation. Everyone has the right to be rich, allowing individuals to live fully, support their families, and contribute to society. Aligning with this purpose attracts wealth and prosperity since the universe supports life's expansion. To attract wealth, align your thoughts and actions with this purpose. Just as water flows naturally in a river, wealth follows when aligned with the universe. True wealth comes from making a positive impact. When actions help others grow, wealth follows. Develop a growth mindset by nurturing thoughts of expansion and abundance. This shapes how we see opportunities. For example, Andrew Carnegie started with nothing and built a steel empire through continuous growth.

By embracing these principles, we align with the universe's laws, positioning ourselves for true wealth and success. It all starts with a single thought envisioning a better future and igniting a passion to strive for more. Stay tuned for the grand unveiling of the other parts of the VICTORY model—a framework, a blueprint, and a roadmap that will guide you through the exhilarating journey of business evolution. Your adventure has just begun, and the best is yet to come. Now, let's explore the next phase known as "Transform".

Chapter 6.5

Transformative Journey of Market Dominance from startup to Scaleup with Micro Creation

Success is not just about having big dreams or making plans; it requires taking consistent and purposeful action towards our goals.

Think about the last time you achieved something significant—whether in your career, relationships, or personal and professional pursuits. What set you apart from others? It was your ability to take decisive action, to persevere in the face of challenges, and to adapt your strategies as needed. This is the essence of Transform Stage—to inspire you to take bold and strategic action in pursuit of your dreams.

Transitioning from the Curate phase, characterised by refined ideas and strategic planning, to the Transform phase, marked by the spotlight on implementation and adaptation, signifies a significant shift in the startup's journey, propelling it towards unlocking its ultimate potential.

Imagine waking up each day with clarity and determination, knowing that every action you take brings you closer to your goals. By aligning your actions with your aspirations, you harness the creative power of the universe to attract opportunities, resources, and people that support your journey.

But effective action is more than just effort; it is a disciplined approach to achieving our goals. Transform stage teaches us to prioritise our tasks, to focus on high-impact activities, and to persist in the face of challenges. It encourages us to learn from failures, to adapt our strategies as needed, and to embrace innovation and creativity in our pursuits.

Consider the stories of achievers and trailblazers who made their mark through strategic action—entrepreneurs who launched successful ventures, activists who drove social change, and artists who captured the imagination of millions. Their stories remind us that effective action is the catalyst for transformation and the key to achieving our highest aspirations.

The Transform stage within the Visions to Victory Model, represents a critical juncture where businesses undergo significant evolution and growth. It is during this transformative stage that I introduce the Micro Creation programme, a strategic initiative designed to propel the startup enterprises towards unparalleled success toward scaleup.

T - The Transform Stage: A Journey of Micro Venture Evolution for Market Domination

The Transform stage of the Visions to Victory Model marks a turning point in the entrepreneurial journey for you. It is a phase characterised by significant growth, change, and expansion, where your businesses transition from modest beginnings to establishing a strong foothold in the market. At this stage, your focus shifts towards achieving operational efficiency, expanding market reach, building a strong team, and attaining financial stability.

The T for Transform stage of the Victory Model represents a pivotal phase in your entrepreneurial journey, where your businesses undergo significant changes to achieve market dominance.

In the rhythmic progression of your entrepreneurial saga, the letter T beckons, ushering us into the exhilarating act of "Transform the Micro Venture for Market Domination." This phase is the climax of your collective efforts, dedicated to achieving a competitive edge, diversifying products or services, and potentially entering international markets. The objective is crystal clear—sustained growth and the optimisation of market share.

Imagine this period not just as a phase but as the grand transformation where your venture, campaign or product evolve into giants within their respective industries. It's not merely about growth; it's about crafting a competitive edge that sets your venture apart from the rest. Picture your business becoming the go-to choice in your industry, offering something unique and unparalleled.

The Significance of the Transform Stage

In the Transform stage, your businesses undergo profound changes that lay the groundwork for future success. This stage is characterised by a series of strategic initiatives aimed at enhancing operational efficiency, expanding market reach, building a strong team, and ensuring financial stability.

At the heart of the Transform stage lies the pursuit of operational efficiency. This entails streamlining processes, optimising workflows, and effectively allocating resources to boost productivity and reduce costs. By embracing new technologies, refining existing systems, and automating repetitive tasks, your businesses can unlock efficiency gains that propel them forward. Operational efficiency not only enhances competitiveness but also lays the foundation for sustainable growth and profitability.

In tandem with operational efficiency, the Transform stage presents an opportunity for market expansion. It is a time to broaden your horizons, explore new customer segments, geographic regions, and product/service offerings. Through strategic partnerships, targeted marketing campaigns, and innovative approaches, your businesses can attract and retain customers, thereby opening doors to new growth opportunities. Market expansion is essential for diversification and resilience against market fluctuations.

No business can thrive without a strong and cohesive team. Hence, team building takes centre stage during the Transform stage. By recruiting top talent, fostering a positive work culture, and investing in employee development, your businesses can cultivate a team that drives organisational success and innovation. Empowering employees and fostering a sense of belonging not only boosts morale but also enhances productivity and creativity, fuelling your business growth.

Financial stability serves as the bedrock upon which your businesses stand. During the Transform stage, the focus shifts towards managing your cash flow, reducing debt, and achieving profitability. By ensuring sound financial practices, your businesses can weather economic uncertainties and invest in future growth initiatives. Financial stability provides the foundation for long-term success, enabling your businesses to withstand challenges and seize opportunities in the market.

The Transform stage is not just a phase; it's a narrative of market dominance and strategic growth. The focus is on achieving a competitive edge, diversifying products or services, and possibly entering international markets or forming strategic partnerships. The objective by the end of this transformative phase is sustained growth and optimisation of market share.

In other words, the Transform stage is a critical phase in the evolution of your businesses, where strategic initiatives are undertaken to enhance efficiency, expand market reach, build a strong team, and ensure financial stability. By embracing the opportunities presented during this stage, businesses can position themselves for sustainable growth and prosperity in an ever-evolving business landscape. The Transform stage is not just a phase; it's a catalyst for transformative change and future success.

However, understanding the Transform stage in isolation is incomplete without considering the role of the Micro Creation framework.

By embracing the Micro Creation framework alongside the Transform stage, your businesses can unlock their full potential. They can cultivate a culture of continuous improvement, strategically allocate resources, and innovate to stay ahead in the market. In essence, the two frameworks work hand in hand to propel businesses towards market dominance and long-term success. Thus, understanding the significance of Micro Creation within the Transform stage is essential for entrepreneurs like you and me seeking to navigate the complexities of business growth effectively.

Introducing the Micro Creation System

The Micro Creation framework represents a strategic approach to nurturing and developing small-scale enterprises into thriving micro businesses. It encompasses deliberate cultivation, resource optimisation, continuous improvement, and strategic focus to propel your ventures towards success.

In alignment with the objectives of the Transform stage, we introduce the Micro Creation programme as a transformative catalyst for you. This programme represents a strategic framework aimed at empowering you to unlock your full potential and achieve exceptional results. Grounded in principles of intentional cultivation, strategic focus, and continuous improvement, the Micro Creation programme provides your businesses with the tools and strategies they need to thrive in today's competitive business landscape.

In the process of business domination, the concept of Micro Creation is a powerful narrative. It celebrates the journey of your enterprises intentionally and strategically built, nurtured, and optimised by successful entrepreneurs for exceptional results. Micro creation involves the deliberate cultivation and development of your businesses, going beyond survival to intentionally craft success.

As you delve into the intricacies of "Transform the Micro Venture for Market Domination," envision your venture as the architect of its success. It's a narrative of resilience, innovation, and outperformance where intentional cultivation propels your business toward exceptional heights within the intricate tapestry of the business landscape.

One of the key aspects In the micro creation framework is diversification. By expanding your range of products or services, your businesses can appeal to a wider audience and reduce their reliance on a single revenue stream. This not only helps mitigate risks but also opens up new opportunities for growth and innovation.

This stage is crucial because it marks the transition from being a small venture to establishing a strong foothold in the market. In the micro creation framework, your businesses focus on gaining a competitive edge, diversifying their product or service offerings, and potentially expanding into new markets. This phase is essential for sustained growth and the optimisation of market share, allowing businesses to solidify their position and thrive in the long term.

Moreover, the micro creation framework often involves venturing into international markets or forming strategic partnerships. This expansion allows your businesses to extend their reach beyond their domestic market, tapping into new sources of revenue and gaining access to a larger customer base. By establishing your presence in global markets, your businesses can position themselves for long-term success and sustainability.

Unlocking Business Growth with Micro Creation

Micro Creation framework emerges as a catalyst for transformative growth for millions of entrepreneurs like you and me. This strategic approach propels your businesses through a pivotal phase in their journey, fostering evolution and expansion. At the heart of this framework lies a focus on operational efficiency, market expansion, team building, and financial stability, each playing a vital role in driving sustainable success.

Operational efficiency stands as a cornerstone of your business effectiveness. It involves the optimisation of processes, resources, and productivity to deliver greater value to customers. By identifying inefficiencies and implementing best practices, your businesses can streamline operations, reduce costs, and enhance overall performance.

Market expansion is another crucial component of the Micro Creation framework. It empowers your businesses to reach new customers, explore untapped markets, and increase brand awareness. Through strategic marketing initiatives and partnerships, your businesses can broaden their market presence, driving growth opportunities and strengthening their competitive position.

Team building is essential for fostering a culture of innovation and collaboration within organisations. By recruiting top talent, fostering a positive work culture, and providing ongoing training opportunities, your businesses can build a motivated team capable of executing strategies effectively. A strong team not only drives business success but also fuels creativity and innovation, essential elements for staying ahead in today's competitive landscape.

Financial stability serves as the bedrock for long-term sustainability and growth. It involves managing cash flow, reducing debt, and achieving profitability. By maintaining healthy financial practices, your businesses can weather economic uncertainties and invest in future growth initiatives. Financial stability provides the foundation upon which businesses can build resilience and navigate challenges effectively.

Scaling and growing your startup involves optimising operations to improve efficiency and exploring new markets and customer segments. Continuous innovation is key; invest in research and development to enhance your offerings.

As your businesses progress through the Transform stage, they aim to build a capable and motivated team, increase market reach and awareness, develop a solid understanding of market dynamics, and achieve enhanced financial stability. By focusing on these key areas, businesses can position themselves for sustainable growth, profitability, and long-term success in an ever-changing business landscape.

The Micro Creation framework aligns with the objectives of the Transform stage, emphasising market expansion as a critical phase in the evolution of your business. By transitioning from operating solely in domestic markets to expanding globally, your businesses can tap into new avenues for growth, diversify their revenue streams, and gain a competitive advantage. In other words, the Micro Creation framework represents a strategic approach to nurturing and developing small-scale enterprises into thriving businesses. By focusing on operational efficiency, market expansion, team building, and financial stability, your businesses can unlock their full potential and achieve exceptional results in today's dynamic business environment.

Nurturing the Inspiring Journey of Micro Venture Creation

Micro-businesses stand as the embodiment of resilience, innovation, and the unwavering spirit of the entrepreneurial journey in the vast landscape of entrepreneurship. These small-scale enterprises may start with modest beginnings, but they possess the potential to blossom into thriving entities that leave a lasting impact on their industries and communities. Let's embark on a journey through the Micro Business Growth Life Cycle—a journey marked by challenges, triumphs, and the relentless pursuit of success.

Micro Creation Inception Phase: Planting Seeds of Potential - In the Inception Phase, your business takes its first steps towards formalising its step up journey. Basic market research is conducted, and initial operations commence. It's a pivotal moment—a stepping stone from campaign ideation to action, from vision to reality. Transformation Phase is focussed on Nurturing Growth and Expansion

In this transformation Phase from start up to scale up, your business is undergoing a significant evolution, transitioning from its infancy into a more established entity. Multiple campaigns are underway, each strategically designed to propel the business to new heights. Building upon the foundation laid during its formative years, you are now focused on fostering growth and expansion.

This phase represents a period of intense activity and strategic planning, where you harness the lessons learned from your early years to drive innovation and adaptability. Through targeted market research and refined operational strategies, you are positioning yourselves for sustainable success in the years to come.

As you embark on this transformative journey, you remain committed to your core values and vision while embracing change and embracing new opportunities. It's an exciting time for your micro-business as you embark on the next chapter of your growth story.

This phase lays the groundwork for a more structured and organised approach to business, setting the stage for future growth and development.

Micro Creation Survival Phase: Navigating the Waters of Uncertainty - As your business sets sail into the Survival Phase, building a customer base becomes the cornerstone of its journey. Optimising processes and operations becomes essential to ensure stability and sustainability in the dynamic business ecosystem. In this phase, every decision is guided by the goal of not just surviving, but thriving amidst the challenges and uncertainties that come their way.

Micro Creation Sustain Phase: Strengthening Foundations for Growth - With survival comes the opportunity to grow, and thus begins the Sustain Phase. Your business enhances its offerings, gaining a stronger foothold in the market. Solidifying the brand identity becomes more than just an ambition—it becomes a strategic necessity for long-term success. This phase is characterised by strategic investments, innovative marketing strategies, and a relentless focus on delivering value to customers.

Micro Creation Success Phase: Paving the Way for Regional Leadership - In the Success Phase, the your business achieves a significant milestone—regional market leadership. This achievement paves the way for strategic partnerships, collaborations, and sustainable growth opportunities. It's a phase marked by recognition, validation, and the realisation of the micro-business's full potential as a formidable player in its industry.

Micro Creation Thrive Phase: Embracing Innovation and Community Impact - Finally, your business enters the Thrive Phase—a phase where diversification becomes a strategic move, innovative practices fuel growth, and contributing to community development marks the ascent to a thriving existence. Here, the focus shifts beyond mere profitability to creating a meaningful impact on society and the environment. It's a phase of empowerment, inspiration, and the realisation of your business's role as a catalyst for positive change.

Micro Business Growth Life Cycle is not just a roadmap—it's a journey of growth, transformation, and making a difference in the world. As your businesses navigate through each phase of this cycle, they embody the spirit of entrepreneurship and pave the way for a brighter, more prosperous future for all. It's a celebration of the unsung heroes of entrepreneurship—who dare to dream big, defy the odds, and leave an indelible mark on the world.

Startup to Scale-Up - Navigating the Path to Sustainable Growth

Turning a startup into a thriving scale-up is a journey that requires strategic planning, operational finesse, and a relentless focus on sustainable growth. Let me guide you on how to transform your budding business into an industry leader.

First, it's crucial to solidify your foundation. Ensure your product or service genuinely meets a market need by validating your business model. Gather and act on customer feedback to refine what you offer. Clearly differentiate your product from competitors and align your value proposition with your customers' needs and desires.

As you prepare to grow, you need to build a robust framework that can handle increased demand. Upgrade your technology and processes with scalable systems and automation tools to streamline operations. Regularly review and optimise these processes to maintain efficiency. Recruit talented professionals who can support and drive growth, while also fostering a company culture that encourages innovation and collaboration.

Growth doesn't happen by chance; it requires deliberate actions and strategies. Explore new geographical markets and diversify your customer base to expand your market reach. Use market research to identify and target new opportunities. Invest in high-impact marketing campaigns that resonate with your target audience and strengthen your sales team with training and data-driven strategies.

Securing the right financial backing is imperative for fuelling your expansion. Prepare compelling pitches for venture capitalists, angel investors, or consider taking out loans to provide the necessary funds. Explore crowdfunding or strategic partnerships for additional funding sources. Maintain a clear budget and realistic financial projections while diligently monitoring cash flow to ensure sustainable spending and avoid pitfalls.

Staying agile and responsive to the ever-changing business landscape is key to maintaining momentum. Regularly measure key performance indicators related to growth, customer acquisition, and retention to gather valuable insights. Use this data to make informed adjustments, keeping your strategies relevant and effective. Be ready to pivot or adapt based on market trends and feedback. Foster a culture of continuous innovation to stay ahead of the competition.

Loyal customers are the bedrock of a successful scale-up. Deliver exceptional customer service consistently and implement feedback loops to continuously improve your offerings. Develop loyalty programmes and personalised incentives, and engage with customers through targeted marketing efforts to build a loyal customer base that supports sustained growth.

Harness the power of collaboration and mentorship to amplify your efforts. Collaborate with other businesses to leverage each other's strengths. Join industry networks and associations for support and resources. Engage with mentors who have successfully scaled businesses and apply their insights and advice to navigate challenges and seize opportunities.

Transitioning from a startup to a scale-up is a strategic journey that requires careful planning, relentless execution, and a focus on sustainable growth. Consider the transform stage model to assemble the building blocks of scale up organisation. Leverage available resources such as online courses and workshops and master mind programme offered under micro creation framework to solidify the foundation of your venture. By solidifying your foundation, developing a scalable infrastructure, implementing growth strategies, securing the right funding, monitoring progress, strengthening customer relationships, and leveraging partnerships, your venture can achieve new heights. By following these steps and guidelines, you can transform your startup into a successful scale up venture and embrace the challenge to drive your business towards lasting success.

Conclusion & Recap

This is the foundation of your scale up entrepreneurial journey. As you transition from startup to scale-up, let your ambition drive your venture forward. Embrace the Transform stage with its opportunities and challenges. Focus on operational efficiency, market expansion, team building, and financial stability to position yourself for success and market dominance. Together, let's chart a path to prosperity, turning your dreams into reality and forging a brighter future for your business.

As you embark on this visionary journey and explore the Transform stage and Micro Creation framework, ignite your entrepreneurial spirit. Discover inspiration to transform your venture into a force to be reckoned with. Stay tuned for the upcoming TRANSFORM stage and the unveiling of the VICTORY model—a blueprint to guide you through this exhilarating business evolution. Your adventure has just begun, and the best is yet to come.

As your venture progresses from a micro business to an SME through the Optimise phase, focus on expanded operations, streamlined processes, and enhanced efficiency. Lay the groundwork for sustainable growth and enduring success.

The Micro Creation framework is pivotal, marking a critical phase in your business evolution. It's a time of growth, change, and expansion where you can establish leadership and pave the way for future dominance in your industry.

If you seek further insights, connect with me through the resources provided. Stay tuned for the next volume where we delve deeper into MICRO CREATION strategies, exploring actions and mindsets that propel small ventures towards market leadership.

Chapter 6.6

Optimise Stage - Empowering SME Creation in V2V Model

Optimise stage represents a crucial juncture where your businesses refine their operations, enhance their competitive stance, and foster a culture of continuous improvement. It is a stage marked by strategic decision-making, meticulous planning, and unwavering commitment to excellence.

Transitioning from a promising scale-up to a thriving Small and Medium Enterprise (SME) marks a significant milestone in business growth. This chapter explores the strategic steps involved in this transformation, guiding you through key aspects of scaling operations effectively.

Central to this journey is the need to scale operations while maintaining efficiency and sustainability. We delve into strategic planning, financial management, and operational scalability—essential pillars that underpin a successful transition. By optimising processes, adopting scalable technologies, and fortifying infrastructure, your businesses prepare to meet increased demand and expand their market footprint.

Financial prudence is crucial. From managing cash flow to seeking funding or investment, your businesses must navigate these waters to execute growth plans while ensuring profitability and stability.

Effective marketing and sales strategies play a pivotal role in extending market reach and enhancing brand visibility. Tailoring marketing efforts and forging strategic alliances enable your businesses to penetrate new markets and capitalise on growth opportunities.

Human resources development is equally vital. Investing in talent acquisition, training, and retention strategies builds a skilled workforce aligned with the organisation's growth trajectory.

Compliance with legal and regulatory frameworks is emphasised as essential. Staying updated with regulations and protecting intellectual property mitigate risks and ensure business operations are secure.

Throughout, fostering innovation and continuous improvement is key. By leveraging customer feedback, monitoring performance metrics, and adapting to market dynamics, your businesses sustain growth momentum and navigate challenges effectively.

This chapter equips you with insights and tools to navigate the journey from scale-up to successful SME. Through proactive planning, meticulous execution, and a commitment to excellence, your businesses can achieve sustainable growth and enduring success in competitive markets.

In this chapter, you will explore the significance of the Optimise Stage and its impact on SME creation. You will delve into the key components of this stage, including maximising profits, strengthening competitive position, enhancing agility, fostering innovation, and driving sustained growth.

The Essence of the Optimise Stage

Venturing into the Optimise stage of the VICTORY MODEL, witness the business with a fortified market presence and refined operations. This phase magnifies the focus on innovations and efficiency improvements, aiming to maximise profits and solidify its competitive position.

Imagine this stage as more than just achieving financial gains; it's about strategically extracting the full potential from every facet of the business. The business transcends mere survival, shifting towards a thriving state of maximising profits. Solidifying the competitive position becomes imperative as your businesses evolve. This is about creating a stronghold in the market, ensuring not just meeting but surpassing the competition. It's the foundation for sustained success in the dynamic business landscape.

As you enter the Optimise stage, innovations and efficiency improvements become the focal points. It's not just about doing things differently; it's about doing them better. Your businesses leverage creativity and strategic thinking to enhance operations, respond to market dynamics, and stay ahead of the curve. In the symphony of business orchestration, SME creation plays a dynamic and enriching melody. It's not just about establishing your businesses; it's about nurturing them to become vibrant contributors to the harmonious progression of economies and communities alike. SMEs are the unsung heroes, creating ripples of impact far beyond their size.

O – Optimise Business with Operational Excellence and Innovation

The O for Optimise Stage in the Victory Model focuses on enhancing operational efficiency and fostering innovation within a business. Embark with us into the vibrant realm of the "Optimise" stage, a phase where operational excellence and innovation seamlessly dance to the rhythm of entrepreneurial success. Your journey is dedicated to maximising profits and fortifying your competitive stance, where innovations and efficiency improvements take centre stage, ensuring agility and responsiveness to the dynamic market landscape. This unfolds under the umbrella of SME CREATION.

In the dynamic tapestry of the business landscape, Small and Medium Enterprises (SMEs) emerge as vibrant threads, weaving significant contributions to economic growth and innovation. SME CREATION encapsulates intentional efforts and strategic manoeuvres by entrepreneurs to nurture these enterprises, elevating them to sustainable success levels.

As you unravel the essence of SME creation, I invite you to explore its significance and anticipate the unveiling of strategies for triumph in the SME domain in our next volume. Picture SME creation as a symphony, playing a dynamic and enriching melody that harmoniously progresses economies and communities.

Venturing into the O or OPTIMISE STAGE of the VICTORY MODEL, witness the business with a fortified market presence and refined operations. This phase magnifies the focus on innovations and efficiency improvements, aiming to maximise profits and solidify its competitive position.

Picture this as more than just financial gains; it's strategically extracting the full potential from every facet of the business. The business transcends mere survival, shifting towards a thriving state of maximising profits.

Solidifying the competitive position becomes imperative as your businesses evolve. This is about creating a stronghold in the market, ensuring not just meeting but surpassing the competition. It's the foundation for sustained success in the dynamic business landscape.

As you enter the Optimise stage, innovations and efficiency improvements become the focal points. It's not just about doing things differently; it's about doing them better. Your businesses leverage creativity and strategic thinking to enhance operations, respond to market dynamics, and stay ahead of the curve.

In the symphony of your business orchestration, SME creation plays a dynamic and enriching melody. It's not just about establishing your businesses; it's about nurturing them to become vibrant contributors to the harmonious progression of economies and communities alike. SMEs are the unsung heroes, creating ripples of impact far beyond their size.

The Optimise stage represents a critical juncture in the entrepreneurial journey, where your businesses aim to maximise their potential for growth and success. This stage is characterised by a focus on your Small Business Growth with Market Diversification, Revenue Stream Diversification, Global Expansion, and Capacity for Growth.

Small Business Growth with Market Diversification: At the heart of the Optimise stage is the pursuit of sustainable growth for your small businesses. This involves expanding beyond traditional markets and diversifying customer bases to reduce dependency on any single market segment. By tapping into new markets and customer demographics, your businesses can mitigate risks and capitalise on emerging opportunities for growth.

Revenue Stream Diversification: Revenue stream diversification is essential for long-term viability and resilience. This entails exploring multiple revenue streams, such as product sales, subscription services, licensing agreements, and partnerships. By diversifying revenue streams, your businesses can create more stable and predictable income streams, mitigate revenue fluctuations, and enhance overall financial sustainability.

Global Expansion: Global expansion represents a significant growth opportunity for your businesses looking to scale beyond domestic markets. This involves strategically entering international markets, establishing a presence in key regions, and adapting products or services to meet the needs of diverse cultural and regulatory environments. By expanding globally, your businesses can access new customer bases, tap into global supply chains, and unlock new sources of revenue and growth.

Capacity for Growth: Capacity for growth refers to a business's ability to scale operations, infrastructure, and resources to accommodate increased demand and expansion opportunities. This may involve investing in technology, upgrading facilities, hiring additional staff, and optimising supply chain logistics. By building scalable and flexible systems, your businesses can effectively manage growth trajectories and capitalise on new opportunities without compromising quality or efficiency.

In the dynamic landscape of business, where challenges and opportunities intersect, the Optimise Stage stands as a beacon of strategic importance within the framework of Vision to Victory Model and SME Creation. This pivotal phase acts as a catalyst for growth, innovation, and sustained success, shaping the trajectory of your businesses in their pursuit of excellence. At the heart of the Optimise Stage lies a multifaceted approach aimed at maximising operational efficiency and fostering innovation. This stage is not merely a checkpoint but a transformative journey for your businesses, offering a multitude of benefits that are essential for their long-term viability and prosperity.

The Significance: Why is Optimise Stage so Crucial?

One of the key pillars of the Optimise Stage is the maximisation of profits. By optimising operations, your businesses can significantly reduce costs, improve productivity, and ultimately increase their profitability. This financial stability is fundamental for the sustainability and growth of your businesses, providing them with the resources necessary to reinvest in further development and expansion.

Furthermore, the Optimise Stage plays a pivotal role in strengthening the competitive position of your businesses in the market. Through operational optimisation, companies can deliver products or services more efficiently and effectively, gaining a competitive edge over their rivals. By offering superior value to customers at a lower cost, your businesses can solidify their position in the market and defend against potential threats from competitors.

In today's fast-paced business environment, agility is paramount. The Optimise Stage equips your businesses with the agility needed to respond quickly to changes in the market, customer demands, and industry trends. By optimising operations, your businesses can become more agile and adaptable, enabling them to seize opportunities and navigate challenges with ease. Moreover, the Optimise Stage serves as a catalyst for innovation. By freeing up resources through operational efficiencies, businesses can create a culture that encourages and supports innovation. This culture of innovation is essential for staying relevant and competitive in the marketplace, driving product development, and enhancing overall competitiveness.

Crucially, the Optimise Stage lays the foundation for sustained growth. By streamlining processes, improving customer satisfaction, and identifying new opportunities for expansion, your businesses can set themselves on a trajectory of continuous growth and development. This sustained growth is essential for long-term success, ensuring that your businesses remain resilient and relevant in an ever-evolving business landscape.

In other words, the Optimise Stage is of paramount importance in the journey of SME creation. It empowers your businesses to become more efficient, innovative, and competitive, leading to long-term success and growth. As you conclude your exploration of SME creation and the Optimise Stage, it is evident that this phase is not just a checkpoint but a transformative journey towards operational excellence and innovation. As businesses embark on this journey, they must remain committed to continuous improvement, embracing change, and seizing opportunities for growth and development.

The Optimise stage focuses on elevating your small business, diversifying income sources, expanding internationally, and progressing from small to medium-sized operations. This framework highlights entrepreneurship, diversifying revenue, measuring success, and managing growth. These aspects are bolstered by a robust framework and the SME Creation program detailed in the next segment of this chapter. Also explore Volume 2 of this series for an in-depth exploration of these concepts. Discover practical insights, strategies, and best practices that empower entrepreneurs on their path to success.

What is SME Creation

SME creation, or the process of transitioning a micro business into a small-scale enterprise, involves a strategic and intentional approach to growth, expansion, and development. It encompasses a series of steps aimed at transforming a small business with limited resources and operations into a more robust and scalable entity. This transformation typically involves increasing the size of the workforce, expanding market reach, and aiming for higher revenue targets.

At its core, SME creation framework is about seizing opportunities and addressing challenges inherent in the small business landscape. It begins with a thorough assessment of the current state of the business, including its strengths, weaknesses, opportunities, and threats. This evaluation serves as the foundation for developing a comprehensive business plan that outlines the roadmap for growth and expansion.

One of the key aspects of SME creation framework is market analysis and expansion. This involves conducting in-depth research to identify new opportunities for growth, whether through diversifying product offerings, entering new geographic markets, or targeting different customer segments. By expanding the market reach, your businesses can tap into new revenue streams and increase their overall profitability.

Operational optimisation is another critical component of SME creation framework. This entails streamlining internal processes and workflows to improve efficiency and productivity. Investing in technology, upgrading infrastructure, and implementing best practices can help support growth and scalability, ensuring that the business is well-equipped to handle increased demand and expansion.

Financial planning and investment are also essential aspects of SME creation framework. Developing a sound financial strategy that aligns with the goals of the business is crucial for securing additional funding or investment to support expansion initiatives. Effective cost management strategies can help optimise profitability and ensure long-term financial sustainability.

Building a skilled and capable workforce is another key element of SME creation. Investing in talent acquisition and development programmes can help attract and retain top talent, ensuring that the business has the resources it needs to support growth and expansion. Creating a positive work culture is also essential for fostering employee engagement and productivity.

Marketing and branding play a vital role in SME creation as well. Enhancing brand awareness and visibility can help attract new customers and drive sales growth. Developing a comprehensive marketing strategy, leveraging digital channels, and implementing targeted advertising campaigns can help reach key audiences and generate interest in the business.

Finally, ensuring compliance with relevant laws, regulations, and industry standards is essential for mitigating risks and protecting the business from potential liabilities. Establishing robust compliance processes and implementing risk management strategies can help ensure that the business operates ethically and responsibly. SME creation is a strategic and intentional process aimed at transforming a micro business into a small-scale enterprise that is well-equipped to tackle the challenges and capitalise on the opportunities of the small business landscape. By focusing on market expansion, operational optimisation, financial planning, talent acquisition, marketing, and compliance, your businesses can successfully navigate the journey of SME creation and position themselves for long-term success and growth.

Elevating SME Creation: Optimising Growth within the Vision to Victory Model

SME creation, within the context of the Optimise stage of the Vision to Victory Model, represents a critical juncture in the journey of a business's growth and development. This stage marks the transition from the initial stages of establishment to a phase of strategic optimisation and innovation, where your businesses aim to maximise their potential for success and sustainability.

At the heart of SME creation within the Optimise stage lies the pursuit of operational excellence and efficiency. This involves streamlining processes, optimising resources, and enhancing productivity to drive profitability and competitiveness. By focusing on operational optimisation, your businesses can reduce costs, improve efficiency, and ultimately increase their bottom line. Moreover, SME creation within the Optimise stage emphasises the importance of market diversification and expansion. Your businesses explore new markets, customer segments, and revenue streams to reduce dependency on any single market segment and mitigate risks. This strategic approach to market diversification not only fosters resilience but also opens up new growth opportunities for your businesses.

Additionally, the Optimise stage of the Vision to Victory Model places a strong emphasis on innovation and agility. SME creation involves fostering a culture of innovation within the organisation, where creativity and experimentation are encouraged to drive continuous improvement and adaptability. By embracing innovation, your businesses can stay ahead of the curve, anticipate market trends, and respond swiftly to changing customer demands.

Furthermore, SME creation within the Optimise stage is closely intertwined with the concept of sustained growth. Your businesses focus on laying the foundation for long-term success by enhancing customer satisfaction, identifying new opportunities for expansion, and building scalable systems and processes. This proactive approach to growth management ensures that your businesses are well-positioned to capitalise on emerging opportunities and navigate challenges effectively. In other words, SME creation framework within the Optimise stage of the Vision to Victory Model is a strategic imperative for your businesses seeking to maximise their potential for success and growth. By focusing on operational excellence, market diversification, innovation, and sustained growth, your businesses can unlock new opportunities, drive profitability, and position themselves as leaders in their respective industries.

Soaring Beyond Boundaries - SMEs Inspiring Journey

In the vast and ever-evolving landscape of business, Small and Medium-sized Enterprises (SMEs) stand as beacons of innovation, resilience, and the unwavering spirit of entrepreneurship. These dynamic entities may start as modest ventures, but they possess the potential to grow into industry leaders, shaping markets and leaving a lasting impact on the global economy. Let's embark on a journey through the SME Growth Life Cycle—a journey marked by determination, adaptability, and the relentless pursuit of success.

SME Creation Inception Phase: Laying the Foundation for Growth - In the Inception Phase, strategic planning becomes the SME's compass, guiding its course through uncharted waters. Market entry strategies are meticulously crafted, and securing initial funding forms the bedrock of operations. It's a phase of anticipation, excitement, and laying the groundwork for future success.

SME Creation Survival Phase: Navigating Challenges with Resilience - As the SME navigates through the Survival Phase, market penetration becomes not just a goal, but a necessity for survival. Adapting to competition, refining operational efficiency, and staying agile in the face of uncertainty become the ethos of the business. It's a phase characterised by resilience, resourcefulness, and the ability to weather storms with grace.

SME Creation Sustain Phase: Pioneering Growth and Sustainability -With survival comes the opportunity for growth, and thus begins the Sustain Phase. Diversification becomes the SME's anthem as it explores new markets, products, and services. Regional expansion and establishing a robust brand presence become keystones of sustainability. This phase is marked by strategic investments, innovative marketing strategies, and a relentless focus on delivering value to customers.

SME Creation Success Phase: Ascending to Market Leadership - In the Success Phase, the SME rises to new heights as market leadership becomes not just a dream, but a reality. Strategic collaborations, partnerships, and industry recognition become the hallmarks of success. It's a phase of validation, affirmation, and the realisation of the SME's full potential as a leader in its industry.

SME Creation Thrive Phase: Embracing Global Opportunities and Sustainability - Finally, the SME enters the Thrive Phase—a phase where international expansion beckons, and mergers and acquisitions become strategic moves to further fuel growth. Leading in sustainable business practices becomes the zenith of thriving, as the SME cements its position as a global leader in its field. It's a phase of empowerment, innovation, and making a meaningful impact on the world.

SME Growth Life Cycle is a journey of growth, transformation, and making a difference in the world. As SMEs navigate through each phase of this cycle, they embody the spirit of entrepreneurship and pave the way for a brighter, more prosperous future for all. It's a celebration of journey to leave an indelible mark on the global stage.

Turning Your Business to Become a Successful SME

Turning your venture from scale up into a successful SME is all about growing strategically and making continuous improvements. It starts with really understanding your business model—figuring out what works well and where you can do better. Setting clear goals is crucial. These should be specific, measurable, achievable, relevant, and time-bound—goals that make sense for your business and have a deadline to keep you focused.

Managing your finances well is key. You need to keep a tight grip on cash flow, ensuring money comes in on time and expenses are managed efficiently. If you need extra funds to expand, look into options like loans or investments. Regularly checking your financial performance helps you understand where you're making money and where you might need to adjust your strategy.

Making your operations run smoothly is essential. Streamline your processes to cut costs and boost productivity. Using technology to automate tasks can save time and effort. Make sure your business is set up to handle more work as you grow—having scalable systems in place is vital.

When it comes to marketing and sales, be strategic. Clearly define what makes your business stand out and use this to target your marketing efforts effectively. Building a loyal customer base is key. Invest in relationships with your customers to keep them coming back and recommending you to others.

Your team is the heart of your business. Hiring the right people and helping them develop their skills is crucial. Establish clear HR policies to create a positive working environment and ensure everyone knows what's expected of them.

Staying on top of legal requirements is important. Make sure you understand and comply with the rules that apply to your industry. Protecting your intellectual property, like trademarks or inventions, safeguards your business's unique ideas and creations.

Networking and forming partnerships can open up new opportunities. Get involved with industry groups and collaborate with other businesses to learn from each other and explore new ventures.

Being adaptable is vital in business. Keep an eye on how things are going, listen to feedback from customers and employees, and be ready to change tack if needed. Being able to move quickly and respond to changes in the market will help your business stay competitive.

Listening to your customers is essential for success. Take their feedback on board and use it to improve your products or services. Innovation is key to staying ahead of the game and meeting the needs of your customers.

Celebrate your achievements and learn from your mistakes. Every success and setback is a chance to grow and improve. Keep pushing forward and learning along the way—this is how you'll turn your venture into a thriving SME.

Turning your venture into a successful SME demands meticulous planning, dedicated effort, and an unwavering commitment to continuous improvement. It's a journey that requires leveraging every available resource and opportunity.

To begin, consider diving into resources such as online courses and workshops provided through the SME creation framework. These tools can significantly bolster your understanding and skills, helping to solidify the foundation of your business. By enhancing your knowledge and capabilities in areas like strategic planning, financial management, and operational efficiency, you pave the way for sustainable growth.

Establishing a robust foundation involves more than just acquiring knowledge—it requires action. Develop scalable infrastructure that can support increased demand and expansion into new markets. Implement growth strategies tailored to your business's unique strengths and market opportunities. Secure the necessary funding through strategic partnerships or investment to fuel your growth trajectory effectively.

Monitoring your progress is essential. Regularly assess key performance indicators (KPIs) to gauge the effectiveness of your strategies and make informed adjustments as needed. Nurture strong relationships with your customers by delivering exceptional value and service. Their feedback will be invaluable in refining your offerings and maintaining customer loyalty.

Lastly, strategic partnerships can provide access to new resources, markets, or technologies that accelerate your growth. Collaborate with like-minded businesses and industry leaders to leverage collective strengths and seize growth opportunities together.

By following these steps and embracing a mindset of continual learning and adaptation, you position your venture not just to survive, but to thrive in the competitive landscape of SMEs.

Conclusion & Recap

The Optimise Stage emerges as a cornerstone within the Vision to Victory Model and SME Creation framework. This pivotal phase acts as a catalyst for growth, innovation, and sustained success, shaping the trajectory of businesses as they strive for excellence.

Central to the Optimise Stage is a comprehensive approach aimed at enhancing operational efficiency and fostering innovation. It represents more than a mere checkpoint; it signifies a transformative journey for businesses, offering indispensable benefits for their long-term viability and prosperity.

Join us as we delve deeper into the intricacies of the Optimise Stage in the next volume of the Vision to Victory Model. Discover the secrets to success and chart a course towards a future brimming with possibilities. Together, let us embark on this transformative journey, unlocking pathways to operational excellence and innovation in SME creation.

Embark on the journey of SME creation, where your efforts resonate with the essence of innovation, resilience, and sustained success within the vibrant realm of Small and Medium Enterprises. This journey is about cultivating an ecosystem where entrepreneurship thrives, communities prosper, and economies flourish.

For more in-depth insights, connect with me through the available resources. Stay tuned for the upcoming volume where we will delve deeper into SME creation strategies, uncovering actionable steps and mindsets that propel small ventures towards achieving market leadership.

Chapter 6.7

Rise Stage - Empowering SMEs to Achieve Large-Scale Success

Expanding a Small and Medium-sized Enterprise (SME) into a large business demands careful planning and strategic execution. This chapter explores essential strategies and practical steps to navigate this transformational journey successfully. Whether your goal is to increase revenue, expand market reach, or enhance operational capabilities, the path to becoming a large business requires a deliberate approach across multiple facets of your organisation.

Navigating this journey towards success requires a strategic approach and a clear roadmap. Among the various stages of business growth, the Rise Stage stands out as a pivotal phase where your businesses transition from small-scale operations to significant players in the market. The Visions to Victory Model isn't just another framework; it's a roadmap that guides your businesses through the complexities of growth and evolution. At its core lies the Rise Stage, a phase where dreams turn into reality, and aspirations are transformed into achievements.

Diversification, the heartbeat of sustained growth, will take centre stage in the Triumph phase. Ventures evolve by expanding their product or service offerings, catering to a broader audience and mitigating risks by reducing dependence on a single revenue stream. It's a metamorphosis from a specialised niche to a comprehensive solution provider.

From setting ambitious growth objectives and securing financial resources to optimising operations and leveraging technology, each step plays a crucial role in scaling your business effectively. Moreover, fostering a culture of innovation, nurturing strategic partnerships, and prioritising customer relationships are key factors that contribute to sustainable growth.

By delving into these topics, this chapter aims to equip you with actionable insights and best practices to propel your SME towards becoming a thriving large business. Embrace the challenges and opportunities ahead, and leverage strategic planning to realise your business's full potential in the competitive landscape.

R – Rise in Public Ownership and Leadership

As you venture into the R or RISE stage of the VICTORY MODEL, representing the culmination of the entrepreneurial odyssey, you will anticipate a momentous event—an IPO. This is not just a financial transition; it's a strategic move that unlocks new dimensions for your business, turning it into a powerhouse.

Journey with us through the penultimate will act, a transformative stage where your businesses ascend to new heights—Revelling in Public Ownership and Leadership. This will mark the commencement of an extraordinary phase, with considerations of an Initial Public Offering (IPO) and entry into the public market. Picture access to capital markets, potential acquisitions, and sustained growth, all converging towards the ultimate goal of market leadership.

Going public will be more than a financial event; it's a strategic leap that transforms your business into a cash-generating machine. The decision to embrace public ownership will signify maturity and success, providing access to capital markets, enhancing visibility, and creating avenues for expansion.

Public ownership will bring the advantage of tapping into capital markets, offering your businesses the means to fund strategic initiatives—expanding operations, investing in research and development, or exploring new markets. The capital market will become a wellspring for continued growth and innovation.

With public ownership will come the potential for strategic acquisitions, enabling your businesses to consolidate their industry position and expand their market presence. The RISE STAGE will become a platform for strategic manoeuvres that redefine the business landscape.

The overarching theme of the RISE stage is sustained growth and market leadership. Going public is not merely a one-time event; it will be about setting the stage for enduring success. Beyond thriving in the public domain, your businesses will aspire to lead their industries, becoming beacons of inspiration.

The Rise Framework marks a significant milestone in the entrepreneurial journey, dedicated to facilitating the growth and expansion of medium-scale businesses.

What exactly is the Rise Stage?

The Rise Stage is a critical phase within the framework of the Visions to Victory Model—a strategic roadmap designed to guide your businesses through the complexities of growth and evolution. It represents a period of dynamic expansion, strategic innovation, and preparation for future success. In essence, the Rise Stage marks the point where your businesses ascend to new heights, propelled by a relentless pursuit of excellence and a commitment to realising their strategic objectives.

The Rise Stage is more than just a phase; it's a journey of transformation—a journey where your businesses transition from small beginnings to significant players in the market. It's a phase characterised by dynamic growth, strategic expansion, and visionary leadership. In the Rise Stage, your businesses don't just aim to survive; they strive to thrive, to excel, and to become market leaders.

It's the strategic imperatives, the organisational capabilities, and the unwavering commitment to excellence that define this stage. It's about seizing opportunities, leveraging strengths, and charting a course towards sustainable success.

What are the key components of the Rise Stage?

Strategic expansion is at the forefront—a strategic move to expand market presence, diversify product offerings, and explore new territories. Resource expansion follows suit, with investments in infrastructure, technology, and human capital to support the growing demands of a burgeoning business.

But the Rise Stage isn't just about expansion; it's also about innovation and differentiation. It's about fostering a culture of creativity, experimentation, and continuous improvement. It's about staying ahead of the curve, embracing new technologies, and redefining industry standards.

Of course, financial planning and capital raising are integral to navigating the complexities of the Rise Stage. Robust financial strategies, capital infusion, and preparation for future financial needs are paramount for sustainable growth and success.

And let's not forget about preparation for future growth and leadership—a strategic endeavour to position the business for sustained success and market leadership. It's about laying the groundwork for the future, nurturing talent, and fostering a culture of excellence.

In essence, the Rise Stage of the Visions to Victory Model is more than just a phase; it's a journey—a journey of growth, transformation, and triumph. It's about seizing opportunities, overcoming challenges, and realising the full potential of your businesses. So let us embrace the Rise Stage with open arms, for it is not just a phase in your journey; it is the pathway to victory.

Shaping the trajectory of your businesses

At the heart of the Rise Stage lie several key characteristics that define this transformative phase and set the stage for business success. These characteristics are crucial in shaping the trajectory of your businesses during this phase.

First and Foremost, The Rise Stage is characterised by dynamic growth—a period marked by significant expansion in market presence, customer base, and revenue streams. During this phase, your businesses seize strategic opportunities, capitalise on emerging trends, and explore new avenues for growth. It's a time of rapid expansion and scaling as your businesses strive to establish themselves as key players in their respective industries.

Strategic expansion is another hallmark of the Rise Stage. Your businesses focus on scaling operations, diversifying product offerings, and entering new markets to capture untapped opportunities. This expansion is driven by a deep understanding of market dynamics, customer needs, and competitive landscapes. It's about making calculated moves that position the business for sustainable growth and market leadership.

Third key characteristic, Innovation, is paramount in the Rise Stage, driving differentiation and competitive advantage. Your businesses foster a culture of creativity, experimentation, and continuous improvement to stay ahead of the curve and meet evolving customer demands. It's about thinking outside the box, embracing new technologies, and disrupting the status quo to carve out a unique position in the market.

To support their growth trajectory, your businesses invest in expanding their resources, including infrastructure, technology, and human capital which is the next characteristics of this phase. This enables them to scale operations, improve efficiency, and meet the evolving demands of a growing organisation. Resource expansion is essential for laying a solid foundation for future growth and ensuring operational excellence.

Fifth element is Financial Planning and Capital Raising. Sound financial planning is crucial for navigating the complexities of the Rise Stage. Your businesses develop robust financial strategies, raise capital through various means, and prepare for future financial needs, including potential IPOs or other forms of public offerings. It's about securing the necessary funding to fuel growth initiatives and strategic expansion plans.

And last but not the least is Preparation for Future Growth. As your businesses evolve through the Rise Stage, they lay the groundwork for future growth and leadership. This involves strategic planning, talent development, and organisational restructuring to position the business for sustained success and market leadership. It's about building a strong foundation for long-term growth and ensuring that the business is well-equipped to thrive in a competitive market landscape.

In other words, the Rise Stage is a transformative phase in the entrepreneurial journey—a phase characterised by dynamic growth, strategic expansion, and relentless innovation. By embracing these key characteristics, your businesses can navigate the complexities of this phase and position themselves for long-term success and market leadership.

The Rise Framework is designed to propel medium-scale businesses to new heights by expanding reach and resources, fostering innovation, enhancing customer satisfaction, and diversifying income streams. In Volume 2 of this series, you will explore these concepts in detail, providing practical insights, strategies, and best practices to empower medium-scale businesses on their journey to success.

The Rise Stage is important as it represents a significant milestone in the entrepreneurial journey, signifying the transition towards market leadership and sustained growth. By embracing public ownership and leadership, your businesses unlock new opportunities for expansion, innovation, and market dominance, positioning themselves for long-term success and creating value for shareholders and stakeholders alike.

Significance of RISE stage

The R for Rise Stage of the Victory Model represents a significant milestone in the entrepreneurial journey, where your businesses transition towards public ownership and leadership. This stage is crucial as it marks the culmination of efforts to establish a strong market presence and signals the readiness of the business to expand its horizons. RISE stage signifies more than just a milestone; it represents a transformative phase where your businesses transition towards public ownership and leadership. The journey towards the Rise Stage is marked by relentless dedication, strategic planning, and unwavering commitment. It is the culmination of efforts to establish a strong market presence and signals the readiness of the business to expand its horizons. At this juncture, your businesses contemplate a significant decision—the consideration of an Initial Public Offering (IPO). This transformative step not only raises capital but also opens doors to a broader investor base, enhancing visibility and credibility in the market.

The Rise Stage is not just another phase in the entrepreneurial journey—it is a pathway to business growth and success. It represents a strategic inflection point where your businesses harness their potential, overcome challenges, and prepare for future opportunities. By navigating the Rise Stage effectively, your businesses can position themselves for sustained success, market leadership, and the realisation of their strategic objectives.

One of the key aspects of the Rise Stage is the attainment of market dominance. Going public signifies that a business has reached a level of maturity and success where it can compete with established players in the industry. By consolidating its position through public ownership, the business aims to solidify its competitive stance and establish itself as a market leader.

Access to capital is another crucial benefit of public ownership. It opens doors to capital markets, enabling your businesses to raise funds for expansion, innovation, and strategic initiatives. This access to capital fuels the growth trajectory, allowing companies to pursue acquisitions, invest in research and development, and explore new markets or product lines.

Strategic acquisitions become a viable option with the infusion of capital from public markets. Your businesses can strategically acquire other companies to strengthen their market position, expand their customer base, or diversify their offerings. These acquisitions play a significant role in accelerating growth and achieving market dominance.

Moreover, going public elevates the profile of the business, increasing its visibility and credibility among customers, partners, and stakeholders. As a publicly traded company, it gains recognition in the industry and has the opportunity to influence market trends and set industry standards, establishing itself as a leader in its field.

In essence, the Rise Stage is not just a milestone; it is a testament to the resilience, determination, and vision of entrepreneurs and business leaders. It represents a significant transition towards market leadership and sustained growth. By embracing public ownership and leadership, your businesses unlock new opportunities for expansion, innovation, and market dominance, positioning themselves for long-term success and creating value for shareholders and stakeholders alike.

As you embark on this journey through the Rise Stage, let us embrace the challenges and opportunities that lie ahead. Let us chart a course towards success, guided by the principles of integrity, innovation, and excellence. Together, let us rise to new heights and redefine the future of business.

As entrepreneurs and business leaders, understanding the significance of the Rise Stage is essential for charting a course towards sustainable growth and long-term success. By embracing the opportunities and challenges of the Rise Stage, your businesses can unlock their full potential and emerge as leaders in their respective industries.

In other words, the Rise Stage is a critical phase in the journey of every business—a phase where dreams are transformed into reality, and aspirations are turned into achievements. It is a period of growth, innovation, and preparation—a period where your businesses rise to new heights and embark on a journey towards success. However, the Rise Stage discussion is incomplete without mentioning the Business Creation framework. Together, these elements form a synergistic pathway, equipping businesses with the tools, strategies, and support needed to navigate the complexities of expansion and ultimately achieve success.

What is Business Creation

The Business Creation Programme represents a transformative initiative tailored to empower small and medium-sized enterprises (SMEs) on their journey towards substantial growth and evolution into large-scale organisations. This programme is meticulously crafted with the aim of equipping SMEs with the necessary tools, strategies, and support to navigate the intricate landscape of expansion, ultimately culminating in a successful public offering.

The relationship between the Business Creation Framework and the RISE Stage within the Visions to Victory model is symbiotic and indispensable. Each element complements and reinforces the other, creating a synergistic pathway for your businesses to achieve substantial growth and transformation. Let's delve into how these two components intertwine and why they cannot stand alone:

Interdependence of Business Creation Framework and RISE Stage

The journey from a small and medium-sized enterprise (SME) to a large organisation is both challenging and rewarding. It requires strategic planning, resource optimisation, and a clear roadmap for growth. Recognising the complexities of this journey, the Business Creation Programme offered by Visions to Victory Models provides SMEs with the tools, guidance, and support needed to navigate their path to success. Let's explore how this programme empowers SMEs to rise to the status of large organisations.

At the core of the Business Creation Programme is strategic planning. SMEs are guided through the process of defining their vision, mission, and long-term goals. They learn how to conduct market research, analyse industry trends, and identify growth opportunities. By developing a comprehensive business plan, SMEs set the foundation for their future expansion and success. One of the key challenges SMEs faces on their journey to becoming large organisations is resource management. The Business Creation Programme helps SMEs optimise their resources by identifying areas of inefficiency and implementing strategies for improvement. Whether it's streamlining operational processes, leveraging technology, or enhancing workforce productivity, SMEs learn how to make the most of their available resources.

Access to capital is crucial for fuelling growth and expansion. Through the Business Creation Programme, SMEs learn about different funding options available to them, including loans, venture capital, angel investors, and government grants. They receive guidance on how to prepare funding proposals, pitch to investors, and secure the necessary financing to support their growth initiatives.

Operational excellence is a hallmark of successful large organisations. The Business Creation Programme helps SMEs optimise their operations by adopting best practices, implementing efficient workflows, and investing in technology. By improving operational efficiency, SMEs can reduce costs, increase productivity, and enhance their competitive advantage in the market.

Innovation is essential for staying ahead of the curve in today's fast-paced business environment. The Business Creation Programme encourages SMEs to foster a culture of innovation within their organisations. They learn how to identify emerging trends, anticipate customer needs, and develop innovative products and services that set them apart from the competition. Additionally, SMEs are taught the importance of adaptability and resilience in responding to market changes and disruptions.

As SMEs prepare to transition into large organisations, the Business Creation Programme equips them with the necessary tools and strategies for expansion and scaling. They learn how to develop growth strategies, enter new markets, and diversify their product offerings. By planning for expansion in advance, SMEs can position themselves for sustainable growth and long-term success.

The journey from an SME to a large organisation is filled with challenges, but it is also brimming with opportunities. The Business Creation Programme offered by Visions to Victory Models serves as a guiding light for SMEs embarking on this transformational journey. By providing strategic planning, resource optimisation, access to capital, operational excellence, innovation, and preparation for expansion, the programme empowers SMEs to rise to the status of large organisations and achieve their full potential in the market. Through dedication, perseverance, and the right support system, SMEs can overcome obstacles, seize opportunities, and emerge as leaders in their industries. With the Business Creation Programme as their roadmap, the possibilities for growth and success are endless.

Reaching New Heights - Growth Cycle of Large Businesses

In the dynamic world of business, Large Businesses stand as towering pillars of innovation, resilience, and unwavering ambition. From humble beginnings to global giants, these enterprises navigate through the intricate stages of the Growth Life Cycle, leaving an indelible mark on industries and economies around the world. Let's embark on a journey through the Large Business Growth Life Cycle—a journey marked by strategic vision, operational excellence, and the relentless pursuit of success.

Business Creation Inception Phase: Building Foundations for Success - In the idea or Inception phase, your large businesses strategically enter the market with a clear vision and significant capitalisation. Establishing a robust corporate structure becomes the blueprint for growth, laying the groundwork for future success. It's a phase of ambition, innovation, and setting the stage for industry disruption.

Business Creation Survival Phase: Navigating Challenges with Resilience - As the large business navigates through the Survival Phase, industry consolidation becomes a mantra for success. Optimising operational efficiency, managing shareholder expectations, and weathering market fluctuations become second nature. It's a phase characterised by resilience, adaptability, and the ability to thrive in the face of adversity.

Business Creation Sustain Phase: Pioneering Global Presence and Innovation - With survival comes the opportunity for expansion, and thus begins the Sustain Phase. A global market presence is no longer an aspiration but a testament to success. Continual innovation becomes the driving force behind the large business, contributing to industry standards and shaping the future of the market. This phase is marked by strategic investments, transformative initiatives, and a relentless commitment to excellence.

Business Creation Success Phase: Ascending to Industry Leadership - In the Success Phase, the large business ascends to new heights as industry leadership becomes the crown jewel of achievement. Strategic acquisitions become stepping stones for growth, and being a benchmark for competitors becomes the emblem of triumph. It's a phase of recognition, validation, and the realisation of the large business's full potential as a leader in its field.

Business Creation Thrive Phase: Shaping the Future of Global Industries - Finally, the large business enters the Thrive Phase—a phase where it stands at the pinnacle of success, shaping global industry trends and setting standards for corporate responsibility. Transformative innovation becomes the driving force, as the large business cements its position as a beacon of progress and innovation. It's a phase of empowerment, influence, and making a meaningful impact on the world.

Large Business Growth Life Cycle is a testament to the vision, leadership, and determination of your large businesses. It's a journey of growth, transformation, and making a difference on a global scale. As your large businesses navigate through each phase of this cycle, they embody the spirit of innovation and pave the way for a brighter, more prosperous future for all leading by example and leaving a lasting legacy for generations to come.

From Ambition to Achievement: Transforming Your SME into a Thriving Large Business

A journey from small and medium-sized enterprise to a thriving, large-scale business is a journey of transformation. It's not just a path of growth but a strategic evolution that demands foresight, determination, and adaptability at every step.

Firstly, define your destination: what does "large business" mean for you? It's about setting ambitious goals—increasing revenue, expanding market presence, and strengthening your workforce. These goals will guide you through the challenges and triumphs of growth.

Securing the financial foundation is crucial. Whether through investments, reinvesting profits, or a smart combination of both, robust financial management will steer your course towards sustainable expansion.

Operational excellence is your compass. Refine your processes to accommodate greater demand without compromising on quality. Rigorous quality control ensures we consistently deliver excellence, vital for nurturing customer loyalty.

Exploring new horizons is essential. By identifying untapped markets and tailoring your strategies, You'll broaden your reach and establish a compelling brand presence that resonates with a diverse audience.

Investing in your team fuels your ascent. Through training and development, You empower your workforce to innovate and excel. Experienced hires enrich your capabilities, driving forward your collective vision.

Technology is your ally in this digital age. Embracing digital transformation enhances efficiency, enriches customer experiences, and provides invaluable insights through data-driven strategies.

Navigating regulatory landscapes ensures your growth is grounded in compliance and integrity. Partnering strategically amplifies your strengths, propelling you towards new opportunities and fostering innovation.

Above all, nurturing customer relationships is paramount. By delivering exceptional value and maintaining transparent communication, you forge enduring connections that sustain your growth.

Continuous improvement is your rhythm. Feedback loops refine your strategies, ensuring you evolve dynamically amidst market fluctuations.

With strong leadership and a cohesive culture, you inspire resilience and unity—essential ingredients for weathering uncertainties and seizing new heights.

Anticipate and mitigate risks, fortifying your foundation against potential challenges.

In essence, converting your SME into a large business is more than a goal—it's a commitment to excellence, innovation, and unwavering customer focus. Embrace this journey with courage and determination, knowing that each stride forward brings you closer to your vision of sustainable success in the competitive landscape.

Conclusion and Next Steps

As you conclude your exploration of the Rise stage, anticipate the release of the next volume in this series. In the upcoming volume, you will delve into intricate strategies contributing to the success of your businesses Revelling in Public Ownership and Leadership. Uncover specific actions, mindset shifts, and tactical manoeuvres propelling ventures toward market leadership and sustained growth in the public domain. In the next volume of this 3-book series, along with the Startup Creation, Micro Creation, SME creation and Business Creation you will explore further about

The Dynamics of an IPO - Uncover the nuances of planning and executing a successful Initial Public Offering, ensuring a seamless transition into the public market.

Leveraging Public Ownership for Growth - Explore how your businesses can strategically use public ownership to access capital, explore new markets, and drive innovation.

Navigating Challenges in the Public Domain - Delve into the realities of being a publicly owned entity, understanding the challenges and opportunities that come with this transformative stage.

The Leadership Mindset - Uncover the mindset shifts required for your businesses to thrive in the public domain, emerging as leaders in their industries.

As you journey through the RISE stage and explore the strategies of public ownership and leadership, may your entrepreneurial spirit be ignited. This will not just be a stage; it's the next level upon which your entire entrepreneurial saga stands. May your IPO creation be as boundless as your ambition, and may your vision be the guiding light propelling you toward triumph and the creation of a lasting legacy.

Stay tuned for the RISE stage for LEGACY or IPO CREATION & grand unveiling of the VICTORY model—a framework, a blueprint, and a roadmap that will guide you through the exhilarating journey of business evolution. Your adventure has just begun, and the best is yet to come.

The next chapter is dedicated to unravelling the mysteries and unveiling the profound significance of the Yield Stage in the entrepreneurial journey. In next chapter, you delve deep into the essence of the Yield Stage, exploring its transformative power, its strategic importance, and its role in shaping the legacy of successful ventures. Let's dive in.

Chapter 6.8

Yielding the Fruits of Legacy

The pursuit of wealth is natural and necessary for personal growth and the fulfilment of one's potential. I believe that every individual has the right to be rich. But what if we extend this notion beyond ourselves? What if we view our businesses not only as vehicles for personal success but also as instruments for creating a legacy that benefits our families, our communities, and future generations?

The true purpose of wealth goes beyond personal gain; it has the potential to make a meaningful impact on the world.

One such principle is the Universal Growth Principle. I believe that the purpose of nature is the continuous expansion and increase of life. Whether it's plants, water, or human beings, we all strive for growth naturally and effortlessly. Aligning with this purpose is essential for attracting wealth. By aligning ourselves with this universal purpose, we can attract wealth and prosperity. Imagine using your business to contribute to this continuous growth—not just for yourself, but for others as well. When we build businesses that aim to uplift and empower, we align with this universal purpose, and our efforts are naturally supported by the abundance of the universe.

The Yield Stage represents a pivotal moment in the evolution of a business, a juncture where years of dedication, innovation, and strategic planning culminate in tangible success. It's a phase marked not only by financial achievement but also by the profound impact businesses have on their industries, communities, and the entrepreneurial landscape as a whole. This entices us to embark on a journey of discovery, unlocking the hidden potential of the Yield Stage and uncovering the secrets to creating a legacy that transcends time in the next segment of this chapter.

Y –Yield, Yielding the Fruits of Legacy

The letter Y symbolises "Yield the Fruits of Legacy." At this stage, your narrative transforms into a celebration of enduring success, where your businesses not only grow and adapt but leave a lasting mark on their industry. It's about building a legacy that inspires future generations of entrepreneurs.

The venture transitions into "Yielding the Fruits of Legacy," celebrating enduring success as your businesses grow and make an indelible mark on their industry. This phase showcases a legacy that transcends time and inspires tomorrow's entrepreneurs. Under the LEGACY CREATION Framework, ventures mark the culmination of a transformative journey, celebrating enduring success and constructing a timeless legacy.

The VICTORY model provides a strategic roadmap for your businesses to navigate each development stage. Through the LEGACY CREATION Framework, entrepreneurs build a strong foundation, overcome market challenges, and savour victory in their industries. The Yield stage is a jubilation—a time to reflect and celebrate sustained effort and strategic vision. Your businesses embracing the VICTORY model craft a legacy that resonates through time.

"Yielding the Fruits of Legacy" goes beyond financial success; it's about leaving an enduring impact on the industry and the entrepreneurial landscape. In this stage, your businesses transition from market players to architects of a legacy that inspires future generations.

This stage acknowledges enduring success achieved through resilience, strategic acumen, and commitment—a moment to recognise the collective efforts of teams, leaders, and stakeholders. Building a legacy goes beyond financial metrics; it's about creating something that transcends time. As your businesses enter the Yield stage, the focus shifts to being revered for the lasting impact on the industry and entrepreneurial spirit.

Entering the Yield stage of the VICTORY MODEL symbolises a pivotal moment. Your businesses can celebrate enduring success, construct a legacy, and inspire future entrepreneurs. The Yield stage invites reflection on a journey that began with a vision and navigated challenges. It's a moment to acknowledge the collective efforts that propelled ventures through growth phases.

Legacy building surpasses financial success—it encompasses values, culture, and impact. As ventures move into the Yield stage, the focus shifts towards creating a legacy beyond the balance sheet. The true measure of success lies in inspiring future entrepreneurs. Your businesses become beacons of inspiration, showing that enduring success is a continuous journey.

The Y for YIELD Stage of the Victory Model represents the culmination of the entrepreneurial journey, where your businesses transition from achieving success to leaving a lasting legacy. This stage signifies enduring success and the creation of a legacy that transcends time.

In the YIELD stage, your businesses have navigated growth and development phases, established market presence, achieved profitability, and demonstrated resilience. Now, they aim to make a significant, lasting impact. The Yield stage represents a milestone characterised by exponential growth, brand recognition, and financial stability. Focus areas include:

Brand Exposure: Increasing visibility, attracting customers, and establishing brand authority through targeted marketing and public relations efforts.

Growth Acceleration: Capitalising on momentum to scale operations rapidly, leveraging resources, and expanding into new markets.

Strategic Partnerships: Forming alliances to access new markets, technologies, and distribution channels, leveraging shared resources and expertise.

Financial Resources: Securing funding through equity financing, debt financing, or strategic investments to support expansion and sustainability.

Volume 2 delves deeper into brand exposure, growth acceleration, strategic partnerships, and financial resources in the Yield stage, offering case studies, practical insights, and strategic guidance for sustainable growth and success.

Here's why the YIELD stage is important:

Celebration of Success - The YIELD stage allows your businesses to pause and celebrate their achievements. It's a moment of reflection on the journey they have undertaken and the milestones they have reached. Recognising and celebrating success is essential for boosting morale and motivation among team members.

Building a Lasting Legacy - Beyond financial success, the YIELD stage focuses on creating a legacy. Your businesses aim to leave behind a positive impact on their industry, community, and society as a whole. This legacy becomes part of the business's identity and contributes to its long-term reputation and influence.

Inspiring Future Generations - By achieving enduring success and leaving a lasting legacy, your businesses inspire future generations of entrepreneurs. Their stories of resilience, innovation, and impact serve as a source of motivation and guidance for aspiring business leaders, driving continued entrepreneurship and economic growth.

Recognition of Collective Efforts - The YIELD stage acknowledges the collective efforts of teams, leaders, and stakeholders who contributed to the business's success. It's an opportunity to express gratitude and appreciation for everyone involved in the entrepreneurial journey.

Focus on Values and Impact - Legacy building in the YIELD stage goes beyond financial metrics. Your businesses focus on upholding their core values, fostering a positive company culture, and making a meaningful impact on society. This emphasis on values and impact ensures that the legacy created is not only enduring but also purposeful.

The Y for YIELD Stage of the Victory Model represents the pinnacle of entrepreneurial achievement, where your businesses transition from success to legacy. It's a time of celebration, reflection, and inspiration, marking the culmination of a transformative journey and the beginning of a lasting impact on the business world and beyond.

Transformative Power of the Yield Stage

At the heart of the Yield stage lies its transformative power—the ability to turn dreams into reality, challenges into opportunities, and aspirations into achievements. This stage represents a culmination of years of hard work, strategic planning, and unwavering dedication, culminating in a moment of celebration and reflection.

One of the most significant aspects of the Yield stage is its capacity to redefine the narrative of success. No longer is success measured solely by financial metrics; rather, it encompasses a broader spectrum of impact, influence, and inspiration. For example, companies like Microsoft have established philanthropic initiatives such as the Bill & Melinda Gates Foundation, which focus on global health, education, and poverty alleviation. Such initiatives demonstrate how businesses in the Yield stage can become architects of change, leaving an indelible mark on their industries and inspiring future generations of entrepreneurs.

Moreover, the Yield stage serves as a catalyst for personal and professional growth. It demands resilience in the face of adversity, adaptability in the midst of uncertainty, and creativity in the pursuit of innovation. Through the challenges encountered and overcome in this stage, entrepreneurs emerge stronger, wiser, and more capable of navigating the complexities of the business world.

But perhaps most importantly, the Yield stage offers a moment of introspection—a chance for entrepreneurs to reflect on their journey, acknowledge their accomplishments, and express gratitude for the collective efforts that have propelled them forward.

Another great example of lasting legacy Founded by Andrew Carnegie, the Carnegie Corporation of New York in 1911 has been dedicated to promoting the advancement and diffusion of knowledge and understanding. Over the past century, it has supported a wide range of educational, cultural, and social initiatives, including libraries, universities, scientific research, and international peace efforts.

It's a time to celebrate not only individual success but also the shared triumphs of teams, leaders, and stakeholders who have contributed to the venture's ascent.

In essence, the Yield stage is a testament to the transformative power of entrepreneurship—the ability to turn dreams into reality, challenges into opportunities, and ventures into legacies. As you delve deeper into its mysteries and uncover its secrets, you unlock a profound understanding of the journey from vision to victory, and the enduring impact of those who dare to embark on it.

The Strategic Importance of the Yield Stage

The Yield Stage stands as a pivotal phase in the entrepreneurial journey, crucial for achieving enduring success and establishing a lasting legacy. It involves strategic decisions and actions that profoundly shape the trajectory of your business, emphasising long-term value creation and influence.

For instance, companies like Google have exemplified this by launching philanthropic initiatives such as Google.org, focusing on global challenges like climate change, education, and economic opportunity. These initiatives highlight how businesses in the Yield Stage can consolidate efforts and resources to maximise impact and sustainability, transitioning from a focus solely on growth and profitability.

Businesses in the Yield Stage not only evaluate strategies but also align with core values and position themselves as industry leaders. They foster expansion and diversification through strategic partnerships, tapping into new markets and embracing innovative opportunities.

Ford foundation Established in 1936 by Edsel Ford and Henry Ford, is one of the largest private philanthropic foundations globally. It focuses on addressing inequality and advancing human welfare through grants and initiatives in areas such as economic development, education, human rights, and democratic governance.

Strategic planning, foresight, and adaptability are critical during this phase to navigate complexities and capitalise on emerging opportunities. Moreover, cultivating a culture of innovation and continuous improvement through investments in research, technology, and workforce development helps businesses maintain a competitive edge.

Ultimately, the Yield Stage represents a strategic inflection point where businesses consolidate their gains, plan for future growth, and aim to leave a lasting legacy that transcends mere financial success.

Shaping a Lasting Legacy

The Yield Stage represents a pivotal juncture for successful ventures, where strategic efforts and steadfast commitment lay the foundation for creating a legacy that extends beyond mere financial success. This phase marks the culmination of a business's impact on industries, communities, and society, focusing on values, innovation, and positive change.

For instance, Patagonia, a renowned outdoor apparel company, exemplifies this by prioritising environmental sustainability through initiatives like "1% for the Planet," where they donate one percent of their sales to environmental causes. Such initiatives underscore how businesses in the Yield Stage can define their legacy by aligning actions with core values, fostering integrity, and prioritising initiatives that contribute to the greater good.

Strategic partnerships further amplify impact and reach, enhancing visibility and credibility while fostering a legacy rooted in collaboration and shared purpose. By forging alliances with like-minded organisations and stakeholders, ventures can broaden their influence and effect meaningful change on a larger scale.

Moreover, the Yield Stage serves as an inspiration to future generations of entrepreneurs, showcasing resilience, innovation, and excellence. By demonstrating a commitment to social responsibility and sustainability, ventures not only set a precedent for success but also contribute to an entrepreneurial ecosystem that values creativity, innovation, and community impact.

The Peabody Trust, founded in 1862 by George Peabody, is one of the oldest housing associations in the world. It was established to provide affordable housing for the working poor in London. Over the years, it has expanded its mission to include community development and support services, aiming to improve the quality of life for residents of its housing estates.

In essence, the Yield Stage shapes the legacy of successful ventures through impactful initiatives, reflective practices, collaborative efforts, and inspirational leadership, leaving an enduring mark on both the business world and society at large.

Yielding the Fruits of Hard Work

The Yield stage in the entrepreneurial journey represents a significant milestone, where years of dedication, strategic planning, and perseverance culminate in a moment of celebration and reflection. It's a time to pause and recognise the collective efforts that have propelled ventures forward and to savour the sweet taste of success.

For example, Unilever, a global consumer goods company, exemplifies this by committing to sustainable living through initiatives like the Unilever Sustainable Living Plan. This plan focuses on improving health and well-being, reducing environmental impact, and enhancing livelihoods, demonstrating how businesses can integrate philanthropic initiatives into their core operations.

At its heart, the Yield stage celebrates the milestones achieved, challenges overcome, and goals realised. Entrepreneurs take pride in their accomplishments, acknowledging the sacrifices made, and expressing gratitude to their teams, leaders, and stakeholders whose contributions have been invaluable to their success.

Gratitude plays a transformative role, not only fostering positive relationships and boosting morale but also encouraging continued growth and innovation. It serves as a reminder of the journey taken, the obstacles surmounted, and the individuals who supported along the way.

Moreover, the Yield stage signifies the culmination of strategic efforts, resulting in financial success and establishing ventures as leaders within their industries. It's a time for introspection as entrepreneurs reflect on their experiences, learn from past challenges, and chart a course for future growth and sustainability.

Rods Scholarship established in 1902 through the will of Cecil Rhodes, fund exceptional students from around the world to study at the University of Oxford. The scholarships aim to nurture future leaders who will contribute to the betterment of society through their academic pursuits and leadership capabilities.

In essence, the Yield stage embodies a celebration of achievement, the realisation of hard-earned rewards, and a moment for gratitude and reflection. By embracing these principles, businesses can not only mark their success but also pave the way for a promising future built on integrity, innovation, and meaningful impact.

Celebrating Success and Achieving Big Dreams

The Yield stage in the entrepreneurial journey marks a pivotal moment of both celebration and the realisation of ambitious dreams. It's a time for entrepreneurs to not only acknowledge their achievements but also to strategise for future growth.

For instance, Salesforce, a global leader in CRM solutions, has established the Salesforce.org Foundation, which focuses on leveraging technology for social good. Through initiatives like the 1-1-1 model (donating 1% of Salesforce's equity, time, and products to charitable causes), Salesforce demonstrates a commitment to using its success to create positive change.

Celebrating success in the Yield stage is vital. Recognising milestones reached and hurdles overcome fosters a culture of positivity, resilience, and motivation within teams. These celebrations serve as reminders of the progress made and the collective effort that has propelled ventures forward.

Moreover, the Yield stage provides entrepreneurs with a moment to reflect on their big dreams and ambitious goals. It's a time to assess progress, reaffirm commitments, and ignite passion for achieving even greater success. By revisiting their initial vision, entrepreneurs can realign their strategies and drive towards new objectives.

This stage also serves as a launchpad for setting bold new goals. Ventures can capitalise on their momentum to explore new markets, innovate with product offerings, or deepen their impact through community engagement initiatives. The Yield stage encourages dreaming big and turning aspirations into concrete actions.

Additionally, it offers an opportunity to inspire others. Sharing success stories and lessons learned not only motivates aspiring entrepreneurs but also strengthens the entrepreneurial ecosystem. By showcasing achievements and the journey behind them, entrepreneurs can instill courage and determination in others to pursue their own ventures.

Founded in 1913 by John D. Rockefeller, the Rockefeller Foundation was established with a singular mission: to promote the well-being of humanity. From its inception, it has pursued this mission with unwavering commitment, pioneering groundbreaking initiatives that have shaped the course of history. The Rockefeller Foundation stands as a testament to the power of philanthropy and visionary leadership. Its century-long commitment to improving lives and creating enduring impact serves as an inspiration to us all. As we reflect on its achievements, let us recommit ourselves to the ideals of innovation, compassion, and equity that define the Rockefeller legacy.

In essence, the Yield stage represents a powerful opportunity for entrepreneurs to celebrate their accomplishments, pursue ambitious goals, and inspire others along the way. By embracing reflection, strategic planning, and a commitment to making a positive impact, ventures can leverage this stage to propel themselves to new heights of success and significance.

Empowering Communities and Loved Ones

The Yield stage in the entrepreneurial journey transcends individual success; it serves as a catalyst for making a positive impact on communities and supporting loved ones. As entrepreneurs celebrate achievements and enjoy the fruits of their labour, they also seize the opportunity to give back and uplift those around them.

For example, Tesla, known for its innovative approach to sustainable energy, has established the Tesla Foundation to promote environmental stewardship and support sustainable energy initiatives globally. This philanthropic initiative aligns with Tesla's core values and demonstrates their commitment to creating lasting change beyond their business success.

Philanthropy and corporate social responsibility initiatives enable thriving businesses to contribute to causes that resonate with their values. Whether through investments in education, healthcare, environmental conservation, or poverty alleviation, ventures in the Yield stage can make significant and meaningful contributions to society.

Supporting loved ones is another crucial aspect of the Yield stage. Entrepreneurs can provide financial assistance to family members, invest in children's education, or support the dreams and aspirations of friends and loved ones. This support not only enriches the lives of individuals but also reinforces the entrepreneurial journey's impact on personal relationships and community ties.

From its inception, the Rockefeller Foundation has been actively involved since 1910 till today in improving global health outcomes. They funded the research that led to the discovery of the yellow fever vaccine in the early 20th century, saving countless lives in tropical regions. More recently, they have focused on initiatives to combat diseases like malaria and tuberculosis, as well as promoting maternal and child health.

Furthermore, the Yield stage offers opportunities to create employment and economic opportunities within communities. By expanding operations, hiring local talent, and investing in skills development programs, businesses can stimulate economic growth, foster job creation, and empower individuals to build brighter futures for themselves and their families.

Moreover, entrepreneurs can serve as role models and mentors, sharing their knowledge, experiences, and insights with others. By inspiring aspiring entrepreneurs to pursue their dreams and overcome challenges, they contribute to a culture of entrepreneurship, innovation, and social responsibility within their communities.

In essence, the Yield stage empowers entrepreneurs to make a lasting impact on communities and support loved ones. By leveraging their success to give back, create opportunities, and inspire others, they can cultivate a legacy of generosity, compassion, and social responsibility that extends far beyond their immediate achievements.

Crafting a Legacy and Shaping Mindsets

In the entrepreneurial journey, the Yield stage serves as a pivotal opportunity for ventures to leave a lasting legacy and influence society's collective mindset. As businesses celebrate their accomplishments, they also have the power to inspire future generations to pursue ambitious goals.

For instance, Starbucks, renowned for its commitment to social responsibility, established the Starbucks Foundation to support communities by investing in education and economic development initiatives globally. This philanthropic endeavour reflects their dedication to creating positive, lasting impacts beyond their business success.

During the Yield stage, ventures can establish a timeless legacy by embodying values such as integrity, innovation, and social responsibility. By setting high standards of excellence, these ventures inspire aspiring entrepreneurs to strive for greatness. Through mentorship programs, speaking engagements, or thought leadership initiatives, successful entrepreneurs pass on invaluable lessons and insights, equipping the next generation with the knowledge and inspiration needed for success.

Moreover, the Yield stage presents an opportunity to challenge conventional notions of success. By prioritising purpose-driven outcomes over mere profitability, advocating for sustainability practices, and fostering collaborative efforts, ventures can promote a more inclusive and holistic approach to achieving meaningful goals. This stage also serves as a catalyst for cultural and social change, advocating for diversity, equity, and inclusion, thereby contributing to a fairer and more equitable society.

In response to urbanisation and climate change challenges, the Rockefeller Foundation launched the 100 Resilient Cities initiative in 2013 till today. This program aimed to help cities around the world become more resilient to physical, social, and economic challenges. It provided support to cities to develop comprehensive resilience strategies, enhancing their capacity to withstand and recover from shocks and stresses.

In summary, the Yield stage is not only a time for celebrating achievements but also a crucial tool for leaving a legacy and shaping mindsets. By embodying core values and leveraging their influence, ventures can inspire others to dream big, embrace innovation, and positively impact the world around them. This stage allows businesses to craft a legacy that extends far beyond immediate success, leaving an enduring mark on society.

From Ambition to Achievement: Transforming Your SME into a Thriving Large Business

Everything in the universe is geared towards growth and advancement. Just as plants, animals, and ecosystems constantly evolve and expand, our businesses should strive for continuous improvement and innovation. This relentless drive for growth is not just about financial success; it's about creating value, fostering development, and leaving a positive impact on the world.

The journey of transformation from small and medium-sized enterprise to a thriving, large-scale business is not just a path of growth but a strategic evolution that demands foresight, determination, and adaptability at every step.

Firstly, define your destination: what does "large business" mean for you? It's about setting ambitious goals—increasing revenue, expanding market presence, and strengthening our workforce. These goals will guide you through the challenges and triumphs of growth.

Securing the financial foundation is crucial. Whether through investments, reinvesting profits, or a smart combination of both, robust financial management will steer our course towards sustainable expansion.

Operational excellence is your compass. You'll refine your processes to accommodate greater demand without compromising on quality. Rigorous quality control ensures you consistently deliver excellence, vital for nurturing customer loyalty.

Exploring new horizons is essential. By identifying untapped markets and tailoring your strategies, you'll broaden your reach and establish a compelling brand presence that resonates with a diverse audience.

Investing in your team fuels your ascent. Through training and development, you empower your workforce to innovate and excel. Experienced hires enrich your capabilities, driving forward your collective vision.

Technology is your ally in this digital age. Embracing digital transformation enhances efficiency, enriches customer experiences, and provides invaluable insights through data-driven strategies.

Navigating regulatory landscapes ensures your growth is grounded in compliance and integrity. Partnering strategically amplifies your strengths, propelling you towards new opportunities and fostering innovation.

Above all, nurturing customer relationships is paramount. By delivering exceptional value and maintaining transparent communication, you forge enduring connections that sustain your growth.

Continuous improvement is your rhythm. Feedback loops refine your strategies, ensuring you evolve dynamically amidst market fluctuations.

With strong leadership and a cohesive culture, you inspire resilience and unity—essential ingredients for weathering uncertainties and seizing new heights.

Together, you'll anticipate and mitigate risks, fortifying your foundation against potential challenges.

True wealth and success come from making a positive impact. When our actions contribute to the growth and betterment of others, we are rewarded with wealth—not just in financial terms, but in the form of a lasting legacy. True success is measured by the positive change we bring to the world.

Think of great visionaries and entrepreneurs like Thomas Edison, Steve Jobs, and Andrew Carnegie. They didn't just build successful businesses; they created legacies that continue to influence and inspire. Their stories teach us that the purpose of wealth is to enable us to live fully, support our families, and contribute to society.

As we build our businesses, let us remember that we have the power to create a legacy. By aligning our efforts with the universal purpose of growth and expansion, and by focusing on creating value and making a positive impact, we can ensure that our businesses become instruments of lasting change.

Let us dare to dream big, to define our purpose with clarity, and to pursue our vision with unwavering commitment. By doing so, we will not only achieve personal success but also leave a legacy that inspires and uplifts future generations.

Building Legacies: The Pathway to Lasting Impact

Establishing a legacy transcends mere profitability and involves creating a lasting impact that extends into the community and society at large. The Visions to Victory Model serves as a pivotal platform for business development and collaboration, uniquely positioned to foster this impact through structured philanthropic initiatives. This segment explores the Legacy Creation Framework tailored for the Visions to Victory Model, outlining how organisations can strategically harness their resources to drive sustainable philanthropy.

The journey towards legacy creation begins with a thorough assessment of core values and available resources within the Visions to Victory Model. Understanding these foundational elements helps align philanthropic efforts with the organisation's overarching mission and vision. By identifying priorities and feasible goals, organisations lay the groundwork for impactful initiatives that resonate with stakeholders.

Strategic Planning

Strategic planning within the Legacy Creation programme involves defining clear, measurable goals and objectives that underscore its commitment to social responsibility and community engagement.

By identifying key impact areas such as education, environmental sustainability, or economic empowerment, the programme focuses its efforts where you can achieve the greatest impact and align philanthropic activities with organisational strengths.

Developing a visionary outlook ensures that philanthropic efforts extend beyond immediate gains, aiming to create enduring legacies that benefit society for generations.

This forward-thinking approach inspires stakeholders and fosters sustained support for philanthropic initiatives.

Implementation

In the realm of implementation, the Legacy Creation programme of Visions to victory Model focuses on selecting projects that closely align with identified impact areas and strategic goals. This careful selection process ensures that resources are efficiently utilised to maximise social impact while enhancing overall effectiveness.

Collaborating with nonprofit organisations, NGOs, and local communities expands the reach and effectiveness of philanthropic initiatives, leveraging external expertise and fostering innovative solutions to address social challenges.

Thoughtful allocation of financial, human, and intellectual resources is prioritised to ensure sustainable philanthropy, balancing long-term investments that yield measurable social returns with operational and financial sustainability.

Establishing clear metrics for assessing philanthropic outcomes promotes accountability and enables continuous improvement, allowing the Visions to Victory Model to refine strategies, replicate successful approaches, and adapt to evolving community needs effectively.

Engagement and Communication

In terms of engagement and communication, the Legacy Creation programme of Visions to victory Model prioritises internal involvement by engaging employees, leaders, and stakeholders to cultivate a shared commitment to philanthropy.

Fostering a culture of social responsibility encourages active participation and support for philanthropic initiatives within the organisation.

Externally, transparent and authentic communication about philanthropic efforts strengthens relationships with stakeholders and enhances the overall reputation of the Visions to Victory Model.

Sharing success stories and impact metrics inspires trust and attracts like-minded partners and clients who are aligned with the model's goals.

Additionally, storytelling plays a crucial role in humanising the organisation's philanthropic endeavours and resonating with a wider audience.

By effectively narrating the impact of its initiatives through compelling stories, the Visions to Victory Model amplifies the reach of its philanthropic messages, motivating others to contribute to positive change.

Adaptation and Growth

Adaptation and growth are integral to the Visions to Victory Model, enabling it to respond effectively to evolving societal challenges through continuous improvement and learning.

By iterating on philanthropic strategies, the model enhances its relevance and impact over time. Additionally, successful initiatives can be scaled up or replicated in new contexts to extend their reach and deepen their effectiveness.

Maintaining fidelity to core values and mission while exploring opportunities for expansion is crucial for scalability.

Embracing innovation in philanthropy, such as leveraging technology, data analytics, and collaborative partnerships, fosters creativity and enhances the model's ability to address complex social issues.

In essence, The Legacy Creation Framework of the Visions to Victory Model represents a strategic pathway to harness organisational influence and resources for sustainable philanthropy. By aligning values, setting clear objectives, fostering partnerships, and measuring impact, organisations can leave a lasting legacy of social responsibility and community empowerment. Through deliberate action and collective commitment, the Visions to Victory Model can shape a future where business success is synonymous with positive societal impact.

Conclusion & Recap

In conclusion, converting your SME into a large business is more than a goal—it's a commitment to excellence, innovation, and unwavering customer focus. Let's embrace this journey with courage and determination, knowing that each stride forward brings us closer to our vision of sustainable success in the competitive landscape.

Also, To create a legacy through business, we must adopt a mindset and actions focused on growth and contribution. This involves several key principles:

Firstly, operational efficiency is crucial. Streamlining processes and optimising resources ensure that our businesses run smoothly and sustainably, allowing us to focus on creating lasting value.

Secondly, expanding market reach is vital. Reaching broader audiences and entering new markets not only increases our influence but also extends the benefits of our products and services to more people, improving lives and communities.

Thirdly, building a strong team is essential. By nurturing talented individuals and fostering a collaborative culture, we create an environment where innovation thrives and collective success becomes possible. A strong team is essential for driving forward a vision that transcends individual achievement.

Lastly, attaining financial stability is fundamental. Financial planning and strategic investments lay the foundation for sustainable growth, ensuring that our businesses can continue to operate and contribute positively, even in challenging times.

As you conclude your exploration of the Yield stage, I extend an invitation to anticipate the release of the next volume in this transformative series. In the upcoming volume, you will delve into intricate strategies contributing to the success of your businesses "Yielding the Fruits of Legacy." You will uncover specific actions, mindset shifts, and tactical manoeuvres propelling ventures toward a legacy that stands the test of time. As you journey through the Yield stage and explore the strategies of legacy building, may your entrepreneurial spirit be ignited, and may you find inspiration to yield not just success but a legacy that shapes the future.

Your journey doesn't end here; in fact, you're gearing up for the grand unveiling of the next volume of our book. And let me tell you, it's going to be an adventure like no other.

Let's explore this further in next chapter.

Chapter 6.9

Winning the Battle with VICTORY Model in VOLUME 2

VOL 2: THE MIDDLE GAME
WINNING THE BATTLE
VISIONS
TO
VICTORY
UNLOCKING THE OPPORTUNITIES:
Strategies and Insights for Business
Brilliance
SANTOSH KUMAR

This volume isn't just another book – it's the foundation upon which your entire entrepreneurial saga progresses. As you navigate this transformative journey, may your entrepreneurial spirit be ignited, and may you find inspiration to optimise your business for triumph.

You'll also be uncovering the secrets behind maximising profits without compromising sustainability, solidifying your competitive position in your industry, and leveraging innovation and efficiency for success. Plus, you'll take a closer look at the broader impact of business on job creation, community development, and overall economic well-being.

Stay tuned for the grand unveiling of the VICTORY model – a framework, a blueprint, and a roadmap that will guide you through the exhilarating journey of business evolution to the next level. Your business adventure has just begun, and believe me when I say, the best is yet to come!

But that's not all you have in store. In Volume 2, you'll delve deep into the evolution from visionary entrepreneur to mentor, offering personal insights and reflections gleaned from years of experience navigating the ever-changing landscape of entrepreneurship. As you journey through the pages of Visions to Victory Volume 2 – The Middle game, you'll accompany me on a voyage of self-discovery and growth, uncovering invaluable lessons that transcend mere business acumen. From the highs of triumph to the lows of uncertainty, each experience serves as a compass guiding us toward a deeper understanding of leadership, resilience, and adaptability.

In this upcoming installment, you're diving even deeper into the framework, strategies, blueprints, and roadmap for transforming lives and solving problems. You'll be peeling back the layers of the VICTORY MODEL, providing you with a comprehensive understanding of its principles and applications.

Legacy Building Strategies that go beyond just financial success. You'll be exploring how to create a legacy that resonates with stakeholders and the industry, leaving a lasting impact for generations to come. You'll also delve into Leadership in the Legacy Stage, uncovering the qualities and principles that drive businesses to thrive and leave their mark on the world.

But that's not all – you'll be delving into how businesses can inspire future generations of entrepreneurs and navigate the challenges of transitioning into legacy-building mode. And that's just the beginning. Volume 2 is more than just a recounting of past experiences; it's a call to action – a call to embrace mentorship and empower the next generation of entrepreneurs. Through the insights shared in this volume, I aim to offer guidance and support to aspiring business leaders, equipping them with the tools and strategies needed to navigate the complexities of entrepreneurship with confidence and clarity.

So, are you ready to embark on this transformative journey with us? The road ahead may be challenging, but together, you'll navigate every twist and turn, emerging stronger and more resilient than ever before. Let's make Volume 2 of Visions to Victory your greatest adventure yet!

Decoding the Entrepreneurial Success Journey

I am penning down today with an electrifying announcement—one that is sure to ignite your entrepreneurial spirit and propel you toward unprecedented success. Prepare yourselves for the release of "Visions to Victory - Volume 2" around winning the battle. I am thrilled to introduce you to the advanced version of the VICTORY Model—a strategic framework, the blueprint, the model which is designed to empower you to achieve unparalleled success in today's competitive landscape by unlocking the opportunities.

In this eagerly anticipated volume, I will delve deeper into the heart of entrepreneurship, unveiling an advanced concept that promises to revolutionise the way you approach business growth and development. The Advanced VICTORY Model represents a culmination of years of research, experience, and insights gathered from successful entrepreneurs around the globe. It serves as a comprehensive roadmap that guides entrepreneurs through the intricacies of business growth, equipping them with the tools and strategies needed to overcome obstacles and achieve victory in their endeavours.

Imagine an extensive roadmap—a blueprint—that guides you through the complexities of multiple cogs required for business growth, equipping you with the tools and strategies needed to overcome obstacles and achieve victory in your endeavours. That's exactly what the Advanced VICTORY Model offers. It's a comprehensive framework explanation that encapsulates visionary leadership, innovation, customer-centricity, strategic thinking, operational excellence, resilience, and yielding bigger and better tangible results.

As entrepreneurs, you embark on a journey filled with excitement, challenges, and opportunities. In the upcoming Volume 2 of "Visions to Victory," you delve even deeper into the intricacies of entrepreneurial success, unveiling an advanced concept that promises to revolutionise the way you approach business growth and development. At the heart of this groundbreaking volume lies the VICTORY Model—a strategic framework designed to empower entrepreneurs to achieve unparalleled success in today's competitive landscape.

So, I urge you—reserve your interest today. Be among the first to embark on this exhilarating journey toward victory. By reserving your interest, you're not just securing a copy of Volume 2; you're declaring your commitment to your own success. You're signalling to the world that you're ready to rise to the challenge, overcome obstacles, and achieve greatness.

From Failure to Success: A Riveting Success Journey

Volume 2 of Visions to Victory is on its way, and let me tell you, it's not just another book – it's a journey, an adventure that will ignite your spirit, fuel your ambitions, and propel you towards the success you've always dreamed of. So, get ready to embark on the thrilling ride that is "Visions to Victory - Volume 2."

In this upcoming volume, you're delving deep into the heart of entrepreneurship, uncovering a tale of resilience, determination, and the unyielding pursuit of victory. It's a story that begins in the depths of failure, where challenges and setbacks loom large, threatening to extinguish the flames of ambition.

But fear not, my friend, for this is not a story of defeat. No, it's a story of triumph – a riveting success journey that will inspire and empower you to overcome any obstacle that stands in your way. "Visions to Victory – Volume 2" is a transformative journey that takes readers from the depths of failure to the pinnacle of success.

Imagine this: You find yourself in the trenches of failure, surrounded by doubt and uncertainty. But instead of succumbing to despair, you rise. You rise with an unwavering belief in your vision, a determination to defy the odds, and a resilience that knows no bounds. As the story unfolds, you witness the entrepreneur's gradual ascent from the depths of failure to the pinnacle of success. You see how each setback becomes a stepping stone, each challenge a catalyst for growth, and each triumph a testament to the power of perseverance.

But "Visions to Victory - Volume 2" is more than just a story; it's a call to action. It's an invitation for you to join us on a transformative journey of exploration and discovery. It's an opportunity for you to unlock the secrets of success, embrace failure as a necessary part of the journey, and chart your own course towards victory.

So, my fellow adventurers, I urge you – reserve your interest today. Be among the first to embark on this exhilarating journey towards success. By reserving your interest, you're not just securing a copy of Volume 2; you're declaring your commitment to your own greatness. You're showing the world that you're ready to rise to the challenge, overcome obstacles, and achieve your wildest dreams.

Join us as you unveil the advanced concept of the VICTORY Model in "Visions to Victory - Volume 2." Together, let's ignite your spirits, inspire greatness, and pave the way for a future filled with triumphs, successes, and victories beyond your imagination. And remember, my friend, no matter how dark the night may seem, dawn always breaks. With resilience, determination, and unwavering belief, victory is within reach. So, let's embark on this journey together and write your own stories of triumph.

Top Secrets of Business Success Unveiled

In your upcoming volume, you're not just presenting another book – you're unveiling a treasure trove of wisdom, a roadmap to success forged from the collective experiences and proven strategies of thriving businesses. "Top Secrets of Business Success Unveiled" isn't just a title; it's a promise – a promise to uncover the closely-guarded secrets that lie at the heart of flourishing enterprises.

Now, picture this: You hold in your hands not just a book, but a blueprint – a guide that distills the essence of business success into actionable insights. That's precisely what "Top Secrets of Business Success Unveiled" offers. Inside its pages, you'll find the keys to unlocking your full potential and achieving unparalleled success in today's competitive landscape.

But success isn't just about making decisions; it's about making the right decisions. And that's where strategic decision-making comes into play. In this book, you arm you with the tools and strategies to make informed decisions that drive growth and profitability. Through relatable case studies and practical examples, you'll learn how to navigate the complexities of business and steer your company towards success.

Now, resilience – that's the backbone of success. It's about weathering storms and emerging stronger on the other side. "Top Secrets of Business Success Unveiled" delves into the mindset shifts and resilience-building techniques that empower entrepreneurs to overcome obstacles and thrive amidst adversity. But success isn't just built on resilience alone; it's built on strong foundations. And that's what you explore in this book – the fundamental elements that lay the groundwork for sustainable success. From fostering innovative cultures to building trust and credibility with customers and stakeholders, you delve into what it takes to build a solid foundation for success.

And let's not forget about innovation and adaptation – essential ingredients for staying ahead in today's ever-evolving business landscape. Through insights from successful enterprises, you'll discover how to embrace change, leverage emerging opportunities, and drive growth through innovation.

So, my friend, I invite you to join us on this journey of discovery. Let's unlock the secrets of business success together and pave the way for a future filled with triumphs, successes, and victories beyond your wildest dreams.

Expanding the Top 3 Key Elements Behind Running a Successful Business

You're about to embark on a voyage through the essential elements that propel successful businesses forward. Today, I want to shed light on the top three key elements that define thriving ventures – elements that will revolutionise the way you approach entrepreneurship and business management.

First and foremost, effective leadership. Leadership isn't just about giving orders; it's about inspiring, motivating, and guiding teams towards a shared vision. "Visions to Victory" champions visionary leaders who embody integrity, empathy, and decisiveness. Through captivating stories and practical insights, you'll explore what it takes to be a successful leader – qualities that empower us to overcome obstacles and foster sustainable growth within your teams.

Next, strategic vision. A clear vision acts as a compass, steering businesses towards their desired destination. "Visions to Victory" underscores the importance of strategic vision in setting the course for success. Together, you'll learn how to craft a vision that reflects your values and long-term objectives. By articulating a compelling vision, you not only inspire others but also attract top talent and navigate the ever-changing business landscape with unwavering confidence.

And finally, a culture of innovation. Innovation is the lifeblood of business growth and differentiation. "Visions to Victory" highlights the significance of nurturing a culture of innovation within organisations. Through real-world examples and practical strategies, you'll uncover how to foster creativity, experimentation, and continuous improvement. By instilling a culture of innovation, you position ourselves to adapt to market changes and seize new opportunities for growth.

My friend, as you embark on this journey together, let us embrace the power of effective leadership, strategic vision, and a culture of innovation. Let us pave the way for a future filled with boundless possibilities and unparalleled success. The adventure awaits – are you ready to join me on this transformative voyage to victory?

Seeing the Framework in Action

In this transformative volume, you're not just sharing stories; you're providing you with real-world case studies and practical examples that will ignite your spirit and empower you on your own journey to success.

Picture this: Immersive case studies that transport you into the shoes of successful entrepreneurs who have weathered the storms of the business world using the principles of the VICTORY Model. Volume 2 of Visions to Victory offers you a front-row seat to these real-life scenarios, allowing you to experience firsthand how strategic planning and execution can lead to triumph in the face of challenges.

But you're not stopping at storytelling. Oh no, Volume 2 goes above and beyond, providing you with practical examples that demonstrate how the VICTORY Model can be applied in various entrepreneurial contexts. Whether you're a budding startup founder with a revolutionary idea or a seasoned business leader navigating a changing market, these examples offer actionable insights that you can implement in your own ventures.

At the heart of it all lies strategic planning – the cornerstone of success. The VICTORY Model serves as a powerful tool for strategic planning and execution, and Volume 2 illustrates this beautifully through real-world examples. Witness how entrepreneurs leverage this framework to identify opportunities, innovate products or services, and build sustainable business models. By seeing strategic planning in action, you'll gain a deeper understanding of how to navigate the complexities of the business landscape with unwavering confidence and clarity.

But Volume 2 is more than just inspiration; it's empowerment. By witnessing the VICTORY Model in action, you'll be equipped with the knowledge and tools to apply these same principles and strategies to your own entrepreneurial endeavours. Whether you're just starting out on your journey or facing a new challenge, these practical insights will serve as your guiding light, leading you towards the success you've always dreamed of. So, my friend, I urge you to seize this opportunity. Dive into Volume 2 of Visions to Victory, and let its immersive case studies, practical examples, and empowering insights propel you towards greatness. The journey awaits – are you ready to embark on it?

Chapter 6.10

Beliefs that Fuels your Success.

"Whatever your mind can conceive, and you can Believe, you can achieve." This statement, coined by Napoleon Hill in 1937 mentioned in his book "Think and Grow Rich", still holds true in today's modern digital age. Beliefs form the fundamental floorboard for your success.

Your belief systems are at the heart of who you are. They shape how you see the world and guide the choices you make every day. These beliefs come from various places like your upbringing, culture, education, and personal experiences. They're like the foundation of your identity, shaping your thoughts and actions.

Belief systems help you make sense of life. They give you a sense of what's right and wrong and connect you to something bigger than yourselves. When things feel uncertain, your beliefs act as a compass, pointing you in the right direction.

They also influence how you see society and interact with others. Whether you're more liberal, conservative, socialist, or libertarian, your beliefs shape your views on politics and social issues.

Your beliefs also make you ponder life's big questions. They make you think about reality, knowledge, ethics, and the meaning of your existence, offering deep insights into what it means to be human.

They represent the shared values, traditions, and customs of your society, giving you a sense of belonging and guiding how you interact with others.

Your belief systems provide you with meaning and purpose, guiding you through life and connecting you to your communities. They also serve as the roadmap for business success.

let's delve into the common beliefs that entrepreneurs often hold before starting a business. They have shaped countless business professionals like you and me. Let's embrace them as integral parts of your journey to success and examine how these beliefs influence your actions, decisions, and, ultimately, your outcomes.

Belief 01 – Positive contribution

The topmost rule for a business to achieve success is to focus on the community and serve them well before prioritising anything else.

By focusing on community needs and contributing positively, businesses build strong, supportive relationships and foster goodwill. This community-oriented approach creates a loyal customer base and enhances the company's reputation. Moreover, businesses that serve their communities are seen as responsible and ethical, attracting customers who value these principles. Ultimately, prioritising community service helps businesses grow sustainably by ensuring they are aligned with the values and needs of the people they serve, leading to mutual prosperity and long-term success.

Belief 02 – Vision, the north star

A clear vision not only provides direction but also inspires and motivates yourself and your team members, instilling a sense of purpose and focus that drives you forward, even in the face of uncertainty.

A compelling vision serves as a guiding star, aligning efforts and decisions towards common goals. It energises the team, fostering unity and commitment to achieving the desired outcomes. This sense of purpose helps navigate challenges and maintain momentum, ensuring that everyone remains dedicated to the mission, regardless of obstacles. Ultimately, a clear vision is crucial for sustaining motivation and achieving long-term success.

Belief 03 – Passion, the driving force

Passion fuels the determination to bring your vision to life. The driving force behind your venture's success is your passion.

Love what you do with passion. The driving force behind your venture's success is your passion. It inspires relentless effort, creativity, and resilience, enabling you to overcome obstacles and stay committed to your goals. It ignites enthusiasm, motivating both you and your team to strive for excellence. It also resonates with customers, who can sense and appreciate the genuine dedication behind your products or services. Ultimately, passion transforms challenges into opportunities, propelling your business forward and turning your vision into a thriving reality.

Belief 04 – Fundamental Belief for growth

The master key to doors of success is prioritising the needs of the customers and solving their problems.

This belief underscores the essence of a customer-centric approach, which is fundamental for achieving long-term success and sustainability. Prioritising the needs of the customers and solving their problems is the cornerstone of business success. It fosters trust, loyalty, and value creation, drives innovation, enhances the customer experience, boosts financial performance, and ensures adaptability in a dynamic market. Adopting a customer-centric mindset is not just a strategy but a fundamental belief that paves the way for long-term success and growth.

Belief 05 –Confidence Fuels the courage

The self-assurance and trust in your own abilities and skills empower you to take bold risks, pursue ambitious goals, and persevere in the face of doubt or criticism.

Confidence in yourself is a crucial foundation for entrepreneurial success, as it fuels the courage to venture into the unknown and tackle challenges head-on. This inner belief helps you remain resilient and focused, even when faced with setbacks or scepticism. Self-assurance encourages proactive decision-making and innovation, driving you to achieve your vision and turn ambitious goals into reality, regardless of external obstacles.

Belief 06 – Maintain your commitment

The road to success will be daunting, stay focusses and remain steadfast in the face of adversity.

Maintain your commitment to seeing your vision through and refuse to be deterred by temporary failures or setbacks, no matter how challenging the road ahead may seem. Embrace resilience and perseverance as your allies, understanding that setbacks are merely stepping stones on the path to achievement. By staying focused on your goals and remaining steadfast in the face of adversity, you can navigate the most challenging terrains and emerge victorious in the pursuit of your dreams.

Belief 07 – Exceed Customer Expectations

Striving to deliver the exceptional value at every touchpoint of the customer journey is the best way to prioritise customer focus and build success.

By exceeding expectations, businesses foster strong relationships and loyalty. This approach not only differentiates your company from competitors but also cultivates a positive brand reputation. By continuously striving to exceed expectations and improve the customer experience, businesses can enhance customer satisfaction and drive long-term success. Ultimately, prioritising customer focus is essential for building trust, loyalty, and sustainable growth in today's competitive marketplace.

Belief 08 – leverage the knowledge and insights earned by others

Life is too short to learn everything from firsthand

experience, so learn from other people experiences and evolve your journey to success.

Life's brevity underscores the importance of leveraging the knowledge and insights amassed by those who have traversed similar paths. Embracing this principle allows for accelerated learning and growth, as one can benefit from the successes and failures of others. By humbly seeking guidance and drawing from diverse perspectives, individuals can refine their strategies, avoid common pitfalls, and chart a more informed course towards success.

Belief 08 – Understand your Customers

At the heart of every successful business is a deep understanding of its customers.

Understanding your customers is crucial for the success of any business. It involves delving into the intricacies of their needs, preferences, and behaviours. By truly comprehending what makes your customers tick, you can tailor your products or services to meet their specific requirements, thereby enhancing customer satisfaction and loyalty. Moreover, understanding your customers allows you to anticipate their future needs and stay ahead of the competition. Ultimately, this deep understanding fosters stronger relationships with customers, leading to increased sales, positive word-of-mouth referrals, and sustainable business growth. In essence, knowing your customers inside out forms the bedrock upon which successful businesses are built.

Belief 09 – Continuous Learning should never stop

Embrace continuous learning and approach every experience, whether success or failure, as an opportunity to learn, adapt, and improve.

Stay curious, open-minded, and receptive to feedback. Life and business success is all about learning, and hence continuous learning should never stop. By continuously seeking new insights and adapting to evolving circumstances, individuals and businesses can stay ahead in a dynamic world, fostering innovation, resilience, and long-term success.

Belief 10 – Staying attuned & maintain a competitive edge

Staying ahead means continuously monitoring industry trends. Successful ventures quickly pivot and take advantage of new technologies and market trends.

Staying attuned and maintaining a competitive edge in the market is essential for the long-term success of any business. This involves continuously monitoring industry trends, customer preferences, and technological advancements to ensure that your offerings remain relevant and appealing to your target audience. By staying ahead of the curve, businesses can capitalise on emerging opportunities and proactively address potential threats, thereby maintaining their competitive advantage. This proactive approach enables companies to stay one step ahead of their competitors, positioning themselves as industry leaders and driving sustainable growth in the long run.

Belief 11 – Build Loyal Customer Base

loyal customer base forms the foundation for steady revenue streams and long-term growth.

Building a loyal customer base is the cornerstone of sustainable success. By providing genuine value, you can build a loyal customer base that drives your success. Satisfied customers not only return for repeat purchases but also become advocates, spreading positive word-of-mouth and attracting new business. This loyal customer base forms the foundation for steady revenue streams and long-term growth. By prioritising customer satisfaction and continuously innovating to meet their needs, businesses can cultivate a loyal following that propels their success in the marketplace.

Belief 12 – Business Ethics and Integrity

Ethical practices and integrity are non-negotiable.

Trust is the cornerstone of long-term success. Conducting business with integrity and adhering to ethical practices build trust with customers, employees, and partners. A reputation for honesty and fairness is invaluable. A strong reputation for ethical conduct enhances brand value and attracts stakeholders who share similar values. By adhering to ethical principles, businesses establish themselves as reliable and trustworthy entities, ensuring sustained success and positive relationships within their ecosystem.

Belief 13 – Recognise the importance of agility

Embracing innovation and adaptability is the Key to stay ahead.

The business world is always changing, and staying ahead means being innovative and adaptable. By fostering a culture of innovation and adaptability, you can lead the way in your industry. Those that continuously innovate and adapt are better positioned to ensure their relevance and success in the long run. Recognising the importance of agility in business means understanding the need to be flexible and responsive to change. It involves embracing innovation and adaptability as essential strategies for staying ahead in a dynamic and competitive market. By being agile, businesses can quickly pivot their strategies, processes, and products in response to shifting customer preferences. This enables them to seize new opportunities, address emerging challenges, and maintain their relevance and competitiveness over time. Ultimately, prioritising agility allows businesses to remain resilient and responsive in the face of uncertainty, positioning them for sustained success and growth in the ever-evolving business landscape.

Belief 14 – Push Forward

Building a successful venture is rarely a smooth journey.

Setbacks and challenges are inevitable. The crucial factor lies in the unwavering commitment to learn from failures and forge ahead with renewed determination. Persistence and resilience are key. The important thing is to remain persistent and resilient, learning from failures and continuing to push forward. Embracing setbacks as opportunities for growth and refinement, entrepreneurs cultivate the resilience needed to weather storms and emerge stronger. Through persistence and an indomitable spirit, they navigate adversity and ultimately propel their ventures towards success.

Belief 15 – Learn the valuable insights offered by Setback

Setbacks are not roadblocks but opportunities for growth and learning.

Each setback offers valuable insights into what went wrong and why, providing a chance to refine strategies and approaches. By viewing setbacks as learning experiences, entrepreneurs can identify weaknesses, make necessary adjustments, and emerge stronger. This perspective encourages resilience and perseverance, essential traits for navigating the challenges of business. Setbacks also foster innovation, as overcoming obstacles often requires creative problem-solving. Ultimately, treating setbacks as opportunities helps entrepreneurs to continuously improve, adapt, and progress towards their goals, turning potential failures into stepping stones for success.

Belief 16 – Flexibility allows to evolve

A fixed course of action will hinder progress; hence, remain flexible and pivot your plans and strategies in response to feedback and changing market dynamics. Flexibility is paramount here.

By staying adaptable, businesses can respond effectively to new challenges and opportunities, ensuring they remain competitive and relevant. Flexibility allows for quick adjustments to evolving customer needs and market trends, fostering innovation and resilience. Embracing a flexible approach also encourages continuous improvement and agile decision-making, which are crucial for long-term success in an ever-changing business environment.

Belief 17 – People Power

No one builds a successful business alone.

Effective leadership and team building are essential. It's important to gather a strong, diverse team and foster a culture of collaboration and trust. Effective leadership inspires and motivates the team to work towards shared objectives. By fostering a supportive environment where individuals thrive and collaborate, businesses harness the collective power of their people. Together, they navigate challenges, drive innovation, and achieve collective success, proving that the strength of a business lies in its people.

Belief 18 – Informed Decision Making.

Making informed decisions is better than guessing.

Data-driven decision making helps businesses understand market trends, customer behaviour, and operational efficiencies. Using data and analytics leads to more strategic and effective actions. This information enables more strategic and effective actions, ensuring resources are allocated optimally and initiatives are aligned with overarching objectives. Embracing data-driven decision-making not only enhances business agility but also minimises risks associated with uncertainty. Ultimately, businesses equipped with actionable insights can adapt swiftly, capitalise on opportunities, and sustain competitive advantage in dynamic market environments.

Belief 19 – Failure provides valuable lessons

Embracing failure is an integral part of entrepreneurial success.

Failure provides valuable lessons and insights that drive improvement and innovation. Entrepreneurs who view failures as learning opportunities can adapt their strategies, refine their approaches, and build resilience. This mindset fosters a culture of experimentation and growth, encouraging risk-taking and creative problem-solving. By accepting and learning from failures, entrepreneurs can navigate the complexities of business more effectively, ultimately leading to greater success. In essence, embracing failure transforms setbacks into stepping stones, paving the way for continuous development and long-term achievement.

Belief 20 – Planning helps mitigate risks and seize opportunities

Financial planning and Budgeting are the backbone of any successful venture.

Maintaining strict financial discipline, budgeting carefully, forecasting accurately, and managing cash flow are critical to ensuring sustainability and growth. By prioritising sound financial planning, businesses can mitigate risks, seize opportunities, and foster long-term sustainability and growth. Maintaining a steadfast commitment to financial discipline provides the necessary framework for strategic decision-making and enables businesses to navigate challenges with resilience and confidence.

Belief 21 – Branding and Marketing serve as a powerful tool

Developing a strong brand identity & robust marketing strategy helps businesses stand out in a crowded marketplace.

A strong brand identity and effective marketing are key to attracting and retaining customers. Through strategic marketing initiatives, companies can effectively communicate their value proposition and engage target audiences. A well-crafted marketing strategy not only attracts new customers but also fosters loyalty among existing ones. By consistently delivering compelling messaging and experiences, businesses can reinforce their brand presence and drive sustained growth in competitive markets. Effective branding and marketing efforts serve as powerful tools for businesses to connect with their audience and drive long-term success.

Belief 22 – Seek Feedback

Embracing a culture of seeking feedback, and learning from both successes and failures help businesses evolve and stay competitive.

The most successful ventures never stop learning. Continuous learning and improvement are vital. This commitment to ongoing learning empowers teams to stay ahead of evolving trends and emerging challenges, ensuring sustained relevance and competitiveness. Embracing a philosophy of lifelong learning not only fosters individual growth but also drives organisational excellence, positioning businesses to thrive in an ever-changing landscape.

Belief 23 – Choose your network carefully

Scanning your hand-held device for 5 minutes, I can tell you what your bank balance would be in 5 years.

It's important to note that the top 5 or 10 people you talk to regularly play a big role in your current and future personal, financial and social situation. You can look at the device in your hand which is the most powerful tool you have, displaying both positions of where you are now and where you would be in the next 5 years. So, it's wise to choose your contacts carefully. Interact with the right people, especially considering your circumstances and where you aim to be in the future. These interactions can greatly impact your journey and help you achieve your desired goals.

Belief 24 – Follow the footprints

Following the footprints of individuals who have traversed similar journeys provides invaluable guidance, wisdom, and inspiration.

Embrace the power of learning from those who have trodden the path before you. Their experiences serve as beacons, illuminating the way forward and offering insights to navigate challenges and seize opportunities. By honouring the lessons and successes of those who have gone before you, you gain a deeper understanding of the road ahead, accelerate your growth, and increase the likelihood of achieving your aspirations. Embracing the wisdom of predecessors empowers you to forge your own paths with confidence, resilience, and purpose.

Belief 25 – Follow a Framework

Frameworks are essential guiding structures for success that empower individuals and organisations to navigate complexities, achieve clarity, and drive meaningful progress.

Embracing the power of frameworks enables us to approach challenges systematically, break down complex problems into manageable components, and develop strategic pathways towards success. By adopting and refining frameworks tailored to your unique objectives and circumstances, you unlock the potential for innovation, efficiency, and sustainable growth. You firmly believe that frameworks serve as invaluable tools for shaping your understanding, facilitating decision-making, and fostering continuous improvement in pursuit of your goals."

Belief 26 – Don't Spend but embrace the principle of Investing for growth

Money spent is lost, but money invested fuels growth and delivers a better return on investment.

Believe in the principle of investing rather than spending. Investing, whether in assets, education, or relationships, cultivates growth, security, and opportunity. You believe in the power of thoughtful and strategic investing to enhance your financial well-being. By directing your resources towards opportunities that promise growth, you not only secure your future but also create value that multiplies over time. Investing wisely ensures that your money works for us, fostering stability, prosperity, and long-term success. Embracing the ethos of investing not only enriches your lives but also paves the way for a more fulfilling and purpose-driven future. Before making any buying decision, it is crucial to analyse and understand that the money you are committing is not just spent, but invested, contributing to your growth.

Belief 27 –Self Development

Self-development is the bridge between where you are and where you want to be.

Success is not an accident; it's the result of continuous self-development and hard work. Self-improvement helps you overcome obstacles, unlock your full potential, and achieve your goals. It involves continuous learning, skill enhancement, and personal growth, all of which help you move from your current state to your desired future. This journey of self-development empowers you to adapt to new challenges, seize opportunities, and create a more fulfilling and successful life. Ultimately, self-development is the key to transforming your dreams into reality.

Belief 28 – You are all products of your own Environment

Choose your environment wisely as your surroundings, experiences, and interactions with others in that environment shape who you are and influence your perspectives, values, and actions.

Recognising the profound impact of your environment empowers us to cultivate environments that foster growth, positivity, and opportunity. By nurturing supportive, inclusive, and inspiring environments, you can unlock your full potential and empower others to do the same. Embracing the idea that your environment plays a pivotal role in shaping your identity motivates us to create spaces that promote personal and collective well-being, fostering a culture of growth and resilience."

Belief 29 – Embrace Long term planning

Ninety-five percent of your short-term goals planned for the next 12 months may not be achieved, but ninety-five percent of your goals will be accomplished once you have a long-term vision and plan your goals for five years or more.

This belief highlights the vital role of patience, persistence, and strategic vision in attaining meaningful success. Short-term plans are prone to disruption by unforeseen challenges, but adopting a longer-term perspective enables better adaptation and resilience. Long-term planning facilitates adjustments in strategy, enhancing the likelihood of success. It involves breaking down the long-term vision into manageable milestones, promoting continuous improvement and growth. By setting a horizon of five years or more, you establish a flexible framework that accommodates fluctuations in progress, fostering alignment with broader objectives. Embracing long-term planning nurtures a mindset of continual advancement, leading to substantial and sustainable achievements. While many goals set for the next 12 months may go unrealised, planning for a longer period significantly increases the chances of attainment. Therefore, it's essential to look ahead, exercise patience, and work towards objectives for lasting success.

Belief 30 – Build trust and credibility

Trust and credibility are the keys to success, and these can be built by consistently adding value to your customers.

Adding value fosters customer loyalty and satisfaction, as clients feel appreciated and well-served. This approach not only differentiates a business from its competitors but also encourages positive word-of-mouth referrals. In essence, continuously adding value is fundamental for building strong, lasting relationships with customers, which are crucial for long-term success and growth.

Belief 31 – Risk empowers progress

Risk is part of the entrepreneur's journey, but it should be an informed and calculated risk, not gambling. Approach risk-taking with a sense of optimism and adventure,

viewing each new opportunity as a chance to grow and succeed.

While mindful of potential pitfalls, adopt a proactive approach to risk management, leveraging insights and data to make well-informed decisions. Viewing risk as a catalyst for innovation and progress empowers entrepreneurs to navigate uncertainties with confidence and resilience, ultimately driving them towards greater achievements.

Belief 32 – The Purpose

Finding your purpose gives meaning to your existence and fuels your passion. It transforms the ordinary into the extraordinary.

Many people simply exist, go about their lives, and eventually depart from this world without leaving much of a mark. The true essence of life lies not merely in its beginning and end, but in uncovering the unique purpose for your existence. It's about understanding why you are here and the impact you can make on humanity and the world around us. How can you contribute to something greater than ourselves? What actions can you take to leave a lasting legacy that others will remember? These questions compel us to search for your purpose and strive to make a meaningful difference during your time on this planet. Purpose is the fundamental reason for existence or the underlying motivation that drives actions and decisions. Finding your purpose is crucial because it provides clarity, direction, and meaning to your work.

Belief 33 – Opportunity to Learn and Grow

Approach risk-taking with a sense of optimism and adventure, viewing each new opportunity as a chance to Learn, grow and succeed.

Opportunity to Learn and Grow emphasises a positive, adventurous mindset towards risk-taking. View challenges as opportunities for growth, fostering a continuous improvement mentality. Approach new opportunities with optimism, seeing them as chances to learn and succeed. Act decisively, trusting that you can adapt and learn on the go. Celebrate small wins, stay flexible, and seek feedback to enhance learning. This belief encourages turning uncertainties into stepping stones for personal and professional development, building resilience and fostering creativity through proactive engagement and hands-on experience.

Conclusion

Success is not solely determined by the viability of a business idea or the strength of a business plan. Rather, it is the mindset—the beliefs and attitudes—that entrepreneurs bring to their endeavours that ultimately shape their success. By embracing beliefs such as passion, resilience, flexibility, and vision, aspiring entrepreneurs can navigate the challenges of entrepreneurship with confidence, determination, and purpose, paving the way for long-term success and fulfillment.

In your next volume, "Visions to Victory Volume 2," I am excited to delve deeper into some of the key foundational beliefs discussed here. Building upon the insights shared here, next Volume of the series is bringing a comprehensive exploration of each belief, offering practical strategies, frameworks, and roadmaps to support you as an entrepreneurs on your journey to success. From harnessing the power of passion to mastering the art of resilience, each belief will be dissected and illuminated to equip readers with the tools and knowledge needed to navigate the complexities of your entrepreneurship with confidence and clarity. Whether you're a budding entrepreneur or a seasoned business leader, "Visions to Victory Volume 2" promises to be an invaluable resource for unlocking your potential and achieving your goals. Stay tuned for an inspiring and transformative journey ahead.

As you eagerly await the release of Volume 2, I invite you to reserve your interest and join me on this transformative journey. Together, let's turn visions into resounding victories in the world of business.

Chapter 6.11

Why Volume 2 of "Visions to Victory" Matters

Have you ever faced the daunting challenges of navigating today's fiercely competitive business landscape? Whether you're a seasoned entrepreneur with years of experience or just embarking on your entrepreneurial journey, the complexities of venture creation can seem overwhelming. Understanding market dynamics, staying ahead of evolving trends—these are the demands that require clarity, confidence, and actionable strategies. Visions to Victory is a framework and roadmap to greatness—a guide that empowers you to unlock your full potential and achieve your wildest dreams.

In this section 6 of visions to victory, you embarked on an exploration of the VICTORY Model, which served as a roadmap for entrepreneurial success. You began by understanding the importance of having a clear vision (V). Then, you delved into the process of idea inception and launch (I), emphasising the significance of strategic planning and execution in turning ideas into viable products or services. Next, you explored the concept of curating and cultivating the startup (C). You then discussed the transformation of micro ventures for market domination (T). Furthermore, you examined the optimisation of SME businesses with operational excellence and innovation (O). You also discussed rising in public ownership and leadership (R) and finally, you explored yielding the fruits of legacy (Y), where you discussed leaving a lasting impact on society and future generations through entrepreneurial endeavours.

In conclusion, the Visions to Victory Model is not just a framework; it's a 360-degree mindset – a mindset that empowers you to dream big, think innovatively, plan strategically, and act decisively. By implementing the Visions to Victory Model in their business journey, you can navigate the complexities of the business landscape with confidence and clarity, driving sustainable growth, and achieving their goals. So, whether you're a seasoned entrepreneur or just starting out on your business journey, embrace the Visions to Victory Model and set sail towards success. I urge you to embrace the Visions to Victory Model in your business success journey. Let it be your guiding light, your strategic compass, and your source of inspiration. Together, let us set sail towards the horizon of success, fuelled by vision, guided by strategy, and propelled by resilience. With the Visions to Victory Model as your map, there is no limit to what you can achieve.

Why Volume 2 of "Visions to Victory" Matters

Have you ever sought a resource that not only offers theoretical insights but also provides practical steps that you can implement immediately? Through the power of the VICTORY Model, illustrated with compelling case studies and real-world examples, you'll gain invaluable lessons from successful entrepreneurs who have turned their visions into reality.

Whether you're tackling a new business challenge or striving to elevate your enterprise to the next level, this framework equips you with the latest tools and knowledge needed to thrive in today's dynamic business environment. It offers actionable insights and practical strategies within the framework that is aimed to propel you towards success in today's fiercely competitive business landscape.

Volume 2 provides insights and strategies that you can implement right away. These are not theoretical concepts but practical steps designed to transform your entrepreneurial dreams into reality. It's an opportunity to take immediate action and see tangible results in your business.

By reserving your copy of Volume 2 today, you're not just securing a book; you're taking the first step towards transforming your business and your life. Join us as you unveil the secrets of the Venture Creation Framework and embark on a journey of discovery, empowerment, and success. Volume 2 of "Visions to Victory" is more than a guide; it's a transformative experience that will inspire, educate, and empower you to achieve your entrepreneurial aspirations. I urge you to seize this opportunity and reserve your copy today. Embrace the journey towards greatness and let this resource be your companion in achieving your wildest dreams.

Guidance with real life success stories

Have you ever wished you could learn directly from those who have conquered the business world? In Volume 2 of "Visions to Victory," you'll get just that – real-life success stories from entrepreneurs who have faced and overcome the toughest challenges.

Have you ever wanted a practical guide, not just theory, to help you elevate your leadership, sharpen your vision, and ignite innovation in your own venture? This book delivers actionable tips and tricks you can immediately apply.

These stories of triumph are not just to impress; they are designed to inspire and guide you on your own journey. They demonstrate how the VICTORY Model is put into practice, proving that smart planning and decisive action can lead to success, no matter the obstacles.

"Visions to Victory" is more than just bedtime reading; it is a testament to grit, determination, and perseverance. It invites you to join a community of like-minded entrepreneurs who share ideas, learn from each other, and celebrate each other's successes. These tales of real-world achievements show how the VICTORY Model gets results in various situations.

Moreover, "Visions to Victory" redefines failure, turning it from a setback into a stepping stone. It encourages embracing challenges, taking risks, and pursuing your goals with unwavering determination. By seeing the VICTORY Model in action, you'll gain the knowledge and confidence to elevate your entrepreneurial dreams. Whether you're aiming to stand out in a crowded market or adapting your business to changing times, the VICTORY Model is your roadmap to success.

So, what are you waiting for? Let's embark on this journey to greatness together and discover how to transform challenges into opportunities for victory.

Inspiration in Adversity

In a world where things are never easy and challenges are lurking around every corner, "Visions to Victory" is like a shining light in the darkness. It's here to remind you that no matter how tough things get, success is still within reach. This book is all about showing you that, even when the odds are stacked against you, there's still a way to come out on top. It's about lifting your spirits and giving you the push you need to chase your dreams, no matter what stands in your way.

And let me tell you, "Visions to Victory – Volume 2" is packed with stories that'll light a fire under you. It's full of tales of people just like you who've stared down their fears, tackled their problems head-on, and come out on the other side stronger than ever. These stories aren't just here to entertain you; they're here to inspire you to reach for the stars and grab hold of your own greatness, both in business and in life.

So, if you're feeling a bit down and out, if you're struggling to see the light at the end of the tunnel, just remember this: "Visions to Victory" is here to remind you that you've got what it takes to overcome any obstacle that comes your way. All you've got to do is keep pushing forward and never give up on your dreams.

Holistic Approach

"Visions to Victory – Volume 2" is all about covering the essential bases of successful business management, focusing on the top three key elements that really make a difference.

Now, my dear friends, the launch of Volume 2 of Visions to Victory isn't just any old event—it's a golden chance to completely change up your journey as an entrepreneur. Come along with us as you dig deep into the Venture Creation Framework and set off on a path that leads straight to success.

This book isn't just something else to stick on your reading list; it's more like a treasure map to greatness—a trusty guide that'll help you unlock every ounce of your potential and make those big dreams of yours a reality. So, don't waste a moment – reserve your copy now and be one of the first to set sail towards greatness with Volume 2 of "Visions to Victory."

Immersive Experiences Await

Alright, folks, let me tell you about what awaits you in Volume 2 of Visions to Victory. It's not just a book; it's like stepping into a whole new world—a world where you get to see the VICTORY Model in action. You're talking about immersive experiences that'll grab hold of you and show you exactly how real entrepreneurs have used the VICTORY Model to turn their dreams into reality.

Picture this: captivating case studies and real-life examples that'll whisk you away into the worlds of these entrepreneurs. You'll see firsthand how they've used the principles laid out in the VICTORY Model to create ventures that are nothing short of victorious.

But hold on, you're not stopping at just inspiring you. Volume 2 is also packed with practical examples that you can actually use in your own journey as an entrepreneur. Whether you're just dipping your toes in the water or you're facing a brand-new challenge in your business, these insights will give you the power to make smart decisions and drive your venture towards success.

And let's not forget about the VICTORY Model itself. It's not just some fancy theory; it's a practical framework that you can start using right away. It'll guide you through all the twists and turns of growing your business, giving you the confidence and clarity you need to keep moving forward.

So, if you're ready for an immersive experience that'll change the way you think about entrepreneurship, then Volume 2 of Visions to Victory is where it's at. Dive in, and let's start turning those dreams into reality, shall you?

Resilience and Determination

let's talk about resilience and determination. As you journey through the world of entrepreneurship, you're not just learning about business – you're learning some vital life lessons too. You're learning about picking ourselves up when you're knocked down, about staying determined even when the going gets tough, and about never, ever giving up on those dreams of ours.

Now, whether you're a seasoned pro or you're just dipping your toe into the entrepreneurial waters, Volume 2 of Visions to Victory is your guide and a formula book to success. It's like having a roadmap right in front of you, showing you every strategic step, you need to take to turn your dreams into reality. It's about giving you the tools and the know-how to make your entrepreneurial vision come to life.

So, my dear friends, the release of Volume 2 isn't just some run-of-the-mill event – it's a chance for you to completely transform your journey as an entrepreneur. Come join us as you dive deep into the Venture Creation Framework and set off on a path that leads straight to success.

Strategic Guidance

When you see the model in action, it's like a big thumbs-up, confirming that what you've been learning is the real deal. It's about boosting your understanding and giving you that extra dose of confidence to put those concepts into practice.

Now, I'm buzzing to share something truly revolutionary with you all – the Venture Creation Framework. This game-changer, at the heart of Volume 2 of Visions to Victory, is like your strategic GPS, guiding you from your initial vision right through to smashing success in business. So, join me as you dive deep into this framework, uncovering all its hidden gems.

Volume 2 is your roadmap to success, meticulously designed to guide you from dreamer to triumphant business owner. Inside, you'll find the Venture Creation Framework – a goldmine of wisdom and strategies to help you tackle the entrepreneurial world with confidence.

Now, let's get to the crux of it – turning dreams into action. That's what the Venture Creation Framework is all about. It's about taking that lightbulb moment and turning it into a clear plan of action that drives your business forward. In Volume 2, you're going to dig into this framework, learning its secrets and figuring out how to make it work for your own ventures.

You all know that the world of entrepreneurship is like a rollercoaster ride – full of ups, downs, and unexpected twists. But with the Venture Creation Framework by your side, you can navigate this terrain with ease. Through real-life examples and practical strategies, Volume 2 will arm you with the tools you need to spot opportunities, tackle challenges, and make smart decisions that lead to success.

So, let's unveil this strategic blueprint together. The Venture Creation Framework isn't just a set of rules; it's a carefully crafted roadmap to success. And in Volume 2, you're going to explore every nook and cranny, discovering the principles and strategies that drive successful venture creation.

At its core, the Venture Creation Framework is all about turning vision into action. In Volume 2 of Visions to Victory, you'll dive deep into this framework, uncovering how it can guide entrepreneurs like you at every step of the journey. Whether you're just starting out or looking to take your business to the next level, this framework offers a systematic approach to turning your ideas into reality. Seeing the model in action validates the concepts presented in Volume 2, reinforcing your understanding and confidence in applying them to your own ventures.

From Visionary to Mentor: My Perspective

So why does Volume 2 matter?

Volume 2 of "Visions to Victory" matters profoundly because matters because it offers a personal connection—a connection that transcends the pages of a book and resonates deeply with each and every one of us. It matters because it empowers us to overcome challenges, seize opportunities, and unlock your full potential. It matters because it inspires us to dream big, take risks, and turn your visions into reality.

The release of Volume 2 of Visions to Victory is not just an event but an opportunity to witness the transformative power of the VICTORY Model and chart your course towards entrepreneurial success. Join us on this journey of discovery, and unlock the secrets to turning your visions into victorious ventures.

Prepare to embark on a transformative journey with the advanced concepts revealed in Volume 2 of "Visions to Victory." Reserve your interest today and be among the first to transform your entrepreneurial journey.

Let me make an electrifying announcement—one that promises to ignite your entrepreneurial spirit and propel you towards unprecedented success. Get ready to embark on a transformative journey as you unveil the advanced concepts of the VICTORY Model in Volume 2 of the Visions to Victory book series.

So join us as you uncover the secrets of the Venture Creation Framework and embark on a path towards entrepreneurial success. Reserve your interest today and be among the first to transform your entrepreneurial journey with Volume 2 of "Visions to Victory."

Thank you for your attention, and I look forward to embarking on this transformative journey with you. Whether you're at the beginning of your journey or facing a new challenge, these practical insights are penning down to guide you towards success.

Join the “Visions to Victory” LinkedIn Group

What Do I Bring To You with LinkedIn Visions to Victory group?

Today, I'd like to talk to you about why joining the Visions to Victory LinkedIn group could be one of the best decisions you make for your career and personal growth.

Imagine a place where you can expand your professional network with ease. Our LinkedIn group connects you with entrepreneurs, industry leaders, and experts from diverse fields. These connections aren't just virtual; they're opportunities to collaborate, share insights, and potentially open doors to new ventures and partnerships.

Being part of our LinkedIn group means staying informed. You'll gain access to exclusive content—articles, discussions, and thought-provoking posts—that keep you up-to-date with industry trends and best practices. Whether it's learning about the latest strategies in entrepreneurship or leadership tips from seasoned professionals, there's always something valuable to discover.

Career development is at the heart of what we do. Through webinars, workshops, and interactive discussions, we provide you with the tools and knowledge to enhance your skills and advance your career. It's about equipping yourself with the expertise needed to excel in today's competitive business landscape.

Visibility matters. By joining our LinkedIn group, you can showcase your achievements, share your expertise, and build your personal brand among a targeted audience. It's a platform where your voice can be heard and your contributions recognised, fostering professional growth and credibility.

But it's not just about professional benefits. Our group is a supportive community where you can find inspiration, seek advice, and receive mentorship from peers and industry leaders. It's about connecting with like-minded individuals who share your drive for success and are ready to support you on your journey.

In summary, the Visions to Victory LinkedIn group isn't just another networking platform—it's a gateway to opportunities, knowledge, and growth. Whether you're starting out in your career or aiming to elevate your professional status, joining our community could be the catalyst for your next big breakthrough.

So, why not take that step today? Join us on LinkedIn and let's embark together on a journey of learning, achievement, and success.

Thank you for your time.

NEXT STEPS

CHARTING YOUR CONTINUED JOURNEY

As you delve into the final section, "Next Steps," it's crucial to acknowledge that the entrepreneurial journey is a dynamic, ever-evolving expedition. This chapter isn't just a conclusion; it's an open door to new opportunities, growth, and a deeper connection with the vast entrepreneurial ecosystem. Charting your continued journey involves a commitment to growth, learning, and innovation.

By embracing the next steps, you not only enhance your chances of success but also ensure that your entrepreneurial journey is dynamic and fulfilling. Stay informed, build strong networks, refine your strategies, enhance your problem-solving skills, foster sustainable growth, and maintain a visionary mindset.

Your journey is just beginning, and the possibilities are endless. The path to victory is paved with continuous effort and unwavering determination. Embrace it, and let your entrepreneurial spirit soar.

Here's why you should consider the next steps and how they can propel your entrepreneurial journey forward.

Embrace Continuous Learning and Adaptation - The entrepreneurial landscape is constantly changing. By taking the next steps, you commit to continuous learning and adaptation. This involves staying updated with market trends, embracing new technologies, and refining your business strategies. Engaging with Volume 2 of "Visions to Victory" will provide you with the latest insights and practical tools to navigate these changes effectively.

Access to a Wealth of Knowledge and Experience - By moving forward, you gain access to the collective wisdom of mentors, industry experts, and fellow entrepreneurs. Their experiences, challenges, and successes offer invaluable lessons that can help you avoid common pitfalls and capitalise on opportunities. The next volume will delve into real-life success stories and provide actionable insights that can inspire and guide your journey.

Refine Your Strategic Approach - The VICTORY model is a comprehensive framework designed to enhance every aspect of your entrepreneurial venture. Each stage of the model offers specific strategies and techniques to ensure your business is aligned with market needs and poised for success. By exploring Volume 2, you'll gain a deeper understanding of each stage, allowing you to refine your strategic approach and make informed decisions.

Strengthen Your Network - Networking is a cornerstone of entrepreneurial success. The next steps involve building and strengthening relationships with other entrepreneurs, investors, and industry professionals. These connections can open doors to new opportunities, collaborations, and resources. Volume 2 will highlight networking strategies and success stories, showing you how to leverage your network effectively.

Enhance Your Problem-Solving Skills - Every entrepreneurial journey is fraught with challenges. Developing robust problem-solving skills is essential for overcoming obstacles and turning challenges into opportunities. The next volume of "Visions to Victory" will provide case studies and scenarios that illustrate effective problem-solving techniques, helping you build resilience and adaptability.

Foster Sustainable Growth - Sustainable growth is the hallmark of a successful business. The next steps will focus on strategies for scaling your business while maintaining its core values and mission. By understanding the intricacies of sustainable growth, you can ensure that your business not only survives but thrives in the long term.

Cultivate a Visionary Mindset - A visionary mindset is crucial for driving innovation and staying ahead of the competition. The next steps will encourage you to think creatively, challenge the status quo, and envision the future of your industry. Volume 2 will provide inspiration and practical advice on cultivating a visionary mindset that can transform your business.

Taking the next step is not just a progression; it's a commitment to your entrepreneurial success. The entrepreneurial journey is a continuous path of growth, learning, and adaptation. Embracing the next steps with the "Visions to Victory" series will equip you with the tools, knowledge, and network to transform your vision into a successful reality. Don't just conclude this chapter—open the doors to new possibilities and let your entrepreneurial journey flourish.

As you conclude this section, consider it a prelude to the grand symphony that awaits in Volume 2 of your series, "Visions to Victory." In the upcoming release, you will delve into each stage of the VICTORY model, unravelling the intricacies, exploring real-life success stories, and providing actionable insights for your entrepreneurial journey.

Stay tuned, for a deeper dive into the strategic realms of VICTORY. Let the anticipation build, the excitement rise, and the motivation soar. The journey to triumph awaits in the next volume, where Vision evolves into Victory. Get ready to embrace the complete VICTORY model – a roadmap to unparalleled success. Get ready to claim your copy and be part of the entrepreneurial revolution. The path to victory begins here!

01 - Join My Facebook Group

Facebook Groups create microcosms of communities cantered around shared interests. Joining a Facebook Group connects you with a tribe of individuals navigating similar entrepreneurial landscapes. It's a space for discussions, resource-sharing, and a support system as you continue your journey. Facebook Groups offer a sense of belonging, facilitate knowledge exchange, and provide a platform for seeking advice from a community of peers.

02 - Join My Weekly Tips for Free

Receive our weekly tips. Simple, fun and free - join our smart subscribers. Newsletters are a curated compilation of insights, updates, and valuable resources. Subscribing to a weekly newsletter ensures a steady influx of relevant information directly to your inbox. It's a convenient way to stay informed, inspired, and connected with the latest developments. Newsletters offer a structured and comprehensive source of information, keeping you updated and providing actionable insights on a regular basis.

03- Become Part of My Power Team

A Power Team is a collective of individuals with diverse skills and expertise who collaborate to achieve common goals. Becoming part of a Power Team amplifies your capabilities, leveraging the strengths of each member. It's a synergistic approach to overcoming challenges and driving collective success. Joining a Power Team enhances your capabilities, fosters collaboration, and provides a support system for tackling challenges collectively.

04 - Join My Global Community

The entrepreneurial journey is not confined to local boundaries. Joining a global community broadens your horizons, offering exposure to diverse perspectives, cultures, and market dynamics. It's an opportunity to connect with entrepreneurs worldwide, expanding your network and fostering a global mindset. Joining a global community enriches your entrepreneurial journey, provides access to international opportunities, and fosters a global perspective.

05 - Visit My Webpage

A webpage is a centralised space that encapsulates the essence of an entrepreneurial brand. Visiting the webpage offers a deeper dive into the journey, insights, and the offerings available. It's a comprehensive resource that allows you to explore, engage, and connect on a more substantial level. Visiting the webpage provides a holistic understanding of the entrepreneurial journey, offerings, and additional resources available for your ongoing growth.

06 - Book a FREE Discovery Call

A discovery call is an opportunity for personalised engagement. Booking a free discovery call allows you to connect directly, discuss your specific challenges, and explore how tailored insights and guidance can propel your journey forward. It's a bespoke approach to addressing your unique entrepreneurial needs. A discovery call offers personalised guidance, clarity on challenges, and a roadmap for your continued success, tailored to your specific circumstances.

07 - Attend a Workshop for FREE

Workshops are immersive learning experiences that delve into specific aspects of the entrepreneurial journey. Attending a free workshop provides hands-on insights, practical strategies, and the opportunity to interact with experts. It's a dynamic way to enhance your skills and gain actionable takeaways. Workshops offer practical knowledge, skill-building opportunities, and a platform to interact with experts in a focused and immersive setting.

08 - Join the 3 Day Bootcamp

A bootcamp is an intensive, short-duration programme designed to catalyse growth and transformation. Joining a 3-day bootcamp provides a concentrated burst of learning, skill development, and networking. It's an efficient way to gain impactful insights and strategies in a condensed timeframe. A 3-day bootcamp accelerates your learning, fosters intensive skill development, and offers a concentrated burst of entrepreneurial insights.

09 - Join Your Flagship Programme

Your mastermind programme is a structured platform for peer-to-peer learning, brainstorming, and collective problem-solving. Joining a mastermind programme positions you among a group of high-achieving individuals who share insights, offer guidance, and contribute to each other's success. This mastermind programme provides a supportive network, collective problem-solving, and a structured platform for ongoing learning and growth.

10 - Join Your Retreat Programme

The Visions to Victory Retreat Programme offers a structured environment for personal and professional development. Participants step away from their usual routines to focus on growth and introspection through tailored workshops and activities. The programme aims to provide clarity, recharge energy, and foster skills like leadership, creativity, and mindfulness. It serves various purposes: for corporate teams to enhance cohesion and strategic planning, wellness seekers to boost health, spiritual enthusiasts to deepen practice, creatives to nurture talents, and individuals pursuing personal growth to explore new possibilities. Ultimately, the retreat empowers participants to return refreshed, inspired, and ready to achieve their goals.

11 - Join The Speakers Academy Programme

The Visions to Victory Speakers Academy Programme equips individuals with essential skills and confidence for effective public speaking and communication. Participants learn foundational communication principles, clarity of thought, and articulation, progressing to crafting compelling stories and mastering presentation techniques. The programme emphasises practical skills like Q&A handling, effective visuals, and engaging diverse audiences. It aims to empower individuals to communicate ideas persuasively, inspire others, and lead effectively. Mastering public speaking boosts career prospects, leadership capabilities, and personal growth by enhancing confidence and credibility. Participants can articulate visions, influence others positively, and succeed in professional and personal endeavours.

12 - Join Academy Award Night and Annual Gala Dinner

The Visions to Victory Academy Awards Programme celebrates entrepreneurship, leadership, and personal growth with categories like Visionary Entrepreneur and Leadership Excellence. Winners are selected by industry experts and celebrated at a Gala Dinner and Award Ceremony. Participation offers recognition, networking opportunities, and inspiration for excellence, fostering a culture of achievement and community impact. Join us in celebrating success and leadership through this programme, where aspirations thrive. "In From Visions to Victory," these steps are pathways to growth, learning, and success, offering tangible benefits such as networking, guidance, and immersive learning for ongoing success.

May these steps be the catalysts for your continued entrepreneurial triumphs.

About the AUTHOR – Santosh Kumar

Santosh Kumar, a dynamic figure in the entrepreneurial landscape, renowned for his multifaceted roles as an author, thought leader, serial entrepreneur, speaker around personal and professional development and esteemed member of the Forbes Business Council. His latest edition, "Visions to Victory," stands as a testament to his passion for sharing knowledge and empowering aspiring entrepreneurs worldwide for personal and professional growth and success.

Santosh Kumar is considered as a beacon of inspiration and a creative thinker, driving innovation and success in personal, professional, entrepreneurship and thought leadership. His multifaceted career spans authorship, serial entrepreneurship and visionary leadership, leaving an indelible mark on the global business community. With a keen eye for emerging trends and a relentless drive for innovation, he has spearheaded numerous successful ventures across diverse industries. From pioneering technology startups to groundbreaking renewable energy initiatives, Santosh's entrepreneurial endeavours consistently redefine industry standards and push the boundaries of possibility.

What distinguishes Santosh as an entrepreneur is not just his knack for identifying lucrative opportunities but also his unwavering commitment to creating value and driving positive change. Each venture he undertakes is driven by a vision to address pressing global challenges while delivering sustainable growth and profitability. Through his leadership and strategic acumen, Santosh inspires a new generation of entrepreneurs to pursue their dreams with passion and purpose for personal and professional growth and success. Beyond his entrepreneurial pursuits, he is revered as a thought leader and visionary author. His seminal work, "Visions to Victory," serves as a manifesto for aspiring entrepreneurs, offering a roadmap for navigating the complexities of the business world. Through compelling narratives and actionable advice, Santosh shares invaluable insights on strategy, leadership, resilience, and the relentless pursuit of excellence. "Visions to Victory" transcends mere literature; it is a guidebook for shaping the future of entrepreneurship and thought leadership. Santosh challenges conventional wisdom and inspires readers to think boldly, dream big, and chart their own path towards success and growth. His visionary approach underscores the importance of sustainability, social responsibility, and ethical practices, setting a new standard for success in the business world.

Looking ahead, Santosh Kumar remains steadfast in his commitment to shaping the future of entrepreneurship and thought leadership. Through ongoing ventures, mentorship initiatives, and thought-provoking writings, he continues to drive innovation and foster positive change in society. Santosh envisions a future where entrepreneurship becomes a catalyst for economic growth, social progress, and environmental sustainability.

Santosh Kumar's journey as an entrepreneur, thought leader, and visionary author exemplifies the transformative power of vision, determination, and perseverance. His contributions inspire countless individuals to unlock their full potential and pursue their dreams with unwavering conviction for personal and professional growth and success. As you embark on this journey with Santosh, you are reminded that with vision and passion, victory is not just a destination but a way of life. His journey embodies the essence of entrepreneurship and thought leadership. With a wealth of experience in founding and leading successful ventures across diverse industries, he has earned recognition as a visionary entrepreneur. Beyond his entrepreneurial endeavours, Santosh is revered as a thought leader, challenging conventional norms and championing innovation in the business community.

As a member of the esteemed Forbes Business Council, Santosh Kumar is part of a select group of influential business leaders shaping the future of entrepreneurship. His insights and contributions to the council underscore his commitment to driving positive change and fostering collaboration in the global business landscape. His latest venture into authorship with "Visions to Victory" reflects his desire to share the lessons learned from his entrepreneurial journey. Through this book, he aims to provide aspiring entrepreneurs with a roadmap for success, offering invaluable insights and practical advice on strategy, leadership, and resilience. Driven by a passion for empowering others and making a positive impact, Santosh wrote "Visions to Victory" to serve as a guiding light for aspiring entrepreneurs worldwide. His vision is to inspire individuals to pursue their dreams with confidence, overcome challenges, and achieve success in the ever-evolving world of business.

Printed in Great Britain
by Amazon

44904814R00269